A FIRST LOOK AT COMMUNICATION THEORY

NINTH EDITION

EM GRIFFIN

ANDREW LEDBETTER

GLENN SPARKS

A FIRST LOOK AT COMMUNICATION THEORY

NINTH EDITION

EM GRIFFIN

Wheaton College

ANDREW LEDBETTER

Texas Christian University

GLENN SPARKS

Purdue University

Mc Graw Hill Education

A FIRST LOOK AT COMMUNICATION THEORY, NINTH EDITION

This book is printed on acid-free paper.

1 2 3 4 5 6 7 8 9 0 QVS/QVS 1 0 9 8 7 6 5 4

ISBN: 978-1-25-944536-1
MHID: 1-25-944536-4

Previous ISBN: 978-0-07-352392-7
Previous MHID: 0-07-352392-5

Senior Vice President, Products & Markets: *Kurt L. Strand*
Vice President, General Manager, Products & Markets: *Michael Ryan*
Vice President, Content Production & Technology Services: *Kimberly Meriwether David*
Managing Director: *David S. Patterson*
Executive Director of Development: *Lisa Pinto*
Managing Editor: *Penina Braffman*
Associate Marketing Manager: *Alexandra Schultz*
Development Editor: *Adina Lonn*
Director, Content Production: *Terri Schiesl*
Content Project Manager: *Jessica Portz*
Buyer: *Nichole Birkenholz*
Cover Designer: *Studio Montage, St. Louis, MO*
Media Project Manager: *Jennifer Bartell*
Compositor: *Laserwords Private Limited*
Typeface: *10/12 Palatino LT Std Roman*
Printer: *Quad/Graphics*

Library of Congress Cataloging-in-Publication Data

CIP APPLIED FOR

www.mhhe.com

ABOUT THE AUTHORS

Em Griffin is Professor Emeritus of Communication at Wheaton College in Illinois, where he taught for over 35 years and was chosen Teacher of the Year. He received his M.A. and Ph.D. in communication from Northwestern University; his research interest is in the development of close friendships. Em is the author of three applied communication books: *The Mind Changers* (persuasion), *Getting Together* (group dynamics), and *Making Friends* (close relationships). For three decades, Em has been an active volunteer with Opportunity International, a nonprofit development organization providing financial solutions and training to empower people living in poverty to transform their lives. He also serves as a mediator and coach at the Center for Conflict Resolution in Chicago. Em's wife, Jean, is an artist and a musician. They recently celebrated 50 years of marriage and have two adult children, Jim and Sharon, and six grandchildren, Josh, Amy, Sam, Kyle, Alison, and Dan. You can reach Em at em.griffin@wheaton.edu.

Andrew Ledbetter is an Associate Professor of Communication Studies at Texas Christian University. He received his M.A. and Ph.D. in communication studies from the University of Kansas. His research addresses how people use communication technology to maintain their interpersonal relationships. A related interest concerns how parent–child communication predicts health and well-being. Andrew has published more than 35 articles and received recognition for teaching excellence from both the National Communication Association and Central States Communication Association. His wife, Jessica, is a former attorney who teaches business law at Texas Christian University. With their daughters, Sydney and Kira, they enjoy involvement in their church, playing board and card games, reading, cooking, and following the TCU Horned Frogs and Kansas Jayhawks. You can reach Andrew at a.ledbetter@tcu.edu, visit his blog at www.andrewledbetter.com, or follow him on Twitter via @dr_ledbetter.

Glenn Sparks is a professor in the Brian Lamb School of Communication at Purdue University in Indiana, where he has taught for 28 years. He received his Ph.D. in communication arts from the University of Wisconsin–Madison; his research focuses on the effects of media. Glenn is the author of *Media Effects Research: A Basic Overview* and a personal memoir, *Rolling in Dough: Lessons I Learned in a Doughnut Shop.* He's co-author of *Refrigerator Rights: Our Crucial Need for Close Connection.* Glenn is an avid sports fan and also enjoys trying to increase his skill playing the theremin. He is married to Cheri, a developmental therapist; they have three adult children, David, Erin, and Jordan, and one grandchild, Caleb. You can reach Glenn at sparks@purdue.edu.

DEDICATION

We dedicate this book to our wives, Jeanie, Jessica, and Cheri, who encouraged us to work together, celebrated with us when the process went well, and comforted us when it didn't. Just as they lovingly supported us in this project, we commit to being there for them in what they feel called to do.

Em, Andrew, Glenn

CONTENTS

PREFACE FOR INSTRUCTORS

If you're already familiar with *A First Look at Communication Theory* and understand the approach, organization, and main features of the book, you may want to jump ahead to the "Major Changes in the Ninth Edition" section. For those who are new to the text, reading the entire preface will give you a good grasp of what you and your students can expect.

A Balanced Approach to Theory Selection. We've written *A First Look* for students who have no background in communication theory. It's designed for undergraduates enrolled in an entry-level course, regardless of the students' classification. The trend in the field is to offer students a broad introduction to theory relatively early in their program. But if a department chooses to offer its first theory course on the junior or senior level, the course will still be the students' first comprehensive look at theory, so the book will meet them where they are.

Our goal in this text is to present 32 communication theories in a clear and interesting way. After reading about a given theory, students should understand the theory, know the research that supports it, see useful applications in their lives, and be aware of the theory's possible flaws. We hope readers will discover relationships among theories located across the communication landscape—a clear indication that they grasp what they're reading. But that kind of integrative thinking only takes place when students first comprehend what a theorist claims.

With the help of more than 200 instructors, we've selected a range of theories that reflect the diversity within the discipline. Some theories are proven candidates for a Communication Theory Hall of Fame. For example, Aristotle's analysis of logical, emotional, and ethical appeals continues to set the agenda for many public-speaking courses. Mead's symbolic interactionism is formative for interpretive theorists who are dealing with language, thought, self-concept, or the effect of society upon the individual. Berger's uncertainty reduction theory was the first objective theory to be crafted by a social scientist trained in the field. And no student of mediated communication should be ignorant of Gerbner's cultivation theory, which explains why heavy television viewing cultivates fear of a mean and scary world.

It would be shortsighted, however, to limit the selection to the classics of communication. Some of the discipline's most creative approaches are its newest. For example, Sandra Petronio's theory of communication privacy management undergirds much of the research conducted in the field of health communication. Leslie Baxter and Barbara Montgomery's theory of relational dialectics offers insight into the ongoing tensions inherent in personal relationships. And Robert McPhee's communicative constitution of organizations describes how the principle of social construction works in an organizational context.

Organizational Plan of the Book. Each chapter introduces a single theory in 10 to 15 pages. We've found that most undergraduates think in terms of discrete packets of information, so the concentrated coverage gives them a chance to focus their thoughts while reading a single chapter. This way, students can gain an in-depth understanding of important theories rather than acquire only a vague familiarity with a jumble of related ideas. The one-chapter–one-theory arrangement also gives teachers the opportunity to drop theories or rearrange the order of presentation without tearing apart the fabric of the text.

The first four chapters provide a framework for understanding the theories to come. The opening chapter, "Launching Your Study of Communication Theory," presents working definitions of both *theory* and *communication*, and also prepares students for the arrangement of the chapters and the features within them. Chapter 2, "Talk About Theory," lays the groundwork for understanding the differences between objective and interpretive theories. Chapter 3, "Weighing the Words," presents two sets of criteria for determining a good objective or interpretive theory. Based on Robert Craig's (University of Colorado) conception, Chapter 4, "Mapping the Territory," introduces seven traditions within the field of communication theory.

Following this integrative framework, we feature 32 theories in 32 self-contained chapters. Each theory is discussed within the context of a communication topic: interpersonal messages, relationship development, relationship maintenance, influence, group communication, organizational communication, public rhetoric, media and culture, media effects, intercultural communication, or gender and communication. These communication context sections usually contain three theories. Each section's two-page introduction outlines a crucial issue that theorists working in this area address. The placement of theories in familiar contexts helps students recognize that theories are answers to questions they've been asking all along. The final chapter, "Common Threads in Comm Theories," offers students a novel form of integration that will help them discern order in the tapestry of communication theory that might otherwise seem chaotic.

Because all theory and practice has value implications, we briefly explore a dozen ethical principles throughout the book. Consistent with the focus of this text, each principle is the central tenet of a specific ethical theory. Other disciplines may ignore these thorny issues, but to discuss communication as a process that is untouched by questions of good and bad, right and wrong, or questions of character would be to disregard an ongoing concern in our field.

Features of Each Chapter. Most people think in pictures. Students will have a rough time understanding a theory unless they apply its explanations and interpretations to concrete situations. The typical chapter uses an extended example to illustrate the "truth" a theory proposes. We encourage readers to try out ideas by visualizing a first meeting of freshman roommates, responding to conflict in a dysfunctional family, trying to persuade other students to support a zero-tolerance policy on driving after drinking, and many others. We also use speeches of Martin Luther King Jr. and Malcolm X, and scenes from *Mad Men, The Office, The Help, Bend It Like Beckham,* and *Thank You for Smoking* to illustrate principles of the theories. The case study in each chapter follows the pedagogical principle of explaining what students don't yet know in terms of ideas and images already within their experience.

Some theories are tightly linked with an extensive research project. For example, the impact of cognitive dissonance theory was greatly spurred by Festinger's surprising finding in his now classic $1/$20 experiment. And Philipsen's speech codes theory began with a three-year ethnographic study of what it means to speak like a man in "Teamsterville." When such exemplars exist, we describe the research in detail so that students can learn from and appreciate the benefits of grounding theory in systematic observation. In this way, readers of *A First Look* are led through a variety of research designs and data analyses.

Students will encounter the names of Baxter, Berger, Bormann, Burgoon, Burke, Deetz, Fisher, Giles, Kramarae, Pacanowsky, Pearce, Philipsen, Ting-Toomey, Walther, Wood, and many others in later communication courses. We therefore make a concerted effort to link theory and theorist. By pairing a particular theory with its originator, we try to promote both recall and respect for a given scholar's effort.

The text of each chapter concludes with a section that critiques the theory. This represents a hard look at the ideas presented in light of the criteria for a good theory outlined in Chapter 3. Some theorists have suggested that we are "friends" of their theory. We appreciate that because we want to present all of the theories in a constructive way. But after we summarize a theory's strengths, we then discuss its weaknesses, unanswered questions, and possible errors that remain. We try to stimulate a "That makes sense, and yet I wonder . . ." response among students.

We include a short list of thought questions at the end of each chapter. Labeled "Questions to Sharpen Your Focus," these probes encourage students to make connections among ideas in the chapter and also to apply the theory to their everyday communication experience. As part of this feature, words printed in italics remind students of the key terms of a given theory.

Each chapter ends with a short list of annotated readings entitled "A Second Look." The heading refers to resources for students who are interested in a theory and want to go further than a 10- to 15-page introduction allows. The top item is the resource we recommend as the starting point for further study. The other listings identify places to look for material about each of the major issues raised in the chapter. The format is designed to offer practical encouragement and guidance for further study without overwhelming the novice with multiple citations. The sources of quotations and citations of evidence are listed in an "Endnotes" section at the end of the book.

We think professors and students alike will get a good chuckle out of the cartoons we've selected for each chapter and section introduction. The art's main function, however, is to illustrate significant points in the text. As in other editions, we're committed to using quality cartoon art from *The New Yorker* and *Punch* magazines, as well as comic strips such as "Calvin and Hobbes" and "Dilbert." Perceptive cartoonists are modern-day prophets—their humor serves the education process well when it slips through mental barriers or attitudinal defenses that didactic prose can't penetrate.

While no author considers his or her style ponderous or dull, we believe we've presented the theories in a clear and lively fashion. Accuracy alone does not communicate. We've tried to remain faithful to the vocabulary each theorist uses so that the student can consider the theory in the author's own terms, but we also translate technical language into more familiar words. Students and reviewers cite readability and interest as particular strengths of the text. We encourage you to sample a chapter so you can decide for yourself.

In 13 of the chapters, you'll see photographs of the theorists who appear in "Conversations with Communication Theorists," eight-minute video clips of our discussions together. The text that accompanies each picture previews intriguing comments the theorists made so students can watch the interview with a specific purpose in mind. You can find these videos, as well as auto-graded quizzes, theory abstracts, web links, and crossword puzzles on the book's two websites, *www.mhhe.com/griffin9e* and the author-driven *www.afirstlook.com.*

Both sites offer password-protected features for instructors. The most selected resource is Emily Langan's world-class Instructor's Manual, which offers additional commentary, discussion questions, and classroom activities for each chapter. In addition, the McGraw-Hill Online Learning Center contains a test bank, flashcards, and PowerPoint presentations. The *First Look* site offers annotated movie clips that illustrate theories, a comparison chart showing theories covered in major communication theory texts, and chapter-by-chapter changes from the previous edition.

Major Changes in the Ninth Edition. Andrew Ledbetter and Glenn Sparks have become co-authors with Em. They were special consultants for the previous edition, but we now join together as equal partners. Both men are highly recognized scholars in their field—Andrew in computer-mediated communication and family communication; Glenn in media effects and interpersonal communication. Glenn was a student in Em's first persuasion course at Wheaton; Andrew aced the last communication theory class Em taught before he retired from full-time teaching. Despite differences in our ages of up to 45 years, the three of us are close friends and colleagues who have published together before. Each of us vets and edits what the other two write and offers advice on what to cover. We believe this interactive process ensures that students will read up-to-date information presented in the same "voice" that has characterized the book throughout eight editions.

Responding to instructors' desire to have at least one more organizational theory, we've added a chapter on Robert McPhee's theory, the *communicative constitution of organizations.* McPhee's conception of four flows of communication that create and sustain an organization is just one of several versions of CCO, but we think it's the account easiest to understand and most useful for students. In order to make room for McPhee's theory, we've moved our coverage of Delia's *constructivism* to the theory archive at *www.afirstlook.com.*

We've made a concerted effort to update examples that no longer have the explanatory power or appeal they did when introduced in previous editions. References to old films are a case in point. As apt as these movies are to illustrate *symbolic interactionism* or *critical theory of communication in organizations,* the majority of college students aren't familiar with *Nell* or *Erin Brockovich.* We've replaced many of these examples with cultural material more relevant to students.

Half the chapters in the book have undergone major additions, deletions, or alterations. Here's a sample:

- In the **"Talk About Theory"** chapter, Glenn's and Marty's analyses of the most popular commercial of the 2013 Super Bowl telecast highlight the differences between objective and interpretive scholarship.
- In the **"Weighing the Words"** chapter, a discussion of communication apprehension now illustrates the explanation-of-data standard for objective theories.
- The chapter on the ***coordinated management of meaning*** has been completely rewritten. It's shorter, less complex, and faithful to the new direction the theory has taken. The CMM Institute will use it on its website to introduce the theory.
- In the **"Uncertainty Reduction Theory"** chapter, the section on *anxiety/uncertainty management theory* has been replaced with an in-depth section on the *relational turbulence model*, which is on the cutting-edge of research in the URT tradition.
- The revised chapter on ***social information processing theory*** begins by referencing the hit 2010 movie *The Social Network* and then uses an ongoing example of a Facebook friendship to illustrate key components of the theory. Walther's hyperpersonal perspective is applied to online dating.
- The "Three State-of-the-Art Revisions" section of the **"Cognitive Dissonance"** chapter has been largely rewritten. The edits more clearly differentiate among the three revisions and use the example of President Obama's struggle with smoking to illustrate those differences.
- In Deetz' **"Critical Theory of Communication"** chapter, there's an extensive elaboration of his Politically Attentive Relational Constructivism (PARC). This is followed by an account of how Deetz applies the theory to his work with the International Atomic Energy Agency to prevent nuclear plant meltdowns.
- We've made a major reorganization of the chapter on Burke's ***dramatism***. The order of the first four sections is now (1) an expanded presentation of the dramatistic pentad, (2) a new section on language as the genesis of guilt, (3) the guilt–redemption cycle, and (4) identification as the necessary condition for persuasion to occur.
- In the chapter on ***cultural studies***, we rewrote the section on broadcast and print news supporting dominant ideology, using Obamacare as a case study. We then discussed satire as a possible form of resistance to the dominant ideology, using *The Daily Show* and *The Colbert Report* as examples.
- In the **"Genderlect Styles"** chapter, we replaced the *When Harry Met Sally* example with new material on rules of conversation that boys and girls learn early in life, and discuss how childhood speech communities may be the origin of genderlect.
- The revised chapter on ***muted group theory*** introduces Orbe's co-cultural theory, which charts how muted groups desire assimilation, separation, or accommodation.

Bottom-line numbers on important features of the text are an index of additional changes we've made in this edition. We've created **two** new "Conversations with Communication Theorists" videos—Glenn interviewing Sandra Petronio about her *communication privacy management theory* and Andrew discussing *communication accommodation theory* with Howie Giles. We've selected **six** new application logs that show how students use theories in their lives, and captured **seven** new cartoons that cleverly highlight a crucial claim of a particular theory. You'll also find **50** new annotated citations in the "Second Look" feature at the end of the chapters.

McGraw-Hill Education offers a robust custom publishing program, Create, that you may want to consider. Create enables you to build a book with only the chapters you need, and arrange them in the order you'll teach them. There's also the option of adding materials you prepare or using chapters from other McGraw-Hill books or resources from their library. When you build a Create book, you will receive a complimentary print review copy in just a few days or a complimentary eBook via email in about one hour.

Acknowledgments. We gratefully acknowledge the wisdom and counsel of many generous scholars whose intellectual capital is embedded in every page you'll read. Over the last 27 years, hundreds of communication scholars have gone out of their way to make the book better. People who have made direct contributions to this edition include Ron Adler, Santa Barbara City College; Ed Appel, Lock Haven University; Ryan Bisel, University of Oklahoma; Dan Brown, Grove City College; Kristen Carr, Texas Christian University; Ken Chase, Wheaton College; Stan Deetz, University of Colorado; Chip Eveland, Ohio State University; Darin Garard, Santa Barbara City College; Howard Giles, University of California, Santa Barbara; Cheris Kramarae, University of Oregon; Glen McClish, San Diego State University; Max McCombs, University of Texas; Marty Medhurst, Baylor University; Rebecca Meisenbach, University of Missouri; Melanie Mills, Eastern Illinois University; James Olufowote, Boston College; Mark Orbe, Western Michigan University; Doug Osman, Purdue University; Kim Pearce, CMM Institute for Personal and Social Evolution; Sandra Petronio, University of Indiana–Purdue University Indianapolis; Gerry Philipsen, University of Washington; Russ Proctor, Northern Kentucky University; Linda Putnam, University of California, Santa Barbara; Derrick Rosenoir, Vanguard University; Alan Rubin, Hebrew University of Jerusalem; Christa Sloan, Pepperdine University; Jordan Soliz, University of Nebraska; Stella Ting-Toomey, California State University, Fullerton; Mina Tsay, Boston University; Paul Witt, Texas Christian University; Robert Woods Jr., Spring Arbor University. Without their help, this edition would be less accurate and certainly less interesting.

Em has great appreciation for two Wheaton undergraduate research assistants. David Washko juggled his responsibilities while playing two seasons of varsity football at Wheaton. Laurel Porter constructed the comprehensive index that contains thousands of entries—a task no one should do more than once in life. Glenn is grateful for Lewis Day and Beth Stanley, two Purdue student production assistants who made recording his conversation with Sandra Petronio possible.

Our relationships with the professionals at McGraw-Hill have been highly satisfactory. Susan Gouijnstook was our initial Development Editor, but a maternity leave and well-deserved promotion to Director of Communication brought Adina Lonn to the Development Editor role. Both women were incredibly responsive to our needs, and their care for the entire project matched ours. They were backed up by Lisa Pinto, Executive Director of Development; David Patterson, Managing

Director; Penina Braffman, Managing Editor; Jessica Portz, Project Manager; and Jamie Daron, Brand Coordinator. Other authors are envious when they hear of our experience working with these professionals.

We've been fortunate to work closely with four outside contractors: Jenn Meyer, a commercial computer artist, created and revised figures on 24-hour notice; Judy Brody achieved the impossible by making the extensive permissions process enjoyable; Robyn Tellefsen, freelance writer and editor, was my student research assistant for the fourth edition of the book and proofreader for editions six through eight. When others saw her abilities and thoroughness, they recommended she be the copy editor for this edition. She also edited a book Glenn wrote. Robyn is quite familiar with communication theory and is someone whose edits we trust implicitly. Thus, the book your students read is better than the one we wrote. Rebecca Lazure is a project manager at SPi Global who took our comments on Robyn's edits and guided the manuscript and images through the production process and ultimately turned over the final digital package to the printer. She did it well and with grace.

We offer a special word of appreciation to Emily Langan, Em's former student who now teaches the courses he taught at Wheaton. This edition is Emily's fourth as writer of the ever-evolving Instructor's Manual that is famous among communication theory instructors. Em recalls the time when he first introduced Emily at a National Communication Association short course on teaching communication theory. The participants stood and applauded. Now, at the NCA short courses, she introduces Em. The three of us are grateful for her wisdom, dedication, creativity, and friendship.

Em Griffin
Andrew Ledbetter
Glenn Sparks

Overview

DIVISION ONE

Overview

CHAPTER 1

Launching Your Study of Communication Theory

This is a book about theories—communication theories. After that statement you may already be stifling a yawn. Many college students, after all, regard theory as obscure, dull, and irrelevant. People outside the classroom are even less charitable. An aircraft mechanic once chided a professor: "You academic types are all alike. Your heads are crammed so full of theory, you wouldn't know which end of a socket wrench to grab. Any plane you touched would crash and burn. All Ph.D. stands for is 'piled higher and deeper.'"

The mechanic could be right. Yet it's ironic that even in the process of knocking theory, he resorts to his own theory of cognitive overload to explain what he sees as the mechanical stupidity of scholars. I appreciate his desire to make sense of his world. Here's a man who spends a hunk of his life making sure that planes stay safely in the air until pilots are ready to land. When we really care about something, we should seek to answer the *why* and *what if* questions that always emerge. That was the message I heard from University of Arizona communication theorist Judee Burgoon when I talked with her in my series of interviews, *Conversations with Communication Theorists.*[1] If we care about the fascinating subject of communication, she suggested, we've got to "do theory."

WHAT IS A THEORY AND WHAT DOES IT DO?

In earlier editions I've used *theory* as "an umbrella term for all careful, systematic, and self-conscious discussion and analysis of communication phenomena," a definition offered by the late University of Minnesota communication professor Ernest Bormann.[2] I like this definition because it's general enough to cover the diverse theories presented in this book. Yet the description is so broad that it doesn't give us any direction on how we might construct a theory, nor does it offer a way to figure out when thoughts or statements about communication haven't attained that status. If I call any idea a "theory," does saying it's so make it so?

In my discussion with Judee Burgoon, she suggested that a theory is nothing more than a "set of systematic hunches about the way things operate."[3] Since Burgoon is the most frequently cited female scholar in the field of communication,

I was intrigued by her unexpected use of the nontechnical term *hunch.* Would it therefore be legitimate to entitle the book you're reading *Communication Hunches?* She assured me that it would, quickly adding that they should be "informed hunches." So for Burgoon, a theory consists of *a set of systematic, informed hunches about the way things work.* In the rest of this section, I'll examine the three key features of Burgoon's notion of a theory. First, I'll focus on the idea that theory consists of a *set of hunches.* But a set of hunches is only a starting point. Second, I'll discuss what it means to say that those hunches have to be *informed.* Last, I'll highlight the notion that the hunches have to be *systematic.* Let's look briefly at the meaning of each of these core concepts of theory.

A Set of Hunches

If a theory is a set of hunches, it means we aren't yet sure we have the answer. When there's no puzzle to be solved or the explanation is obvious, there's no need to develop a theory. Theories always involve an element of speculation, or conjecture. Being a theorist is risky business because theories go beyond accepted wisdom. Once you become a theorist, you probably hope that all thinking people will eventually embrace the trial balloon you've launched. When you first float your theory, however, it's definitely in the hunch category.

Theory
A set of systematic, informed hunches about the way things work.

By referring to a plural "set of hunches" rather than a single "hunch," Burgoon makes it clear that a theory is not just one inspired thought or an isolated idea. The young theorist in the cartoon may be quite sure that dogs and bees can smell fear, but that isolated conviction isn't a theory. A developed theory offers some sort of explanation. For example, how are bees and dogs able to sniff out fright? Perhaps the scent of sweaty palms that comes from high anxiety is qualitatively different than the odor of people perspiring from hard work. A theory will also give some indication of scope. Do only dogs and bees possess this keen sense of smell, or do butterflies and kittens have it as well? Theory construction involves multiple hunches.

Informed Hunches

Bormann's description of creating communication theory calls for a careful, self-conscious analysis of communication phenomena, but Burgoon's definition asks for more. It's not enough to think carefully about an idea; a theorist's hunches should be *informed.* Working on a hunch that a penny thrown from the Empire State Building will become deeply embedded in the sidewalk, the young theorist has a responsibility to check it out. Before developing a theory, there are articles to read, people to talk to, actions to observe, or experiments to run, all of which can cast light on the subject. At the very least, communication theorists should be familiar with alternative explanations and interpretations of the type of communication they are studying. (Young Theorist, have you heard the story of Galileo dropping balls from the Leaning Tower of Pisa?)

Pepperdine University communication professor Fred Casmir's description of theory parallels Burgoon's call for multiple informed hunches:

> Theories are sometimes defined as guesses—but significantly as "educated" guesses. Theories are not merely based on vague impressions nor are they accidental by-products of life. Theories tend to result when their creators have prepared themselves to discover something in their environment, which triggers the process of theory construction.[4]

Hunches That Are Systematic

Most scholars reserve the term *theory* for an integrated *system* of concepts. A theory not only lays out multiple ideas, but also specifies the relationships

• Can a theory ever become more than just a theory?

among them. In common parlance, it connects the dots. The links among the informed hunches are clearly drawn so that a pattern emerges.

None of the young theories in the cartoon rise to this standard. Since most of the nine are presented as one-shot claims, they aren't part of a conceptual framework. One possible exception is the dual speculation that "adults are really Martians, and they're up to no good." But the connecting word *and* doesn't really show the relationship between grown-ups' unsavory activity and their hypothesized other-world origin. To do that, the young theorist could speculate about the basic character of Martians, how they got here, why their behavior is suspicious, and whether today's youth will turn into aliens when they become parents. A theory would then tie all of these ideas together into a unified whole. As you read about any theory covered in this book, you have a right to expect a set of *systematic,* informed hunches.

Images of Theory

In response to the question *What is a theory?* I've presented a verbal definition. Many of us are visual learners as well and would appreciate a concrete image that helps us understand what a theory is and does. So I'll present three metaphors that I find helpful, but will also note how an over-reliance on these representations of theory might lead us astray.

Theories as Nets: Philosopher of science Karl Popper said that "theories are nets cast to catch what we call 'the world'. . . . We endeavor to make the mesh ever finer and finer."[5] I appreciate this metaphor because it highlights the ongoing labor of the theorist as a type of deep-sea angler. For serious scholars, theories are the tools of the trade. The term *the world* can be interpreted as everything that goes on under the sun—thus requiring a *grand* theory that applies to all communication, all the time. Conversely, catching the world could be construed as calling for numerous *special* theories—different kinds of small nets to capture distinct types of communication in local situations. Either way, the quest for finer-meshed nets is somewhat disturbing because the study of communication is about people rather than schools of fish. The idea that theories could be woven so tightly that they'd snag everything humans think, say, or do strikes me as naive. The possibility also raises questions about our freedom to choose some actions and reject others.

Theories as Lenses: Many scholars see their theoretical constructions as similar to the lens of a camera or a pair of glasses, as opposed to a mirror that accurately reflects the world out there. The lens imagery highlights the idea that theories shape our perception by focusing attention on some features of communication while ignoring other features, or at least pushing them into the background. Two theorists could analyze the same communication event—an argument, perhaps—and, depending on the lens each uses, one theorist may view the speech act as a breakdown of communication or the breakup of a relationship, while the other theorist will see it as democracy in action. For me, the danger of the lens metaphor is that we might regard what is seen through the glass as so dependent on the theoretical stance of the viewer that we abandon any attempt to discern what is real or true.

Theories as Maps: I use this image when I describe the *First Look* text to others. Within this analogy, communication theories are maps of the way communication works. The truth they depict may have to do with objective behaviors "out there" or subjective meanings inside our heads. Either way, we need to have theory to guide us through unfamiliar territory. In that sense, this book of theories is like a scenic atlas that pulls together 32 must-see locations. It's the kind of travel guide that presents a close-up view of each site. I would caution, however, that the map is not the territory.[6] A static theory, like a still photograph, can never fully portray the richness of interaction between people that is constantly changing, always more varied, and inevitably more complicated than what any theory can chart. As a person intrigued with communication, aren't you glad it's this way?

WHAT IS COMMUNICATION?

To ask this question is to invite controversy and raise expectations that can't be met. Frank Dance, the University of Denver scholar credited for publishing the first comprehensive book on communication theory, cataloged more than 120 definitions of *communication*—and that was more than 40 years ago.[7] Communication scholars have suggested many more since then, yet no single definition has risen to the top and become the standard within the field of communication. When it comes to defining what it is we study, there's little discipline in the discipline.

At the conclusion of his study, Dance suggested that we're "trying to make the concept of communication do too much work for us."[8] Other communication theorists agree, noting that when the term is used to describe almost every kind of human interaction, it's seriously overburdened. Michigan Tech University communication professor Jennifer Slack brings a splash of reality to attempts to draw definitive lines around what it is that our theories and research cover. She declares that "there is no single, absolute essence of communication that adequately explains the phenomena we study. Such a definition does not exist; neither is it merely awaiting the next brightest communication scholar to nail it down once and for all."[9]

Despite the pitfalls of trying to define *communication* in an all-inclusive way, it seems to me that students who are willing to spend a big chunk of their college education studying communication deserve a description of what it is they're looking at. Rather than giving the final word on what human activities can be legitimately referred to as *communication,* this designation would highlight the essential features of communication that shouldn't be missed. So for starters, I offer this working definition:

> *Communication is the relational process of creating and interpreting messages that elicit a response.*

To the extent that there is redeeming value in this statement, it lies in drawing your attention to five features of communication that you'll run across repeatedly as you read about the theories in the field. I'll flesh out these concepts in the rest of this section.

Communication
The relational process of creating and interpreting messages that elicit a response.

1. Messages

Messages are at the core of communication study. University of Colorado communication professor Robert Craig says that communication involves "talking and listening, writing and reading, performing and witnessing, or, more generally, doing anything that involves 'messages' in any medium or situation."[10]

When academic areas such as psychology, sociology, anthropology, political science, literature, and philosophy deal with human symbolic activity, they intersect with the study of communication. The visual image of this intersection of interests has prompted some to refer to communication as a *crossroads discipline.* The difference is that communication scholars are parked at the junction focusing on messages, whereas other disciplines are just passing through on their way to other destinations. All of the theories covered in this book deal specifically with messages.

Communication theorists use the word *text* as a synonym for a message that can be studied, regardless of the medium. This book is a text. So is a verbatim transcript of a conversation with your instructor, a recorded presidential news conference, a silent YouTube video, or a Justin Timberlake song on your iPod. To illustrate the following four parts of the definition, suppose you received this cryptic text message from a close, same-sex friend: "Pat and I spent the night together." You immediately know that the name Pat refers to the person with whom you have an ongoing romantic relationship. An analysis of this text and the context surrounding its transmission provides a useful case study for examining the essential features of communication.

Text
A record of a message that can be analyzed by others; for example, a book, film, photograph, or any transcript or recording of a speech or broadcast.

2. Creation of Messages

This phrase in the working definition of communication indicates that the content and form of a text are usually *constructed, invented, planned, crafted, constituted, selected,* or *adopted* by the communicator. Each of these terms is used in one or more of the theories I describe, and they all imply that the communicator is making a conscious choice of message form and substance. For whatever reason, your friend sent a text message rather than meeting face-to-face, calling you on the phone, sending an email, or writing a note. Your friend also chose the seven words that were transmitted to your cell phone. There is a long history of textual analysis in the field of communication, wherein the rhetorical critic looks for clues in the message to discern the motivation and strategy of the person who created the message.

There are, of course, many times when we speak, write, or gesture in seemingly mindless ways—activities that are like driving on cruise control. These are preprogrammed responses that were selected earlier and stored for later use. In like manner, our repertoire of stock phrases such as *thank you, no problem, whatever,* or a string of swear words were chosen sometime in the past to express our feelings, and over time have become habitual responses. Only when we become more mindful of the nature and impact of our messages will we have the ability to alter them. That's why consciousness-raising is a goal of five or six of the theories I'll present—each one seeks to increase our communication choices.

3. Interpretation of Messages

Messages do not interpret themselves. The meaning that a message holds for the creators and receivers doesn't reside in the words that are spoken, written, or acted out. A truism among communication scholars is that *words don't mean things, people mean things.* Symbolic interactionist Herbert Blumer stated its implication: "Humans act toward people or things on the basis of the meanings they assign to those people or things."[11]

What is the meaning of your friend's text message? Does "spent the night together" mean *talking until all hours? Pulling an all-night study session? Sleeping on the sofa? Making love?* If it's the latter, was Pat a *willing* or *unwilling partner* (perhaps drunk or the victim of acquaintance rape)? How would your friend characterize their sexual liaison? *Recreational sex? A chance hookup? Friends with benefits? Developing a close relationship? Falling in love? The start of a long-term commitment?* Perhaps of more importance to you, how does Pat view it? What emotional meaning is behind the message for each of them? *Satisfaction? Disappointment? Surprise? The morning-after-the-night-before blahs? Gratefulness? Guilt? Ecstasy?* And finally, what does receiving this message through a digital channel mean for you, your friendship, and your relationship with Pat? None of these answers are in the message. Words and other symbols are polysemic—they're open to multiple interpretations.

4. A Relational Process

The Greek philosopher Heraclitus observed that "one cannot step into the same river twice."[12] These words illustrate the widespread acceptance among communication scholars that communication is a *process*. Much like a river, the flow of communication is always in flux, never completely the same, and can only be described with reference to what went before and what is yet to come. This means that the text message "Pat and I spent the night together" is not the whole story. You'll probably contact both your friend and Pat to ask the clarifying questions raised earlier. As they are answered or avoided, you'll interpret the message in a different way. That's because communication is a process, not a freeze-frame snapshot.

In the opening lines of her essay "Communication as Relationality," University of Georgia rhetorical theorist Celeste Condit suggests that the communication process is more about relationships than it is about content.

> Communication is a process of relating. This means it is not primarily or essentially a process of transferring information or of disseminating or circulating signs (though these things can be identified as happening within the process of relating).[13]

Communication is a relational process not only because it takes place between two or more persons, but also because it affects the nature of the connections among those people. It's obvious that the text message you received will influence the triangle of relationships among you, Pat, and your (former?) friend. But this is true in other forms of mediated communication as well. Television viewers and moviegoers have emotional responses to people they see on-screen. And as businesses are discovering, even the impersonal recorded announcement that "this call may be monitored for quality assurance purposes" has an impact on how we regard their corporate persona.

5. Messages That Elicit a Response

This final component of communication deals with the effect of the message upon people who receive it. At the end of his groundbreaking book on communication theory, Dance concludes, "'Communication,' in its broadest interpretation, may be defined as the eliciting of a response."[14] If a message fails to stimulate any cognitive, emotional, or behavioral reaction, it seems pointless to refer to it as *communication.* We often refer to such situations as a message "falling on deaf ears" or the other person "turning a blind eye."

Picture a mother driving her 10-year-old son home from school. He's strapped in the seat behind her playing *Angry Birds* on his smartphone, equipped with earbuds. His mother asks if he has any homework. Is that communication? Not if he doesn't hear the question or see her lips moving. What if he isn't wired for sound and hears her voice? It depends. If he's glued to the screen and totally engrossed in wiping out pigs before they eat eggs, he may literally tune her out—still no communication.

Suppose, however, the boy hears her words and feels *bad* that he has homework, *sad* that his mom's so nosy, *mad* that she broke his game-playing concentration, or *glad* that he finished the assignment in study hall. Although these are internal feelings that his mother may miss, each response would have been triggered by Mom's question and would therefore qualify as communication. And of course any vocal response, even a noncommittal grunt, indicates that some form of communication has occurred.

In like manner, surely you would respond to your friend's cryptic message about the night spent with Pat—one way or another. In fact, the text seems to have been crafted and sent to provoke a response. How closely your thoughts, feelings, words, or actions would match what your friend expected or intended is another matter. Successful or not, the whole situation surrounding the text and context of the message fits the working definition of communication that we hope will help you frame your study of communication theory. *Communication is the relational process of creating and interpreting messages that elicit a response.*

AN ARRANGEMENT OF IDEAS TO AID COMPREHENSION

Now that you have a basic understanding of what a communication theory is, knowing how we've structured the book and arranged the theories can help you grasp their content. That's because we've organized the text to place a given theory in a conceptual framework and situational context before we present it. After this chapter, there are three more integrative chapters in the "Overview" division. For Chapter 2, I've asked co-author Glenn Sparks and another leading communication scholar to analyze a highly acclaimed TV ad in order to illustrate how half the theories in the book are based on *objective* assumptions, while the other half are constructed using an *interpretive* set of principles. Chapter 3 presents criteria for judging both kinds of theory so you can make an informed evaluation of a theory's worth rather than relying solely on your gut reaction. Finally, Chapter 4 describes seven traditions of communication theory and research. When you know the family tree of a theory, you can explain why it has a strong affinity with some theories but doesn't speak the same language as others.

Following this overview, there are 32 chapters that run 10–15 pages apiece, each concentrating on a single theory. we think you'll find that the one-chapter, one-theory format is user-friendly because it gives you a chance to focus on a single theory at a time. This way, they won't all blur together in your mind. These chapters are arranged into four major divisions according to the primary communication context that they address. The theories in Division Two, "Interpersonal Communication," consider one-on-one interaction. Division Three, "Group and Public Communication," deals with face-to-face involvement in collective settings. Division Four, "Mass Communication," pulls together theories that explore electronic and print media. Division Five, "Cultural Context," explores systems of shared meaning that are so all-encompassing that we often fail to realize their impact upon us.

These four divisions are based on the fact that theories are tentative answers to questions that occur to people as they mull over practical problems in specific situations. It therefore makes sense to group them according to the different communication settings that usually prompt those questions. This organizational plan is like having four separately indexed file cabinets. Although there is no natural progression from one division to another, the plan provides a convenient way to classify and retrieve the 32 theories.

Finally, Division Six, "Integration," seeks to distill core ideas that are common to a number of theories. Ideas have power, and each theory is driven by one or more ideas that may be shared by other theories from different communication contexts. For example, in each of the four context divisions, there's at least one theory committed to the force of narrative. They each declare that people respond to stories and dramatic imagery with which they can identify. Reading about key concepts that cut across multiple theories wouldn't mean much to you now, but after you become familiar with a number of communication theories, it can be an eye-opening experience that also helps you review what you've learned.

CHAPTER FEATURES TO ENLIVEN THEORY

In many of the chapters ahead, we use an extended example from life on a college campus, a well-known communication event, or the conversations of characters in movies, books, or TV shows. The main purpose of these illustrations is to provide a mind's-eye picture of how the theory works. The imagery will also make the basic thrust of the theory easier to recall. But if you can think of a situation in your own life where the theory is relevant, that personal application will make it doubly interesting and memorable for you.

You might also want to see how others put the theories into practice. With our students' permission, we've weaved in their accounts of application for almost all the theories featured in the text. We're intrigued by the rich connections these students make—ones we wouldn't have thought of on our own. Some students draw on scenes from short stories, novels, or movies. To see an annotated list of feature film scenes that illustrate the theories, go to the book's website, www.afirstlook.com, and under Theory Resources, click on Suggested Movie Clips. As co-authors of this book, we'll draw upon our life experiences as well. We've been professional colleagues for years and are close friends, so we'd like that warmth to extend to readers by writing in a direct, personal voice. That means using *I*, *my*, and *me* when referring to individual thoughts or stories from our lives. We think that's much better than stating them in the passive voice or referring to ourselves in an arms-length, third-person way. We don't use personal references in every chapter, but when we do, we want you to know whose voice you're "hearing."

The three of us contributed to every chapter and jointly edited the final version. But in each case one of us took the lead and wrote most of the words.

For the first four introductory chapters and more than half of the theory chapters, that was me. So unless you see a reference in a chapter that Andrew or Glenn is sharing his own ideas, feelings, or experiences, you can assume that the "I" refers to Em—just as it does in this chapter.

We also make a consistent effort to link each theory with its author. It takes both wisdom and courage to successfully plant a theoretical flag. In a process similar to the childhood game king-of-the-hill, as soon as a theorist constructs a theory of communication, critics try to pull it down. That's OK, because the value of a theory is discerned by survival in the rough-and-tumble world of competitive ideas. For this reason we always include a section in theory chapters labeled "Critique." Theorists who prevail deserve to have their names associated with their creations.

There is a second reason for tying a theory to its author. Many of you will do further study in communication, and a mastery of names like Deetz, Giles, Walther, Baxter, Berger, and Burke will allow you to enter into the dialogue without being at a disadvantage. Ignoring the names of theorists could prove to be false economy in the long run.

Don't overlook the three features at the end of each chapter. The queries under the title "Questions to Sharpen Your Focus" will help you mull over key points of the theory. They can be answered by pulling together information from this text and from the text of your life. The italicized words in each question highlight terms you need to know in order to understand the theory. Whenever you see a picture of the theorist, it's captured from one of our *Conversations with Communication Theorists* and shown alongside a brief description of what we talked about. You can view these 6- to 8-minute interviews at www.afirstlook.com. And the feature entitled "A Second Look" offers an annotated bibliography of resources should you desire to know more about the theory. You'll find it a good place to start if you are writing a research paper on the theory or are intrigued with a particular aspect of it.

You've already seen the last feature we'll mention. In every chapter and section introduction we include a cartoon for your learning and enjoyment. Cartoonists are often modern-day prophets. Their incisive wit can illustrate a feature of the theory in a way that's more instructive and memorable than a few extra paragraphs would be. In addition to enjoying their humor, you can use the cartoons as minitests of comprehension. Unlike my comments on "Young Theories" earlier in this chapter, we usually don't refer to the art or the caption that goes with it. So if you can't figure out why a particular cartoon appears where it does, make a renewed effort to grasp the theorist's ideas.

Some students are afraid to try. Like travelers whose eyes glaze over at the sight of a road map, they have a phobia about theories that seek to explain human intentions and behavior. We sympathize with their qualms and misgivings, but find that the theories in this book haven't dehydrated life or made it more confusing. On the contrary, they add clarity and provide a sense of competence as we communicate with others. We hope they do that for you as well.

Every so often a student will ask me, "Do you really think about communication theory when you're talking to someone?" My answer is "Yes, but not all the time." Like everyone else, I often speak on autopilot—words, phrases, sentences, descriptions rolling off my tongue without conscious thought. Old habits die hard. But when I'm in a new setting or the conversational stakes are high, I start to think strategically. And that's when the applied wisdom of theories that fit the situation comes to mind. By midterm, many of our students discover they're thinking that way as well. That's our wish for you as you launch your study of communication theory.

QUESTIONS TO SHARPEN YOUR FOCUS

1. Suppose you share the aircraft mechanic's suspicion that scholars who create theories would be all thumbs working on a plane's ailerons or engine. What would it take to transform your *hunch* into a *theory?*
2. Which *metaphor* of theory do you find most helpful—theory as a *net,* a *lens,* or a *map?* Can you think of another image that you could use to explain to a friend what this course is about?
3. Suppose you want to study the effects of yawns during intimate conversations. Would your research fall under *communication* as defined as the *relational process of creating and interpreting messages to elicit a response?* If not, how would you change the definition to make it include your interest?
4. You come to this course with a vast array of communication experiences in *interpersonal, group and public, mass media,* and *intercultural contexts.* What are the communication *questions* you want to answer, *puzzles* you want to solve, *problems* you want to fix?

A SECOND LOOK

Recommended resource: Gregory Shepherd, Jeffrey St. John, and Ted Striphas (eds.), *Communication as . . . Perspectives on Theory,* Sage, Thousand Oaks, CA, 2006.

Diverse definitions of communication: Frank E. X. Dance, "The Concept of Communication," *Journal of Communication,* Vol. 20, 1970, pp. 201–210.

Communication as human symbolic interaction: Gary Cronkhite, "On the Focus, Scope and Coherence of the Study of Human Communication," *Quarterly Journal of Speech,* Vol. 72, No. 3, 1986, pp. 231–246.

Theories of communication as practical: J. Kevin Barge, "Practical Theory as Mapping, Engaged Reflection, and Transformative Practice," *Communication Theory,* Vol. 11, 2001, pp. 5–13.

Multidimensional view of theory: James A. Anderson and Geoffrey Baym, "Philosophies and Philosophic Issues in Communication, 1995–2004," *Journal of Communication,* Vol. 54, 2004, pp. 589–615.

To access 50 word summaries of theories featured in the book, see Appendix A or click on Theory Overview under Theory Resources at *www.afirstlook.com.*

CHAPTER 2

Talk About Theory

I met Glenn Sparks and Marty Medhurst my first year teaching at Wheaton College. Glenn and Marty were friends who signed up for my undergraduate persuasion course. As students, both men were interested in broadcast media. After graduating from Wheaton, each went on for a master's degree at Northern Illinois University. Each earned a doctorate at a different university, and both are now nationally recognized communication scholars. Marty is on the faculty at Baylor University; Glenn is at Purdue University and is a co-author of this book.

Despite their similar backgrounds and interests, Glenn and Marty are quite different in their approaches to communication. Glenn calls himself a *behavioral scientist*, while Marty refers to himself as a *rhetorician*. Glenn's training was in empirical research; Marty was schooled in rhetorical theory and criticism. Glenn conducts experiments; Marty interprets texts.

Behavioral scientist
A scholar who applies the scientific method to describe, predict, and explain recurring forms of human behavior.

Rhetorician
A scholar who studies the ways in which symbolic forms can be used to identify with people, or to persuade them toward a certain point of view.

To understand the theories ahead, you need to first grasp the crucial differences between the objective and interpretive approaches to communication. As a way to introduce the distinctions, I asked Glenn and Marty to bring their scholarship to bear on a television commercial that first aired during Super Bowl XLVII, the game where the lights went out. It's a stealth ad for beer that doesn't show booze on a beach, men in a bar flirting with a waitress serving brew, or a guy tapping a keg yelling, "Party all night!" These are typical images that turn off a significant portion of viewers who see them as silly, distasteful, or unethical. That's because those ads appear to promote the dangerous practice of binge drinking among young adults as a way to gain acceptance or get a buzz. Instead, this ad portrays the bond that develops between a shaggy-hooved Clydesdale horse and his young trainer.[1]

TWO COMMUNICATION SCHOLARS VIEW A HEARTWARMING AD

Using no dialogue or voice-over, the Super Bowl commercial tells a visual story in 60 seconds. We see scenes of the newborn foal, his trainer asleep in the sick colt's stall, horseplay between them as the animal gains stature, and the fully grown animal running free alongside the trainer's truck. When it's time for this magnificent animal to become part of a working team of Clydesdales promoting beer, the trainer leads him into the company's horse van and gazes wistfully as it disappears down the road.

Three years later, the man discovers the Clydesdales will be in a Chicago parade and drives to the city to reconnect with his horse. He smiles with pride as the horse prances by, but blinders keep the animal from seeing him. As the trainer walks sadly back to his truck, the harness is removed and the horse catches a glimpse of him. The final shots show the Clydesdale galloping down the street to catch up with his human friend, who then buries his face in the horse's mane as they are reunited.

Since the sponsor spent $7 million to air this one-minute commercial—and more than that to film it—its marketing department obviously believed that featuring this huge draft horse would sell huge amounts of draft beer. There's no doubt that most critics and viewers liked the ad. *Advertising Age* analyst Ken Wheaton concludes, "Weepy, sentimental, nostalgic. I don't care. This is everything I want from a Budweiser Super Bowl spot."[2] Yet as you'll see, social scientist Glenn and rhetorical critic Marty take different theoretical approaches as they analyze the intent of the ad and how it works.

Glenn: An Objective Approach

Objective approach The assumption that truth is singular and is accessible through unbiased sensory observation; committed to uncovering cause-and-effect relationships.

After the 2013 Super Bowl ended, a research company announced that the Clydesdale ad was the year's commercial winner.[3] The researchers tracked 400 viewers who used a phone app to express their feelings during the broadcast. Viewers' liking for the Clydesdale ad was on par with what they felt when their favorite team scored a touchdown. Social scientists wonder why the commercial produced so much positive sentiment and whether it resulted in action. They want to explain and predict human behavior.

How do scientists satisfy these interests? After observing behavior, we identify or construct a theory that offers insight into what we've observed. In this case, advertising guru Tony Schwartz' *resonance principle of communication* is a promising theoretical idea.[4] Although Schwartz passed away in 2008, his theory lives on.

According to Schwartz, successful persuasive messages evoke past experiences that create *resonance* between the message content and a person's thoughts or feelings. Schwartz believed that resonance leads to persuasion. It's not *arguments* that persuade people as much as it is *memories* of personal experiences triggered by the message.

The heartwarming story of a worker dedicated to a horse he loves may tap into viewers' deep memories of their own devotion to animals they once nurtured. The emotional scene at the end of the ad might stir reminiscence of your pet's excitement when you would return home or the tremendous relief at being reunited with one you thought lost. Once these good feelings are evoked, Schwartz believed people associate them with the advertised product. For beer drinkers, those good feelings may lead to more sales. For viewers who see drinking beer as a health risk, the good feelings may lead to positive thoughts about a company that seems to care not only about selling beer, but also about taking good care of those splendid Clydesdales. In this case, persuasion may be measured both in beer sales and positive thoughts about Budweiser—a company well aware that its success may lead to alcohol abuse among consumers and a bad corporate reputation.

Theories need to be validated. For scientists, it's not enough to identify a theory that seems to apply to the situation. We want an objective test to find out if a theory is faulty. For example, I'd want to discover if commercials that trigger warm emotional memories are better than other ads at selling products or generating good feelings toward the sponsor. Testing audience response is a crucial scientific enterprise. Even though a theory might sound plausible, we can't be sure it's valid until it's been tested. In science, theory and research walk hand in hand.

Marty: An Interpretive Approach

Interpretive approach The linguistic work of assigning meaning or value to communicative texts; assumes that multiple meanings or truths are possible.

There is more going on here than a simple reunion of man and horse. The entire ad is structured by an archetypal mythic pattern of birth-death-rebirth. Archetypal myths are those that draw upon a universal experience—what psychoanalyst Carl Jung called the "collective unconscious."[5] Deep within the mental makeup of all human beings is the archetype of the birth-death-rebirth cycle. The use of such archetypes, according to rhetorical theorist Michael Osborn, touches off "depth responses" that emotionally resonate at the core of our being.[6] The ad activates these emotions by incorporating the form of the cycle within a mini-narrative.

We first see the newborn colt in the barn as the breeder feeds him, strokes his coat, and even sleeps next to him in the stall. Birth naturally leads to growth, as we watch the colt mature before our eyes. But just as this Clydesdale grows to full stature, the Budweiser 18-wheeler arrives to take away the treasured horse. Symbolically, this is a death because it represents an absence or void. What once was is no more. Then, three years later, the breeder and his horse are reunited in an act of rebirth. The former relationship, which had been shattered by the symbolic death, is now restored with the reunion of man and horse.

It is significant that the passage of time is three years. Just as Christians believe Jesus lay in the tomb for three days before his resurrection, so the horse is gone for three years before he reappears. But once he reemerges, it is as though he never left. That which was lost has been found. The emotions evoked by this ad are strong because we are dealing with life and death, with loss and restoration. All of us unconsciously long for a reunion with those people or things in our lives that have been most important to us. Even the music—"Landslide" by Fleetwood Mac—underscores the archetypal pattern, as it speaks of love, loss, change, and being afraid. Fear of death is a primordial human instinct. It is only through a rebirth that we can reclaim what time and change have taken from us.

The ad subtly suggests that Budweiser beer is our constant mainstay. Life changes and losses happen, but Bud never changes, never disappears. We see that in the shots of the beer bottle on the breeder's table as he reads about the upcoming parade in Chicago. Bud is portrayed as our companion and our comforter, something that will be with us through the dark nights of separation and loss.

OBJECTIVE OR INTERPRETIVE WORLDVIEWS: SORTING OUT THE LABELS

Although both of these scholars focus on the warm feelings viewers have when seeing the Budweiser Clydesdale ad, Glenn's and Marty's approaches to communication study clearly differ in starting point, method, and conclusion. Glenn is a social *scientist* who works hard to be *objective.* When I refer to theorists and researchers like Glenn throughout the book, I'll use the terms *scientist* and *objective scholar* interchangeably. Marty is a *rhetorical critic* who does *interpretive* study. Here the labels get tricky.

While it's true that all rhetorical critics do interpretive analysis, not all interpretive scholars are rhetoricians. Most (including Marty) are *humanists* who study what it's like to be another person in a specific time and place. But a growing number of postmodern communication theorists reject that tradition. These interpretive scholars refer to themselves with a bewildering variety of brand names: hermeneuticists, poststructuralists, deconstructivists, phenomenologists, cultural studies researchers, and social action theorists, as well as combinations of these terms. Writing from this postmodernist perspective, University of Utah theorist James Anderson observes:

Humanistic scholarship
Study of what it's like to be another person in a specific time and place; assumes there are few important panhuman similarities.

> With this very large number of interpretive communities, names are contentious, border patrol is hopeless and crossovers continuous. Members, however, often see real differences.[7]

All of these scholars, including Marty, do interpretive analysis—scholarship concerned with meaning—yet there's no common term like *scientist* that includes them all. So from this point on I'll use the designation *interpretive scholars* or the noun form *interpreters* to refer to the entire group, and use *rhetoricians, humanists, postmodernists,* or *critical scholars* only when I'm singling out a particular subgroup.

The separate worldviews of interpretive scholars and scientists reflect contrasting assumptions about ways of arriving at knowledge, the core of human nature, questions of value, and the purpose of having theory. The rest of this chapter sketches out these differences.

WAYS OF KNOWING: DISCOVERING TRUTH OR CREATING MULTIPLE REALITIES?

How do we know what we know, if we know it at all? This is the central question addressed by a branch of philosophy known as *epistemology*. You may have been in school for a dozen-plus years, read assignments, written papers, and taken tests without ever delving into the issue *What is truth?* With or without in-depth study of the issue, however, we all inevitably make assumptions about the nature of knowledge.

Epistemology
The study of the origin, nature, method, and limits of knowledge.

Scientists assume that Truth is singular. They see a single, timeless reality "out there" that's not dependent on local conditions. It's waiting to be discovered through the five senses of sight, sound, touch, taste, and smell. Since the raw sensory data of the world is accessible to any competent observer, science seeks to be bias-free, with no ax to grind. The evidence speaks for itself. As Galileo observed, anyone could see through his telescope. Of course, no one person can know it all, so individual researchers pool their findings and build a collective body of knowledge about how the world works.

Scientists consider good theories to be those that are faithful representations of the way the world really is. Of the metaphors introduced in Chapter 1, they like the image of theory as a mirror that reflects reality, or a net that captures part of it. Objective theorists are confident that once a principle is discovered and validated, it will continue to hold true as long as conditions remain relatively the same. That's why Glenn believes the theory of resonance can explain why other media messages succeed or fail.

Interpretive scholars seek truth as well, but many interpreters regard that truth as socially constructed through communication. They believe language creates social realities that are always in flux rather than revealing or representing fixed principles or relationships in a world that doesn't change. Knowledge is always viewed from a particular standpoint. A word, a gesture, or an act may have constancy within a given community, but it's dangerous to assume that interpretations can cross lines of time and space.

Texts never interpret themselves. Most of these scholars, in fact, hold that truth is largely subjective—that meaning is highly interpretive. But rhetorical critics like Marty are not relativists, arbitrarily assigning meaning on a whim. They do maintain, however, that objectivity is a myth; we can never entirely separate the knower from the known.

Convinced that meaning is in the mind rather than in the verbal sign, interpreters are comfortable with the notion that a text may have multiple meanings. Rhetorical critics are successful when they get others to view a text through their interpretive lens—to adopt a new perspective on the world. For example, did Marty convince you that the Budweiser ad draws upon a deep-seated pattern of birth-death-rebirth ingrained in all of us? As Anderson notes, "Truth is a struggle, not a status."[8]

HUMAN NATURE: DETERMINISM OR FREE WILL?

One of the great philosophical debates throughout history revolves around the question of human choice.[9] Hard-line *determinists* claim that every move we make is the result of heredity ("biology is destiny") and environment ("pleasure stamps in, pain stamps out"). On the other hand, free-will purists insist that every human act is ultimately voluntary ("I am the master of my fate: I am the captain of my soul"[10]). Although few communication theorists are comfortable with either extreme, most tend to line up on one side or the other. Scientists stress the forces that shape human behavior; interpretive scholars focus on conscious choices made by individuals.

Determinism
The assumption that behavior is caused by heredity and environment.

The difference between these two views of human nature inevitably creeps into the language people use to explain what they do. Individuals who feel like puppets on strings say, "I *had* to . . . ," whereas people who feel they pull their own strings say, "I *decided* to. . . ." The first group speaks in a passive voice: "I was distracted from studying by the argument at the next table." The second group speaks in an active voice: "I stopped studying to listen to the argument at the next table."

In the same way, the language of scholarship often reflects theorists' views of human nature. Behavioral scientists usually describe human conduct as occurring *because of* forces outside the individual's awareness. Their causal explanations tend not to include appeals to mental reasoning or conscious choice. They usually describe behavior as the response to a prior stimulus. Schwartz' theory of resonance posits that messages triggering emotional memories from our past will inevitably affect us. We *will* be swayed by an ad that strikes a responsive chord.

In contrast, interpretive scholars tend to use explanatory phrases such as *in order to* and *so that* because they attribute a person's action to conscious intent. Their word selection suggests that people are free agents who could decide to respond differently under an identical set of circumstances. Marty, for example, uses the language of voluntary *action* rather than knee-jerk *behavior* when he writes, "It is only through a rebirth that we can reclaim what time and change have taken from us." If someone *reclaims* what was lost, it is an act of volition. The trainer decided to go to Chicago. Others who felt loss might not. The consistent interpreter

doesn't ask why this man made that choice. As Anderson explains, "True choice demands to be its own cause and its own explanation."[11]

Human choice is problematic for the behavioral scientist because as individual freedom goes up, predictability of behavior goes down. Conversely, the roots of humanism are threatened by a highly restricted view of human choice. In an impassioned plea, British author C. S. Lewis exposes the paradox of stripping away people's freedom and yet expecting them to exercise responsible choice:

> In a sort of ghastly simplicity we remove the organ and expect of them virtue and enterprise. We laugh at honor and are shocked to find traitors in our midst. We castrate and bid the geldings be fruitful.[12]

Lewis assumes that significant decisions are value laden; interpretive scholars would agree.

THE HIGHEST VALUE: OBJECTIVITY OR EMANCIPATION?

When we talk about values, we are discussing priorities, questions of relative worth.[13] Values are the traffic lights of our lives that guide what we think, feel, and do. The professional values of communication theorists reflect the commitments they've made concerning knowledge and human nature. Since most social scientists hold to a distinction between the "knower" and the "known," they place value on objectivity that's not biased by ideological commitments. Because humanists and others in the interpretive camp believe that the ability to choose is what separates humanity from the rest of creation, they value scholarship that expands the range of free choice.

As a behavioral scientist, Glenn works hard to maintain his objectivity. He is a man with strong moral and spiritual convictions, and these may influence the topics he studies. But he doesn't want his personal values to distort reality or confuse what *is* with what he thinks *ought to be.* As you can see from Glenn's call for objective testing, he is frustrated when theorists offer no *empirical evidence* for their claims or don't even suggest a way in which their ideas could be validated by an independent observer. He is even more upset when he hears of researchers who fudge the findings of their studies to shore up questionable hypotheses. Glenn shares the research values of Harvard sociologist George Homans—to let the evidence speak for itself: "When nature, however stretched out on the rack, still has a chance to say 'no'—then the subject is science."[14]

Empirical evidence
Data collected through direct observation.

Marty is aware of his own ideology and is not afraid to bring his values to bear upon a communication text and come under scrutiny. He doesn't take an overtly critical stance toward advertising or the capitalist system. But his insight of Bud framed as a constant companion and comforter gives us the resource to laugh at the irony of hugging a bottle of beer whenever we feel lonely or a sense of loss.

Critical interpreters value socially relevant research that seeks to liberate people from oppression of any sort—economic, political, religious, emotional, or any other. They decry the detached stance of scientists who refuse to take responsibility for the results of their work. Whatever the pursuit—a Manhattan Project to split the atom, a Genome Project to map human genes, or a class project to analyze the effectiveness of an ad—critical interpreters insist that knowledge is never neutral. "There is no safe harbor in which researchers can avoid the power structure."[15]

In the heading for this section, I've contrasted the primary values of scientific and interpretive scholars by using the labels *objectivity* and *emancipation.* University of Colorado communication professor Stan Deetz frames the issue somewhat differently. He says that every general communication theory has two priorities—*effectiveness* and *participation.*[16] Effectiveness is concerned with successfully communicating information, ideas, and meaning to others. It also includes persuasion. Participation is concerned with increasing the possibility that all points of view will affect collective decisions and individuals being open to new ideas. It also encourages difference, opposition, and independence. The value question is *Which concern has higher priority?* Objective theorists usually foreground effectiveness and relegate participation to the background. Interpretive theorists tend to focus on participation and downplay effectiveness.

Emancipation
Liberation from any form of political, economic, racial, religious, or sexual oppression; empowerment.

PURPOSE OF THEORY: UNIVERSAL LAWS OR INTERPRETIVE GUIDES?

Even if Glenn and Marty could agree on the nature of knowledge, the extent of human autonomy, and the ultimate values of scholarship, their words would still sound strange to each other because they use distinct vocabularies to accomplish different goals. As a behavioral scientist, Glenn is working to pin down universal laws of human behavior that cover a variety of situations. As a rhetorical critic, Marty strives to interpret a particular communication text in a specific context.

If these two scholars were engaged in fashion design rather than research design, Glenn would probably tailor a coat suitable for many occasions that covers everybody well—one size fits all. Marty might apply principles of fashion design to style a coat that makes an individual statement for a single client—a one-of-a-kind, custom creation. Glenn adopts a theory and then tests it to see if it covers everyone. Marty uses theory to make sense of unique communication events.

Since theory testing is the basic activity of the behavioral scientist, Glenn starts with a hunch about how the world works—perhaps the idea that stories are more persuasive than arguments. He then crafts a tightly worded hypothesis that temporarily commits him to a specific prediction. As an empiricist, he can never completely "prove" that he has made the right gamble; he can only show in test after test that his behavioral bet pays off. If repeated studies uphold his hypothesis, he can more confidently predict which media ads will be effective, explain why, and make recommendations on how practitioners can craft messages that stir up memories.

The interpretive scholar explores the web of meaning that constitutes human existence. When Marty creates scholarship, he isn't trying to prove theory. However, he sometimes uses the work of rhetorical theorists like Michael Osborn to inform his interpretation of the aural and visual texts of people's lives. Robert Ivie, former editor of the *Quarterly Journal of Speech,* suggests that rhetorical critics ought to use theory this way:

> We cannot conduct rhetorical criticism of social reality without benefit of a guiding rhetorical theory that tells us generally what to look for in social practice, what to make of it, and whether to consider it significant.[17]

OBJECTIVE OR INTERPRETIVE: WHY IS IT IMPORTANT?

Why is it important to grasp the differences between objective and interpretive scholarship? The first answer is because you can't fully understand a theory if you aren't familiar with its underlying assumptions about *truth, human nature,* the *purpose of the theory,* and its *values.* If you're clueless, things can get confusing fast. It's like the time my wife, Jeanie, and I were walking around the Art Institute of Chicago, enjoying the work of French impressionists who painted realistic scenes that I could recognize. Then I wandered into a room dedicated to abstract expressionism. The paintings seemed bizarre and made no sense to me. I was bewildered and somewhat disdainful until Jeanie, who is an artist, explained the goals these painters had and the techniques they used to achieve them. So too with interpretive and objective communication theories. Right now you are probably more familiar and comfortable with one approach than you are with the other. But when you understand what each type of theorist is about, your comfort zone will expand and your confusion will diminish.

Metatheory
Theory about theory; the stated or inherent assumptions made when creating a theory.

There's another reason to master these *metatheoretical* differences. After exposure to a dozen or more theories, you may find that they begin to blur together in your mind. Classifying them as scientific or interpretive is a good way to keep them straight. It's somewhat like sorting 52 cards into suits—spades, hearts, diamonds, and clubs. In most sophisticated card games, the distinction is crucial. By the end of this course you could have up to 32 cards in your deck of communication theories. Being able to sort them in multiple combinations is a good way to show yourself and your professor that you've mastered the material. When you can compare and contrast theories on the basis of their interpretive or objective worldview, you've begun an integration that's more impressive than rote memorization.

Understanding the objective/interpretive choice points I've described can also help you decide the direction you want to take in your remaining course work. Some concentrations in the field of communication tend to have either a scientific or an interpretive bias. For example, all the theories we present in the relationship development, influence, and media effects sections of the book are proposed by objective scholars. Conversely, most of the theories we cover in the public rhetoric, media and culture, organizational communication, and gender and communication sections are interpretive. You'll want to see if this is true at your school before you choose the specific route you'll take.

Finally, theorists in both camps hope you'll care because each group believes that its brand of work holds promise for improving relationships and society. The scientist is convinced that knowing the truth about how communication works will give us a clearer picture of social reality. The interpreter is equally sure that unearthing communicator motivation and hidden ideologies will improve society by increasing free choice and discouraging unjust practices.

PLOTTING THEORIES ON AN OBJECTIVE–INTERPRETIVE SCALE

In this chapter I've introduced four important areas of difference between objective and interpretive communication scholars and the theories they create. A basic appreciation of these distinctions will help you understand where like-minded thinkers are going and why they've chosen a particular path to get there. But once you grasp how they differ, it will be helpful for you to realize that not all theorists fall neatly into one category or the other. Many have a foot in both camps. It's more accurate to picture the *objective* and *interpretive* labels as anchoring the ends of a continuum, with theorists spread out along the scale.

Objective ____ **Interpretive**

Figure 2–1 displays our evaluation of where each theory we feature fits on an objective–interpretive continuum. For easier reference to positions on the scale, we've numbered the five columns at the bottom of the chart. In placing a theory, we've tried to factor in choices the theorists have made about ways of knowing, human nature, what they value most, and the purpose of theory. We've consulted a number of scholars in the field to get their "read" on appropriate placements. They didn't always agree, but in most cases the discussion has sharpened our understanding of theory and the issues to be considered in the process of creating one. What we learned is reflected in the chapters ahead.

Of course, the position of each dot won't make much sense to you until you've read about the theory. But by looking at the pattern of distribution, you can see that roughly half the theories have an objective orientation, while the other half reflect an interpretive commitment. This 50–50 split matches the mix of scholarship we see in the field. When talking about relationships among the theories and the common assumptions made by a group of

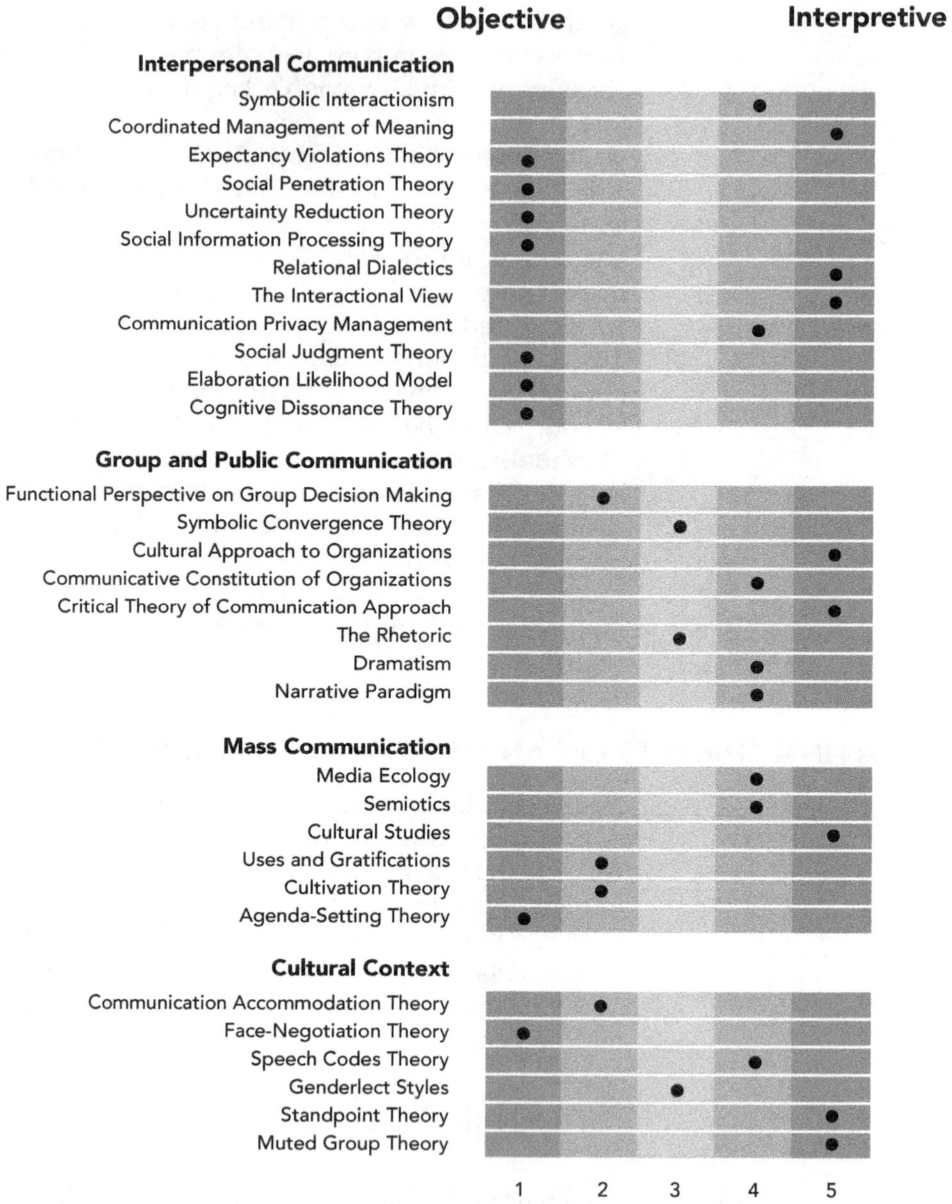

FIGURE 2–1 Classification of Communication Theories According to Objective/Interpretive Worldview

theorists, your instructor may frequently refer back to this chart. So for easy reference, we reproduce the appropriate "slice" of the chart on the first page of each chapter.

Now that you have an idea of the differences between objective and interpretive theories, you may wonder whether some of these theories are better than others. We think so. Chapter 3, "Weighing the Words," offers a set of six standards you can use to judge the quality of objective theories, and a half dozen alternative criteria to discern the worth of interpretive theories. By applying the appropriate criteria, you can see if you agree with our evaluations.

QUESTIONS TO SHARPEN YOUR FOCUS

1. Compare Glenn Sparks' and Marty Medhurst's approaches to the Clydesdale commercial. Which analysis makes the most sense to you? Why?
2. How do scientists and interpretive scholars differ in their answers to the question *What is truth?* Which perspective do you find more satisfying?
3. How do you account for the wide-ranging diversity among types of interpretive theories (*rhetorical, critical, humanistic, postmodern,* etc.) as compared to the relative uniformity of objective theories?
4. Think of the communication classes you've taken. Did an *objective* or *interpretive* orientation undergird each course? Was this due more to the nature of the subject matter or to the professor's point of view?

A SECOND LOOK

Recommended resource: James A. Anderson and Geoffrey Baym, "Philosophies and Philosophic Issues in Communication 1995–2004," *Journal of Communication,* Vol. 54, 2004, pp. 589–615.

Metatheoretical overview: James A. Anderson, *Communication Theory: Epistemological Foundations,* Guilford, New York, 1996, pp. 13–77.

Metatheory: Robert T. Craig, "Metatheory," in *Encyclopedia of Communication Theory,* Sage, Los Angeles, CA, 2009, pp. 657–661.

Contemporary scientific scholarship: Charles Berger, Michael Roloff, and David Roskos-Ewoldsen (eds.), *Handbook of Communication Science,* 2nd ed., Sage, Los Angeles, CA, 2010.

Contemporary rhetorical scholarship: Sonja Foss, Karen Foss, and Robert Trapp, *Contemporary Perspectives on Rhetoric,* 3rd ed., Waveland, Prospect Heights, IL, 2000.

Defense of empirical scholarship: Robert Bostrom and Lewis Donohew, "The Case for Empiricism: Clarifying Fundamental Issues in Communication Theory," *Communication Monographs,* Vol. 59, 1992, pp. 109–129.

Defense of interpretive scholarship: Arthur Bochner, "Perspectives on Inquiry II: Theories and Stories," in *Handbook of Interpersonal Communication,* 2nd ed., Mark Knapp and Gerald Miller (eds.), Sage, Thousand Oaks, CA, 1994, pp. 21–41.

Scientific research: Glenn Sparks, *Media Effects Research: A Basic Overview,* 4th ed., Wadsworth, Belmont, CA, 2013.

Rhetorical analysis: Martin J. Medhurst, "Mitt Romney, 'Faith in America,' and the Dance of Religion and Politics in American Culture," *Rhetoric & Public Affairs,* Vol. 12, 2009, pp. 195–221.

For a historical perspective on the place of objective and interpretive theory in the field of communication, click on Talk about Theory in the Archive under Theory Resources at *www.afirstlook.com.*

CHAPTER 3

Weighing the Words

In Chapter 2 we looked at two distinct approaches to communication theory—objective and interpretive. Because the work of social scientists and interpreters is so different, they often have trouble understanding and valuing their counterparts' scholarship. This workplace tension parallels the struggle between Democrats and Republicans. Members of both political parties study the same financial reports, projected statistics, and potential solutions for fixing the nation's economic woes. Nevertheless, when it comes to proposing a plan of action, the two parties are often miles apart. The distance is usually due to the different assumptions each party uses to guide its thinking. Their philosophies can be so divergent that significant agreement seems impossible, and meaningful compromise only a pipe dream.

In politics, when it gets down to the nitty-gritty of adopting specific proposals and passing concrete laws, the partisan bickering can make the conversation tense. The same can be said of the disputes that are common between objective and interpretive communication scholars. Differences in ways of knowing, views of human nature, values, goals of theory building, and research methods seem to ensure tension and misunderstanding.

Friendly attitudes between empiricists and interpreters are particularly hard to come by when each group insists on applying its own standards of judgment to the work of the other group. As a first-time reader of communication theory, you could easily get sucked into making the same mistake. If you've had training in the scientific method and judge the value of every communication theory by whether it predicts human behavior, you'll automatically reject 50 percent of the theories presented in this book. On the other hand, if you've been steeped in the humanities and expect every theory to help unmask the meaning of a text, you'll easily dismiss the other half.

Regardless of which approach you favor, not all objective or interpretive communication theories are equally good. For each type, some are better than others. Like family members trying to decide which pizza to order, you'll want a way to separate the good, the bad, and the nasty. Since we've included theories originating in the social sciences as well as the humanities, you need to have two separate lenses through which to view their respective claims. This chapter offers that pair of bifocals. We hope by the time you finish you'll be on friendly terms with the separate criteria that behavioral scientists and a wide range of interpretive scholars use to weigh the words of their colleagues. We'll start with the standards that social scientists use to judge the worth of objective theories, and then turn to the criteria that interpretive scholars employ to evaluate their communication theories.

WHAT MAKES AN OBJECTIVE THEORY GOOD?

An objective theory is credible because it fulfills the twin objectives of scientific knowledge. The theory *predicts* some future outcome, and it *explains* the reasons for that outcome. Social scientists of all kinds agree on four additional criteria a theory must meet to be good—*relative simplicity, testability, practical utility,* and *quantifiable research.* As we discuss these standards, we will use the terms *objective* and *scientific* interchangeably.

Scientific Standard 1: Prediction of Future Events

A good objective theory predicts what will happen. Prediction is possible only when we are dealing with things we can see, hear, touch, smell, and taste over and over again. As we repeatedly notice the same things happening in similar situations, we begin to speak of invariable patterns or universal laws. In the realm of the physical sciences, we are seldom embarrassed. Objects don't have a choice about how to respond to a stimulus. The sun can't choose to rise in the west instead of the east.

The social sciences are another matter. Although theories of human behavior often cast their predictions with confidence, a good measure of humility on the part of the theorist is advisable. Even the best theory may only be able to speak about people in general, rather than about specific individuals—and these only in terms of probability and tendencies, not absolute certainty.

What do good scientific communication theories forecast? Some predict that a specific type of communication triggers a particular response. (Mutual self-disclosure creates interpersonal intimacy.) Other theories predict that people will use different types of communication depending upon some pre-existing factor. (People avoid messages that they think will be disagreeable so they won't experience cognitive dissonance.) These claims may or may not be true, but you should regard the scientific theories presented in this book as valuable to the extent that theorists are willing to make confident predictions about communication behavior.

Scientific Standard 2: Explanation of the Data

A good objective theory explains an event or human behavior. Philosopher of science Abraham Kaplan said that theory is a way of making sense out of a disturbing situation.[1] An objective theory should bring clarity to an otherwise jumbled state of affairs; it should draw order out of chaos.

A good social science theory describes the process, focuses our attention on what's crucial, and helps us ignore that which makes little difference. But it also goes beyond raw data and explains *why.* When Willie Sutton was asked why he robbed banks, urban legend says the Depression-era bandit replied, "Because that's where the money is." It's a great line, but as a theory of motivation, it lacks explanatory power. There's nothing in the words that casts light on the internal processes or environmental forces that led Sutton to crack a safe while others tried to crack the stock market.

Sometimes a communication theory can sound great but, upon closer inspection, it doesn't explain much. Years ago, researchers discovered that by having people answer a few key questions about the emotions they felt prior to giving a speech, they could predict which people would be the most nervous or apprehensive during the talk itself. A theory based on the research claimed that *communication apprehension* was a trait only some people possess. The theory had great predictive power in identifying nervous public speakers, but it lacked a good explanation for why some people became nervous and others didn't.[2] It merely suggested that nervous speakers possessed the trait of communication apprehension.

You can probably sense that this circular thinking leaves something to be desired. How do people acquire the trait? Are they born with it? Can they get rid of it through some type of intervention? Over the past few decades, theorists have grappled with the question of how well "trait" theories explain behavior.[3] If the rationale behind why people engage in certain behaviors is simply *That's the kind of people they are,* objective scholars won't be happy with the theory's explanatory power. As a student of communication theory, you shouldn't be either. When you evaluate an objective theory, keep in mind that the *reason* something happens becomes as important as the fact that it does.

Scientific Standard 3: Relative Simplicity

A good objective theory is as simple as possible—no more complex than it has to be. A few decades ago a cartoonist named Rube Goldberg made people laugh by sketching plans for complicated machines that performed simple tasks. His "better mousetrap" went through a sequence of 15 mechanical steps that were triggered by turning a crank and ended with a bird cage dropping over a cheese-eating mouse.

Goldberg's designs were funny because the machines were so needlessly convoluted. They violated the scientific principle called Occam's razor, so named because philosopher William of Occam implored theorists to "shave off" any assumptions, variables, or concepts that aren't really necessary to explain what's going on.[4] When you've concentrated on a subject for a long time, it's easy to get caught up in the grandeur of a theoretical construction. Yet the *rule of parsimony*—another label for the same principle—states that

given two plausible explanations for the same event, we should accept the less complex version. Theoretical physicist Albert Einstein put it this way: "Any intelligent fool can make things bigger and more complex. . . . It takes a touch of genius—and a lot of courage—to move in the opposite direction."[5]

Rule of parsimony (Occam's razor) Given two plausible explanations for the same event, we should accept the simpler version.

Einstein practiced what he preached. His elegant formula ($E = mc^2$) explains the relationships among energy, mass, time, and the speed of light using just three terms, and history credits him with more than a touch of genius. But relative simplicity doesn't necessarily mean *easy to understand.* Trained physicists admit they're still struggling to fully comprehend the theory of relativity. That theory is parsimonious not because it's a no-brainer, but because it doesn't carry the extraneous baggage rival theories carry as they try to explain why time stands still when you approach the speed of light.

Scientific Standard 4: Hypotheses That Can Be Tested

A good objective theory is testable. If a prediction is wrong, there ought to be a way to demonstrate the error. Karl Popper called this requirement *falsifiability,* and saw it as the defining feature of scientific theory.[6] But some theories are so loosely stated that it's impossible to imagine empirical results that could disprove their hypotheses. And if there is no way to prove a theory false, then any claim that it's true seems hollow. A boyhood example may help illustrate this point.

Falsifiability The requirement that a scientific theory be stated in such a way that it can be tested and disproved if it is indeed wrong.

When I was 12 years old I had a friend named Mike. We spent many hours shooting baskets in his driveway. The backboard was mounted on an old-fashioned, single-car garage with double doors that opened outward like the doors on a cabinet. In order to avoid crashing into them on a drive for a layup, we'd open the doors during play. But since the doors would only swing through a 90-degree arc, they extended about 4 feet onto the court along the baseline.

One day Mike announced that he'd developed a "never-miss" shot. He took the ball at the top of the free-throw circle, drove toward the basket, then cut to the right corner. When he got to the baseline, he took a fade-away jump shot, blindly arcing the ball over the top of the big door. I was greatly impressed as the ball swished through the net. When he boasted that he never missed, I challenged him to do it again, which he did. But his third shot was an air ball—it completely missed the rim.

Before I could make the kind of bratty comment junior high school boys make, he quickly told me that the attempt had not been his never-miss shot. He claimed to have slipped as he cut to the right and therefore jumped from the wrong place. Grabbing the ball, he drove behind the door again and launched a blind arcing shot. Swish. *That,* he assured me, was his never-miss shot.

I knew something was wrong. I soon figured out that any missed attempt was, by definition, not the ballyhooed never-miss shot. When the ball went in, however, Mike heralded the success as added evidence of 100 percent accuracy. I now know that I could have called his bluff by removing the net from the basket so he couldn't hear whether the shot went through. This would have forced him to declare from behind the door whether the attempt was of the never-miss variety. But as long as I played by his rules, there was no way to disprove his claim.

Unfortunately, some theories are stated in a way that makes it impossible to prove them false. They shy away from the put-up-or-shut-up standard—they aren't testable. If it isn't possible to gather clear evidence that goes against a theory's claims, then it's also impossible to collect evidence that clearly supports those claims.

Scientific Standard 5: Practical Utility

Over time, a good objective theory is useful. Since an oft-cited goal of social science is to help people have more control over their daily lives, people facing the type of thorny social situations that the theory addresses should be able to benefit from its wisdom. This requirement is consistent with social psychologist Kurt Lewin's claim that there is nothing as practical as a good theory. A theory that communication practitioners find helpful may not be more valid than one to which few folks turn for guidance, but because of its influence, it may prove to be more valuable.

As you read about theories crafted from an objective perspective, let usefulness be one measure of their worth. A word of caution, however: Most of us can be a bit lazy or shortsighted, having a tendency to consider unimportant anything that's hard to grasp or can't be applied to our lives right now. Before considering a theory irrelevant, make certain you understand it and consider how others have made use of its insight. We'll try to do our part by presenting each theory as clearly as possible and suggesting potential applications. Perhaps you'll be even more interested in how other students have found a theory useful in their lives. That's why we've included a student-written application in almost all of the 32 chapters that feature a specific theory.

Scientific Standard 6: Quantitative Research

As the heading suggests, scientists tend to appeal to *numbers* as they gather evidence to support their theories. Almost all scientific research depends on a *comparison of differences*—this group compared to that group, this treatment as opposed to that treatment, these results versus those results. Since objective theorists aim to mirror reality, it makes sense for them to measure and report what they discover in precise numerical terms rather than in linguistic terms, which are open to interpretation. Enlightenment philosopher David Hume insisted on the superiority of quantitative methods over qualitative research:

> If we take in our hand any volume . . . let us ask: Does it contain any abstract reasoning concerning quantity or number? No. Does it contain any experimental reasoning concerning the matter of fact or existence? No. Commit it then to the flames, for it can contain nothing but sophistry and illusion.[7]

Given the radical nature of Hume's over-the-top pronouncement, we can wryly imagine the English philosopher making daily trips to a used bookstore for fuel to heat his home in winter. But the idea that numbers are more reliable than words does run deep in the scientific community. More than other quantitative methods, objective theorists use *experiments* and *surveys* to test their predictions.

Experiments. Working under the assumption that human behavior is not random, an experimenter tries to establish a cause-and-effect relationship by

"Are you just pissing and moaning, or can you verify what you're saying with data?"

systematically manipulating one factor (the independent variable) in a tightly controlled situation to learn its effect on another factor (the dependent variable). A laboratory experiment would be an appropriate way to answer the question, *Does greater perceived attitude similarity lead to increased interpersonal attraction?* The experimenter might first identify a range of attitudes held by the participating subjects and then systematically alter the attitude information provided about an experimental confederate before they met. A similarity-causes-attraction hypothesis would be supported if the subjects whose attitudes meshed with what they thought the confederate believed ended up liking that person better than did those who thought they were quite different from the confederate.[8]

Experiment
A research method that manipulates a variable in a tightly controlled situation in order to find out if it has the predicted effect.

Surveys. Whether using questionnaires or structured interviews, survey researchers rely on self-reported data to discover people's past behavior and what they now think, feel, or intend to do. For example, media-effects researchers have used survey methodology to answer the research question, *Do people who watch a high amount of dramatic violence on television hold an exaggerated belief that the world is a mean and scary place?* They asked the number of hours a day the respondents watched TV and then gave a series of forced-choice options that tapped into respondents' perceived odds of becoming a victim of violence. The researchers discovered a positive relationship between the amount of viewing and the amount of fear.[9]

Survey
A research method that uses questionnaires and structured interviews to collect self-reported data that reflects what respondents think, feel, or intend to do.

Although the presence of a correlation doesn't necessarily imply a causal relationship, it keeps that possibility alive. It's also the case that if a survey shows two variables *aren't* correlated, that's a powerful clue that one of the variables *isn't* a cause of the other. A survey can save valuable time that would otherwise be needed to establish cause-and-effect by conducting an experiment. In addition to the clues they provide about causal relationships, surveys are often the most convenient way to discover what people are thinking, feeling, and intending to do—the key components of our attitudes.

WHAT MAKES AN INTERPRETIVE THEORY GOOD?

Unlike scientists, interpretive scholars don't have an agreed-on, six-point set of criteria for evaluating their theories. But, even though there is no universally approved model, rhetoricians, critical theorists, and other interpreters repeatedly urge that interpretive theories should accomplish some or all of the following functions: *identify values, create understanding, inspire aesthetic appreciation, stimulate agreement, reform society,* and *conduct qualitative research.* The rest of this chapter examines these oft-mentioned ideals.

Interpretive Standard 1: Clarification of Values

A good interpretive theory brings people's values into the open. The theorist actively seeks to acknowledge, identify, or unmask the ideology behind the message under scrutiny.

Interpretive theorists should also be willing to reveal their own ethical commitments. As Webster University dean of communication Eric Rothenbuhler states, "Theoretical positions have moral implications, and when we teach them, advocate their use by others, or promote policies based upon them they have moral consequences."[10] Of course, not all interpretive scholars occupy the same moral ground, but there are core values most of them share. For example, humanists usually place a premium on individual liberty. Klaus Krippendorff of the Annenberg School for Communication at the University of Pennsylvania wants to make sure that scholars' drive for personal freedom extends to the people they study. His *ethical imperative* directs the theorist to "grant others that occur in your construction the same autonomy you practice constructing them."[11] When theorists follow this rule, scholarly monologue gives way to collegial dialogue. In this way people have a say in what's said about them. This kind of communal assessment requires reporting multiple voices rather than relying on one or two informants.

Ethical imperative
Grant others that occur in your construction the same autonomy you practice constructing them.

Some interpretive scholars value equality as highly as they do freedom. This commitment leads to continual examination of the power relationships inherent in all communication. Critical theorists, in particular, insist that scholars can no longer remain ethically detached from the people they are studying or from the political and economic implications of their work. For critical theorists, "There is no safe harbor in which researchers can avoid the power structure."[12]

Interpretive Standard 2: New Understanding of People

Interpretive scholarship is good when it offers fresh insight into the human condition. Rhetorical critics, ethnographers, and other humanistic researchers seek to gain new understanding by analyzing the activity that they regard as uniquely human—symbolic interaction. As opposed to social science theorists who attempt to identify communication patterns common to all people, an interpretive scholar typically examines a one-of-a-kind speech community that exhibits a specific language style. By analyzing this group's communication practice, the researcher hopes to develop an understanding of local knowledge or members' unique rules for interaction. Interpretive theories are tools to aid this search for situated meaning.

Some critics fear that by relying on rhetorical theory, we will read our preconceived ideas into the text rather than letting the words speak for themselves. They suggest that there are times when we should "just say no" to theory. But University of Minnesota communication theorist Ernest Bormann noted that rhetorical theory works best when it suggests universal patterns of symbol-using: "A powerful explanatory structure is what makes a work of humanistic scholarship live on through time."[13]

Self-referential imperative
Include yourself as a constituent of your own construction.

Bormann's claim is akin to the behavioral scientist's insistence that theory explains why people do what they do. But the two notions are somewhat different. Science wants an objective explanation; humanism desires subjective understanding. Krippendorff urges us to recognize that we, as theorists, are both the cause and the consequence of what we observe. His *self-referential imperative* for building theory states, "Include yourself as a constituent of your own construction."[14]

Interpretive Standard 3: Aesthetic Appeal

The way a theorist presents ideas can capture the imagination of a reader just as much as the wisdom and originality of the theory he or she has created. As with any type of communication, both content and style make a difference. Objective theorists are constrained by the standard format for acceptable scientific writing—propositions, hypotheses, operationalized constructs, and the like. But interpretive theorists have more room for creativity, so aesthetic appeal becomes an issue. Although the elegance of a theory is in the eye of the beholder, clarity and artistry seem to be the two qualities needed to satisfy this aesthetic requirement.

No matter how great the insights the theory contains, if the essay describing them is disorganized, overwritten, or opaque, the theorist's ideas will come across murky rather than clear. A student of mine who fought through a theorist's monograph filled with esoteric jargon likened the experience to "scuba diving in fudge."

According to University of Pittsburgh professor Barbara Warnick, a rhetorical critic can fill one or more of four roles—artist, analyst, audience, and advocate.[15] As an artist, the critic's job is to spark appreciation. Along with clarity, it's another way to construct an interpretive theory with aesthetic appeal. By artfully incorporating imagery, metaphor, illustration, and story into the core of the theory, the theorist can make his or her creation come alive for others. We can't illustrate all of these artful devices in a single paragraph, but many students of rhetoric are moved by the way University of Wisconsin rhetorical critic Edwin Black summed up his analysis of Lincoln's Gettysburg address:

> The Gettysburg Address is, finally and inevitably, a projection of Lincoln himself, of his discretion, of his modesty on an occasion which invited him to don the mantle of the prophet, of his meticulous measure of how far he ought to go, of the assurance of his self-knowledge: his impeccable discernment of his own competence, his flawless sense of its depth and its limits. As an actor in history and a force in the world, Lincoln does not hesitate to comprehend history and the

> world. But he never presumes to cast his mind beyond human dimensions. He does not recite divine intentions; he does not issue cosmic judgments. He knows, to the bottom, what he knows. Of the rest, he is silent.[16]

Interpretive Standard 4: Community of Agreement

We can identify a good interpretive theory by the amount of support it generates within a community of scholars who are interested and knowledgeable about the same type of communication. Interpretation of meaning is subjective, but whether the interpreter's case is reasonable or totally off the wall is ultimately decided by others in the field. Their acceptance or rejection is an objective fact that helps verify or vilify a theorist's ideas.

Sometimes interpretive theorists present a controversial thesis to an audience restricted to true believers—those who already agree with the author's position. But an interpretive theory can't meet the community of agreement standard unless it becomes the subject of widespread analysis. For example, former National Communication Association president David Zarefsky warns that rhetorical validity can be established only when a work is debated in the broad marketplace of ideas. For this Northwestern University rhetorical critic, sound arguments differ from unsound ones in that "sound arguments are addressed to the general audience of critical readers, not just to the adherents of a particular 'school' or perspective. . . . They open their own reasoning process to scrutiny."[17]

John Stewart is the editor of *Bridges, Not Walls,* a collection of humanistic articles on interpersonal communication. As the book has progressed through 11 editions, Stewart's judgment to keep, drop, or add a theoretical work has been made possible by the fact that interpretive scholarship is "not a solitary enterprise carried out in a vacuum." It is instead, he says, "the effort of a community of scholars who routinely subject their findings to the scrutiny of editors, referees, and readers."[18]

Interpretive Standard 5: Reform of Society

A good interpretive theory often generates change. Some interpretive scholars, but by no means all, aren't content merely to interpret the intended meanings of a text. Contrary to the notion that we can dismiss calls for social justice or emancipation as *mere rhetoric,* critical interpreters are reformers who can have an impact on society. They want to expose and publicly resist the ideology that permeates the accepted wisdom of a culture. Kenneth Gergen, a Swarthmore College social psychologist, states that theory has the capacity to challenge the guiding assumptions of the culture, to raise fundamental questions regarding contemporary social life, to foster reconsideration of that which is "taken for granted," and thereby to generate fresh alternatives for social action.[19]

Along with many interpretive scholars, *critical theorists* tend to reject any notion of permanent truth or meaning. They see society's economic, political, social, religious, and educational institutions as socially constructed by unjust communication practices that create or perpetuate gross imbalances of power. The aim of their scholarship is to unmask these communication practices in an

Critical theorists
Scholars who use theory to reveal unjust communication practices that create or perpetuate an imbalance of power.

attempt to stimulate change. To traditional thinkers, their activity looks like a few angry children in kindergarten knocking over other kids' blocks, but they are intentionally using theory to carve out a space where people without power can be heard. For example, a critical theorist working from a Marxist, feminist, or postmodern perspective might craft a theory to support an alternative interpretation of the Golden Rule, namely, *He who has the gold, rules.* The theorist would then apply this reinterpretation to a specific practice, perhaps the publishing and pricing of required textbooks such as the one you're reading. To the extent that the theory stimulates students to rethink, respond, and react to this "free-market" process, it is a good interpretive theory.

Interpretive Standard 6: Qualitative Research

While scientists use *numbers* to support their theories, interpretive scholars use *words*. That's the basic difference between quantitative and qualitative research. As the editors of the *Handbook of Qualitative Research* describe the process, "Qualitative researchers study things in their natural settings, attempting to make sense of, or to interpret, phenomena in terms of the meaning people bring to them."[20] A focus on meaning and significance is consistent with the maxim that once hung on the wall of Einstein's Princeton University office:[21]

> Not everything that can be counted counts, and
> not everything that counts can be counted.

The interpretive scholar's qualitative tools include open-ended interviews, focus groups, visual texts, artifacts, and introspection. But *textual analysis* and *ethnography* are the two methods most often used to study how humans use signs and symbols to create and infer meaning.

Textual Analysis. The aim of *textual analysis* is to describe and interpret the characteristics of a message. Communication theorists use this term to refer to the intensive study of a single message grounded in a humanistic perspective.

Textual analysis
A research method that describes and interprets the characteristics of any text.

Rhetorical criticism is the most common form of textual research in the communication discipline. For example, rhetorical critics have asked, *What does Martin Luther King's choice of language in his "I Have a Dream" speech on the Washington mall reveal about his strategic intent?* They've then undertaken a close reading of the text and context of that famous speech and concluded that King was trying to simultaneously appeal to multiple audiences without alienating any of them.[22]

Ethnography. The late Princeton anthropologist Clifford Geertz said that *ethnography* is "not an experimental science in search of law, but an interpretive [approach] in search of meaning."[23] As a sensitive observer of the human scene, Geertz was loath to impose his way of thinking onto a society's construction of reality. He wanted his theory of communication grounded in the meanings that people within a culture share. Getting it right means seeing it from their point of view.

Ethnography
A method of participant observation designed to help a researcher experience a culture's complex web of meaning.

When Stan Musial—one of the greatest baseball players in history—passed away in January 2013 at the age of 92, his many admirers took the opportunity to share their memories. One story that circulated revealed that Musial was an amateur ethnographer. After baseball was desegregated in 1945, Musial noticed a group of black players on his all-star team congregating in the back corner of the dugout to play poker. In an effort to start dialogue, foster team spirit, and begin friendships, Musial cautiously approached the table and sat down. He felt like he had entered another world. In order to befriend his black teammates, he had to learn their group rituals, linguistic expressions, and cultural experiences that were all unfamiliar to him. His task was even more difficult because he didn't know the first thing about poker. Gradually, through listening and making careful mental notes, Musial began to understand his teammates and see the game of baseball through their eyes instead of his. That's ethnography.[24]

CONTESTED TURF AND COMMON GROUND AMONG THEORISTS

Throughout this chapter we have urged using separate measures for weighing the merits of objective and interpretive theories. That's because the two sets of criteria reflect the divergent mindsets of scientists and interpretive scholars as outlined in Chapter 2. Perhaps the field of personality assessment offers a way to understand how deeply these differences run. Some of you have taken the Myers-Briggs Type Indicator, a test that measures individual preferences on four bipolar scales. The *sensing–intuition* scale shows how people perceive or acquire information—how they seek to find out about things. As you read through the descriptions of *sensing* and *intuition* below, consider how closely they reflect the contrast of objective and interpretive epistemology—different ways of knowing.[25]

Sensing. One way to "find out" is to use your sensing function. Your eyes, ears, and other senses tell you what is actually there and actually happening, both inside and outside of yourself. Sensing is especially useful for appreciating the realities of a situation.

Intuition. The other way to "find out" is through intuition, which reveals the meanings, relationships, and possibilities that go beyond the information from your senses. Intuition looks at the big picture and tries to grasp the essential patterns.

These are differences that make a difference. It's hard to imagine two theorists becoming intellectual soul mates if each discounts or disdains the other's starting point, method, and conclusion. Does that mean they can't be friends? Not necessarily. There are at least three reasons for guarded optimism.

A firm foundation for their friendship would be a mutual respect for each other's curiosity about the communication process and a recognition that they are both bringing the very best of their intellect to bear on what they study. A second basis for mutual appreciation would be an understanding that the strong point of science is a rigorous comparison of multiple messages or groups, while the forte of humanism is its imaginative, in-depth analysis of a single message or group. Anthropologist Gregory Bateson described *rigor* and *imagination* as the two great contraries of the mind. He wrote that either "by itself is lethal. Rigor alone is paralytic death, but imagination alone is insanity."[26]

A third reason for mutual appreciation can be seen in a side-by-side comparison of the two sets of criteria in Figure 3–1. The chart suggests that the standards set by scientists and the evaluative criteria used by interpretive theorists

Scientific Theory	Interpretive Theory
Prediction of Future	Clarification of Values
Explanation of Data	Understanding of People
Relative Simplicity	Aesthetic Appeal
Testable Hypothesis	Community of Agreement
Practical Utility	Reform of Society
Quantitative Research	Qualitative Research

FIGURE 3–1 Summary of Criteria for Evaluating Communication Theory

share some similarities. Work down through the chart line-by-line and note a bit of overlap for each pair of terms. Here are the points of contact we see:

1. Both *prediction* and *value clarification* look to the future. The first suggests what *will* happen, the second, what *ought* to happen.
2. An *explanation* of communication behavior can lead to further *understanding* of people's motivation.
3. For many students of theory, *simplicity* has an *aesthetic appeal.*
4. *Testing hypotheses* is a way of achieving a *community of agreement.*
5. What could be more *practical* than a theory that *reforms* unjust practices?
6. Both *quantitative research* and *qualitative research* reflect a commitment to learn more about communication.

Identifying reasons for mutual appreciation doesn't guarantee respect. Republicans and Democrats have a common goal to bring about a more perfect union, but it's often impossible to see anything more than political gridlock when members of the two parties get together. Similarly, when objective and interpretive theorists work in the same academic department, tensions can run high. At the very least, the two scholarly communities should have a familiarity with each other's work. That's one reason we've elected to present objective as well as interpretive theories in this book.

You'll find that we often refer to these requirements for good theory in the critique sections at the end of each chapter. As you might expect, the 32 theories stack up rather well—otherwise we wouldn't have picked them in the first place. But constructing theory is difficult, and most theories have an Achilles' heel that makes them vulnerable to criticism. All of the theorists readily admit a need for fine-tuning their work, and some even call for major overhauls. We encourage you to weigh their words by the standards you think are important before reading the critique at the end of each chapter.

QUESTIONS TO SHARPEN YOUR FOCUS

1. How can we call a scientific theory good if it is *capable of being proved wrong?*
2. How can we decide when a *rhetorical critic* provides a *reasonable interpretation?*

3. All theories involve trade-offs; no theory can meet every standard of quality equally well. Of the 12 *criteria* discussed, which two or three are most important to you? Which one is least important?
4. Do you think objective scholars have any room in their approach for *intuition?* If so, how might that work? Do interpretive scholars have any space for *sensing?*

A SECOND LOOK

Scientific evaluation: Steven Chaffee, "Thinking About Theory," in *An Integrated Approach to Communication Theory and Research,* 2nd ed., Don Stacks and Michael Salwen (eds.), Routledge, NY, 2009, pp. 13–29.

Interpretive evaluation: Klaus Krippendorff, "On the Ethics of Constructing Communication," in *Rethinking Communication: Vol. 1,* Brenda Dervin, Lawrence Grossberg, Barbara O'Keefe, and Ellen Wartella (eds.), Sage, Newbury Park, CA, 1989, pp. 66–96.

Progress in scientific research: Franklin Boster, "On Making Progress in Communication," *Human Communication Research,* Vol. 28, 2002, pp. 473–490.

Quantitative theory: Michael Beatty, "Thinking Quantitatively," in Stacks and Salwen, pp. 30–39.

Qualitative theory: James A. Anderson, "Thinking Qualitatively," in Stacks and Salwen, pp. 40–58.

Quantitative methods: Franklin Boster and John Sherry, "Alternative Methodological Approaches to Communication Science," in *The Handbook of Communication Science,* 2nd ed., Charles Berger, Michael Roloff, and David Roskos-Ewoldsen (eds.), Sage, Los Angeles, CA, 2010, pp. 55–71.

Qualitative methods: Norman Denzin and Yvonna Lincoln, *Collecting and Interpreting Qualitative Materials,* Sage, Thousand Oaks, CA, 1998.

To view a chapter-by-chapter list of changes from the previous edition, click on Changes under Theory Resources at *www.afirstlook.com.*

CHAPTER 4

Mapping the Territory

(Seven Traditions in the Field of Communication Theory)

In Chapter 1, we presented working definitions for the concepts of *communication* and *theory*. In Chapters 2 and 3, we outlined the basic differences between objective and interpretive communication theories. These distinctions should help bring order out of chaos when your study of theory seems confusing. And it may seem confusing. University of Colorado communication professor Robert Craig describes the field of communication theory as awash with hundreds of unrelated theories that differ in starting point, method, and conclusion. He suggests that our field of study resembles "a pest control device called the Roach Motel that used to be advertised on TV: Theories check in, but they never check out."[1]

My mind conjures up a different image when I try to make sense of the often baffling landscape of communication theory. I picture a scene from the film *Harry Potter and the Chamber of Secrets* in which the boy wizard ventures into the Forbidden Forest. Inside, he finds it teeming with all kinds of spiders. Some are big, others small, but all look like they might want to eat him for lunch. He's overwhelmed at the sight of them—perhaps not unlike how you felt when you first saw the table of contents for this book. Harry discovers that the spiders momentarily retreat from the bright light of his wand, letting him secure a safe place to stand. It's my hope that the core ideas of Chapters 1–3 will provide you with that kind of space. The fantasy nature of the film is such that I could even imagine Harry emerging from the forest with all the spiders bound together in two sticky webs—the objective batch in his right hand and the interpretive batch in his left. But that's an overly simplistic fantasy. Craig offers a more sophisticated solution.

Craig agrees that the terrain is confusing if we insist on looking for some kind of grand theoretical overview that brings all communication study into focus—a top-down, satellite picture of the communication theory landscape. He suggests, however, that communication theory is a coherent field when we understand communication as a practical discipline.[2] He's convinced that our search for different types of theory should be grounded where real people grapple with everyday problems and practices of communication. Craig explains that "all communication theories are relevant to a common practical lifeworld in which *communication* is already a richly meaningful term."[3] Communication theory is the systematic and thoughtful response of communication scholars to questions posed as humans interact with one another—the best thinking within a practical discipline.

Craig thinks it's reasonable to talk about a *field of communication theory* if we take a collective look at the actual approaches researchers have used to study communication problems and practices. He identifies seven established traditions of communication theory that include most, if not all, of what theorists have done. These already established traditions offer "distinct, alternative vocabularies" that describe different "ways of conceptualizing communication problems and practices."[4] This means that scholars within a given tradition talk comfortably with one another but often take potshots at those who work in other camps. As Craig suggests, we shouldn't try to smooth over these between-group battles. Theorists argue because they have something important to argue about.

In the rest of the chapter I'll outline the seven traditions Craig describes. Taken together, they reveal the breadth and diversity that span the field of communication theory. The classifications will also help you understand why some theories share common ground, while others are effectively fenced off from each other by conflicting goals and assumptions. As I introduce each tradition, I'll highlight how its advocates tend to define communication, suggest a practical communication problem that this kind of theory addresses, and provide an example of research that the tradition has inspired.[5] Since I find that the topic of friendship is of great interest to most college students, the seven research studies I describe will show how each tradition approaches this type of close relationship.

THE SOCIO-PSYCHOLOGICAL TRADITION

Communication as Interpersonal Interaction and Influence

The socio-psychological tradition epitomizes the scientific or objective perspective described in Chapter 2. Scholars in this tradition believe there are communication truths that can be discovered by careful, systematic observation. They look for cause-and-effect relationships that will predict the results when people communicate. When they find causal links, they are well on the way to answering the ever-present question that relationship and persuasion practitioners ask: *How can I get others to change?* In terms of generating theory, the socio-psychological tradition is by far the most prolific of the seven that Craig names. This disciplinary fact of life is reflected in the many theories of this type that we present in the book.

When researchers search for universal laws of communication, they try to focus on what *is* without being biased by their personal view of what *ought to be.* As social scientists, they heed the warning of the skeptical newspaper editor: "You think your mother loves you? Check it out—at least two sources." For communication theorists in the socio-psychological tradition, checking it out usually means designing a series of surveys or controlled experiments. That's been our approach.

Teaching at a small liberal arts college where I've had the opportunity to be personally involved in the lives of my students, I've always wondered if there's a way to predict which college friendships will survive and thrive after graduation. As someone trained in the socio-psychological tradition, I began a longitudinal study spanning two decades to find out the answer.[6] I asked 45 pairs of best friends to respond to questions about (1) when they became close friends; (2) the similarity of their academic majors; (3) their range of mutual-touch behavior;

(4) their perceived status difference; and (5) the extent to which they avoided discussing awkward topics. I also (6) assessed their self-disclosure to each other and (7) measured their communication efficiency by watching them play two rounds of the cooperative word game *Password*. Would any of these measures forecast who would be friends forever?

In order to determine the answer, I needed a reliable and valid measure of relational closeness. Based on social psychologist Harold Kelley's interactional theory, which suggests that close relationships are characterized by "strength, frequency, diversity, and duration," Glenn and I developed a composite measure that assessed these properties.[7] For example, we gauged *relative strength* by asking the pair how many friends they now have to whom they feel closer than their college best friend. And we assessed *frequency of contact* by counting the number of times over the last year that the pair communicated face-to-face, over the phone, by letter, and through email.

Nineteen years after the initial study, Andrew helped me locate the study participants and asked them to respond to the measures of relational closeness mentioned above. We weren't surprised that participants with a longer history as best friends when they came to the study were most likely to remain close two decades later. Past behavior tends to be a good predictor of future behavior. Of more interest to us as communication scholars was the fact that those with similar academic majors and those with better scores on the *Password* game also remained close.[8] Remember that participants' choice of major and the *Password* game occurred about two decades earlier, yet these factors still predicted friendship long after college. It appears that communicating on the same wavelength and sharing common academic interests is a boon to long-lasting friendship. Maybe it's no surprise, then, that working together on this research project solidified our friendship with each other. Eventually, that friendship led to the three of us joining together to write the book you're reading now.

Theorists and researchers working within the socio-psychological tradition often call for longitudinal empirical studies. Only by using this type of research design could we predict which pairs were likely to be friends forever.

THE CYBERNETIC TRADITION

Communication as a System of Information Processing

MIT scientist Norbert Wiener coined the word *cybernetics* to describe the field of artificial intelligence.[9] The term is a transliteration of the Greek word for "steersman" or "governor," and it illustrates the way feedback makes information processing possible in our heads and on our laptops. During World War II, Wiener developed an anti-aircraft firing system that adjusted future trajectory by taking into account the results of past performance. His concept of feedback anchored the cybernetic tradition, which regards communication as the link connecting the separate parts of any system, such as a computer system, a family system, a media system, or a system of social support. Theorists in the cybernetic tradition seek to answer such questions as *How does the system work? What could change it?* and *How can we get the bugs out?*

Cybernetics
The study of information processing, feedback, and control in communication systems.

University of Washington communication professor Malcolm Parks studies personal relationships by asking both partners to describe their social network. In one major study of college students' same-sex friendships, he separately asked each partner to prepare a list of his or her closest relationships, including four family members and eight non-family ties.[10] In almost all cases, the eight people who weren't family were other friends or romantic partners rather than co-workers, coaches, or teachers. Parks then had the two friends trade their lists and asked them questions that probed their relationship with the key people in their *friend's* social network. These included:

1. Prior contact: Which people did you know before you met your friend?
2. Range of contact: How many of them have you now met face-to-face?
3. Communication: How often do you communicate with each of them?
4. Liking: How much do you like or dislike each of the ones you know?
5. Support: To what extent does each of them support your friendship?
6. Support: To what extent does *your own* network support your friendship?

Note that the first four questions establish the links within and between the friends' social networks. Both support questions reveal the feedback friends receive from these support systems.

Using a number of traditional measures that assess personal relationships, Parks measured the amount of *communication* between the friends, the *closeness* of their relationship, and their *commitment* to see it continue. When he compared these three measures to the quantity and quality of links to their friend's social network, the results were striking. Friends who had multiple and positive interactions with their partner's social networks had more communication with, closeness to, and commitment toward their partner than friends who had little involvement and felt little support from these folks. Friendships don't exist in a vacuum; they are embedded in a network that processes social information.

THE RHETORICAL TRADITION

Communication as Artful Public Address

Whether speaking to a crowd, congregation, legislative assembly, or jury, public speakers have sought practical advice on how to best present their case. Well into the twentieth century, the rhetorical theory and advice from Plato, Aristotle, Cicero, Quintilian, and other Greco-Roman rhetors served as the main source of wisdom about public speaking. There are a half-dozen features that characterize this influential tradition of rhetorical communication:

Rhetoric
The art of using all available means of persuasion, focusing on lines of argument, organization of ideas, language use, and delivery in public speaking.

- A conviction that speech distinguishes humans from other animals. Cicero suggested that only oral communication had the power to lead humanity out of its brutish existence and establish communities with rights of citizenship.[11]
- A confidence that public address delivered in a democratic forum is a more effective way to solve political problems than rule by decree or resorting to force. Within this tradition, the phrase *mere rhetoric* is a contradiction in terms.
- A setting in which a single speaker attempts to influence multiple listeners through persuasive discourse. Effective communication requires audience adaptation.
- Oratorical training as the cornerstone of a leader's education. Speakers learn to deliver strong arguments in powerful voices that carry to the edge of a crowd.

- An emphasis on the power and beauty of language to move people emotionally and stir them to action. Rhetoric is more art than science.
- Oral public persuasion as the province of males. A key feature of the women's movement has been the struggle for the right to speak in public.

Readers of Aristotle's *The Rhetoric* may be surprised to find a systematic analysis of friendship. He defines a friend as "one who loves and is loved in return."[12] The Greek word for this kind of love is *philia,* as in Philadelphia (the city of brotherly love). Based on this mutual love, Aristotle says a friend takes pleasure when good things happen to the other and feels distress when the other goes through bad times—emotions experienced for no other reason than the fact that they are friends. Aristotle then catalogs more than 20 personal qualities that make people attractive to us as friends. For example, we have friendly feelings toward those who are pleasant to deal with, share our interests, aren't critical of others, are willing to make or take a joke, and show that they "are very fond of their friends and not inclined to leave them in the lurch."[13] Although Aristotle wrote 2,500 years ago, this last quality resonates with Bill Withers' classic song "Lean On Me," recently covered by the cast of the hit Fox comedy *Glee.* A good friend helps you make it through tough times.[14]

You might have trouble seeing the link between the main features of the rhetorical tradition and Aristotle's comments on friendship. After an in-depth study on Aristotle's entire body of work—not just *The Rhetoric*—St. John's University philosopher Eugene Garver concluded that Aristotle didn't analyze friendship as a way to help Greek citizens develop close relationships.[15] Rather, he was instructing orators on how to make their case seem more probable by creating a feeling of goodwill among the audience. If by word and deed a speaker appears friendly, listeners will be more open to the message.

Twenty-five years ago I wrote a book on friendship and suggested the title *Making Friends.* The publisher liked my proposal, but at the last minute added a phrase. I was startled when the book came out entitled *Making Friends (and Making Them Count).*[16] I'm uncomfortable with the idea of using friends as a means to achieve other goals. According to Garver, Aristotle had no such qualms. Rhetoric is the discovery of all available means of persuasion.

THE SEMIOTIC TRADITION

Communication as the Process of Sharing Meaning Through Signs

Semiotics
The study of verbal and nonverbal signs that can stand for something else, and how their interpretation impacts society.

Symbols
Arbitrary words and nonverbal signs that bear no natural connection with the things they describe; their meaning is learned within a given culture.

Semiotics is the study of signs. A *sign* is anything that can stand for something else. High body temperature is a sign of infection. Birds flying south signal the coming of winter. A white cane signifies blindness. An arrow designates which direction to go.

Words are also signs, but of a special kind. They are *symbols.* Unlike the examples I've just cited, words are arbitrary symbols that have no inherent meaning, no natural connection with the things they describe. For example, there's nothing in the sound of the word *share* or anything visual in the letters *h-u-g* that signifies a good friendship. One could just as easily coin the term *snarf* or *clag* to symbolize a close relationship between friends. The same thing is true for nonverbal symbols like *winks* or *waves.*

Cambridge University literary critic I. A. Richards railed against the semantic trap that he labeled "the proper meaning superstition"—the mistaken belief

that words have a precise definition. For Richards and other semiologists, meaning doesn't reside in words or other symbols; meaning resides in people. Most theorists grounded in the semiotic tradition are trying to explain and reduce the misunderstanding created by the use of ambiguous symbols.

Communication professor Michael Monsour (Metropolitan State University of Denver) recognized that the word *intimacy* used in the context of friendship might mean different things to different people, and the disparity could lead to confusion or misunderstanding. So he asked 164 communication students what they meant by intimacy when used in reference to their same-sex and their opposite-sex friends. Roughly two-thirds of the respondents were female, two-thirds were single, and two-thirds were under the age of 30. Participants offered 27 distinct interpretations of intimacy between friends, and the number of meanings suggested by each respondent ranged from 1–5, with an average of two different meanings per person.[17]

Seven meanings were mentioned often enough to include them in the final analysis. Self-disclosure was by far the meaning of intimacy mentioned most. In rank-order of frequency, the seven interpretations were:

1. Self-disclosure: Revelations about self that the friend didn't know
2. Emotional expressiveness: Closeness, warmth, affection, and caring

3. Physical contact: Nonsexual touch
4. Trust: Confidence that the other is reliable
5. Unconditional support: Being there for the other in good times and bad
6. Sexual contact: Overt sexual activity
7. Activities: Doing things together of a nonsexual nature

The content and order of the top five interpretations of intimacy held relatively constant for both opposite-sex and same-sex friendships, whether the respondent was a man or a woman. The notable deviations were that a few more men in opposite-sex friendships thought of intimacy as sexual contact, but in same-sex relationships characterized intimacy as activities together. For Monsour, the major contribution of this study is that for friends in both kinds of relationships, the word *intimacy* is multidimensional—a polysemic linguistic sign. A symbol like this can easily be misunderstood. Yet if two of the students in Monsour's study referred to intimacy in a conversation, with a few exceptions, it's likely that they'd understand what the other was talking about.

THE SOCIO-CULTURAL TRADITION

Communication as the Creation and Enactment of Social Reality

The socio-cultural tradition is based on the premise that as people talk, they produce and reproduce culture. Most of us assume that words reflect what actually exists. However, theorists in this tradition suggest that the process often works the other way around. Our view of reality is strongly shaped by the language we've used since we were infants.

University of Chicago linguist Edward Sapir and his student Benjamin Lee Whorf were pioneers in the socio-cultural tradition. The Sapir–Whorf hypothesis of linguistic relativity states that the structure of a culture's language shapes what people think and do.[18] "The 'real world' is to a large extent unconsciously built upon the language habits of the group."[19] Their theory of linguistic relativity counters the assumption that words merely act as neutral vehicles to carry meaning. Language actually structures our perception of reality.

Sapir–Whorf hypothesis of linguistic relativity
The claim that the structure of a language shapes what people think and do; the social construction of reality.

Contemporary socio-cultural theorists grant even more power to language. They claim that it is through the process of communication that "reality is produced, maintained, repaired, and transformed."[20] Or, stated in the active voice, *persons-in-conversation co-construct their own social worlds*.[21] When these worlds collide, the socio-cultural tradition offers help in bridging the culture gap that exists between "us" and "them."

Patricia Sias, a communication professor at the University of Arizona, takes a socio-cultural approach when studying friendships that form and dissolve in organizational settings. She writes that "relationships are not entities external to the relationship partners, but are mental creations that depend on communication for their existence and form. . . . If relationships are constituted in communication they are also *changed* through communication."[22] Sias uses a social construction lens through which to view deteriorating friendships in the workplace.

Sias located 25 people in a variety of jobs who were willing to talk about their failing workplace friendships. Some relationships were between peer co-workers, others between a supervisor and a subordinate. All the workers spontaneously told stories about their deteriorating friendship that revealed how communication between the two co-workers had changed. Although the friendships went sour for a variety of reasons—personality problems, distracting life events, conflicting expectations, betrayal, and promotion—the *way* the friendships dissolved was remarkably similar. Almost all workers told stories of using indirect communication to change the relationship.

While their friendships were deteriorating, the former friends still had to talk with each other in order to accomplish their work. But these co-workers stopped eating lunch together and spending time together outside the office. While on the job they avoided personal topics and almost never talked about the declining state of their relationship. Even seemingly safe topics such as sports or movies were no longer discussed; small talk and watercooler chitchat disappeared.

Although linguistic connection was sparse, nonverbal communication spoke loudly. The workers who talked with Sias recalled the lack of eye contact, snappy or condescending tones of voice, and physically backing away from the other. Ideally, social construction research in the office would capture the real-time communication of co-workers, but that would require a video-recorded account of office conversations when the friendship was in the process of deteriorating—a high hurdle for Sias to clear. As for contrasting narratives, she notes that "the damaged nature of the relationships made it difficult to recruit both partners in each friendship."[23] Yet without the actual dialogue of both conversational partners to examine, any statement about their co-creation of social reality must remain tentative.

THE CRITICAL TRADITION

Communication as a Reflective Challenge to Unjust Discourse

The term *critical theory* comes from the work of a group of German scholars known as the "Frankfurt School" because they were part of the independent Institute for Social Research at Frankfurt University. Originally set up to test the ideas of Karl Marx, the Frankfurt School rejected the economic determinism of orthodox Marxism yet carried on the Marxist tradition of critiquing society.

What types of communication practice and research are critical theorists *against?* Although there is no single set of abuses that all of them denounce, critical theorists consistently challenge three features of contemporary society:

1. *The control of language to perpetuate power imbalances.* Critical theorists condemn any use of words that inhibits emancipation.
2. *The role of mass media in dulling sensitivity to repression.* Critical theorists see the "culture industries" of television, film, music, and print media as reproducing the dominant ideology of a culture and distracting people from recognizing the unjust distribution of power within society.
3. *Blind reliance on the scientific method and uncritical acceptance of empirical findings.* Critical theorists are suspicious of empirical work that scientists say is ideologically free, because science is not the value-free pursuit of knowledge that it claims to be.

Culture industries
Entertainment businesses that reproduce the dominant ideology of a culture and distract people from recognizing unjust distribution of power within society; e.g., film, television, music, and advertising.

University of Louisville communication professor Kathy Werking agrees that personal relationship research decisions aren't neutral. In a chapter titled "Cross-Sex Friendship Research as Ideological Practice," Werking acknowledges that the reigning cultural model of relationships between women and men is one of romance. Yet she is critical of scholars for continually reproducing this heterosexual ideology to the point where it seems natural or just common sense to assume that all close male–female relationships are about sex and romance.[24]

In support of her ideological critique, Werking notes that academic journals devoted to the study of personal relationships publish vastly more articles on dating, courtship, and marriage than they do on opposite-sex friendships. Even when a rare study of opposite-sex friendship is reported, the author usually compares this type of relationship unfavorably with romantic ties that "may or may not include equality, are passionate, and have the goal of marriage."[25] Friendship, Werking claims, is best "based on equality, affection, communion, and is an end in itself."[26] This disconnect puts opposite-sex friends in a bind. They have no language that adequately describes or legitimizes their relationship. The term *just friends* downplays its importance, *platonic friends* has an archaic connotation, and if they use the word *love,* it must be qualified so that no one gets the wrong idea.

Werking also criticizes Western scholars for the individualistic ideology that permeates their opposite-sex research. She says they equate biological sex characteristics with gender identity—an assumption that precludes the possibility that masculine and feminine orientations are socially created and can change over time. They also assume that the perceptions of one friend adequately represent the complexity of what's going on in the relationship. And rather than observe friends' actual interactions over time, they naively rely on freeze-frame responses on a structured survey to provide sufficient information to understand a relationship. Werking claims that all of these research practices do an injustice to men and women in opposite-sex relationships.

THE PHENOMENOLOGICAL TRADITION

Communication as the Experience of Self and Others Through Dialogue

Although *phenomenology* is an imposing philosophical term, it basically refers to the intentional analysis of everyday life from the standpoint of the person who is living it. Thus, the phenomenological tradition places great emphasis on people's perception and their interpretation of their own experience. For the phenomenologist, an individual's story is more important, and more authoritative, than any research hypothesis or communication axiom. As psychologist Carl Rogers asserted, "Neither the Bible nor the prophets—neither Freud nor research—neither the revelations of God nor man—can take precedence over my own direct experience."[27]

Phenomenology
Intentional analysis of everyday experience from the standpoint of the person who is living it; explores the possibility of understanding the experience of self and others.

The problem, of course, is that no two people have the same life story. Since we cannot experience another person's experience, we tend to talk past each other and then lament, "Nobody understands what it's like to be me." Thus, theorists who work within the phenomenological tradition seek to answer two questions: *Why is it so hard to establish and sustain authentic human relationships?* and *How can this problem be overcome?*

Communication professor Bill Rawlins (Ohio University) works within this tradition as he studies friendship by taking an in-depth look at the actual conversations between friends. In his book *The Compass of Friendship: Narratives, Identities, and Dialogues,* he devotes an entire chapter to a 90-minute recorded conversation between Chris and Karen, two women who agree they've been friends for "30 years and counting."[28] Rawlins provided no guidelines or instructions. The women only know that he is interested in their friendship. After an hour of recounting stories about shared experiences, Chris brings up Karen's slow retreat into silence the past winter. Obviously bothered by losing contact, Chris continues . . .

> CHRIS: And I thought, "Well that's okay; everybody has these times when they feel this way." But I feel like you should *alert* people that *care* about you [laughs] to the fact that this is what is goin' on—
>
> KAREN: [laughs] Yeah . . .
>
> CHRIS: "I'm going into my cave. See ya in the spring," or whatever. Or "I don't wish to have anything, writing or any communications for a while. Not to worry. Adios. Bye to everybody. Hasta la vista or whatever."
>
> KAREN: Yeah.
>
> CHRIS: Or something, because I [pause], I [pause], I . . .
>
> KAREN: You were worried.[29]

The dialogue above is less than a minute of the women's conversation, yet it provides a rich resource for Rawlins' insight into their friendship. Chris says to herself at the time that such feelings are commonplace and "OK." Even so, she believes that Karen "should *alert* people that *care* about you to the fact that this is going on. . . ." They both laugh at this paradoxical recommendation that Karen communicate to significant others that she does not intend to communicate with them. Chris rehearses two voices for Karen here: a humorous one that trades on a hibernation metaphor, and then a more serious, explicit statement with Spanish flourishes at the end that seem to add a comical flavor. As Karen affirms this idea, however, Chris surrenders her comic tone and makes the frank request, "Or something," haltingly trying to offer her reasons, "I [pause], I [pause], I . . . ," which Karen completes for her: "You were worried." In short, Karen again recognizes the emotional basis of Chris' concerns and legitimates Chris' suggested policy for communicating social withdrawal.[30]

Rawlins' reconstruction of this segment reveals how *he* experiences the women's friendship. After reading his interpretation of the entire conversation, the women independently tell him that he was "right on" and had "nailed it."[31] That's because he paid attention to *their* interpretation of their experience.

FENCING THE FIELD OF COMMUNICATION THEORY

The seven traditions I've described have deep roots in the field of communication theory. Team loyalties run strong, so theorists, researchers, and practitioners working within one tradition often hear criticism from those in other traditions that their particular approach has no legitimacy. In addition to whatever arguments each group might muster to defend their choice, they can also claim "squatters' rights" because scholars who went before had already established the right to occupy that portion of land. Taking the real estate metaphor seriously, in Figure 4–1, I've charted the seven traditions as equal-area parcels of land that collectively make up the larger field of study. A few explanations are in order.

First, it's important to realize that the location of each tradition on the map is far from random. My rationale for placing them where they are is based on the distinction between objective and interpretive theories outlined in Chapter 2. According to the scientific assumptions presented in that chapter, the socio-psychological tradition is the most objective, and so it occupies the far left position on the map—solidly rooted in objective territory. Moving across the map from left to right, the traditions become more interpretive and less objective. Some students wonder why rhetoric is rated more objective than semiotics. It's because rhetoricians have traditionally regarded what language refers to as "real," whereas semiologists perceive the relationship between a word and its referent as more tenuous. I see the phenomenological tradition as the most subjective of the seven traditions, and so it occupies the position farthest to the right—firmly grounded in interpretive territory. The order of presentation in this chapter followed the same progression—a gradual shift from objective to interpretive concerns. Scholars working in adjacent traditions usually have an easier time appreciating each other's work. On the map they share a common border. Professionally, they are closer together in their basic assumptions.

Second, hybrids are possible across traditions. You've seen throughout this chapter that each tradition has its own way of defining communication and its own distinct vocabulary. Thus, it's fair to think of the dividing lines on the map as fences built to keep out strange ideas. Scholars, however, are an independent bunch. They climb fences, read journals, and fly to faraway conferences. This cross-pollination sometimes results in theory grounded in two or three traditions.

Finally, the seven charted traditions might not cover every approach to communication theory. Craig recently suggested the possibility of a *pragmatist tradition*—a pluralistic land where different perspectives on truth could all be

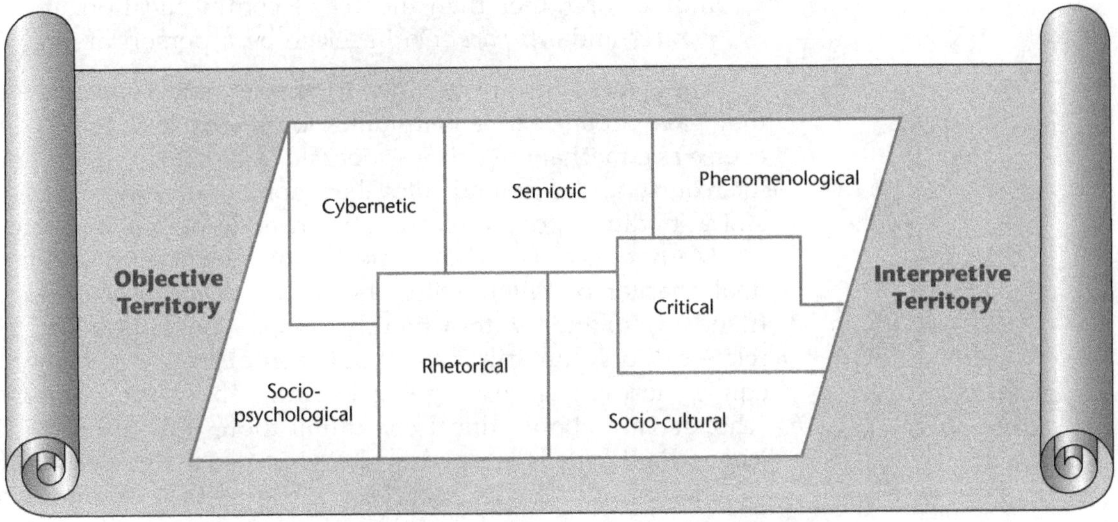

FIGURE 4–1 A Survey Map of Traditions in the Field of Communication Theory

Pragmatism
An applied approach to knowledge; the philosophy that true understanding of an idea or situation has practical implications for action.

legitimate in different ways. He pictures it as a tradition that "orients to practical problems, and evaluates ideas according to their usefulness rather than by an absolute standard of truth."[32] It would be a location where he sees his own work fitting in well. Craig's openness to considering new territories leads us to offer a quite different stream of theory running through the field of communication. Our candidate is an *ethical tradition.*

THE ETHICAL TRADITION

Communication as People of Character Interacting in Just and Beneficial Ways

More than many academic disciplines, the field of communication has been concerned with ethical responsibility. Since the time of Plato and Aristotle, communication scholars have grappled with the obligations that go along with the opportunities we have to communicate. Contemporary discussions of morality are increasingly beleaguered by the rise of ethical relativism.[33] Yet despite the postmodern challenge to all claims of Truth, at the turn of the century, the National Communication Association (NCA) adopted a "Credo for Ethical Communication" (see Appendix C).[34] Like most attempts to deal with communication ethics, it addresses the problem of what is ethical and starts with the issue of honesty versus lying. I'll cite three of the creed's nine principles in order to illustrate the major streams of thought within the ethical tradition:[35]

1. *We advocate truthfulness, accuracy, honesty, and reason as essential to the integrity of communication.* This principle centers on the *rightness* or *wrongness* of a communication act regardless of whether it benefits the people involved. It speaks to the question of *obligation.* Is it always our *duty* to be honest?
2. *We accept responsibility for the short- and long-term consequences of our own communication and expect the same of others.* This principle is concerned with the *harm* or *benefit* that results from our words. It raises the question of *outcomes.* Will a lie promote *well-being* or prevent *injury?*
3. *We strive to understand and respect other communicators before evaluating and responding to their messages.* This principle focuses on the *character* of the communicator rather than the act of communication. It bids us to look at our *motives* and *attitudes.* Do I seek to be a person of *integrity* and *virtue?*

These are difficult questions to answer, and some readers might suggest that they have no place in a communication theory text. But to deal with human intercourse as a mechanical process separate from values would be like discussing sexual intercourse under ground rules that prohibit any reference to love. And within the ethical tradition, communication theorists do offer answers to these questions.

Many ethical theorists come out of interpretive traditions. For example, the final chapter of Bill Rawlins' book *The Compass of Friendship* suggests what a friendship aligned with a moral compass looks like. The friends negotiate their relationship voluntarily, care about each other's well-being, respect each other as equals, and engage in ongoing learning about each other.[36] But some objective scholars care about ethical communication, too. Andrew's TCU friend and colleague Paul Witt is steeped in the socio-psychological tradition. He also teaches "Communication and Character," a course that examines honesty, compassion, courage, patience, and humility—important ingredients for ethical friendships. Thus, we won't try to locate the ethical tradition in any single spot on the objective–interpretive landscape in Figure 4–1. We have, however, encapsuled the thoughts of some influential ethical theorists into 13 summary statements. Each of these *ethical reflections* appears in this book alongside a theory with which it naturally resonates.

With or without our addition of an ethical tradition, Craig's framework can help make sense of the great diversity in the field of communication theory. As you read about a theory in the section on media effects, remember that it may have the same ancestry as a theory you studied earlier in the section on relationship development. On the first page of each of the next 32 chapters, we'll tie each theory to one or more traditions. Hopefully this label will make it easier for you to understand why the theorist has made certain choices. The labels are signposts that will help you navigate the world of communication theory.

QUESTIONS TO SHARPEN YOUR FOCUS

1. Considering the differences between *objective* and *interpretive* theory, can you make a case that the *rhetorical* tradition is less objective than the *semiotic* one or that the *socio-cultural* tradition is more interpretive than the *critical* one?
2. Suppose you and your best friend have recently been on an emotional roller coaster. Which of the seven highlighted *definitions of communication* offers the most promise of helping you achieve a stable relationship? Why?
3. Communication departments rarely have a faculty representing all seven traditions. In order to create specialties and minimize conflict, some recruit from just one or two. What tradition(s) seems well-represented in your department?
4. The map in Figure 4–1 represents seven traditions in the field of communication theory. In which region do you feel most at home? What other areas would you like to explore? Where would you be uncomfortable? Why?

A SECOND LOOK

Recommended resource: Robert T. Craig, "Communication Theory as a Field," *Communication Theory,* Vol. 9, 1999, pp. 119–161.

Communication as a practical discipline: Robert T. Craig, "Communication as a Practical Discipline," in *Rethinking Communication: Vol. 1,* Brenda Dervin, Lawrence Grossberg, Barbara O'Keefe, and Ellen Wartella (eds.), Sage, Newbury Park, CA, 1989, pp. 97–122.

Anthology of primary resources for each tradition: Heidi L. Muller and Robert T. Craig (eds.), *Theorizing Communication: Readings Across Traditions,* Sage, Los Angeles, CA, 2007.

Socio-psychological tradition: Carl Hovland, Irving Janis, and Harold Kelley, *Communication and Persuasion,* Yale University, New Haven, CT, 1953, pp. 1–55.

Cybernetic tradition: Norbert Wiener, *The Human Use of Human Beings,* Avon, New York, 1967, pp. 23–100.

Rhetorical tradition: Thomas M. Conley, *Rhetoric in the European Tradition,* Longman, New York, 1990, pp. 1–52.

Semiotic tradition: C. K. Ogden and I. A. Richards, *The Meaning of Meaning,* Harcourt, Brace & World, New York, 1946, pp. 1–23.

Phenomenological tradition: Carl Rogers, "The Characteristics of a Helping Relationship," in *On Becoming a Person,* Houghton Mifflin, Boston, MA, 1961, pp. 39–58.

Socio-cultural tradition: Benjamin Lee Whorf, "The Relation of Habitual Thought and Behaviour to Language," in *Language, Culture, and Personality: Essays in Memory of Edward Sapir,* University of Utah, Salt Lake City, UT, 1941, pp. 123–149.

Critical tradition: Raymond Morrow with David Brown, *Critical Theory and Methodology,* Sage, Thousand Oaks, CA, 1994, pp. 3–34, 85–112.

Ethical tradition: Richard L. Johannesen, "Communication Ethics: Centrality, Trends, and Controversies," in *Communication Yearbook 25,* William B. Gudykunst (ed.), Lawrence Erlbaum, Mahwah, NJ, 2001, pp. 201–235.

Pragmatic tradition: Robert T. Craig, "Pragmatism in the Field of Communication Theory," *Communication Theory,* Vol. 17, 2007, pp. 125–145.

Critique of Craig's model and his response: David Myers, "A Pox on All Compromises: Reply to Craig (1999)," and Robert T. Craig, "Minding My Metamodel, Mending Myers," *Communication Theory,* Vol. 11, 2001, pp. 218–230, 231–240.

To access three-level sentence outlines for all 37 chapters,
click on Outline under Theory Resources at
www.afirstlook.com.

Interpersonal Communication

DIVISION TWO

Interpersonal Communication

Interpersonal Messages

Communication theorists often use the image of a game to describe interpersonal communication. Various scholars refer to *language games, rules of the game, gamelike behavior,* and even *game theory.* I'll use three specific game metaphors to illustrate what interpersonal communication *is,* and what it *is not.*[1]

Communication as Bowling The bowling model of message delivery is likely the most widely held view of communication. I think that's unfortunate.

This model sees the bowler as the sender, who delivers the ball, which is the message. As it rolls down the lane (the channel), clutter on the boards (noise) may deflect the ball (the message). Yet if it is aimed well, the ball strikes the passive pins (the target audience) with a predictable effect.

In this one-way model of communication, the speaker (bowler) must take care to select a precisely crafted message (ball) and practice diligently to deliver it the same way every time. Of course, that makes sense only if target listeners are static, interchangeable pins waiting to be bowled over by our words—which they aren't. Communication theory that emphasizes message content to the neglect of relational factors simply isn't realistic. Real-life interpersonal communication is sometimes confusing, often unpredictable, and always involves more than just the speaker's action. This realization has led some observers to propose an interactive model for interpersonal communication.

Communication as Ping-Pong Unlike bowling, Ping-Pong is not a solo game. This fact alone makes it a better analogy for interpersonal communication. One party puts the conversational ball in play, and the other gets into position to receive. It takes more concentration and skill to receive than to serve because while the speaker (server) knows where the message is going, the listener (receiver) doesn't. Like a verbal or nonverbal message, the ball may appear straightforward yet have a deceptive spin.

Ping-Pong is a back-and-forth game; players switch roles continuously. One moment the person holding the paddle is an initiator; the next second the same player is a responder, gauging the effectiveness of his or her shot by the way the ball comes back. The repeated adjustment essential for good play closely parallels the feedback process described in a number of interpersonal communication theories. There are, however, two inherent flaws in the table-tennis analogy.

The first defect is that the game is played with one ball, which at any point in time is headed in a single direction. A true model of interpersonal encounters would have people sending and receiving multiple balls at the same time. The other problem is that table tennis is a competitive game—there's a winner and a loser. In successful dialogue, both people win.

Communication as Charades The game of charades best captures the simultaneous and collaborative nature of interpersonal communication. A charade is neither an action, like bowling a strike, nor an interaction, like a rally in Ping-Pong. It's a *transaction.*

Charades is a mutual game; the actual play is cooperative. One member draws a title or slogan from a batch of possibilities and then tries to act it out visually for teammates in a silent minidrama. The goal is to get at least one partner to say the exact words that are on the slip of paper. Of course, the actor is prohibited from talking out loud.

Suppose you drew the saying "God helps those who help themselves." For *God* you might try folding your hands and gazing upward. For *helps* you could act out offering a helping hand or giving a leg-up boost over a fence. By pointing at a number of real or imaginary people you may elicit a response of *them,* and by this point a partner may shout out, "God helps those who help themselves." Success.

Like charades, interpersonal communication is a mutual, ongoing process of sending, receiving, and adapting verbal and nonverbal messages with another person to create and alter the images in both our minds. Communication between us begins when there is some overlap between two images, and is effective to the extent that overlap increases. But even if our mental pictures are congruent, communication will be partial as long as we interpret them differently. The idea that "God helps those who help themselves" could strike one person as a hollow promise, while the other might regard it as a divine stamp of approval for hard work.

The three theories in this section reject a simplistic, one-way bowling analogy and an interactive Ping-Pong model of interpersonal communication. Instead, they view interpersonal communication in a way more akin to charades—a complex transaction in which overlapping messages simultaneously affect and are affected by the other person and multiple other factors.

© John O'Brien/The New Yorker Collection/www.cartoonbank.com

CHAPTER 5

Objective — Interpretive

Socio-cultural tradition

Symbolic Interactionism

of George Herbert Mead

George Herbert Mead was an early *social constructionist*. Mead believed that our thoughts, self-concept, and the wider community we live in are created through communication—symbolic interaction. The book that lays out his theory, *Mind, Self, and Society*, describes how language is essential for these three critical human characteristics to develop.[1] Without symbolic interaction, humanity as we know it wouldn't exist.

Symbolic interaction isn't just talk. The term refers to the language and gestures a person uses in anticipation of the way others will respond. The verbal and nonverbal responses that a listener then provides are likewise crafted in expectation of how the original speaker will react. The continuing process is like the game of charades described in the introduction to this section; it's a full-fledged conversation.

Symbolic interaction
The ongoing use of language and gestures in anticipation of how the other will react; a conversation.

Mead was a philosophy professor at the University of Chicago for the first three decades of the twentieth century. As a close personal friend of renowned pragmatist John Dewey, he shared Dewey's applied approach to knowledge. Mead thought the true test of any theory is whether it is useful in solving complex social problems. If it doesn't work in practice, forget it! He was a social activist who marched for women's suffrage, championed labor unions in an era of robber-baron capitalism, and helped launch the urban settlement house movement with pioneer social worker Jane Addams.

Although Mead taught in a philosophy department, he is best known by sociologists as the professor who trained a generation of the best minds in their field. Strangely, he never set forth his wide-ranging ideas in a book or systematic treatise. After he died, his students pulled together class notes and conversations with their mentor and published *Mind, Self, and Society* in his name. It was only then that his chief disciple, Herbert Blumer at the University of California, Berkeley, coined the term *symbolic interactionism*. This phrase captures what Mead claimed is the most human and humanizing activity that people can engage in—talking to each other.

Blumer stated three core principles of symbolic interactionism that deal with *meaning*, *language*, and *thinking*.[2] These premises lead to conclusions about the creation of a person's *self* and socialization into the larger *society*. The rest of this chapter discusses these five related topics one by one. I'll offer a variety of interactionist stories and qualitative research to illustrate Mead's claims.

MEANING: THE CONSTRUCTION OF SOCIAL REALITY

Blumer started with the premise that *humans act toward people or things on the basis of the meanings they assign to those people or things.* Facts don't speak for themselves; it's our interpretation that counts. And once people define a situation as real, it's very real in its consequences.[3]

For Mead, meaning-making isn't an individual undertaking. Interpretations are a joint venture. This idea is illustrated in Jane Wagner's one-woman play *The Search for Signs of Intelligent Life in the Universe,* in which Trudy, an urban bag lady, views society from her perspective on the street. Her words underscore the interactionist position that social reality is created and validated within community:

> It's my belief we all, at one time or another,
> secretly ask ourselves the question,
> "Am *I* crazy?"
> In my case, the answer came back: A resounding
> YES!
>
> You're thinkin': How does a person know if they're crazy or not? Well, sometimes you don't know. Sometimes you can go through life suspecting you *are* but never really knowing for sure. Sometimes you know for sure 'cause you got so many people tellin' you you're crazy that it's your word against everyone else's. . . .
>
> After all, what is reality anyway? Nothin' but a collective hunch.[4]

What causes people to react this way toward Trudy? For followers of Mead that's a loaded question, one that reflects the stimulus–response thinking of behavioral scientists. Interactionists are united in their disdain for deterministic thinking. The closest they come to the idea of causality is to argue that humans act on their definition of the situation.[5] An interactionist revision of the way scientists diagram stimulus–response causality might look like this:

Stimulus ➔ Interpretation ➔ Response

The middle term in the chain shows that it's the meaning that matters. As Trudy notes, however, when those interpretations are shared throughout society, they become hard to resist.

LANGUAGE: THE SOURCE OF MEANING

Blumer's second premise is that *meaning arises out of the social interaction that people have with each other.* In other words, meaning is not inherent in objects; it's not pre-existent in a state of nature. Meaning is negotiated through the use of *language*—hence the term *symbolic interactionism.*

As human beings, we have the ability to name things. We can designate a specific object *(person),* identify an action *(scream),* or refer to an abstract idea *(crazy).* Occasionally a word sounds like the thing it describes *(smack, thud, crash),* but usually the names we use have no logical connection with the object at hand. Symbols are arbitrary signs. There's nothing inherently small, soft, or lovable in the word *kitten.*[6] It's only by talking with others—symbolic interaction—that we come to ascribe that meaning and develop a universe of discourse.

Mead believed that symbolic naming is the basis for human society. The book of Genesis in the Judeo-Christian Scriptures states that Adam's first task was to name the animals—the dawn of civilization. Interactionists claim that the extent of knowing is dependent on the extent of naming. Although language can be a prison that confines us, we have the potential to push back the walls and bars as we master more words. From your experience taking the SAT or ACT college entrance exams, you probably recall a major focus on linguistic aptitude. The construction of the test obviously reflects agreement with the interactionist claim that human intelligence is the ability to symbolically identify much of what we encounter.

But symbolic interaction is not just a means for intelligent expression; it's also the way we learn to interpret the world. A symbol is "a stimulus that has a learned meaning and value for people."[7] A symbol conveys messages of how we are to feel about and respond to the object, event, or person to which it refers.[8] Consider the puzzle posed by the following story:

> A father and his son were driving to a ball game when their car stalled on the railroad tracks. In the distance a train whistle blew a warning. Frantically, the father tried to start the engine, but in his panic, he couldn't turn the key, and the car was hit by the onrushing train. An ambulance sped to the scene and picked them up. On the way to the hospital, the father died. The son was still alive but his condition was very serious, and he needed immediate surgery. The moment they arrived at the hospital, he was wheeled into an emergency operating room, and the surgeon came in, expecting a routine case. However, on seeing the boy the surgeon blanched and muttered, "I can't operate on this boy—he's my son."[9]

How can this be? How do you explain the surgeon's dilemma? If the answer isn't immediately obvious, I encourage you to close the book and think it through.

This puzzle is the opening paragraph of an article that appears in a fascinating book of readings that is my Second Look resource for applications of symbolic interactionism. Douglas Hofstadter, the man who poses the problem, is adamant that readers mull it over until they figure out the answer. There's no doubt, he assures us, that we'll know it when we get it.

I first heard this puzzle in a slightly different form about a decade ago. I'm ashamed to admit that it took me a few minutes to figure out the answer. My chagrin is heightened by the fact that my doctor is the wife of a departmental colleague and my daughter-in-law is a physician as well. How could I have been taken in?

Hofstadter's answer to my question is that the words we use have *default assumptions*. Since the story contains no reference to the doctor's gender, and the majority of surgeons in America are men, we'll likely assume that the surgeon in the story is male. While such an assumption may have some basis in fact, the subtle tyranny of symbols is that we usually don't consciously think about the mental jump we're making. Unless we're brought up short by some obvious glitch in our taken-for-granted logic, we'll probably conjure up a male figure every time we read or hear the word *surgeon*. What's more, we'll probably assume that the way we think things are is the way they ought to be.

Significant symbols can of course be nonverbal as well as linguistic. When I asked my students to apply a feature of symbolic interaction to their own experience, Glynka wrote the following:

> A ring. A class ring. A guy's class ring. In high school it was the ultimate symbol of status, whether dangling from a chain or wrapped with a quarter inch of yarn.

> Without ever speaking a word, a girl could tell everybody that she was loved (and trusted with expensive jewelry), that she had a protector (and how big that protector was, based, of course, on ring size—the bigger the better), the guy's status (preferably senior), and his varsity sport (preferably football). Yes, if you had the (right) class ring, you were really somebody.

She then noted it was only through hundreds of conversations among students at her school that the privileges and responsibilities that went with wearing the ring became something "everyone knows." Without symbolic interaction, there's no shared meaning.

THINKING: THE PROCESS OF TAKING THE ROLE OF THE OTHER

Blumer's third premise is that *an individual's interpretation of symbols is modified by his or her own thought processes.* Symbolic interactionists describe thinking as an inner conversation. Mead called this inner dialogue *minding*.

Minding is the pause that's reflective. It's the two-second delay while we mentally rehearse our next move, test alternatives, anticipate others' reactions. Mead said we don't need any encouragement to look before we leap. We naturally talk to ourselves in order to sort out the meaning of a difficult situation. But first, we need language. Before we can think, we must be able to interact symbolically.

Minding
An inner dialogue used to test alternatives, rehearse actions, and anticipate reactions before responding; self-talk.

The Lion King, *Finding Nemo*, and *Dr. Dolittle* movies aside, Mead believed that animals act "instinctively" and "without deliberation."[10] They are unable to think reflectively because, with few exceptions, they are unable to communicate symbolically. The human animal comes equipped with a brain that is wired for thought. But that alone is not sufficient for thinking. Interactionists maintain that "humans require social stimulation and exposure to abstract symbol systems to embark upon conceptual thought processes that characterize our species."[11] Language is the software that activates the mind, but it doesn't come pre-installed. Without the symbolic interaction that learning a language requires, we wouldn't be able to think through our responses—we'd only react.[12]

If the idea that language is required for mulling over ideas or interpersonal situations strikes you as far-fetched, consider the plight of a baby born deaf. If the condition isn't spotted early and the infant isn't taught sign language, the result is a case of arrested cognitive development that is often misdiagnosed as retardation or autism. That's how the phrase *deaf and dumb* came to carry the unfortunate connotation of *stupid*. But as psychologist Oliver Sacks documents in his book *Seeing Voices*, if the child is immersed in a signing community early on, by age three he or she will develop cognitive skills equal to or better than those of kids who have normal hearing.[13] It appears Mead had it right. Symbolic interaction—whether verbal or nonverbal—activates our cognitive ability for inner dialogue that, once switched on, won't shut down.

Mead's greatest contribution to our understanding of the way we think is his notion that human beings have the unique capacity to *take the role of the other.* Early in life, kids role-play the activities of their parents, talk with imaginary friends, and take constant delight in pretending to be someone else. As adults, we continue to put ourselves in the place of others and act as they would act, although the process may be less conscious. Mead was convinced that thinking is the mental conversation we hold with others, always with an eye toward how they might see us and react to what we might do.

Taking the role of the other
The process of mentally imagining that you are someone else who is viewing you.

In Harper Lee's novel *To Kill a Mockingbird,* Scout stands on Boo Radley's porch and recalls her father's words, "You never really know a man until you stand in his shoes and walk around in them."[14] That's a clear statement of what symbolic interactionism means by role-taking. The young, impulsive girl takes the perspective of a painfully shy, emotionally fragile man. Note that she doesn't *become* him—that would be *Invasion of the Body Snatchers.* She does, however, look out at the world through his eyes. More than anything else, what she sees is herself.

THE SELF: REFLECTIONS IN A LOOKING GLASS

Once we understand that *meaning, language,* and *thinking* are tightly interconnected, we're able to grasp Mead's concept of the *self.* Mead dismissed the idea that we could get glimpses of who we are through introspection. He claimed, instead, that we paint our self-portrait with brush strokes that come from *taking the role of the other*—imagining how we look to another person. Interactionists call this mental image the *looking-glass self* and insist that it's socially constructed. Mead borrowed the phrase from sociologist Charles Cooley, who adapted it from a poem by Ralph Waldo Emerson. Emerson wrote that each close companion . . .

> Is to his friend a looking-glass
> Reflects his figure that doth pass.[15]

Looking-glass self
The mental self-image that results from taking the role of the other; the objective self; me.

Stated more formally, the Mead–Cooley hypothesis claims that "individuals' self-conceptions result from assimilating the judgments of significant others."[16]

Symbolic interactionists are convinced that the self is a function of language. Without talk there would be no self-concept. "We are not born with senses of self. Rather, selves arise in interaction with others. I can only experience myself in relation to others; absent interaction with others, I cannot be a self—I cannot emerge as someone."[17] To the extent that we interact with new acquaintances or have novel conversations with significant others, the self is always in flux. This means that there is no etched-in-stone Em Griffin inside my body waiting to be discovered or set free.

I
The subjective self; the spontaneous driving force that fosters all that is novel, unpredictable, and unorganized in the self.

According to Mead, the self is an ongoing process combining the "I" and the "me." The "I" is the spontaneous, driving force that fosters all that is novel, unpredictable, and unorganized in the self. For those of you intrigued with brain hemisphere research, the "I" is akin to right-brain creativity. We know little about the "I" because it's forever elusive. Trying to examine the "I" part of the self is like viewing a snowflake through a lighted microscope. The very act causes it to vanish. Put another way, you can never know your "I," because once it is known it becomes your "me."[18]

Me
The objective self; the image of self seen when one takes the role of the other.

The "me" is viewed as an object—the image of self seen in the looking glass of other people's reactions. Do you remember in grammar school how you learned to identify the personal pronoun *me* in a sentence as the *object* of a verb? Because of the role-taking capacity of the human race, we can stand outside our bodies and view ourselves as objects. This reflexive experience is like having the Goodyear blimp hover overhead, sending back video images of ourselves while we act. Mead described the process this way: "If the 'I' speaks, the

'me' hears."[19] And "the 'I' of this moment is present in the 'me' of the next moment."[20]

Sociologist Thomas Scheff uses Mead's distinction between the "I" and the "me" to explain the creative genius of Beethoven, Bach, Brahms, and other renowned composers. In each case, the creative impulse of their subjective "I" was tutored and nurtured by a close relative who himself was a gifted musician. The abundance of positive feedback they received early on as opposed to ridicule for any errors they might make created an objective "me" with a high level of self-esteem. Thus, each composer could later trust his creative impulses when audiences were critical.

Scheff defines self-esteem as "freedom from chronic shame."[21] Even if w don't share the musical genius of these classical composers, Scheff suggests th affectionate or good-humored laughter almost always dispels shame and boos s our evaluation of the "me" we perceive.

SOCIETY: THE SOCIALIZING EFFECT OF OTHERS' EXPECTATIONS

Mead and other symbolic interactionists refer to the composite person in our mind with whom we are in dialogue as our *generalized other.* Our conversational partner is a blend of not only significant others—family, close friends, an outside authority figure—but also voices from the broader society. Although Mead died before the impact of television and the Internet, I believe he'd regard the hours we're glued to a screen and the responses we receive through social media as playing a big part in shaping the content of that inner dialogue.[22] Those mental conversations are important because:

> The generalized other is an organized set of information that the individual carries in her or his head about what the general expectation and attitudes of the social group are. We refer to this generalized other whenever we try to figure out how to behave or how to evaluate our behavior in a social situation. We take the position of the generalized other and assign meaning to ourselves and our actions.[23]

Generalized other
The composite mental image a person has of his or her self based on societal expectations and responses.

Unlike most sociologists, Mead saw society as consisting of individual actors who make their own choices—society-in-the-making rather than society-by-previous-design.[24] Yet these individuals align their actions with what others are doing to form education systems, health care systems, legal systems, economic systems, and all the other societal institutions in which they take part. It is unclear from *Mind, Self, and Society* whether Mead regarded the *generalized other* as (1) an overarching looking-glass self that we put together from the reflections we see in everyone we know or (2) the institutional expectations, rules of the game, or accepted practices within society that influence every conversation that takes place in people's minds. Either way, the generalized other shapes how we think and interact within the community.

To summarize, there is no "me" at birth. The "me" is formed only through continual symbolic interaction—first with family, next with playmates, then in institutions such as schools. As the generalized other develops, this imaginary composite person becomes the conversational partner in an ongoing mental dialogue. In this way, kids participate in their own socialization. The child gradually acquires the roles of those in the surrounding community. Mead would have us think of the "me" as the organized society within the individual.

But society does not always speak in a single, consistent voice. The application log of Andrew's student Cody strikingly reveals how a person's generalized other can change in a short period of time when a single group holds sway.

> I joined the military at age 18 and in three hellish months of basic training witnessed firsthand how the Army used language to create a new reality and alter my self-concept. I was told to stand in line and "shut my mouth." My orders were to follow orders. I was not to ask why, or question the judgment of my leaders. As one of my drill sergeants so eloquently stated, "You were not issued an opinion." All of the sergeants made us repeat mantras such as "BLOOD, BLOOD, BLOOD, MAKES THE GREEN GRASS GROW" and "Two in the chest, one in the head, KILL, KILL, KILL."
>
> The Army created a new social reality. The drill sergeants were the models for what we as soldiers were to become. They would recite tales of killing like normal men would recall catching a touchdown pass in high school. I was told over and over, "Killing is what we do; it is a privilege. You all will learn to do so efficiently

and without remorse." Only through killing the enemy could we neutralize any threat our republic deemed dangerous.

Where previously I thought of killing as a practice reserved for villains and tyrants, I came to see it as not only acceptable but something worthy of praise. I thirsted for the opportunity to prove myself worthy of the task; I longed to belong to the hall of hallowed combat vets. When my father looked me in the eyes and my drill sergeant shook my hand at my graduation from Basic Combat Training, I knew that I had changed. I was able to define myself by what others expected and the way others treated me. In Mead's terms, I had become a new "me." I later served as a drill sergeant.

A SAMPLER OF APPLIED SYMBOLIC INTERACTION

Since Mead believed that a theory is valuable to the extent that it is useful, I've pulled together six separate applications of symbolic interactionism. Not only will this provide a taste of the practical insights the theory has generated, it will give you a chance to review some of the theoretical ideas covered in the chapter.

Creating Reality. Shakespeare wrote, "All the world's a stage, and all the men and women merely players."[25] In his book *The Presentation of Self in Everyday Life,* University of California, Berkeley, sociologist Erving Goffman described social interaction as a dramaturgical performance.[26] Consistent with that character-in-a-play metaphor, Goffman claimed that we are all involved in a constant negotiation with others to publicly define our identity and the nature of the situation. He warned that "the impression of reality fostered by a performance is a delicate, fragile thing that can be shattered by minor mishaps."[27] His colleague Joan Emerson outlines the cooperative effort required to sustain the definition of a gynecological exam as a routine medical procedure.[28] The doctor and nurse enact their roles in a medical setting to assure patients that "everything is normal, no one is embarrassed, no one is thinking in sexual terms." The audience of one is reassured only when the actors give a consistent performance.

Meaning-ful Research. Mead advocated research through participant observation, a form of ethnography in which researchers systematically set out to share in the lives of the people they study. The participant observer adopts the stance of an interested—yet ignorant—visitor who listens carefully to what people say in order to discover how they interpret their world. Mead had little sympathy for tightly controlled behavioral experiments or checklist surveys. The results might be quantifiable, but the lifeless numbers are void of the meaning the experience had for the person. Mead would have liked the wrangler who said that the only way to understand horses is to smell like a horse, eat from a trough, and sleep in a stall. That's participant observation.

Participant observation
A method of adopting the stance of an ignorant yet interested visitor who carefully notes what people say and do in order to discover how they interpret their world.

Generalized Other. The sobering short story "Cipher in the Snow" tells the true account of a boy who is treated as a nonentity by his parents, his teachers, and other children. Their negative responses gradually reduce him to what they perceive him to be—nothing. He eventually collapses and dies in a snowbank for no apparent reason. The interactionist would describe his death as symbolic manslaughter.[29] This sad outcome brings to mind the 2012 Sandy Hook school massacre and many other events where a single shooter turns a gun on a group of people and then commits suicide. In the bloody aftermath, the authorities discover that the killer was a detached soul who lived a life of social isolation and alienation after years of verbal and nonverbal put-downs. Interactionists might call this symbolic destruction.

Naming. Here's a partial list of epithets I heard in public places over a one-year period; they were all spoken in a demeaning voice: *dummy, ugly, slob, fag, nigger, retard, fundamentalist, liberal, Neanderthal, slut, liar.* Sticks and stones can break my bones, but names can *really* hurt me. Name-calling can be devastating because the labels force us to view ourselves in a warped mirror. The grotesque images aren't easily dismissed.

Self-Fulfilling Prophecy. One implication of the looking-glass-self hypothesis is that each of us has a significant impact on how others view themselves. That kind of interpersonal power is often referred to as *self-fulfilling prophecy,* the tendency for our expectations to evoke responses in others that confirm what we originally anticipated. The process is nicely summed up by Eliza Doolittle, a woman from the gutter in George Bernard Shaw's play *Pygmalion,* the inspiration for the musical *My Fair Lady:* "The difference between a lady and a flower girl is not how she behaves, but how she's treated."[30]

Self-fulfilling prophecy
The tendency for our expectations to evoke responses that confirm what we originally anticipated.

Symbol Manipulation. Saul Alinsky was a product of the "Chicago School" of sociology at a time when Mead was having his greatest influence. Similar to Barack Obama, Alinsky became a community organizer in Chicago when he finished grad school, and applied what he learned to empower the urban poor. For example, in the early 1960s he helped found The Woodlawn Organization (TWO) to oppose his alma mater's complicity in substandard neighborhood housing. He searched for a symbol that would galvanize Woodlawn residents into united action and stir the sympathies of other Chicago residents. He had previously described his technique for selecting a symbolic issue:

> You start with the people, their traditions, their prejudices, their habits, their attitudes and all of those other circumstances that make up their lives. It should always be remembered that a real organization of the people . . . must be rooted in the experiences of the people themselves.[31]

Alinsky found his symbol in the rats that infested the squalid apartments. TWO's rallying cry became "Rats as big as cats." Not only did the city start to crack down on slum landlords, but for the first time Woodlawn residents gained a sense of identity, pride, and political clout.

ETHICAL REFLECTION: LEVINAS' RESPONSIVE "I"

European Jewish philosopher Emmanuel Levinas agreed with Mead that the self is socially constructed. He stated that "without the Other, there is no 'I.' "[32] (Note that Levinas used the term "*I*" to refer to what Mead called the *self*—the "I" and the "me.") But there's a striking difference between how the two theorists thought this construction project takes place. Mead contended that the looking-glass self develops through the way *others respond to us;* Levinas insisted that the identity of our "I" is formed by the way *we respond to others.*

Responsive "I"
The self created by the way we respond to others.

Ethical echo
The reminder that we are responsible to take care of each other; I am my brother's keeper.

Face of the "Other"
A human signpost that points to our ethical obligation to care for the other before we care for self.

Levinas used the term *ethical echo* to designate the responsibility he believed we all have to take care of each other. That ethical echo has existed since the beginning of human history and is summed up in the words, *"I am my brother's keeper."* The way each of us meets that obligation shapes our "I." Levinas said that every time we gaze at *the face of the Other,* we are reminded of our caretaking responsibility. Thus, each person's face is a signpost pointing to the panhuman ethical requirement to actively care for all people. Since the "I" finds its identity in responding to and caring for the Other, not allowing the humanity of that face to register puts our identity at risk.

Levinas was clear about the burden that comes with looking at the face of the Other:

> My world is ruptured, my contentment interrupted. I am already obligated. Here is an appeal from which there is no escape, a responsibility, a state of being hostage. It is looking into the face of the Other that reveals the call to a responsibility that is before any beginning, decision or initiative on my part. . . . I am responsible for the Other without waiting for reciprocity, [even if I were] to die for it. Reciprocity is *his* affair.[33]

Duquesne University communication ethicist Ron Arnett regards Levinas as the premier ethical voice of the twentieth century. Arnett acknowledges that urging others to adopt a responsive "I" ethical standard is not an easy sell in this postmodern age, with its quest for comfort and self-actualization.[34] Yet Levinas noted that even in his dark hours as a prisoner in a World War II German concentration camp, he found joy in embracing the human responsibility of being for the Other before oneself. To the extent that we follow Levinas' lead, Arnett suggests that our interpersonal communication will be characterized more by listening than telling.[35]

CRITIQUE: SETTING THE GOLD STANDARD FOR FOUR INTERPRETIVE CRITERIA

"Viewing theory as testable explanations of directly or indirectly observable social regularities, Mead's ideas are seriously flawed."[36] That's the judgment of Indiana University sociologist Sheldon Stryker, and I agree. If we treat symbolic interactionism as an objective theory that must meet scientific standards of prediction and testability, it's a poor theory. But Mead's work was highly interpretive and deserves to be evaluated on the six criteria for good interpretive theories offered in Chapter 3, "Weighing the Words."

Let's start with *clarification of values,* which Mead did exceedingly well. Drawing upon William James, John Dewey, and other pragmatists, Mead proclaimed that humans are free to make meaningful choices on how to act when facing problems. In his critique, Stryker reveals, "What fascinated me as an undergraduate and graduate student was in part the dignity accorded humans by seeing them as important determiners of their lives rather than the pure product of conditioning."[37] Of course, this freedom and dignity are dependent upon our ability to communicate.

Certainly Mead offered a marvelous new *understanding of people* by showing how humans socially construct their concept of self as well as the way society influences—yet doesn't dictate—that construction project. We also can gain a new appreciation of human diversity from extensive, theory-inspired *ethnographic research* that describes individuals in similar situations responding in strikingly different ways.

Both the theory and the theorist have more than satisfied a fourth interpretive requirement for a good theory—the emergence of a *community of agreement*. The once-radical Mead–Cooley looking-glass-self hypothesis has now become a truism in the field of sociology.[38] Mead, a philosopher who saw communication as the most human thing people do, has been called "America's greatest sociological thinker."[39] Even if the text you use in your interpersonal course doesn't mention the theorist or the theory by name, you can spot Mead's pervasive influence by the way the book treats the topic of self-concept.

Symbolic interactionism doesn't meet the other two criteria for an interpretive theory nearly as well as the four discussed above. Given Mead's personal efforts to help the displaced and distressed amid urban industrialization, it's puzzling that Mead's theory doesn't call for *reform of society*. His theory says little about power or emotion—realities that a community organizer deals with every day.

In contrast to *aesthetic appeal*, most readers of *Mind, Self, and Society* get bogged down in the baffling array of ideas Mead tried to cover. The theory's fluid boundaries, vague concepts, and undisciplined approach don't lend themselves to an elegant summary. There are no *CliffsNotes* for this one. Perhaps Mead was precise when he presented his ideas in class, but their exact meaning became blurred in the years before his students compiled the manuscript. Whatever the explanation, the theory suffers from a lack of clarity.

A final note: Symbolic interactionism may also suffer from overstatement. Mead repeatedly declared that our capacity for language—the ability to use and interpret abstract symbols—is what distinguishes humans from other animals. My former graduate assistant is the mother of a son who has a permanent peripheral nerve disorder. His eyes, ears, and other sense receptors work fine, but the messages they send get scrambled on the way to his brain. Doctors say that he is, and always will be, unable to talk or interact with others on a symbolic level. After reading an early draft of this chapter, my assistant asked, "So this means that Caleb is less than human?" Her haunting question serves as a caution to any theorist who claims to have captured the essence of humanity.

QUESTIONS TO SHARPEN YOUR FOCUS

1. Blumer's three core *premises of symbolic interactionism* deal with *meaning, language,* and *thinking*. According to Blumer, which comes first? Can you make a case for an alternative sequence?
2. What do interactionists believe are the crucial differences between *human beings* and *animals?* What would you add to or subtract from the list?
3. As Mead used the terms, are the *looking-glass self,* the *objective self,* a person's *"me,"* and the *generalized other* all referring to the same thing? Why or why not?
4. Think of a time in your life when your self-concept changed in a significant way. Do you think the shift occurred because *others viewed you differently* or because *you treated others differently?* Could Mead and Levinas both be right?

SELF-QUIZ

For chapter self-quizzes, go to the book's Online Learning Center at *www.mhhe.com/griffin9e.*

A SECOND LOOK

Recommended resource: Larry T. Reynolds and Nancy J. Herman-Kinney (eds.), *Handbook of Symbolic Interactionism,* AltaMira, Walnut Creek, CA, 2003:

Gil Musolf, "The Chicago School," pp. 91–117.

Bernard Meltzer, "Mind," pp. 253–266.

Andrew Weigert and Viktor Gecas, "Self," pp. 267–288.

Michael Katovich and David Maines, "Society," pp. 289–306.

Primary source: George Herbert Mead, *Mind, Self, and Society,* University of Chicago, Chicago, IL, 1934.

Development of Mead's ideas: Herbert Blumer, *Symbolic Interactionism,* Prentice-Hall, Englewood Cliffs, NJ, 1969, pp. 1–89.

Summary statement: Herbert Blumer, "Symbolic Interaction: An Approach to Human Communication," in *Approaches to Human Communication,* Richard W. Budd and Brent Ruben (eds.), Spartan Books, New York, 1972, pp. 401–419.

Basic concepts of symbolic interactionism: John Hewitt, *Self and Society: A Symbolic Interactionist Social Psychology,* 10th ed., Allyn and Bacon, Boston, MA, 2006, pp. 36–81.

The self as a social construction: Susan Harter, "Symbolic Interactionism Revisited: Potential Liabilities for the Self Constructed in the Crucible of Interpersonal Relationships," *Merrill-Palmer Quarterly,* Vol. 45, 1999, pp. 677–703.

Looking-glass self—a research review: David Lundgren, "Social Feedback and Self-Appraisals: Current Status of the Mead–Cooley Hypothesis," *Symbolic Interaction,* Vol. 27, 2004, pp. 267–286.

Generalized other: Clare Holdsworth and David Morgan, "Revisiting the Generalized Other: An Exploration," *Sociology,* Vol. 41, 2007, pp. 401–417.

Theory application: Jodi O'Brien (ed.), *The Production of Reality,* 5th ed., Pine Forge, Thousand Oaks, CA, 2011.

Levinas' responsive "I": Ronald C. Arnett, "The Responsive 'I': Levinas' Derivative Argument," *Argumentation and Advocacy,* Vol. 40, 2003, pp. 39–50.

Critique: Peter Hull, "Structuring Symbolic Interaction: Communication and Power," *Communication Yearbook 4,* Dan Nimmo (ed.), Transaction Books, New Brunswick, NJ, 1980, pp. 49–60.

Critique: Sheldon Stryker, "From Mead to a Structural Symbolic Interactionism and Beyond," *Annual Review of Sociology,* Vol. 34, 2008, p. 18.

For self-scoring quizzes for this and all other chapters, click on Self-Help Quizzes under Theory Resources at *www.afirstlook.com.*

CHAPTER 6

Objective — Interpretive

Socio-cultural tradition
Phenomenological tradition

Coordinated Management of Meaning (CMM)

of W. Barnett Pearce & Vernon Cronen

Barnett Pearce and Vernon Cronen bemoan the fact that most communication theorists and practitioners hold to a *transmission model* of communication. This model depicts a source that sends a message through a channel to one or more receivers.

Transmission model
Picturing communication as a transfer of meaning by a source sending a message through a channel to a receiver.

Source → Message → Channel → Receiver

In this model, communication is considered successful to the extent that a high-fidelity version of the message gets through the channel and the receiver's interpretation of it closely matches what the sender meant. People who picture communication this way tend to focus either on the message content or on what each party is thinking, but CMM says that they lose sight of the pattern of communication and what that pattern creates.

Pearce, a communication professor at the Fielding Graduate Institute before he died in 2010, and Cronen (University of North Carolina Wilmington) would undoubtedly extend their critique to the definition of communication we offer in Chapter 1. We suggested that *communication is the relational process of creating and interpreting messages that elicit a response.* What's wrong with this description? Although the two theorists would appreciate our concern for relationship and response, they would note that our definition continues to treat communication as merely a means of exchanging ideas. They'd say that our definition looks *through* communication rather than directly *at* it. It renders the ongoing process invisible.

In contrast, Pearce and Cronen offer the *coordinated management of meaning* (CMM) as a theory that looks directly at the communication process and what it's doing. Because that process is complicated, the theory offers multiple insights into what communication is creating and a number of tools for changing our communication patterns. This way, we can grasp the essentials of the theory without being overwhelmed. Kimberly Pearce, Barnett's wife and president of the CMM Institute for Personal and Social Evolution, boils down CMM into four claims about communication.

FIRST CLAIM: OUR COMMUNICATION CREATES OUR SOCIAL WORLDS

Kim Pearce starts with what we've just covered and then adds what communication does: "Communication is not just a tool for exchanging ideas and information. . . . It 'makes' selves, relationships, organizations, communities, cultures, etc. This is what I've referred to as taking the *communication perspective.*"[1]

Communication perspective
An ongoing focus on how communication makes our social worlds.

Selves, relationships, organizations, communities, and cultures are the "stuff" that makes up our social worlds. For CMM theorists, our social worlds are not something we find or discover. Instead, we create them. For most of his professional life, Barnett Pearce summed up this core concept of the theory by asserting that *persons-in-conversation co-construct their own social realities and are simultaneously shaped by the worlds they create.*[2] Figure 6–1 presents artist M. C. Escher's 1955 lithograph *Bond of Union,* which strikingly illustrates a number of CMM's notions of how persons-in-conversation are making the social worlds of which they are a part. I see three parallels between the picture and the theory.

First, Escher's art foregrounds interpersonal communication as the primary activity that's going on in the social universe. This squares with CMM's claim that *the experience of persons-in-conversation is the primary social process of human life.*[3] Barnett Pearce said this idea runs counter to the prevailing intellectual view of "communication as an odorless, colorless vehicle of thought that is interesting or important only when it is done poorly or breaks down."[4] He saw the ribbon in Escher's drawing as representing patterns of communication that literally form who the persons-in-conversation are and create their relationship. Their conversation does something to them quite apart from the issue they're discussing.

FIGURE 6–1 M. C. Escher's *Bond of Union*

Second, the figures in the lithograph are bound together regardless of what they are talking about. This reflects Barnett Pearce's belief that the way people communicate is often more important than the content of what they say. The mood and manner that persons-in-conversation adopt play a large role in the process of social construction. He pointed out that the faces in *Bond of Union* have no substance; they consist in the twists and turns of the spiraling ribbon:

> Were the ribbon straightened or tied in another shape, there would be no loss of matter, but the faces would no longer exist. This image works for us as a model of the way the process of communication (the ribbon) creates the events and objects of our social worlds (the faces), not by its substance but by its form.[5]

Third, the endless ribbon in *Bond of Union* loops back to *re*form both persons-in-conversation. If Escher's figures were in conflict, each person would be wise to ask, "If I win this argument, what kind of person will I become?" Barnett Pearce said it's the same for us. Our actions are reflexively reproduced as the interaction continues; any action we take will bounce back and affect us. That's also true with the social worlds we create. Pearce wrote, "When we communicate, we are not just talking about the world, we are literally participating in the creation of the social universe."[6] And, like the figures in the lithograph, we then have to live in it.

Social constructionists Curious participants in a pluralistic world who believe that persons-in-conversation co-construct their own social realities and are simultaneously shaped by the worlds they create.

These ideas identify CMM theorists and practitioners as *social constructionists*—curious participants in a pluralistic world. Barnett Pearce said they are *curious* because they think it's folly to profess certainty when dealing with individuals acting out their lives under ever-changing conditions. They are *participants* rather than spectators because they seek to be actively involved in what they study. They live in a *pluralistic world* because they assume that people make multiple truths rather than find a singular Truth.[7] So Escher's *Bond of Union* is an apt representation of persons-in-conversation even when one or both of the parties are CMM advocates.

SECOND CLAIM: THE STORIES WE TELL DIFFER FROM THE STORIES WE LIVE

CMM uses the term *story* to refer to much of what we say when we talk with others about our social worlds—ourselves, others, relationships, organizations, or the larger community. Pearce and Cronen claim that communication is a two-sided process of *stories told* and *stories lived*.[8] Stories told are tales we tell to make sense of the world and tame the terrors that go bump in the night. CMM calls this *making and managing meaning*. Stories lived are the ongoing patterns of interaction we enact as we seek to mesh our lives with others around us. CMM calls this effort *coordinating our actions together*. Pearce and Cronen labeled their theory *coordinated management of meaning* to encompass both types of stories.

Stories Told: Making and Managing Meaning

The stories we tell or hear are never as simple as they seem. Take, for example, the story that appeared in my inbox a month before my high school reunion. Decades earlier, the writer (Bea) and I had been in the same 7th and 8th grade class where we engaged in what I would describe as mild flirtation. Here's what I read:

> I'm writing because I still think about the mystery of you not speaking to me all the way through high school. You may not even remember that you ignored me,

> but I do. What did I do to make you so angry? My mother always wondered if someone had said something to you about me that wasn't true. I just never knew. I would feel better if we could say "hello" at least at the gathering.

This seems to be a rather straightforward tale of a young girl who felt bad when a guy ignored her. If so, you might expect a *that-was-years-ago* reaction, a *get-a-life* response, or a quick mouse click on *delete*. Pearce and Cronen suggest, however, that there's always much more to stories told that could enrich or alter their meaning. Emphasizing that CMM is a practical theory, they offer a number of analytical tools to help the listener consider alternative or additional interpretations. When I got this message from Bea, I used their LUUUUTT model pictured in Figure 6–2 to help me expand the story and possibly narrow the disparity between her account of me in the distant past and the stories each of us might want to live now.

LUUUUTT is an acronym to label the seven types of stories identified in the model.[9] The focus of the model depicts the tension between our stories lived and our stories told. That tension can be increased or decreased by the manner in which the stories are presented. The four descriptions of non-obvious stories radiating toward the corners remind us there's always more to the situation that we haven't seen or heard. Barnett and Kim Pearce use the term *mystery* to cover everything relevant that is not, or cannot, be said. As I reread Bea's message, I tried to imagine what each of those seven interrelated stories in the LUUUUTT model might be.

1. **Lived stories**—*what we actually did or are doing.* I have no reason to doubt Bea's claim. Although I can't recall intentionally avoiding conversation with her in high school, neither do I have a mental image of us talking together, even though we were both cast members in the school play. In contrast, I know we chatted in junior high.
2. Unknown stories—*information that's missing.* Bea's mother suggested that I was turned off by lies I heard about her daughter. Not so. But the multiple possibilities that Bea imagined and couldn't discount would surely be distressing.

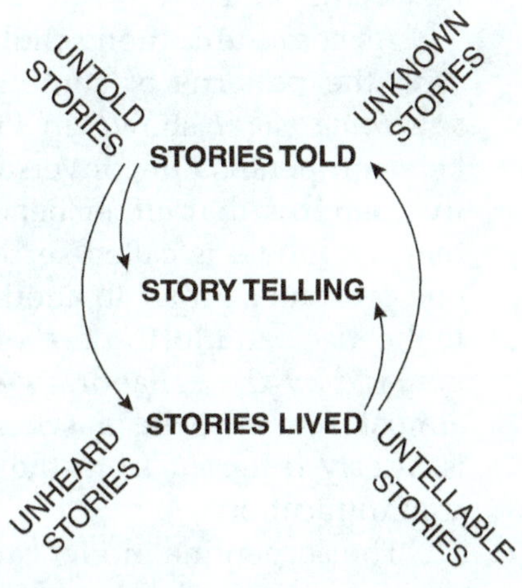

FIGURE 6–2 CMM's LUUUUTT Model

3. **U**ntold stories—*what we choose not to say.* There was nothing in Bea's message about the attention I paid to her in junior high or anger she might have felt at the abrupt change in my behavior. Nor did she say anything about her current life.
4. **U**nheard stories—*what we say that isn't heard or acknowledged.* Did Bea try to reach out to me during those four years of silence and, if so, did I snub her? To ignore her email message now would add insult to injury.
5. **U**ntellable stories—*stories that are forbidden or too painful for us to tell.* It would be the height of arrogance on my part to think that I had the power to ruin Bea's life back then. Yet I did wonder what she couldn't say.
6. Story **T**elling—*the manner in which we communicate.* "Why" questions often impute blame, but the tone of Bea's message struck me as a mix of curiosity, sadness, courage, and an honest effort to clear the air before the class reunion.
7. Stories **T**old—*what we say we are doing.* With Bea's permission, I've already cited the story she told in her email. The additional six stories that the LUUUUTT model generated don't negate what she expressed. As Kim Pearce explains,

> The point of the LUUUUTT model is not to "find the correct story" or "the correct interpretation" as much as enlarging your awareness of how complex our social worlds are. The more aware we are of the complexity of our social worlds, the greater our capacity for holding frustrating situations and people more compassionately.[10]

I'll revisit these stories told and my response to Bea when we examine the third claim of CMM.

Stories Lived: Coordinating Our Patterns of Interaction

There's almost always a difference or tension between our stories told and stories lived. That's because we can craft the stories we tell to be coherent and consistent, but the stories we live intersect with the actions and reactions of others. That makes them messy.

As communication scholars, Pearce and Cronen were particularly concerned with the patterns of communication we create with others. They offered the *serpentine model* shown in Figure 6–3 as a tool to capture what's taking place between persons-in-conversation. Without such a tool, we may miss the repetitive patterns that either benefit or pollute the social environment. Pearce wrote that the model is called serpentine because it "looks like a snake crawling from one person or group to another and back again. This model directs our attention to the 'back and forth-ness' of social interaction. Every aspect of our social worlds is made by the collaborative action of multiple people."[11] Note that the model almost seems to be a schematic drawing of Escher's *Bond of Union,* which is utterly different from the standard one-way message transmission model of communication.

The serpentine model can analyze any conversation and map out its history. The conversation between Wilson and Larry has only six turns and clearly reveals the deterioration of their stories lived. Turns 1 and 2 show an honest difference of opinion, each stated vehemently. In turn 3, Wilson's comment about the film director expands on his enthusiasm. But he also shows disdain for anyone who doesn't agree with him, lumping Larry with a class of people who are mentally

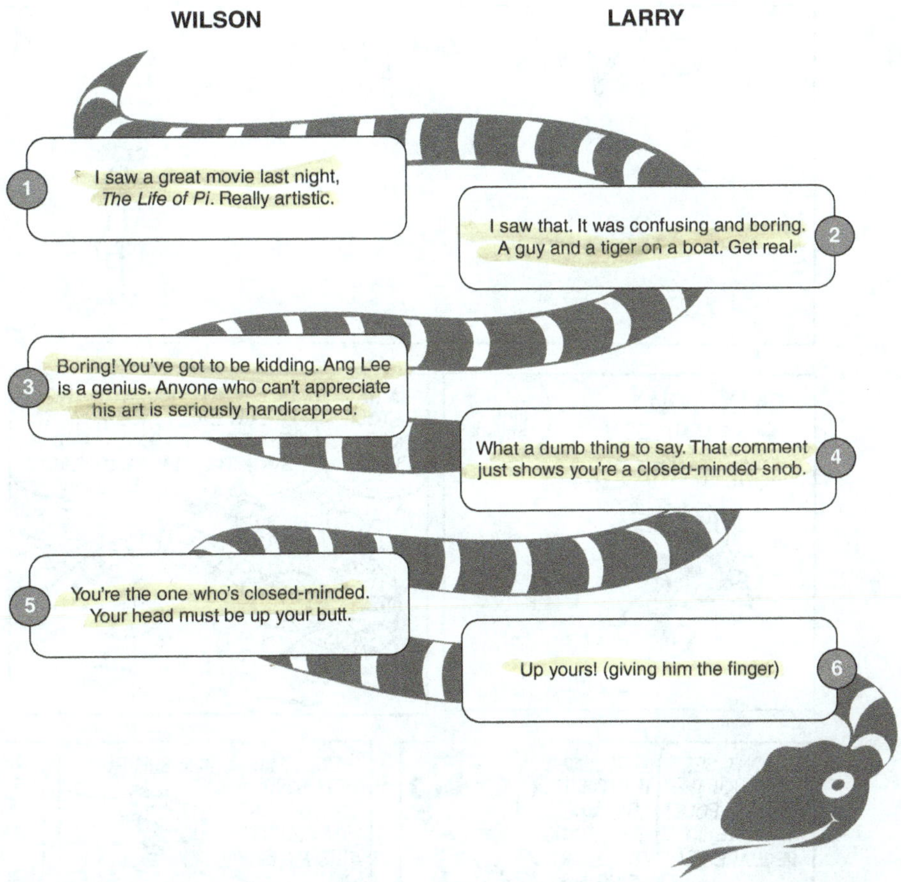

FIGURE 6–3 Serpentine Model of a Deteriorating Conversation

handicapped. Larry then goes on the attack—no surprise. Note that in just four turns the guys have moved into an escalating pattern in which both are competing to see who can say the most hurtful things to the other. The original topic of conversation has become irrelevant. Trapped in a sense of oughtness that has them in its grip, they can continue this feud forever, fueled only by the *logical force* of the interaction.[12]

Logical force
The moral pressure or sense of obligation a person feels to respond in a given way to what someone else has just said or done—"I had no choice."

CMM describes this type of conversational sequence as an *unwanted repetitive pattern (URP)*.[13] It's likely that neither party wants it, yet both seem compelled to relive it over and over. Those who've seen Bill Murray's classic film *Groundhog Day* will appreciate the irony. And all Americans have seen this URP reenacted in the reciprocated diatribe between Republicans and Democrats.[14] Yet Pearce and Cronen maintained that it's possible for people to mesh their stories lived without agreeing on the meaning of their stories told. That's the coordination part of CMM.

Coordination
People collaborating in an attempt to bring into being their vision of what is necessary, noble, and good, and to preclude the enactment of what they fear, hate, or despise.

According to Barnett Pearce, *coordination* refers to the "process by which persons collaborate in an attempt to bring into being their vision of what is necessary, noble, and good, and to preclude the enactment of what they fear, hate, or despise."[15] This intentional meshing of stories lived doesn't require people to reach agreement on the meaning of their joint action. They can decide to coordinate their behavior without sharing a common interpretation of the event. For example, conservative activists and staunch feminists could temporarily join forces to protest the public showing of a hardcore pornographic movie. Although

Calvin and HOBBES
by WATTERSON
OLLY-WOLLY POLLIWOGGY UMP-BUMP FIZZ!
HEY!
HA HA! I STOLE YOUR FLAG!
BUT I HIT YOU WITH THE CALVIN BALL! YOU HAVE TO PUT THE FLAG BACK AND SING THE "I'M VERY SORRY" SONG!
I DON'T HAVE TO SING THE SONG! I WAS IN THE "NO SONG" ZONE!
NO YOU WEREN'T. I TOUCHED THE "OPPOSITE POLE", SO THE "NO SONG ZONE" IS NOW A "SONG ZONE"!
I DIDN'T SEE YOU TOUCH THE OPPOSITE POLE! YOU HAVE TO DECLARE IT!
I DECLARED IT OPPOSITELY BY NOT DECLARING IT. START SINGING.
"HERE'S THE 'VERY SORRY SONGG.' WON'T YOU HELP AND SING ALONGG?"
BUM BUM BUM
I BLEW IT! ..... I KNEW IT! ..... I'M VERY VERY SORRY THAT I TOOK YOUR PRECIOUS FLAAGGG!
HE'S SORRY! SO SORRY! JUST DON'T DO IT ANY MORE, YOU SCURVY SCALAWAAGGG!
I'M FREE! I GET FREE PASSAGE TO WICKET FIVE!
NO, THAT'S WHAT WE DID LAST TIME, REMEMBER?
OH YEAH. HMM.
OK, THE NEW RULE IS WE HAVE TO JUMP EVERYWHERE UNTIL SOMEONE FINDS THE BONUS BOX!
THAT'S GOOD!
THE ONLY PERMANENT RULE IN CALVINBALL IS THAT YOU CAN'T PLAY IT THE SAME WAY TWICE!
THE SCORE IS STILL Q TO 12!
5-27
WATTERSON

they have discrepant views of social justice and different reasons for condemning the film, they might agree on a unified course of action.

Pearce used the phrase *coordination without coherence* to refer to people cooperating for quite different reasons. Sarah's application log for CMM provides a striking example:

> CMM suggests that people may synchronize their actions even if they don't share the other's motives. This was the case with my core group of friends in high school. Our group consisted of Colin—a gay atheist, Stephany—a non-practicing Jewish girl, Aliza—a devout Jewish girl, and me—a Christian. We all abstained from drinking, drugs, and sex, but the reasons for our behavior were extremely different.

In light of the way real groups of people coordinate their actions without a great amount of mutual understanding, Calvin and Hobbes' game of "Calvinball" on page 72 doesn't seem that strange.

THIRD CLAIM: WE GET WHAT WE MAKE

Since CMM claims we create our social worlds through our patterns of communication, it follows that we get what we make. Kim Pearce explains, "If your patterns of interaction contain destructive accusations and reactive anger, you will most likely make a defensive relationship; if your patterns contain genuine questions and curiosity, you will have a better chance of making a more open relationship."[16]

In the last major article he wrote before his death, Barnett Pearce urged that we ask three questions when we reflect on past interactions, are in the midst of a current conversation, or contemplate what we might say in the future:[17]

> *How did that get made?*
> *What are we making?*
> *What can we do to make better social worlds?*

These questions motivated me to do the LUUUUTT analysis of Bea's email message that I outlined in the "Stories Told" section. The *How did that get made?* question is easy to figure out, although I don't like the answer. Bea's angst seemed to be the product of my total disregard over a four-year period. My behavior may not have been the sole cause of the confusion and hurt she felt, but after reading the story she told I wished I had lived a story back then that created something positive.

The second question was more pressing. What were Bea and I making through the pattern of our email exchange? You've already read Bea's query and request expressed below in turn 3. But CMM theorists believe you can only come to understand what we were creating by looking at the twists and turns of the whole serpentine flow.

A Digital Conversation between Bea and Em

#1 BEA: Hi Emory. Are you the Emory Griffin that went to Morgan Park High School? If so, I saw your name on the list as coming to the reunion.

#2 EM: Hi Bea. That's me. I look forward to seeing you and everyone else next month.

#3 BEA: I'm writing because I still think about the mystery of you not speaking to me all the way through high school. You may not even remember that you ignored me, but I do. What did I do to make you so angry? My mother always wondered if someone had said something to you about me that wasn't true. I just never knew. I would feel better if we could say "hello" at least at the gathering.

#4 EM: Wow, I am so sorry. Please forgive me for this hurtful behavior, and even more so that I'm not even conscious that I didn't speak. Thank you for having the courage to raise the issue. I feel bad that on the basis of my stupid behavior, for decades you've thought there was something wrong with you. Obviously the problem was in me. Was I too conceited, insecure, insensitive, or oblivious? Probably all of the above.

No, you didn't say or do anything to make me angry and I never heard anything derogatory about you from others. So why didn't I talk to you? I honestly don't know. And I feel bad that I wasn't approachable enough that you could say something back then. ("Excuse me, Em. Why aren't you talking to me?") Not likely I guess. I'd like to spend some time together at the reunion catching up, if you're willing. But I'd understand if "Hello" is all you want. Again, thanks so much for writing.

#5 BEA: Was that ever nice! I've been doing computer stuff all day and receiving your email was the best part. Thanks for your response, it felt so good. Yes, I'll enjoy catching up at the reunion. What is it that you teach?

#6 EM: You'll laugh! I teach communication. I'm even supposed to be an expert.

An additional four turns set up where and when we'd meet at the reunion. We ate dinner together with other friends at the table and swapped stories and pictures. That night our stories told and our stories lived seemed to mesh well. I had the rest of the night and breakfast in the morning to enjoy the company of old friends.

A CMM Interpretation

Turns 1 and 2 are noteworthy for their guarded tone. Bea is checking to see if I'm the right guy—a reasonable caution because it was only in high school that friends started to call me Em. I respond that it's me, but my "looking forward" statement covers all who come to the party. I've expressed no special encouragement or excitement to Bea. If the pattern continued in that noncommittal tone, Barnett Pearce would have called it a "dead snake."

Bea then shares her bewilderment, desire for online clarity, and a request for face-to-face civility at the reunion. Given my lack of responsiveness throughout high school, it struck me as a gutsy move. After reading this message I sat back and mulled over how I wanted to respond. This is when I did the LUUUUTT analysis described earlier. We were at the crucial place in our email exchange that Barnett and Kim Pearce called a *bifurcation point*. They said it's the turn "in a conversation where what happens next will affect the unfolding pattern of interaction and take it in a different direction."[18]

Bifurcation point
A critical point in a conversation where what one says next will affect the unfolding pattern of interaction and potentially take it in a different direction.

I was at a fork in the road. I could deny that I had ignored Bea, stonewall her query, or casually reply that I would "of course say hello" when we met. That kind of response would likely have created more tension, hurt, anger, guilt, fear, and all the other yucky stuff that pollutes the social environment. And for sure it would take away any desire to attend the class reunion. Instead, I chose the route shown in turn 4. As Bea's and my comments in turns 5 and 6 reveal, we created a social world more to our liking—one that may have even benefitted others at the reunion.

I was fortunate that Bea raised these issues through email rather than confronting me with the same words face-to-face at the reunion. The time lag possible in computer-mediated communication offered me an opportunity to do the LUUUUTT analysis, which got me in touch with the depth and complexity of the story Bea told. That gap gave me a chance to craft what I hoped would be a thoughtful and caring response. The privacy also made it possible for me to convey my apology without a bunch of onlookers weighing in or taking sides. But it was Barnett Pearce's hope that every student majoring in communication would become adept at spotting the bifurcation points in the midst of tough discussions and have the desire and skill to craft a response on the fly that would make better social worlds. If the current crop of more than 400,000 undergraduate communication majors developed that mindset and ability, he was convinced we could make a radically different social world.[19]

FOURTH CLAIM: GET THE PATTERN RIGHT, CREATE BETTER OUTCOMES

What do the best social worlds look like? Barnett Pearce admitted he couldn't be specific, because each situation is different. He also feared that those who have a precise image of what the ideal social world should be will try to compel others to live within their vision and end up making things worse.[20] But throughout their most recent publications on CMM, Barnett and Kim Pearce described better social worlds as replete with *caring, compassion, love,* and *grace* among its inhabitants—not the stated goal of most communication theories.[21] And Kim stresses that these are not just internal emotional experiences. Rather, they are "a way of being with others that makes a space for something new to emerge."[22]

This interpersonal goal of CMM raises a serious question for students of communication. What personal characteristics or abilities does it take for a person to create conversational patterns that will change the social world for the better? The theorists' answer is that one does not need to be a saint, a genius, or an orator. The communicator, however, must be *mindful.*[23]

Mindfulness
The presence or awareness of what participants are making in the midst of their own conversation.

Mindfulness is a presence or awareness of what participants are making in the midst of a difficult conversation. It's paying less attention to what they are talking about and focusing on what they are *doing*. Mindful participants don't speak on mental automatic pilot or cognitive cruise control. They are participant observers willing to step back and look for places in the conversational flow where they can say or do something that will make the situation better for everyone involved. For example, are you willing and able to be mindful when

. . . talking to your roommate about the mess in your apartment?
. . . replying to your mom's phone plea to spend spring break at home?
. . . listening to your teammates complain about the coach?
. . . responding to a sarcastic comment posted on Facebook?
. . . dealing with a demanding customer at your minimum-wage McJob?
. . . fending off unwelcome advances during a Friday night pub crawl?

To the extent that your answer is *yes,* CMM claims you have the capacity to make better social worlds.

Once the mindful communicator spots a bifurcation point in a pattern of communication that's deteriorating, what should he or she say? Barnett Pearce found it helpful to respond to challenging or boorish statements with phrases that showed curiosity rather than offense.[24] *Tell me more about that. What else was going on at the time? What experiences have led you to that position? Why don't people understand?* Those familiar with Hebrew wisdom literature will recognize the parallel with Proverbs 15:1, "A gentle answer turns away wrath."

Even a single word like *yes* can change the direction of the conversational pattern. In her autobiography, *Bossypants,* actress, comedian, writer, and producer Tina Fey offers "The Rules of Improvisation That Will Change Your Life . . ."

> The first rule of improvisation is **AGREE.** Always agree and SAY YES. When you're improvising, this means you are required to agree with whatever your partner has created. So if we're improvising and I say, "Freeze, I have a gun," and you say, "That's not a gun. It's your finger. You're pointing your finger at me," our improvised scene has ground to a halt. But if I say, "Freeze, I have a gun!" and you say, "The gun I gave you for Christmas. You bastard!" then we have started a scene because we have AGREED that my finger is in fact a Christmas gun.
>
> Now, obviously in real life you're not always going to agree with everything everyone says. But the Rule of Agreement reminds you to respect what your partner has created and to at least start from an open-minded place. Start with a YES and see where it takes you.
>
> As an improviser, I always find it jarring when I meet someone in real life whose first answer is no. "No we can't do that." "No that's not in the budget . . ." What kind of way is that to live?[25]

For an overall remedy to unsatisfactory or destructive patterns of interaction, CMM theorists advocate *dialogue,* a specific form of communication that they believe will create a social world where we can live with dignity, honor, joy, and love.[26] Although the term is used in multiple ways within our discipline, Barnett and Kim Pearce have adopted the perspective of Jewish philosopher Martin Buber.

Dialogic communication
Conversation in which parties remain in the tension between holding their own perspective while being profoundly open to the other.

For Buber, dialogue "involves remaining in the tension between holding our own perspective while being profoundly open to the other."[27] This of course takes "courage because it means giving up a person-position of clarity, certainty, or moral/intellectual superiority."[28] We might actually learn something new that will change what we think, or even who we are.[29] The following ethical reflection expands on Buber's concept of dialogue.

ETHICAL REFLECTION: MARTIN BUBER'S DIALOGIC ETHICS

Martin Buber was a German Jewish philosopher and theologian who immigrated to Palestine before World War II and died in 1965. His ethical approach focuses on relationships between people rather than on moral codes of conduct. "In the beginning is the relation," Buber wrote. "The relation is the cradle of actual life."[30]

Buber contrasted two types of relationships—*I-It* versus *I-Thou.* In an I-It relationship we treat the other person as a thing to be used, an object to be manipulated. Created by monologue, an I-It relationship lacks mutuality. Parties come together as individuals intent on creating only an impression. Deceit is a way to maintain appearances.

In an I-Thou relationship we regard our partner as the very one we are. We see the other as created in the image of God and resolve to treat him or her as a valued end rather than a means to our own end. This implies that we will seek to experience the relationship as it appears to the other person. Buber said we can do this only through dialogue.

For Buber, *dialogue* was a synonym for ethical communication. Dialogue is mutuality in conversation that creates the *Between*, through which we help each other to be more human. Dialogue is not only a morally appropriate act, but it is also a way to discover what is ethical in our relationship. It thus requires self-disclosure to, confirmation of, and vulnerability with the other person.

Buber used the image of the *narrow ridge* to illustrate the tension of dialogic living. On one side of the moral path is the gulf of relativism, where there are no standards. On the other side is the plateau of absolutism, where rules are etched in stone:

> On the far side of the subjective, on this side of the objective, on the narrow ridge, where I and Thou meet, there is the realm of the Between.[31]

Narrow ridge
A metaphor of I-Thou living in the dialogic tension between ethical relativism and rigid absolutism.

Duquesne University communication ethicist Ron Arnett notes that "living the narrow-ridge philosophy requires a life of personal and interpersonal concern, which is likely to generate a more complicated existence than that of the egoist or the selfless martyr."[32] Despite that tension, many interpersonal theorists and practitioners have carved out ethical positions similar to Buber's philosophy. Consistent with CMM's foundational belief that persons-in-conversation co-construct their own social realities, Barnett and Kim Pearce were attracted to Buber's core belief that dialogue is a joint achievement that cannot be produced on demand, but occurs among people who seek it and are prepared for it.

CRITIQUE: HIGHLY PRACTICAL AS IT MOVES FROM CONFUSION TO CLARITY

Because CMM is an interpretive theory, I'll apply the six criteria suggested in Chapter 3 as I did when evaluating Mead's theory of *symbolic interactionism* in the previous chapter.

New understanding of people. By offering such diagnostic tools as the serpentine and LUUUUTT models of communication, CMM promotes a deeper *understanding of people* and of the social worlds they create through their conversation. Those models are just two of the tools the theorists offer. Students who take a further look at the theory will find the daisy model, the hierarchical model, and strange loops equally helpful.

Clarification of values. For interpretive scholars, CMM leaves no doubt as to the commitments and practices that make better social worlds. Barnett and Kim Pearce are clearly on record as valuing curiosity, caring, compassion, mindfulness, gratitude, grace, and love. They have invited us to join them in an ongoing effort to enact these qualities in our stories lived. Some objective theorists may personally share these values, but believe a communication theory holding out the promise of making *better social worlds* should describe that goal in terms of specific behaviors and outcomes.

Community of agreement. Although many objectivist theorists dismiss CMM because of its social constructionist assumptions, CMM has generated widespread interest and *acceptance within the community* of interpretive communication scholars. For example, when Robert Craig proposed that a pragmatic tradition be added to his original list of seven traditions of communication theory (see Chapter 4), he cited CMM as the exemplar of a practical theory.[33]

Reform of society. If changing destructive patterns of communication in whole communities strikes you as a bit of a stretch, you should know that pursuit of this goal is why Barnett and Kim Pearce founded the Public Dialogue Consortium and the CMM Institute.[34] Not only have many associates signed on to the cause, but these groups have also demonstrated that a dialogic form of communication is "learnable, teachable, and contagious."[35]

Qualitative research. CMM scholars and practitioners use a wide range of qualitative research methods—textual and narrative analyses, case studies, interviews, participant observation, ethnography, and collaborative action research.[36] It's not clear that this research has spawned new theoretical development,[37] but these studies have definitely helped refine the models of communication that practitioners use in their training and consulting.

Aesthetic appeal. Despite meeting the previous five criteria with ease, lack of clarity has seriously limited CMM's wider use. The theory has a reputation of being a confusing mix of ideas that are hard to pin down because they're expressed in convoluted language. In 2001, when Pearce asked those who use CMM in their teaching, training, counseling, and consulting what changes or additions they thought should be made to the theory, the most frequent plea was for user-friendly explanations expressed in easy-to-understand terms. The following story from the field underscores why this call for clarity is so crucial:

> My counseling trainees often find CMM ideas exciting, but its language daunting or too full of jargon. Some trainees connect with the ideas but most feel intimidated by the language and the concepts—diminished in some way or excluded! One trainee sat in a posture of physically cringing because she did not understand. This was a competent woman who had successfully completed counselor training three years ago and was doing a "refresher" with us. I don't think she found it too refreshing at that moment. CMM ideas would be more useful if they were available in everyday language—perhaps via examples and storytelling.[38]

I've tried to heed this advice while writing about CMM. Hopefully, you haven't cringed. But in order to reduce the wince factor, I've had to leave out many of the valued terms, tools, and models that are the working vocabulary of this complex theory. I've been guided by Kim Pearce's new book, *Compassionate Communicating Because Moments Matter,* where she lays out the essentials of CMM in the way the advocate requested.[39] This little volume, which is my recommended resource, is a clear statement of CMM's four core claims. In user-friendly language, Kim illustrates them with stories from her work and life together with her husband, Barnett. CMM's aesthetic appeal is on the rise.

QUESTIONS TO SHARPEN YOUR FOCUS

1. *Social constructionists* see themselves as curious participants in a pluralistic world. Are you willing to accept uncertainty, abandon a detached perspective, and not insist on a singular view of Truth so that you can join them?
2. Can you provide a rationale for placing this chapter on CMM immediately after the chapter on *symbolic interactionism?*
3. CMM suggests that we can take part in joint action without a common understanding—*coordination* without *shared meaning.* Can you think of examples from your own life?
4. Can you recall an important conversation in which you were *mindful* of what you were making and you spotted a *bifurcation point* where you could change the *pattern of conversation* so as to create a *better social world?*

CONVERSATIONS

View this segment online at www.mhhe.com/griffin9e or www.afirstlook.com.

As you watch my conversation with Barnett Pearce, you might think of us as the persons-in-conversation pictured in Escher's *Bond of Union.* What kind of social world do you see us creating as we talk? I like to think that our conversation displays a few examples of dialogic communication. If so, was Pearce right in thinking that you'll find this kind of talk contagious? At one point I repeat my "Questions to Sharpen Your Focus" query about how social constructionists must give up claims of certainty, objectivity, and Truth. I then ask if that's a fair question. See if you agree with Pearce's response and the reason he gave.

A SECOND LOOK

Recommended resource: Kimberly Pearce, *Compassionate Communicating Because Moments Matter: Poetry, Prose, and Practices,* Lulu, 2012. www.lulu.com

Brief overview: W. Barnett Pearce, "The Coordinated Management of Meaning (CMM)," in *Theorizing About Intercultural Communication,* William Gudykunst (ed.), Sage, Thousand Oaks, CA, 2004, pp. 35–54.

Comprehensive statement: W. Barnett Pearce, *Making Social Worlds: A Communication Perspective,* Blackwell, Malden, MA, 2008.

Original statement: W. Barnett Pearce and Vernon E. Cronen, *Communication, Action, and Meaning: The Creation of Social Realities,* Praeger, New York, 1980; also www.cios.org/www/opentext.htm.

Evolution of the theory: W. Barnett Pearce, "Evolution and Transformation: A Brief History of CMM and a Meditation on What Using It Does to Us," in *The Reflective, Facilitative, and Interpretative Practice of the Coordinated Management of Meaning: Making Lives, Making Meaning,* Catherine Creede, Beth Fisher-Yoshida, and Placida Gallegos (eds.), Fairleigh Dickinson, Madison, NJ, 2012, pp. 1–21.

Social construction: W. Barnett Pearce, "Communication as Social Construction: Reclaiming Our Birthright," in *Socially Constructing Communication,* Gloria J. Galanes and Wendy Leeds-Hurwitz (eds.), Hampton, Cresskill, NJ, 2009, pp. 33–56.

Making meaning and coordinating actions: W. Barnett Pearce, *Communication and the Human Condition,* Southern Illinois University, Carbondale, IL, 1989, pp. 32–87.

Intellectual heritage: Vernon E. Cronen, "Coordinated Management of Meaning: The Consequentiality of Communication and the Recapturing of Experience," in *The Consequentiality of Communication,* Stuart Sigman (ed.), Lawrence Erlbaum, Hillsdale, NJ, 1995, pp. 17–65.

Peacemaking: W. Barnett Pearce and Stephen W. Littlejohn, *Moral Conflict: When Social Worlds Collide,* Sage, Thousand Oaks, CA, 1997.

Dialogic communication: W. Barnett Pearce and Kimberly A. Pearce, "Combining Passions and Abilities: Toward Dialogic Virtuosity," *Southern Communication Journal,* Vol. 65, 2000, pp. 161–175.

Buber's dialogic ethics: Martin Buber, *I and Thou,* 2nd ed., R. G. Smith (trans.), Scribner, New York, 1958.

Research review of CMM: J. Kevin Barge and W. Barnett Pearce, "A Reconnaissance of CMM Research," *Human Systems,* Vol. 15, 2004, pp. 13–32.

CMM as a practical theory: J. Kevin Barge, "Articulating CMM as a Practical Theory," *Human Systems,* Vol. 15, 2004, pp. 193–204.

To access scenes from feature films that illustrate CMM and other theories, click on Suggested Movie Clips under Theory Resources at *www.afirstlook.com.*

CHAPTER 7

Objective — Interpretive

Socio-psychological tradition

Expectancy Violations Theory

of Judee Burgoon

Early in my teaching career, I was walking back to my office, puzzling over classroom conversations with four students. All four had made requests. Why, I wondered, had I readily agreed to two requests but just as quickly turned down two others? Each of the four students had spoken to me individually during the class break. Andre wanted my endorsement for a graduate scholarship, and Dawn invited me to eat lunch with her the next day. I said yes to both of them. Belinda asked me to help her on a term paper for a class with another professor, and Charlie encouraged me to play water polo that night with guys from his house, something I had done before. I said no to those requests.

Sitting down at my desk, I idly flipped through the pages of *Human Communication Research (HCR)*, a relatively new behavioral science journal that had arrived in the morning mail. I was still mulling over my uneven response to the students when my eyes zeroed in on an article entitled "A Communication Model of Personal Space Violations."[1] "That's it," I blurted out to our surprised department secretary. I suddenly realized that in each case my response to the student may have been influenced by the conversational distance between us.

I mentally pictured the four students making their requests—each from a distance that struck me as inappropriate in one way or another. Andre was literally in my face, less than a foot away. Belinda's 2-foot interval invaded my personal space, but not as much. Charlie stood about 7 feet away—just outside the range I would have expected for a let's-get-together-and-have-some-fun-that-has-nothing-to-do-with-school type of conversation. Dawn offered her luncheon invitation from across the room. At the time, each of these interactions had seemed somewhat strange. Now I realized that all four students had violated my expectation of an appropriate interpersonal distance.

Because I describe my impressions and reactions to these students, I've changed their names, and replaced them with names that start with the letters *A, B, C,* and *D* to represent the increasing distance between us when we spoke. (Andre was the closest; Dawn, the farthest away.) Figure 7–1 plots the intervals relative to my expectations.

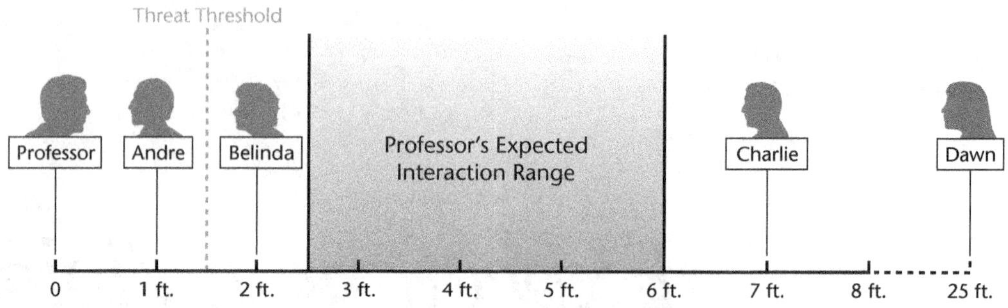

FIGURE 7–1 Expectancy Violations in a Classroom Setting

Judee Burgoon, a communication scholar at the University of Arizona, wrote the journal article that stimulated my thinking. The article was a follow-up piece on the *nonverbal expectancy violations model* that she had introduced in *HCR* two years earlier. Since my own dissertation research focused on interpersonal distance, I knew firsthand how little social science theory existed to guide researchers studying nonverbal communication. I was therefore excited to see Burgoon offering a sophisticated theory of personal space. The fact that she was teaching in a communication department and had published her work in a communication journal was value added. I eagerly read Burgoon's description of her nonverbal expectancy violations model to see whether it could account for my mixed response to the various conversational distances chosen by the four students.

PERSONAL SPACE EXPECTATIONS: CONFORM OR DEVIATE?

Personal space
The invisible, variable volume of space surrounding an individual that defines that individual's preferred distance from others.

Burgoon defined *personal space* as the "invisible, variable volume of space surrounding an individual that defines that individual's preferred distance from others."[2] She claimed that the size and shape of our personal space depend on our cultural norms and individual preferences, but our space always reflects a compromise between the conflicting approach–avoidance needs that we as humans have for affiliation and privacy.

Proxemics
The study of people's use of space as a special elaboration of culture.

The idea of personal space wasn't original with Burgoon. In the 1960s, Illinois Institute of Technology anthropologist Edward Hall coined the term *proxemics* to refer to the study of people's use of space as a special elaboration of culture.[3] He entitled his book *The Hidden Dimension* because he was convinced that most spatial interpretation is outside our awareness. He claimed that Americans have four proxemic zones, which nicely correspond with the four interpersonal distances selected by my students:

1. Intimate distance: 0 to 18 inches (Andre)
2. Personal distance: 18 inches to 4 feet (Belinda)
3. Social distance: 4 to 12 feet (Charlie)
4. Public distance: 12 to 25 feet (Dawn)

Hall's book is filled with examples of "ugly Americans" who were insensitive to the spatial customs of other cultures. He strongly recommended that in order to be effective, we learn to adjust our nonverbal behavior to conform to the communication rules of our partner. We shouldn't cross a distance boundary uninvited.

Cartoon by Peter Steiner. Reprinted with permission.

In his poem "Prologue: The Birth of Architecture," poet W. H. Auden echoes Hall's analysis and puts us on notice that we violate his personal space at our peril:

> Some thirty inches from my nose
> The frontier of my Person goes,
> And all the untilled air between
> Is private pagus or demesne.
> Stranger, unless with bedroom eyes
> I beckon you to fraternize,
> Beware of rudely crossing it:
> I have no gun, but I can spit.[4]

Burgoon's nonverbal expectancy violations model offered a counterpoint to Hall's and Auden's advice. She didn't argue with the idea that people have definite expectations about how close others should come. In fact, she would explain Auden's 30-inch rule as based on well-established American norms, plus the poet's own idiosyncracies. But contrary to popular go-along-to-get-along wisdom, Burgoon suggested that there are times when it's best to break the rules. She believed that under some circumstances, violating social norms and personal expectations is "a superior strategy to conformity."[5]

AN APPLIED TEST OF THE ORIGINAL MODEL

Whether knowingly or not, each of the four students making a request deviated from my proxemic expectation. How well did Burgoon's initial model predict my responses to these four different violations? Not very well. To help you capture the flavor of Burgoon's early speculation and recognize how far her current theory has come, I'll outline what the model predicted my responses would be and, in each case, compare that forecast to what I actually did.

Threat threshold
The hypothetical outer boundary of intimate space; a breach by an uninvited other occasions fight or flight.

Andre. According to Burgoon's early model, Andre made a mistake when he crossed my invisible *threat threshold* and spoke with me at an intimate eyeball-to-eyeball distance. The physical and psychological discomfort I'd feel would hurt his cause. But the model missed on that prediction, since I wrote the recommendation later that day.

Belinda. In the follow-up article I read that day, Burgoon suggested that noticeable deviations from what we expect cause us to experience a heightened state of arousal. She wasn't necessarily referring to the heart-pounding, sweaty-palms reaction that drives us to fight or flight. Instead, she pictured violations stimulating us to mentally review the nature of our relationship with the person who acted in a curious way. That would be good news for Belinda if I thought of her as a highly rewarding person. But every comment she made in class seemed to me a direct challenge, dripping with sarcasm. Just as Burgoon predicted, the narrow, 2-foot gap Belinda chose focused my attention on our rocky relationship, and I declined her request for help in another course. Score one for the nonverbal expectancy violations model.

Charlie. Charlie was a nice guy who cared more about having a good time than he did about studies. He knew I'd played water polo in college, but he may not have realized that his casual attitude toward the class was a constant reminder that I wasn't as good a teacher as I wanted to be. In her 1978 *HRC* article, Burgoon wrote that a person with "punishing power" (like Charlie) would do best to observe proxemic conventions or, better yet, stand slightly farther away than expected. Without ever hearing Burgoon's advice, Charlie did it right. He backed off to a distance of 7 feet—just outside the range of interaction I anticipated. Even so, I declined his offer to swim with the guys.

Dawn. According to this nonverbal expectancy violations model, Dawn blew it. Because she was an attractive communicator, a warm, close approach would have been a pleasant surprise. Her decision to issue an invitation from across the room, however, would seem to guarantee a poor response. The farther she backed off, the worse the effect would be. There's only one problem with this analysis: Dawn and I had lunch together in the student union the following day.

Obviously, my attempt to apply Burgoon's original model to conversational distance between me and my students didn't meet with much success. The theoretical scoreboard read:

Nonverbal expectancy violations model: **1**
Unpredicted random behavior: **3**

Burgoon's first controlled experiments didn't fare much better. But where I was ready to dismiss the whole model as flawed, she was unwilling to abandon *expectancy violation* as a key concept in human interaction. At the end of her journal article she hinted that some of her basic assumptions might need to be tested and reevaluated.

Of course, that was then; this is now. For more than three decades, Judee Burgoon and her students have crafted a series of sophisticated laboratory experiments and field studies to discover and explain the effects of expectancy violations. One of the reasons I chose to write about her theory is that the current version is an excellent example of ideas continually revised as a result of empirical disconfirmation. As she has demonstrated, in science, failure can lead to success.

A CONVOLUTED MODEL BECOMES AN ELEGANT THEORY

When applied to theories, the term *elegant* suggests "gracefully concise and simple; admirably succinct."[6] That's what expectancy violations theory has become. Burgoon has dropped concepts that were central in earlier versions but never panned out. Early on, for example, she abandoned the idea of a "threat threshold." Even though that hypothetical boundary made intuitive sense, repeated experimentation failed to confirm its existence.

Burgoon's retreat from *arousal* as an explanatory mechanism has been more gradual. She originally stated that people felt physiologically aroused when their proxemic expectations were violated. Later she softened the concept to "an orienting response" or a mental "alertness" that focuses attention on the violator. She now views arousal as a side effect of a partner's deviation and no longer considers it a necessary link between expectancy violation and communication outcomes such as attraction, credibility, persuasion, and involvement.

Arousal, relational
A heightened state of awareness, orienting response, or mental alertness that stimulates a review of the relationship.

By removing extraneous features, Burgoon has streamlined her model. By extending its scope, she has produced a complete theory. Her original nonverbal expectancy violations model was concerned only with spatial violations—a rather narrow focus. But by the mid-1980s, Burgoon concluded that proxemic behavior is part of an interconnected system of nonlinguistic cues. It no longer made sense to study interpersonal distance in isolation. She began to apply the model to a host of other nonverbal variables—facial expression, eye contact, touch, and body lean, for example. Burgoon continues to expand the range of expectancy violations. While not losing interest in nonverbal communication, she now applies the theory to what's said in emotional, marital, and intercultural communication as well. Consistent with this broad sweep, she has dropped the *nonverbal* qualifier and refers to her theory as "expectancy violations theory," or EVT. From this point on, so will I.

What does EVT predict? Burgoon sums up her empirically driven conclusions in a single paragraph. I hope that my long narrative of the theory's development will help you appreciate the 30 years of work that lie behind these simple lines.

> Expectancies exert significant influence on people's interaction patterns, on their impressions of one another, and on the outcomes of their interactions. Violations of expectations in turn may arouse and distract their recipients, shifting greater attention to the violator and the meaning of the violation itself. People who can assume that they are well regarded by their audience are safer engaging in violations and more likely to profit from doing so than are those who are poorly regarded. When the violation act is one that is likely to be ambiguous in its meaning or to carry multiple interpretations that are not uniformly positive or negative, then the reward valence of the communicator can be especially significant in moderating interpretations, evaluations, and subsequent outcomes. . . . In other cases, violations

have relatively consensual meanings and valences associated with them, so that engaging in them produces similar effects for positive- and negative-valenced communicators.[7]

CORE CONCEPTS OF EVT

A close reading of Burgoon's summary suggests that EVT offers a "soft determinism" rather than hard-core universal laws (see Chapter 2). The qualifying terms *may, more likely, can be,* and *relatively* reflect her belief that too many factors affect communication to ever allow us to discover simple cause-and-effect relationships. She does, however, hope to show a link among surprising interpersonal behavior and attraction, credibility, influence, and involvement. These are the potential outcomes of expectancy violation that Burgoon and her students explore. In order for us to appreciate the connection, we need to understand three core concepts of EVT: *expectancy, violation valence,* and *communicator reward valence.* I'll illustrate these three variables by referring back to my students' proxemic behavior and to another form of nonverbal communication—touch.

Expectancy

When I was a kid, my mother frequently gave notice that she *expected* me to be on my best behavior. I considered her words to be a wish or a warning rather than a forecast of my future actions. That's not how Burgoon uses the word. She and her colleagues "prefer to reserve the term *expectancy* for what is predicted to occur rather than what is desired."[8] Figure 7–1 shows that I anticipated conversations with students to take place at a distance of 2½ to 6 feet. How did this expectation arise? Burgoon suggests that I processed the context, type of relationship, and characteristics of the others automatically in my mind so that I could gauge what they might do.

Expectancy
What people predict will happen, rather than what they desire.

Context begins with cultural norms. Three feet is too close in England or Germany yet too far removed in Saudi Arabia, where you can't trust people who won't let you smell their breath. Context also includes the setting of the conversation. A classroom environment dictates a greater speaking distance than would be appropriate for a private chat in my office.

Relationship factors include similarity, familiarity, liking, and relative status. In one study, Burgoon discovered that people of all ages and stations in life anticipate that lower-status people will keep their distance. Because of our age difference and teacher–student relationship, I was more surprised by Andre's and Belinda's invasion of my personal space than I was by Charlie's and Dawn's remote location.

Communicator characteristics include all of the age/sex/place-of-birth demographic facts requested on applications, but they also include personal features that may affect expectation even more—physical appearance, personality, and communication style. Dawn's warm smile was a counterpoint to Belinda's caustic comments. Given this difference, I would have assumed that Dawn would be the one to draw close and Belinda the one to keep her distance. That's why I was especially curious when each woman's spatial "transgression" was the opposite of what I would have predicted.

We can do a similar analysis of my expectation for touch in that classroom situation. Edward Hall claimed that the United States is a "noncontact culture," so I wouldn't anticipate touch during the course of normal conversation.[9] Does this mean that Latin American or Southern European "contact cultures" wouldn't have tight expectations for nonverbal interaction? By no means; Burgoon is convinced that all cultures have a similar *structure* of expected communication behavior, but that the *content* of those expectations can differ markedly from culture to culture. Touch is fraught with meaning in every society, but the who, when, where, and how of touching are a matter of culture-specific standards and customs.

As a male in a role relationship, it never occurred to me that students might make physical contact while voicing their requests. If it had, Dawn would have been the likely candidate. But at her chosen distance of 25 feet, she'd need to be a bionic woman to reach me. As it was, I would have been shocked if she'd violated my expectation and walked over to give me a hug. (As a lead-in to the next two sections, note that I didn't say I would have been disturbed, distressed, or disgusted.)

Violation Valence

The term *violation valence* refers to the positive or negative value we place on a specific unexpected behavior, regardless of who does it. Do we find the act itself pleasing or distressing, and to what extent? With her commitment to the scientific method, Burgoon may have borrowed the concept of valence from chemistry, where the valence of a substance is indicated by a number and its sign (+3 or −2, for example). The term *net worth* from the field of accounting seems to capture the same idea.

Violation valence
The perceived positive or negative value assigned to a breach of expectations, regardless of who the violator is.

We usually give others a bit of wiggle room to deviate from what we regard as standard operating procedure. But once we deal with someone who acts outside the range of expected behavior, we switch into evaluation mode. According to Burgoon, we first try to interpret the meaning of the violation, and then figure out whether we like it.

The meaning of some violations is easy to spot. As a case in point, no one would agonize over how to interpret a purposeful poke in the eye with a sharp stick. It's a hostile act, and if it happened to us, we'd be livid. Many nonverbal behaviors are that straightforward. For example, moderate to prolonged eye contact in Western cultures usually communicates awareness, interest, affection, and trust. A level gaze is welcome; shifty eyes are not. With the exception of a riveting stare, we value eye contact. Even Emerson, a man of letters, wrote, "The eyes of men converse as much as their tongues, with the advantage that the ocular dialect needs no dictionary. . . ."[10]

When a behavior has a socially recognized meaning, communicators can usually figure out whether to go beyond what others expect. If the valence is negative, do less than expected. If the valence is positive, go further. Burgoon validated this advice when she studied the effect of expectancy on marital satisfaction.[11] She questioned people about how much intimate communication they expected from their partner compared to how much focused conversation they actually got. Not surprisingly, intimacy was ranked as positive. Partners who received about as much intimacy as they expected were moderately satisfied with their marriages. But people were highly satisfied with their marriages when they had more good talks with their husbands or wives than they originally thought they would.

On the other hand, many expectancy violations are ambiguous and open to multiple interpretations. For example, the meaning of unexpected touch can be puzzling. Is it a mark of total involvement in the conversation, a sign of warmth and affection, a display of dominance, or a sexual move? Distance violations can also be confusing. Andre isn't from the Middle East, so why was he standing so close? I don't bark or bite, so why did Dawn issue her invitation from across the room? According to EVT, it's at times like these that we consider the reward valence of the communicator as well as the valence of the violation.

Before we look at the way communicator reward valence fits into the theory, you should know that Burgoon has found few nonverbal behaviors that are ambiguous when seen in a larger context. A touch on the arm might be enigmatic in isolation, but when experienced along with close proximity, forward body lean, a direct gaze, facial animation, and verbal fluency, almost everyone interprets the physical contact as a sign of high involvement in the conversation.[12] Or consider actor Eric Idle's words and nonverbal manner in a *Monty Python* sketch. He punctuates his question about Terry Gilliam's wife with a burlesque wink, a leering tone of voice, and gestures to accompany his words: "Nudge nudge. Know what I mean? Say no more . . . know what I mean?"[13] Taken alone, an exaggerated wink or a dig with the elbow might have many possible meanings, but as part of a coordinated routine, both gestures clearly transform a questionable remark into a lewd comment.

There are times, however, when nonverbal expectancy violations are truly equivocal. The personal space deviations of my students are cases in point. Perhaps I just wasn't sensitive enough to pick up the cues that would help me make sense of their proxemic violations. But when the meaning of an action is unclear, EVT says that we interpret the violation in light of how the violator can affect our lives.

Communicator Reward Valence

EVT is not the only theory that describes the tendency to size up other people in terms of the potential rewards they have to offer. *Social penetration theory* suggests that we live in an interpersonal economy in which we all "take stock" of the relational value of others we meet (see Chapter 8). The questions *What can you do for me?* and *What can you do to me?* often cross our minds. Burgoon is not a cynic, but she thinks the issue of reward potential moves from the background to the foreground of our minds when someone violates our expectation and there's no social consensus on the meaning of the act. She uses the term *communicator reward valence* to label the results of our mental audit of likely gains and losses.

The reward valence of a communicator is the sum of the positive and negative attributes the person brings to the encounter plus the potential he or she has to reward or punish in the future. The resulting perception is usually a mix of good and bad and falls somewhere on a scale between those two poles. I'll illustrate communicator characteristics that Burgoon frequently mentions by reviewing one feature of each student that I thought about immediately after their perplexing spatial violations.

Communicator reward valence
The sum of positive and negative attributes brought to the encounter plus the potential to reward or punish in the future.

Andre was a brilliant student. Although writing recommendations is low on my list of fun things to do, I would bask in reflected glory if he were accepted into a top graduate program.

Belinda had a razor-sharp mind and a tongue to match. I'd already felt the sting of her verbal barbs and thought that thinly veiled criticism in the future was a distinct possibility.

Charlie was the classic goof-off—seldom in class and never prepared. I try to be evenhanded with everyone who signs up for my classes, but in Charlie's case I had to struggle not to take his casual attitude toward the course as a personal snub.

Dawn was a beautiful young woman with a warm smile. I felt great pleasure when she openly announced that I was her favorite teacher.

My views of Andre, Belinda, Charlie, and Dawn probably say more about me than they do about the four students. I'm not particularly proud of my stereotyped assessments, but apparently I have plenty of company in the criteria I used. Burgoon notes that the features that impressed me also weigh heavily with others when they compute a reward valence for someone who is violating their expectations. Status, ability, and good looks are standard "goodies" that enhance the other person's reward potential. The thrust of the conversation is even more important. Most of us value words that communicate acceptance, liking, appreciation, and trust. We're turned off by talk that conveys disinterest, disapproval, distrust, and rejection.

Why does Burgoon think that the expectancy violator's power to reward or punish is so crucial? Because puzzling violations force victims to search the social context for clues to their meaning.[14] Thus, an ambiguous violation embedded in a host of relationally warm signals takes on a positive cast. An equivocal violation from a punishing communicator stiffens our resistance.

Now that I've outlined EVT's core concepts of expectancy, violation valence, and communicator reward valence, you can better understand the bottom-line advice that Burgoon's theory offers. Should you communicate in a totally unexpected way? If you're certain that the novelty will be a pleasant surprise, the answer is yes. But if you know that your outlandish behavior will offend, don't do it.

When you aren't sure how others will interpret your far-out behavior, let their overall attitude toward you dictate your verbal and nonverbal actions. So if, like Belinda and Charlie, you have reason to suspect a strained relationship, and the meaning of a violation might be unclear, stifle your deviant tendencies and do your best to conform to expectations. But when you know you've already created a positive personal impression (like Andre or Dawn), a surprise move is not only safe, it will probably enhance the positive effect of your message.

INTERACTION ADAPTATION—ADJUSTING EXPECTATIONS

As evidence of its predictive power, EVT has been used to explain and predict attitudes and behaviors in a wide variety of communication contexts. These include students' perceptions of their instructors, patients' responses to health care providers, and individuals' actions in romantic relationships. For example, Arizona State University communication professor Paul Mongeau has studied men's and women's expectations for first dates and compared those expectations with their actual experiences.[15] He discovered that men are pleasantly surprised when a woman initiates a first date, and that they usually interpret such a request as a sign that she's interested in sexual activity. But there's a second surprise in store for most of these guys when it turns out that they have less physical intimacy than they do on the traditional male-initiated first date. We might expect that the men's disappointment would put a damper on future dates together but, surprisingly, it doesn't.

For Mongeau, EVT explains how dating partners' expectations are affected by who asks out whom. Yet unlike early tests of EVT, Mongeau's work considers how one person's actions might reshape a dating partner's perceptions after their time together—a morning-after-the-night-before adjustment of expectations. In the same way, Burgoon has reassessed EVT's single-sided view and now favors a dyadic model of adaptation. That's because she regards conversations as more akin to duets than solos. Interpersonal interactions involve synchronized actions rather than unilateral moves. Along with her former students Lesa Stern and Leesa Dillman, Burgoon has crafted *interaction adaptation theory (IAT)* as an extension and expansion of EVT.[16]

Interaction adaptation theory
A systematic analysis of how people adjust their approach when another's behavior doesn't mesh with what's needed, anticipated, or preferred.

Interaction position
A person's initial stance toward an interaction as determined by a blend of personal requirements, expectations, and desires (RED).

Burgoon states that human beings are predisposed to adapt to each other. That's often necessary, she says, because another person's actions may not square with the thoughts and feelings we bring to the interaction. She sees this initial *interaction position* as made up of three factors: requirements, expectations, and desires. *Requirements (R)* are the outcomes that fulfill our basic needs to survive, be safe, belong, and have a sense of self-worth. These are the panhuman motivations that Abraham Maslow outlined in his famous hierarchy of needs.[17] As opposed to requirements that represent what we need to happen, *expectations (E)* as defined in EVT are what we think really will happen. Finally, *desires (D)* are what we personally would like to see happen. These RED factors coalesce or meld into our interaction position of what's needed, anticipated, and preferred. I'll continue to use touch behavior to show how Burgoon uses this composite mindset to predict how we adjust to another person's behavior.

In her course application log, Lindi briefly describes a roommate's unanticipated interaction with a casual friend:

> At the end of last year my roommate was hanging out with a bunch of our friends late at night and one of the guys started playing with her hair and continued to do so for the rest of the night. This unexpected violation of her personal space surprised her, but turned out to be a very pleasant experience. She was forced then to reevaluate their relationship. Even though they didn't develop a romantic relationship, this violation brought them closer together and helped them redefine their friendship.

Although details are sparse, it's possible to approximate the roommate's interactional position at the start of the evening. Her willingness to spend the night hanging around with a group of friends suggests that she has a high need or requirement for affiliation and belongingness (R). Given her surprise at the fellow fiddling with her hair, we can assume that this ongoing touch was definitely not the behavioral norm of the group, nor what she expected based on the guy's past behavior (E). Yet her pleasure with this fellow's continual touch indicates that she had a strong desire for this kind of personal attention from him (D). Her initial interaction position would therefore be an amalgam of what she needed, expected, and preferred.

With the help of hindsight, we can see that the valence of the guy playing with her hair was more positive than her interaction position. According to IAT, the pattern of response would therefore be one of reciprocity or convergence. Reciprocity would mean that she then ran her fingers through his hair. There's no hint that this happened. Yet since the whole group of friends could monitor her response, it's unlikely he would have continued with this form of touch unless she encouraged him with a smile or words indicating pleasure. That would be convergence. If, on the other hand, the valence she assigned to him messing with her hair was more negative than her interaction position, Burgoon predicts some form of compensation or divergent behavior. She might lean away from him, excuse herself to comb her hair, or simply look at him and say, "Cut it out." Unlike EVT, IAT addresses how people adjust their behavior when others violate their expectations.

Burgoon outlined two shortcomings of expectancy violations theory that she found particularly troubling:

Reciprocity
A strong human tendency to respond to another's action with similar behavior.

> First, EVT does not fully account for the overwhelming prevalence of reciprocity that has been found in interpersonal interactions. Second, it is silent on whether communicator reward valence supersedes behavior valence or vice versa when the two are incongruent (such as when a disliked partner engages in a positive violation).[18]

Interaction adaptation theory is Burgoon's attempt to address these problems within the broader framework of ongoing behavioral adjustments. There's obviously more to the theory than I've been able to present, but hopefully this brief sketch lets you see that for Burgoon, one theory leads to another.

CRITIQUE: A WELL-REGARDED WORK IN PROGRESS

I have a friend who fixes my all-terrain cycle whenever I bend it or break it. "What do you think?" I ask Bill. "Can it be repaired?" His response is always the same: "Man made it. Man can fix it!"

Judee Burgoon shows the same resolve as she seeks to adjust and redesign an expectancy violations model that never quite works as well in practice as its theoretical blueprint says it should. Almost every empirical test she runs seems to yield mixed results. For example, her early work on physical contact suggested that touch violations were often ambiguous. However, a sophisticated experiment she ran in 1992 showed that unexpected touch in a problem-solving situation was almost always welcomed as a positive violation, regardless of the status, gender, or attractiveness of the violator.

Do repeated failures to predict outcomes when a person stands far away, moves in too close, or reaches out to touch someone imply that Burgoon ought to trade in her expectancy violations theory for a new model? Does IAT render EVT obsolete? From my perspective, the answer is no.

Taken as a whole, Burgoon's expectancy violations theory continues to meet five of the six criteria of a good scientific theory as presented in Chapter 3. Her theory advances a reasonable *explanation* for the effects of expectancy violations during communication. The explanation she offers is *relatively simple* and has actually become less complex over time. The theory has *testable hypotheses* that the theorist is willing to adjust when her *quantitative research* doesn't support the prediction. Finally, the model offers *practical advice* on how to better achieve important communication goals of increased credibility, influence, and attraction. Could we ask for anything more? Of course.

We could wish for *predictions* that prove more reliable than the *Farmer's Almanac* long-range forecast of weather trends. A review of expectancy violations research suggests that EVT may have reached that point. For example, a comparative empirical study tested how well three leading theories predict interpersonal responses to nonverbal immediacy—close proximity, touch, direct gaze, direct body orientation, and forward lean.[19] None of the theories proved to be right all of the time, but EVT did better than the other two. And based on what a revised EVT now predicts, the scoreboard for my responses to the proxemic violations of Andre, Belinda, Charlie, and Dawn shows four hits and no misses.

ETHICAL REFLECTION: KANT'S CATEGORICAL IMPERATIVE

EVT focuses on what's *effective.* But, according to German philosopher Immanuel Kant, before we knowingly violate another's expectation we should consider what's *ethical.* Kant believed that any time we speak or act, we have a moral obligation to be truthful. He wrote that "truthfulness in statements which cannot be avoided is the formal duty of an individual to everyone, however great may be the disadvantage accruing to himself or another."[20] Others might wink at white lies, justify deception for the other's own good, or warn of the dire consequences that can result from total honesty. But from Kant's perspective, there are no mitigating circumstances. Lying is wrong—always. So is breaking a promise. He'd regard nonverbal deception the same way.

Categorical imperative Duty without exception; act only on that maxim which you can will to become a universal law.

Kant came to this absolutist position through the logic of his *categorical imperative,* a term that means duty without exception. He stated the categorical imperative as an ethical absolute: "Act only on that maxim which you can will to become a universal law."[21] In terms of EVT, Kant would have us look at the violation we are considering and ask, *What if everybody did that all the time?* If we don't like the answer, we have a solemn duty not to do the deed.

The categorical imperative is a method of determining right from wrong by thinking through the ethical valence of an act, regardless of motive. Suppose we're thinking about touching someone in a way he or she doesn't expect and hasn't clearly let us know is welcome. Perhaps the other person, like Lindi's roommate, might be pleasantly surprised. But unless we can embrace the idea of everyone—no matter what their communication reward valence—having that kind of unbidden access to everybody, the categorical imperative says don't do it. No exceptions. In the words of a sports-minded colleague who teaches ethics, "Kant plays ethical hardball without a mitt." If we say, *I "Kant" play in that league,* what ethical scorecard will we use in place of his categorical imperative?

QUESTIONS TO SHARPEN YOUR FOCUS

1. What *proxemic* advice would you give to communicators who believe they are seen as *unrewarding?*
2. EVT suggests that *violation valence* is especially important when it's clearly positive or negative. What verbal or nonverbal expectancy violations would be confusing to you even when experienced in context?
3. Using the concepts of *expectancy, violation valence,* and *communicator reward valence,* can you explain how the final version of EVT accurately predicts Em's response to the four requests made by Andre, Belinda, Charlie, and Dawn?
4. EVT and coordinated management of meaning (see Chapter 6) hold divergent views about the nature of *ways of knowing, human nature,* and *communication research.* Can you spot the different assumptions?

CONVERSATIONS

View this segment online at www.mhhe.com/griffin9e or www.afirstlook.com.

A few minutes into my discussion with Judee Burgoon, you'll notice that one of us violates a communication expectation of the other. See if you think the violation is accidental or strategic. How does this event affect the rest of the conversation? Burgoon's love of theory is apparent throughout the segment. Do you think her enthusiasm is bolstered by a view of theories as systematic hunches rather than timeless principles chiseled in stone? As a scientist, Burgoon believes that much of human behavior is genetically programmed, yet she insists that communication is also a choice-driven, strategic behavior. As you watch, decide whether you think these beliefs are compatible.

A SECOND LOOK

Recommended resource: Judee K. Burgoon and Jerold Hale, "Nonverbal Expectancy Violations: Model Elaboration and Application to Immediacy Behaviors," *Communication Monographs,* Vol. 55, 1988, pp. 58–79.

Original model: Judee K. Burgoon, "A Communication Model of Personal Space Violations: Explication and an Initial Test," *Human Communication Research,* Vol. 4, 1978, pp. 129–142.

Expectancy: Judee K. Burgoon and Beth A. LePoire, "Effects of Communication Expectancies, Actual Communication, and Expectancy Disconfirmation on Evaluations of Communicators and Their Communication Behavior," *Human Communication Research,* Vol. 20, 1993, pp. 67–96.

Communicator reward valence: Judee K. Burgoon, "Relational Message Interpretations of Touch, Conversational Distance, and Posture," *Journal of Nonverbal Behavior,* Vol. 15, 1991, pp. 233–259.

Extension of the theory: Walid A. Afifi and Judee K. Burgoon, "The Impact of Violations on Uncertainty and the Consequences for Attractiveness," *Human Communication Research,* Vol. 26, 2000, pp. 203–233.

Cultural violations: Judee K. Burgoon and Amy Ebesu Hubbard, "Cross-Cultural and Intercultural Applications of Expectancy Violations Theory and Interaction Adaptation Theory," in *Theorizing About Intercultural Communication,* William B. Gudykunst (ed.), Sage, Thousand Oaks, CA, 2004, pp. 149–171.

Interaction adaptation theory: Judee K. Burgoon, Lesa Stern, and Leesa Dillman, *Interpersonal Adaptation: Dyadic Interaction Patterns,* Cambridge University, Cambridge, 1995.

Interaction adaptation theory application: Keri K. Stephens, Marian L. Houser, and Renee L. Cowan, "R U Able to Meat Me: The Impact of Students' Overly Casual Email Messages to Instructors," *Communication Education,* Vol. 58, 2009, pp. 303–326.

Explanation and comparison of EVT and IAT: Cindy H. White, "Expectancy Violations Theory and Interaction Adaptation Theory: From Expectations to Adaptation," in *Engaging Theories in Interpersonal Communication: Multiple Perspectives,* Leslie A. Baxter and Dawn O. Braithwaite (eds.), Sage, Thousand Oaks, CA, 2008, pp. 189–202.

Kant's categorical imperative: Immanuel Kant, *Groundwork of the Metaphysics of Morals,* H. J. Paton (trans.), Harper Torchbooks, New York, 1964, pp. 60–88.

Critique: Peter A. Andersen, Laura K. Guerrero, David B. Buller, and Peter F. Jorgensen, "An Empirical Comparison of Three Theories of Nonverbal Immediacy Exchange," *Human Communication Research,* Vol. 24, 1998, pp. 501–535.

Relationship Development

Think about your closest personal relationship. Is it one of "strong, frequent and diverse interdependence that lasts over a considerable period of time?"[1] That's how UCLA psychologist Harold Kelley and eight co-authors defined the concept of close relationship. Though their definition could apply to parties who don't even like each other, most theorists reserve the term *close* for relationships that include a positive bond—usually romantic, friend, and family. All three types of intimacy can provide enjoyment, trust, sharing of confidences, respect, mutual assistance, and spontaneity.[2] The question is, *How do we develop a close relationship?*

Two distinct approaches have dominated the theory and practice of relational development. One *experiential approach* is typified by humanistic psychologist Carl Rogers. Based upon his years of nondirective counseling, Rogers described three necessary and sufficient conditions for relationship growth. When partners perceived (1) congruence; (2) unconditional positive regard; and (3) empathic understanding of each other, they could and would draw closer.[3]

Congruence is the match or fit between an individual's inner feelings and outer display. The congruent person is genuine, real, integrated, whole, transparent. The noncongruent person tries to impress, plays a role, puts up a front, hides behind a facade. "In my relationship with persons," Rogers wrote, "I've found that it does not help, in the long run, to act as though I was something I was not."[4]

Unconditional positive regard is an attitude of acceptance that isn't contingent upon performance. Rogers asked, "Can I let myself experience positive attitudes toward this other person—attitudes of warmth, caring, liking, interest, and respect?"[5] When the answer was *yes,* both he and his clients matured as human beings. They also liked each other.

Empathic understanding is the caring skill of temporarily laying aside our views and values and entering into another's world without prejudice. It is an active process of seeking to hear the other's thoughts, feelings, tones, and meanings as if they were our own. Rogers thought it was a waste of time to be suspicious or to wonder, *What does she really mean?* He believed that we help people most when we accept what they say at face value. We should assume that they describe their world as it really appears to them.

Rogerian ideas have permeated the textbooks and teaching of interpersonal communication.[6] The topics of self-disclosure, nonverbal warmth, empathic listening, and trust are mainstays of an introductory course.

The other approach assumes that relationship behavior is shaped by the *rewards and costs of interaction.* In 1992, University of Chicago economist Gary Becker won the Nobel Prize in economics on the basis of his application of supply-and-demand market models to predict the behavior of everyday living, including love and marriage.[7] News commentators expressed skepticism that matters of the heart could be reduced to cold numbers, but the economic metaphor has dominated social science discussions of interpersonal attraction and behavior for the last five decades. It's also the approach of popular dating websites like eHarmony, where customers complete a questionnaire that matches them to "singles who have been prescreened on 29 Dimensions of Compatibility:

scientific predictors of long-term relationship success."[8] Like such dating services, the basic assumption of many relational theorists is that people interact with others in a way that maximizes their personal benefits and minimizes their personal costs.

Numerous parallels exist between the stock market and relationship market:

Law of supply and demand. A rare, desirable characteristic commands higher value on the exchange.

Courting a buyer. Most parties in the market prepare a prospectus that highlights their assets and downplays their liabilities.

Laissez-faire rules. Let the buyer beware. All's fair in love and war. It's a jungle out there.

Investors and traders. Investors commit for the long haul; traders try to make an overnight killing.

Even from these brief summaries, you can tell that a humanistic model of relational development is quite different from an economic model of social exchange. Yet both models affect each of the theories presented in this section.

All three theories regard communication as the means by which people can draw close to one another. Each considers instant intimacy a myth; relationships take time to develop and they don't always proceed on a straight-line trajectory toward that goal. In fact, most relationships never even get close. Yet some people do have deep, satisfying, long-lasting relationships. Why do they develop close ties when others don't? Each of the theories in this section offers an answer.

"I've done the numbers, and I will marry you."

CHAPTER 8

Objective — Interpretive

Socio-psychological tradition

Social Penetration Theory

of Irwin Altman & Dalmas Taylor

> A friend in need is a friend indeed.
> Neither a borrower nor a lender be.
>
> A soft answer turns away wrath.
> Don't get mad, get even.
>
> To know him is to love him.
> Familiarity breeds contempt.

Proverbs are the wisdom of the ages boiled down into short, easy-to-remember phrases. There are probably more maxims about interpersonal relationships than about any other topic. But are these truisms dependable? As we can see in the pairings above, the advice they give often seems contradictory.

Consider the plight of Pete, a freshman at a residential college, as he enters the dorm to meet his roommate face-to-face for the first time. Pete has just waved good-bye to his folks and already feels pangs of loneliness as he thinks of his girlfriend back home. He worries how she'll feel about him when he goes home at Thanksgiving. Will she illustrate the reliability of the old adage "absence makes the heart grow fonder," or will "out of sight, out of mind" be a better way to describe the next few months?

Pete finds his room and immediately spots the familiar shape of a lacrosse stick. He's initially encouraged by what appears to be a common interest, but he also can't forget that his roommate's Facebook profile expressed enthusiasm for several candidates on the opposite end of the political spectrum from Pete. Will "birds of a feather flock together" hold true in their relationship, or will "opposites attract" better describe their interaction?

Just then Jon, his roommate, comes in. For a few minutes they trade the stock phrases that give them a chance to size up each other. Something in Pete makes him want to tell Jon how much he misses his girlfriend, but a deeper sense of what is an appropriate topic of conversation when first meeting someone prevents him from sharing his feelings. On a subconscious level, perhaps even a conscious one, Pete is torn between acting on the old adage "misery loves company" or on the more macho "big boys don't cry."

Pete obviously needs something more than pithy proverbs to help him understand relational dynamics. More than two decades before Pete was born, social psychologists Irwin Altman and Dalmas Taylor proposed a *social penetration process* that explains how relational closeness develops. Altman is distinguished professor emeritus of psychology at the University of Utah, and Taylor, now deceased, was provost and professor of psychology at Lincoln University in Pennsylvania. They predicted that Pete and Jon would end up best friends only if they proceeded in a "gradual and orderly fashion from superficial to intimate levels of exchange as a function of both immediate and forecast outcomes."[1] In order to capture the process, we first have to understand the complexity of people.

Social penetration
The process of developing deeper intimacy with another person through mutual self-disclosure and other forms of vulnerability.

PERSONALITY STRUCTURE: A MULTILAYERED ONION

Altman and Taylor compared people to onions. This isn't a commentary on the human capacity to offend. Like the self-description that the ogre in *Shrek* shares with his donkey sidekick in the original film, it is a depiction of the multilayered *structure* of personality. Peel the outer skin from an onion, and you'll find another beneath it. Remove that layer and you'll expose a third, and so on. Pete's outer layer is his public self that's accessible to anyone who cares to look. The outer layer includes a myriad of details that certainly help describe who he is but are held in common with others at the school. On the surface, people see a tall, 18-year-old male business major from Michigan who lifts weights and gets lots of Facebook posts from friends back home. If Jon can look beneath the surface, he'll discover the semiprivate attitudes that Pete reveals only to some people. Pete is sympathetic to liberal social causes, deeply religious, and prejudiced against overweight people.

Personality structure
Onion-like layers of beliefs and feelings about self, others, and the world; deeper layers are more vulnerable, protected, and central to self-image.

Pete's inner core is made up of his values, self-concept, unresolved conflicts, and deeply felt emotions—things he'd never dream of posting on Facebook. This is his unique private domain, which is invisible to the world but has a significant impact on the areas of his life that are closer to the surface. Perhaps not even his girlfriend or parents know his most closely guarded secrets about himself.

CLOSENESS THROUGH SELF-DISCLOSURE

Pete becomes accessible to others as he relaxes the tight boundaries that protect him and makes himself vulnerable. This can be a scary process, but Altman and Taylor believed it's only by allowing Jon to penetrate well below the surface that Pete can truly draw close to his roommate. Nonverbal paths to closeness include mock roughhousing, eye contact, and smiling. But the main route to deep social penetration is through verbal *self-disclosure.*

Figure 8–1 illustrates a wedge being pulled into an onion. It's as if a strong magnetic force were drawing it toward the center. The depth of penetration represents the degree of personal disclosure. To get to the center, the wedge must first separate the outer layers. Altman and Taylor claimed that on the surface level this kind of biographical information exchange takes place easily, perhaps at the first meeting. But they pictured the layers of onion skin tougher and more tightly wrapped as the wedge nears the center.

Self-disclosure
The voluntary sharing of personal history, preferences, attitudes, feelings, values, secrets, etc., with another person; transparency.

Recall that Pete is hesitant to share his longing for his girlfriend with Jon. If he admits these feelings, he's opening himself up for some heavy-handed

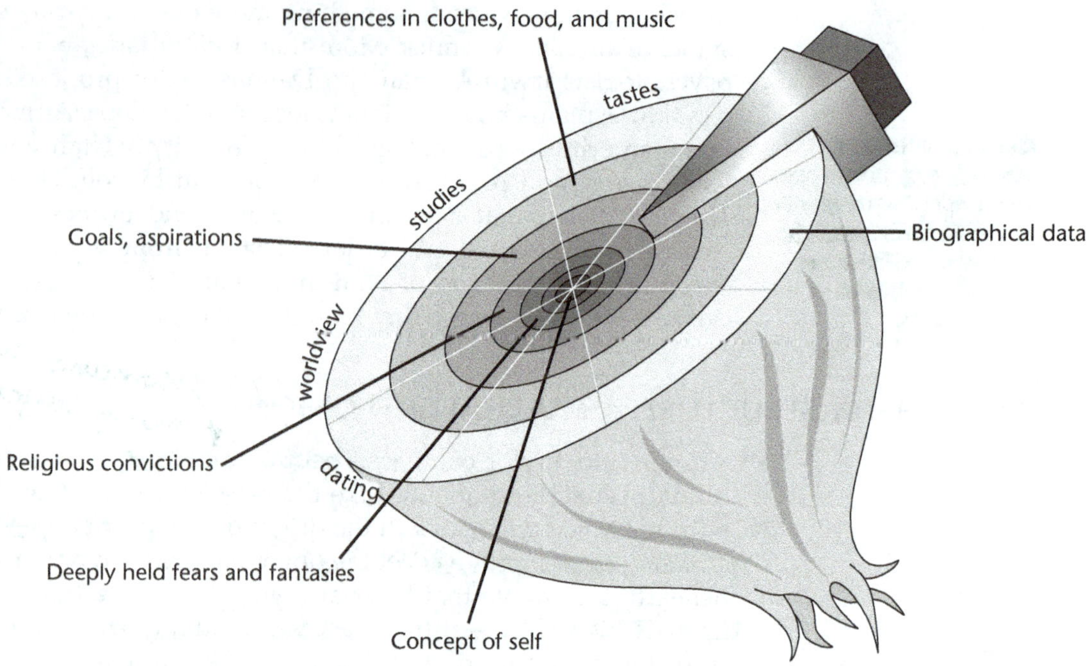

FIGURE 8–1 Penetration of Pete's Personality Structure

kidding or emotional blackmail. In addition, once the wedge has penetrated deeply, it will have cut a passage through which it can return again and again with little resistance. Future privacy will be difficult. Realizing both of these factors, Pete may be extra cautious about exposing his true feelings. Perhaps he'll fence off this part of his life for the whole school term. According to social penetration theory, a permanent guard will limit the closeness these two young men can achieve.

THE DEPTH AND BREADTH OF SELF-DISCLOSURE

Depth of penetration The degree of disclosure in a specific area of an individual's life.

The *depth of penetration* is the degree of intimacy. Although Altman and Taylor's penetration analogy strikes some readers as sexual, this was not their intent. The analogy applies equally to intimacy in friendship and romance. Figure 8–1 diagrams the closeness Jon gains if he and Pete become friends during the year. In their framework of social penetration theory, Altman and Taylor outlined four observations about the process that will bring Pete and Jon to this point:

1. *Peripheral items are exchanged sooner and more frequently than private information.* When the sharp edge of the wedge has barely reached the intimate area, the thicker part has cut a wide path through the outer rings. The relationship is still at a relatively impersonal level ("big boys don't cry"). University of Connecticut communication professor Arthur VanLear analyzed the content of conversations in developing relationships. His study showed that 14 percent of talk revealed nothing about the speaker, 65 percent dwelled on public items, 19 percent shared semiprivate details, and only 2 percent disclosed intimate confidences.[2] Further penetration will bring Pete to the point where he can share deeper feelings ("misery loves company").

2. *Self-disclosure is reciprocal, especially in the early stages of relationship development.* The theory predicts that new acquaintances like Pete and Jon will reach roughly equal levels of openness, but it doesn't explain why. Pete's vulnerability could make him seem more trustworthy, or perhaps his initial openness makes transparency seem more attractive. The young men might also feel a need for emotional equity, so a disclosure by Pete leaves Jon feeling uneasy until he's balanced the account with his own payment—a give-and-take exchange in which each party is sharing deeper levels of feeling with the other. Whatever the reason, social penetration theory asserts a *law of reciprocity.*

Law of reciprocity
A paced and orderly process in which openness in one person leads to openness in the other; "You tell me your dream; I'll tell you mine."

3. *Penetration is rapid at the start but slows down quickly as the tightly wrapped inner layers are reached.* Instant intimacy is a myth. Not only is there internal resistance to quick forays into the soul, but there are societal norms against telling too much too fast. Most relationships stall before a stable intimate exchange is established. For this reason, these relationships fade or die easily after a separation or a slight strain. A comfortable sharing of positive and negative reactions is rare. When it is achieved, relationships become more important to both parties, more meaningful, and more enduring.
4. *Depenetration is a gradual process of layer-by-layer withdrawal.* A warm friendship between Pete and Jon will deteriorate if they begin to close off areas of their lives that had previously been opened. Relational retreat is a sort of taking back of what has already been exchanged in the building of a relationship. Altman and Taylor compared the process to a movie shown in reverse. Surface talk still goes on long after deep disclosure is avoided. Relationships are likely to terminate not in an explosive flash of anger but in a gradual cooling off of enjoyment and care.

While depth is crucial to the process of social penetration, *breadth* is equally important. Note that in Figure 8–1 I have segmented the onion much like an orange to represent how Pete's life is cut into different areas—dating, studies, and so forth. It's quite possible for Pete to be candid about every intimate detail of his romance yet remain secretive about his father's alcoholism or his own minor dyslexia. Because only one area is accessed, the relationship depicted in the onion drawing is typical of a summer romance—depth without breadth. Of course, breadth without depth describes the typical "Hi, how are you?" casual friendship. A model of true intimacy would show multiple wedges inserted deeply into every area.

Breadth of penetration
The range of areas in an individual's life over which disclosure takes place.

REGULATING CLOSENESS ON THE BASIS OF REWARDS AND COSTS

Will Pete and Jon become good friends? To answer that question, Altman and Taylor borrowed ideas from another theory called *social exchange theory,* developed by psychologists John Thibaut (University of North Carolina at Chapel Hill) and Harold Kelley (University of California, Los Angeles).[3] If you want to know more about social exchange theory, I encourage you to visit www.afirstlook.com to read a chapter on the theory from a previous edition of this book. Here, I'll focus on the ideas from the theory that Altman and Taylor thought are useful for understanding the process of self-disclosure.

Investors choose where to put their money in the stock market. College freshmen like Pete and Jon choose where to put their time in friendships. Social exchange theory claims we make both decisions in similar ways. Whether finance or friendship, we want a good return on our investment, so we do a cost-benefit analysis beforehand. For the financial investor, that might involve combing the pages of *The Wall Street Journal* for tips about which stocks might increase in value. Pete and Jon don't have a newspaper with that kind of expert interpersonal advice, so instead they'll think about whether they'll enjoy interacting in the future. Right after their first encounter, Pete will sort out the pluses and minuses of friendship with Jon, computing a bottom-line index of relational satisfaction. Jon will do the same regarding Pete. If the perceived mutual benefits outweigh the costs of greater vulnerability, the process of social penetration will proceed.

Social exchange
Relationship behavior and status regulated by both parties' evaluations of perceived rewards and costs of interaction with each other.

Social exchange theory identifies three key components of this mental calculation: relational outcome, relational satisfaction, and relational stability. Altman and Taylor agreed these factors are important, and therefore included them in social penetration theory. I'll describe each of the three concepts below.

Relational Outcome: Rewards Minus Costs

Thibaut and Kelley suggested that people try to predict the *outcome* of an interaction before it takes place. Thus, when Pete first meets his roommate, he mentally gauges the potential rewards and costs of friendship with Jon. He perceives a number of benefits. As a newcomer to campus, Pete strongly desires someone to talk to, eat with, and just hang out with when he's not in class or studying. His roommate's interest in lacrosse, easy laugh, and laid-back style make Jon an attractive candidate.

Outcome
The perceived rewards minus the costs of interpersonal interaction.

Pete is also aware that there's a potential downside to getting to know each other better. If he reveals some of his inner life, his roommate may scoff at his faith in God or ridicule his liberal "do-gooder" values. Pete isn't ashamed of his convictions, but he hates to argue, and he regards the risk of conflict as real. Factoring in all the likely pluses and minuses, reaching out in friendship to Jon strikes Pete as net positive, so he makes the first move.

The idea of totaling potential benefits and losses to determine behavior isn't new. Since the nineteenth century, when philosopher John Stuart Mill first stated his principle of utility,[4] there's been a compelling logic to the *minimax principle of human behavior*. The minimax principle claims that people seek to maximize their benefits and minimize their costs. Thus, the higher we rate a relational outcome, the more attractive we find the behavior that might make it happen.

Minimax principle of human behavior
People seek to maximize their benefits and minimize their costs.

Social exchange theorists assume that we can accurately gauge the payoffs of a variety of interactions and that we have the good sense to choose the action that will provide the best result. Altman and Taylor weren't sure that we always base such decisions on reliable information, but that's not the issue. What mattered to them is that we decide to open up with another person using the perceived benefit-minus-cost outcome.

Lee, a former student of Em's, shared how he calculated cost–benefit ratios in one of his friendships. For him, self-disclosure has a higher emotional cost than it does for the average person:

> Self-disclosure makes me uncomfortable. However, the medium of music makes me a bit more comfortable and my desire to write a good song forces me to open up in ways I wouldn't otherwise. For example, I wrote a song for my friend John's birthday party where I put together a series of verses that commemorated all the

things in the last year that John and I shared or thought were funny. John and I still had a relatively superficial relationship at that point, but I think by showing that I cared through the song, another layer of the onion was peeled away.

Early in a relationship, we tend to see physical appearance, similar backgrounds, and mutual agreement as benefits ("birds of a feather flock together"). Disagreement and deviance from the norm are negatives. But as the relationship changes, so does the nature of interaction that friends find rewarding. Deeper friendships thrive on common values and spoken appreciation, and we can even enjoy surface diversity ("opposites attract").

If Pete sees much more benefit than cost in a relationship with Jon, he'll start to reveal more of who he is. If the negatives outweigh the positives, he'll try to avoid contact with Jon as much as possible. Even though they're stuck together physically in the same dorm room, a negative assessment could cause him to hold back emotionally for the rest of the year.

Gauging Relational Satisfaction—The Comparison Level (CL)

Evaluating outcomes is a tricky business. Even if we mentally convert intangible benefits and costs into a bottom-line measure of overall effect, its psychological impact upon us may vary. A relational result has meaning only when we contrast

it with other real or imagined outcomes. Social exchange theory offers two standards of comparison that Pete and others use to evaluate their interpersonal outcomes. The first point of reference deals with relative *satisfaction*—how happy or sad an interpersonal outcome makes a participant feel. Thibaut and Kelley called this the *comparison level*.

Comparison level (CL) The threshold above which an interpersonal outcome seems attractive; a standard for relational satisfaction.

A person's comparison level (CL) is the threshold above which an outcome seems attractive. Suppose, for example, that Pete is looking forward to his regular Sunday night phone call with his girlfriend. Since they usually talk for about a half hour, 30 minutes is Pete's comparison level for what makes a pleasing conversation. If he's not in a hurry, a 45-minute call will seem especially gratifying, while a 15-minute chat would be quite disappointing. Of course, the length of the call is only one factor that affects Pete's positive or negative feelings when he hangs up the phone. He has also developed expectations for the topics they'll discuss, his girlfriend's tone of voice, and the warmth of her words when she says good-bye. These are benchmarks that Pete uses to gauge his relative satisfaction with the interaction.

To a big extent, our relational history establishes our CLs for friendship, romance, and family ties. We judge the value of a relationship by comparing it to the baseline of past experience. If Pete had little history of close friendship in high school, a relationship with Jon would look quite attractive. If, on the other hand, he's accustomed to being part of a close-knit group of intimate friends, hanging out with Jon could pale by comparison.

Sequence plays a large part in evaluating a relationship. The result from each interaction is stored in the individual's memory. Experiences that take place early in a relationship can have a huge impact because they make up a large proportion of the total relational history. One unpleasant experience out of 10 is merely troublesome, but 1 out of 2 can end a relationship before it really begins. Trends are also important. If Pete first senses coolness from Jon yet later feels warmth and approval, the shift will raise Jon's attractiveness to a level higher than it would be if Pete had perceived positive vibes from the very beginning.

Gauging Relational Stability—The Comparison Level of Alternatives (CL_{alt})

Thibaut and Kelley suggested that there is a second standard by which we evaluate the outcomes we receive. They called it the *comparison level of alternatives* (*CL_{alt}*). Don't let the similarity of the names confuse you—CL and CL_{alt} are two entirely different concepts. CL is your overall standard for a specific type of relationship, and it remains fairly stable over time. In contrast, CL_{alt} represents your evaluation of other relational options at the moment. For Pete, it's the result of thinking about his interactions with other people in his dorm. As he considers whether to invest his limited time in getting to know Jon, he'll ask, *Would my relational payoffs be better with another person?* His CL_{alt} is his *best available alternative* to a friendship with Jon. If CL_{alt} is less than Pete's current outcomes, his friendship with Jon will be *stable*. But if more attractive friendship possibilities become available, or roommate squabbles drive his outcomes below the established CL_{alt}, the instability of their friendship will increase.

Comparison level of alternatives (CL_{alt}) The best outcome available in other relationships; a standard for relational stability.

Taken together, CL and CL_{alt} explain why some people remain in relationships that aren't satisfying. For example, social workers describe the plight of a physically abused wife as "high cost, low reward." Despite her anguish, the woman feels trapped in the distressing situation because being alone in the world appears even worse. As dreadful as her outcomes are, she can't imagine a better alternative. She won't leave until she perceives an outside alternative that promises a better life. Her relationship is very unsatisfying because her outcomes are far below her CL, but also quite stable because her outcomes are above her CL_{alt}.

The relative values of outcome, CL, and CL_{alt} go a long way in determining whether a person is willing to become vulnerable in order to have a deeper relationship. The optimum situation is when both parties find

$$\text{Outcome} > CL_{alt} > CL$$

Using Pete as an example, this notation shows that he forecasts a friendship with Jon that will be more than *satisfying*. The tie with Jon will be *stable* because there's no other relationship on campus that is more attractive. Yet Pete won't feel trapped, because he has other satisfying options available should this one turn sour. We see, therefore, that social exchange theory explains why Pete is primed for social penetration. If Jon's calculations are similar, the roommates will begin the process of mutual vulnerability that Altman and Taylor described, and reciprocal self-disclosure will draw them close.

ETHICAL REFLECTION: EPICURUS' ETHICAL EGOISM

The minimax principle that undergirds social exchange theory—and therefore social penetration theory as well—is also referred to as *psychological egoism*. The term reflects many social scientists' conviction that all of us are motivated by self-interest. Unlike most social scientists who limit their study to what *is* rather than what *ought* to be, *ethical egoists* claim we *should* act selfishly. It's right and it's good for us to look out for number one.

Epicurus, a Greek philosopher who wrote a few years after Aristotle's death, defined the good life as getting as much pleasure as possible: "I spit on the noble and its idle admirers when it contains no element of pleasure."[5] Although his position is often associated with the adage "Eat, drink, and be merry," Epicurus actually emphasized the passive pleasures of friendship and good digestion, and above all, the absence of pain. He cautioned that "no pleasure is in itself evil, but the things which produce certain pleasures entail annoyances many times greater than the pleasures themselves."[6] The Greek philosopher put lying in that category. He said that the wise person is prepared to lie if there is no risk of detection, but since we can never be certain our falsehoods won't be discovered, he didn't recommend deception.

Ethical egoism
The belief that individuals should live their lives so as to maximize their own pleasure and minimize their own pain.

A few other philosophers have echoed the Epicurean call for selfish concern. Thomas Hobbes described life as "nasty, brutish and short" and advocated political trade-offs that would gain a measure of security. Adam Smith, the spiritual father of capitalism, advised every person to seek his or her own profit. Friedrich Nietzsche announced the death of God and stated that the noble soul has reverence for itself. Egoist writer Ayn Rand dedicated her novel *The Fountainhead* to "the exultation of man's self-esteem and the sacredness of his happiness on earth."[7] Of course, the moral advice of Epicurus, Hobbes, Nietzsche, and Rand may be suspect. If their counsel consistently reflects their beliefs, their words are spoken for their own benefit, not ours.

Most ethical and religious thinkers denounce the selfishness of egoism as morally repugnant. How can one embrace a philosophy that advocates terrorism as long as it brings joy to the terrorist? When the egoistic pleasure principle is compared to a life lived to reduce the suffering of others, as with the late Mother Teresa, ethical egoism seems to be no ethic at all. Yet the egoist would claim that the Nobel Peace Prize winner was leading a sacrificial life because she took pleasure in serving the poor. If charity becomes a burden, she should stop.

DIALECTICS AND THE ENVIRONMENT

Viewing increased self-disclosure as the path to intimacy is a simple idea—one that's easily portrayed in the onion model of Figure 8–1. It can also be summarized in less than 40 words:

> Interpersonal closeness proceeds in a gradual and orderly fashion from superficial to intimate levels of exchange, motivated by current and projected future outcomes. Lasting intimacy requires continual and mutual vulnerability through breadth and depth of self-disclosure.

But Altman later had second thoughts about his basic assumption that openness is the predominant quality of relationship development. He began to speculate that the desire for privacy may counteract what he first thought was a unidirectional quest for intimacy. He now proposes a *dialectical model,* which assumes that "human social relationships are characterized by openness or contact and closedness or separateness between participants."[8] He believes that the tension between openness and closedness results in cycles of disclosure or withdrawal.

Altman also identifies the *environment* as a factor in social penetration.[9] Sometimes the environment guides our decision to disclose—a quiet, dimly lit sit-down restaurant might make us more willing to open up than when sitting on stools under the harsh lights of a noisy fast food joint. Other times we actively manipulate our environment to meet our privacy and disclosure goals. Thus, we might choose a quiet booth in the corner if we don't want others to overhear a sensitive conversation.

Dialectical model
The assumption that people want both privacy and intimacy in their social relationships; they experience a tension between disclosure and withdrawal.

Pete and Jon face choices about how to manage their room's environment. For Altman, this is more than just deciding whether to put a mini-fridge under the desk or next to the bed. He believes the way the two manage their dorm room says a lot about their relationship with each other and with their peers. Will they keep the door open on weeknights? Will they lock the room when they're away? Will they split the room down the middle, or will their possessions intermingle? Each decision shapes how the roommates manage the ongoing tension between openness and closedness during the year.

Because college freshmen face so many decisions about disclosure, privacy, and their physical environment, Altman studied social penetration in dorm living at the University of Utah.[10] He asked college freshmen how they used their environment to seek out and avoid others. To probe deeper into how students managed their space, he visited their rooms and photographed the wall above their beds. Two years later he examined school records to see if students' choices about their physical space predicted success and satisfaction at college. Overall, Altman found that students were more likely to remain at the university when they honored their need for *territoriality,* the human (and animalistic) tendency to claim a physical location or object as our own. This need shows that the onion of social penetration includes both our mind and our physical space.

Territoriality
The tendency to claim a physical location or object as our own.

Some students in Altman's study crafted a dorm room environment that welcomed others. They kept their doors open, invited others to visit, and even used music to draw people into the room. Their wall decorations promoted mutual self-disclosure by showing multiple facets of their identity, ranging from calendars and schedules to hobbies and photographs of friends. Just like verbal disclosure, environmental disclosure can vary in its breadth. If Pete and Jon decorate their room with several facets of their identities, the law of reciprocity suggests that visitors might feel more comfortable disclosing verbally as well. The students who created this kind of warm atmosphere tended to succeed at college.

The students who later dropped out used wall decorations that didn't reveal a range of interests, like one student who only displayed ballet-related images, or another with only ski posters. Such students tended to shut out potential visitors and play loud music that discouraged discussion. Also, students who eventually left the university didn't honor their need for personal territory. Compared to those who remained, they were less likely to arrange the furniture to create some private spaces or occasionally retreat from the dorm room for time alone. To explain this curious finding, Altman reasoned that "the dormitory environment inherently provides many opportunities for social contact," and therefore "it may be more important to develop effective avoidance techniques in such a setting."[11] Consequently, Pete and Jon would be wise to recognize each other's need for clearly defined territory. Each of them might be unwilling to let the other penetrate his physical space until they've first penetrated each other's psychological space—their onion.

Altman's results demonstrate the importance of both psychological and territorial boundaries in the process of social penetration. Students who were successful at college honored their dialectical needs for both contact and separateness. Sandra Petronio, a communication theorist at Indiana University–Purdue University Indianapolis, was intrigued by Altman's use of territoriality to explain dialectical forces. She later crafted *communication privacy management theory* to further explain the intricate ways people manage boundaries around their personal information. You can read about her insights in Chapter 12.

CRITIQUE: PULLING BACK FROM SOCIAL PENETRATION

Social penetration theory is an established and familiar explanation of how closeness develops in ongoing relationships. Altman and Taylor's image of multiple wedges penetrating deeply into a multilayered onion has proved to be a helpful model of growing intimacy. But just as these theorists described people continually reappraising their relationships in light of new experiences, it makes sense for us to reconsider the basic assumptions and claims of their theory. Social penetration theory has many critics.

As you will read in Chapter 12, Petronio challenges some core assumptions of social penetration theory. She thinks it's simplistic to equate self-disclosure with relational closeness. It can *lead* to intimacy, but a person may reveal private information merely to express oneself, to release tension, or to gain relational control. In these cases the speaker doesn't necessarily desire nor achieve a stronger bond with the confidant. And if the listener is turned off or disgusted by what was said, depenetration can be swift. Petronio also questions Altman and Taylor's view of personality structure. The onion-layer model of social penetration theory posits fixed boundaries that become increasingly thick as one penetrates toward the inner core of personality. In contrast, for Petronio, our privacy boundaries are personally created, often shifting, and frequently permeable.

Other personal relationship scholars are uncomfortable with Altman and Taylor's wholesale use of a reward–cost analysis to explain the differential drive for penetration. Can a complex blend of advantages and disadvantages be reduced to a single numerical index? And assuming that we can forecast the value of relational outcomes, are we so consistently selfish that we always opt for what we calculate is in our own best interest? Julia Wood, a communication theorist associated with standpoint theory (see Chapter 35), is skeptical. She argues, "The focus in exchange theories is one's own gains and outcomes; this focus is incapable of addressing matters such as compassion, caring, altruism, fairness, and other ethical issues that should be central to personal relationships."[12] To her and like-minded scholars, relational life has a human core that pure economic calculus cannot touch.

University of North Dakota psychologist Paul Wright believes Pete and Jon could draw close enough that their relationship would no longer be driven by a self-centered concern for personal gain. When friendships have what Wright calls "an intrinsic, end-in-themselves quality," people regard good things happening to their friends as rewards in themselves.[13] When that happens, Jon would get just as excited if Pete had a successful employment interview as if he himself had been offered the job. This rare kind of selfless love involves a relational transformation, not just more self-disclosure.[14] Altman and Taylor's theory doesn't speak about the transition from *me* to *we*, but that apparently takes place only after an extended process of social penetration.

QUESTIONS TO SHARPEN YOUR FOCUS

1. The onion model in Figure 8–1 is sectioned into eight parts, representing the *breadth* of a person's life. How would you label eight regions of interest in your life?
2. Jesus said, "There is no greater love than this: to lay down one's life for one's friends."[15] Given the *minimax principle* of human behavior used in a *social exchange* analysis, how is such a sacrifice possible?
3. Altman conducted his study of first-year students in the 1970s. How have subsequent technological advances changed the ways students manage contact and privacy in their personal territory?
4. The romantic truism "to know her is to love her" seems to contradict the relational adage "familiarity breeds contempt." Given the principles of social penetration theory, can you think of a way both statements might be true?

A SECOND LOOK

Recommended resource: Irwin Altman and Dalmas Taylor, *Social Penetration: The Development of Interpersonal Relationships,* Holt, New York, 1973.

Altman's reflective research summary: Irwin Altman, "Toward a Transactional Perspective: A Personal Journey," in *Environment and Behavior Studies: Emergence of Intellectual Traditions: Advances in Theory and Research, Vol. 11, Human Behavior and Environment, Environment and Behavior Studies,* Irwin Altman and Kathleen Christensen (eds.), Plenum, New York, 1990, pp. 225–255.

Social penetration in intercultural and interracial friendships: Yea-Wen Chen and Masato Nakazawa, "Influences of Culture on Self-Disclosure as Relationally Situated in Intercultural and Interracial Friendships from a Social Penetration Perspective," *Journal of Intercultural Communication Research,* Vol. 38, 2009, pp. 77–98.

Social exchange theory: John W. Thibaut and Harold H. Kelley, *The Social Psychology of Groups,* John Wiley & Sons, New York, 1952.

Dialectic revision: Irwin Altman, Anne Vinsel, and Barbara Brown, "Dialectic Conceptions in Social Psychology: An Application to Social Penetration and Privacy Regulation," in *Advances in Experimental Social Psychology, Vol. 14,* Leonard Berkowitz (ed.), Academic Press, New York, 1981, pp. 107–160.

Cost-benefit analysis: Dalmas Taylor and Irwin Altman, "Self-Disclosure as a Function of Reward–Cost Outcomes," *Sociometry,* Vol. 38, 1975, pp. 18–31.

Online self-disclosure in the United States, Japan, and South Korea: Young-ok Yum and Kazuya Hara, "Computer-Mediated Relationship Development: A Cross-Cultural Comparison," *Journal of Computer-Mediated Communication,* Vol. 11, 2005, pp. 133–152.

Effects of environment on relationship closeness: Carol Werner, Irwin Altman, and Barbara B. Brown, "A Transactional Approach to Interpersonal Relations: Physical Environment, Social Context and Temporal Qualities," *Journal of Social and Personal Relationships,* Vol. 9, 1992, pp. 297–323.

Environmental study of first-year roommates: Anne Vinsel, Barbara B. Brown, Irwin Altman, and Carolyn Foss, "Privacy Regulation, Territorial Displays, and Effectiveness of Individual Functioning," *Journal of Personality and Social Psychology,* Vol. 39, 1980, pp. 1104–1115.

Ethical egoism: Edward Gegis, "What Is Ethical Egoism?" *Ethics,* Vol. 91, 1980, pp. 50–62.

To access a chapter on social exchange driven by rewards and costs, click on Social Exchange Theory in Archive under Theory Resources at *www.afirstlook.com.*

CHAPTER 9

Objective — Interpretive

Socio-psychological tradition

Uncertainty Reduction Theory

of Charles Berger

No matter how close two people eventually become, they always begin as strangers. Let's say you've just taken a job as a driver for a delivery service over the winter break. After talking with the other drivers, you conclude that your income and peace of mind will depend on working out a good relationship with Heather, the radio dispatcher. All you know for sure about Heather is her attachment to Hannah, a 100-pound Labrador retriever that never lets Heather out of her sight. The veteran drivers joke that it's hard to tell the difference between the voices of Heather and Hannah over the radio. With some qualms you make arrangements to meet Heather (and Hannah) over coffee and donuts before your first day of work. You really have no idea what to expect.

Chuck Berger believes it's natural to have doubts about our ability to predict the outcome of initial encounters. Berger, professor emeritus of communication at the University of California, Davis, notes that "the beginnings of personal relationships are fraught with uncertainties."[1] Unlike social penetration theory, which tries to forecast the future of a relationship on the basis of projected rewards and costs (see Chapter 8), Berger's uncertainty reduction theory (URT) focuses on how human communication is used to gain knowledge and create understanding.

> Central to the present theory is the assumption that when strangers meet, their primary concern is one of uncertainty reduction or increasing predictability about the behavior of both themselves and others in the interaction.[2]

Interpersonal ignorance is not bliss; it's frustrating! Berger contends that our drive to reduce uncertainty about new acquaintances gets a boost from any of three prior conditions:[3]

1. *Anticipation of future interaction:* We know we will see them again.
2. *Incentive value:* They have something we want.
3. *Deviance:* They act in a weird way.

Heather hooks you on all three counts. You know you're going to be dealing with her for the next few weeks, she can make or break you financially according to the routes she assigns, and she has this strange attachment to Hannah. According to Berger, when you add these three factors to your natural curiosity, you'll *really* want to solve the puzzle of who she is.

Berger believes that our main purpose in talking to people is to "make sense" of our interpersonal world. That's why you're having breakfast with a stranger and her dog. If you brought your own hound to the meeting, chances are the two dogs would circle and sniff each other, trying to get some idea of what their counterpart was like. Humans are no different; we're just a bit more subtle, using symbols instead of smells to reach our conclusions.

UNCERTAINTY REDUCTION: TO PREDICT AND EXPLAIN

Berger focuses on predictability, which he sees as the opposite of uncertainty. "As the ability of persons to predict which alternative or alternatives are likely to occur next decreases, uncertainty increases."[4] He owes a debt to Fritz Heider's view of people as intuitive psychologists. Heider, the father of *attribution theory*, believed that we constantly draw inferences about why people do what they do.[5] We need to predict *and* explain. If Heather's going to bark at you on the radio, you want to understand why.

Attribution theory
A systematic explanation of how people draw inferences about the character of others based upon observed behavior.

Berger notes that there are at least two kinds of uncertainty you face as you set out for your first meeting with Heather. Because you aren't sure how you

"What say we find another way to say hello?"

© Peter Steiner/The New Yorker Collection/www.cartoonbank.com

should act, one kind of uncertainty deals with *behavioral* questions. Should you shake hands? Who pays for the donuts? Do you pet the dog? Often there are accepted procedural protocols to ease the stress that behavioral uncertainty can cause. Good manners go beyond common sense.

Uncertainty reduction
Increased knowledge of what kind of person another is, which provides an improved forecast of how a future interaction will turn out.

A second kind of uncertainty focuses on *cognitive* questions aimed at discovering who the other person is as a unique individual. What does Heather like about her job? What makes her glad, sad, or mad? Does she have other friends, or does she lavish all her attention on Hannah? When you first meet a person, your mind may conjure up a wild mix of potential traits and characteristics. Reducing cognitive uncertainty means acquiring information that allows you to discard many of these possibilities. That's the kind of uncertainty reduction Berger's theory addresses—cognitive rather than behavioral uncertainty.

AN AXIOMATIC THEORY: CERTAINTY ABOUT UNCERTAINTY

Berger proposes a series of axioms to explain the connection between his central concept of uncertainty and eight key variables of relationship development: *verbal communication, nonverbal warmth, information seeking, self-disclosure, reciprocity, similarity, liking,* and *shared networks.*[6] *Axioms* are traditionally regarded as self-evident truths that require no additional proof. (All people are created equal. The shortest distance between two points is a straight line. What goes up must come down.) Here are Berger's eight truths about initial uncertainty.

Axiom
A self-evident truth that requires no additional proof.

> ***Axiom 1, Verbal Communication:*** Given the high level of uncertainty present at the onset of the entry phase, as the amount of verbal communication between strangers increases, the level of uncertainty for each interactant in the relationship will decrease. As uncertainty is further reduced, the amount of verbal communication will increase.

When you first sit down with Heather, the conversation will be halting and somewhat stilted. But as words begin to flow, you'll discover things about each other that make you feel more confident in each other's presence. When your comfort level rises, the pace of the conversation will pick up.

> ***Axiom 2, Nonverbal Warmth:*** As nonverbal affiliative expressiveness increases, uncertainty levels will decrease in an initial interaction situation. In addition, decreases in uncertainty level will cause increases in nonverbal affiliative expressiveness.

When initial stiffness gives way to head nods and tentative smiles, you'll have a better idea of who Heather is. This assurance leads to further signs of warmth, such as prolonged eye contact, forward body lean, and pleasant tone of voice.

> ***Axiom 3, Information Seeking:*** High levels of uncertainty cause increases in information-seeking behavior. As uncertainty levels decline, information-seeking behavior decreases.

What is it about Heather that prompted the other drivers to warn you not to start off on the wrong foot? You simply have no idea. Like a bug with its antennae twitching, you carefully monitor what she says and how she acts in order to gather clues about her personality. But you become less vigilant after she explains that her pet peeve is drivers who complain about their assignments on the radio. Whether or not you think her irritation is justified, you begin to relax because you have a better idea of how to stay on her good side.

> ***Axiom 4, Self-Disclosure:*** High levels of uncertainty in a relationship cause decreases in the intimacy level of communication content. Low levels of uncertainty produce high levels of intimacy.

Like Altman and Taylor (see Chapter 8), Berger equates intimacy of communication with depth of self-disclosure. Demographic data revealing that Heather was raised in Toledo and that you are a communication major are relatively nonintimate. They typify the opening gambits of new acquaintances who are still feeling each other out. But Heather's comment that she feels more loyalty from Hannah than from any person she knows is a gutsy admission that raises the intimacy level of the conversation to a new plane. Most people wait to express attitudes, values, and feelings until they have a good idea what the listener's response will be.

> ***Axiom 5, Reciprocity:*** High levels of uncertainty produce high rates of reciprocity. Low levels of uncertainty produce low levels of reciprocity.

Self-disclosure research confirms the notion that people tend to mete out the personal details of their lives at a rate that closely matches their partner's willingness to share intimate information.[7] Reciprocal vulnerability is especially important in the early stages of a relationship. The issue seems to be one of power. When knowledge of each other is minimal, we're careful not to let the other person one-up us by being the exclusive holder of potentially embarrassing information. But when we already know some of the ups and downs of a person's life, an even flow of information seems less crucial. Berger would not anticipate long monologues at your first get-together with Heather; future meetings might be a different story.

> ***Axiom 6, Similarity:*** Similarities between persons reduce uncertainty, while dissimilarities produce increases in uncertainty.

The more points of contact you establish with Heather, the more you'll feel you understand her inside and out. If you are a dog lover, the two of you will click. If, however, you are partial to purring kittens, Heather's devotion to this servile beast will cause you to wonder if you'll ever be able to figure out what makes her tick.

> ***Axiom 7, Liking:*** Increases in uncertainty level produce decreases in liking; decreases in uncertainty produce increases in liking.

This axiom suggests that the more you find out about Heather, the more you'll appreciate who she is. It directly contradicts the cynical opinion that "familiarity breeds contempt" and affirms instead the relational maxim that "to know her is to love her."

> ***Axiom 8, Shared Networks:*** Shared communication networks reduce uncertainty, while lack of shared networks increases uncertainty.

This axiom was not part of Berger's original theory, but his ideas triggered extensive research by other communication scholars who soon moved uncertainty reduction theory beyond the confines of two strangers meeting for the first time. Berger applauds this extension: "The broadening of the theory's scope suggests the potential usefulness of reconceptualizing and extending the original formulation."[8] For example, Malcolm Parks (University of Washington) and Mara Adelman (Seattle University) discovered that men and women who communicate more often with their romantic partners' family and friends have less uncertainty about the person they love than do those whose relationships exist in relative isolation.[9] Networking couples also tend to stay together. On the basis of these findings, Berger incorporated this axiom into his formal design.

THEOREMS: THE LOGICAL FORCE OF UNCERTAINTY AXIOMS

Once we grant the validity of the eight axioms, it makes sense to pair two of them together to produce additional insight into relational dynamics. The combined axioms yield an inevitable conclusion when inserted in the well-known pattern of deductive logic:

Theorem
A proposition that logically and necessarily follows from two axioms.

If $A = B$
and $B = C$
then $A = C$

Berger does this for all possible combinations, thereby generating 28 theorems—for example:

If similarity reduces uncertainty (axiom 6)
and reduced uncertainty increases liking (axiom 7)
then similarity and liking are positively related (theorem 21)

In this case, the result isn't exactly earthshaking. The connection between similarity and liking is a long-established finding in research on interpersonal attraction.[10] When viewed as a whole, however, these 28 logical extensions sketch out a rather comprehensive theory of interpersonal development—all based on the importance of reducing uncertainty in human interaction.

Instead of listing all 28 theorems, I've plotted the relationships they predict in Figure 9–1. The chart reads like a mileage table you might find in a road atlas.

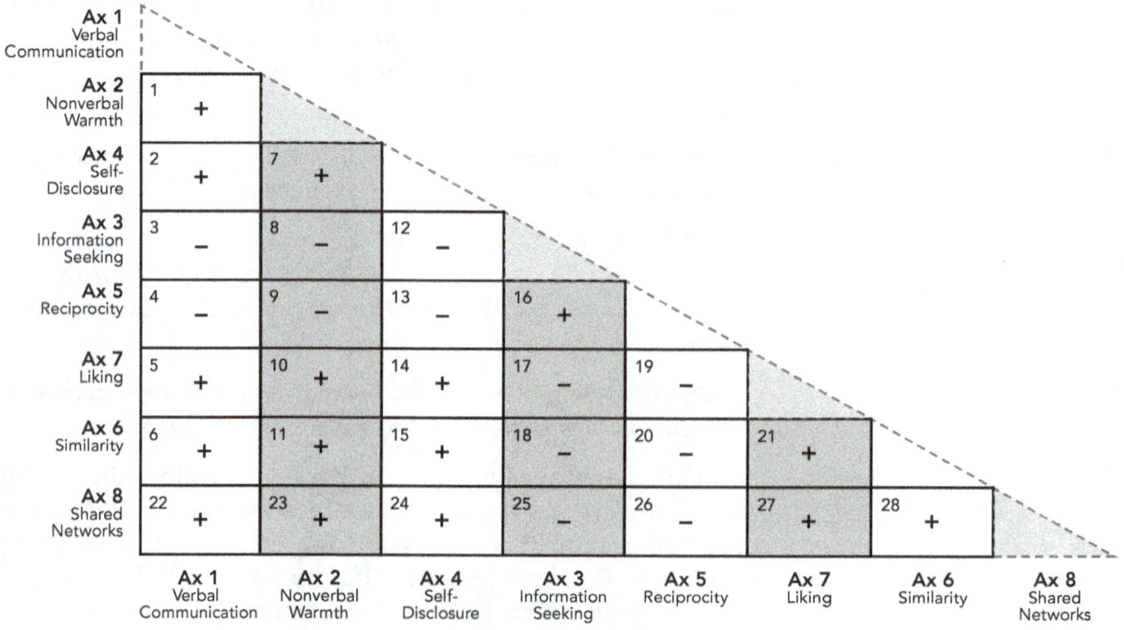

FIGURE 9–1 Theorems of Uncertainty Reduction Theory
Adapted from Berger and Calabrese, "Some Explorations in Initial Interaction and Beyond"

Select one axiom along the bottom and another down the side. The intersection between the two shows the number of Berger's theorem and the type of correlation it asserts. A plus sign (+) shows that the two interpersonal variables rise or fall together. A minus sign (−) indicates that as one increases, the other decreases. Will the warmth of Heather's nonverbal communication increase as the intimacy of her self-disclosure deepens? Theorem 7 says it will. Suppose you grow fond of Heather as a friend. Will you seek to find out more about her? Theorem 17 makes the surprising prediction that you won't (more on this later).

Recall from Malcolm Parks' research that good friends who have overlapping social networks communicate more frequently with each other than those who don't have those connections (see the cybernetic tradition in Chapter 4). You and Heather aren't good friends, but suppose you unexpectedly discover that her parents and your folks attend the same church service and sometimes play cards together. Does URT predict you'll be talking with each other more in the future? Check the intersection between axioms 1 and 8 on the chart for Berger's prediction.

MESSAGE PLANS TO COPE WITH UNCERTAIN RESPONSES

Berger believes most social interaction is goal-driven; we have reasons for saying what we say. So after developing the core axioms and theorems of uncertainty reduction theory, he devoted his attention to explaining *how* we communicate to reduce uncertainty. Berger labeled his work "A Plan-Based Theory of Strategic Communication" because he was convinced we continually construct cognitive plans to guide our communication.[11] According to Berger, "*plans* are mental representations of action sequences that may be used to achieve goals."[12] Figure 9–2 offers a possible example of a strategic plan for your breakfast with Heather.

Your main reason for getting together with the dispatcher is to maximize your income over the holidays. Your overall strategy to reach that goal is to build a good working relationship with Heather, since she assigns the routes. The term *overall* is appropriate because Berger claims that plans are "hierarchi-

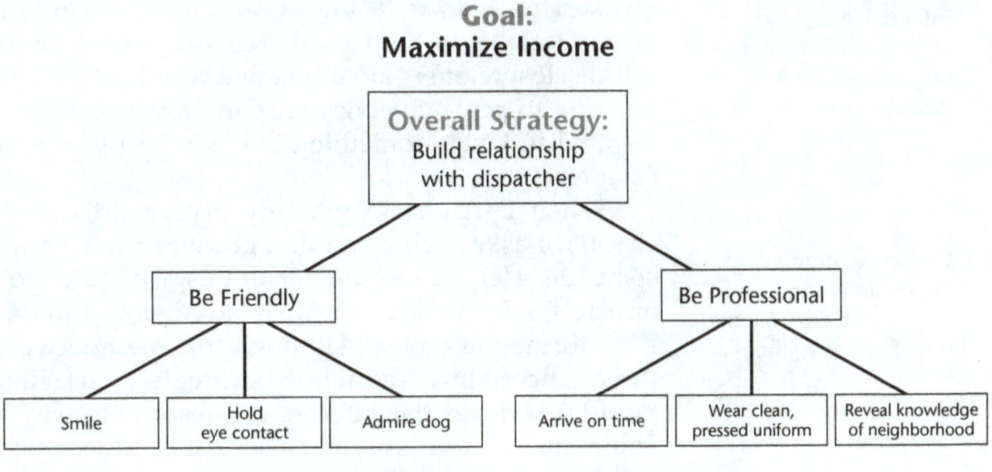

FIGURE 9–2 A Hierarchical Plan of Goal-Directed Communication

cally organized with abstract action representations at the top of the hierarchy and progressively more concrete representations toward the bottom."[13] In order to build that relationship, you intend to converse in a *friendly* and *professional* manner. In this case, friendly means smiling, holding eye contact when she speaks, and admiring her dog. You'll show professionalism by arriving on time; wearing a clean, pressed uniform; and revealing knowledge of the neighborhood.

If you switch strategies at the top—seeking pity for a poor, struggling college student in the midst of a recession, for example—the alteration will cascade down the hierarchy, requiring changes in many of the behaviors below. Thus, a top-down revision of an action plan requires great amounts of cognitive capacity.

Even if you think carefully about your plan, Berger claims you can't be sure you'll reach your goal. You may have a great plan but execute it poorly. Heather may interpret words that you meant one way to mean something else. Or she may have her own goals and plans that will inevitably thwart yours. Berger has come to the conclusion that uncertainty is central to *all* social interaction: "The probability of perfect communication is zero."[14] Thus he asks, "How do individuals cope with the inevitable uncertainties they must face when constructing messages?"[15] The following strategies are some of his answers.

Seeking Information. Uncertainty reduction theorists have outlined four approaches we can use to reduce uncertainty. Using a *passive strategy,* we unobtrusively observe others from a distance. This fly-on-the-wall tactic works best when we spot others reacting to people in informal, or "backstage," settings. (The strategy sounds like normal "scoping" behavior on any college campus.) Unless Heather lives in your neighborhood or hangs out in the same places, you might not have an opportunity to simply observe her behavior.

Passive strategy
Impression formation by observing a person interacting with others.

In an *active strategy,* we ask a third party for information. We realize that our mutual acquaintance will probably give a somewhat slanted view, but most of us have confidence in our ability to filter out the bias and gain valuable information. Regarding Heather, you've already used the active strategy by querying other drivers for their opinions about her.

Active strategy
Impression formation by asking a third party about a person.

With an *interactive strategy,* we talk face-to-face with the other person and ask specific questions—just what you're planning to do with Heather. This is the quickest route to reducing uncertainty, but continual probing in social settings begins to take on the feel of a cross-examination or the third degree. Our own self-disclosure offers an alternative way to elicit information from others without seeming to pry. By being transparent, we create a safe atmosphere for others to respond in kind—something the "law of reciprocity" suggests they will do (see Chapter 8).

Interactive strategy
Impression formation through face-to-face discussion with a person.

When I (Andrew) told my 5-year-old daughter I was working on this chapter, I asked what she thought was the best way to find information about someone. Her answer demonstrates she's a child of the 21st century: "Check on Facebook!" Clearly she's already learned the *extractive strategy* of searching for information online. Although this method was not part of Berger's original three uncertainty reduction strategies, Art Ramirez (University of South Florida) believes the Internet creates a new way for us to reduce uncertainty. Sometimes a name is all that's necessary to search for blogs, archived newspaper articles, tweets, and more—an unobtrusive process that is something like

Extractive strategy
Impression formation by searching the Internet for information about a person.

"conducting a personalized background check."[16] If you discover Heather writes a blog about her dog, you might reduce a lot of uncertainty even before you meet.

Plan complexity
A characteristic of a message plan based on the level of detail it provides and the number of contingencies it covers.

Choosing Plan Complexity. The complexity of a message plan is measured in two ways—the level of detail the plan includes and the number of contingency plans prepared in case the original one doesn't work. If it's crucial that you make top dollar in your holiday delivery job, you're likely to draw upon a plan from memory or create a new one far more complex than the sample shown in Figure 9–2. You're also likely to have a fallback plan in case the first one fails. On the other hand, you don't know much about Heather's goals or feelings, and high uncertainty argues for a less complex plan that you can adjust in the moment, once you get a feel for who she is and what she wants. This simpler approach is preferred for another reason. Enacting a complex plan takes so much cognitive effort that there's usually a deterioration in verbal and nonverbal fluency, with a resultant loss in credibility. Jeff, a student athlete, used an interactive strategy that has low complexity:

> I thought of URT this afternoon in the trainer's room where I again made eye contact with a girl I'd never met. We were the only two people in the room and I realized I needed a plan of action. I quickly ran through several strategies to reduce uncertainty. I chose a tried-and-true icebreaker line: "Hi, I know I've seen you around a ton of times, but I don't think I've ever met you. What's your name?" I hoped for the best, but prepared for a negative reaction. My contingency plan was to simply end the attempt at conversation and seem preoccupied with my treatment. Fortunately she responded with a look of relief, her name, and then a smile. Let the conversation begin. As Berger said, "Uncertainty is central to all social interaction." It sure makes life interesting.

Hedging
Use of strategic ambiguity and humor to provide a way for both parties to save face when a message fails to achieve its goal.

Hedging. The possibility of plan failure suggests the wisdom of providing ways for both parties to save face when at least one of them has miscalculated. Berger catalogs a series of planned hedges that allow a somewhat gracious retreat. For instance, you may be quite certain about what you want to accomplish in your meeting with Heather, yet choose words that are *ambiguous* so as not to tip your hand before you find out more about her. You might also choose to be equivocal in order to avoid the embarrassment that would come from her refusing your specific request for preferred treatment in route assignment. *Humor* can provide the same way out. You could blatantly propose to use a portion of the saved time and good tips that come from prime assignments to stop at the butcher shop for a juicy bone for Hannah—but make the offer in a joking tone of voice. If Heather takes offense, you can respond, "Hey, I was just kidding."

Hierarchy hypothesis
The prediction that when people are thwarted in their attempts to achieve goals, their first tendency is to alter lower-level elements of their message.

The Hierarchy Hypothesis. What happens to action choices when plans are frustrated? Berger's *hierarchy hypothesis* asserts that "when individuals are thwarted in their attempts to achieve goals, their first tendency is to alter lower level elements of their message."[17] For example, when it's obvious the person we're talking to has failed to grasp what we are saying, our inclination is to repeat the same message—but this time louder. The tactic seldom works, but it takes less mental effort than altering strategic features higher up in the action plan. Berger describes people as "cognitive misers" who would rather try a quick fix than expend the effort to repair faulty plans.[18] There's no doubt that in-the-moment modifications are taxing, but when the issue is important, the chance to be effective makes it worth the effort. An additional hedge against failure is to practice in front of a friend who will critique your action plan before you put it into effect.[19] As a Hebrew proverb warns, "Without counsel, plans go wrong."[20]

THE RELATIONAL TURBULENCE MODEL

Berger developed uncertainty reduction theory to explain first-time encounters. Can uncertainty also wreak havoc in ongoing relationships? Leanne Knobloch at the University of Illinois believes the answer is yes, although the uncertainty differs from what we experience with new acquaintances. After the get-to-know-you phase has passed, we're unlikely to wonder about someone's age, hobbies, or hometown. Instead, uncertainty in close relationships arises from whether we're sure about our own thoughts (*Am I really in love?*), those of the other person (*Does he really enjoy spending time together?*), and the future of the relationship (*Are we headed for a breakup?*).[21] Since Knobloch's work has focused on romantic relationships, I'll describe such *relational uncertainty* in that context, although we can experience uncertainty with friends and family, too.

Relational uncertainty
Doubts about our own thoughts, the thoughts of the other person, or the future of the relationship.

Like the common cold, romantic partners might "catch" relational uncertainty at any time. But just as colds occur more often in cooler weather and enclosed spaces, some life circumstances tend to generate relational uncertainty. Knobloch's initial research focused on romantic couples' transition from casual to serious dating—a time when couples negotiate what the relationship means and whether it's likely to continue.[22] Not only can this phase produce feelings of uncertainty, but couples also experience *partner interference* as they learn to coordinate their individual goals, plans, and activities in ways that don't annoy each other. The learning process isn't always smooth.

Partner interference
Occurs when a relational partner hinders goals, plans, and activities.

Knobloch believes uncertainty leads close partners to experience *relational turbulence.* If you've flown in an airplane, you've probably felt the bumps and lurches caused by turbulent air. Knobloch thinks that's a good metaphor for partners facing uncertainty and interference:

Relational turbulence
Negative emotions arising from perceived problems in a close relationship.

> When an aircraft encounters a dramatic change in weather conditions, passengers feel turbulence as the plane is jostled, jerked, and jolted erratically. Similarly, when a [couple] undergoes a period of transition that alters the climate of the relationship, partners experience turbulence as sudden intense reactions to their circumstances. Just as turbulence during a flight may make passengers [reconsider] their safety, fear a crash, or grip their seat, turbulence in a relationship may make partners ruminate about hurt, cry over jealousy, or scream during conflict.[23]

In times of relational turbulence, we're likely to feel unsettling emotions like anger, sadness, and fear. It's a bumpy emotional ride that makes us more *reactive,* or sensitive, to our partner's actions. Let's say your dating partner asks you to pick up a candy bar while you're at the store. If you forget, your partner might be bothered but probably won't make a big deal about the brief lapse in memory. When couples are already experiencing relational turbulence, however, the same gaffe could ignite a ridiculously big argument. Over time, turbulence leads to even more uncertainty and interference, which then creates more turbulence—a vicious cycle that could threaten the health of the relationship.

Knobloch's research supports her relational turbulence model across many types of romantic relationships, ranging from couples facing clinical depression[24] to military spouses returning from deployment.[25] Throughout these studies, Knobloch has focused more on diagnosing the causes and symptoms of relational uncertainty than prescribing a cure. Like Berger, she suspects direct attempts to reduce uncertainty (such as the interactive strategy) may help resolve relational turbulence. She believes we're most likely to talk directly when the relationship has high intimacy and equal power. The talk still may produce pain, but intimacy and power equality provide stability in the face of relational turbulence.[26]

CRITIQUE: NAGGING DOUBTS ABOUT UNCERTAINTY

Within the communication discipline, Berger's uncertainty reduction theory was an early prototype of what an objective theory should be and it continues to inspire a new generation of scholars today. His theory makes specific testable predictions, and offers the human need to reduce interpersonal uncertainty as the engine that drives its axioms. Although combining the axioms generates a slew of theorems, they are straightforward, logically consistent, and simple to understand. As for practical utility, readers interested in promoting interpersonal ties can regard the linkages the theorems describe as a blueprint for constructing solid relationships. Subsequent survey and experimental research supports most of URT's axioms and has expanded the scope of the theory to cover development of established relationships. There are, however, continuing questions about Berger's reliance on the concept of *uncertainty* and his assumption that we're motivated to reduce it.

A dozen years after publishing the theory, Berger admitted that his original statement contained "some propositions of dubious validity."[27] Critics quickly point to theorem 17, which predicts that the more you like people, the less you'll seek information about them.

> Frankly, it is not clear why information-seeking would decrease as liking increased other than being required by deductive inference from the axiomatic structure of uncertainty reduction theory. In fact, it seems more reasonable to suggest that persons will seek information about and from those they like rather than those they dislike.[28]

That's the blunt assessment of Kathy Kellermann at ComCon consulting, who originally participated in Berger's research program. We might be willing to dismiss this apparent error as only one glitch out of 28 theorems, but the tight logical structure that is the genius of the theory doesn't give us that option. Theorem 17 is dictated by axioms 3 and 7. If the theorem is wrong, one of the axioms is suspect. Kellermann targets the motivational assumption of axiom 3 as the problem.

Axiom 3 assumes that lack of information triggers a search for knowledge. But as Kellermann and Rodney Reynolds at California Lutheran University discovered when they studied motivation to reduce uncertainty in more than a thousand students at 10 universities, "wanting knowledge rather than lacking knowledge is what promotes information-seeking in initial encounters with others."[29] The distinction is illustrated by the story of a teacher who asked a boy, "What's the difference between *ignorance* and *apathy?*" The student replied, "I don't know, and I don't care." (He was right.)

Kellermann and Reynolds also failed to find that anticipated future interaction, incentive value, or deviance gave any motivational kick to information seeking, as Berger claimed they would. Thus, it seems that Berger's suggestion of a universal drive to reduce uncertainty during initial interaction is questionable at best. Yet along with the suspect third axiom, it, too, remains part of the theory.

Another attack on the theory comes from Michael Sunnafrank at the University of Minnesota Duluth. He challenges Berger's claim that uncertainty reduction is the key to understanding early encounters. Consistent with Altman and Taylor's social penetration model (see Chapter 8) is Sunnafrank's insistence that the early course of a relationship is guided by its *predicted outcome value (POV)*.[30] He's convinced that the primary goal of our initial interaction with another is maximizing our relational outcomes rather than finding out who he or she is. If this is true, you'll be more concerned with establishing a smooth working relationship with Heather at your initial meeting than you will be in figuring out why she does what she does.

Predicted outcome value
A forecast of future benefits and costs of interaction based on limited experience with the other.

Who's right—Berger or Sunnafrank? Berger thinks there's no contest. He maintains that any predictions you make about the rewards and costs of working with Heather are only as good as the quality of your current knowledge. To the extent that you are uncertain of how an action will affect the relationship, predicted outcome value has no meaning. Walid Afifi (University of Iowa) thinks *both* theories are too narrow.[31] In his *theory of motivated information management,* he suggests we're most motivated to reduce anxiety rather than uncertainty. So when uncertainty doesn't make us feel anxious, we won't seek to reduce it—like a couple enjoying the mystery of a date planned by one person for the other. As relational dialectics suggests (see Chapter 11), complete certainty is complete boredom.

Even though the validity of Berger's theory is in question, his analysis of initial interaction is a major contribution to communication scholarship. Berger notes that "the field of communication has been suffering and continues to suffer from an intellectual trade deficit with respect to related disciplines; the field imports much more than it exports."[32] Uncertainty reduction theory was an early attempt by a scholar trained within the discipline to reverse that trend. His success at stimulating critical thinking among his peers can be seen in the fact that every scholar cited in this chapter has been a member of a communication faculty.

Although some of Berger's axioms may not perfectly reflect the acquaintance process, his focus on the issue of reducing uncertainty is at the heart of communication inquiry. Appealing for further dialogue and modification rather than wholesale rejection of the theory, Berger asks:

> What could be more basic to the study of communication than the propositions that (1) adaptation is essential for survival, (2) adaptation is only possible through the reduction of uncertainty, and (3) uncertainty can be both reduced and produced by communicative activity?[33]

It's a sound rhetorical question.

QUESTIONS TO SHARPEN YOUR FOCUS

1. An *axiom* is a self-evident truth. Which one of Berger's axioms seems least self-evident to you?
2. Check out *theorem 13* in Figure 9–1. Does the predicted relationship between *self-disclosure* and *reciprocity* match the forecast of social penetration theory?
3. What is your goal for the class period when *uncertainty reduction theory* will be discussed? What is your *hierarchical action plan* to achieve that goal?
4. When are you most likely to feel *relational turbulence* in your close relationships? Does anything other than *partner interference* or *relational uncertainty* help explain why you experience a bumpy emotional ride?

CONVERSATIONS

View this segment online at www.mhhe.com/griffin9e or www.afirstlook.com.

Chuck Berger would not be surprised if you were confused by the mid-chapter switch from axioms of uncertainty reduction to plan-based strategic communication. In his conversation with Em he describes why he originally viewed the two lines of research as separate but now sees them as tightly linked. Many students find this interview especially fascinating because of Berger's strongly stated opinions. For example, he dismisses CMM's idea of co-creation of social reality (see Chapter 6) because it offers a "total amnesia model." He also criticizes social scientists who purposely create ambiguity so that they can never be proved wrong. Berger's explicit and forthright statements show that he's willing to take that risk.

A SECOND LOOK

Recommended resource: Leanne K. Knobloch, "Uncertainty Reduction Theory," in *Engaging Theories in Interpersonal Communication: Multiple Perspectives,* Leslie A. Baxter and Dawn O. Braithwaite (eds.), Sage, Thousand Oaks, CA, 2008, pp. 133–144.

Original statement: Charles R. Berger and Richard Calabrese, "Some Explorations in Initial Interaction and Beyond: Toward a Developmental Theory of Interpersonal Communication," *Human Communication Research,* Vol. 1, 1975, pp. 99–112.

Comparison with other uncertainty theories: Walid A. Afifi, "Uncertainty and Information Management in Interpersonal Contexts," in *New Directions in Interpersonal Communication Research,* Sandi W. Smith and Steven R. Wilson (eds.), Sage, Thousand Oaks, CA, 2010, pp. 94–114.

Uncertainty reduction and online dating: Jennifer L. Gibbs, Nicole B. Ellison, and Chih-Hui Lai, "First Comes Love, Then Comes Google: An Investigation of Uncertainty Reduction Strategies and Self-Disclosure in Online Dating," *Communication Research,* Vol. 38, 2011, pp. 70–100.

Goals and plans in message production: Charles R. Berger, "Message Production Skill in Social Interaction," in *Handbook of Communication and Social Interaction Skills,* John O. Greene and Brant R. Burleson (eds.), Lawrence Erlbaum, Mahwah, NJ, 2003, pp. 257–290.

Uncertainty reduction in close relationships: Leanne K. Knobloch and Denise H. Solomon, "Information Seeking Beyond Initial Interaction: Negotiating Relational Uncertainty Within Close Relationships," *Human Communication Research,* Vol. 28, 2002, pp. 243–257.

Relational turbulence and military couples: Leanne K. Knobloch and Jennifer A. Theiss, "Experiences of U.S. Military Couples During the Post-Deployment Transition: Applying the Relational Turbulence Model," *Journal of Social and Personal Relationships,* Vol. 29, 2012, pp. 423–450.

Critique of axiom 3: Kathy Kellermann and Rodney Reynolds, "When Ignorance Is Bliss: The Role of Motivation to Reduce Uncertainty in Uncertainty Reduction Theory," *Human Communication Research,* Vol. 17, 1990, pp. 5–75.

Predicted outcome value theory: Artemio Ramirez Jr., Michael Sunnafrank, and Ryan Goei, "Predicted Outcome Value Theory in Ongoing Relationships," *Communication Monographs,* Vol. 77, 2010, pp. 27–50.

To access a chapter on reducing uncertainty when communicating across cultures, click on Anxiety/Uncertainty Management Theory in Archive under Theory Resources at *www.afirstlook.com.*

CHAPTER 10

Objective — Interpretive

Socio-psychological tradition

Social Information Processing Theory

of Joseph Walther

As depicted in the hit movie *The Social Network,* in 2003 Mark Zuckerberg created "Facemash"—a website allowing Harvard students to compare the physical attractiveness of their female peers.[1] Although Harvard's administration quickly shut down Facemash and nearly expelled Zuckerberg, Facemash soon led to Facebook, now by far the most popular social networking site. According to a Pew Internet & American Life Project survey, 65 percent of online adults use social networking sites such as Facebook, Twitter, and LinkedIn, with 43 percent having accessed a site in the last day.[2] Young and middle-aged adults are particularly avid users, but even 33 percent of adults over 65 use social networking sites. Why does social networking have such appeal? A separate Pew study suggests much of the motivation is social—commenting on another person's post is the most frequent daily Facebook activity.[3]

Chances are, social networking is part of your life, too. Consider the technological changes you've seen in your lifetime. If you're a typical college student, you probably remember a time when you didn't have text messaging or Facebook to get ahold of a friend. Perhaps you used instant messaging or email, but you probably have relatives who remember when those technologies weren't available either. From telephone to smartphone, the rapid changes in communication technology have frustrated communication scholars seeking to understand what all of this means for interpersonal relationships.

Amid this flood of cyber-innovation, Joe Walther's social information processing (SIP) theory has stood the test of time. Building on *social penetration theory* (Chapter 8), *uncertainty reduction theory* (Chapter 9), and other relationship development theories, the Michigan State University communication professor initially developed SIP to explain how people form relationships across the communication technologies that became popular in the early 1990s, such as email. Now, even after two decades of rapid technological development, the theory remains one of the most helpful explanations for why and how people form relationships online. To appreciate the theory's staying power, we need to review its history.

A BRIEF HISTORY OF SIP THEORY

From the 1980s through the early 1990s, many communication scholars expressed strong skepticism about building close relationships online through computer-mediated communication (CMC). They thought CMC might be fine for task-related purposes such as data processing, news dissemination, and long-distance business conferencing. But as a place to bond with others, cyberspace seemed like a relational wasteland—stark and barren. Scholars who studied new electronic media had already offered a variety of theories to explain the inherent differences between CMC and face-to-face communication. I'll mention three.

CMC
Computer-mediated communication, often referring to text-based messages, which filter out nonverbal cues.

Social presence theory suggests that text-based messages deprive CMC users of the sense that other warm bodies are jointly involved in the interaction.[4] To the extent that we no longer feel that anyone is *there,* our communication becomes more impersonal, individualistic, and task-oriented.

Social presence theory
Suggests that CMC deprives users of the sense that another actual person is involved in the interaction.

Media richness theory classifies each communication medium according to the complexity of the messages it can handle efficiently.[5] For example, the theory suggests that face-to-face communication provides a rich mix of verbal and nonverbal cue systems that can convey highly nuanced emotions, and even double meanings. By contrast, the limited bandwidth of CMC makes it rather lean—appropriate for transacting everyday business, but not for negotiating social relations.

Media richness theory
Purports that CMC bandwidth is too narrow to convey rich relational messages.

A third theory concentrates on the *lack of social context cues* in online communication.[6] It claims CMC users have no clue as to their relative status, and norms for interaction aren't clear, so people tend to become more self-absorbed and less inhibited. The result is increased *flaming*—hostile language that zings its target and creates a toxic climate for relational growth on the Internet. Early in *The Social Network,* Mark Zuckerberg writes a blog post criticizing his ex-girlfriend's last name and bra size. Though it may be a fictional or exaggerated account of what actually happened, one suspects he wouldn't have had the gall to say those things face-to-face.

Cues filtered out
Interpretation of CMC that regards lack of nonverbal cues as a fatal flaw for using the medium for relationship development.

All of these theories share a *cues filtered out* interpretation of CMC. In other words, they assume that most online communication is text-only, without visual or auditory cues, which limits its usefulness for developing interpersonal relationships.[7] To users accustomed to watching YouTube videos, browsing Pinterest boards, or playing the latest multiplayer game on *Xbox LIVE,* this no doubt sounds like a strange assumption. But in the early 1990s, text ruled the online world. At that time, the Internet was the province of scientific and academic users—the relatively few home users connected with slow dial-up modems that couldn't transmit images or sound quickly. In this historical context, it's not surprising that users and communication theorists were skeptical about close relationships online.

Yet in 1992, Walther countered this conventional wisdom with social information processing theory. He claimed CMC users can adapt to cue-limited media and use them effectively to develop close relationships. He argued that given the opportunity for a sufficient exchange of social messages and subsequent relational growth, *as goes face-to-face communication, so goes CMC.* Although many technologies you use today weren't invented when Walther first developed the theory, communication scholars have found SIP quite useful for understanding why and how people use cell phones, instant messaging, and social networking sites to build close relationships.

CMC VERSUS FACE-TO-FACE: A SIP INSTEAD OF A GULP

Michelle is one of my (Andrew) wife's close college friends. I didn't meet her until we moved to my first full-time job in Ohio, where Michelle lived just two hours away. It was close enough to eat dinner together a few times, but far enough that we didn't see her often. By the time she moved overseas, I'd discovered a bit about her from our handful of meals, such as her Tennessee roots and passion for studying chemistry. I enjoyed those face-to-face meetings, but still felt like I had a lot more to learn about her before I could consider her a good friend. Since our future communication would be through Facebook, I wasn't sure how our friendship would progress when she moved away. According to Walther's SIP, not a problem.

Walther labeled his theory *social information processing* because he believes relationships grow only to the extent that parties first gain information about each other and use that information to form interpersonal impressions of who they are. In taking this view, SIP theory is consistent with *social penetration theory* and *uncertainty reduction theory* (see Chapters 8 and 9). With these more or less defined impressions in mind, the interacting parties draw closer if they both like the image of the other that they've formed. SIP focuses on the first link of the chain—the personal information available through CMC and its effect on the composite mental image of the other that each one creates.

Social Information → Impression Formation → Relationship Development

Impression formation
The composite mental image one person forms of another.

At its heart, the theory recognizes that the information we receive depends on the communication medium we're using. When I first met Michelle face-to-face, we had a range of nonverbal cues available to form impressions of each other. When she moved to England, we began connecting exclusively through Facebook, and those cues disappeared from our communication. On Facebook, we can't observe each other's physical context, facial expression, tone of voice, interpersonal distance, body position, appearance, gestures, or smell. According to the *cues filtered out* interpretation, that should mean interpersonal disaster.

Walther disagrees. He doesn't think the loss of nonverbal cues is necessarily fatal or even injurious to a well-defined impression of the other or the relational development it triggers. Walther highlights two features of CMC that provide a rationale for SIP theory:[8]

1. *Verbal cues.* When motivated to form impressions and develop relationships, communicators employ any cue system that's available. Thus, CMC users can create fully formed impressions of others based solely on the linguistic content of online messages. Because Michelle posts frequently on Facebook, I've learned more about her on many topics, ranging from her love of travel to her adventures in learning to cook.
2. *Extended time.* The exchange of social information through text-only CMC is much slower than it is face-to-face, so communicators form impressions at a reduced rate. Yet given enough time, there's no reason to believe that CMC relationships will be weaker or more fragile than those developed with the benefit of nonverbal cues.

The SIP acronym suggests a liquid analogy that can help us understand Walther's thinking.[9] Suppose someone hands you a 12-ounce glass of water, cola, or beer—whatever drink you find refreshing. You could hoist the glass and chug the contents in a matter of seconds. That big gulp is similar to being face-to-face with someone you've just met and want to know better. For just a few hours of face-to-face meetings in Ohio over the course of two years, Michelle and I had this large amount of social information available.

But what if you had to drink your beverage through a straw—one *sip* at a time? You'd still be able to drain the entire 12 ounces, however, it would take much longer. That's the situation for CMC users who are thirsty for social information. They end up with the same quantity and quality of interpersonal knowledge, but it accumulates at a slower rate. It's been three years since Michelle left the country. Since then, our Facebook conversations have ranged from political debates to discussions about Asian cuisine. I now consider her a good friend and, although I'm sure we could've built the same depth of friendship more quickly face-to-face, Facebook messages have worked just fine over a longer period of time.

VERBAL CUES OF AFFINITY REPLACE NONVERBAL CUES

Walther claims that the human need for affiliation is just as active when people communicate online as when they are face-to-face. For example, a Nielsen report found that the average American teenager sends 3,339 text messages per month—more than 100 per day.[10] Evidently, teens believe a deluge of 160-character messages can quench their thirst for social information, even without the nonverbal cues that typically signal friendship or romantic attraction.

When it comes to building impressions of others, Walther is convinced that verbal and nonverbal cues can be used interchangeably. If this claim strikes you as far-fetched, remember that prior to electronic communication, people developed pen-pal relationships by discovering similarities and expressing affection through the written word alone. Long-distance romantic relationships thrived as the casual exchange of friendly notes progressed to a stream of passionate love letters. During World War II, postal letters so powerfully boosted soldier morale that the United States government launched a campaign encouraging citizens to write to loved ones serving abroad. When the mass of letters became too expensive to transport, a technology known as *v-mail* reduced letters to small pieces of film that were expanded to readable size upon reaching soldiers.[11] History supports SIP's claim that people creatively adapt their communication to connect across cue-limited media.

Experimental Support for a Counterintuitive Idea

The examples of teen texters and soldiers abroad suggest that people can express affinity just as well through a digital medium as when face-to-face. But as a communication theorist steeped in the socio-psychological tradition, Walther isn't content to rely on such anecdotes to support his theory. Over the course of the past two decades, he's performed numerous controlled experiments (see Chapter 3) to put his ideas to the test. After reading my description of the following study, see if you can identify how it provides evidence that humans are creative communicators, able to use text-only channels to convey a level of relational warmth that can equal face-to-face communication.[12]

Walther asked 28 pairs of students who didn't know each other to discuss moral dilemmas—a communication task used in many previous experiments. Half the pairs talked face-to-face, while the other half communicated online. In both cases, one member of each pair was a student accomplice—someone the researchers recruited ahead of time. Half of these confederates were asked to communicate in a friendly, positive way, while the other half were told to act unfriendly. During the experiment, video cameras recorded the face-to-face conversations from behind a one-way mirror, and all computer messages were saved. Afterward, trained raters categorized the different ways confederates communicated both verbal and nonverbal emotion. The naïve participants rated their partners on the degree of affection expressed during the discussion.

Results of the experiment indicated that the method of communication made no difference in the emotional tone perceived by naïve participants. Any discrepancy in warmth was due to the intention of each confederate—nice confederates successfully conveyed warmth, and grouchy confederates were perceived as mean. What verbal behaviors did confederates use in CMC to show they were friendly? As you might expect, self-disclosure, praise, and statements of affection topped the list. These are core strategies of making an impression by reducing uncertainty and drawing close through social penetration. Yet surprisingly, indirect disagreement, a change of subject, and compliments offered while proposing a contrasting idea were also associated with friendliness. When discussing a controversial topic, each of these verbal techniques allows a partner to save face and defuse potential conflict.

Of course, face-to-face confederates could have used these same verbal behaviors—and indeed, some of them did. But *what* confederates said when physically present seemed insignificant compared to *how* they showed it nonverbally. Consistent with previous research, confederates relied on facial expression, eye contact, tone of voice, body position, and other nonverbal cues to convey how they felt about their partners.[13] Walther believes these results support SIP's claim that people meeting online can begin a relationship just as effectively as if they had met face-to-face, using the words they write rather than nonverbal cues.

EXTENDED TIME: THE CRUCIAL VARIABLE IN CMC

Our closest relationships, such as with a best friend, tend to be *multimodal*, meaning we use a variety of media to sustain them. But like my friendship with Michelle, you may have friends you communicate with only through one medium. In such relationships, Walther is convinced that the length of time CMC users have to send their messages is the key factor that determines whether their online messages can achieve the level of intimacy that others develop face-to-face.

Multimodal
Using multiple media to maintain a relationship.

Over an extended period, the issue is not the *amount* of social information that can be conveyed online; rather, it's the *rate* at which that information mounts up. Because typing is slower than talking, text-based messages take longer to compose. How much longer? Walther finds that any message spoken in person will take at least four times longer to say through CMC.[14] This four-to-one time differential explains why many early experiments seemed to show that CMC is task-oriented and impersonal. In the experiment described above, Walther compared 10 minutes of face-to-face time with 40 minutes of CMC. There was no difference in partner affinity between the two modes.

As a senior Nielsen executive notes, "Despite the almost unlimited nature of what you can do on the Web, nearly half of U.S. online time is spent on three activities—social networking, playing games and e-mailing."[15] Perhaps the additional time necessary to convey an impression explains why people invest so much time in online socializing. Since CMC conveys social information more slowly than face-to-face communication does, Walther advises online users to make up for the rate difference by sending messages more often. Not only does this practice help impression formation in personal relationships, but it's also reassuring to virtual group partners who naturally wonder who their colleagues are, what they're thinking, and if they're going to do the work they've promised. I've found this to make a critical difference in my friendship with Michelle. We each update our Facebook status at least once a day. Without those updates, I doubt our friendship would've grown much closer.

Two other time factors can contribute to intimacy on the Internet—anticipated future interaction and chronemic cues. *Anticipated future interaction* wasn't part of Walther's original conception of SIP, but he now sees it as a way of extending psychological time. Recall that Chuck Berger claims our drive to reduce uncertainty about someone we've just met gets an added boost when we think we're going to see each other again (see Chapter 9). Through his empirical research, Walther's discovered that members of an online conference or task group start to trade relational messages when they are scheduled for multiple meetings. It's as if the "shadow of the future" motivates them to encounter others on a personal level.[16]

Anticipated future interaction
A way of extending psychological time; the likelihood of future interaction motivates CMC users to develop a relationship.

Chronemics is the label nonverbal researchers use to describe how people perceive, use, and respond to issues of time in their interaction with others. Unlike other nonverbal cues, no form of online communication can completely filter out time. A recipient can note the time of day a message was sent and then gauge the elapsed time until the reply. Does this knowledge really affect a relationship? Walther's work inspired me to investigate how college students evaluate email reply rate between friends. In the study, participants read an email message and a reply to that message. The text of the email exchange was the same for each participant, but the time stamp varied randomly. The study revealed that replying quickly (such as within an hour) yielded the most positive impressions, with some evidence that women are more attuned to reply rate than are men.[17] So if you want to convey a positive impression, a fast reply is probably best.

Chronemics
The study of people's systematic handling of time in their interaction with others.

You now have the basic predictions of social information processing theory. SIP claims that CMC users can get to know each other and develop a mutual affinity by using the medium's available cues to manage relational development. The process will probably take longer than face-to-face bonding, but there's no reason to believe the relationship will be any less personal. After offering a similar summary, Walther asks, "Is this the best that one can hope to attain when communicating electronically—the mere potential for intimacy where time permits?"[18] His answer is no—sometimes, CMC actually surpasses the quality of relational communication that's available when parties talk face-to-face. Walther's hyperpersonal perspective shows how this works.

HYPERPERSONAL PERSPECTIVE: CLOSER THROUGH CMC THAN IN PERSON

Walther uses the term *hyperpersonal* to label CMC relationships that are more intimate than if partners were physically together. Under the familiar *sender-receiver-channel-feedback* categories, he classifies four types of media effects that occur precisely because CMC users aren't face-to-face and don't have a full range of nonverbal cues available. In an interview with fellow CMC researcher Nicole Ellison at the University of Michigan, Walther explained how these four characteristics shape the nature of online dating—a method more than 20 percent of Americans believe is a good way to find a significant other.[19] I'll draw on his insights as I explain the four elements of the hyperpersonal perspective.

Hyperpersonal perspective
The claim that CMC relationships are often more intimate than those developed when partners are physically together.

Sender: Selective Self-Presentation

Walther claims that through *selective self-presentation,* people who meet online have an opportunity to make and sustain an overwhelmingly positive impression. That's because they can write about their most attractive traits, accomplishments, and actions without fear of contradiction from their physical appearance, their inconsistent actions, or the objections of third parties who know their dark side. As a relationship develops, they can carefully edit the breadth and depth of their self-disclosure to conform to their cyber image, without worrying that nonverbal leakage will shatter their projected persona For dating site users, Walther notes that "selective self-presentation is a process that is probably very much involved in how people put together the profile" because they want people to find them attractive.[20] But Walther's colleague Jeff Hancock at Cornell University notes that the viewer of the profile sees it as a promise—and if online self-presentation differs too much from offline reality, partners will be disappointed if they meet face-to-face.[21]

Selective self-presentation
An online positive portrayal without fear of contradiction, which enables people to create an overwhelmingly favorable impression.

Receiver: Overattribution of Similarity

Attribution is a perceptual process whereby we observe what people do and then try to figure out what they're really like. Our basic interpretive bias is to assume that the specific action we see reflects the personality of the person who did it. People who *do* things like that *are* like that. But when it comes to reading a text message or tweet, we have very little to go on. Our only basis for judgment is the verbal behavior of the person who sent the message. Walther says the absence of other cues doesn't keep us from jumping to conclusions. On the contrary, someone viewing an online dating profile will tend to overattribute the information on the profile and create an idealized image of the owner.

My student Taylor described how a new boyfriend's Facebook and text messages helped her build a positive impression of him:

> Joseph Walther claims that communicators use whatever cues are available to form an impression, and I could tell by the frequency with which my boyfriend talked about his family and music that those were two things he really cared about. Because he was always on Facebook and quickly responded to my texts, I knew he was just as excited to talk to me as I was to talk to him, and his insightful questions meant he really was interested in who I was as a person.

"I can't wait to see what you're like online."

© Paul Noth/The New Yorker Collection/www.cartoonbank.com

Channel: Communicating on Your Own Time

Many forms of interpersonal communication require that parties synchronize their schedules in order to talk with each other. Although face-to-face interaction and phone conversations offer a sense of immediacy, co-presence is achieved at a high price. One partner's desire to communicate often comes at a bad time for the other. Parties may make a date to talk, of course, but locking in a time for communication raises expectations for significance that may be hard to meet.

Asynchronous channel A nonsimultaneous medium of communication that each individual can use when he or she desires.

In contrast, many forms of online communication are *asynchronous* channels of communication, meaning that parties can use them nonsimultaneously—at different times. With time constraints relaxed, CMC users are free to write when they are able to do so, knowing that the recipient will read the message at a convenient time. That's a big plus, especially when they are communicating across time zones or their waking hours are out of sync. Even within the same time zone, online communication helps busy people maximize their time, as Glenn's daughter Jordan described when explaining how she and her boyfriend met through online dating: "How do you get a date when you know about four people in town and have to spend most of your 'free' time studying or working?

We were both totally alone in a new city and had precious few avenues to meet people who shared our values. This is what led us to seek romance on the Internet."

Walther notes an added benefit of nonsimultaneous CMC over face-to-face communication: "In asynchronous interaction one may plan, contemplate, and edit one's comments more mindfully and deliberatively than one can in more spontaneous, simultaneous talk."[22] This is a tremendous advantage when dealing with touchy issues, misunderstandings, or conflict between parties.

Feedback: Self-Fulfilling Prophecy

Self-fulfilling prophecy is the tendency for a person's expectation of others to evoke a response from them that confirms what he or she anticipated. Believing it's so can make it so. This process creates hyperpersonal relationships only if CMC parties first form highly favorable impressions of each other. When an online romantic relationship doesn't work out, daters might use that feedback to further revise their profiles with an eye toward better self-presentation. Then the process starts again: *Senders* self-select what they reveal, *receivers* create an idealized image of their partner, and the *channel* lets users express themselves the way they want, when they want. What's not to like?

Self-fulfilling prophecy
The tendency for a person's expectation of others to evoke a response from them that confirms what was originally anticipated.

Beyond online dating, Walther suggests hyperpersonal communication may improve relationships between groups with a strong history of tension and conflict, such as Israeli Jews and Palestinian Muslims. As Walther asks, "In CMC, when the turban and the yarmulke need not be visible during interactions, can [similarities] be made more [meaningful] than differences?"[23] A recent test in the Israeli education system suggests the answer can be yes, as one Jewish student reported after spending more than a year communicating online in a multicultural course: "This coming year, I will begin teaching . . . and when I use the word 'Arab' in my class, it will sound different than it would have before the course."[24] Walther also points to similar successful online interaction between hostile groups in Northern Ireland.[25]

Of course, CMC itself isn't a magical cure for intergroup hostility. For CMC to ease tensions, Walther recommends focusing on common tasks rather than group differences, allowing plenty of time for communication, and exclusively using text-only channels.[26] If that last suggestion surprises you, remember Walther's claim that fewer nonverbal cues means more positive sender self-presentation and receiver attribution. Walther hopes hyperpersonal effects might change the attitudes of hostile groups toward each other—changes that could persist even when they eventually communicate offline.

THE WARRANTING VALUE OF INFORMATION: WHAT TO TRUST?

Walther's recent work examines how people process social information on social networking sites. One thing that sets social networking sites apart from other CMC forms is the ability to add information to other people's pages—other users can supplement, or even contradict, the account owner's claims. For Facebook users, such added information might include friends' comments on posts or tags on pictures and videos. In other words, sites such as Facebook display two types of information—that controlled by the profile owner and that beyond the owner's direct control. Walther believes this is a difference that truly makes a difference in how Facebook users process social information.

As an example, let's say you view a new classmate's Facebook profile for the first time. The classmate describes herself as "quiet and studious," lists her interests as "reading philosophy" and "playing solitaire," and is part of a group titled "I'd rather stay in and read a good book." Yet many of her friends' comments describe her as "the life of the party," with tags on photographs of her socializing with large groups of people. If you think these messages contradict each other, who are you likely to believe—your classmate or her friends? Answering this question is at the heart of Walther's investigation of the *warranting value* of personal information, or what he describes as "the perceived validity of information presented online with respect to illuminating someone's offline characteristics."[27] For both Walther and scholars of debate, the word "warrant" has a similar meaning to the word "reason": If the information we're reading has warranting value, then it gives us reason to believe the information is true.

Warranting value
Reason to believe that information is accurate, typically because the target of the information cannot manipulate it.

If communicating via CMC is like sipping through a straw, SIP has assumed that "all water passing through the [straw] is the same sort of water."[28] But now Walther believes Facebook lets users sip two different kinds of liquid at the same time. Like email messages, whose content is under the sole control of the sender, information posted by a profile owner is *low warrant information* because he or she can manipulate it with ease. Walther argues that we may not trust this information: "Because online impressions are controllable, they are often suspect."[29] Since the profile owner can't as easily manipulate what's posted by friends, we're more likely to accept such *high warrant information* as true. As Walther notes, this happens offline, too: You might believe a classmate who says he'll work hard with you on a group project, but you'll probably give even greater weight to the testimony of his lab partner last term. For the purpose of impression formation, low warrant information is like a sip of grape juice, but high warrant information is like a taste of fine wine.

Walther and his colleagues have tested warranting value through a series of experiments, with participants randomly assigned to view different versions of fake Facebook profiles. These experiments confirm that people trust high warrant information. In one study, the content of friends' posts altered evaluations of the profile owner's credibility and social attractiveness.[30] Another experiment directly compared low and high warrant information, finding that friends' comments overrode the profile owner's claims when forming impressions of physical attractiveness and extroversion.[31] These studies suggest that, unlike email, interpersonal information on Facebook comes from both the self and other site users. An outside observer won't give those two sources equal weight.

CRITIQUE: WALTHER'S CANDID ASSESSMENT

Because technology changes so rapidly, a valid CMC theory is difficult to craft and defend. Just as theorists begin to understand one technology, along comes the next.[32] Yet in this train of high-tech innovation, Walther's theory stands strong. SIP remains popular among communication scholars because it stacks up well against all the criteria for a good social science theory (Chapter 3). It offers specific, *quantitatively testable hypotheses* about a *relatively simple* set of variables. It clearly *explains* differences and similarities between face-to-face and online communication. The theory *predicts* communication behavior across media that didn't even exist when the theory was born, and SIP's advice is *useful* to many, ranging from spatially separated soulmates to international business partners.

However, communication theorists Tom Postmes (University of Groningen) and Nancy Baym (Microsoft Research, New England) believe SIP possesses two weaknesses.[33] First, they argue that the theory falls into the common socio-psychological ideology of *determinism.* If our interpersonal relationships are simply a product of the number of nonverbal cues afforded by the communication medium, are we really free to choose how and with whom we develop relationships? Second, they argue that the theory does not fully account for how group identification structures CMC relationship development.

Walther's response to these critiques suggests he's willing to consider the possibility that some elements of technology are deterministic. He takes Postmes and Baym to task for "accusing other approaches of determinism as though determinism is something to scrape off one's shoe," and argues that they "have ignored scrutiny of methodological features among studies" that might suggest how both intergroup and interpersonal processes explain CMC relationship development.[34] Clearly, Walther is committed to discovering cause-and-effect relationships, while Postmes and Baym are committed to human choice. Their debate may remind you of the tension between determinism and free will (see Chapter 2), and your reaction to their claims probably has something to do with whether you prefer an objective or interpretive worldview.

But perhaps the harshest critic of Walther's theory is Walther himself. For all the theory's success, he openly admits the existence of gaps and weaknesses in his analysis of CMC. For example, when referencing his four-factor hyperpersonal perspective, Walther takes pains to label the sender-receiver-channel-feedback model a *perspective* rather than a *theory.* As a rigorous social scientist, he understands that a good theory should offer a central explanatory mechanism to drive a synthesis of the observed effects. Walther doesn't believe the hyperpersonal perspective has reached that state, because "certain aspects of the model remain underresearched," including how the components of the model fit together and why feedback increases attraction.[35] Two recent experiments have begun to test the associations among the components of the hyperpersonal perspective, with results providing support for the model.[36] Nevertheless, Walther candidly acknowledges that only additional work can discover the theoretical glue that would bind the hyperpersonal perspective's four components into a coherent whole.

Walther's exploration of warranting value represents one attempt to expand SIP to newer forms of CMC. Like the core of SIP, a strength of Walther's warranting work is its relative simplicity—but perhaps it is too simple. One series of experiments suggests warranting may differ depending on the kind of information under scrutiny. For example, Walther speculates that warranting might depend on the information's *social desirability,* or value in the eyes of society. Physical attractiveness is one such socially desirable trait, and so we may suspect some Facebook members alter their profile pictures, erasing wrinkles and facial blemishes.[37] But society doesn't care as much about other characteristics, like favorite restaurants or TV shows. For such qualities, Walther suspects that "the warranting principle may not as strongly apply."[38] And so the idea of warranting remains a work in progress.

Rather than being disheartened by Walther's assessment of his theory, I'm encouraged by his candor:

> CMC research has generated a good amount of information about how groups of relative strangers can be coaxed into quite positive relationships. The challenge remains to integrate and synthesize the research . . . and ultimately propose strategies that facilitate the use of sociotechnical arrangements to overcoming animosity, and apply generalizable theoretically-based strategies in applied contexts of dire importance.[39]

All theories have flaws and limitations. Walther's honest evaluation gives me confidence in his optimistic belief that computer technology can help build truly human relationships.

QUESTIONS TO SHARPEN YOUR FOCUS

1. *SIP* proposes that *CMC* conveys relational information just as well as *face-to-face communication,* with only one difference. What is that difference?
2. Recall a time when you felt particularly drawn to another person when communicating through email, Facebook, or some other type of CMC. Why did you feel drawn to this person? Does the presence (or absence) of verbal cues or extended time explain your attraction?
3. The *hyperpersonal perspective* suggests that CMC effects of *sender, receiver, channel,* and *feedback* promote greater intimacy. Which factor do you think has the greatest relational impact? Which has the least?
4. Your online partner seems wonderful—but, because it's possible to create a *fictitious persona* through CMC, you want to make sure he or she is "for real." How would you find out? What might the warranting principle suggest you do to get trustworthy information?

CONVERSATIONS

View this segment online at www.mhhe.com/griffin9e or www.afirstlook.com.

Most of Em's conversation with Joe Walther centers on CMC users who have a great affinity for the Internet. Granted, they can develop strong impressions of others online, but does true intimacy require face-to-face communication? Are heavy CMC users more in love with the medium than with their partners? Can those who are socially shy develop better relationships through CMC? What code of ethical online behavior would Walther suggest? Walther offers advice to CMC partners who want to meet in person. He also discusses the scope of SIP and how building theory is a risky business.

A SECOND LOOK

Recommended resource: Joseph B. Walther, "Social Information Processing Theory: Impressions and Relationship Development Online," in *Engaging Theories in Interpersonal Communication: Multiple Perspectives,* Leslie A. Baxter and Dawn O. Braithwaite (eds.), Sage, Thousand Oaks, CA, 2008, pp. 391–404.

Original statement: Joseph B. Walther, "Interpersonal Effects in Computer-Mediated Interaction: A Relational Perspective," *Communication Research,* Vol. 19, 1992, pp. 52–90.

Hyperpersonal perspective: Joseph B. Walther, "Computer-Mediated Communication: Impersonal, Interpersonal, and Hyperpersonal Interaction," *Communication Research,* Vol. 23, 1996, pp. 3–43.

Overview of major CMC theories: Joseph B. Walther, "Theories of Computer-Mediated Communication and Interpersonal Relations," in *The Handbook of Interpersonal Communication,* 4th ed., Mark L. Knapp and John A. Daly (eds.), Sage, Thousand Oaks, CA, 2011, pp. 443–479.

Testing hyperpersonal communication: L. Crystal Jiang, Natalie N. Bazarova, and Jeffrey T. Hancock, "The Disclosure-Intimacy Link in Computer-Mediated Communication: An Attributional Extension of the Hyperpersonal Model," *Human Communication Research,* Vol. 37, 2011, pp. 58–77.

Verbal cues of affection in CMC: Joseph B. Walther, Tracy Loh, and Laura Granka, "The Interchange of Verbal and Nonverbal Cues in Computer-Mediated and Face-to-Face Affinity," *Journal of Language and Social Psychology,* Vol. 24, 2005, pp. 36–65.

Time effects in CMC: Joseph B. Walther, "Time Effects in Computer-Mediated Groups: Past, Present, and Future," in *Distributed Work,* Pamela J. Hinds and Sara Kiesler (eds.), MIT, Cambridge, MA, 2002, pp. 235–257.

Warranting: Joseph B. Walther, Brandon Van Der Heide, Lauren M. Hamel, and Hillary C. Shulman, "Self-Generated Versus Other-Generated Statements and Impressions in Computer-Mediated Communication: A Test of Warranting Theory Using Facebook," *Communication Research,* Vol. 36, 2009, pp. 229–253.

CMC and group conflict: Joseph B. Walther, "Computer-Mediated Communication and Virtual Groups: Applications to Interethnic Conflict," *Journal of Applied Communication Research,* Vol. 37, 2009, pp. 225–238.

Online dating: Catalina L. Toma, Jeffrey T. Hancock, and Nicole B. Ellison, "Separating Fact from Fiction: Deceptive Self-Presentation in Online Dating Profiles," *Personality and Social Psychology Bulletin,* Vol. 34, 2008, pp. 1023–1036.

For self-scoring quizzes for this and all other chapters, click on Self-Help Quizzes under Theory Resources at *www.afirstlook.com.*

Relationship Maintenance

The term *maintenance* may call to mind an auto repair shop where workers with oil-stained coveralls and grease under their fingernails struggle to service or fix a well-worn engine. The work is hard, the conditions are messy, and the repair is best performed by mechanics who have a good idea what they're doing.

This image of rugged work is appropriate when thinking about the ongoing effort required to maintain a close relationship. Forming a relational bond is often easier than sustaining it. The beginning stages of intimacy are typically filled with excitement at discovering another human being who sees the world as we do, with the added touch of wonder that the person we like likes us as well. As the relationship becomes more established, however, irritating habits, conflict, jealousy, and boredom can be the friction that threatens to pull the engine apart. The owner's manual of a new "Intimacy" should warn that periodic maintenance is necessary for friends, romantic partners, and even blood relatives to make it for the long haul.

Of course, personal relationships aren't inanimate machines with interchangeable parts that can be adjusted with a wrench. Expanding the *maintenance* metaphor to living organisms underscores the importance of individualized attention in relational health. Humanist communication writer John Stewart refers to a pair's

"They're a perfect match—she's high-maintenance, and he can fix anything."

personal relationship as a "spiritual child," born as the result of their coming together.[1] His analogy stresses that a relationship requires continual care and nurture for sustained growth. Stewart thinks it's impossible to totally kill a relationship as long as one of the "parents" is still alive. Yet when people ignore or abuse the spiritual children they've created, the results are stunted or maimed relationships.

What does a healthy relationship look like? Through an extensive research program on relationship maintenance, Dan Canary (Arizona State University) and Laura Stafford (Bowling Green State University) conclude that long-term satisfying relationships have at least four characteristics—*liking, trust, commitment,* and *control mutuality.*[2] The first three seem like old relational friends. But control mutuality is a less familiar concept. According to Canary and Stafford, it is "the degree to which partners agree about which of them should decide relational goals and behavioral routines."[3] They may have an egalitarian relationship, or perhaps one person regularly defers to the other but is genuinely happy to do so. Either way, they could each embrace the following statement: *Both of us are satisfied with the way we handle decisions.*

Stafford and Canary surveyed 662 people involved in extended romantic relationships to find out what maintenance behaviors promoted liking, trust, commitment, and control mutuality. They discovered five interpersonal actions that contribute to long-term relational satisfaction:[4]

Positivity—Cheerful, courteous talk, avoiding criticism.

Openness—Self-disclosure and frank talk about their relationship.

Assurances—Affirming talk about the future of their relationship.

Networking—Spending time together with mutual friends and family.

Sharing tasks—Working together on routine jobs, chores, and assignments.

Researchers have found that friends and family members use these maintenance behaviors, too.[5] But why do we maintain some relationships and not others? Scholars have suggested two possible answers. First, the *exchange-oriented* perspective appeals to social exchange theory (see Chapter 9). Theorists in this tradition, including Canary and Stafford, believe we maintain relationships when costs and rewards are distributed fairly between partners. In contrast, the *communally oriented* perspective argues that maintenance doesn't involve such economic calculations. Rather, theorists in this tradition believe we maintain relationships when we see the other person as part of who we are—cost/reward ratio doesn't influence that choice.[6]

I (Andrew) recently conducted a study comparing the exchange and communal explanations. The results weren't simple—although communal orientation was the strongest predictor of couples' maintenance communication, cost/reward ratio was a significant predictor as well.[7] How could rewards and costs matter to partners, yet also *not* matter to them? It's a theoretical puzzle that wouldn't surprise the scholars who developed the three theories presented in this section. All three theories claim that the essence of relational maintenance is dialogue about *me, you,* and *we.* Sometimes that dialogue involves contradiction, confusion, and frustration—in other words, balancing relational needs is harder than balancing tires. Although maintaining relationships is tricky, these theorists agree that smooth-running, long-lasting relationships are worth the effort.

CHAPTER 11

Objective — Interpretive

Phenomenological tradition

Relational Dialectics

of Leslie Baxter & Barbara Montgomery

Leslie Baxter and Barbara Montgomery are central figures in a growing group of scholars who study how communication creates and constantly changes close relationships. Baxter directs an extensive program of research at the University of Iowa. Montgomery is former provost and vice president for academic affairs at Colorado State University–Pueblo.

The first time Baxter conducted a series of in-depth interviews with people about their personal relationships, she quickly gave up any hope of discovering scientific laws that neatly ordered the experiences of friends and lovers.

> I was struck by the contradictions, contingencies, non-rationalities, and multiple realities to which people gave voice in their narrative sense-making of their relational lives.[1]

Baxter saw no law of gravitational pull to predict interpersonal attraction, no coefficient of friction that would explain human conflict. She found, instead, people struggling to interpret the mixed messages about their relationship that they both spoke and heard. Although Montgomery worked independently of Baxter, her experience was much the same.

Baxter and Montgomery each analyzed tensions inherent in romantic relationships and began to catalog the contradictions that couples voiced. They soon recognized the commonality of their work and co-authored a book on relating based on the premise that personal relationships are indeterminate processes of ongoing flux.[2]

Both scholars make it clear that the forces that strain romantic relationships are also at work among close friends and family members. They applaud the work of William Rawlins at Ohio University, who concentrates on the "communicative predicaments of friendship," and the narrative analysis of Art Bochner at the University of South Florida, who focuses on the complex contradictions within family systems. Whatever the form of intimacy, Baxter and Montgomery's basic claim is that "social life is a dynamic knot of contradictions, a ceaseless interplay between contrary or opposing tendencies."[3]

Relational dialectics
A dynamic knot of contradictions in personal relationships; an unceasing interplay between contrary or opposing tendencies.

Relational dialectics highlight the tension, struggle, and general messiness of close personal ties. According to Baxter, the best way we can grasp relational dialectics is to look at a narrative in which competing discourses are etched in bold relief. The popular movie *Bend It Like Beckham* is especially helpful in illustrating tensions within family, friendship, and romantic ties. Audiences of all ages and every ethnicity can identify with the relational struggles of Jesminder Bhamra (who goes by "Jess"), an Indian teenage girl brought up in the west end of London.

Like many British teenage males, Jess is passionate about soccer, but she's better than any of the guys she plays with in pickup games at the park. A poster of England's football superstar David Beckham hangs on her bedroom wall and she often talks to his image about her game and her life. In the close-knit Indian expat community, Jess is at an age where girls are supposed to focus on marrying a well-regarded Indian boy—a union often arranged by their parents. Her mother insists that Jess quit "running around half-naked in front of men." Her dad reluctantly agrees. "Jess, your mother's right. It's not nice. You must start behaving as a proper woman. OK?"

Jules, an English girl who sees Jess play, recruits her to play for an amateur women's soccer team. Jess and Jules quickly become "mates," bonded together by their goal-scoring ability and joint efforts to keep Jess' participation a secret from her mom and dad. Their friendship is soon ruptured by Jules' jealousy over a romantic interest between Jess and Joe, the team's coach. Of course, that kind of relationship is out of bounds for Jess. The resulting tensions in Jess' conversations with her dad, best friend, and admired coach allow us to see the oppositional pull of contrasting forces, which is relational dialectics at work.

THE TUG-OF-WAR DIALECTICS OF CLOSE RELATIONSHIPS

Some viewers might assume that Jess' up-again, down-again relationships with Joe, Jules, and her dad are due to her age, sex, birth order, ethnicity, or obsession with soccer. But Baxter and Montgomery caution us not to look at demographics or personal traits when we want to understand the nature of close relationships. Neither biology nor biography can account for the struggle of contradictory tendencies that Jess and her significant others experience in this story. The tensions they face are common to all personal relationships, and those opposing pulls never quit.

Contradiction is a core concept of relational dialectics. *Contradiction* refers to "the dynamic interplay between unified oppositions."[4] A contradiction is formed "whenever two tendencies or forces are interdependent (the dialectical principle of unity) yet mutually negate one another (the dialectical principle of negation)."[5] According to Baxter, every personal relationship faces the same tension. Rather than bemoaning this relational fact of life, Baxter and Montgomery suggest that couples take advantage of the opportunity it provides: "From a relational dialectics perspective, bonding occurs in both interdependence with the other and independence from the other."[6] One without the other diminishes the relationship.

Baxter and Montgomery draw heavily on the thinking of Mikhail Bakhtin, a Russian intellectual who survived the Stalinist regime. Bakhtin saw dialectical tension as the "deep structure" of all human experience. On the one hand, a centripetal, or centralizing, force pulls us together with others. On the other hand, a centrifugal, or decentralizing, force pushes us apart.

In order to picture Bakhtin's simultaneous and conflicting forces, imagine yourself playing "crack the whip" while skating with a group of friends. You volunteer to be the outermost person on a pinwheeling chain of skaters. As you accelerate, you feel the centripetal pull from the skater beside you, who has a viselike grip on your wrist. You also feel the opposing centrifugal force that threatens to rip you from your friend's grasp and slingshot you away from the group. Skill at skating doesn't reduce the conflicting pressures. In fact, the more speed you can handle, the greater the opposing forces.

Baxter emphasizes that Bakhtin's fusion-fission opposites have no ultimate resolution. Unlike the thesis-antithesis-synthesis stages of Hegelian or Marxist dialectics, there is no final synthesis or end stage of equilibrium. Relationships are always in flux; the only certainty is certain change. For Bakhtin, this wasn't bad news. He saw dialectical tension as providing an opportunity for dialogue, an occasion when partners could work out ways to mutually embrace the conflict between unity *with* and differentiation *from* each other.

Many Westerners are bothered by the idea of paradox, so Baxter and Montgomery work hard to translate the concept into familiar terms. At the start of her research interviews, Baxter introduces a dialectical perspective without ever using the phrase itself. She talks about people experiencing certain "pulls" or "tugs" in different directions. Her words call up the image of parties engaged in an ongoing *tug-of-war* created through their conversations. Within this metaphor, their communication exerts simultaneous pulls on both ends of a taut line—a relational rope under tension.

It's important to understand that when Baxter uses the term *relational dialectics,* she is not referring to *being of two minds*—the cognitive dilemma within the head of an individual who is grappling with conflicting desires. Instead, she's describing the contradictions that are "located in the relationship between parties, produced and reproduced through the parties' joint communicative activity."[7] So dialectical tension is the natural product or unavoidable result of our conversations rather than the motive force guiding what we say in them. And despite the fact that we tend to think of any kind of conflict as detrimental to our relationships, Baxter and Montgomery believe these contradictions can be constructive. That's fortunate, because these theorists are convinced that dialectics in relationships are inevitable.

THREE DIALECTICS THAT AFFECT RELATIONSHIPS

While listening to hundreds of people talk about their relationships, Baxter spotted three recurring contradictions that challenge the traditional wisdom of the theories described in the relationship development section. Recall that Rogers' phenomenological approach assumes that *closeness* is the relational ideal, Berger's uncertainty reduction theory posits a quest for interpersonal *certainty,* and Altman and Taylor's social penetration theory valorizes the *transparent* or *open self* (see the introduction to Relationship Development, Chapter 9, and Chapter 8). But from the accounts she heard, Baxter concluded that these pursuits are only part of the story.

Although most of us embrace the traditional ideals of closeness, certainty, and openness in our relationships, our actual communication within family, friendship, and romance seldom follows a straight path toward these goals. Baxter and Montgomery believe this is the case because we are also drawn toward the exact opposite—autonomy, novelty, and privacy. These conflicting forces can't be resolved by simple "either/or" decisions. The "both/and" nature of

	Internal Dialectic (within the relationship)	**External Dialectic** (between couple and community)
Integration – Separation	Connection – Autonomy	Inclusion – Seclusion
Stability – Change	Certainty – Uncertainty	Conventionality – Uniqueness
Expression – Nonexpression	Openness – Closedness	Revelation – Concealment

FIGURE 11–1 Typical Dialectical Tensions Experienced by Relational Partners
Based on Baxter and Montgomery, *Relating: Dialogues and Dialectics*

dialectical pressures guarantees that our relationships will be complex, messy, and always somewhat on edge.

Baxter and Montgomery's research has focused on three overarching relational dialectics that affect almost every close relationship: *integration–separation, stability–change,* and *expression–nonexpression.* These oppositional pairs are listed on the left side of Figure 11–1. The terms within the chart label these contrasting forces as they are experienced in two different contexts. The Internal Dialectic column describes the three dialectics as they play out *within a relationship.* The External Dialectic column lists similar pulls that cause tension *between a couple and their community.* Unlike a typical Hollywood love story, the portrayals of Jess' key relationships in *Bend It Like Beckham* are credible due to each pair's continual struggles with these contradictions. Since Baxter insists that dialectics are created through conversation, I'll quote extensively from the characters' dialogue in the film.

Internal dialectics
Ongoing tensions played out within a relationship.

External dialectics
Ongoing tensions between a couple and their community.

Most researchers who explore contradictions in close relationships agree that there is no finite list of relational dialectics. This is a very important point, and the dialectical theorists mentioned in this chapter would be disappointed if you thought the three tensions in Figure 11-1 were an exhaustive inventory. Accordingly, the ragged edge at the bottom of the figure suggests that these opposing forces are just the start of a longer list of contradictions that confront partners as they live out their relationship in real time and space. For example, Rawlins finds that friends continually have to deal with the paradox of judgment and acceptance. In this section, however, I'll limit my review to the "Big Three" contradictions that Baxter and Montgomery discuss.

Integration and Separation

Baxter and Montgomery regard the contradiction between connection and autonomy as a primary strain within all relationships. If one side wins this *me–we* tug-of-war, the relationship loses:

Integration–separation
A class of relational dialectics that includes connection–autonomy, inclusion–seclusion, and intimacy–independence.

> No relationship can exist by definition unless the parties sacrifice some individual autonomy. However, too much connection paradoxically destroys the relationship because the individual identities become lost.[8]

Throughout *Bend It Like Beckham,* Jess and her father portray a "stay-away close" ambivalence toward each other that illustrates the connection–autonomy dialectic. Through much of the story she defies his "no soccer" ban, going so far as taking a stealthy overnight trip with the team to play in Germany. As for her father, his words to her suggest that he's more worried about what the Indian community thinks than he is about her—an external dialectic. Yet when an Indian friend offers to rush her away from her sister's wedding reception to play in the championship game, Jess turns to her father and says, "Dad, it doesn't matter. This is much more important. I don't want to spoil the day for you." He in turn tells her to go and "play well and make us proud." Later that night at home with the extended family, he strengthens his connection with Jess by defending his decision to his irate wife: "Maybe you could handle her long face. I could not. I didn't have the heart to stop her."

Bakhtin wrote that dialectical moments are occasions for dialogue. Perhaps the best example in the film comes after Jess receives a red card penalty in a tournament game for retaliating against an opponent who fouled her. Although her shorthanded team holds on to win, Joe reads her the riot act in the locker room: "What the hell is wrong with you, Bhamra? I don't ever want to see anything like that from you ever again. Do you hear me?" Without waiting for an answer, he turns and marches out. Jess runs after him and their dialogue reflects the ongoing tension between connection and autonomy in their relationship:

JESS: Why did you yell at me like that? You knew that the ref was out of order.

JOE: You could have cost us the tournament.

JESS: But it wasn't my fault! You didn't have to shout at me.

JOE: Jess, I am your coach. I have to treat you the same as everyone else. Look, Jess, I saw it. She fouled you. She tugged your shirt. You just overreacted. That's all.

JESS: That's not all. She called me a Paki, but I guess you wouldn't understand what that feels like, would you?

JOE: Jess, I'm Irish. Of course I'd understand what that feels like. [Joe then holds a sobbing Jess against his chest, a long hug witnessed by her father.]

Baxter and Montgomery maintain that even as partners struggle with the stresses of intimacy in their relationship vis-à-vis each other, as a couple they also face parallel yin–yang tensions with people in their social networks. The seclusion of private togetherness that is necessary for a relationship to gel runs counter to the inclusion of the couple with others in the community. The observed embrace certainly complicates Jess and Joe's relationship. And unless they find a way to work through the dilemma between inclusion with outsiders and seclusion for themselves, the future of their relationship is in doubt. These opposing external forces surface again when Jess runs into Joe's arms on a dimly lit soccer field to tell him that her parents will allow her to go to an American university on a soccer scholarship. But as Joe seeks their first kiss, she stops him, saying, "I'm sorry, Joe. I can't." To a baffled Joe she explains, "Letting me go is a really big step for my mum and dad. I don't know how they'd survive if I told them about you."

Stability and Change

Berger's uncertainty reduction theory makes a strong case for the idea that people strive for predictability in their relationships (see Chapter 9). Baxter and

"Would you guys mind if I slept alone for a change?"

Montgomery don't question our human search for interpersonal certainty, but they are convinced that Berger makes a mistake by ignoring our simultaneous efforts toward its opposite: novelty. We seek the bit of mystery, the touch of spontaneity, the occasional surprise that is necessary for having fun. Without the spice of variety to season our time together, the relationship becomes bland, boring, and, ultimately, emotionally dead.

Stability–change
A class of relational dialectics that includes certainty–uncertainty, conventionality–uniqueness, predictability–surprise, and routine–novelty.

Early in their friendship, Jess asks about Jules' romantic interest in Joe. Their brief conversation can be seen as a *novel* fantasy expressed in the imagery of the *familiar*—a conventional marriage to a partner who is out of bounds:

JESS: Jules . . . you know Joe, do you like him?

JULES: Nah, he'd get sacked if he was caught shagging one of his players.

JESS: Really?

JULES: I wish I could find a bloke like him. Everyone I know is a prat. They think girls can't play as well as them, except Joe of course.

JESS: Yeah, I hope I marry an Indian boy like him, too.

The girls then laugh together—a tension release—and hug before they part. But dealing with dialectics is always tenuous. When the romantically unthinkable becomes possible for Jess, Jules lashes out: "You knew he was off-limits. Don't pretend to be so innocent. . . . You've really hurt me, Jess! . . . You've betrayed me."

It would be easy to see Jess' family relationships as a simplistic face-off between the *conventionality* of life in their culture versus the shocking *uniqueness* of an Indian girl playing soccer. That's because so much of what Jesminder's sister and parents say reproduces time-honored Indian norms and practices. As her sister warns, "Look, Jess . . . do you want to be the one that everyone stares at, at every family [gathering], 'cause you've married the English bloke?" And Jess' dream to go to college in California, play pro soccer, and have the freedom to fall in love with her Irish coach seem a unified pull in the opposite direction.

But neither Jess nor her father speak in a single voice. In conversations with friends, Jess depicts herself as a dutiful daughter who gets top grades and doesn't sleep around with guys. She also describes her parents' real care for her, her desire not to hurt them, and her fear that her dad might no longer talk with her. And despite his apparently firm stance against Jess playing English football, her father goes to watch her play and says he doesn't want to see her disappointed. In compelling drama and in real life, the contradictory forces created through dialogue are quite complex.

Expression and Nonexpression

Recall that Irwin Altman, one of the founders of social penetration theory, ultimately came to the conclusion that self-disclosure and privacy operate in a cyclical, or wavelike, fashion over time.[9] Baxter and Montgomery pick up on Altman's recognition that relationships aren't on a straight-line path to intimacy. They see the pressures for openness and closedness waxing and waning like phases of the moon. If Jess' communication to her parents seems somewhat schizophrenic, it's because the dialectical forces for transparency and discretion are hard to juggle.

Expression–nonexpression
A class of relational dialectics that includes openness–closedness, revelation–concealment, candor–secrecy, and transparency–privacy.

Through most of the movie, Jess is closemouthed with her parents about the extent of her soccer playing and her romantic attraction to Joe, even after her dad discovers both secrets. But on the night following her sister's wedding (and the tournament final) she decides to come clean about one of them:

> Mum, Dad . . . I played in the final today, and we won! . . . I played the best ever. And I was happy because I wasn't sneaking off and lying to you. . . . Anyway, there was a scout from America today, and he's offered me a place at a top university with a free scholarship and a chance to play football professionally. And I really want to go. And if I can't tell you what I want now then I'll never be happy whatever I do.

Just as the openness–closedness dialectic is a source of ongoing tension within a relationship, a couple also faces the *revelation* and *concealment* dilemma of what to tell others. Baxter and Montgomery note that each possible advantage of "going public" is offset by a corresponding potential danger. For example, public disclosure is a relational rite of passage signaling partners and others that the tie that binds them together is strong. Jess seems to sense this relational fact of life when she tells Joe on the soccer field that her parents wouldn't be able to handle the news of their attraction for each other. She doesn't buy much time for their romance to develop because she's leaving for school, and Joe can't stand the uncertainty. As Jess and Jules say goodbye to their families before boarding the plane to America, Joe comes running down the concourse calling to Jess. They move a few feet away from the others and Joe implores, "Look. I can't let you go without knowin'. . . . that even with the distance—and the concerns of your family—we still might have something. Don't you think?" She gives Joe (and her parents, if they turn to look) the answer through a long first kiss. At this climactic point in the film, the viewer realizes that the force field of dialectics has irrevocably changed, but will never disappear.

RDT 2.0: DRILLING DOWN ON BAKHTIN'S CONCEPT OF DIALOGUE

Baxter says theories are like relationships—they aren't stagnant. The good ones change and mature over time. As you know, Baxter's early emphasis with Montgomery was on contradictory forces inherent in all relationships. But without abandoning anything said so far, Baxter now backgrounds the language of *contradiction* and *dialectics,* even to the point of referring to the second generation of the theory as RDT 2.0 rather than *relational dialectics.*

Dialogue
Communication that is constitutive, always in flux, capable of achieving aesthetic moments.

In her recent book *Voicing Relationships: A Dialogic Perspective,* Baxter focuses on the relational implications of Mikhail Bakhtin's concept of *dialogue.* She explains that she uses the verb form of the word *voice* in the title "to suggest that relationships achieve meaning through the active interplay of multiple, competing discourses or voices."[10] RDT 2.0 highlights five dialogic strands within Bakhtin's thought, as the Russian writer insisted that without dialogue, there is no relationship.

Dialogue as Constitutive—Relationships in Communication

Baxter states that a "constitutive approach to communication asks how communication defines or constructs the social world, including our selves and our personal relationships."[11] This dialogical notion is akin to the core commitments of *symbolic interactionism* and *coordinated management of meaning* (see Chapters 5 and 6). Recall that Mead claimed our concept of self is formed by interaction with others. Pearce and Cronen state that persons-in-conversation co-construct their own social realities and are simultaneously shaped by the worlds they create. If Baxter and these other theorists are right, it's confusing to talk about "communication in relationships," as if communication were just a feature of a couple's relationship. A constitutive approach suggests that it works the other way around—communication creates and sustains the relationship. If a pair's communication practices change, so does their relationship.

Constitutive dialogue
Communication that creates, sustains, and alters relationships and the social world; social construction.

Perhaps nowhere is the constitutive nature of dialogue more fascinating than in the study of interpersonal similarities and differences.[12] Traditional scholarship concentrates on similarities, regarding common attitudes, backgrounds, and interests as the positive glue that helps people stick together. ("My idea of an agreeable person is a person who agrees with me.") Within this framework, self-disclosure is seen as the most valuable form of communication because, by mutual revelation, people can discover similarities that already exist.

In contrast, a dialogic view considers differences to be just as important as similarities and claims that both are created and evaluated through a couple's dialogue. For example, a relative of mine married a man who is 20 years older than she is. The difference in their age is a chronological fact. But whether she and her husband regard their diverse dates of birth as a difference that makes a difference is the result of the language they use to talk about it. So is the extent to which they see that age gap as either positive or negative. Meaning is created through dialogue. Amber, a student in my communication theory class, gives voice to the tension created by conflicting discourses.

> My boyfriend Tyler is on the swim team and I know most of the guys well. The exceptions are the new freshmen, who Tyler said refer to me as "the girlfriend." When I heard this I was surprised how much it irritated me. I obviously value my connection with him, otherwise we wouldn't be dating. But as I told Tyler, I also have my own separate, independent identity outside of our relationship. This has become a very real tension.

Dialogue as Utterance Chain—Building Block of Meaning

An utterance is what a person says in one conversational turn. For example, we've already looked at the statement Jess makes to her friend Jules about her coach, Joe: "I hope I marry an Indian boy like him." According to Bakhtin and Baxter, that's an utterance. But it isn't simply a statement reflecting her autonomous desire for a certain type of man. The utterance is embedded in an utterance chain that includes things Jess has heard in the past and responses she anticipates hearing in the future. In that sense, the utterance chain that Baxter describes looks something like the CMM serpentine model of communication shown on page 71. Baxter highlights four links on the chain where the struggle of competing discourses can be heard.

Utterance chains
The central building blocks of meaning-making, where utterances are linked to competing discourses already heard as well as those yet to be spoken.

1. Cultural ideologies (throughout Jess' past):
   Collectivism says, *Marry an Indian man; honor your family's wishes.*
   Individualism says, *It's your choice; marry the man who makes you happy.*
   Romanticism says, *Marry for love; only one man is right for you.*
   Rationalism says, *Cross-cultural marriages are risky; don't be impulsive.*
2. Relational history (from the immediate past):
   Jules is a friend, a valued teammate.
   Jules is a co-conspirator, keeping your soccer secret from your folks.
   Jules is your rival for Joe's affection.
3. Not-yet spoken response of partner to utterance (immediate future):
   Jules says I'm silly and laughs at me.
   Jules tells me to stay away from Joe.
   Jules swears that she'll keep my secrets.
   Jules shares her frustration that Joe is off-limits.
4. Normative evaluation of third party to utterance (further in future):
   Mother may say, *Jesminder was selfish.*
   Sister may say, *Jess was setting herself up for a fall.*
   Her children may say, *Jess was courageous.*

All of these competing voices within the utterance chain are in play with Jess' statement about the man she hopes to marry. It's as if she's had an inner dialogue with all of these discourses, probably listening more to some than to others. Baxter regards the utterance chain as the basic building block in the construction project of creating meaning through dialogue. That's why she says, "The core premise of dialogically grounded RDT is that meanings are wrought from the struggle of competing, often contradictory discourses."[13]

Dialogue as Dialectical Flux—The Complexity of Close Relationships

We've already explored Bakhtin's and Baxter's conviction that all social life is the product of "a contradiction-ridden, tension-filled unity of two embattled tendencies."[14] The existence of these contrasting forces means that developing and sustaining a relationship is bound to be an unpredictable, unfinalizable, indeterminate process—more like playing improvisational jazz than following the score of a familiar song. Since a relationship is created through dialogue that's always in flux, Baxter thinks we shouldn't be surprised that the construction project moves "by fits and starts, in what can be an erratic process of backward-forward, up-and-down motion."[15] It's messy.

Dialectical flux
The unpredictable, unfinalizable, indeterminate nature of personal relationships.

Figure 11–2 is an attempt to capture the complexity of relationships as seen through the lens of dialectical flux. Note that each of the relational forces discussed in the chapter is shown in tension with every other pole. For example, *autonomy* is in opposition not only with *connection* but also with *certainty* and all the other relational forces. This chaotic jumble of contradictions is far removed from such idyllic notions of communication as a one-way route to *interpersonal closeness, shared meaning,* or *increased certainty.*

Simultaneous expression of opposing voices is the exception rather than the rule, according to Baxter. At any given time, most relationship partners bring one voice to the foreground while pushing the other one to the background. Baxter and Montgomery have identified two typical conversational strategies for responding to relational dialectics:

Spiraling inversion
Switching back and forth between two contrasting voices, responding first to one pull, then the other.

1. ***Spiraling inversion*** is switching back and forth across time between two contrasting voices, responding first to one pull, then the other. This spiraling shift describes the inconsistency of Jess' communication with her family. Her lies about what she's doing are followed by incredible candor. Her open admissions precede times of silence and deception.

Segmentation
A compartmentalizing tactic by which partners isolate different aspects of their relationship.

2. ***Segmentation*** is a compartmentalizing tactic by which partners isolate different aspects of their relationship. Some issues and activities resonate with one dialectical tug, while other concerns and actions resonate with the opposing pull. For example, Joe seeks to separate his roles as coach and boyfriend, a distinction Jess tries to duplicate. His "I am your coach" statement makes a clear-cut distinction. When Jules asks Jess whether Joe is treating her too hard, her response is more mixed. "He was really nice. Just really professional." Viewers may smile at this mixed message, but from a dialogical perspective, her answer is a healthy reflection of the multiple discourses that create her ever-changing relationship with Joe.

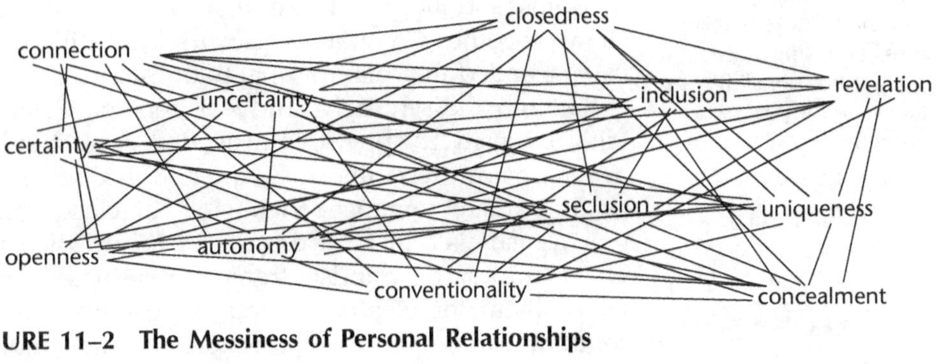

FIGURE 11–2 The Messiness of Personal Relationships

Dialogue as Aesthetic Moment—Creating Unity in Diversity

Aesthetic moment
A fleeting sense of unity through a profound respect for disparate voices in dialogue.

Taking her lead from Bakhtin's work, Baxter describes dialogue as an *aesthetic accomplishment,* "a momentary sense of unity through a profound respect for the disparate voices in dialogue."[16] Parties are fully aware of their discursive struggle and create something new out of it. That mutual sense of completion or wholeness in the midst of fragmented experience doesn't last. It's a fleeting moment that can't be sustained. Yet memories of that magic moment can support a couple through the turbulence that goes with the territory of any close relationship.

For romantic partners, turning points such as the relationship-defining talk or the first time they make love may be aesthetic moments. Baxter suggests that a meaningful ritual can be an aesthetic moment for all participants because it's "a joint performance in which competing, contradictory voices in everyday social life are brought together simultaneously."[17] For example, a marriage renewal ceremony where a couple exchanges newly crafted vows is often the occasion of an aesthetic moment for all participants.[18] So too the communion rail where people with diverse beliefs and practices may feel that they are one before the same God.

The turning point in *Bend It Like Beckham* occurs in a moving scene in the Bhamra home after Jess has fervently made known her dream of playing soccer in America. Hers is a desire that clearly rejects the traditional role of women in this close-knit Indian enclave—a role that her sister enthusiastically embraced in her wedding earlier that day. As one family friend whispers to another after Jess' declaration, "She's dead meat." Yet the sisters' father takes these polar-opposite visions of life and integrates them into a unified whole. He recounts a story of his own timidity and suffering when he experienced rejection, and then says:

> I don't want Jessie to suffer. I don't want her to make the same mistakes her father made of accepting life, or accepting situations. I want her to fight. I want her to win. Because I've seen her playing. She's—She's brilliant. I don't think anybody has the right stopping her. Two daughters made happy on one day. What else could a father ask for?

Dialogue as Critical Sensibility—A Critique of Dominant Voices

Critical sensibility
An obligation to critique dominant voices, especially those that suppress opposing viewpoints; a responsibility to advocate for those who are muted.

The fifth sense of dialogue is an obligation to critique dominant voices, especially those that suppress opposing viewpoints. Bakhtin's analysis of a medieval carnival laid the groundwork for Baxter's understanding of this function.[19] Much like the court jester, the carnivalesque eye is characterized by "mockery of all serious, 'closed' attitudes about the world."[20] Power imbalances, hierarchal relationships, and judgments are set aside. The lofty and low, the wise and the foolish all mix together. Competing discourses are still present, but opposition is temporarily suspended in a playful quality of interplay.

Within the scholarly study of personal relationships, Baxter believes that a critical sensitivity provides a needed correction to the theories of relationship development presented in Chapters 8 through 10. Each of these theories offers a single path to romance, friendship, or close family ties. And within relational practice, she is critical of those who regard their partners as objects of influence. This manipulative mindset frames a relationship as one of power and domination, which then ridicules or silences opposing points of view.[21] Baxter opposes any communication practice that ignores or gags another's voice.

Consistent with this multivocal emphasis, the entirety of *Bend It Like Beckham* can be seen as the triumphant story of a young girl who resists traditional forces that would keep her silenced—a journey from monologue to dialogue. The director and co-writer of the film, Gurinder Chadha, admits it's autobiographical. She notes that "Beckham's uncanny ability to 'bend' the ball around a wall of players into the goal is a great metaphor for what young girls (and film directors) go through. You see your goal, you know where you want to go, but you've got to twist and turn and bend the rules to get there."[22]

ETHICAL REFLECTION: SISSELA BOK'S PRINCIPLE OF VERACITY

Does lying only bend the rules, or does it break and trash them as well? By looking at lies from the perspective of all who are affected by them, philosopher Sissela Bok hopes to establish when, or if, lies can be justified.

Bok rejects an absolute prohibition of lying. She believes that "there are at least some circumstances which warrant a lie . . . foremost among them, when innocent lives are at stake, and where only a lie can deflect the danger."[23] But she also rejects *consequentialist ethics,* which judge acts on the basis of whether we think they will result in harm or benefit. That approach represents a kind of bottom-line accounting that treats an act as morally neutral until we figure out if it will have positive or negative outcomes. Bok doesn't view lies as neutral. She is convinced that all lies drag around an initial negative weight that must be factored into any ethical equation. Her *principle of veracity* asserts that "truthful statements are preferable to lies in the absence of special considerations."[24]

Consequentialist ethics
Judging actions solely on the basis of their beneficial or harmful outcomes.

Bok contends that we need the principle of veracity because liars engage in a tragic self-delusion. When they count the cost of deceit, they usually anticipate only their own short-term losses. Liars downplay the impact of their falsehood on the persons deceived and almost always ignore the long-term effects on themselves and everyone else. Bok warns, "Trust and integrity are precious resources, easily squandered, hard to regain. They can thrive only on a foundation of respect for veracity."[25] Jess may not be dead meat, but the things she says to her folks in the future might be tough for them to swallow.

Principle of veracity
Truthful statements are preferable to lies in the absence of special circumstances that overcome the negative weight.

CRITIQUE: MEETING THE CRITERIA FOR A GOOD INTERPRETIVE THEORY

Some communication scholars question whether relational dialectics should be considered a theory at all:

> It lacks the structural intricacies of formal theories of prediction and explanation; it offers no extensive hierarchical array of axiomatic or propositional arguments. It does not represent a single unitary statement of generalizable predictions.[26]

You may be surprised that Baxter and Montgomery agree with that judgment. In fact, they're the ones who wrote those words. That's because the traditional goals of a scientific theory that they mention are not at all what these theorists are trying to accomplish. They don't even think these goals are plausible when theorizing about relationships. Instead, they offer relational dialectics as a *sensitizing theory,* one that should be judged on the basis of its ability to help us see close relationships in a new light.[27] So an appropriate critique of their theory should apply the standards for evaluating an *interpretive* theory that I introduced in Chapter 3. As

I briefly address these six criteria, you'll find that I think relational dialectics stacks up quite well.

1. A new understanding of people. Baxter and Montgomery offer readers a whole new way to make sense of their close relationships. I find that many students feel a tremendous sense of relief when they read about relational dialectics. That's because the theory helps them realize that the ongoing tensions they experience with their friend, family member, or romantic partner are an inevitable part of relational life. Competing discourses aren't necessarily a warning sign that something is terribly wrong with their partner or themselves.

2. A community of agreement. Leslie Baxter's two decades of work in relational dialectics has received high acclaim from scholars who study close personal ties. The International Association for Relationship Research designated her monograph "Relationships as Dialogues" as its 2004 Distinguished Scholar Article, an honor bestowed only once a year. Baxter's research has changed the landscape within the field of study known as *personal relationships.*

3. Clarification of values. By encouraging a diverse group of people to talk about their relationships, and taking what they say seriously, Baxter and Montgomery model the high value that Bakhtin placed on hearing multiple voices. Yet Baxter continues to critique her own research for heavy reliance on self-report data from surveys and interviews, and she laments the relative lack of dialogue studies focusing on talk between relational parties. Given her increasing emphasis on dialogue, however, this disconnect between theory and research methodology will hopefully soon be bridged.[28]

4. Reform of society. Not only does Baxter listen to multiple voices, but her theory seeks to carve out a space where muted or ignored voices can be heard. Relational dialectics creates a *critical sensibility* that encourages dialogue rather than monologue. In this way the theory is a force for change—not only in personal relationships, but in the public sphere as well.

5. Qualitative research. The first version of the theory employed a variety of methodological approaches. In contrast, RDT 2.0 emphasizes the importance of qualitative work when using the theory. In fact, Baxter's 2011 book includes an entire chapter that explains how to analyze the discourses present in relationship talk. The theory takes the power and potential of qualitative research seriously.

6. Aesthetic appeal. Figure 11–2 illustrates the difficulty of crafting an artistic representation when the objects of study—in this case, relationships—are inherently messy. Baxter's task becomes even more difficult given her commitment to unraveling Bakhtin's multistranded conception of dialogue. Since the Russian philosopher wrote in his native language, it's difficult to translate his nuanced ideas into English in an elegant way. Accuracy has to come before artistry. Baxter's *Voicing Relationships* is a tough read as well. Yet in describing *fleeting moments of wholeness,* Baxter holds out the promise of an aesthetic ideal to which all of us can aspire—an image that could make slogging through the morass of relational contradictions feel less frustrating. And Montgomery's imagery suggests that dealing with dialectics can actually be fun:

> I have been told that riding a unicycle becomes enjoyable when you accept that you are constantly in the process of falling. The task then becomes one of

continually playing one force against another, countering one pull with an opposing motion and adapting the wheel under you so that you remain in movement by maintaining and controlling the fall. If successful, one is propelled along in a state of sustained imbalance that is sometimes awkward and sometimes elegant. From a dialectical perspective, sustaining a relationship seems to be a very similar process.[29]

QUESTIONS TO SHARPEN YOUR FOCUS

1. How many different synonyms and equivalent phrases can you list that come close to capturing what Baxter and Montgomery mean by the word *dialectic?* What do these words have in common?
2. Which of the six theories discussed in previous chapters would Baxter and Montgomery consider simplistic or nondialogical?
3. What *conflicting pulls* place the most strain on your closest personal relationship? To what extent do you and your partner use *spiraling inversion, segmentation,* and *dialogue* to deal with that *tension?*
4. Why wouldn't typical scale items like the following reveal opposing discourses in a close relationship, even if they exist?

What characterizes your relationship?

Intimacy :____:____:____:____:____:____:____: Independence

SELF-QUIZ

For chapter self-quizzes, go to the book's Online Learning Center at *www.mhhe.com/griffin9e*

CONVERSATIONS

View this segment online at www.mhhe.com/griffin9e or www.afirstlook.com.

At the start of her conversation with Em, Leslie Baxter states that all communication involves the interplay of differences, which are often competing or in opposition to each other. She explains why this dialectic tension isn't a problem to be solved, but an occasion for a relationship to change and grow. Baxter cautions that we've been seduced into thinking relating is easy, when in fact it's hard work. Most of our discussion centers on ways to cope with the interplay of differences we experience. She urges partners to reflect carefully on rituals that celebrate both their unity and diversity, and offers other practical suggestions as well.

A SECOND LOOK

Recommended resource: Leslie A. Baxter and Barbara M. Montgomery, *Relating: Dialogues and Dialectics,* Guilford, New York, 1996.

RDT 2.0: Leslie A. Baxter, *Voicing Relationships: A Dialogical Perspective,* Sage, Thousand Oaks, CA, 2011.

Dialogue: Leslie A. Baxter, "Relationships as Dialogues," *Personal Relationships,* Vol. 11, 2004, pp. 1–22.

Summary statement: Leslie A. Baxter and Dawn O. Braithwaite, "Relational Dialectics Theory," in *Engaging Theories in Interpersonal Communication: Multiple Perspectives,* Leslie A. Baxter and Dawn O. Braithwaite (eds.), Sage, Thousand Oaks, CA, 2008, pp. 349–361.

Personal narrative of the theory's development: Leslie A. Baxter, "A Tale of Two Voices," *Journal of Family Communication,* Vol. 4, 2004, pp. 181–192.

Bakhtin on dialectics: Mikhail Bakhtin, "Discourse in the Novel," in *The Dialogic Imagination: Four Essays by M. M. Bakhtin,* Cary Emerson and Michael Holquist (trans.), University of Texas, Austin, TX, 1981, pp. 259–422.

Bakhtin on utterance chains: Mikhail Bakhtin, "The Problem of Speech Genres," in *Speech Genres & Other Late Essays,* Caryl Emerson and Michael Holquist (eds.), V. W. McGee (trans.), University of Texas, Austin, TX, 1986, pp. 60–102.

Friendship dialectics: William Rawlins, *Friendship Matters: Communication, Dialectics, and the Life Course,* Aldine de Gruyter, New York, 1992.

Comparing and contrasting different dialectical approaches: Leslie A. Baxter and Dawn O. Braithwaite, "Social Dialectics: The Contradictions of Relating," in *Explaining Communication: Contemporary Theories and Exemplars,* Bryan B. Whaley and Wendy Samter (eds.), Lawrence Erlbaum, Mahwah, NJ, 2007, pp. 305–324.

Critique: Leslie A. Baxter, "Relational Dialectics Theory: Multivocal Dialogues of Family Communication," in *Engaging Theories in Family Communication: Multiple Perspectives,* Dawn O. Braithwaite and Leslie A. Baxter (eds.), Sage, Thousand Oaks, CA, 2006, pp. 130–145.

To access scenes from feature films that illustrate Relational Dialectics, click on Suggested Movie Clips under Theory Resources at *www.afirstlook.com.*

CHAPTER 12

Objective ——— Interpretive

Socio-cultural tradition
Cybernetic tradition

Communication Privacy Management Theory

of Sandra Petronio

Altman and Taylor's *social penetration theory* focused on self-disclosure as the primary way to develop close relationships (see Chapter 8). Yet Altman, as well as Baxter and Montgomery, eventually concluded that openness is only part of the story. We also have a desire for privacy (see Chapter 11). Suppose you visit your school's health center because you're concerned about abnormal bleeding or a suspicious lump below the belt. Upon careful examination, the doctor says that you may have cervical or testicular cancer; exploratory surgery will be necessary. While not life-threatening if caught in time, it is cancer, and you fear that it could put at risk your ability to have children. Who will you tell right away—an immediate family member, a romantic partner, a good friend, maybe all three, or perhaps none of them?

Sandra Petronio, a communication professor at Indiana University–Purdue University Indianapolis, agrees with Altman that revealing this private information might strengthen your relationships with significant people in your life. The disclosure would also give them a chance to offer you comfort and perhaps help you figure out a course of action to deal with the disturbing diagnosis. However, disclosing your medical condition could stress your relationships if it turns out that people can't handle your scary and potentially embarrassing news, or if they carelessly blab about it to others. And even if people you confide in respond well, sharing confidential information always reduces your privacy.

Privacy boundaries
A metaphor to show how people think of the borders between private and public information.

Petronio sees *communication privacy management theory* (CPM) as a description of a privacy management system that contains three main parts. The first part of the system, *privacy ownership*, contains our privacy boundaries that encompass information we have but others don't know. Privacy boundaries can range from thin and porous filters to thick, impenetrable barriers that shield deep, dark secrets.

Privacy control, the second part of the system, involves our decision to share private information with another person. Petronio considers this the engine of privacy management. Decisions to share information or relinquish some control also reshape the boundaries contained in the privacy ownership part of the system.

Privacy turbulence, the third part of the privacy management system, comes into play when managing private information doesn't go the way we expect.[1] Perhaps your friend revealed your secret after you laid down a strict-confidence rule. The decisions you make in the aftermath of the breach are directed at reducing turbulence. Having a mental image of these three parts of the privacy management system is helpful in understanding the five core principles of Petronio's CPM.[2] The first four principles deal with issues of privacy ownership and control; the fifth involves privacy turbulence—the turmoil that erupts when rules are broken. The principles are:

1. People believe they own and have a right to control their private information.
2. People control their private information through the use of personal privacy rules.
3. When others are told or given access to a person's private information, they become co-owners of that information.
4. Co-owners of private information need to negotiate mutually agreeable privacy rules about telling others.
5. When co-owners of private information don't effectively negotiate and follow mutually held privacy rules, boundary turbulence is the likely result.

Although these five statements seem deceptively simple, the management processes they describe are often quite complex. In the rest of the chapter I'll unpack the mental considerations and communication behaviors that each principle summarizes. The evidence for their validity comes from more than 100 research studies over a wide range of face-to-face situations where there's a dialectical tension between privacy and disclosure. Since Petronio's own research has cut across interpersonal, family, and health communication contexts, I'll continue to use a variety of medical issues to illustrate how people manage their private information.

1. OWNERSHIP AND CONTROL OF PRIVATE INFORMATION

People believe they own and have a right to control their private information.

Instead of talking about *self-disclosure* as many relational theorists do, Petronio refers to the *disclosure of private information.* There are four reasons she favors this term. In the first place, a lot of the private information we tell others isn't about ourselves. The revelation may be about other people or convey news of an impersonal nature. Another reason she avoids the self-disclosure label is that it's usually associated with interpersonal intimacy. For example, all three theories in the Relationship Development section assume that self-disclosure is a primary way to develop close personal ties (see Chapters 8–10). Yet Petronio notes that there are many other motives for disclosing private information.[3] For example, we could desire to relieve a burden, prevent a wrong, make an impression, gain control, or simply enjoy self-expression.

Private information
The content of potential disclosures; information that can be owned.

A third reason Petronio chooses to talk about the *disclosure of private information* is that the phrase has a neutral connotation, as opposed to *self-disclosure,* which has a positive feel. The outcome of disclosing private information may turn out well, but as bartenders and hairdressers can attest, it might be unwelcome—a real downer. Finally, while the term *self-disclosure* focuses on the unilateral act of the discloser, Petronio's preferred description directs attention to the content of what's said and how the confidant handles this now not-so-private information. In that sense it's a more complete communication theory.

How do we regard the private information we manage? The first principle of communication privacy management theory is quite clear: We see it as ours; we believe it belongs to us. Whether that perception is accurate isn't the issue. Our conviction is so strong that Petronio defines *privacy* as "the feeling one has the right to own private information."[4] You may feel that way about your overall GPA or even the grade you get in this course.

Privacy
The feeling that one has the right to own private information.

Ownership conveys rights as well as obligations. Privacy bolsters our sense of autonomy and makes us feel less vulnerable. That's the upside. But Petronio also suggests that ownership of private information can be a liability. She claims that when we are privy to something others don't know, we understand that we are responsible for that information and will be held accountable for how we handle it. That's why we seek to control who else gets to know.

Within the context of medical privacy, probably no group faces more pressure for disclosure than those who have an observable stigma. For example, complete strangers often ask intrusive questions of those who are paralyzed that they wouldn't think of asking an able-bodied person. In a research study entitled "Just How Much Did That Wheelchair Cost?" University of Nebraska communication professor Dawn Braithwaite reports how the physically disabled manage their privacy boundaries. She found that in most cases paraplegics will answer a question if they deem it appropriate to the discussion or if it's posed by a kid. But if they think the question comes out of sheer nosiness or morbid curiosity, they avoid answering or respond with anger. One person confined to a wheelchair admitted, "I'm not beyond rolling over toes, really. I have been in situations where . . . there's really no other alternative."[5]

The people Braithwaite interviewed obviously believe they own their private information, and they actively work to maintain control of what, when, and with whom it is shared. The first principle of CPM says that's true for all of us. Our sense of ownership motivates us to create boundaries that will control the spread of what we know. The second principle of CPM addresses how thick those boundaries might be.

2. RULES FOR CONCEALING AND REVEALING

People control their private information through the use of personal privacy rules.

Rule-based theory
A theory that assumes we can best understand people's freely chosen actions if we study the system of rules they use to interpret and manage their lives.

Petronio refers to communication privacy management theory as a *rule-based theory.*[6] An easy way to grasp what she means is to remember that people usually have rules for managing their private information. When Petronio spots a pattern of disclosure within a group of people and these folks offer similar explanations for their actions, she articulates the internalized rules that appear to guide their decisions. These rules are guides for interpretation rather than ironclad laws. Yet in practice, they help people feel they have control over their private information.

CPM maintains that five factors play into the way we develop our own privacy rules: *culture, gender, motivation, context,* and *risk/benefit ratios.* These foundational criteria are evident in a study Petronio conducted among children and adolescents who reported that they were victims of sexual abuse.[7] After gaining permission from their parents, Petronio asked 38 victims between the ages of 7 and 18 to describe how they made the decision to tell someone what had happened. I'll draw upon her findings to illustrate the five constants in rule-making for privacy.

Culture. Cultures differ on the value of openness and disclosure. The United States is a patchwork of many subcultures, but Petronio notes that, overall, U.S. citizens are highly individualistic. This means they have a bias toward locking doors, keeping secrets, and preserving privacy. Regarding victims of sexual abuse, there's no firm evidence among Anglos, Hispanics, African Americans, or Asians that one group is more at risk than the others. But other researchers have found that there is a difference when it comes to who suffers in silence. Presumably because of the Asian emphasis on submissiveness, obedience, family loyalty, and sex-talk taboos, Asian American children who are sexually abused are less likely than other kids to tell their mothers.[8]

Gender. Popular wisdom suggests that women disclose more than men, yet research on this issue is mixed at best. What is clear, however, is that both men and women more easily reveal private information to a woman than to a man.[9] Perhaps this is especially true when a young girl is sexually abused by an older man. As one female victim explained why she chose to tell her mother, "She's my mom and she's a grown-up, you know, and she's a girl."[10]

Motivation. Petronio emphasizes attraction and liking as interpersonal motives that can loosen privacy boundaries that could not otherwise be breached. That's certainly the case when a sexual perpetrator has sworn the victim to secrecy under threat of dire consequences. Some victims lowered their barriers and provided access when they felt the additional force of reciprocity. As one girl reported, "A sudden bond formed between [us by] her saying, you know, 'I was molested' and knowing that all of a sudden I wasn't all by myself. . . . I could trust her because I knew that she could feel the scariness. . . ."[11]

Context. Traumatic events can temporarily or permanently disrupt the influence of culture, gender, and motivation when people craft their rules for privacy. Petronio has in mind the diagnosis of AIDS, the suicide or murder of a loved one, the loss of a limb, physical paralysis, experiencing the carnage of war or natural disaster, and sexual abuse as a child. Any of these events can generate privacy boundaries that are initially impenetrable. The sufferer first struggles to cope; talk may come later. The abused children who spoke to Petronio often shared what it took for them to feel secure before they were willing to be open about their experience. The abuser had to be away from the home or out of the car and doors had to be locked, with just the abused child and confidant together. Disclosure usually came while doing ordinary things together such as cooking, washing dishes, watching TV, or shopping. These mundane activities, which require no eye contact, seemed to offer the child a sense of normalcy and control that made a very abnormal conversation possible.

Risk/benefit ratio. Think back to the mental calculations that social exchange theory claims we make before deciding how we'll act (see Chapter 8). We add up the benefits and subtract the costs of each option in order to do what we think will have the best outcome. Risk/benefit ratios do the math for revealing as well as concealing private information. Typical benefits for revealing are relief from stress, gaining social support, drawing closer to the person we tell, and the chance to influence others. Realistic risks are embarrassment, rejection, diminished power, and everyone finding out our secret. All of these benefits and risks can come into play when sexually abused children adopt a rule that will guide their decision to speak out or keep silent. Because the stakes are high and it's so hard for them to know what response they'll get, many of these kids use partial disclosure to test the waters before fully diving in. For example, one girl in Petronio's study said to her mother, "Mom, I've got to tell you something. He's been walking around the house with no clothes on."[12] When the mother showed that she believed her daughter, the girl then told her what her stepfather had done.

3. DISCLOSURE CREATES A CONFIDANT AND CO-OWNER

When others are told or discover a person's private information, they become co-owners of that information.

Sandra Petronio regards CPM as a full-fledged communication theory. By this she means that a person can't just consider self in deciding whether to conceal or reveal. The act of disclosing private information creates a confidant and draws that person into a *collective privacy boundary,* whether willingly or reluctantly.

What does co-ownership mean? First, the discloser must realize that the personal privacy boundary encompassing the information has morphed into a collective boundary that seldom shrinks back to being solely personal. That would only be possible if the confidant were to die or suffer loss of memory. Once you let the cat out of the bag, it's hard to stuff him back in. Thus, those who own private information should consider carefully before sharing it with others. Second, as co-owners, people tend to feel a sense of responsibility for the information. That doesn't mean, however, that they perceive an equal responsibility. For example, the original owner may still feel like the sole titleholder and assume that others will follow his or her lead when access to the information is an issue. Despite this perception, "once the information is known, others 'in the know' may have their own interpretation of how the information should be managed."[13] Finally, those who had the information foisted upon them may be much more casual about protecting it than those who sought it.

Collective privacy boundary
An intersection of personal privacy boundaries of co-owners of private information, all of whom are responsible for the information.

Communication professors Paige Toller (University of Nebraska Omaha) and Chad McBride (Creighton University) explored the complexities of co-owning private information within families. Specifically, they studied how parents manage privacy boundaries with their children when a family member dies or has a terminal illness.[14] Based on their interviews, they found that parents usually wanted to share information about a family member's death or illness with a young child in the interest of being open and honest. On the other hand, they often withheld information out of concern for the child's emotional welfare. They also concealed the news because they were afraid that their children might not make the most responsible judgments as co-owners of the information. Parents who choose to share sensitive information with a young child often discover that their own privacy boundary may be thick, but the child's is paper-thin or nonexistent.

4. COORDINATING MUTUAL PRIVACY BOUNDARIES

Co-owners of private information need to negotiate mutually agreeable privacy rules about telling others.

Mutual privacy boundary
A synchronized collective privacy boundary that co-owners share because they have negotiated common privacy rules.

This pivotal fourth principle of CPM is where Petronio moves from being descriptive to prescriptive. With the first three principles she's been mapping out how people handle their private information—they think they own it and they control it (Principle 1) through the use of privacy rules (Principle 2). If they disclose some of that private information, the recipients become co-owners of a patch of common informational territory, which entails rights as well as responsibilities (Principle 3). Principle 4 assumes that the privacy boundaries co-owners place around this particular piece of information won't necessarily look the same. But Petronio thinks that for the sake of relational harmony they ought to be congruent, so this principle is a plea for co-owners to negotiate *mutual privacy boundaries.* Or, using the map metaphor, she urges parties to collaboratively draw the same borders around their common piece of informational real estate. If you receive private information from someone, Petronio believes it's best to think of yourself as a good steward or protective guardian over that information. This way, there's less of a chance for disagreement about how the information gets handled. Just as good real estate stewards protect the property entrusted to them, good stewards over private information are on guard to protect that information from falling into the wrong hands.

The overall process of co-managing collective boundaries that Petronio envisions isn't simple. These negotiations focus on *boundary ownership, boundary linkage,* and *boundary permeability.* In order to illustrate what's involved in coordinating boundary management rules, I'll use the privacy/disclosure issue that's received the most attention from health communication practitioners and scholars—HIV status.

Consider the plight of Nate, who goes to see his doctor because of a persistent fever and swollen glands. After running a series of tests, the doctor regretfully informs Nate that he's HIV positive. She assures Nate that this isn't a death sentence. With the advent of HAART—highly active anti-retroviral therapy—Nate may never have to experience the worsening, telltale symptoms of AIDS. But the news comes as a real blow. When he was in college, Nate engaged in risky sexual behavior that his wife, Becky, knows nothing about. He's embarrassed and dreads telling her. Yet even if his state didn't have a mandatory partner notification program, he feels morally bound to tell her if for no other reason than she needs to be tested and protected from his infection. He believes Becky will "stand by her man," but fears rejection from anyone else who hears about his condition. He doesn't want his extended family, friends, or co-workers to find out. But once he tells Becky, she may have different ideas about who else should hear and how much they should be told. For the sake of their relationship, Petronio believes they need to synchronize their privacy rules.

You might be wondering about the question of timing. Should Nate try to get Becky to agree about who she can or can't share the news with *before* he drops the bombshell, or does he need to share the news first and trust that *afterward* they can reach an agreement on how to handle the information? Petronio isn't too concerned about the timing. Whether the rules are worked out before or after the information is shared, she thinks Nate and Becky's relationship will be healthier *whenever* they reach a mutual agreement about how to handle the private information.

Boundary Ownership—Who Should Decide?

We've already seen that co-ownership of private information involves a joint responsibility for its containment or release. But not all *boundary ownership* is 50–50. One person may have a greater stake in how the information is handled or feel that he or she should have total control of how it's used. If so, that person is usually the original owner. When the confidant agrees that the original owner has the right to call the shots, Petronio refers to that recipient as a *shareholder* who is "fully vested in keeping the information according to the original owner's privacy rules."[15] Nate obviously hopes this will be the case, but it doesn't seem that Becky fits well into the shareholder role. So if Nate clings to the belief that he alone should make the rules about how to manage the information, he will lose the chance to negotiate a mutually satisfying agreement with Becky, almost guaranteeing a turbulent future.

Boundary ownership
The rights and responsibilities that co-owners of private information have to control its spread.

Shareholder
A confidant fully committed to handling private information according to the original owner's privacy rules.

Deliberate confidant
A recipient who sought out private information.

Petronio's description of how a person becomes a confidant sheds light on the degree of control this recipient has.[16] The *deliberate confidant* intentionally seeks private information, often in order to help others out. For example, doctors, counselors, attorneys, and clergy solicit personal information only after they assure clients that they have a privacy policy that severely limits their right to reveal the information to others. As a general rule of thumb, the more eager people are to take on the role of confidant, the less control they have over what they hear.

Conversely, a *reluctant confidant* doesn't want the disclosure, doesn't expect it, and may find the revealed information an unwelcome burden. Picture the hapless airplane travelers who must listen to their seatmates' life stories. This sort of reluctant confidant usually doesn't feel a strong obligation to follow the privacy guidelines of the discloser. If the reluctant recipient comes across the

Reluctant confidant
A co-owner of private information who did not seek it nor want it.

information by accident, he or she will be even less likely to cede control of revealing/concealing to the original owner. So if someone comes across our private thoughts jotted in a journal or encoded in an email, those thoughts may become quite public.

As for Becky, her role as Nate's confidant probably shifts when he makes his startling revelation. She didn't initiate this health conversation and, like many long-term partners, she may at first listen with half an ear out of a sense of obligation. But once he drops the bombshell, she'll be all ears and deliberately probe for more details. Given Becky's probable fear, hurt, and anger that Nate never told her of his possible exposure to HIV, we might expect her to follow her own privacy rules rather than be constrained by his. If she later discovers that Nate has infected her with HIV, his rules will be history.

Boundary Linkage—Who Else Gets to Know?

Boundary linkage is the process of the confidant being linked into the privacy boundary of the person who revealed the information. When Nate discloses his HIV status to Becky, she'll share responsibility for what happens in the future with that information. As for Nate, his privacy boundary will morph into an expanded, joint boundary of a different shape. He clearly wants his condition to remain the couple's secret, but will that happen?

The major consideration in boundary linkage is the nature of the pair's relationship. When the revealer and recipient have a close, trusting relationship, there's a good chance that the recipient will deal with the new information the way the discloser wants. But even though Nate and Becky would both say they've had five years of a loving marriage, news that her husband is HIV positive is likely to rock Becky's world. Her first question will probably be, *How did this happen?* and she won't be satisfied with a vague answer or a claim that it came from a blood transfusion. As Nate reveals a sexual past that he always felt he alone owned, Becky's trust in Nate may take a big hit. From her perspective, she had a right to know about anything that could so profoundly affect her life and their relationship. She might indeed be committed to stay with Nate "in sickness and in health as long as we both shall live," but that doesn't mean she'll agree to a shroud of secrecy.

Boundary linkage
An alliance formed by co-owners of private information as to who else should be able to know.

If the couple follows Petronio's advice to negotiate who else gets to know, they might bring up the following considerations, each of which is supported by research on the privacy and disclosure of HIV status.[17] Becky might insist that she can't live with the stress of keeping Nate's infection secret; she's willing to keep her father in the dark but needs to tell her mother. She also wants the ongoing social support of at least one close friend who knows what she's living with and can help her cope.

For his part, Nate voices his fear of the prejudice that he knows HIV victims encounter.[18] When people find out he has HIV, he's apt to lose his job, his insurance, his buddies, and the respect of others. He can't possibly tell his folks about the diagnosis because they know nothing of his sexual past. Nate imagines his shocked father bemoaning, "I can't even think about this," and then slamming the door on him forever. As for Becky telling her mother, he's seen her close-knit family in action. If his mother-in-law finds out, he's sure the rest of the family will know by the end of the day. At this point, Nate and Becky aren't even close to agreeing on who else can know what they know.

Boundary Permeability—How Much Information Can Flow?

Boundary permeability
The extent to which a boundary permits private information to flow to third parties.

Boundary permeability refers to the degree that privacy boundaries are porous. Some boundaries are protected by ironclad rules, with those in the know sworn to secrecy. These barriers are impervious to penetration. Petronio refers to such informational barriers as *closed, thick,* or *stretched tight.* Often that information is quarantined because public revelation would be highly embarrassing for those in the inner circle.

At the other extreme, some boundaries are quite porous. Petronio describes them as *open, thin,* or *loosely held.* Information permeates them easily. As barriers to disclosure, they are a façade. To the extent that privacy rules are supposed to check the flow of insider information, they are honored in the breach. As the movie *Mean Girls* illustrates, some confidences are meant to be spread.

Permeability is a matter of degree. Many coordinated access rules are crafted to be filters, letting some private information seep through, while other related facts are closely guarded. You may wonder how this could apply to Nate and Becky's situation. Isn't HIV infection like pregnancy—an either/or thing? Biologically, yes, but Petronio describes a number of ways that disclosure could be partial. For example, Nate might talk about movies that sympathetically portray AIDS victims, enthusing about the Oscar-winning performance of Sean Penn in *Milk.* Or, similar to the sexually abused children that Petronio interviewed, he could drop hints about his condition and watch for signs that others would handle further disclosure well. Along that line, some gay and lesbian victims reveal their sexual orientation to others first, later speaking of their HIV status only if the response to the first disclosure is nonjudgmental. As with boundary linkage and boundary ownership, collaborative boundary permeability doesn't happen by accident.

5. BOUNDARY TURBULENCE—RELATIONSHIPS AT RISK

When co-owners of private information don't effectively negotiate and follow jointly held privacy rules, boundary turbulence is the likely result.

Boundary turbulence
Disruption of privacy management and relational trust that occurs when collective privacy boundaries aren't synchronized.

When boundary coordination fails, turbulence is the result. Petronio uses the metaphor of *boundary turbulence* to refer to "disruptions in the way that co-owners control and regulate the flow of private information to third parties."[19] The examples she offers make it clear that turbulence can quickly destroy the trust between revealers and recipients that has built up over time. Petronio likes to describe turbulence with a boat metaphor. Imagine sitting in a sailboat on a placid lake. A speedboat passes by and creates a wake that smacks the side of your boat and rocks it back and forth. Similarly, boundary turbulence can rock your relationships with the havoc it creates. Just as you might seek to steady the boat's rocking while hanging on to keep your balance, Petronio predicts that people will react to turbulence in an attempt to regulate the disturbed relationships left in its wake.

Petronio lists a variety of factors that can lead to boundary turbulence, which I'll lump into three categories—fuzzy boundaries, intentional breaches, and mistakes.[20] I'll illustrate the first two from research she's conducted on family and friends as health care advocates—the triangular interactions that occur when patients bring someone with them to their doctor appointments.[21]

Fuzzy Boundaries

Petronio has found that patients and the advocates they bring with them have rarely discussed what can and can't be revealed—typical of many interactions where private information is shared. She places the onus on the friend or family member: "Curiously, these informal advocates did not appear to confer with the patient before entering the medical situation to find out when or if the advocate should disclose private medical information."[22] Having no recognized mutual boundaries and only a vague idea of the patient's expectations, advocates resort to using their own privacy rules to guide what they say. The result is turbulence and a patient who is often embarrassed or unhappy.

In like manner, doctor–patient confidentiality can be compromised. As one doctor admitted, "When the patient is accompanied by a friend or relative, we're often unclear about that companion's function in the interview."[23] From the legal standpoint, once the patient invites someone else into the mix, the physician no longer has to be concerned about confidentiality. But the patient may be shocked when his wife hears the doctor reveal alarming test results, offer a depressing prognosis, or refer to a previous medical condition she knew nothing about.

Intentional Breaches

Sometimes those who are now in the know understand that the original owner will be horrified if they blab the secret about, yet they reveal it anyway. They may do so to purposely hurt the original owner or simply because breaking the confidence works to their personal advantage. A painful romantic breakup is the classic case when the spurned partner lashes out by revealing intimate details that make the other look bad. Petronio didn't run across disloyal breaches in her study of unofficial health advocates, but she did discover intentional boundary crossings when advocates faced a *confidentiality dilemma.* These occurred when patients said things to their doctor that advocates knew weren't true or avoided revealing embarrassing medical information that advocates knew was important for the physician to know.

Petronio cites the example of a man who tells his cardiologist that he quit smoking after his heart surgery. His daughter who's present is in a quandary. She could respect her father's privacy but by her silence put his health at risk. Or she could violate family privacy rules by revealing his continued smoking so that the doctor can make an informed medical decision. She faces a tragic moral choice where whatever she does is wrong. Petronio found that advocates placed in this position opt for health over privacy, and speculates, "Perhaps in cases when safety or well-being is at stake, privacy issues seem less significant for those trying to help."[24] In support of this interpretation, she notes that one man poignantly explained why he breached his wife's privacy boundary—*because I did not want my wife to die.*

Confidentiality dilemma The tragic moral choice confidants face when they must breach a collective privacy boundary in order to promote the original owner's welfare.

Mistakes

Not all boundary and relational turbulence comes from privacy rules out of sync or the intentional breach of boundaries. Sometimes people create turmoil by making mistakes, such as letting secrets slip out when their guard is down or simply forgetting who might have access to the information. Many young Facebook users have gone back to their pages in a panic, attempting to scrub a piece of information they posted for their friends without thinking about the fact that their parents could also see the post. Other users make errors of judgment by discussing private information in the public arena of many Facebook friends. Another kind of mistake is a *miscalculation in timing.* Doctors and nurses have been known to phone people in the middle of the workday to tell them that they have cancer. There's no good way to deliver that devastating news. But to do it at a time when the person may be interacting with co-workers takes away the chance to process the stark reality in private.

David's application log suggests that it may not make much difference whether a barrier breach is a mistake or intentional. The harm is done and the relationship suffers.

> When I was a freshman I had just broken up with my longtime girlfriend and it was affecting my play on the football field. The quarterback coach called me into his office and asked me what was wrong. As I didn't have anyone else to confide in, I told him the situation. I expected our privacy boundaries to be ruled by player–coach confidentiality. However, that same day at practice, he created boundary turbulence after I threw a bad pass. He asked me if I was "thinking about my girlfriend taking body shots off frat boys while doing keg stands." He said this in front of everyone. I can't say if it was an intentional breach or a mistake, but I now refuse to disclose any of my private information to that man.

CRITIQUE: KEEN DIAGNOSIS, GOOD PRESCRIPTION, LESS AMBIGUITY

CPM nicely fulfills five of the six criteria for a good interpretive theory. Petronio painstakingly maps out the different ways people handle private information and discerns why they make the choices they do. This *understanding of people* is furthered by the *qualitative research* she and other communication scholars conduct to expand their knowledge of privacy management. Typically their research takes the form of open-ended interviews such as those Petronio conducted with sexually abused children, but Petronio also draws on the results of quantitative research to support the theory's conclusions. This extensive research and the fact that CPM provides a needed focus on privacy, where there was previously a theoretical void, has created a *community of agreement* on the worth of the theory among communication scholars. In medical terms, CPM provides an astute diagnosis of the use and abuse of privacy rules.

As for *clarification of values,* CPM presents privacy as valuable in its own right, not relationally inferior to openness, transparency, or self-disclosure. Additionally, Petronio upholds mutually coordinated privacy rules as the best way to establish effective boundaries that protect co-owned private information. It's a bit of a stretch to say that the theory calls for a radical *reform of society* the way some critical theories do, but Petronio clearly believes that healthy relationships within a community depend on trust and that they'll be less at risk when people follow her research-based prescription for the prevention of turbulence.

The interpretive criterion that CPM does not meet well is *aesthetic appeal,* which is a matter of both style and clarity. Petronio's organizational style is one of arranging insights into multiple lists that result in a confusing array of classifications. Clarity is a problem as well. For example, in Principle 4 and throughout much of her writing, Petronio indicates that people who co-own private information should negotiate mutual privacy rules. Yet in another summary version of CPM, Petronio seems to directly contradict this principle. She writes, "As co-owners, the recipients have a responsibility to care for the information in the way that the original owner desires."[25] That sounds more like acquiescence or submission than negotiation. It's also confusing, as is Petronio's frequent use of qualifiers such as *may be, tend to be, possibly, perhaps,* and *sometimes.*

Petronio is aware of these problems. In her 35 years of work with the theory, she's acknowledged its ambiguities[26] and repackaged concepts for improved clarity. Her efforts have made writing this chapter easier.[27] In 2013, an entire issue of the *Journal of Family Communication* was devoted to CPM. In a preview to the issue's articles, Petronio provided a brief status report on the theory, noting the trend in CPM research to make "theoretical refinements."[28] We hope this trend continues and results in more clarity and less ambiguity.

Two gaps in the theory coverage bear mentioning. Petronio writes convincingly about the value of co-owner negotiation and how quickly trust can be lost when privacy rules are breached.[29] Yet she doesn't offer insight on how to conduct those negotiations, nor does she describe after-the-fact remedies for the mistrust that boundary turbulence stirs up. Petronio needs to expand CPM to suggest *how* to effectively negotiate mutual boundaries, and to offer *ways and means* to settle the turbulence that occurs when collective privacy boundaries are violated. She's been working on a new book about CPM that she promises will address these thorny issues. Petronio has a habit, however, of responding to the theory's critics by encouraging them to wait around for improvement. In 2004 she instructed readers to "please stand by,"[30] and in her 2013 report she encouraged us to "stay tuned."[31] Hopefully, after the next revision appears, there will be less need for a "new and improved" version of CPM.

QUESTIONS TO SHARPEN YOUR FOCUS

1. In Principle 2, Petronio cites five foundational criteria that affect our *personal privacy rules.* Which factor most shapes the rules you adopt? Is there one factor that seems to include or trump the other four?
2. Petronio states that *ownership* and *control of private information* don't always go together. Can you imagine a situation where you are the sole owner of a secret yet have no control over its disclosure or discovery?
3. CPM states that those who are privy to private information can avoid *boundary turbulence* by *negotiating mutual privacy rules.* Why do you think many *disclosers* and their *confidants* fail to have this discussion?
4. CPM is a *rules theory* that is supported by *qualitative research.* Why would a *quantitative* researcher have a problem testing the theory using an experimental design?

CONVERSATIONS

View this segment online at www.mhhe.com/griffin9e or www.afirstlook.com.

In her conversation with Glenn, Sandra Petronio says that people believe they own and control their private information. When information is shared, it's crucial for the original owner to set expectations and negotiate with the co-owner as to how that information ought to be managed. When those expectations are violated or aren't negotiated at all, turbulence results. Petronio reflects on how turbulence can sometimes lead to complete privacy breakdowns, and how difficult it can be to manage relationships after that occurs. She also shares what she thinks is missing from the theory.

A SECOND LOOK

Recommended resource: Sandra Petronio, *Boundaries of Privacy: Dialectics of Discourse,* State University of New York, Albany, NY, 2002.

Summary statement: Sandra Petronio, "Communication Privacy Management Theory," in *Engaging Theories in Interpersonal Communication: Multiple Perspectives,* Leslie A. Baxter and Dawn O. Braithwaite (eds.), Sage, Thousand Oaks, CA, 2008, pp. 309–322.

Summary statement: Mary Claire Morr Serewicz and Sandra Petronio, "Communication Privacy Management Theory," in *Explaining Communication: Contemporary Theories and Exemplars,* Bryan Whaley and Wendy Samter (eds.), Lawrence Erlbaum, Mahwah, NJ, 2007, pp. 257–273.

Current state of the art: Special Issue on Communication Privacy Management Theory, *Journal of Family Communication,* Vol. 13, 2013, pp. 1–75.

Five principles of CPM applied: Ashley Duggan and Sandra Petronio, "When Your Child Is in Crisis: Navigating Medical Needs with Issues of Privacy Management," in *Parent and Children Communicating with Society,* Thomas J. Socha (ed.), Routledge, New York, 2009, pp. 117–132.

Initial version: Sandra Petronio, "Communication Boundary Management: A Theoretical Model of Managing Disclosure of Private Information Between Married Couples," *Communication Theory,* Vol. 1, 1991, pp. 311–335.

Research review on secrecy: Sandra Petronio (ed.), *Balancing the Secrets of Private Disclosure,* Lawrence Erlbaum, Mahwah, NJ, 2000.

Development of CPM: Sandra Petronio, "Road to Developing Communication Privacy Management Theory: Narrative in Process, Please Stand By," *Journal of Family Communication,* Vol. 4, 2004, pp. 193–207.

Confidants: Sandra Petronio and Jennifer Reierson, "Regulating the Privacy of Confidentiality: Grasping the Complexities through Communication Privacy Management Theory," in *Uncertainty, Information Management, and Disclosure Decisions: Theories and Applications,* Tamara D. Afifi and Walid A. Afifi (eds.), Routledge, New York, 2009, pp. 365–383.

CHAPTER 13

Objective — Interpretive

Cybernetic tradition
Socio-cultural tradition

The Interactional View

of Paul Watzlawick

The Franklin family is in trouble. A perceptive observer could spot their difficulties despite their successful façade. Sonia Franklin is an accomplished pianist who teaches advanced music theory and keyboard technique in her home. Her husband, Stan, will soon become a partner in a Big Four accounting firm. Their daughter, Laurie, is an honor student, an officer in her high school class, and the number two player on the tennis team. But Laurie's younger brother, Mike, has dropped all pretense of interest in studies, sports, or social life. His only passion is drinking beer and smoking pot.

Each of the Franklins reacts to Mike's substance abuse in different but less than helpful ways. Stan denies that his son has a problem. Boys will be boys, and he's sure Mike will grow out of this phase. The only time he and Mike actually talked about the problem, Stan said, "I want you to cut back on your drinking—not for me and your mother—but for your own sake."

Laurie has always felt responsible for her kid brother and is scared because Mike is getting wasted every few days. She makes him promise he'll quit using, and continues to introduce him to her straightlaced friends in the hope that he'll get in with a good crowd.

Sonia worries that alcohol and drugs will ruin her son's future. One weekday morning when he woke up with a hangover, she wrote a note to the school saying Mike had the flu. She also called a lawyer to help Mike when he was stopped for drunk driving. Although she promised never to tell his father about these incidents, she chides Stan for his lack of concern. The more she nags, the more he withdraws.

Mike feels caught in a vicious circle. Smoking pot helps him relax, but then his family gets more upset, which makes him want to smoke more, which. . . . During a tense dinner-table discussion he lashes out: "You want to know why I use? Go look in a mirror." Although the rest of the family sees Mike as "the problem," psychotherapist Paul Watzlawick would have described the whole family system as disturbed. He formed his theory of social interaction by looking at dysfunctional patterns within families in order to gain insight into healthy communication.

THE FAMILY AS A SYSTEM

Picture a family as a mobile suspended from the ceiling. Each figure is connected to the rest of the structure by a strong thread tied at exactly the right place to keep the system in balance. Tug on any string and the force sends a shock wave throughout the whole network. Sever a thread and the entire system tilts in disequilibrium.

The threads in the mobile analogy represent communication rules that hold the family together. Paul Watzlawick believed that in order to understand the movement of any single figure in the *family system,* one has to examine the communication patterns among all its members. He regarded the communication that family members have among themselves about their relationships as especially important.

Family system
A self-regulating, interdependent network of feedback loops guided by members' rules; the behavior of each person affects and is affected by the behavior of another.

Watzlawick (pronounced VAHT-sla-vick) was a senior research fellow at the Mental Research Institute of Palo Alto, California, and clinical professor of psychiatry at Stanford University. He was one of about 20 scholars and therapists who were inspired by and worked with anthropologist Gregory Bateson. The common denominator that continues to draw the Palo Alto Group together is a commitment to studying interpersonal interaction as part of an entire system. This sets their thinking apart from the widespread conception that communication is a linear process of a source sending a message through a channel to a receiver. In place of that transmission model, they picture communication as akin to an orchestra playing without a conductor.[1] Each person plays a part, affecting and being affected by all the others. It's impossible to isolate what causes what. It's interactional—so Watzlawick and his colleagues referred to their theory as the *interactional view.*

This systems approach suggests that interpersonal relationships are complicated, defying simplistic explanations of why family members do what they do. The Palo Alto Group rejects the notion that individual motives, personality traits, or DNA determines the nature of communication within a family or with others. In fact, these therapists care little about *why* a person acts a certain way, but they have great interest in *how* that behavior affects everyone in the group. For example, some pop psychology books on body language claim that a listener standing in a hands-on-hips position is skeptical about what the speaker is saying. Watzlawick was certainly interested in the reaction others have to this posture, but he didn't think that a particular way of standing should be viewed as part of a cause-and-effect chain of events:

$$a \rightarrow b \rightarrow c \rightarrow d$$

Relationships are not simple, nor are they "things," as suggested by the statement "We have a good relationship." Relationships are complex functions in the same sense that mathematical functions link multiple variables:

$$x = b^2 + \frac{2c}{a} - 5d$$

Just as x will be affected by the value of a, b, c, or d, so the hands-on-hips stance can be due to a variety of attitudes, emotions, or physical conditions. Maybe the stance does show skepticism. But it also might reflect boredom, a feeling of awkwardness, aching shoulder muscles, or self-consciousness about middle-aged love handles.

Watzlawick used the math metaphor throughout his book *Pragmatics of Human Communication.*[2] Along with co-authors Janet Beavin Bavelas and Don

Jackson, he presented key axioms that describe the "tentative calculus of human communication." These axioms make up the *grammar of conversation*, or, to use another analogy that runs through the book, the *rules of the game*.

There is nothing particularly playful about the game the Franklins are playing. Psychologist Alan Watts said that "life is a game where rule No. 1 is: This is no game, this is serious."[3] Watzlawick defined *games* as sequences of behavior governed by rules. Even though Sonia and Stan are involved in an unhealthy *game without end* of nag-withdrawal-nag-withdrawal, they continue to play because it serves a function for both of them. (Sonia feels superior; Stan avoids hassles with his son.) Neither party may recognize what's going on, but their rules are a something-for-something bargain. Mike's drinking and his family's distress may fit into the same category. (Getting drunk not only relieves tension temporarily, it's also a great excuse for sidestepping the pressure to excel, which is the name of the game in the Franklin family.)

Games
Sequences of behavior governed by rules.

Lest we be tempted to see the Franklins' relationships as typical of all families dealing with addiction, Watzlawick warned that each family plays a one-of-a-kind game with homemade rules. Just as CMM claims that persons-in-conversation co-construct their own social worlds (see Chapter 6), the Palo Alto Group insists that each family system creates its own reality. That conviction shapes its approach to family therapy:

> In the systemic approach, we try to understand as quickly as possible the functioning of this system: What kind of reality has this particular system constructed for itself? Incidentally, this rules out categorizations because one of the basic principles of systems theory is that "every system is its own best explanation."[4]

AXIOMS OF INTERPERSONAL COMMUNICATIONS

As therapists who met with a wide variety of clients, the Palo Alto Group spotted regularly occurring features of communication among family members. Watzlawick stated these interactional trends in the form of axioms—the preferred way to present academic scholarship 50 years ago. He cautioned that these maxims were tentative and open for revision after further study. Despite the preliminary nature of these axioms, their publication played a key role in launching the study of interpersonal communication within our discipline.[5]

One Cannot Not Communicate

You've undoubtedly been caught in situations where you've felt obliged to talk but would rather avoid the commitment to respond that's inherent in all communication. Perhaps you currently need to study but your roommate wants to chat. In an attempt to avoid communication, you could bluntly state that your test tomorrow morning makes studying more important than socializing. But voicing your desire for privacy can stretch the rules of good behavior and result in awkward silence that speaks loudly about the relationship.

Symptom strategy
Ascribing our silence to something beyond our control that renders communication justifiably impossible—sleepiness, headache, drunkenness, etc.

Or what if you come home from a date or a party and your mother meets you inside the door and says, "Tell me all about it." You could flood her with a torrent of meaningless words about the evening, merely say it was "fine" as you duck into your room, or plead fatigue, a headache, or a sore throat. Watzlawick called this the *symptom strategy* and said it suggests, "*I* wouldn't mind talking to you, but something stronger than *I*, for which I cannot be blamed, prevents me."

Whatever you do, however, it would be naïve not to realize that your mother will analyze your behavior for clues about the evening's activities. His face an immobile mask, Mike Franklin may mutely encounter his parents. But he communicates in spite of himself by his facial expression and his silence. Communication is inevitable. Those nonverbal messages will obviously have an impact on the rest of his family. A corollary to the first axiom is that "one cannot *not* influence."[6]

Communication = Content + Relationship

The heading is a shorthand version of the formal axiom "Every communication has a content and relationship aspect such that the latter classifies the former and is therefore metacommunication."[7] Watzlawick chose to rename the two aspects of communication that Gregory Bateson had originally called *report* and *command*. Report, or *content*, is *what* is said. Command, or *relationship*, is *how* it's said. Edna Rogers, University of Utah communication professor emerita and early interpreter of the interactional view, illustrates the difference with a two-word message:

Content
The report part of a message; *what* is said verbally.

Relationship
The command part of the message; *how* it's said nonverbally.

> The content level provides information based on what the message is about, while the relational level "gives off" information on how the message is to be interpreted. For example, the content of the comment "You're late" refers to time, but at the relational level the comment typically implies a form of criticism of the other's lack of responsibility or concern.[8]

Figure 13–1 outlines the content–relationship distinction that is crucial to the interactional model. Yet neither the equation in the heading above nor the terms in the figure quite capture the way relationship surrounds content and provides a context, frame, or atmosphere for interpretation. It's the difference between data fed into a computer and the program that directs how the data should be processed. In written communication, punctuation gives direction as to how the words should be understood. Shifting a question mark to an exclamation point alters the meaning of the message. Right? Right! In spoken communication, however, tone of voice, emphasis on certain words, facial cues, and so forth direct how the message was meant to be interpreted.

Metacommunication
Communication about communication.

Watzlawick referred to the relational aspect of interaction as *metacommunication*. It's communication about communication. Metacommunication says, "This is how I see myself, this is how I see you, this is how I see you seeing me. . . ." According to Watzlawick, relationship messages are always the most important

Content	Relationship
Report	Command
What is said	How it is said
Computer data	Computer program
Words	Punctuation
Verbal channel	Nonverbal channel
Communication	Metacommunication

FIGURE 13–1 The Content and Relationship Levels of Communication

element in any communication—healthy or otherwise. But when a family is in trouble, metacommunication dominates the discussion. Mike Franklin's dinner-table outburst is an example of pathological metacommunication that shakes the entire family system. The Palo Alto Group is convinced it would be a mistake for the Franklins to ignore Mike's attack in the hope that the tension will go away. Sick family relationships get better only when family members are willing to talk with each other about their patterns of communication.

The Nature of a Relationship Depends on How Both Parties Punctuate the Communication Sequence

Watzlawick uses the term *punctuate* to refer to the mental process of interpreting an ongoing sequence of events, labeling one event as the cause and the following event as the response. The fact that participants might view the sequence radically differently is captured in a classic cartoon displayed in many experimental psychology labs. One rat in a cage brags to another, "I've got my experimenter trained. Whenever I push this lever he gives me food."

Punctuate
Interpreting an ongoing sequence of events by labeling one event as the cause and the following event as the response.

In human relationships, divergent views of what-causes-what can give rise to great conflict. Consider the contrasting realities reflected in a typical argument between Sonia and Stan.

SONIA: Talk to Mike. The boy needs a father.

STAN: Mike's going to be OK.

SONIA: Don't be so passive. You'd never do anything if I didn't push you.

STAN: Quit harping on me all the time. It's because you nag that I withdraw.

SONIA: It's because you withdraw that I nag.

An outsider who observes the interaction diagrammed below will spot a reciprocal pattern of nagging and withdrawal that has no beginning or end. But Sonia, who is enmeshed in the system, *punctuates* or cleaves the sequence with *P, R,* or *T* as the starting point. She's convinced that Stan's passivity is the cause of her nagging.

Equally ensnared in the system, Stan punctuates the sequence by designating Sonia's nagging at point *Q* or *S* as the initial event. He's quite sure that her constant scolding is the reason he backs away. Asking either of them *Who started it?* wouldn't help because the question merely feeds into their fruitless struggle for control.

Watzlawick suggested that "what is typical about the sequence and makes it a problem of punctuation is that the individual concerned conceives of him or herself only as reacting to, but not as provoking, these attitudes."[9] Stan sees himself detaching from Sonia and Mike only because of his wife's constant nagging. Sonia feels certain that she wouldn't harp on the issue if Stan would face the problem of Mike's drinking. The couple will be trapped in this vicious circle

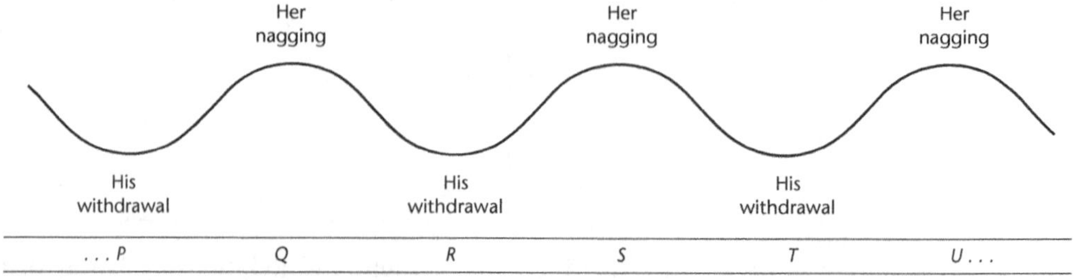

until they engage in a better brand of metacommunication—communication about their communication.

All Communication Is Either Symmetrical or Complementary

This axiom continues to focus on metacommunication. While definitions of relationships include the issues of belongingness, affection, trust, and intimacy, the interactional view pays particular attention to questions of control, status, and power. Remember that Bateson's original label for relationship communication was *command*. According to Watzlawick, *symmetrical* interchange is based on equal power; *complementary* communication is based on differences in power. He makes no attempt to label one type as good and the other as bad. Healthy relationships have both kinds of communication.

Symmetrical interchange Interaction based on equal power.

In terms of ability, the women in the Franklin family have a *symmetrical* relationship; neither one tries to control the other. Sonia has expertise on the piano; Laurie excels on the tennis court. Each of them performs without the other claiming dominance. Fortunately, their skills are in separate arenas. Too much similarity can set the stage for an anything-you-can-do-I-can-do-better competition.

Complementary interchange Interaction based on accepted differences of power.

Sonia's relationship with Mike is *complementary*. Her type of mothering is strong on control. She hides the extent of Mike's drinking from his father, lies to school officials, and hires a lawyer on the sly to bail her son out of trouble with the police. By continuing to treat Mike as a child, she maintains their dominant–submissive relationship. Although complementary relationships aren't always destructive, the status difference between Mike and the rest of the Franklins is stressing the family system.

The interactional view holds that there is no way to label a relationship on the basis of a single verbal statement. Judgments that an interaction is either symmetrical or complementary require a sequence of at least two messages—a statement from one person and a response from the other. While at Michigan State University, communication researchers Edna Rogers and Richard Farace devised a coding scheme to categorize ongoing marital interaction on the crucial issue of who controls the relationship.

One-up communication A conversational move to gain control of the exchange; attempted domination.

One-down communication A conversational move to yield control of the exchange; attempted submission.

One-across communication A conversational move to neutralize or level control within the exchange; when just one party uses it, the interchange is labeled *transitory*.

One-up communication (↑) is movement to *gain* control of the exchange. A bid for dominance includes messages that instruct, order, interrupt, contradict, change topics, or fail to support what the other person said. *One-down communication* (↓) is movement to *yield* control of the exchange. The bid for submission is evidenced by agreement with what the other person said. Despite Watzlawick's contention that all discourse is either symmetrical or complementary, Rogers and Farace code *one-across communication* (→) as well. They define it as *transitory* communication that moves toward *neutralizing* control.

Figure 13–2 presents the matrix of possible relational transactions. The pairs that are circled show a symmetrical interaction. The pairs in triangles indicate complementary relations. The pairs in squares reveal transitory communication. As Rogers' later research shows, bids for dominance (↑) don't necessarily result in successful control of the interaction (↑↓).[10] Matt, a student in my comm theory class, gained new insight about his relationship with his mother when he read this section:

> I'm really pumped on the interactional view. What makes me wide-eyed is how Watzlawick breaks down family communication into symmetrical and

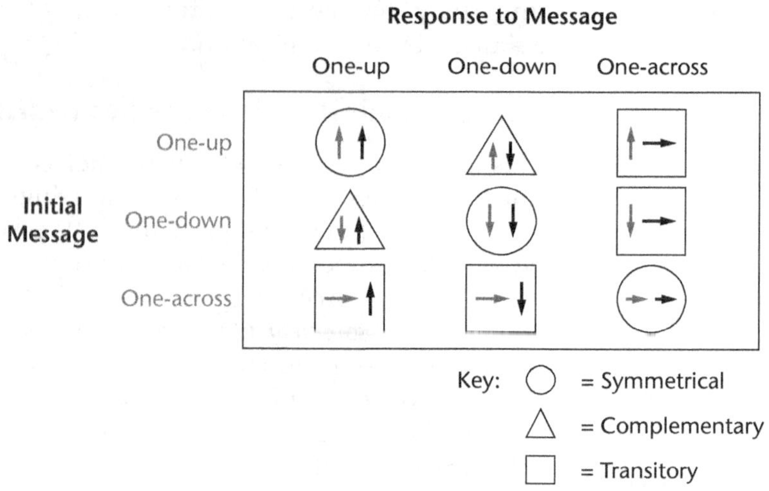

FIGURE 13–2 Matrix of Transactional Types

Adapted from Rogers and Farace, "Analysis of Relational Communication in Dyads: New Measurement Procedures"

complementary. It brings to mind a statement my father would often say: "You and your mother have heated arguments because you are so similar." I usually dismissed this idea as baloney. I'd respond, "What, Mom and I similar? Yeah, right—look how often we disagree!" Looking back through the eyes of Watzlawick, Dad was right. Mom and I were both shooting out one-up messages, thus forming an ongoing symmetrical interaction that wasn't very comfortable.

TRAPPED IN A SYSTEM WITH NO PLACE TO GO

Family systems are highly resistant to change. This inertia is especially apparent in a home where someone has an addiction. Each family member occupies a role that serves the status quo. In the Franklin family, Mike, of course, is the one with "the problem." With the best of intentions, Sonia is the *enabler* who cushions Mike from feeling the pain caused by his chemical abuse. Stan is the "denier," while Laurie is the family "hero" who compensates for her brother's failure. Family therapists note that when one person in a distressed family gets better, another member often gets worse. If Mike stopped drinking and using pot, Laurie might quit the tennis team, ignore her studies, or start smoking marijuana herself. Dysfunctional families confirm the adage "The more things change, the more they stay the same."

Enabler
Within addiction culture, a person whose nonassertive behavior allows others to continue in their substance abuse.

Watzlawick saw family members as often caught in the *double bind* of mutually exclusive expectations, which Bateson originally described. Parental messages such as "You ought to love me" or "Be spontaneous" place children in an untenable position. The children are bound to violate some aspect of the injunction no matter how they respond. (Love can only be freely given; spontaneity on demand is impossible.) The paradox of the double bind is that the high-status party in a complementary relationship insists that the low-status person act as if the relationship were symmetrical—which it isn't. Stan's *demand* that his son stay sober for his *own sake* places Mike in a no-win situation. He can't obey his dad and be autonomous at the same time.

Double bind
A person trapped under mutually exclusive expectations; specifically, the powerful party in a complementary relationship insists that the low-power party act as if it were symmetrical.

REFRAMING: CHANGING THE GAME BY CHANGING THE RULES

How can the members of the Franklin family break out of their never-ending game and experience real change in the way they relate to each other? According to Watzlawick, effective change for the whole family will come about only when members are helped to step outside the system and see the self-defeating nature of the rules under which they're playing. He calls this process *reframing:*

> To reframe . . . means to change the conceptual and/or emotional setting or viewpoint in relation to which a situation is experienced and to place it in another frame which fits the "facts" of the same concrete situation equally well or even better, and thereby changes its entire meaning.[11]

Watzlawick compared reframing to the process of waking up from a bad dream. He pointed out that during a nightmare you may run, hide, fight, scream, jump off a cliff, or try dozens of other things to make the situation better, but nothing really changes. Relief comes only when you step outside the system by waking up. Without the intervention of a timely alarm clock or a caring roommate, relief can be a long time coming.

Reframing
The process of instituting change by stepping outside of a situation and reinterpreting what it means.

Reframing is the sudden "aha" of looking at things in a new light. Suppose you could talk with Watzlawick about your struggles to keep up with the assignments for your comm theory class. You've chosen to be a communication major, so you believe you ought to *like* studying the material. Since you don't, you think there's something wrong with you. You also know that your family is making a financial sacrifice for you to be in college, so you feel guilty that you aren't getting good grades or experiencing deep gratitude for their help. In fact, you resent having to be grateful.

If you described these dilemmas to Watzlawick, he would want you to reframe your attitudes as *unrealistic* and *immature*—nightmarish interpretations for most college students. Even under the best of circumstances, he'd explain, studying is an unpleasant necessity and to believe that it should be fun is ridiculous. As far as your folks are concerned, they have a right to your gratitude, but that doesn't mean you have to *enjoy* being thankful. So it's up to you. You can "continue in these immature outlooks or have the adult courage to reject them and to begin to look at life as a mixture of pleasant and unpleasant things."[12] The *facts* haven't changed, but he's given you a new way to *interpret* them. If you accept Watzlawick's frame, you'll probably cope better and feel less pain.

For the Franklins, reframing means they must radically change their perspective. One way to do this is by adopting the view of Alcoholics Anonymous (AA) that Mike's addiction is a disease over which he has no control. His drinking is not a sign of moral weakness or an intentional rebuff of his family's values—he drinks because he's an alcoholic. The AA interpretation would imply that the Franklins need to abandon their fruitless search for someone to blame. Despite Mike's look-in-the-mirror accusation, the members of his family aren't responsible for his addiction. They didn't cause it, they can't cure it, and they can't control it. It's a disease. Does that mean Mike's not responsible for being chemically dependent? Right . . . but he *is* responsible for putting all of his energy into getting well.

Accepting a new frame implies rejecting the old one. The Franklins must admit that their so-called solutions are as much a problem as their son's drinking.

"Instead of 'It sucks' you could say, 'It doesn't speak to me.'"

Mike will never seek treatment for his illness as long as his family continues to shield him from the consequences of his behavior. Reframing will help Sonia see that writing excuses and hiring lawyers may be less caring than letting her son get kicked out of school or allowing his driver's license to be suspended.

Adopting a tough-love perspective or any new interpretive frame is usually accomplished only with outside help. For Watzlawick, that meant therapy. As a social constructionist, he wouldn't try to discover the "real" reason Mike drinks or worry if it's "true" that some people are genetically predisposed to addiction. In his view, the main goal of therapy is to reduce pain. He would regard the disease model of addiction as an alternative construction—a fiction, perhaps, but for the Franklin family a useful and less painful one.[13]

CRITIQUE: ADJUSTMENTS NEEDED WITHIN THE SYSTEM

Janet Beavin Bavelas co-authored *Pragmatics of Human Communication* with Watzlawick in 1967. Twenty-five years later, she reviewed the status of the axioms that are the central focus of the interactional view.[14] (Recall they were labeled as tentative.) Based on the research program she conducted at the University of Victoria in Canada, Bavelas recommends modifying some axioms of the theory. Her proposal serves as an informed critique of the original theory.

The first axiom claims that *we cannot not communicate.* Perhaps because of the catchy way it's stated, this axiom has been both challenged and defended more than the others. Although Bavelas is fascinated by the way people avoid eye contact or physically position themselves to communicate that they don't want to communicate, she now concedes that not all nonverbal behavior is communication. Observers may draw inferences from what they see, but in the absence of a sender–receiver relationship and the intentional use of a shared code, Bavelas would describe nonverbal behavior as *informative* rather than *communicative.*

As Figure 13–1 shows, the Palo Alto Group treated the verbal and nonverbal channels as providing different kinds of information. Bavelas now thinks that the notion of functionally separate channels dedicated to different uses is wrong. She suggests a *whole-message model* that treats verbal and nonverbal acts as completely integrated and often interchangeable. In effect, she has erased the broken vertical line that divides Figure 13–1 down the middle—a major shift in thinking.

Whole-message model
Regards verbal and nonverbal components of a message as completely integrated and often interchangeable.

The content/relationship distinction of another axiom is still viable for Bavelas. As did Watzlawick, she continues to believe that the content of communication is always embedded in the relationship environment. Looking back, however, she thinks they confused readers by sometimes equating the term *metacommunication* with all communication about a relationship. She now wants to reserve the word for explicit communication about the *process of communicating*. Examples of metacommunication narrowly defined would be Laurie Franklin telling her brother, "Don't talk to me like a kid," and Mike's response, "What do you mean by that?" Laurie's raised eyebrows and Mike's angry tone of voice would also be part of their tightly integrated packages of meaning.

Despite Bavelas' second thoughts, I'm impressed with the lasting impact that Watzlawick and his associates have had on the field of interpersonal communication. The publication of *Pragmatics of Human Communication* marked the beginning of widespread study of the way communication patterns sustain or destroy relationships. The interactional view has also encouraged communication scholars to go beyond narrow cause-and-effect assumptions. The entanglements Watzlawick described reflect the complexities of real-life relationships that most of us know. In that way, the interactional view is similar to the other two interpretive theories covered in this section on relationship maintenance. All of them major in description of communication rather than prediction.

QUESTIONS TO SHARPEN YOUR FOCUS

1. *Systems theorists* compare the family system to a mobile. What part of the mobile represents *metacommunication?* If you were constructing a mobile to model your family, how would you depict *symmetrical* and *complementary* relationships?
2. For decades, the United States and the former Soviet Union were engaged in a nuclear arms race. How does Watzlawick's axiom about the *punctuation of communication sequences* explain the belligerence of both nations?
3. Can you make up something your instructor might say that would place you in a *double bind?* Under what conditions would this be merely laughable rather than frustrating?
4. At the start of this chapter, the interactional view is charted as a highly *interpretive theory* coming from the *cybernetic tradition*—a tradition mapped as relatively *objective* in Chapter 4. Can you resolve this apparent contradiction?

A SECOND LOOK

Recommended resource: Paul Watzlawick, Janet Beavin Bavelas, and Don Jackson, *Pragmatics of Human Communication,* W. W. Norton, New York, 1967.

Commitments of the Palo Alto Group: Codruta Porcar and Cristian Hainic, "The Interactive Dimension of Communication: The Pragmatics of the Palo Alto Group," *Journal for Communication and Culture,* Vol. 1, No. 2, 2011, pp. 4–19.

Original conception of the theory: Gregory Bateson, "Information and Codification," in *Communication,* Jurgen Ruesch and Gregory Bateson (eds.), W. W. Norton, New York, 1951, pp. 168–211.

System theory: B. Aubrey Fisher, "The Pragmatic Perspective of Human Communication: A View from System Theory," in *Human Communication Theory,* Frank E. X. Dance (ed.), Harper & Row, New York, 1982, pp. 192–219.

Relational control: L. Edna Rogers and Richard Farace, "Analysis of Relational Communication in Dyads: New Measurement Procedures," *Human Communication Research,* Vol. 1, 1975, pp. 222–239.

Relational control in families: L. Edna Rogers, "Relational Communication Theory: An Interactional Family Theory," in *Engaging Theories in Family Communication: Multiple Perspectives,* Dawn O. Braithwaite and Leslie A. Baxter (eds.), Sage, Thousand Oaks, CA, 2006, pp. 115–129.

Reframing: Paul Watzlawick, John H. Weakland, and Richard Fisch, *Change,* W. W. Norton, New York, 1974, pp. 92–160.

Whether one cannot not communicate: Theodore Clevenger Jr., "Can One Not Communicate? A Conflict of Models," *Communication Studies,* Vol. 42, 1991, pp. 340–353.

Social construction approach to therapy: Paul Watzlawick and Michael Hoyt, "Constructing Therapeutic Realities: A Conversation with Paul Watzlawick," in *Handbook of Constructive Therapies,* Michael Hoyt (ed.), Jossey-Bass, San Francisco, CA, 1997, pp. 183–196.

Theory adjustments: Janet Beavin Bavelas, "Research into the Pragmatics of Human Communication," *Journal of Strategic and Systemic Therapies,* Vol. 11, No. 2, 1992, pp. 15–29.

Current face of the theory: L. Edna Rogers and Valentin Escudero (eds.), *Relational Communication: An Interactional Perspective to Study Process and Form,* Lawrence Erlbaum, Mahwah, NJ, 2004.

Critique: Carol Wilder, "The Palo Alto Group: Difficulties and Directions of the Interactional View for Human Communication Research," *Human Communication Research,* Vol. 5, 1979, pp. 171–186.

For additional scholarly and artistic resources, click on
Further Resources under Theory Resources at
www.afirstlook.com.

Influence

Getting a person to play a role in an unfamiliar situation can be a powerful method of influence. To explore its effectiveness, Yale social psychologists Irving Janis and Leon Mann surveyed students at a women's college to find out their attitudes and behavior toward smoking—a practice quite resistant to change.[1] They later asked many who smoked to take part in a role play that supposedly assessed their acting ability. Each woman was to take the role of a patient who had gone to the doctor because of a continual cough. She was now back in his office to get the results of a battery of tests the doctor had ordered. She had no script to follow and could respond to the other actor in whatever way she desired.[2]

One researcher then ushered her into a room that was decked out with a scale, sterilizer, fluorescent light for reading X-rays, and a medical school diploma on the wall. The room even smelled of disinfectant. The second experimenter wore a white lab coat with a stethoscope around his neck. Speaking in an authoritative tone of voice, the "doctor" came right to the point. Her chest X-ray gave a positive indication of lung cancer and the diagnosis was confirmed by lab tests. Without question, this condition had developed over a long time. He then paused to let the young woman respond. Often she would say that she'd been smoking too much. Most students eventually asked what they could do.

The doctor wasn't optimistic: "We need to operate immediately. Can you be prepared to check into the hospital tomorrow afternoon?" The surgery only had a 50–50 chance of success of stopping the cancer's spread. At this point the minidrama could go in a number of directions. The student might express fear for her life, anguish over broken plans for graduation, hesitancy over what to tell her parents or fiancé, anger at God, or disbelief that it was happening to her. No matter how the dialogue went, the young woman got caught up in the situation and emotionally involved with the link between smoking and cancer.

Janis and Mann waited two weeks for the effects of the role play to take hold and then rechecked attitudes toward cigarette smoking. They found that role-play students expressed less favorable opinions toward smoking than they had before. They also discovered that the average cigarettes-per-day habit had dropped from 24 (more than a pack a day) to 14—a dramatic decrease in actual smoking behavior. The attitudes of smokers in the control group who didn't have the role-play experience remained the same as before. So did their 24 cigarettes-per-day habit.

Relapse is common when smokers try to cut back or quit cold turkey. Many find the force of nicotine addiction, cigarette advertising, and friends who smoke hard to resist. Yet after eight months the slippage was slight. On average, those who participated in the emotional role play lit up 15 times a day—only one cigarette more.

Why is role play so effective in this case? In their book, *New Techniques of Persuasion,* the late Gerald Miller (Michigan State University) and Michael Burgoon (University of Arizona) suggested three possibilities. Role play makes for *immediacy.* The cigarette–cancer connection becomes more real to the smoker when she can't get the image of the doctor delivering bad news out of her mind. There's also *personal involvement.* The smoker can no longer stand aloof from the threat of cancer when she's actively stating her fears to the doctor. Finally, Miller and Burgoon suggested we consider the effect of *nonverbal messages,* such as the doctor pointing to the patient's X-ray. "The impact of this simple behavioral sequence may well transcend the effects of an extended medical lecture on the dangers of cigarette smoking."[3]

We've recounted this experiment because it illustrates and measures what influence theorists, researchers, and many practitioners value. Will a persuasive approach change people's inner attitudes—their beliefs, their emotional response, and what they intend to do? Will that shift in attitude be matched by a change in actual behavior? Are these changes so deep-seated that they will resist forces that tend to draw them back into old patterns of thinking and behavior? And will they last over time? The three theories that follow suggest different routes to this kind of effective interpersonal influence and, most important, explain why they work.

"I'm through playing doctor.
With insurance forms, co-payments,
and malpractice suits, it's just no fun!"

CHAPTER 14

Objective — Interpretive

Socio-psychological tradition

Social Judgment Theory

of Muzafer Sherif

My son, Jim, is an airline pilot—a job that has changed dramatically since the terrorist acts of September 11, 2001. When he walks through the airport he overhears a variety of comments about the safety of air travel. I've listed 11 statements that reflect the range of attitudes he's heard expressed. Read through these opinions and consider the diversity of viewpoints they represent.

a. Airlines aren't willing to spend money on tight security.
b. All life is risk. Flying is like anything else.
c. Anyone willing to die for a cause can hijack an airplane.
d. Air marshals with guns can deter terrorists.
e. There are old pilots and bold pilots; there are no old, bold pilots.
f. Pilots drink before they fly to quell their fears of skyjacking.
g. Getting there by plane is safer than taking the train or bus.
h. American pilots are trained to handle any in-flight emergency.
i. It's easy to get into the cockpit of a jet airplane.
j. Passenger screening is better with full-body scanners in place.
k. The odds of a plane crash are 1 in 10 million.

Take a few minutes to mark your reactions to these statements. If you follow each instruction before jumping ahead to the next one, you'll have a chance to experience what social judgment theory predicts.

1. To begin, read through the items again and underline the single statement that most closely represents your point of view.
2. Now look and see whether any other items seem reasonable. Circle the letters in front of those acceptable statements.
3. Reread the remaining statements and cross out the letters in front of any that are objectionable to you. After you cross out these unreasonable ideas, you may have marked all 11 statements one way or another. It's also possible that you'll leave some items unmarked.

THREE LATITUDES: ACCEPTANCE, REJECTION, AND NONCOMMITMENT

I've just taken you on paper through what social judgment theory says happens in our heads. We hear a message and immediately judge where it should be placed on the attitude scale in our minds. According to the late Muzafer Sherif, a social psychologist at the University of Oklahoma, this subconscious sorting of ideas occurs at the instant of perception. We weigh every new idea by comparing it with our present point of view. He called his analysis of attitudes the *social judgment–involvement approach,* but most scholars refer to it simply as *social judgment theory.*

Social judgment–involvement
Perception and evaluation of an idea by comparing it with current attitudes.

Sherif believed that the three responses you made on the previous page are necessary to determine your attitude toward airline safety, or any other attitude structure. In all probability you circled a range of statements that seemed reasonable to you and crossed out a number of opinions you couldn't accept. That's why Sherif would see your attitude as a *latitude* rather than any single statement you underlined. He wrote that an "individual's stand is not represented adequately as a point along a continuum. Different persons espousing the same position may differ considerably in their tolerance around this point."[1]

Latitude of acceptance
The range of ideas that a person sees as reasonable or worthy of consideration.

Latitude of rejection
The range of ideas that a person sees as unreasonable or objectionable.

Latitude of noncommitment
The range of ideas that a person sees as neither acceptable nor objectionable.

He saw an attitude as an amalgam of three zones. The first zone is called the *latitude of acceptance.* It's made up of the item you underlined and any others you circled as acceptable. A second zone is the *latitude of rejection.* It consists of the opinions you crossed out as objectionable. The leftover statements, if any, define the *latitude of noncommitment.* These were the items you found neither objectionable nor acceptable. They're akin to marking *undecided* or *no opinion* on a traditional attitude survey. Sherif said we need to know the location and width of each of these interrelated latitudes in order to describe a person's attitude structure.

Suppose Jim encounters Ned, a man in the airport who is complaining about the dangers of flight as evidenced by 9/11 terrorism. Assume Jim would like to persuade Ned that flying is absolutely safe, or at least much less risky than anxious Ned believes. Social judgment theory recommends that Jim try to figure out the location and breadth of the man's three latitudes before presenting his case. Figure 14–1 shows where Ned places those 11 statements along the mental yardstick he uses to gauge safety. As you will discover in the next few pages, if my son has a good idea of this cognitive map, he'll have a much better chance of crafting a message that will persuade Ned to be more optimistic about flying.

EGO-INVOLVEMENT: HOW MUCH DO YOU CARE?

There's one other thing about Ned's attitude structure that Jim needs to know—how *important* the issue of air safety is in Ned's life. Sherif called this concept *ego-involvement. Ego-involvement* refers to how crucial an issue is in our lives. Is it central to our well-being? Do we think about it a lot? Does our attitude on the matter go a long way toward defining who we are? In Figure 14–1, I've used an anchor to represent the position that most closely represents Ned's point of view—that flying is dangerous because fanatics are willing to die for their cause. Sherif said that's what our favored position does; it anchors all our other thoughts about the topic.

If air safety were only a casual concern for Ned, it would be fitting to represent his stance with a small anchor that could easily be dragged to a new position. That's probably the case for some of the nonfliers in the terminal who

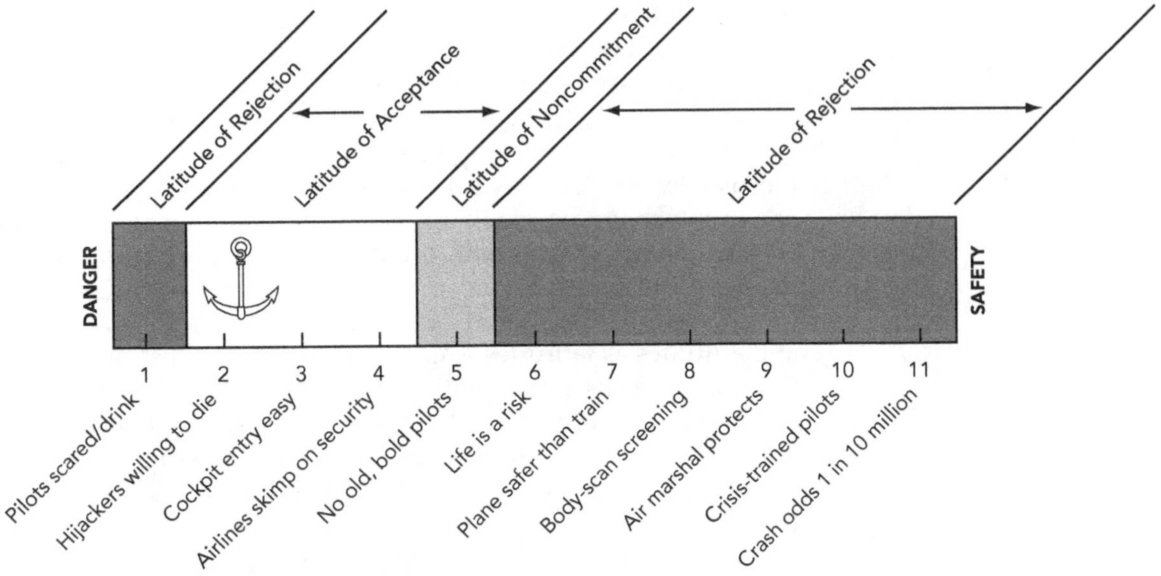

FIGURE 14–1 Ned's Cognitive Map Regarding Air Safety

are simply picking up a rental car, dropping off Aunt Juanita for her flight, or perhaps retrieving a lost bag for a friend. These folks are for safe flights and against crashes, but air safety doesn't present a major personal concern.

Despite the fact that images of airplanes slamming into the twin towers of the World Trade Center are stenciled into most people's minds, not everyone who flies dwells on the topic. Those people don't argue about it, stew over it, or get sweaty palms when their jet roars down the runway. As long as everything seems normal, their ego-involvement is moderate.

But for Ned and others like him, the issue is crucial. They are fearful fliers who swap horror stories of knowing someone who died on a hijacked plane. They experience panic when three swarthy men board their flight to Chicago. Others may experience only passing anxiety about flying, but since Ned's fear is deep-seated, the hefty anchor shown in Figure 14–1 is appropriate.

People with attitude profiles similar to Ned's are highly ego-involved. Some join the International Air Safety Association (IASA), an airline passenger association that lobbies for stricter safety regulations. One way Sherif defined high ego-involvement was *membership in a group with a known stand.* My son's pilot's license, Air Line Pilots Association union card, and employment with a major airline are indications that he's at least as ego-involved in the issue as Ned. Of course, his confidence in airline safety is at the other end of the spectrum.

Ego-involvement
The importance or centrality of an issue to a person's life, often demonstrated by membership in a group with a known stand.

Three features of Ned's attitude structure are typical of people with high ego-involvement in an issue. The first indication is that his latitude of noncommitment is almost nonexistent. People who don't care about an issue usually have a wide latitude of noncommitment, but Ned has only one statement in that category. He may not be sure about old, bold pilots, but he has definite opinions on everything else.

Second, Ned rejects all five statements that offer assurances of safety. According to social judgment theory, a wide latitude of rejection is a typical sign of high ego-involvement. Ned has intense feelings about the potential dangers of flying;

he sees safety as a black-and-white issue. People with low ego-involvement would probably see more gray area.

Finally, people who hold extreme opinions on either side of an issue almost always care deeply. While it's possible to feel passionate about middle-of-the-road positions, social judgment researchers find that massive attitude anchors are usually located toward the ends of the scale. Extreme positions and high ego-involvement go together. That's why religion, sex, and politics are traditionally taboo topics in the wardroom of a U.S. Navy ship at sea. When passions run deep, radical opinions are common, and there's little tolerance for diversity.

Steven Spielberg's film *Lincoln* illustrates Sherif's concepts of ego-involvement and attitudes as latitudes.[2] Against the advice of his cabinet, the president pushes Congress to pass a constitutional amendment abolishing slavery. A *yes* vote falls somewhere within each Republican's latitude of acceptance. But to get the needed two-thirds majority, Lincoln needs to switch the votes of 20 Democrats, whose party publicly opposes the amendment. Abolition appears to fall within their latitude of rejection.

Yet Lincoln's men see a window of opportunity. Leaving Congress are 39 lame-duck Democrats who now have weaker party ties. With that lower ego-involvement, these 39 men may have a wider latitude of noncommitment toward the amendment and could be encouraged to *abstain* rather than vote *no*. Some might be swayed to broaden their latitude of acceptance, making a *yes* vote possible. The film shows Lincoln's political operatives in the House balcony noting which Democrats are sweating or at least not cheering when their leaders lambast the amendment. The aides then use Lincoln's popularity, moral arguments, job offers, threats, and bribes to induce latitude change. The amendment passes and slavery is abolished by a two-vote margin.

Everything I've presented up to this point deals with the way social judgment theory describes the cognitive *structure* of a person's attitude. We now turn to the two-step mental *process* that Sherif said is triggered when a person hears or reads a message. Ned will first evaluate the content of the message to see where it falls vis-à-vis his own position—how far it is from his anchor. That's the *judgment* phase of social judgment theory. In the second stage of the process, Ned will adjust his anchored attitude toward or away from the message he's just encountered. The next two sections explain the way Sherif said the two stages of this influence process work.

JUDGING THE MESSAGE: CONTRAST AND ASSIMILATION ERRORS

Sherif claimed that we use our own anchored attitude as a comparison point when we hear a discrepant message. He believed there's a parallel between systematic biases in the judgments we make in the physical world and the way we determine other people's attitudes. I recently set up three pails of water in my class to illustrate this principle. Even though the contents looked the same, the water in the left bucket was just above freezing, the water in the right bucket was just below scalding, and the water in the middle bucket was lukewarm. A student volunteered to plunge her left hand into the left bucket and her right hand into the right bucket at the same time. Twenty seconds was about all she could take. I then asked her to plunge both hands into the middle bucket and judge the temperature of the water. Of course, this produced a baffling experience, because her left hand told her the water was hot, while her right hand sent a message that it was cold.

Sherif hypothesized a similar *contrast* effect when people who are hot for an idea hear a message on the topic that doesn't have the same fire. Judged by their standard, even warm messages strike them as cold. Sherif's *social judgment–involvement* label nicely captures the idea of a link between ego-involvement and perception. Highly committed people have large latitudes of rejection. Any message that falls within that range will be perceived by them as more discrepant from their anchor than it really is. The message is mentally pushed away to a position that is farther out—not within the latitude of acceptance. So the hearer doesn't have to deal with it as a viable option.

Contrast
A perceptual error whereby people judge messages that fall within their latitude of rejection as farther from their anchor than they really are.

All of this is bad news for Jim as he tries to dispel Ned's fears. He'll probably address Ned's concerns head on:

> Look, Ned, statistics show you're much safer flying than taking the train or bus. In fact, the most dangerous part of flying is the drive to the airport. I know you worry about terrorists, but with the new full-body scanners the TSA is using, there's no way that guns, knives, or explosives can get on board. And you should know there's been an undercover air marshal riding shotgun back in coach on my last three trips.

Jim hopes these points will be reassuring. If Ned hears them as they were intended, they will register at 7, 8, and 9 on his mental scale, where a 1 represents total danger and an 11 indicates complete safety. However, social judgment theory says Ned won't hear them that way. Because the message falls within Ned's latitude of rejection, he's likely to judge the words as even farther from his anchor, perhaps at 9, 10, and 11. The words will strike Ned as unbelievable, self-serving, pilot propaganda—a false guarantee of safety that he'll be quick to reject.

Contrast is a perceptual distortion that leads to polarization of ideas. But according to Sherif, it happens only when a message falls within the latitude of rejection. *Assimilation* is the opposite error of judgment. It's the rubberband effect that draws an idea toward the hearer's anchor so it seems that she and the speaker share the same opinion. Assimilation takes place when a message falls within the latitude of acceptance. For example, suppose Jim tells Ned that his airline isn't willing to spend money on effective security. Although that message is at 4 on Ned's cognitive map, he will hear it as more similar to his anchoring attitude than it really is, perhaps at 3.

Assimilation
A perceptual error whereby people judge messages that fall within their latitude of acceptance as less discrepant from their anchor than they really are.

Sherif was unclear about how people judge a message that falls within their latitude of noncommitment. Most interpreters assume that perceptual bias will not kick in and that the message will be heard roughly as intended.

DISCREPANCY AND ATTITUDE CHANGE

Judging how close or how far a message is from our own anchored position is the first stage of attitude change. Shifting our anchor in response is the second. Sherif thought that both stages of the influence process usually take place below the level of consciousness.

According to social judgment theory, once we've judged a new message to be within our latitude of acceptance, we will adjust our attitude somewhat to accommodate the new input. The persuasive effect will be positive but partial. We won't travel the whole distance, but there will be some measurable movement toward the speaker's perceived position. How much movement? Sherif wasn't specific, but he did claim that *the greater the discrepancy, the more hearers will adjust their attitudes.* Thus, the message that persuades the most is the one that is most discrepant from the listener's position yet falls within his or her *latitude of acceptance* or *latitude of noncommitment.*

If we've judged a message to be within our *latitude of rejection,* we will also adjust our attitude, but in this case *away from* what we think the speaker is advocating. Since people who are highly ego-involved in a topic have a broad range of rejection, most messages aimed to persuade them are in danger of actually driving them further away. This predicted *boomerang effect* suggests that people are often *driven* rather than *drawn* to the attitude positions they occupy.

Boomerang effect
Attitude change in the opposite direction of what the message advocates; listeners driven away from rather than drawn to an idea.

The mental processes Sherif described are automatic. He reduced interpersonal influence to the issue of the distance between the message and the hearer's position:

> Stripped to its bare essential, the problem of attitude change is the problem of the degree of discrepancy from communication and the felt necessity of coping with the discrepancy.[3]

So the only space for volition in social judgment theory is the choice of alternative messages available to the person who's trying to persuade.

PRACTICAL ADVICE FOR THE PERSUADER

Sherif would have advised Jim to avoid messages that claim flying is safer than taking the bus or train. Ned simply won't believe them, and they may push him deeper into his anti-aviation stance. To make sure his words have a positive

"We think you could gain much wider support simply by re-languaging your bigotry."

effect, Jim should select a message that falls at the edge of Ned's latitude of acceptance. Even after the perceptual process of assimilation kicks in, Ned will still judge Jim's message to be discrepant from his point of view and shift his attitude slightly in that direction.

> Ned, you're right. For years the airlines—mine included—didn't invest the money it takes to successfully screen passengers. But 9/11 has changed all that. Every ticket you buy has a surcharge to pay for tight security. And the days of the cowboy pilot are over. Because it's my job to protect hundreds of lives in a $100 million airplane, I do it by the book every flight. I know that if I get my butt there safely, yours will get there that way too.

Jim might try a riskier strategy to produce greater attitude shift. He could use the vague statement about there being no old, bold pilots, since ambiguity can often serve better than clarity. When George W. Bush started campaigning for president, he called himself a "compassionate conservative." Nobody knew exactly what the label meant, so the term stayed out of voters' latitude of rejection. If Jim goes that route and Ned presses for clarification on the absence of old, bold pilots, Jim can explain that rigorous cockpit checkrides weeded out those who take chances. But this approach could backfire and feed Ned's fears if the statement calls to mind an image of reckless pilots about to crash and burn.

The idea of crafting a message to fall within Ned's latitude of acceptance or noncommitment is frustrating to Jim. He wants more change than these strategies offer. But according to social judgment theory, limited change is all he can get in a one-shot attempt. If he were talking to an open-minded person with wide latitudes of acceptance and noncommitment, a bigger shift would be possible. Toby, a student in my class, saw himself that way over a broad range of issues:

> Time and time again I find myself easily persuaded. Afterward I wonder, *How did I get talked into this one?* Credit it to my flexibility, willingness to try, or naïve trust in people's motives. I always pay attention to advice given by a friend or an expert. Social judgment theory would say that I simply have a wide latitude of noncommitment. That's because I have low ego-involvement most of the time. The situation is not a hill to die on, so why should I get my pride involved?

Toby isn't typical. We're more likely to encounter people who are dogmatic on every issue. "Don't confuse me with the facts," they say. "My mind is made up." These cantankerous souls have wide latitudes of rejection. This probably doesn't describe Ned. His deeply skeptical attitude is likely limited to fear of flying. But when Jim is dealing with a highly ego-involved traveler, he has to work within a narrow range. True conversion from one end of the scale to the other is a rare phenomenon. The only way to stimulate large-scale change is through a series of small, successive movements. Persuasion is a gradual process.

Reference groups
Groups that members use to define their identity.

It's also a *social* process. The lack of an interpersonal bond between Jim and Ned limits the amount of influence that's possible. If Ned heard strong reassurances of airline safety from his friends and family, it might occasion a major shift. Sherif noted that "most dramatic cases of attitude change, the most widespread and enduring, are those involving changes in reference groups with differing values."[4]

ATTITUDES ON SLEEP, BOOZE, AND MONEY: EVIDENCE SUPPORTING SJT

Research on the predictions of social judgment theory (SJT) requires highly ego-involving issues where strong resistance to some persuasive messages is likely. The topics of sufficient sleep, alcohol consumption, and asking for money seem ripe for assessing the theory's validity.

Sufficient sleep. In an early experiment testing social judgment theory, psychologists Stephen Bochner (University of New South Wales) and Chester Insko (University of North Carolina at Chapel Hill) queried college students about how much sleep they thought a person should get each night.[5] Before the study, most college students accepted the conventional wisdom that the human body functions best with eight hours of sleep. They then read an article written by an expert in the field that claimed young adults actually need much less. The message was the same for all with one crucial difference. Some students were told they needed eight hours, some seven, some six, and so on, right down the line. The final group actually read that humans need no sleep at all! Then each group had a chance to give their opinions.

Sherif's theory suggests that the fewer hours recommended, the more students will be swayed, until they begin to regard the message as patently ridiculous. The results shown in Figure 14–2 confirm this prediction. Persuasion increased as the hours advocated were reduced to 3, a message that caused students to revise their estimate of optimum sleep down to 6.3 hours. Anything less than 3 hours apparently fell outside their latitude of acceptance and became progressively ineffective. But a highly credible speaker can shrink the hearer's latitude of rejection. When the "expert" in the sleep study was a Nobel Prize-winning physiologist rather than a YMCA director, persuasion increased.

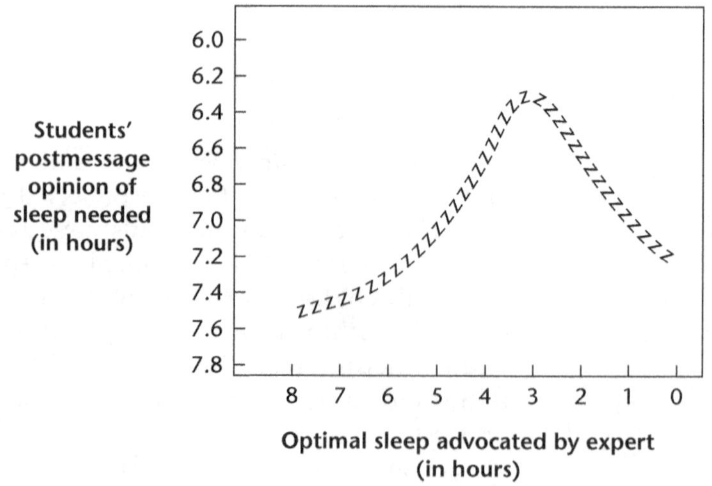

FIGURE 14–2 Sleep Study Results

Adapted from Bochner and Insko, "Communicator Discrepancy, Source Credibility and Opinion Change"

Pluralistic ignorance The mistaken idea that everyone else is doing or thinking something that they aren't.

Alcohol consumption. In the fall of 2004, Michigan State University communication professors Sandi Smith, Charles Atkin, and three other university colleagues measured students' perception of drinking behavior at the school.[6] They found a campus wide *pluralistic ignorance* of the actual amount of booze consumed by students who drink at a party. Whereas reported alcohol consumption averaged 5.3 drinks—with 63 percent downing five drinks or less—students thought the norm was closer to six drinks (5.9 percent). This gap concerned health center officials because perceived social norms affect behavior—in this case, the idea encouraged risky binge drinking. In preparation for a campus wide social norm campaign to correct the misperception and publicize the actual norm, Smith and Atkin measured student body latitudes of acceptance, noncommitment, and rejection of various messages. Based on their research they selected the following true phrase to be included in every communication about student drinking behavior: "Most (63 percent) drink zero to five when they party." The message fell within most students' latitude of noncommitment—as discrepant from campus opinion as possible while still being believable.

The intensive, three-month campaign involved posters across campus, table tents in the cafeteria, and multiple ads in the campus newspaper and in a news magazine handed out at orientation. Almost all students reported seeing the zero-to-five-drinks message many times. The campaign was a success. When Smith and Atkin measured perception of drinking in the spring, they found that students had lowered their estimate to 4.9—one drink less than they had thought in the fall. Even more impressive, the average of number of drinks consumed at a party during that time span fell from 5.3 to 4.5—almost a full glass or mug. Like the lung-cancer role-play experiment reported in the introduction to this section, this research validates an effective strategy to induce lasting change in beliefs and behavior, even when the issue is highly ego-involving.

Asking for money. An anecdotal story of SJT in action comes from a university development director I know who was making a call on a rich alumnus. He anticipated that the prospective donor would give as much as $10,000. He made his pitch and asked what the wealthy businessman could do. The man protested that it had been a lean year and that times were tough—he couldn't possibly contribute more than $20,000. The fundraiser figured that he had seriously underestimated the giver's latitude of acceptance and that $20,000 was on the low end of that range. Without missing a beat he replied, "Trevor, do you really think that's enough?" The alumnus wrote a check for $25,000.

How do you feel about the fundraising ploy just described? The persuasive technique obviously worked, but the application of social judgment theory raises some thorny ethical questions. Is it OK for fundraisers to alter their pitch based on a potential donor's latitude of acceptance? Is it all right for politicians to be intentionally vague so that their message has broad appeal? Or consider my son's genuine desire to allay the fears of the flying public. The theory claims Jim will be more effective by presenting a soft-sell message at mid scale rather than stating his genuine conviction that flying is safer than driving. Are these choices you want to make, or want others to make when they try to influence you?

CRITIQUE: A THEORY WELL WITHIN THE LATITUDE OF ACCEPTANCE

The social norm campaign on alcohol consumption and the college fundraiser's appeal for a generous contribution demonstrate that social judgment theory has *practical utility*—one of the six criteria of a good scientific theory. The trick for the influence practitioner is figuring out where the other person's latitudes of acceptance, noncommitment, and rejection lie. That's what audience analysis, market research, and focus groups are all about, but it's hard to imagine Jim handing a questionnaire to every jittery traveler in the departure lounge.

Social judgment theory offers specific *predictions* about what happens in the mind of someone who hears or reads a message that falls within his or her latitude of acceptance or rejection. Sherif's appeal to the perceptual distortions of assimilation and contrast, as well as the crucial role of ego-involvement, offer a compelling *explanation* of what goes on behind the eyes. Yet like all cognitive explanations put forth in this section of the book, these mental structures and processes can't be seen. We can only infer what's going on inside the head by observing the input and the output—the message and a person's response. The SJT explanation of persuasion is complex, but given Sherif's claim that an attitude can't be identified by a single point on a continuum, it's hard to imagine a *simpler* account of what's happening.

As the studies I've described demonstrate, social judgment theory requires *quantitative research,* and that's the kind social scientists have designed. But compared to the hundreds of empirical studies run to test and refine other leading theories of persuasion, the research base of SJT is relatively small. That may be because it's hard to locate a wide range of experimental subjects who run the gamut of high to low ego-involvement and hold widely different opinions on the same topic. And once they are willing to participate, the process of locating their three latitudes can be tedious for everyone involved. Even so, specific predictions of SJT are *testable;* some have been supported and a few found to fail. For example, Bochner and Insko's sleep experiment confirms that as long as a message remains outside people's latitudes of rejection, the more discrepant it is from the anchor, the greater the attitude shift in the desired direction will be. On the other hand, the boomerang effect that SJT predicts can happen when a message is delivered in the latitude of rejection is not often found. (Students who read the bizarre claim that the body thrives with zero hours of sleep per night didn't then decide that eight hours were too few.)

Despite the questions that surround social judgment theory, it is an elegant conception of the persuasion process that falls well within my latitude of acceptance. There's an intuitive appeal to the idea of crafting a message just short of the latitude of rejection in order to be as effectively discrepant as possible. That would be my message to Jim as he confronts a variety of air travelers. I wonder in what latitude of attitude my advice will fall?

QUESTIONS TO SHARPEN YOUR FOCUS

1. How does the concept of *attitudes as latitudes* help you understand your attitude toward the various requirements of this course?
2. Suppose you find out that the fellow sitting next to you is *highly ego-involved* in the issue of gun control. Based on social judgment theory, what three predictions about his attitude structure would be reasonable to make?

3. What practical advice does social judgment theory offer if you want to ask your boss for a raise?
4. Do you have any *ethical qualms* about applying the wisdom of social judgment theory? Why or why not?

A SECOND LOOK

Recommended resources: Donald Granberg, "Social Judgment Theory," in *Communication Yearbook 6,* Michael Burgoon (ed.), Sage, Beverly Hills, CA, 1982, pp. 304–329; Daniel J. O'Keefe, "Social Judgment Theory," in *Persuasion: Theory and Research,* Sage, Newbury Park, CA, 1990, pp. 29–44.

Original conception: Muzafer Sherif and Carl Hovland, *Social Judgment: Assimilation and Contrast Effects in Communication and Attitude Change,* Yale University, New Haven, CT, 1961.

Further development: Carolyn Sherif, Muzafer Sherif, and Roger Nebergall, *Attitude and Attitude Change: The Social Judgment–Involvement Approach,* W. B. Saunders, Philadelphia, PA, 1965.

Attitudes as latitudes: Kenneth Sereno and Edward Bodaken, "Ego-Involvement and Attitude Change: Toward a Reconceptualization of Persuasive Effect," *Speech Monographs,* Vol. 39, 1972, pp. 151–158.

Ego-involvement: William W. Wilmot, "Ego-Involvement: A Confusing Variable in Speech Communication Research," *Quarterly Journal of Speech,* Vol. 57, 1971, pp. 429–436.

Assimilation and contrast: Alison Ledgerwood and Shelly Chaiken, "Priming Us and Them: Automatic Assimilation and Contrast in Group Attitudes," *Journal of Personality and Social Psychology,* Vol. 93, 2007, pp. 940–956.

Message discrepancy: Stan Kaplowitz and Edward Fink, "Message Discrepancy and Persuasion," in *Progress in Communication Sciences: Advances in Persuasion, Vol. 13,* George Barnett and Frank Boster (eds.), Ablex, Greenwich, CT, 1997, pp. 75–106.

Boomerang effect: Hilobumi Sakaki, "Experimental Studies of Boomerang Effects Following Persuasive Communication," *Psychologia,* Vol. 27, No. 2, 1984, pp. 84–88.

Sleep study: Stephen Bochner and Chester Insko, "Communicator Discrepancy, Source Credibility and Opinion Change," *Journal of Personality and Social Psychology,* Vol. 4, 1966, pp. 614–621.

Changing social norms for drinking on campus: Sandi Smith, Charles Atkin, Dennis Martell, Rebecca Allen, and Larry Hembroff, "A Social Judgment Theory Approach to Conducting Formative Research in a Social Norms Campaign," *Communication Theory,* Vol. 16, 2006, pp. 141–152.

Critique: Hee Sun Park, Timothy Levine, Catherine Y. K. Waterman, Tierney Oregon, and Sarah Forager, "The Effects of Argument Quality and Involvement Type on Attitude Formation and Attitude Change," *Human Communication Research,* Vol. 33, 2007, pp. 81–102.

CHAPTER 15

Objective — Interpretive

Socio-psychological tradition

Elaboration Likelihood Model

of Richard Petty & John Cacioppo

Like a number of women whose children are out of the home, Rita Francisco has gone back to college. Her program isn't an aimless sampling of classes to fill empty hours—she has enrolled in every course that will help her become a more persuasive advocate. Rita is a woman on a mission.

Rita's teenage daughter was killed when the car she was riding in smashed into a stone wall. After drinking three cans of beer at a party, the girl's 18-year-old boyfriend lost control on a curve while driving 80 miles per hour. Rita's son walks with a permanent limp as a result of injuries sustained when a high school girl plowed through the parking lot of a 7-Eleven on a Friday night. When the county prosecutor obtained a DUI (driving under the influence) conviction, it only fueled Rita's resolve to get young drinking drivers off the road. She has become active with Mothers Against Drunk Driving and works to convince anyone who will listen that zero-tolerance laws, which make it illegal for drivers under the age of 21 to have *any* measurable amount of alcohol in their system, should be strictly enforced. Rita also wants to persuade others that young adults caught driving with more than 0.02 percent blood alcohol content should automatically lose their driver's licenses until they are 21.

This is a tough sell on most college campuses. While her classmates can appreciate the tragic reasons underlying her fervor, few subscribe to what they believe is a drastic solution. As a nontraditional, older student, Rita realizes that her younger classmates could easily dismiss her campaign as the ranting of a hysterical parent. She's determined to develop the most effective persuasive strategy possible and wonders if she would have the most success by presenting well-reasoned arguments for enforcing zero-tolerance laws. Then again, couldn't she sway students more by lining up highly credible people to endorse her proposal?

THE CENTRAL AND PERIPHERAL ROUTES TO PERSUASION

Ohio State psychologist Richard Petty thinks Rita is asking the right questions. He conducted his Ph.D. dissertation study using the topic of teenage driving to test the relative effectiveness of strong-message arguments and high source credibility. He found that the results varied depending on which of two mental routes to attitude change a *listener* happened to use. Petty labeled the two cognitive processes the *central route* and the *peripheral route.* He sees the distinction as helpful in reconciling much of the conflicting data of persuasion research. Along with his University of Chicago colleague John Cacioppo, he launched an intensive program of study to discover the best way for a persuader to activate each route.

Central route
Message elaboration; the path of cognitive processing that involves scrutiny of message content.

The central route involves message elaboration. Elaboration is "the extent to which a person carefully thinks about issue-relevant arguments contained in a persuasive communication."[1] In an attempt to process new information rationally, people using the central route carefully scrutinize the ideas, try to figure out if they have true merit, and mull over their implications. Similar to Berger's characterization of strategic message plans, elaboration requires high levels of cognitive effort (see Chapter 9).

Message elaboration
The extent to which a person carefully thinks about issue-relevant arguments contained in a persuasive communication.

The peripheral route offers a mental shortcut path to accepting or rejecting a message "without any active thinking about the attributes of the issue or the object of consideration."[2] Instead of doing extensive cognitive work, recipients rely on a variety of cues that allow them to make quick decisions. Robert Cialdini of Arizona State University lists six cues that trigger a "click, whirr" programmed response.[3] These cues allow people hearing a persuasive appeal to fly the peripheral route on automatic pilot:

1. Reciprocation—"You owe me."
2. Consistency—"We've always done it that way."
3. Social proof—"Everybody's doing it."
4. Liking—"Love me, love my ideas."
5. Authority—"Just because I say so."
6. Scarcity—"Quick, before they're all gone."

Peripheral route
A mental shortcut process that accepts or rejects a message based on irrelevant cues as opposed to actively thinking about the issue.

Figure 15–1 shows a simplified version of Petty and Cacioppo's elaboration likelihood model (ELM) as it applies to Rita's situation. Although their model's twin-route metaphor seems to suggest two mutually exclusive paths to persuasion, the theorists stress that the central route and the peripheral route are poles on a cognitive processing continuum that shows the degree of mental effort a person exerts when evaluating a message.[4] The elaboration scale at the top represents effortful scrutiny of arguments on the left-hand side and mindless reliance on noncontent cues on the right. Most messages receive middle-ground attention between these poles, but there's always a trade-off. The more Rita's listeners work to discern the merits of strict zero-tolerance enforcement, the less they'll be influenced by peripheral factors such as their friends' scoffing laughter at her suggestion. Conversely, the more her hearers are affected by content-irrelevant factors such as Rita's age, accent, or appearance, the less they will be affected by her ideas. We'll work down the model one level at a time in order to understand Petty and Cacioppo's predictions about the likelihood of Rita's message being scrutinized by students at her college.

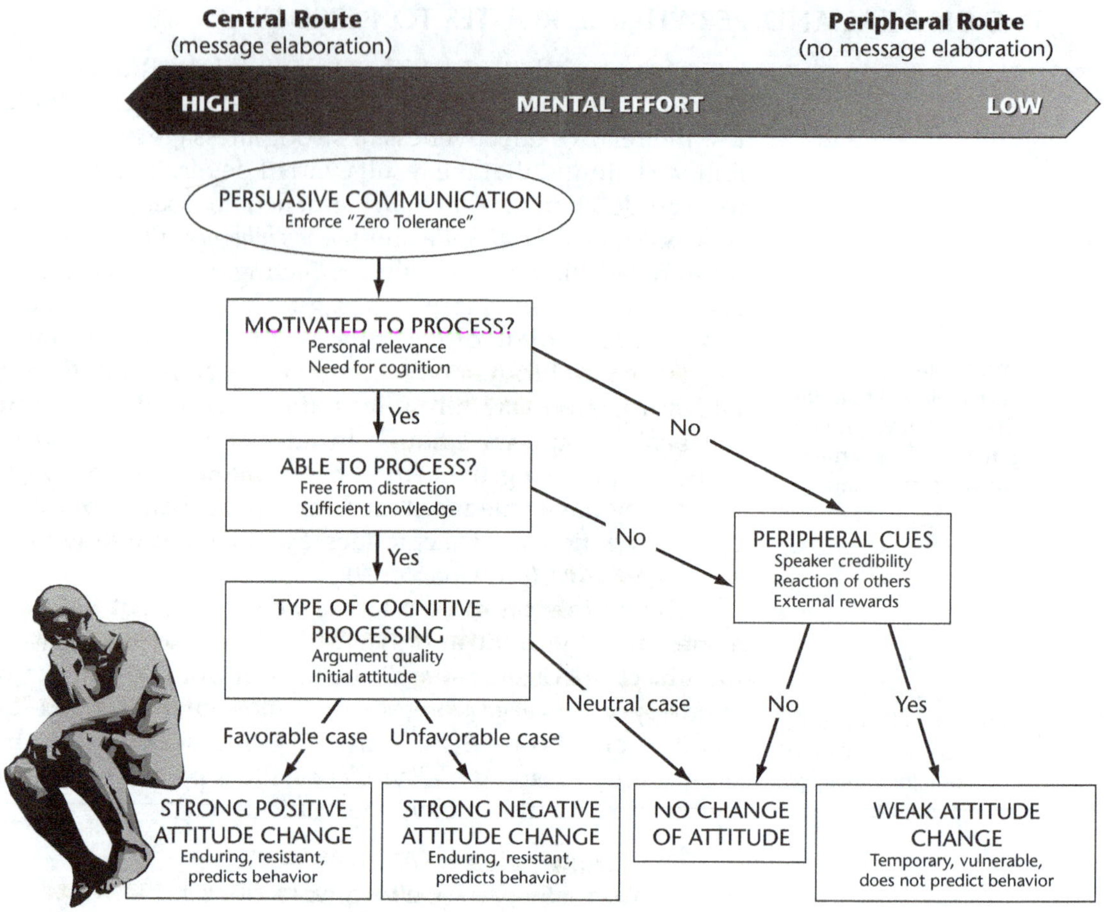

FIGURE 15–1 The Elaboration Likelihood Model

Adapted from Petty and Cacioppo, "The Elaboration Likelihood Model: Current Status and Controversies"

MOTIVATION FOR ELABORATION: IS IT WORTH THE EFFORT?

Petty and Cacioppo assume that people are motivated to hold correct attitudes. The authors admit that we aren't always logical, but they think we make a good effort not to kid ourselves in our search for truth. We want to maintain reasonable positions.

But a person can examine only a limited number of ideas. We are exposed to so many persuasive messages that we would experience a tremendous information overload if we tried to interact with every variant idea we heard or read about. The only way to solve this problem is by being "lazy" toward most issues in life. Petty and Cacioppo claim we have a large-mesh mental filter that allows items we regard as less important to flow through without being carefully processed. But statements about things that are personally relevant get trapped and tested. In the terminology of social judgment theory (see Chapter 14), we're motivated to elaborate only ideas with which we are highly ego-involved.

There are few things in life more important to young Americans than the right to drive. A license is the closest thing our society has to an adolescent rite of passage; for some it is a passport to freedom. It seems unlikely, therefore, that students would regard Rita's zero-tolerance proposal as trivial. Yet threatening the loss of license may have less personal relevance to students who don't drink, or to those who already make sure they don't drive when they drink. And if students over 21 aren't worried about who's driving on the road, they too may feel that Rita's proposal has little to do with them. So ELM's authors would regard teenage students who drive after drinking a few beers as especially motivated to grapple with arguments about automatic driver's license suspension.

Petty and Cacioppo maintain that as long as people have a personal stake in accepting or rejecting an idea, they will be much more influenced by what a message says than by the characteristics of the person who says it. But when a topic is no longer relevant, it gets sidetracked to the periphery of the mind, where credibility cues take on greater importance. Without the motivation of personal relevance, there probably will be little elaboration.

The theorists do recognize, however, that some people have a need for cognitive clarity, regardless of the issue. In fact, they've developed a *Need for Cognition Scale* to identify individuals who are most likely to carefully consider message arguments.[5] Four of the items state:

Need for cognition
Desire for cognitive clarity; an enjoyment of thinking through ideas even when they aren't personally relevant.

I really enjoy a task that involves coming up with new solutions to problems.

I prefer my life to be filled with puzzles that I must solve.

I like tasks that require little thought once I've learned them.

Thinking is not my idea of fun.

If you substantially agree with the first two statements and take issue with the last two, Petty and Cacioppo would anticipate that you'd be a person who works through many of the ideas and arguments you hear.

ABILITY FOR ELABORATION: CAN THEY DO IT?

Once people have shown an inclination to think about the content of a message (motivation), the next issue is whether they are *able* to do so. Since Rita's immediate audience consists of young men and women who have duly impressed a college admissions officer with their ability to think, you would imagine that the question of ability would be moot. But issue-relevant thinking (elaboration) takes more than intelligence. It also requires concentration.

Distraction disrupts elaboration. Rita's classmates will be hard-pressed to think about her point of view if it's expressed amid the din of a student union snack bar where you can't hear yourself think. Or perhaps she presents her solution for highway safety when students are trying to concentrate on something else—an upcoming exam, a letter from home, or a mental replay of the winning shot in an intramural basketball game.

Rita may face the same challenge as television advertisers who have only the fleeting attention of viewers. Like them, Rita can use repetition to ensure that her main point comes across, but too much commotion will short-circuit a reasoned consideration of the message, no matter how much repetition is used. In that case, students will use the peripheral route and judge the message by cues that indicate whether Rita is a competent and trustworthy person.

TYPE OF ELABORATION: OBJECTIVE VERSUS BIASED THINKING

As you can see from the downward flow in the central path of their model (Figure 15–1), Petty and Cacioppo believe motivation and ability strongly increase the likelihood that a message will be elaborated in the minds of listeners. Yet as social judgment theory suggests, they may not process the information in a fair and objective manner. Rita might have the undivided attention of students who care deeply about the right to drive, but discover that they've already built up an organized structure of knowledge concerning the issue.

When Rita claims that the alcohol-related fatal crash rate for young drivers is double that of drivers over 21, a student may counter with the fact that teenagers drive twice as many miles and are therefore just as safe as adults. Whether or not the statistics are true or the argument is valid isn't the issue. The point is that those who have already thought a lot about drinking and driving safety will probably have made up their minds and be biased in the way they process Rita's message.

Biased elaboration
Top-down thinking in which predetermined conclusions color the supporting data.

Petty and Cacioppo refer to biased elaboration as top-down thinking in which a predetermined conclusion colors the supporting data underneath. They contrast this with objective elaboration, or bottom-up thinking, which lets facts speak for themselves. Biased elaboration merely bolsters previous ideas.

Objective elaboration
Bottom-up thinking in which facts are scrutinized without bias; seeking truth wherever it might lead.

Perhaps you've seen a picture of Rodin's famous statue *The Thinker,* a man sitting with his head propped in one hand. If the thinker already has a set of beliefs to contemplate, Petty and Cacioppo's research shows that additional thought will merely fix them in stone. Rita shouldn't assume that audience elaboration will always help her cause; it depends on whether it's biased elaboration or objective elaboration. It also depends on the quality of her arguments.

ELABORATED ARGUMENTS: STRONG, WEAK, AND NEUTRAL

If Rita manages to win an unbiased hearing from students at her school, Petty and Cacioppo say her cause will rise or fall on the perceived strength of her arguments. The two theorists have no absolute standard for what distinguishes a cogent argument from one that's specious. They simply define a strong message as one that generates favorable thoughts when it's heard and scrutinized.

Strong arguments
Claims that generate favorable thoughts when examined.

Petty and Cacioppo predict that thoughtful consideration of strong arguments will produce major shifts in attitude in the direction desired by the persuader. Suppose Rita states the following:

> National Safety Council statistics show that drivers in the 16–20 age group account for 15 percent of the miles driven in the United States, yet they are responsible for 25 percent of the highway deaths that involve alcohol.

This evidence could give students cause for pause. They may not be comfortable with the facts, but some of them might find the statistics compelling and a reason to reconsider their stance. According to ELM, the enhanced thinking of those who respond favorably will cause their change in position to *persist over time, resist counterpersuasion,* and *predict future behavior*—the "triple crown" of interpersonal influence.

However, persuasive attempts that are processed through the central route can have dramatically negative effects as well. If, despite her strong convictions, Rita isn't able to come up with a strong argument for changing the current law, her persuasive attempt might actually backfire. For example, suppose she makes this argument:

> When underage drinkers are arrested for violating zero-tolerance rules of the road, automatic suspension of their licenses would allow the secretary of state's office to reduce its backlog of work. This would give government officials time to check driving records so that they could keep dangerous motorists off the road.

This weak argument is guaranteed to offend the sensibilities of anyone who thinks about it. Rather than compelling listeners to enlist in Rita's cause, it will only give them a reason to oppose her point of view more vigorously. The elaborated idea will cause a boomerang effect that will last over time, defy other efforts to change it, and affect subsequent behavior. These are the same significant effects that the elaborated strong argument produces, but in the opposite direction.

Rita's ideas could also produce an ambivalent reaction. Listeners who carefully examine her ideas may end up feeling neither pro nor con toward her evidence. Their neutral or mixed response obviously means that they won't change their attitudes as a result of processing through the central route. For them, thinking about the pros and cons of the issue reinforces their original attitudes, whatever they may be.

PERIPHERAL CUES: AN ALTERNATIVE ROUTE OF INFLUENCE

Although the majority of this chapter has dealt with the central cognitive route to attitude change, most messages are processed on the less-effortful peripheral path. Signposts along the way direct the hearer to favor or oppose the persuader's point of view without ever engaging in what Petty and Cacioppo call "issue-relevant thinking."[6] There is no inner dialogue about the merits of the proposal.

As explained earlier, the hearer who uses the peripheral route relies on a variety of cues as an aid in reaching a quick decision. The most obvious cues are tangible rewards linked to agreement with the advocate's position. Food, sex, and money are traditional inducements to change. I once overheard the conclusion of a transaction between a young man and a college senior who was trying to persuade him to donate blood in order to fulfill her class assignment. "Ok, it's agreed," she said. "You give blood for me today, and I'll have you over to my place for dinner tomorrow night." Although this type of social exchange has been going on for centuries, Petty and Cacioppo would still describe it as peripheral. Public compliance to the request for blood? Yes. Private acceptance of its importance? Not likely.

For many students of persuasion, source credibility is the most interesting cue on the peripheral route. Four decades of research confirm that people who are likable and have expertise on the issue in question can have a persuasive impact regardless of what arguments they present. Rita's appearance, manner of talking, and background credentials will speak so loudly that some students won't really hear what she says. Which students? According to Petty and Cacioppo, those students who are unmotivated or unable to scrutinize her message and therefore switch to the peripheral path.

Listeners who believe that Rita's twin tragedies have given her wisdom beyond their own will shift to a position more sympathetic to her point of view. The same holds true for those who see her as pleasant and warm. But there are students who will regard her grammatical mistakes as a sign of ignorance, or they'll be turned off by a maternal manner that reminds them of a lecture from mom. These peripheral route critics will become more skeptical of Rita's position.

"In the interest of streamlining the judicial process, we'll skip the evidence and go directly to sentencing."

Note that attitude change on this outside track can be either positive or negative, but it lacks the robust persistence, invulnerability, or link to behavior we see in change that comes from message elaboration.

Nicely illustrating the fragility of peripheral route change, Holly wrote the following entry in her application log:

> In his short story "Salvation," Langston Hughes recounts his childhood experience at a religious revival in his town. For days the old ladies of the church had been praying for the conversion of all the "little lambs" of the congregation. After working the congregation to a fever pitch, the preacher gave an altar call aimed at the children, and one after another they cried and went forward to be saved from hell. The author and his friend didn't feel anything, but after what seemed like forever, his friend went up so all the hubbub would finally stop. Langston knew that his friend hadn't really been converted, but since God didn't smite him for lying, he figured it would be safe for him to fake it as well, which he did. When the revival was over, the congregation calmed down and everyone went home praising the Lord. Langston says that was the day he stopped believing in God.

The preacher relied on peripheral cues. Langston went forward because of the expectation of authority figures, heightened emotion, and conformity pressure. But there was no elaboration of the message, no grappling with the issue, and certainly no encounter with God. The result of this peripheral route processing was as ELM predicts—his "salvation" didn't even last through the night.

PUSHING THE LIMITS OF PERIPHERAL POWER

Understanding the importance of role models for persuasion, Rita scans the pages of *Rolling Stone* to see if singer Dave Matthews might have said something about teenage drivers. The music of the Dave Matthews Band is widely acclaimed by students at her college, and Matthews recently put on a live concert near the school. By somehow associating her message with credible people, she can achieve change in many students' attitudes. But it probably won't last long, stand up to attack, or affect their behavior. Petty and Cacioppo say a fragile change is all that can be expected through the peripheral route.

Yet what if Dave Matthews' tour bus were run off the road by a drunk teenage fan, and a band member met the same fate as Rita's daughter? Would that tragic death and Matthews' avowal that "friends don't let friends drive drunk" cue students to a permanent shift in attitude and behavior? Fortunately, the band is still intact, but a high-profile tragedy in the sports world suggests that even the effect of powerful peripheral cues is short-lived at best.

In 1991, basketball superstar Magic Johnson held a candid press conference to announce that he had tested positive for HIV. At the time, such a diagnosis seemed like a death sentence; the story dominated network news coverage for days. University of South Florida psychologists Louis Penner and Barbara Fritzsche had just completed a study showing that many people had little sympathy for AIDS victims who had contracted the disease through sexual transmission. When asked to volunteer a few hours to help a patient stay in school, a little more than half of the women and none of the men in the study volunteered. Penner and Fritzsche extended their study when they heard of Magic Johnson's illness.[7] They wondered if the tragedy that had befallen this popular star and his pledge to become an advocate for those with the disease would cause students to react more positively toward people with AIDS.

For a while it did. The week after Johnson's announcement, 80 percent of the men offered assistance. That number tapered off to 30 percent, however, within a few months. The proportion of women helping dipped below 40 percent in the same period. Penner and Fritzsche observed that people didn't grapple with the substance of Magic Johnson's message; rather, they paid attention to the man who was presenting it. Consistent with ELM's main thesis, the researchers concluded that "changes that occur because of 'peripheral cues' such as . . . being a well liked celebrity are less permanent than those that occur because of the substantive content of the persuasion attempt."[8]

Penner and Fritzsche could have added that the effects of star performer endorsements are subject to the sharp ups and downs of celebrity status. For example, the Dave Matthews Band has been so environmentally green that a Ben and Jerry's flavor of ice cream was named after one of the band's songs. Yet that image was besmirched when their tour bus dumped 80 gallons of human waste through a grated bridge over the Chicago River. Much of the foul-smelling sewage doused tourists having dinner on the deck of a sightseeing boat passing under the bridge. So any comment by Matthews on safe and sane driving might be treated with derision rather than help Rita's cause.[9] Nike feared the same reaction when Tiger Woods publicly fell from grace.

Although most ELM research has measured the effects of peripheral cues by studying credibility, a speaker's competence or character could also be a stimulus for effortful message elaboration. For example, the high regard that millions of sports fans had for Magic Johnson might for the first time have made it possible to scrutinize proposals for the prevention and treatment of AIDS without a moral stigma biasing each idea. Or the fact that Johnson's magic wasn't strong enough to repel HIV might cause someone to think deeply, "If it happened to a guy like Magic, it could happen to me." Even though Figure 15–1 identifies *speaker credibility, reaction of others,* and *external rewards* as variables that promote mindless acceptance via the peripheral route, Petty and Cacioppo emphasize that it's impossible to compile a list of cues that are strictly peripheral.[10]

Speaker credibility
Audience perception of the message source's expertise, character, and dynamism; typically a peripheral cue.

To illustrate this point, consider the multiple roles that the *mood* of the person listening to Rita's message might play in her attempt to persuade. Rita assumes that her classmate Sam will be a more sympathetic audience if she can present her ideas when he's in a good mood. And she's right, as long as Sam processes her message through the peripheral route without thinking too hard about what she's saying. His positive outlook prompts him to see her proposal in a favorable light.

Yet if Sam is somewhat willing and able to work through her arguments (moderate elaboration), his upbeat mood could actually turn out to be a disadvantage. He was feeling up, but he becomes depressed when he thinks about the death and disfigurement Rita describes. The loss of warm feelings could bias him against Rita's arguments. Petty suggests that Sam might process her arguments more objectively if his original mood had matched the downbeat nature of Rita's experience.[11] Many variables like *perceived credibility* or the *mood of the listener* can act as peripheral cues. Yet if one of them motivates listeners to scrutinize the message or affects their evaluation of arguments, it no longer serves as a no-brainer. There is no variable that's always a shortcut on the peripheral route.

CHOOSING A ROUTE: PRACTICAL ADVICE FOR THE PERSUADER

Petty and Cacioppo's advice for Rita (and the rest of us) is clear. She needs to determine the likelihood that her listeners will give their undivided attention to evaluating her proposal. If it appears that they have the motivation and ability to elaborate the message, she had best come armed with facts and figures to support her case. A pleasant smile, an emotional appeal, or the loss of her daughter won't make any difference.

Since it's only by thoughtful consideration that her listeners can experience a lasting change in attitude, Rita probably hopes they can go the central route. But even if they do, it's still difficult to build a compelling persuasive case. If she fails to do her homework and presents weak arguments, the people who are ready to think will shift their attitude to a more antagonistic position.

If Rita determines that her hearers are unable or unwilling to think through the details of her plan, she'll be more successful choosing a delivery strategy that emphasizes the package rather than the contents. This could include a heartrending account of her daughter's death, a smooth presentation, and an ongoing effort to build friendships with the students. Perhaps bringing homemade cookies to class or offering rides to the mall would aid in making her an attractive source. But as we've already seen, the effects will probably be temporary.

It's not likely that Rita will get many people to elaborate her message in a way that ends up favorable for her cause. Most persuaders avoid the central route because the audience won't go with them or they find it too difficult to generate compelling arguments. But Rita really doesn't have a choice.

Driver's licenses (and perhaps beer) are so important to most of these students that they'll be ready to dissect every part of her plan. They won't be won over by a friendly smile. Rita will have to develop thoughtful and well-reasoned arguments if she is to change their minds. Given the depth of her conviction, she thinks it's worth a try.

ETHICAL REFLECTION: NILSEN'S SIGNIFICANT CHOICE

ELM describes persuasion that's effective. University of Washington professor emeritus Thomas Nilsen is concerned with what's ethical. Consistent with the democratic values of a free society, he proposes that persuasive speech is ethical to the extent that it maximizes people's ability to exercise free choice. Since many political, religious, and commercial messages are routinely designed to bypass rather than appeal to a listener's rational faculties, Nilsen upholds the value of significant choice in unequivocal terms:

> When we communicate to influence the attitudes, beliefs, and actions of others, the ethical touchstone is the degree of free, informed, rational and critical choice—significant choice—that is fostered by our speaking.[12]

For Nilsen, truly free choice is the test of ethical influence because "only a self-determining being can be a moral being; without significant choice, there is no morality."[13] To support his claim, he cites two classic essays on the freedom of speech. John Milton's *Areopagitica*[14] argues against prior restraint of any ideas, no matter how heretical. John Stuart Mill's *On Liberty*[15] advocates a free marketplace of ideas because the only way to test an argument is to hear it presented by a true believer who defends it in earnest.

Philosophers and rhetoricians have compared persuasion to a lover making fervent appeals to his beloved—wooing an audience, for example. Nilsen's ethic of significant choice is nicely captured in the courtship analogy because true love cannot be coerced; it must be freely given. Inspired by Danish philosopher Søren Kierkegaard's description of the ethical religious persuader as lover,[16] I have elsewhere presented a typology of false (unethical) lovers:[17]

> *Smother lovers* won't take no for an answer; their persistence is obnoxious.
> *Legalistic lovers* have a set image of what the other should be.
> *Flirts* are in love with love; they value response, not the other person.

Seducers try deception and flattery to entice the other to submit.
Rapists use force of threats, guilt, or conformity pressure to have their way.

In differing degrees, all five types of unethical persuader violate the human dignity of the people they pursue by taking away choice that is informed and free.

Nilsen obviously would approve of persuasive appeals that encourage message elaboration through ELM's central route. But his standard of significant choice is not always easy to apply. Do emotional appeals seductively short-circuit our ability to make rational choices, or does heightened emotion actually free us to consider new options? Significant choice, like beauty and credibility, may be in the eye of the beholder.

CRITIQUE: ELABORATING THE MODEL

For the last 20 years, ELM has been a leading, if not *the* leading, theory of persuasion and attitude change. Petty, Cacioppo, and their students have published more than 100 articles on the model, and the dual-process conception has stimulated additional research, application, and critique that go beyond what I'm able to capture in a short chapter. Since the time they introduced the theory, Petty and Cacioppo have made it more complex, less predictive, and less able to offer definitive advice to the influence practitioner. This is not the direction in which a scientific theory wants to go.

Arizona State University communication researcher Paul Mongeau and communication consultant James Stiff illustrate one of the specific problems with the theory when they charge that "descriptions of the ELM are sufficiently imprecise and ambiguous as to prevent an adequate test of the entire model."[18] For example, ELM views strong arguments as strong if people are persuaded, but weak if folks remain unmoved. There's no way apart from the persuasive outcome to know whether an argument is strong or weak. Like my childhood friend described in Chapter 3, ELM seems to have its own "never-miss shot." Petty and Cacioppo would say that they never intended to focus on defining factors like strong and weak arguments, high and low source credibility, or highly attractive or unattractive persuaders.[19] That may be true, but it doesn't help much in testing the theory. Objective theories that can't be clearly tested lose some of their luster.

Despite the criticisms, ELM is impressive because it pulls together and makes sense out of diverse research results that have puzzled communication theorists for years. For example, why do most people pay less attention to the communication than they do to the communicator? And if speaker credibility is so important, why does its effect dissipate so quickly? ELM's explanation is that few listeners are motivated and able to do the mental work required for a major shift in attitude. The two-path hypothesis also helps clarify why good evidence and reasoning can sometimes have a life-changing impact, but usually make no difference at all.

Attitude-change research often yields results that seem confusing or contradictory. Petty and Cacioppo's ELM takes many disjointed findings and pulls them together into a unified whole. This integrative function makes it a valuable theory of influence.

QUESTIONS TO SHARPEN YOUR FOCUS

1. Can you think of five different words or phrases that capture the idea of *message elaboration?*
2. What *peripheral cues* do you usually monitor when someone is trying to influence you?
3. Petty and Cacioppo want to persuade you that their elaboration likelihood model is a mirror of reality. Do you process their arguments for its accuracy closer to your *central route* or your *peripheral route?* Why not the other way?
4. Students of persuasion often wonder whether *high credibility* or *strong arguments* sway people more. How would ELM theorists respond to that question?

A SECOND LOOK

Recommended resource: Richard E. Petty, John T. Cacioppo, Alan J. Strathman, and Joseph R. Priester, "To Think or Not to Think: Exploring Two Routes to Persuasion," in *Persuasion: Psychological Insights and Perspectives,* 2nd ed., Timothy Brock and Melanie Green (eds.), Sage, Thousand Oaks, CA, 2005, pp. 81–116.

Full statement: Richard E. Petty and John T. Cacioppo, *Communication and Persuasion: Central and Peripheral Routes to Attitude Change,* Springer-Verlag, New York, 1986.

Major developments in the history of ELM: Richard E. Petty and Pablo Briñol, "The Elaboration Likelihood Model," in *Handbook of Theories of Social Psychology, Vol. 1,* Paul van Lange and Arie Kruglanski (eds.), Sage, London, England, 2012, pp. 224–245.

Effect of involvement: Richard E. Petty and John T. Cacioppo, "Involvement and Persuasion: Tradition Versus Integration," *Psychological Bulletin,* Vol. 107, 1990, pp. 367–374.

Postulates and research: Richard E. Petty and John T. Cacioppo, "The Elaboration Likelihood Model of Persuasion," in *Advances in Experimental Social Psychology, Vol. 19,* Leonard Berkowitz (ed.), Academic Press, Orlando, FL, 1986, pp. 124–205.

Message arguments versus source credibility: Richard E. Petty, John T. Cacioppo, and R. Goldman, "Personal Involvement as a Determinant of Argument-Based Persuasion," *Journal of Personality and Social Psychology,* Vol. 41, 1981, pp. 847–855.

Effects of evidence: John Reinard, "The Empirical Study of the Persuasive Effects of Evidence: The Status After Fifty Years of Research," *Human Communication Research,* Vol. 15, 1988, pp. 3–59.

Effects of credibility: Richard E. Petty, "Multiple Roles for Source Credibility Under High Elaboration: It's All in the Timing," *Social Cognition,* Vol. 25, 2007, pp. 536–552.

Mindless cues: Robert B. Cialdini, *Influence: Science and Practice,* 4th ed., Allyn and Bacon, Needham Heights, MA, 2001.

Cues that affect elaboration: Duane Wegener and Richard E. Petty, "Understanding Effects of Mood Through the Elaboration Likelihood and Flexible Correction Models," in *Theories of Mood and Cognition: A User's Guidebook,* L. L. Martin and G. L. Clore (eds.), Lawrence Erlbaum, Mahwah, NJ, 2001, pp. 177–210.

Status and controversies: Richard E. Petty and Duane Wegener, "The Elaboration Likelihood Model: Current Status and Controversies," in Shelly Chaiken and Yaacov Trope (eds.), *Dual Process Theories in Social Psychology,* Guilford, New York, 1999, pp. 41–72.

Critiques of ELM: "Forum: Specifying the ELM," *Communication Theory,* Vol. 3, 1993. (Paul Mongeau and James Stiff, "Specifying Causal Relationships in the Elaboration Likelihood Model," pp. 65–72; Mike Allen and Rodney Reynolds, "The Elaboration Likelihood Model and the Sleeper Effect: An Assessment of Attitude Change over Time," pp. 73–82.)

CHAPTER 16

Objective — Interpretive

Socio-psychological tradition

Cognitive Dissonance Theory

of Leon Festinger

Aesop told a story about a fox that tried in vain to reach a cluster of grapes dangling from a vine above his head. The fox leaped high to grasp the grapes, but the delicious-looking fruit remained just out of reach of his snapping jaws. After a few attempts the fox gave up and said to himself, "These grapes are sour, and if I had some I would not eat them."[1]

DISSONANCE: DISCORD BETWEEN BEHAVIOR AND BELIEF

Aesop's fable is the source of the phrase *sour grapes*. The story illustrates what former Stanford University social psychologist Leon Festinger called *cognitive dissonance*. It is the distressing mental state that people feel when they "find themselves doing things that don't fit with what they know, or having opinions that do not fit with other opinions they hold."[2]

Cognitive dissonance
The distressing mental state caused by inconsistency between a person's two beliefs or a belief and an action.

The fox's retreat from the grape arbor clashed with his knowledge that the grapes were tasty. By changing his attitude toward the grapes, he provided an acceptable explanation for abandoning his efforts to reach them.

Festinger considered the need to avoid dissonance to be just as basic as the need for safety or the need to satisfy hunger. It is an *aversive drive* that goads us to be consistent. The tension of dissonance motivates us to change either our behavior or our belief in an effort to avoid that distressing feeling. The more important the issue and the greater the discrepancy between our behavior and our belief, the higher the magnitude of dissonance we will feel. In extreme cases cognitive dissonance is like our cringing response to fingernails being scraped on a blackboard—we'll do anything to get away from the awful sound.

HEALTH-CONSCIOUS SMOKERS: DEALING WITH DISSONANCE

When Festinger first published his theory in 1957, he chose the topic of smoking to illustrate the concept of dissonance. Although authoritative medical reports on the link between smoking and lung cancer were just beginning to surface, there was already general concern across the United States that cigarette smoking might cause cancer. Ten years prior, country-and-western singer Tex Williams recorded Capitol Records' first million-seller, "Smoke! Smoke! Smoke! (That Cigarette)." The gravelly voiced vocalist expressed doubt that smoking would affect his health, but the chorus was unambiguous:

> Smoke, smoke, smoke that cigarette
> Puff, puff, puff until you smoke yourself to death
> Tell St. Peter at the Golden Gate
> That you hate to make him wait
> But you just gotta have another cigarette.[3]

At the time, many smokers and nonsmokers alike laughingly referred to cigarettes as "coffin nails." But as the number and certainty of medical reports linking smoking with lung cancer, emphysema, and heart disease increased, humorous references to cigarettes no longer seemed funny. For the first time in their lives, a hundred million Americans had to grapple with two incompatible cognitions:

1. Smoking is dangerous to my health.
2. I smoke cigarettes.

Consider the plight of Cliff, a habitual smoker confronted by medical claims that smoking is hazardous to his health—an idea that strongly conflicts with his pack-a-day practice. Festinger said the contradiction is so clear and uncomfortable that something has to give—either the use of cigarettes or the belief that smoking will hurt him. "Whether the behavior or the cognition changes will be determined by which has the weakest resistance to change."[4] For Cliff it's no contest. He lights up and dismisses the health risk. In his discussion of smoking, Festinger suggested a number of mental gymnastics that Cliff might use to avoid dissonance while he smokes.[5]

Perhaps the most typical way for the smoker to avoid mental anguish is to trivialize or simply deny the link between smoking and cancer. *I think the research is sketchy, the results are mixed, and the warnings are based on junk science.* After the surgeon general's report on smoking was issued in 1964, denial became an uphill cognitive path to climb, but many smokers continue to go that route.

Smokers may counter thoughts of scary health consequences by reminding themselves of other effects they see as positive. *Smoking helps me relax, I like the taste, and it gives me a look of sophistication.* These were the motives cigarette advertising appealed to when Festinger first published his theory. For example, Old Gold was the primary radio sponsor for Chicago Cubs baseball: "We're tobacco men, not medicine men," their ads proclaimed. "For a treat instead of a treatment, try Old Gold. . . . There's not a cough in a carload."

Although it's hard for smokers to pretend they aren't lighting up, they can elude nagging thoughts of trauma by telling themselves that the dire warnings don't apply to them since they are *moderate* smokers, or because they'll soon quit. *My boyfriend is a chain smoker, but I smoke less than a pack a day. As soon as I finish school, I'll have no problem stopping.* Conversely, other smokers manage dissonance by disclaiming any ongoing responsibility for a habit they can't kick. *Let's face it, cigarettes are addictive. I'm hooked.* To be sure, most behaviors are not as difficult to change as the habit of smoking, but Festinger noted that almost all of our actions are more entrenched than the thoughts we have about them. Thus, the focus of his theory is on the belief and attitude changes that take place because of cognitive dissonance.

REDUCING DISSONANCE BETWEEN ACTIONS AND ATTITUDES

Festinger hypothesized three mental mechanisms people use to ensure that their actions and attitudes are in harmony. Dissonance researchers refer to them as *selective exposure, postdecision dissonance,* and *minimal justification*. I'll continue to illustrate these cognitive processes by referring to the practice of smoking, but they are equally applicable to other forms of substance abuse or addiction—alcohol, drugs, food, sex, pornography, gambling, money, shopping, work. Most of us can spot at least one topic on that list where we struggle with an inconsistency between our thoughts and our actions. So if smoking isn't an issue for you, apply these ways of reducing dissonance in an area that is.

Hypothesis 1: Selective Exposure Prevents Dissonance

Selective exposure
The tendency people have to avoid information that would create cognitive dissonance because it's incompatible with their current beliefs.

Festinger claimed that people avoid information that's likely to increase dissonance.[6] This *selective exposure hypothesis* explains why staunch political conservatives watch Sean Hannity on Fox News whereas stalwart liberals catch Rachel Maddow on MSNBC. Not only do we tend to listen to opinions and select reading materials that are consistent with our existing beliefs, we usually choose to be with people who are like us. By taking care to "stick with our own kind," we can maintain the relative comfort of the status quo. Like-minded people buffer us from ideas that could cause discomfort. In that sense, the process of making friends is a way to select our own propaganda.

Two communication researchers looked back over 18 experiments where people were put in dissonant situations and then had to choose what kind of information they would listen to or read. Dave D'Alessio (University of Connecticut–Stamford) and Mike Allen (University of Wisconsin–Milwaukee) discovered that the results consistently supported the selective exposure hypothesis.[7] People tended to select information that lined up with what they already believed and ignored facts or ideas that ran counter to those beliefs. But the strength of this tendency was relatively small. Selective exposure explained only about 5 percent of why they chose the information they did. That leaves 95 percent unexplained.

That modest finding hasn't deterred the sponsors of two media persuasion campaigns from taking the power of selective exposure quite seriously. A University of California–San Francisco survey taken in 2006 documented that 75 percent of Hollywood films show attractive actors smoking, and that this modeling encourages young teens raised in smoke-free homes to adopt the practice. With some success, Harvard School of Public Health researchers are now proactively challenging directors not to introduce smoking into their films. Nevertheless, a follow-up study by the same University of California group found that smoking incidences increased by 36 percent in 2011 for movies rated PG-13 and below. That includes more than 50 smoking incidents apiece in hit movies such as *The Help*, *Rango*, and *X-Men: First Class*.[8]

Entertainment is a tried-and-true way to get around people's selective exposure filters. Another way is humor. The "Don't Pass Gas" broadcast campaign of the American Legacy Foundation uses barnyard comedy to convince the public of the intrusiveness of putrid gas. Presented in the style of a Dr. Seuss rhyme, one ad goes:

> I will not pass gas on a train. I will not pass gas on a plane.
> I will not pass gas in my house. I will not pass gas near my spouse.
> I will not pass gas in a bar. I will not pass gas in a car.
> I will not pass gas where little ones are, no matter how near or how far.
> I will not pass gas in your face, because the gas I pass is worse than mace.[9]

Only after listeners are either laughing or totally grossed out by the image of passing gas are they told that the limerick refers to secondhand smoke. It's a message most people would tune out had it not been for the use of humor with a twist.

German psychologist Dieter Frey surveyed all the pertinent research on selective exposure and concluded that even when we know we're going to hear discrepant ideas, the avoidance mechanism doesn't kick in if we don't regard the dissonant information as a threat.[10] Warm personal relationships are probably the best guarantee that we'll consider ideas that would otherwise seem threatening.

Hypothesis 2: Postdecision Dissonance Creates a Need for Reassurance

According to Festinger, close-call decisions can generate huge amounts of internal tension after the decision has been made. Three conditions heighten *postdecision dissonance:* (1) the more important the issue, (2) the longer an individual delays in choosing between two equally attractive options, and (3) the greater the difficulty involved in reversing the decision once it's been made. To the extent that these conditions are present, the person will agonize over whether he or she made the right choice.[11] Sometimes referred to as "morning-after-the-night-before" regrets, the misgivings or second thoughts that plague us after a tough choice motivate us to seek reassuring information and social support for our decision.

Postdecision dissonance
Strong doubts experienced after making an important, close-call decision that is difficult to reverse.

A classic example of postdecision dissonance is the mental turmoil a person experiences after signing a contract to buy a new car. The cost is high, there are many competing models from which to choose, and the down payment commits the customer to go through with the purchase. It's not unusual to find a customer examining *Consumer Reports* auto ratings *after* placing an order. The buyer is seeking information that confirms the decision already made and quiets nagging doubts.

Many who recover from multiple addictions testify that quitting smoking is harder than giving up booze. Just as countless alcoholics turn to Alcoholics Anonymous for social support, people who try to give up tobacco often need at least one friend, family member, romantic partner, or co-worker who's also going through the pangs of withdrawal. They can remind each other that it's worth the effort. Of course, the decision to stop smoking doesn't fulfill Festinger's third condition of a once-and-for-all, no-going-back, final choice. One can always go back to smoking. In fact, those who swear off cigarettes typically have a few lapses, and total relapses are common. Encouragement and social support are necessary to tamp down the doubts and fears that follow this tough decision.

Smokers who consciously decide *not* to quit face similar qualms and anxieties. They are bombarded with messages telling them they are putting their health at risk. People who care for them deeply urge them to stop, and nonsmokers look down on them because they don't. University of Kentucky communication professor Alan DeSantis describes the camaraderie he found among regular customers at a Kentucky cigar shop. Just as smoke from cigars drives some folks away, DeSantis concludes that the friendship and collective rationalization of those who smoke cigars together hold postdecision dissonance at bay. He also sees *Cigar Aficionado* as serving the same function. He writes that although the magazine professes to simply celebrate the good life, it actually serves "to relieve the cognitive dissonance associated with the consumption of a potentially dangerous product by adding cognitions, trivializing dissonant information, selectively exposing readers to pro-smoking information, and creating a social support network of fellow cigar smokers."[12]

Hypothesis 3: Minimal Justification for Action Induces Attitude Change

Suppose someone wanted to persuade an ex-smoker who is dying of lung cancer to stop publicly bashing the tobacco industry and to respect cigarette companies' right to market their product. That is one of the assignments given to Nick Naylor, chief spokesman for tobacco companies in the movie *Thank You for Smoking*. His job is to convince "Big Tobacco's" former advertising icon—the Marlboro Man—to switch from outspoken critic to silent partner. Before cognitive dissonance theory, conventional wisdom would have suggested that Naylor work first to change the bitter man's *attitude* toward the industry. If he could convince the cowboy that the cigarette companies are well-intentioned, then the man would change his communication *behavior*. It seemed natural to think of attitude and behavior as the beginning and end of a cause-and-effect sequence.

Attitude → Behavior

But Festinger's *minimal justification hypothesis* reversed the sequence. This hypothesis suggests that the best way for Naylor to change the Marlboro Man's attitude toward his former employers is to get him to quit speaking out against them.

Behavior → Attitude

Minimal justification hypothesis
A claim that the best way to stimulate an attitude change in others is to offer just enough incentive to elicit counterattitudinal behavior.

Festinger attached one important condition, however. Instead of giving the cowboy massive incentives to abandon his public critique ($100,000 in cash, lifetime health care for his wife, or a threat to harm his kids), Naylor should offer the minimum enticement necessary to induce him to quietly step off his soapbox. Festinger concluded:

> Thus if one wanted to obtain private change in addition to mere public compliance, the best way to do this would be to offer just enough reward or punishment to elicit overt compliance.[13]

Naylor doesn't follow Festinger's advice. Instead, he does it the old-fashioned way by throwing lots of money at the Marlboro Man. He goes to his rundown ranch with a briefcase filled with bundles of hundred-dollar bills, which he pours out on the floor. He labels the money a gift rather than a bribe, but makes it clear that the cowboy can't keep the money if he continues to denounce the tobacco companies. As it turns out, the offer is more than enough because the dying man is worried about how his family will manage after he's gone. So the Marlboro Man takes both the money and a vow of silence, but his antagonistic attitude toward his former employers hasn't changed. *Compliance* without inner conviction. For Naylor, that's enough.

Compliance
Public conformity to another's expectation without necessarily having a private conviction that matches the behavior.

There is, however, a brief moment in their discussion that suggests the potential of a minimal justification strategy. When the Marlboro Man looks longingly at the cash, he wonders out loud if he might keep half the money and still denounce the tobacco companies. His question reveals that somewhere between 50 percent and 100 percent of the cash on the floor there's a tipping point where the cowboy becomes willing to be bought off. Festinger predicted that if Naylor were to offer that "just-enough" amount, not only would the Marlboro Man alter his communication behavior, but the dissonance he would feel would also cause him to be less angry at the cigarette companies. Festinger's startling $1/$20 experiment shows how this might work.

A CLASSIC EXPERIMENT: "WOULD I LIE FOR A DOLLAR?"

There is nothing particularly radical about Festinger's first two hypotheses. His selective exposure prediction nicely explains why political rallies attract the party faithful and why the audience for religious radio and television tends to be made up of committed believers. As for postdecision dissonance, all of us have tried to convince ourselves that we've made the right choice after facing a close-call decision. But Festinger's minimal justification hypothesis is counterintuitive. Will a small incentive to act really induce a corresponding attitude change when heaping on the benefits won't? Festinger's famous $1/$20 experiment supported his claim that it will.

Festinger and social psychologist James Carlsmith recruited Stanford University men to participate in a psychological study supposedly investigating industrial relations.[14] As each man arrived at the lab, he was assigned the boring and repetitive task of sorting a large batch of spools into sets of 12 and turning square pegs a quarter turn to the right. The procedure was designed to be both monotonous and tiring. At the end of an hour the experimenter approached the subject and made a request. He claimed that a student assistant had failed to show up and that he needed someone to fill in. The experimenter wanted the subject to tell a potential female subject in the waiting room how much fun the experiment was. Dissonance researchers call this *counterattitudinal advocacy*. We'd call it lying.

Counterattitudinal advocacy
Publicly urging others to believe or do something that is opposed to what the advocate actually believes.

Some of the men were promised $20 to express enthusiasm about the task; others were offered only $1. After adjusting for inflation, that's $160 or $8 today.[15] It's comforting to know that six of the men refused to take part in the deception, but most students tried to recruit the young woman. The gist of the typical conversation was similar for both payment conditions:

SHE: "I heard it was boring."

HE: "Oh no, it's really quite fun."

What differed were the men's privately expressed attitudes after the study was over. Students who lied for $20 later confessed that they thought the task of sorting spools was dull. Those who lied for $1 maintained that it was quite enjoyable. (Festinger and Carlsmith practiced their own form of deception in the study—subjects never received the promised money.)

By now you should have a pretty good idea how Festinger analyzed the results. He noted that $20 was a huge sum of money at the time. If a student felt qualms about telling a "white lie," the cash was a ready justification. Thus, the student felt little or no tension between his action and his attitude. But the men who lied for a dollar had lots of cognitive work to do. The logical inconsistency of saying a boring task was interesting had to be explained away through an internal dialogue:

> I'm a Stanford man. Am I the kind of guy who would lie for a dollar? No way. Actually, what I told the girl was true. The experiment was a lot of fun.

Festinger said that $1 was just barely enough to induce compliance to the experimenter's request, and so the students had to create another justification. They changed their attitude toward the task to bring it into line with their behavior—in other words, to eliminate dissonance.

THREE STATE-OF-THE-ART REVISIONS: THE CAUSE AND EFFECT OF DISSONANCE

The $1/$20 study has been replicated and modified many times in an effort to figure out what creates dissonance and how people reduce it. Based on hundreds of experimental studies, most persuasion researchers today subscribe to one of three revisions of Festinger's original theory.

To illustrate these revisions, we'll consider the most famous American to struggle recently with smoking: President Barack Obama. Obama put away his cigarettes before his 2008 presidential bid, but relapsed during the campaign and his first two years in office. In 2011, however, Obama's doctors declared that he had broken his 30-year cigarette habit.[16] According to First Lady Michelle Obama, it seems that dissonance caused the president's decision to stop: "I think he didn't want to look his girls in the eye and tell them that they shouldn't do something that he was still doing."[17] That sounds like a straightforward explanation, but for cognitive dissonance theorists it isn't enough—they want to know what's going on in the mind of the president that generates and eliminates dissonance.

In order to understand each of the options described in the following sections, it will help you to picture the overall dissonance arousal and reduction process. Figure 16–1 shows that four-step sequence. So far we've discussed Festinger's belief that we experience dissonance when we face *logical inconsis-*

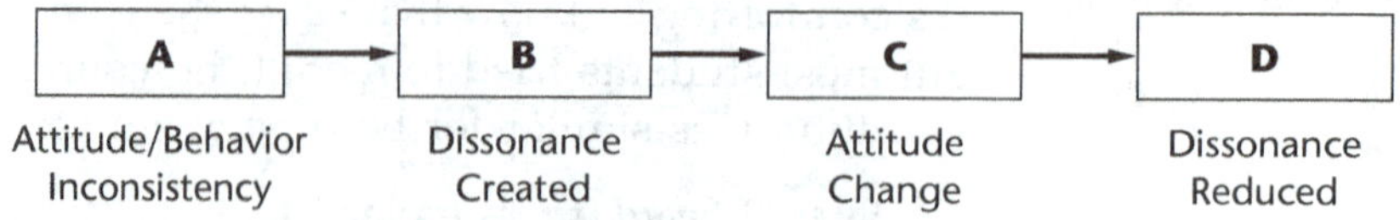

FIGURE 16–1 Festinger's Process Model of Cognitive Dissonance
Based on Festinger, *Cognitive Dissonance Theory*

tency, or beliefs and behaviors that don't quite add up. *(I value my health. My cigarette habit damages my health.)* That's a claim about the A → B link in the figure. Festinger further asserted that the way to reduce dissonance was to remove the logical inconsistency (point D). The three revisions question these assumptions, and each provides a somewhat different explanation for why Obama finally kicked his smoking habit.

1. Self-Consistency: The Rationalizing Animal

One of Festinger's early graduate students, University of California social psychologist Elliot Aronson, wasn't convinced that logical inconsistency produces dissonance. He noted that we sometimes find such inconsistencies curious or even amusing. For example, Andrew once received a university parking ticket in the mail dated several months after he'd graduated and moved out of the state. Two thoughts crossed his mind: *(1) I was not parked at the University of Kansas in October* and *(2) I have a parking ticket that says I was.* That's a logical inconsistency, and it made him feel mildly annoyed—but that's not the aversive discomfort Aronson claims is at the heart of dissonance.

Instead, Aronson thinks what produces dissonance is an inconsistency between a cognition and our *self-concept*—how we perceive ourselves. He interprets the $1/$20 experiment as a study of self-presentation.[18] The Stanford men were in a bind because they regarded themselves as decent, truthful human beings, in contrast to their deceptive behavior. In fact, the higher their opinion of their honesty, the more dissonance they would feel when they told the waiting woman that the study was fun. Conversely, if they had seen themselves as liars, cheats, or jerks, they would have felt no tension. As Aronson puts it, "If a person conceives of himself as a 'schnook,' he will be expected to behave like a 'schnook.'"[19]

Andrew's student Caitlin, a vegetarian, wrote about her feelings of guilt after eating meat. Clearly, she perceived that her choice was inconsistent with her self-concept:

> When I ate meat for the first time in a year, I was at a hibachi grill where the chef gave each of us a sample of steak. At first I tried just one piece, but that provoked my decision to order fried rice and steak. This choice violated my vegetarian beliefs, but I justified it because it was only a small amount of meat. The day after, I experienced postdecision dissonance: I had strong doubts, a guilty conscience about my decision, and a very upset stomach.

If Aronson is right, what's the best way to persuade someone like President Obama to stop smoking? Showing him studies of tobacco's negative health effects might not be the route to go. Even if Obama acknowledges that his cigarette use is inconsistent with that information, Aronson doesn't think logical inconsistency is enough. The president will only feel dissonance if he sees smoking as inconsistent with his self-concept. Given the first lady's explanation ("I think he didn't want to look his girls in the eye . . ."), Aronson might suggest that the president perceived an inconsistency between his smoking and his fatherly image. Maybe Obama also thought that lighting up contradicted his appearance as a health-conscious person who regularly exercises through pickup basketball games. Throwing away his cigarettes reduced dissonance by removing those psychological inconsistencies.

2. Personal Responsibility for Bad Outcomes (the New Look)

For Princeton psychologist Joel Cooper, both Festinger and Aronson miss the true cause of dissonance. He doesn't think inconsistency—whether logical or psychological—is the main motivating factor. In his *new look* model of cognitive dissonance, Cooper argues that we experience dissonance when we believe our actions have unnecessarily hurt another person. For example, in the minimal justification condition of the $1/$20 experiment, the Stanford men willingly "duped a fellow student to look forward to an exciting experience" while knowing "full well that the waiting participant was in for an immense letdown."[20]

Cooper concludes that dissonance is "a state of arousal caused by behaving in such a way as to feel personally responsible for bringing about an aversive event."[21] Note that the acceptance of personal *responsibility* requires that the person know ahead of time that his or her action will have negative consequences for someone else, and yet still choose to do the dirty deed. The reactions of participants in minimal justification experiments show that they often feel bad about the potential effects of their messages.

Purdue University social psychologists Richard Heslin and Michael Amo used a pro-smoking message prepared for junior high kids, but in this case the setup was more involving and potentially more harmful. The researchers encouraged college students in public speaking classes to deliver impromptu speeches to persuade uninformed and uncommitted seventh grade kids that smoking pot wouldn't hurt them. The speakers saw their recorded speeches and were reminded that they'd be identified as actually having pro-marijuana sentiments. The speakers were quite aware that their message might harm kids. One speaker pleaded, "Please don't use my speech. I don't want the course credit; just don't use my speech!"[22] Clearly they felt dissonance, and new look theorists would argue that's because they perceived their actions as harmful (rather than inconsistent). Nevertheless, the speakers actually changed their attitude in the direction of their advocacy—dissonance reduction by concluding that their actions weren't all that harmful.

New look theorists don't think inconsistency is enough to persuade someone like Obama to stop smoking. Sure, he may perceive that his actions are logically inconsistent with scientific research or psychologically inconsistent with his self-image. But if he only lights up in private—and he's never smoked publicly while president—he might believe his actions don't hurt anyone else. For Cooper, the first lady's explanation might suggest that the president thought his smoking could hurt their daughters. If Obama quit smoking because he was afraid Malia and Sasha would imitate him, or because he was concerned about their exposure to secondhand smoke, that's the new look in action.

3. Self-Affirmation to Dissipate Dissonance

While the revisions offered by Aronson (self-consistency) and Cooper (new look) address dissonance *creation* at the front end of Festinger's model (the link from A to B in Figure 16-1), Stanford psychologist Claude Steele's self-affirmation approach speaks to the question of dissonance *reduction* at the back end of the model—point D of the figure. Steele doesn't assume that dissonance always drives people to justify their actions by changing their attitudes. He thinks some fortunate people can call up a host of positive thoughts about themselves that will blot out a concern for restoring consistency. If he's right, high self-esteem is a resource for dissonance reduction.

According to Steele, most people are greatly motivated to maintain an overall self-image of moral adequacy. For a participant in the $1/$20 experiment, there's no question that lying to a fellow student makes it harder to preserve that favorable self-concept. But if the guy ignores the ethical slip and focuses instead on his good grades, athletic ability, social skills, and helpfulness to friends who are hurting, the dissonance will be only a blip on the radar screen of his mind and will quickly fade away. Thus, Steele believes that denial, forgetfulness, and trivialization of the incident are alternatives to attitude change, but only for the person who already has high self-esteem.

According to Steele's self-affirmation approach, Obama might have excused his smoking by reminding himself of his esteem-raising qualities, which include "gifted orator, award winning author, and proven intellect who was the first black president of the *Harvard Law Review*,"[23] not to mention president of the United States, winner of a Nobel Peace Prize, and the commander in chief who stopped Osama bin Laden for good. In light of these accomplishments, Obama might regard relapse as a minor inconsistency rather than a major contradiction. In Steele's view, the first lady's comment suggests that the president eventually couldn't rationalize that way anymore. As the son of a man who ignored his family obligations, perhaps Obama came to believe that smoking is a parenting flaw for which career success can't compensate.

Aronson, Cooper, and Steele offer their respective revisions as more accurate accounts of what goes on in people's heads than Festinger's original theory provided. But we don't have to pick one and trash the others. Self-consistency, personal responsibility for bad outcomes, and self-affirmation aren't mutually exclusive explanations. As Cooper suggests, "They each describe a distinct and important piece of the overall dissonance process and, in doing so, make a unique contribution to our understanding of how cognitions about the self mediate cognitive dissonance and arousal and reduction."[24]

THEORY INTO PRACTICE: PERSUASION THROUGH DISSONANCE

I've placed this chapter in the section on interpersonal influence because Festinger and his followers focused on attitude change as an end product of dissonance. Suppose you know someone named Sam who holds an opinion that you're convinced is harmful or wrong. What practical advice does the theory offer that might help you alter Sam's conviction?

For openers, don't promise lavish benefits if Sam abandons that attitude or warn of dire consequences if he doesn't. A massive reward–punishment strategy may gain behavioral compliance, but the hard sell seldom wins the heart or mind of the person being bribed or pressured. Instead, work to develop a friendly relationship with Sam. That way your own position will tend to bypass the *selective exposure* screen that Sam and the rest of us put up to avoid threatening ideas. And if Sam eventually adopts your viewpoint, an ongoing bond means you'll be around to offer reassurance when *postdecision dissonance* kicks in.

To be an effective agent of change, you should offer just enough encouragement *(minimal justification)* for Sam to try out novel behavior that departs from his usual way of thinking. Avoid making an offer that Sam can't refuse. As long as *counterattitudinal actions* are freely chosen and publicly taken, people are more likely to adopt beliefs that support what they've done. The greater the effort involved in acting this way, the greater the chance that their attitudes will change to match their actions.

Finally, as you seek to *induce compliance,* try to get Sam to count the cost of doing what you want and to grasp the potential downside of that behavior for others *(personal responsibility for negative outcomes).* That kind of understanding will increase the probability that Sam's attitude will shift to be consistent with his actions. And if things turn sour, your relationship won't.

CRITIQUE: DISSONANCE OVER DISSONANCE

When Festinger died in 1989, his obituary in *American Psychologist* testified to the impact of his work:

> Like Dostoyevski and like Picasso, Festinger set in motion a *style* of research and theory in the social sciences that is now the common property of all creative workers in the field. . . . Leon is to social psychology what Freud is to clinical psychology and Piaget to developmental psychology.[25]

As the *Dilbert* cartoon in this chapter suggests, cognitive dissonance is one of the few theories in this book that has achieved name recognition within popular culture. Yet despite this wide influence, Festinger's original theory and its contemporary revisions contain a serious flaw. Like my boyhood friend's never-miss shot in his driveway basketball court (see Chapter 3), it's hard to think of a way the theory can be proved wrong.

Look again at the four stages of the dissonance process diagram in Figure 16–1. Almost all the creative efforts of dissonance researchers have been aimed at inducing counterattitudinal advocacy at point A—getting people to say something in public that is inconsistent with what they believe in private. When researchers find an attitude shift at point C, they automatically *assume* that dissonance was built up at point B and is gone by point D. But they don't test to see whether dissonance is actually there.

Festinger never specified a reliable way to detect the degree of dissonance a person experiences, if any. Psychologist Patricia Devine and her University of Wisconsin–Madison colleagues refer to such an instrument as a *dissonance thermometer.* They applaud researchers' occasional attempts to gauge the *arousal* component of dissonance through physiological measures such as galvanic skin response. (When our drive state increases, we have sweaty palms.) But they are even more encouraged at the possibility of assessing the *psychological discomfort* component of dissonance by means of a self-report measure of affect. Until some kind of dissonance thermometer is a standard part of dissonance research, we will never know if the distressing mental state is for real.

Dissonance thermometer
A hypothetical, reliable gauge of the dissonance a person feels as a result of inconsistency.

Cornell University psychologist Daryl Bem doesn't think it is. He agrees that attitudes change when people act counter to their beliefs with minimal justification, but he claims that *self-perception* is a much simpler explanation than cognitive dissonance. He believes we judge our internal dispositions the same way others do—by observing our behavior.

Bem ran his own $1/$20 study to test his alternative explanation.[26] People heard a recording of a Stanford man's enthusiastic account of the spool-sorting, peg-turning task. Some listeners were told he received $1 for recruiting the female subject. Since he had little obvious reason to lie, they assumed he really liked the task. Other listeners were told the man received $20 to recruit the woman. These folks assumed the man was bored with the task and was lying to get the money. Bem's subjects didn't speculate about what was going on inside the Stanford man's head. They simply judged his attitude by looking at what he did under the circumstances. If people don't need an understanding of cognitive dissonance to forecast how the men would react, Bem asks, why should social scientists? Bem is convinced that cognitive dissonance theory is like the mousetrap pictured on page 26—much too convoluted. He opts for simplicity.

Self-perception theory
The claim that we determine our attitudes the same way outside observers do—by observing our behavior; an alternative to cognitive dissonance theory.

Advocates of cognitive dissonance in the field of communication counter that nothing about mental processes is simple. When we deal with what goes on behind the eyes, we should expect and appreciate complexity. Festinger's theory has energized scientifically oriented communication scholars for more than 50 years. I feel no dissonance by including cognitive dissonance theory in this text.

QUESTIONS TO SHARPEN YOUR FOCUS

1. Cognitive dissonance is a *distressing mental state.* When did you last experience this *aversive drive?* Why might you have trouble answering that question?
2. The results of Festinger's famous *$1/$20 experiment* can be explained in a number of different ways. Which explanation do you find most satisfying?
3. Suppose you want your friends to change their sexist attitudes. What advice does the *minimal justification hypothesis* offer?
4. I see cognitive dissonance theory as a "never-miss shot." What would it take to make the theory *testable?*

A SECOND LOOK

Recommended resource: Joel Cooper, *Cognitive Dissonance: 50 Years of a Classic Theory,* Sage, Thousand Oaks, CA, 2007, (see especially Chapter 1, "Cognitive Dissonance: In the Beginning," pp. 1–27, and Chapter 3, "The Motivational Property of Dissonance," pp. 42–61).

Original statement: Leon Festinger, *A Theory of Cognitive Dissonance,* Stanford University, Stanford, CA, 1957.

Toward a dissonance thermometer: Patricia G. Devine, John M. Turner, et al., "Moving Beyond Attitude Change in the Study of Dissonance Related Processes," Eddie Harmon-Jones and Judson Mills (eds.), *Cognitive Dissonance: Progress on a Pivotal Theory in Social Psychology,* American Psychological Association, Washington, DC, 1999, pp. 297-323.

Engaging account of theory's development: Elliot Aronson, "The Evolution of Cognitive Dissonance Theory: A Personal Appraisal," in *The Science of Social Influence: Advances and Future Progress,* Anthon Prankanis (ed.), Psychology Press, New York, 2007, pp. 115–135.

Selective exposure: Silvia Knobloch-Westerwick and Jingbo Meng, "Looking the Other Way: Selective Exposure to Attitude-Consistent and Counterattitudinal Political Information," *Communication Research,* Vol. 36, 2009, pp. 426–448.

Postdecision dissonance: Dave D'Alessio and Mike Allen, "Selective Exposure and Dissonance after Decisions," *Psychological Reports,* Vol. 91, 2002, pp. 527–532.

$1/$20 experiment: Leon Festinger and James Carlsmith, "Cognitive Consequences of Forced Compliance," *Journal of Abnormal and Social Psychology,* Vol. 58, 1959, pp. 203–210.

Self-consistency revision: Ruth Thibodeau and Elliot Aronson, "Taking a Closer Look: Reasserting the Role of the Self-Concept in Dissonance Theory," *Personality and Social Psychology Bulletin,* Vol. 18, 1992, pp. 591–602.

New-look revision: Joel Cooper and Russell Fazio, "A New Look at Dissonance Theory," in *Advances in Experimental Social Psychology, Vol. 17,* Leonard Berkowitz (ed.), Academic Press, Orlando, FL, 1984, pp. 229–262.

Self-affirmation revision: Claude Steele, "The Psychology of Self-Affirmation: Sustaining the Integrity of the Self," in *Advances in Experimental Social Psychology, Vol. 21,* Leonard Berkowitz (ed.), Lawrence Erlbaum, Hillsdale, NJ, 1988, pp. 261–302.

Role of weapons of mass destruction and dissonance in the invasion of Iraq: Jeff Stone and Nicholas Fernandez, "How Behavior Shapes Attitudes: Cognitive Dissonance Processes," in *Attitudes and Attitude Change,* William Crano and Radmila Prislin (eds.), Psychology Press, New York, 2008, pp. 313–334.

Critique: Daryl Bem, "Self-Perception: An Alternative Interpretation of Cognitive Dissonance Phenomena," *Psychological Review,* Vol. 74, 1967, pp. 183–200.

Critique: Daniel O'Keefe, "Cognitive Dissonance Theory," in *Persuasion: Theory and Research,* 2nd ed., Sage, Thousand Oaks, CA, 2002, pp. 77–100.

Experiencing cognitive dissonance may require a strong need for esteem.
To access a chapter on Abraham Maslow's theory of motivation,
click on Hierarchy of Needs in Archive under Theory Resources at
www.afirstlook.com.

Group and Public Communication

DIVISION THREE

Group and Public Communication

Group Communication

On the morning of January 28, 1986, the space shuttle *Challenger* blasted off from the Kennedy Space Center in Florida. For the first time, the flight carried a civilian schoolteacher, Christa McAuliffe, as part of the crew. Seventy-three seconds after liftoff, millions of schoolchildren watched on television as the rocket disintegrated in a fiery explosion, and the capsule with its crew of seven plunged into the Atlantic Ocean. For many Americans, the *Challenger* disaster marked the end of a love affair with space. As they learned in the months that followed, the tragedy could have been—and should have been—avoided.

An independent presidential commission identified the primary cause of the accident as failure in an O-ring that was supposed to seal a joint, thus allowing volatile rocket fuel to spew out during the "burn." But the commission also concluded that a highly flawed decision process was an important contributing cause of the disaster. Communication, as well as combustion, was responsible for the tragedy. The day before the launch, rocket engineers had talked about the flight being risky. They worried that the O-ring seals had never been tested below 53 degrees Fahrenheit. As one of them later testified, with launch-time temperature in the 20s, getting the O-rings to seal gaps would be like "trying to shove a brick into a crack versus a sponge."[1] Yet during the final "go/no-go" conference, all agreed that the rocket was ready to fly.

Yale social psychologist Irving Janis was convinced that this grievous error wasn't an isolated incident. He had spotted the same group dynamic in other tragic government and corporate decisions. Janis didn't regard chief executives or their advisors as stupid, lazy, or evil. Rather he saw them as victims of "groupthink." He defined *groupthink* as "a mode of thinking that people engage in when they are deeply involved in a cohesive in-group, when the members' strivings for unanimity override their motivation to realistically appraise alternative courses of action."[2] This concurrence-seeking tendency emerges only when the group is characterized by "a warm clubby atmosphere" in which members desire to maintain relationships within the group at all costs. As a result, they automatically apply the "preserve group harmony" test to every decision they face.[3] Janis maintained that the superglue of solidarity that bonds people together can also cause their mental processes to get stuck.

Janis' concept of groupthink highlights the accepted wisdom in the field that there are two functions communication needs to address in any group—a *task function* and a *relationship function.* Task-focused communication moves the group along toward its goal; relational communication holds the group together. Some people concentrate on getting the job done, while others are much more concerned about relationships within the group. Task-oriented individuals are the pistons that drive the group machine. Relationship-oriented members are the lubricant that prevents excessive friction from destroying the group. Good groups require both kinds of people.

Harvard social psychologist Robert Bales was an early theorist who formally made the connection between specific types of communication and accomplishing these two functions.[4] Bales said group locomotion won't happen unless members *ask for* as well as *offer* information, opinions, and suggestions on how the group should proceed. Bales claimed that the most effective groups are those in which the verbal requests and responses are roughly equal in number. If everyone is asking and nobody's offering answers, the group won't make progress toward the goal. If, on the other hand, no one asks and everyone declares, the group will still be stuck.

As for *socio-emotional* communication (Bales' label for relational concern), he regarded showing agreement, showing solidarity, and reducing tension by storytelling as positive forms of communication that make the group cohesive. He saw showing disagreement, antagonism, and tension as negative moves that tend to pull the group apart. Yet Bales found that groups make better decisions when there are a few negative voices. That squares with Janis' recommendation. He suggests that skepticism and blunt critiques are correctives to groupthink. That kind of communication might have saved the lives of the *Challenger* crew and Americans' support for the space shuttle program.[5]

"Now, let's hear it for good old Al, whose idea this Group Think was in the first place."

CHAPTER 17

Objective — Interpretive

Socio-psychological tradition
Cybernetic tradition

Functional Perspective on Group Decision Making

of Randy Hirokawa & Dennis Gouran

A cynic once said that a camel is a horse put together by a committee. Others upset by their experience with group decision making give voice to their frustration with equally disparaging quips:[1]

> "If you want something done, do it yourself."
>
> "Too many cooks spoil the broth."
>
> "A committee is a group that keeps minutes and wastes hours."
>
> "Committees lure fresh ideas down a cul-de-sac and quietly strangle them."

Randy Hirokawa (dean of liberal arts, University of Hawaii at Hilo) and Dennis Gouran (professor of communication, Pennsylvania State University) believe that these pessimistic views are unwarranted. Assuming that group members care about the issue, are reasonably intelligent, and face a challenging task that calls for more facts, new ideas, or clear thinking, Hirokawa and Gouran are convinced that group interaction has a positive effect on the final decision. Hirokawa seeks *quality* solutions.[2] Gouran desires decisions that are *appropriate*.[3] Both scholars regard talk as the social tool that helps groups reach better conclusions than they otherwise would. As the Hebrew proverb suggests, "Without counsel plans go wrong, but with many advisers they succeed."[4]

Functional perspective
A prescriptive approach that describes and predicts task-group performance when four communication functions are fulfilled.

The *functional perspective* specifies what communication must accomplish for jointly made decisions to be wise. Gouran laid the groundwork for the theory with his early writing on group decision making. Hirokawa developed the core principles of the theory during his graduate studies, and for 20 years his research tested and refined the theory. On the chance that you would be intrigued by a behind-the-scenes look at real-life group decisions made by college students living together, I'll illustrate the functional perspective by drawing on my experience conducting a two-week off-campus class that students called the "Island Course."

For 20 years I taught a group dynamics seminar limited to eight students on a remote island in northern Lake Michigan. Travel to and from the island was by a single-engine airplane, and we lived together in a cabin—the only structure on the island. Except when a few of us flew off the island to the mainland to get food, our sole communication was with each other. There's no cell phone service or Internet access on the island. Course alumni look back and consider our isolation as similar to *Survivor*, yet with a cooperative rather than a competitive agenda. No one was ever voted off the island.

The island course was primarily a venture in experiential education. We learned about group dynamics by studying our own interaction. I asked students to adopt the role of participant-observer. Whatever happened among us became a subject for group discussion. Still, the course maintained traditional academic features—four hours of class per day, assigned readings, and final grades. Within that hybrid framework, class members had to decide on a daily schedule, who would do each job necessary for group living, how limited funds for food and fuel would be spent, and on what basis I would assign grades. They understood that they had to live with their decisions for the first half of the course, but could change things for the second week.

As for my role, I let them know that I wouldn't be an active participant in the choices they made—they were free to decide as they saw fit. I'd provide any information they asked for, with the exception of revealing how other island-course groups had handled these issues or disclosing my own personal preferences. In the survey that alums filled out up to two decades after the course, Kelly's response reflected the general consensus:

> I remember Em's role best for what he didn't do. It was my first real experience with a leader who laid back intentionally so that we had to come to our own conclusion—a real democracy. It was refreshing to deal with someone in charge who didn't give all the answers. We were responsible for how things turned out.

As Hirokawa and Gouran predict, how things turned out hinged on the absence or presence of four types of communication.

FOUR FUNCTIONS OF EFFECTIVE DECISION MAKING

Consistent with the approach of Bales and other pioneer researchers, Hirokawa and Gouran draw an analogy between small groups and biological systems. Complex living organisms must satisfy a number of functions, such as respiration, circulation, digestion, and elimination of bodily waste, if they are to survive and thrive in an ever-changing environment. In like manner, Hirokawa and Gouran see the group decision-making process as needing to fulfill four task requirements if members are to reach a high-quality solution. They refer to these conditions as *requisite functions* of effective decision making—thus the "functional perspective" label.[5] The four functions are (1) problem analysis, (2) goal setting, (3) identification of alternatives, and (4) evaluation of positive and negative characteristics of each alternative.

Requisite functions
Requirements for positive group outcome; problem analysis, goal setting, identification of alternatives, and evaluation of pluses and minuses for each.

1. Analysis of the Problem

Is something going on that requires improvement or change? To answer that question, group members must take a realistic look at current conditions. Defenders of the status quo are fond of saying, "If it ain't broke, don't fix it." But, as Hirokawa warns, any misunderstanding of the situation tends to be compounded when the members make their final decision. He also notes that the clearest example of faulty analysis is the failure to recognize a potential threat when one really exists.[6] After people acknowledge a need to be addressed, they still must figure out the nature, extent, and probable cause(s) of the problem that confronts the group.

Problem analysis
Determining the nature, extent, and cause(s) of the problem facing the group.

The first night on the island, students faced the task of drawing up a daily schedule. Because that decision affected other choices, I'll describe how two groups in different summers handled problem analysis and how they fulfilled the other three requisite functions that Hirokawa and Gouran identify. I'll refer to them as the *blue group* and the *green group.*

The blue group never did any overt problem analysis. To them, scheduling seemed a simple matter. They jumped to pooling suggestions for what would make the two weeks ideal without ever considering the unique problems that island living posed. Their conversation centered on building in as much time as possible to go outside to enjoy the island during the day and each other at night. Most class members noted that sleeping in late was also an idea with great appeal.

Conversely, the green group started out by exploring what situational limitations they had to factor into their decision. The close quarters of the small cabin proved to be a problem because it provided no aural—and very little visual—privacy. A few light sleepers admitted that it would be impossible for them to get to sleep at night, or to stay asleep in the morning, if someone was talking or walking around. Before budgeting their limited funds for food and fuel, they also figured out the cost for each member to ride the all-terrain cycle (ATC) around the island for 30 minutes a day—something all were eager to do. Their figures showed that they'd run out of money before the end of the course unless they could limit the use of the diesel generator to no more than 10 hours a day. This problem analysis strongly informed the schedule they finally worked out.

2. Goal Setting

Because group members need to be clear on what they are trying to accomplish, Hirokawa and Gouran regard discussion of goals and objectives as the second requisite function of decision making. A group needs to establish criteria by which to judge proposed solutions. These criteria must set forth the minimal qualities that an acceptable solution must possess. If the group fails to satisfy this task requirement, it's likely that the decision will be driven by power or passion rather than reason.[7]

Goal setting
Establishing criteria by which to judge proposed solutions.

Even before they began discussing alternatives, the green group reached a consensus on the specific criteria their schedule had to meet. They agreed that the schedule should include four hours of class as well as windows wide enough for students to prepare and enjoy decent meals and clean up afterward. Members insisted that there be a minimum of six hours of free time to play, study, or chill out. They also specified a nighttime block of at least seven hours for sleeping, where both the generator and conversation in the cabin would be turned off. And based on their problem analysis, they wanted to craft an energy-sensitive schedule that wouldn't require the generator to be used for more than 10 hours a day. With the possible exceptions of *decent meals* and *energy sensitive,* these were measurable goals that could be used to gauge the quality of their final decision.

Unlike the green group, the blue group never spoke of goals, objectives, standards, targets, or criteria. Their discussion made it clear that fun in the sun and lots of casual time together were high priorities. But these overlapping desires are quite subjective and open to multiple interpretations. With no definitive goals to focus their discussion, it's difficult for group members to know whether they're making an appropriate decision. Or, as sports enthusiasts put it, *You don't know you're winning if you don't keep score.*

3. Identification of Alternatives

Hirokawa and Gouran stress the importance of marshaling a number of alternative solutions from which group members can choose:

Identification of alternatives
Generation of options to sufficiently solve the problem.

> If no one calls attention to the need for generating as many alternatives as is realistically possible, then relatively few may be introduced, and the corresponding possibility of finding the acceptable answer will be low.[8]

Both island-course groups wanted to schedule time when they could enjoy the island. Swimming, sunbathing, stone skipping, playing volleyball or soccer,

"Gentlemen, the fact that all my horses and all my men couldn't put Humpty together again simply proves to me that I must have more horses and more men."

trailblazing, riding the ATC, treasure hunting, bird watching, picking wild raspberries, building tree forts in the woods, and just lolling in the hammock were a few of the daylight activities suggested by blue and green course members alike. But the groups varied greatly on the number of options they generated for scheduling class and meals. The blue group seemed to have tunnel vision and could only picture a schedule with two hours of class in the morning and two hours at night. No other options were seriously considered. They were equally locked into the traditional practice of lunch at noon and dinner at six. One tentatively suggested alternative was shot down before it could be explained.

A girl in the green group had read an article on brainstorming before the course and urged classmates, "Let's see how many different ideas we can think of for when we'll eat." They took her up on it and suggested a dozen meal plans: late breakfast; no breakfast; brunch instead of breakfast and lunch; one big meal a day at noon; dinner at noon and light supper in the evening; a picnic snack to eat in the afternoon; four light meals a day; and a mix of these options.

The green group wasn't quite as creative with alternatives for class, yet they went beyond the two-hours-in-the-morning-and-two-at-night plan that seemed written in stone for the blue group. Different class members suggested three hours in the morning and one at night; four hours in the morning with two breaks; three class sessions of 80 minutes in the morning, afternoon, and night; three hours of class at night when the generator would be on anyway; all classes during daylight hours so the generator wouldn't have to be on. Their final decision turned out to be a combination of these ideas.

4. Evaluation of Positive and Negative Characteristics

After a group has identified alternative solutions, the participants must take care to test the relative merits of each option against the criteria they believe are important. This point-by-point comparison doesn't take place automatically. Hirokawa and Gouran warn that groups get sloppy and often need one member to remind the others to consider both the positive and negative features of each alternative.

Evaluation of positive and negative characteristics
Testing the relative merits of each option against the criteria selected; weighing the benefits and costs.

Because blue group members concentrated on only one schedule option, their evaluation of its characteristics was rather brief. They did a nice job of articulating the benefits they saw in their plan—a similarity to campus schedule, afternoons free for outdoor recreation, late-night opportunity to strengthen relationships, and a chance to sleep in before a late morning class. What's not to like? The blue group never addressed that issue. Hirokawa notes that some group tasks have a negative *bias* in that spotting the downside of each alternative is more important than identifying its positive qualities.[9] Since students were new to island living, it turned out that focusing on the disadvantages inherent in any plan would have been time well spent.

The green group discussed the pluses and minuses of every alternative. They concluded that late-night activity came at the cost of money they'd rather spend on food. They also saw that long class sessions in this idyllic setting could result in boredom and resentment. And for many of the meal plans they were considering, the amount of time spent in preparation, eating, and cleanup struck them as excessive. These realizations led them to adopt the novel schedule displayed on the bottom of Figure 17–1. Note that the three shorter classes meet in daylight hours. Since there are only two sit-down meals with prep and cleanup, there's

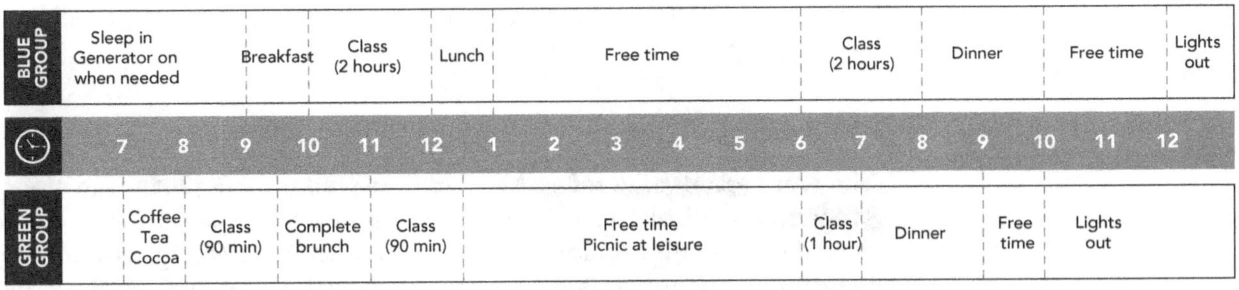

[The Green Group time line depicts their proposal before advancing it an hour to "Island Daylight Saving Time."]

FIGURE 17–1 Blue and Green Group Schedules for the Island Course

more free time for whatever people want to do. And there are more than eight hours of darkness for course members and the generator to be at rest.

When the green group members first looked at their schedule shown in Figure 17–1, some had second thoughts. For them, it seemed bizarre to be going to bed at 10 P.M., with some folks rising at 6:30 in the morning. But one girl suggested advancing all clocks, watches, and times on the schedule ahead by one hour. "We'll feel better about going to bed at 11, and our schedule will still be in sync with the sun," she explained. The others were intrigued by the elegant simplicity of her idea, so before turning in that night, we switched to Island Daylight Saving Time. Our body clocks were quick to adjust as well.

Predictable Outcomes

So what difference did Hirokawa and Gouran's four requisite functions make for these two island groups? Over the course of two weeks, how did these contrasting schedules turn out in practice? Both groups stuck to their plan for the first week, but by the fifth day, the class that didn't address the four functions was struggling. No one in the blue group went to sleep before midnight, and once someone got up early in the morning, no one else could sleep. Students slept only six or seven hours, and those who planned to sleep in were irritated at others who woke them up. The two-hour class at night became a real drag; no one looked forward to that time together.

Perhaps the biggest problem triggered by the blue group's decision was prolonged use of the generator. Extended activity in the cabin resulted in the generator running more than 12 hours a day, at a cost that took a big bite out of the food budget. The blue group made some adjustments the second week, but the menu for our last few meals seemed to consist of grubs and yucca roots. And there was no gas for the ATC.

On the other hand, the eight students in the green group were quite satisfied with the schedule they crafted. They saved time and energy by eating only two meals in the cabin, holding all classes during daylight hours, and preparing the afternoon picnic snack and the brunch at the same time. They had more time for fun in the sun than the blue group did, and looked forward to the abbreviated evening class as a lead-in to a relaxed dinner.

The well-rested green group took great pride in limiting generator use to eight hours per day and celebrated with a T-bone steak dinner the last night with the money they'd saved. In addition, there was enough room in the budget to guarantee unlimited rides on the ATC. As Hirokawa and Gouran suggest, it took discussion of all four requisite functions to hammer out a quality solution that was appropriate for the island course.

PRIORITIZING THE FOUR FUNCTIONS

The word *prioritizing* refers to addressing the four requisite functions in a logical progression. Hirokawa originally thought that no one sequence or group agenda does the job better. As long as the group ends up dealing with all four functions, the route its members take won't make much difference. Yet he's discovered the groups that successfully resolve especially difficult problems usually take a common decision-making path.[10]

The term *prioritizing* in the heading also refers to the question of which function is most important in order for a group to maximize the probability of a high-quality decision. Hirokawa and Gouran originally thought that no single function is inherently more important than any of the others.[11] But as Hirokawa admits, in a paper entitled, "To Err Is Human, To Correct for It Divine," they were wrong. The paper reports on a meta-analysis of 60 empirical research studies on the functional perspective. The study concludes that of the four functions, *evaluation of negative consequences of alternative solutions* is by far the most crucial to ensure a quality decision.[12] Perhaps to stress its importance, Hirokawa now splits up the evaluation of alternatives function into positive outcomes and negative outcomes for each option, and speaks of five requisite functions rather than four.

Figure 17–2 portrays the path that seems to offer the best problem-solving progression. Groups start with problem analysis, then deal with goal setting and identifying alternatives, and end by evaluating the positive and negative characteristics of each alternative before making a final choice. This decision-making flow parallels the advice I once heard on National Public Radio's *Car Talk.* Asked how car owners should handle close-call decisions on auto repair, mechanics Tom and Ray Magliozzi ("Click and Clack, the Tappet Brothers") gave a street-smart answer that ran something like this:

> First, figure out what's broke. Then, make up your mind how good you want to fix it. Or before that ask your mechanic to list the choices you've got. Either way, you gotta do both. Finally, weigh the bang-for-the-buck that each job gives. Then decide.

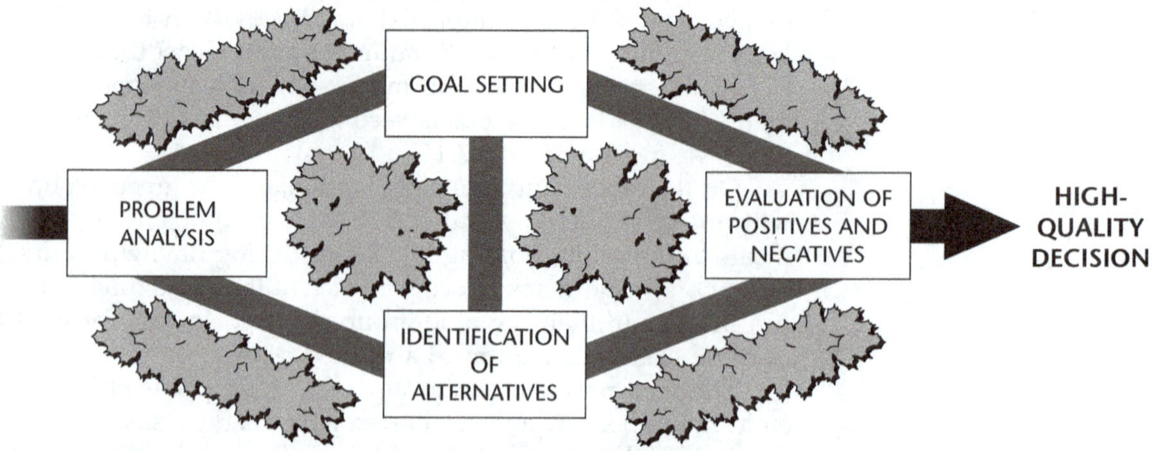

FIGURE 17–2 An Effective Decision-Making Path from the Functional Perspective

THE ROLE OF COMMUNICATION IN FULFILLING THE FUNCTIONS

Most communication scholars believe that discussion among members has a significant effect on the quality of group decisions. Traditional wisdom suggests that talk is the medium, channel, or conduit through which information travels between participants.[13] Verbal interaction makes it possible for members to (1) distribute and pool information, (2) catch and remedy errors, and (3) influence each other. But distractions and nonproductive conversation create channel noise causing a loss of information. Group researcher Ivan Steiner claimed that[14]

$$\text{Actual Group Productivity} = \text{Potential Productivity} - \text{Losses Due to Processes}$$

It follows that communication is best when it doesn't obstruct or distort the free flow of ideas.

While not rejecting this traditional view, Hirokawa believes that communication plays a more active role in crafting quality decisions. Like social constructionists (see Chapters 6, 11, and 13), he regards group discussion as a tool or instrument that group members use to create the social reality in which decisions are made.[15] Discussion exerts its own impact on the end product of the group.

How does this work in practice? Think of the dark, wide lines in Figure 17–2 as safe trails through a dense thicket—paths that connect the four key task functions and lead ultimately to the goal of a high-quality group decision. Members can easily wander off that goal path and get caught up in a tangle of prickerbushes that thwart the group's progress. The bushes in this analogy represent distractions or barriers that hinder movement toward the goal. Hirokawa and Gouran list a number of thorny obstacles—ignorance of the issue, faulty facts, misguided assumptions, sloppy evaluation of options, illogical inferences, disregard of procedural norms, and undue influence by powerful members. They believe that people go astray through talk, but they also believe that communication has the power to pull them back onto the goal-directed path.

Consistent with these convictions, Hirokawa and Gouran outline three types of communication in decision-making groups:

1. **Promotive**—interaction that moves the group along the goal path by calling attention to one of the four requisite decision-making functions.
2. **Disruptive**—interaction that diverts, hinders or frustrates group members' ability to achieve the four task functions.
3. **Counteractive**—interaction that members use to get the group back on track.

Hirokawa and Gouran suggest that most comments from group members disrupt rather than promote progress toward the goal. They conclude, therefore, that "effective group decision-making is perhaps best understood as a consequence of the exercise of counteractive influence."[16] In other words, someone has to say something that will get the group back on track. After reading about these three types of communication in her comm theory course, Lydia recognized that her comments had been disruptive rather than counteractive during a crucial discussion:

> I think group decision making is important, even vital, yet I am the worst at it. When I was in high school, I applied to be a foreign exchange student to

Germany. For our final selection task the six finalists had to come up with a solution to a problem, then present it to the directors. Based on the group process, the directors would select the four of us who would go. Judging by Hirokawa and Gouran's theory, I see why I never went to Germany. I'd like to say it's because I tend to promote different alternatives, however, I can see how my smart/sarcastic comments tend to disrupt and take away from the task of problem analysis and goal setting. I wish I had a chance to do it over—after my big personality change, of course.

FOICS
Function-Oriented Interaction Coding System; a tool to record and classify the function of utterances during a group's discussion.

Hirokawa has made repeated efforts to develop a conversational coding system that classifies the function of specific statements. Much like Bales' interaction categories outlined in the introduction to group communication, Hirokawa's *Function-Oriented Interaction Coding System (FOICS)* requires researchers to categorize each *functional utterance,* which is "an uninterrupted statement of a single member that appears to perform a specified function within the group interaction process."[17]

Figure 17–3 shows a FOICS checklist that researchers might use to analyze communication within a group. As you can see, raters are asked to make two judgments: (1) Which of the four requisite functions, if any, does an utterance address? and (2) Does the remark facilitate (*promote*), inhibit (*disrupt*), or redirect (*counteract*) the group's focus on that function? Ideally, this 4 × 3 classification scheme provides 12 discrete categories of group discussion. With that information, researchers could determine the effect of communication on the quality of the decision the group makes.

Functional utterance
An uninterrupted statement of a single member that appears to perform a specific function.

In practice, however, analyzing the content of group discussion is fraught with difficulty. In the first place, independent raters find it hard to agree on how a statement should be coded. Extensive training boosts the reliability of their judgments, but Hirokawa is keenly aware that a single comment may serve multiple functions. In addition, words that appear helpful on the surface may have hidden power to disrupt, or vice versa. The process of coding comments has turned out to be an ongoing problem for all researchers who want to study the nature and effects of group communication.

	Problem Analysis	Goal Setting	Identification of Alternatives	Evaluation of Positives/Negatives
Promote				
Disrupt				
Counteract				

FIGURE 17–3 Function-Oriented Interaction Coding System (FOICS) Checklist

THOUGHTFUL ADVICE FOR THOSE WHO KNOW THEY ARE RIGHT

How can you and I use the functional perspective to facilitate better group decisions? We can start with a healthy dose of humility concerning the wisdom of our own opinions. Hirokawa and Gouran report that groups often abandon the rational path due to the persuasive efforts of members who are convinced that they alone have the right answer. Their discussion style proclaims, "Don't confuse me with the facts; my mind's made up," and they wear down the opposition. We can make sure we don't come to the table with the sort of closed-minded attitude that torpedoes honest discussion. Additionally, we should be wary of pushing any "intuitive hunch" or "gut feeling" that we can't back up with reasonable evidence. These are errors to avoid.

We can also take proactive measures to promote clear thinking within the group. In almost every article they write, Hirokawa and Gouran acknowledge their intellectual debt to early-twentieth-century American pragmatist philosopher John Dewey.[18] Dewey's pragmatism was based on the hopeful assumption that practical decisions can be brought under more intelligent control through the process of rational inquiry.[19] He advocated a six-step process of *reflective thinking* that parallels a doctor's approach to treating a patient:[20]

1. Recognize symptoms of illness.
2. Diagnose the cause of the ailment.
3. Establish criteria for wellness.
4. Consider possible remedies.
5. Test to determine which solutions will work.
6. Implement or prescribe the best solution.

Reflective thinking
Thinking that favors rational consideration over intuitive hunches or pressure from those with clout.

Note that Hirokawa and Gouran's four requisite functions are almost exact replicas of steps 2, 3, 4, and 5 in Dewey's reflective-thinking process. Both lists recommend that group members discuss issues in a way that promotes problem analysis, goal setting, discovery of alternatives, and evaluation of these options. When we're tempted to make remarks that will detract from the process, Hirokawa and Gouran suggest we bite our tongues. And when others say things that sidetrack the group from fulfilling the four functional requisites, the theorists urge us to counter with a comment aimed at getting the group back on a rational path.

You may be hesitant to counteract the dubious logic of a powerful leader or a high-status member of the group, but Hirokawa and Gouran don't advocate direct criticism. Instead, they recommend a strategy of insisting on a careful process. By raising questions, calling for more alternatives, and urging a thorough evaluation of evidence, a low-status member can have a high-power impact on the quality of the final decision.

ETHICAL REFLECTION: HABERMAS' DISCOURSE ETHICS

German philosopher Jürgen Habermas suggests a rational group process through which people can determine right from wrong—a different kind of decision than Hirokawa and Gouran usually study. In order to develop guidelines for ethical action, the Frankfurt School critical theorist pictures a diverse group of people engaged in public discourse. Habermas' ethical approach seeks an after-the-fact discussion about what we did in a particular situation and why we decided to do it. Being ethical means being accountable.[21]

Habermas assumes that people within a given culture or community can pretty much agree on the good they want to accomplish, and that over time they've built up practical wisdom on how to achieve it. For example, your campus newspaper reporters assume that it's good for students to know more about what's going on within the school's administration ("the people's right to know") and that guaranteeing confidentiality to insiders is the best way to find out ("protecting their sources"). This newsroom common sense is a good place to start doing journalistic ethics, but reporters' justification of the practice typically lacks reflective rigor. It often doesn't take into account the interests of everyone affected by their stories.

Habermas' *discourse ethics* sets up a discursive test for the validity of any moral claim. The person who performed an act must be prepared to discuss in an open forum what he or she did and why he or she did it. This deliberative process is a two-stage process of justification and application. The actor must reveal the general ethical principle that he or she used to justify the action and then show why it was the appropriate thing to do in those particular circumstances. Habermas imagines an *ideal speech situation* where participants are free to listen to reason and speak their minds without fear of constraint or control.[22] He's convinced that the validity of any ethical consensus can be reached only to the extent that three requirements are met:[23]

Discourse ethics
Jürgen Habermas' vision of the ideal speech situation in which diverse participants could rationally reach a consensus on universal ethical standards.

1. *Requirement for access.* All people affected by the ethical norm being debated can attend and be heard, regardless of their status. That means donors, administrators, professors, students, and minimum-wage staff at the school are welcome at the table without prejudice.
2. *Requirement for argument.* All participants are expected to exchange their points of view in the spirit of genuine reciprocity and mutual understanding. They aren't merely trying to advance their own interests but are trying to figure out whether an action serves the common good.
3. *Requirement for justification.* Everyone is committed to a standard of universalization. What makes ethical claims legitimate is their "acceptance not only among those who agree to live with and by them but by anyone *affected* by them."[24]

Ideal speech situation
A discourse on ethical accountability in which discussants represent all who will be affected by the decision, pursue discourse in a spirit of seeking the common good, and are committed to finding universal standards.

Habermas understands that thoroughly noncoercive dialogue is a utopian dream, yet he finds his conception of the ideal speech situation helpful in gauging the degree to which a discussion is rational. This, of course, is a major goal of Hirokawa's, Gouran's, and Dewey's. The trick is getting group members to do it.

CRITIQUE: IS RATIONALITY OVERRATED?

In their review of small-group communication literature, John Cragan and David Wright conclude that there are three leading theories.[25] One is Bormann's *symbolic convergence theory*, discussed in the next chapter. The second is Scott Poole's *adaptive structuration theory*, which you can read about in the theory list section of *www.afirstlook.com*. The third is Hirokawa and Gouran's functional perspective. In their critique of the functional perspective, communication professors Cynthia Stohl (University of California Santa Barbara) and Michael Holmes (Ball State University) explain why it is so highly regarded:

> The basic premise of the perspective, that communication serves task functions and the accomplishment of those functions should be associated with effective group decisions, is intuitively appealing and sensible. It also meets the standards of an objective theory in that it explains, is testable, simple, and practical.[26]

As a result, many communication scholars endorse the theory as a model for group discussion and decision making. One of my students is so convinced that he wrote, "A list of the four functions should be woven into the carpet of every committee room."

Yet Hirokawa's exclusive focus on rational talk may be the reason researchers get mixed results when they test his theory's predictions.[27] Note that the FOICS method of coding conversation all but ignores comments about relationships inside or outside the group. By treating relational statements as a distraction, Hirokawa commits the same mistake that the late Aubrey Fisher admitted he made in his own task-focused research:[28]

> The original purpose of the investigation . . . was to observe verbal task behavior free from the confounding variables of the socioemotional dimension. That purpose, of course, was doomed to failure. The two dimensions are interdependent.[29]

Stohl and Holmes' critique frames the same issue in a slightly different way. They contend that most real-life groups have a prior decision-making history and are embedded within a larger organization. They advocate adding a *historical function* that requires the group to talk about how past decisions were made. They also recommend an *institutional function* that is satisfied when members discuss the reality of power brokers and stakeholders who aren't at the table, but whose views clearly affect and are affected by the group decision.

Dennis Gouran has recently raised doubts about how useful the functional perspective may be for many small-group discussions.[30] He notes that almost all group dynamics research has dealt with decision making and problem solving. Although he and Hirokawa attempted to craft a one-size-fits-all model for group communication, he now believes it's beneficial for members to fulfill the four requisite functions only when they are addressing *questions of policy.* That's not always the case.

Investigative panels and juries deal with *questions of fact* such as "What happened?" or "Who's responsible?" College admission boards and product design teams face *questions of conjecture,* trying to figure out what's likely to happen in an uncertain future without any current way of knowing if their predictions are right. Religious groups and addiction recovery support groups face emotionally loaded *questions of value,* with members sharing or debating what they believe is acceptable, appropriate, ethical, or morally right. None of these questions has a discernable "right" or "high-quality" answer. Gouran doesn't believe that these alternative group goals invalidate the functional perspective, but he does suggest their existence shows that the theory isn't relevant in every situation. The scope of the functional perspective is more limited than first believed.

QUESTIONS TO SHARPEN YOUR FOCUS

1. Hirokawa and Gouran claim that small groups are like living *systems.* Do you see parallels between the four *functional requisites* of task groups and the body's need for respiration, circulation, digestion, and elimination?
2. Given that the functional theory focuses on *decision-making* and *problem-solving* groups, why is its silence on *relationship* issues a problem?

3. Think of a time when you've been part of a task group that strayed from the *goal path.* What *counteractive statement* could you have made that might have brought it back on track?
4. Why might you find it frustrating to use Hirokawa's *Function-Oriented Interaction Coding System (FOICS)* to analyze a group discussion?

SELF-QUIZ

For chapter self-quizzes, go to the book's Online Learning Center at *www.mhhe.com/griffin9e*

CONVERSATIONS

View this segment online at www.mhhe.com/griffin9e or www.afirstlook.com.

As you might expect from an objective theorist discussing a rational theory, Randy Hirokawa gives clear, concise responses to my opening questions about group decision making. Is it possible he will find a yet undiscovered requisite function? Are jokes a form of disruptive communication? But as the conversation continues, Hirokawa voices ideas not usually heard from thoroughgoing empiricists. He refers to the irony of questionable motives producing beneficial actions, a subjective standard to determine whether a decision is good, and his belief that there are no guarantees in life. Many students consider this conversation the best of the bunch.

A SECOND LOOK

Recommended resource: Dennis Gouran, Randy Hirokawa, Kelly Julian, and Geoff Leatham, "The Evolution and Current Status of the Functional Perspective on Communication in Decision-Making and Problem-Solving Groups," in *Communication Yearbook 16,* Stanley Deetz (ed.), Sage, Newbury Park, CA, 1993, pp. 573–600.

Original statement: Dennis Gouran and Randy Hirokawa, "The Role of Communication in Decision-Making Groups: A Functional Perspective," in *Communications in Transition,* Mary Mander (ed.), Praeger, New York, 1983, pp. 168–185.

Research review: Randy Hirokawa, "From the Tiny Pond to the Big Ocean: Studying Communication and Group Decision-Making Effectiveness from a Functional Perspective," 1999 B. Aubrey Fisher Memorial Lecture, Department of Communication, University of Utah, Salt Lake City, UT.

Role of communication: Randy Hirokawa and Dirk Scheerhorn, "Communication in Faulty Group Decision-Making," in *Communication and Group Decision-Making,* Randy Hirokawa and M. Scott Poole (eds.), Sage, Beverly Hills, CA, 1986, pp. 63–80.

Coding group interaction: Randy Hirokawa, "Functional Approaches to the Study of Group Discussion," *Small Group Research,* Vol. 25, 1994, pp. 542–550.

Additional propositions: Dennis Gouran and Randy Hirokawa, "Effective Decision Making and Problem Solving in Groups: A Functional Perspective," in *Small Group Communication: Theory and Practice,* 8th ed., Randy Hirokawa, Robert Cathcart, et al. (eds.), Roxbury, Los Angeles, CA, 2003, pp. 27–38.

Survey of group theories taking a functional perspective: Andrea B. Hollingshead, Gwen Wittenbaum, et al., "A Look at Groups from the Functional Perspective," in *Theories of Small Groups: Interdisciplinary Perspectives,* M. Scott Poole and Andrea B. Hollingshead (eds.), Sage, London, 2005, pp. 21–62.

Requisite functions accomplished face-to-face vs. CMC: Shu-Chu Sarrina Li, "Computer-Mediated Communication and Group Decision Making: A Functional Perspective," *Small Group Research,* Vol. 38, 2007, pp. 593–614.

Equivocal evidence that communication changes group decisions: Dean E. Hewes, "The Influence of Communication Processes on Group Outcomes: Antithesis and Thesis," *Human Communication Research,* Vol. 35, 2009, pp. 249–271.

Critique: Cynthia Stohl and Michael Holmes, "A Functional Perspective for Bona Fide Groups," *Communication Yearbook 16,* 1993, pp. 601–614.

Theorist's assessment of limited scope: Dennis Gouran, "Reflections on the Type of Question as a Determinant of the Form of Interaction in Decision-Making and Problem-Solving Discussions," *Communication Quarterly,* Vol. 53, 2003, pp. 111–125.

To access a chapter on Irving Janis' Groupthink,
click on Archive under Theory Resources at
www.afirstlook.com.

CHAPTER 18

Objective — Interpretive

Rhetorical tradition
Socio-psychological tradition

Symbolic Convergence Theory

of Ernest Bormann

In the introduction to this section on group communication, I refer to Harvard social psychologist Robert Bales' work to categorize comments made in small-group discussions. On the basis of his research with zero-history problem-solving groups in his lab, Bales discovered that *dramatizing* was a significant type of communication that often fostered group cohesiveness.[1] The late University of Minnesota communication professor Ernest Bormann picked up on Bales' finding and undertook a more extensive study of newly formed groups to examine leadership emergence, decision making, norms, cohesiveness, and a number of other features of group life.[2]

Similar to Bales, Bormann and his team of colleagues observed that group members often dramatized events happening outside the group, things that took place at previous meetings, or what might possibly occur among them in the future. Sometimes these stories fell flat and the discussion moved in a different direction. But at other times group members responded enthusiastically by adding on to the story or chiming in with their own matching narratives. When the drama was enhanced in this way, members developed a common group consciousness and drew closer together. On the basis of extensive case studies, Bormann set forth the central explanatory principle of symbolic convergence theory (SCT):

Sharing group fantasies creates symbolic convergence.[3]

When she read about Bormann's theory, Maggie had no difficulty illustrating this core claim. Two weeks before her communication course began, she served as a student leader in the Wheaton Passage program for new freshmen that's held at a camp in Wisconsin's Northwoods. One of the stated goals of this optional offering is to build intentional community. In her application log, Maggie wrote of unplanned communication that achieved this end.

> Cabin 8 was the rustic, run-down cabin that my group of Passage students was assigned to live in for the week. My co-leader and I decked the cabin out with decorations by hanging Christmas lights and origami doves, yet there was no

escaping the massive holes in the screens, sticky messes in the drawers, and the spiders residing in the rafters. The night students arrived, we walked our group of girls past the brand new cabins, arrived at our old cabin, and presented Cabin 8—their home for a week. Needless to say, they were less than pleased.

The next day as our group was trekking to our morning activity, one of the girls brought up what she thought the perfect cabin would look like. Others jumped in with their ideas. For 10 minutes, each girl contributed something to the discussion of the fantasy cabin. Hot tubs, screened-in porches, soft carpet, lounge chairs, and a glass roof for stargazing were all mentioned as features in their ideal cabin. Looking back on this experience, I see how this shared fantasy played a role in our cabin bonding. As the week went on, our dream cabin became a running joke within our group that helped students develop a sense of closeness—what they deemed "hardcoreness." While living in the crummy cabin, they frequently revisited the image of the ideal cabin they created in their conversation.

DRAMATIZING MESSAGES: CREATIVE INTERPRETATIONS OF THERE-AND-THEN

Many comments in task-oriented discussion groups offer lines of argument, factual information, members' opinions, and suggestions for how the group should proceed. That's the kind of member contribution Hirokawa and Gouran's functional perspective values (see Chapter 17). Advocates of rational discussion believe it's usually disruptive and counterproductive when someone cracks a joke, describes a movie, or starts talking about plans for the upcoming weekend. Not so for Bormann. SCT classifies these examples and many other forms of speaking as *dramatizing messages* and believes that conversations about things outside of what's going on right now can often serve the group well.

A dramatizing message is one that contains imaginative language such as a pun or other wordplay, figure of speech (e.g., metaphor, simile, personification), analogy, anecdote, allegory, fable, narrative, story, or other creative expression of ideas. Whatever the form, the dramatizing message describes events occurring somewhere else and/or at some time other than the here-and-now.[4]

Dramatizing message
Imaginative language by a group member describing past, future, or outside events; creative interpretations of there-and-then.

Notice first that a group member's words must paint a picture or call to mind an image in order to be labeled a dramatizing message. A comment that groups need conflict in order to make good decisions might stimulate discussion among members, but that's not dramatizing in the way Bormann used the term. Second, a vivid message qualifies as dramatizing if it either describes something outside the group or portrays an event that has happened within the group in the past or might happen to the group in the future. Comments that have no imagery or those that refer to what's currently going on in the group make up the bulk of most group discussions. They aren't dramatizing messages.

When Maggie's girls started to verbally construct their ideal cabin, they were using imaginative language to talk about what they'd like to see in the future, probably wishing it would magically appear that night. If in a darker tone one of the girls expressed her hope that someone would set fire to the cabin before they returned, that message would also be dramatizing. But if the group of girls sat around in the cabin grousing about the spiders, mosquitoes, and sticky goo in the drawers, those comments would be about the here-and-now and wouldn't be defined as dramatizing messages.

Why is this distinction so important to Bormann and SCT advocates? Because dramatizing messages are interpretive. They aren't knee-jerk responses to experiences of the moment. "Dramatizing accounts of past occurrences artistically organize what are usually more complex, ambiguous, and chaotic experiences."[5] They help the speaker, and sometimes the listeners, make sense out of a confusing situation or bring some clarity to an uncertain future. Whether or not other group members connect with their imagery, dramatizing messages are creative interpretations of the there-and-then.

FANTASY CHAIN REACTIONS: UNPREDICTABLE SYMBOLIC EXPLOSIONS

Some people use the term *fantasy* to refer to children's literature, sexual desire, or things "not true." Bormann, however, reserved the term *fantasy* for dramatizing messages that are enthusiastically embraced by the whole group. Most dramatizing messages don't get that kind of reaction. They often fall on deaf ears, or group members listen but take a ho-hum attitude toward what was said. Of course, an embarrassing silence or a quick change of subject makes it obvious that the dramatizing message has fallen flat. As the cartoon below illustrates, there may even be group members who openly oppose what was said. Yet as Bormann noted, "Some dramatizing messages cause a symbolic explosion in the form of a chain reaction in which members join in until the entire group comes alive."[6] He described what he had seen when a fantasy chains out in this way:

> The tempo of the conversation would pick up. People would grow excited, interrupt one another, blush, laugh, forget their self-consciousness. The tone of the meeting, often quiet and tense immediately prior to the dramatizing, would

"Pardon us, Harrison, if the board fails to share your enthusiasm for the foliage up in Darien."

become lively, animated, and boisterous, the chaining process, involving both the verbal and nonverbal communication, indicating participation in the drama.[7]

A concrete example of a fantasy chain and its results may be helpful. University of Kentucky communication professor Alan DeSantis asks us to picture a group of Kentucky-born, middle-aged white guys sitting around a cigar store smoking hand-rolled imported cigars. As the topic shifts from college basketball to the risk of smoking, the owner tells the story of a heart surgeon who came into the shop after having been on duty for 36 hours. After lighting up, the doctor blew out a big mouthful of smoke and said, "This is the most relaxed I have felt in days. Now how can that be bad for you?"[8]

Whether or not the doctor really said this isn't the issue. Symbolic convergence theory is concerned with the group's response to the tale. In this case the patrons chuckle in appreciation, nod in agreement, or say "You've got it!" to punctuate the narrative. Some vie to tell their own stories that dismiss the harm of cigar smoking, a pastime they consider a benign hobby. Bormann said that we can spot a *fantasy chain* through a common response to the imagery. DeSantis, who was a cigar-smoking participant-observer among the shop's regular customers, affirms that the group's response to the owner's story paralleled Bormann's description above.

Symbolic convergence researchers have had little success predicting when a fantasy will ignite and trigger a chain reaction. They've found there's a better chance of a fantasy chaining out when the group is frustrated (as were Maggie's girls) or when they are bogged down in an effort to solve a thorny problem. Also, members with rhetorical skill seem to have a better chance of providing the spark, but there's no guarantee that their words will ignite others. And even when a skillful image-maker does spark a fantasy chain, he or she has little control over where the conversation will go. Fantasy chains seem to have a life of their own. But once a fantasy chain catches fire, symbolic convergence theory predicts that the group will converge around a fantasy theme.

Fantasy chain
A symbolic explosion of lively agreement within a group in response to a member's dramatizing message.

FANTASY THEMES—CONTENT, MOTIVES, CUES, TYPES

Bormann's technical definition of *fantasy* is "the creative and imaginative shared interpretation of events that fulfills a group's psychological or rhetorical needs."[9]

Think of a *fantasy theme* as the *content* of the dramatizing message that successfully sparks a fantasy chain. As such, it's the theory's basic unit of analysis. Because fantasy themes reflect and create a group's culture, all SCT researchers seek to identify the fantasy theme or themes that group members share. When spotted, fantasy themes are consistently ordered, always interpretive, and they inevitably put the group's slant on things. That is, fantasy themes act as a rhetorical means to sway doubters or naysayers.

Fantasy
The creative and imaginative shared interpretation of events that fulfills a group's psychological or rhetorical needs.

When a fantasy chains out among core patrons in the cigar store, we would expect to see that same theme run throughout multiple narratives. Perhaps the hero of every man's account is a famous cigar smoker who lived into old age without ill effects—think George Burns, Winston Churchill, or Fidel Castro. Or maybe each image reflects a meddling government bureaucrat who wants to limit their right to enjoy a cigar in a public place. Along with examples of long-lived smokers, group fantasies might focus on the difference between cigars and cigarettes, safety in moderation, inconsistent scientific findings concerning

Fantasy theme
Content of the fantasy that has chained out within a group; SCT's basic unit of analysis.

cancer, the greater risks of everyday living, and the health benefits of relaxation that come from smoking a good cigar. All of these fantasies have the same basic theme—*cigar smoking is safe.*

Bormann suggested that group members' *meanings, emotions, motives,* and *actions* are apparent in their fantasy themes. We can see all four of these in DeSantis' description of the angst that the core group of patrons experienced at the premature death of their friend Greg. Like the rest of the store's regulars who sat around smoking, Greg had scoffed at the health risks of their practice. Now they were confronted with the sobering fact of his fatal heart attack. Within a week of the funeral, however, his smoking buddies had constructed a verbal collage of images depicting Greg's stressful lifestyle. The store owner voiced their consensus: "Smoking had nothing to do with his death. He lived, drank and played hard and it took a toll on him at the end."[10] *Meaning:* Hard living killed Greg. *Emotion:* Reduction of fear; relief. *Motive:* Desire to smoke with buddies. *Action:* Not going to quit. Fantasy themes create a group's social reality.

Bormann and symbolic convergence theory advocates have found that many fantasy themes are indexed by a *symbolic cue.* A symbolic cue is "an agreed-upon trigger that sets off the group members to respond as they did when they first shared the fantasy."[11] It could be a code word, nonverbal gesture, phrase, slogan, inside joke, bumper sticker, or any shorthand way of re-establishing the full force of shared fantasy. In the Kentucky smoke shop where these fantasy themes were voiced, any mention of criticism of cigar smoking from family or friends was the cue that set off a new round of protest among store regulars. Their emotional reaction was captured on a T-shirt sold at the store that satirized the surgeon general's cautionary statement: "Warning—Harassing me about my smoking can be hazardous to your health."[12]

Symbolic cue
An agreed-upon trigger that sets off group members to respond as they did when they first shared the fantasy.

The meaning of a given fantasy theme is quite specific. Since clusters of related fantasy themes sometimes surface again and again in different groups, Bormann found it helpful to have a label to classify this phenomenon when it occurs. He used the term *fantasy type* to describe these well-worn symbolic paths. Fantasy types are "greater abstractions incorporating several concrete fantasy themes" and they exist "when shared meaning is taken for granted."[13] The cigar store group's fantasy theme of family and friends criticizing their smoking could be considered part of a larger "get-off-my-case" fantasy type. Perhaps that's a fantasy type that you and your friends have drawn upon when talking about your lifestyle, even if you've never smoked a cigar. Or students at your school may share stock fantasy types about Saturday night parties, the food on campus, professors who never seem to be in their offices, or the guy who always bails out at the last minute on a group project.

Fantasy type
A cluster of related fantasy themes; greater abstractions incorporating several concrete fantasy themes that exist when shared meaning is taken for granted.

SYMBOLIC CONVERGENCE: GROUP CONSCIOUSNESS AND OFTEN COHESIVENESS

The discussion of dramatizing messages, fantasy chains, and fantasy themes has dealt with the first part of SCT's core principle: *Sharing group fantasies creates symbolic convergence.* We're now ready to look at what that sharing creates—symbolic convergence. For Bormann, *symbolic convergence* meant the way in which "two or more private symbol worlds incline toward each other, come more closely together, or even overlap."[14] As those worlds intersect, group members develop a unique group consciousness. No longer do members think in terms of

Symbolic convergence
Two or more private symbol worlds incline toward each other, come more closely together, or even overlap; group consciousness, cohesiveness.

I, me, and *mine.* As symbolic overlap takes place, they begin to think and speak about *we, us,* and *ours.*

Do shared fantasies really cause this group transformation? Bormann insisted they do. Some limited commonality of words and images may naturally occur when group members interact often enough over a long period of time. But the process is accelerated and extended way beyond what otherwise might happen when members participate in one or more fantasy chains that create joint fantasy themes. Bormann used a variety of terms to portray the effect of group consciousness—*common ground, meeting of the minds, mutual understanding, groupiness, common social reality,* and *empathic communion.*

Once a group experiences symbolic convergence, Bormann suggested it's important for members to memorialize their group consciousness with a name and recorded history (*saga*) that recalls moments when fantasies chained out. He did that with his University of Minnesota colleagues who met in the Bormann home every Wednesday night to discuss the ideas that make up symbolic convergence theory. They called themselves the *Turtle Racers*—presumably based on an illustrated poster with the caption "Behold the turtle who makes progress only when he sticks his neck out." The image of a turtle race seemed doubly appropriate to their history of theory building when Bormann described the work going forward in fits and starts.

Symbolic convergence usually results in heightened group *cohesiveness*—members attracted to each other and sticking together through thick and thin. But not always. Bormann regarded symbolic convergence as usually a necessary but not sufficient cause of cohesiveness.

> Groups that do little fantasizing are seldom highly attractive and cohesive. Such groups tend to be boring and ordinary. The cohesive groups have usually done considerable fantasizing, but not all groups that fantasize a lot are rewarding and cohesive. The fantasies that chain may contribute to creating a social reality that is warm, friendly and hard working, that provides the group with a strong identity and self image, and that gives members a sense of purpose and meaning for their group's work. On the other hand, the fantasies may develop a group climate that is fascinating, frustrating, and punishing.[15]

Bormann went on to say that fantasy themes in those negative groups are riddled with conflict and that the humor expressed tends to be satire, ridicule, or sarcasm. I was in such a group my sophomore year of college, and he was right—it was fascinating. Fortunately I had enough sense to bail out.

RHETORICAL VISION: A COMPOSITE DRAMA SHARED BY A RHETORICAL COMMUNITY

Up to this point in the chapter, my description and illustration of symbolic convergence theory has focused on shared fantasies in small-group settings. That's where SCT was spawned. But early in the theory's development, the Turtle Racers discovered that shared fantasies weren't confined to a small-group context. As Bormann explained, "Fantasies that begin in small groups often are worked into public speeches, become picked up by mass media and 'spread out across larger publics.'"[16] Once attuned to the basic concepts of SCT, these scholars spotted swirling batches of related fantasy themes and types in all sorts of communication texts. Bormann coined the term *rhetorical vision* to designate "a composite drama that catches up large groups of people into a common symbolic reality."[17] He called the wide-ranging body of people who share that reality a *rhetorical community.*

Rhetorical vision
A composite drama that catches up large groups of people into a common symbolic reality.

The majority of research conducted using SCT has been aimed at capturing the rhetorical visions of dispersed rhetorical communities and figuring out how their communication created their unified fantasies. Researchers don't have the benefit of sitting in a room with the whole community while waiting for a fantasy to chain out as evidence of a fantasy theme. So Bormann and his colleagues developed a procedure called *fantasy theme analysis* to discover fantasy themes and rhetorical visions that have already been created.

Fantasy Theme Analysis

Fantasy theme analysis is a specific type of rhetorical criticism that's built on two basic assumptions. First, people create their social reality—a premise shared by many interpretive theorists (see Chapters 5, 6, 11, and 13). Second, people's meanings, motives, and emotions can be seen in their rhetoric. So when a dispersed community embraces the same rhetorical vision, that's reality for them. They aren't pretending.

Fantasy theme analysis
A type of rhetorical criticism used to detect fantasy themes and rhetorical visions; the interpretive methodology of SCT.

A rhetorical critic using fantasy theme analysis looks for recurring fantasy themes in the text. If found, the critic should then discern if these shared fantasies are woven together into a rhetorical vision. In addition to using the basic SCT concepts already discussed, Bormann suggested that the critic look for at least four features that are present in all rhetorical visions.[18]

1. **Characters:** Are there heroes to root for and villains to despise?
2. **Plot lines:** Do characters act in a way consistent with the rhetorical vision?
3. **Scene:** How do descriptions of time and place increase the drama's impact?
4. **Sanctioning agent:** Who or what legitimates the rhetorical vision?

I'll describe a fantasy theme analysis of Internet websites to demonstrate how these tools can reveal a rhetorical vision and show how that vision is created and sustained within a dispersed rhetorical community.

The Symbolic Creation of a Pro-Eating Disorder Rhetorical Vision

For those who are anorexic and/or bulimic, the world of face-to-face communication can be a lonely place. Afraid of condemnation if they reveal their eating disorder, they often live a life of secrecy, deception, and guilt. Although 12-step programs extend social support to those who want to overcome their disease, not all people with food disorders want to change. The Internet offers hundreds of pro-eating disorder websites where those who resist recovery can anonymously interact with like-minded others. Wayne State University communication professor Jessi McCabe conducted a fantasy theme analysis to "explore how group exchanges on these websites redefine a reality largely rejected by the cultural norm and what elements contribute to creating this worldview."[19] She chose the 12 most active pro-food disorder sites for her analysis. The message boards on the three most popular sites—Blue Dragon Fly, Pro-Ana Suicide Society, and Fragile Innocence—had a combined membership of more than 25,000 users.

Fantasy types are an SCT category midway between specific fantasy themes and an overall rhetorical vision. McCabe found that two contrasting fantasy types emerged in her analysis—a positive one and a negative one. She labeled the positive fantasy type "The humorous world of Ana and Mia." Within this world, fantasy chains reinforce site users' eating habits and shared reality. Across the message boards, members personify their disorders as characters in an ongoing drama.

> Members depict their own goals, struggles, and emotions through the personification of Ana and Mia. Anorexia and bulimia are given life and attributed human-like emotions and qualities, which are justified by the sanctioning agent, humor. The most favorable depiction is a girl named Ana (anorexia), who represents the goal of the group, the idolization of perfection in this reality. Perfection is about having self-control and being thin. Personified through Ana is a yearning for being untouchable and perfect.[20]

Message-board users write about Ana as their hero. ("Ana knows what to say to make me feel better."[21]) They also confess lapses and seek her forgiveness. ("Dear Ana, I am sorry that I failed you. . . . Not only did I fail you but I binged."[22])

Unlike Ana, Mia (bulimia) isn't seen as perfect. Her role in the drama is to stir up the emotions users feel as they struggle to get down to the elusive perfect weight. Site users rarely describe Mia in positive terms. One post complains, "Mia is SO loud and annoying . . . my Mom heard Mia because she can't keep her [stinking] mouth shut!"[23] Yet other messages reluctantly suggest Mia is needed. "Sometimes she is all right . . . she lets me eat . . . keeps my body pure."[24] The third character in this ongoing drama is the villainous ED (eating disorder). He represents the social norm of moderation and recovery from addiction. McCabe explains why he's so feared: "Members not only try to avoid ED for fear of recovery but the group knows that accepting ED means a loss of community and a reentry into a reality in which eating disorders are a negative attribute."[25]

The discussion of these three characters constructs an alternative world where high-risk dieters aren't hassled. Despite the lurking presence of ED, who reminds everyone of another reality "out there," this positive fantasy type is a closed world where anorexics and bulimics feel safe. McCabe sees humor as the *sanctioning agent* that makes this constructed reality legitimate for site users. The satirical exchange of experiences turns discussion of a deadly disease into a game that validates what these users are doing, saying, and living.

Conversely, the negative fantasy type portrayed on these message boards is "Surviving encounters with The Real World," a distressing place for those who visit these websites. McCabe notes that almost all users log on to get tips on "safe" foods and how to hide their eating habits and symptoms from friends and family. The *scene* of the struggle in "the real world" is almost always part of this fantasy type. Many posts include references to time and space.

> I hate coming home at night. . . . I am with Ana all day and I cannot eat . . . but when I get home Ana stays at the door and I just binge.[26]

> How can I live with Mia if we are sharing community bathrooms in our dorm?[27]

McCabe doesn't explicitly address *plot lines* in her fantasy theme analysis, but from her rich description two plots seem paramount. The first is acting in multiple ways to reduce weight—dieting, exercising, and purging. The second plot is doing whatever one has to do to keep the extent of this obsession with food a secret from those who don't share it.

McCabe concludes that the rhetorical vision of the pro-eating disorder community is the uneasy coexistence of these two contrasting fantasy types—*The humorous world of Ana and Mia* and *Surviving encounters with The Real World.* She writes, "The rhetorical vision shared by this group is the effort to maintain a disease within settings where their belief is challenged and get back to the state where the personification of the disease can proliferate."[28]

THEORY INTO PRACTICE: ADVICE TO IMPROVE YOUR COLLEGE EXPERIENCE

As you've gained an understanding of symbolic convergence theory, you've hopefully thought about its implications for a group in which you take part. No matter what your role in the group, Bormann has offered the following advice:[29]

- When the group begins to share a drama that in your opinion would contribute to a healthy culture, you should pick up the drama and feed the chain.
- If the fantasies are destructive, creating group paranoia or depression, cut the chain off whenever possible.
- To build cohesiveness, use personification to identify your group.
- Be sure to encourage the sharing of dramas depicting your group history early in your meetings.
- Remember that a conscious rhetorical effort on your part can succeed in igniting a chain reaction, but the fantasy may take an unexpected turn.

Bormann and his followers have also used fantasy theme analysis to improve organizational communication, conduct market research, and assess public opinion. To illustrate the pragmatic value of the methodology, John Cragan (University of St. Thomas—Minnesota) and Donald Shields (University of Missouri–St. Louis) require students in their applied research classes to analyze the way high school seniors talk about college. They find that most rhetorical visions employ one of three competing master analogues—a righteous vision, a social vision, or a pragmatic vision.[30]

Potential applicants who embrace a *righteous* vision are interested in a school's academic excellence, the reputation of its faculty, and special programs it offers. Those who adopt a *social* vision view college as a means of getting away from home, meeting new friends, and joining others in a variety of social activities. High school seniors who buy into a *pragmatic* vision are looking for a marketable degree that will help them get a good job. (What was your vision when you entered college?) Knowledge of these distinct visions could help admissions officers at your school develop a strategy to appeal to prospective students who would most appreciate the character of your campus. That knowledge could also help you figure out if you're at a school that can best meet your needs.

CRITIQUE: JUDGING SCT AS BOTH A SCIENTIFIC AND INTERPRETIVE THEORY

Ernest Bormann claimed that symbolic convergence theory is both objective and interpretive. The theory's basic explanatory hypothesis—*sharing group fantasies creates symbolic convergence*—is framed as a universal principle that holds for all people, in any culture, at any time, in any communication context.[31] Definitely objective. But the methodology of determining fantasy themes, fantasy types, and rhetorical visions is rhetorical criticism—a humanistic approach that's undeniably interpretive. Perhaps this unusual mix has stimulated many of the 1,000 original research studies that have examined and applied the theory over the last 40 years.[32] Bormann wryly noted that one positive result from SCT has been the collaboration between "muddleheaded anecdotalists and hardheaded empiricists."[33] When the six standards for judging a social science theory and the six criteria for evaluating an interpretive theory are applied to SCT, the theory stacks up remarkably well. I'll single out four of these benchmarks for further discussion.

1. *A good objective theory explains what occurs and why it happened.* The concept of symbolic convergence can help us make sense of chaotic group discussions. Even though group leaders urge members to *speak one at a time* and *stick to the point,* participants often go off on verbal tangents. According to SCT, graphic digressions and boisterous talk aren't signs of a flawed process; rather, they are evidence that the group is chaining out a fantasy and developing a group consciousness. This explanation of how groups become cohesive is a strength of the theory. However, University of Oklahoma communication professor James Olufowote doesn't believe Bormann's explanation goes far enough. In a sympathetic critique aimed at making the theory better, he contends that "SCT does not sufficiently explain why humans are predisposed to dramatizing reality and sharing fantasy in the first place."[34]

2. *A good objective theory predicts what's going to happen.* SCT clearly predicts that when a fantasy chain erupts among members, symbolic convergence will occur. The theory even suggests that without shared fantasies, there will be little or no cohesiveness. But as discussed earlier in the chapter, SCT researchers have had minimal success predicting when a dramatizing message will trigger a chain reaction. On that point, Bormann noted that uncertainty about the future isn't bothersome in other scientific theories. He saw symbolic convergence theory as similar to Darwin's biological theory of evolution in that respect.

> An evolutionary theory can explain the way modern humans evolved from earlier humanoid individuals. But, such theories cannot predict the future path of evolution. . . . SCT involves a careful cataloguing of group consciousness through time. The theory also includes a description of the dynamic forces that provide a necessary and sufficient set of causes to explain the discovered communication patterns. For an evolution theory the dynamic may be the survival of the fittest. For SCT the dynamic is the process of group sharing.[35]

3. *A good interpretive theory clarifies people's values.* There's no doubt that fantasy theme analysis uncovers the values of a rhetorical community. It does that well. But Olufowote is concerned about the unexamined values that undergird SCT.[36] One concern is an ideology of convergence. The terms that describe its effects—*common ground, meeting of the minds, empathic communion,* etc.—make it clear that the theory has a pro-social bias. Shall we look at the convergence of hate groups or pro-eating disorder websites as a positive outcome?

A second concern Olufowote expresses is an egalitarian assumption that ignores issues of power within groups. For example, do all members of a group benefit equally when a fantasy chains out? Does an *inside joke* become a symbolic cue at the expense of one of the members? A final concern is about the way members of a rhetorical community are characterized. The communities described come across as conflict-free. Differences among members are ignored, and there's little discussion of the inner tension a member feels when the multiple rhetorical visions he or she embraces don't mesh.

4. *A good interpretive theory offers a new understanding of people.* SCT's method of fantasy theme analysis does this exceptionally well by directing rhetorical critics to focus on symbolic language. A few scholars charge that the best fantasy theme analyses are the result of critics' astute perception or acumen rather than the method they use.[37] Bormann acknowledged that some critics do it better than others. But he noted that regardless of how perceptive the critic, the method used makes a huge difference. For example, a Marxist critique looks for economic exploitation; a feminist critique looks for patterns of male dominance. Think how different the analyses of cigar store smokers or pro-eating disorder message-board users would be if DeSantis or McCabe hadn't zeroed in on imaginative language. With that lens in place, fantasy theme analysts uncover rhetorical visions as varied as the communities they study. When I read a well-written fantasy theme analysis, I gain a greater appreciation for the fascinating diversity within the human race.

QUESTIONS TO SHARPEN YOUR FOCUS

1. As a rhetorically sensitive scholar, Bormann defined SCT terms carefully. Can you distinguish between *dramatizing messages* and *fantasies?* Do you understand why it's a difference that makes a difference?
2. Some critics dismiss SCT as a cookie-cutter approach to group analysis. Could this be said of most social science theories? Bormann regarded the charge as a compliment.[38] Can you figure out why he was pleased rather than offended?
3. Bormann insisted that SCT is an objective theory that's valid *any time* and in *any culture,* but that its methodology, *fantasy theme analysis,* is interpretive. Do you regard SCT as a better *objective* or *interpretive* theory? Why?
4. Bormann was intrigued with a T-shirt that proclaims, "I have given up my search for truth. Now I want to find a good fantasy."[39] Based on what you've read, does this slogan reflect the *symbolic world* of SCT advocates? Does it reflect yours?

A SECOND LOOK

Recommended resource: Ernest G. Bormann, John Cragan, and Donald Shields, "Three Decades of Developing, Grounding, and Using Symbolic Convergence Theory (SCT)," in *Communication Yearbook 25,* William Gudykunst (ed.), Lawrence Erlbaum, Mahwah, NJ, 2001, pp. 271–313.

Brief summary: Ernest Bormann, "Symbolic Convergence Theory," in *Small Group Communication Theory & Practice: An Anthology,* 8th ed., Randy Hirokawa, Robert Cathcart, Larry Samovar, and Linda Henman (eds.), Roxbury, Los Angeles, CA, 2003, pp. 39–47.

Early statement of the theory: Ernest G. Bormann, "Fantasy and Rhetorical Vision: The Rhetorical Criticism of Social Reality," *Quarterly Journal of Speech,* Vol. 58, 1972, pp. 396–407.

Small-group context: Ernest G. Bormann and Nancy C. Bormann, *Effective Small Group Communication*, 5th ed., Burgess, Edina, MN, 1992, pp. 105–126.

Organizational context: Ernest G. Bormann, "Symbolic Convergence: Organizational Communication and Culture," in *Communication and Organizations: An Interpretive Approach*, Linda Putnam and Michael Pacanowsky (eds.), Sage, Beverly Hills, CA, 1983, pp. 99–122.

Fantasy theme analysis: Sonja K. Foss, *Rhetorical Criticism: Exploration and Practice*, 4th ed., Waveland, Prospect Heights, IL, 2009, pp. 97–136.

Practical applications of assessing rhetorical visions: John F. Cragan and Donald C. Shields, *Symbolic Theories in Applied Communication Research: Bormann, Burke, and Fisher*, Hampton, Cresskill, NJ, 1995, pp. 161–198.

Cigar store ethnography: Alan D. DeSantis, "Smoke Screen: An Ethnographic Study of a Cigar Shop's Collective Rationalization," *Health Communication*, Vol. 14, 2002, pp. 167–198.

Symbolic convergence in a neighborhood watch group: Cheryl Broom and Susan Avanzino, "The Communication of Community Collaboration: When Rhetorical Visions Collide," *Communication Quarterly*, Vol. 58, 2010, pp. 480–501.

Pro-eating disorder website analysis: Jessi McCabe, "Resisting Alienation: The Social Construction of Internet Communities Supporting Eating Disorders," *Communication Studies*, Vol. 60, 2009, pp. 1–15.

Small-group fantasies becoming rhetorical visions: Ernest Bormann, "The Critical Analysis of Seminal American Fantasies," in *The Force of Fantasy: Restoring the American Dream*, Southern Illinois University, Carbondale, IL, 2001, pp. 1–25.

Early critique: G. P. Mohrmann, "An Essay on Fantasy Theme Criticism" and "Fantasy Theme Criticism: A Peroration," *Quarterly Journal of Speech*, Vol. 68, 1982, pp. 109–132, 306–313.

Response to early critics: Ernest G. Bormann, John Cragan, and Donald Shields, "In Defense of Symbolic Convergence Theory: A Look at the Theory and Its Criticisms After Two Decades," *Communication Theory*, Vol. 4, 1994, pp. 259–294.

Contemporary critique: James O. Olufowote, "Rousing and Redirecting a Sleeping Giant: Symbolic Convergence Theory and Complexities in the Communicative Constitution of Collective Action," *Management Communication Quarterly*, Vol. 19, 2006, pp. 451–492.

Will our group stay like this or will it change?
Poole's Adaptive Structuration Theory answers this question.
Click on Archive under Theory Resources at
www.afirstlook.com.

Organizational Communication

What do the following organizations have in common—the *United States Navy, McDonald's, General Motors,* and the *Green Bay Packers?* The first three are gigantic organizations, the middle two sell a tangible product, and the last three are publicly owned corporations that try to make a profit. But in terms of organizational communication, their most important common feature is that each is a prime example of *classical management theory* in action. Figure OC–1 lists some of the principles of this traditional approach to management.

Classical management theory places a premium on productivity, precision, and efficiency. As York University (Toronto) professor Gareth Morgan notes, these are the very qualities you expect from a well-designed, smoothly running machine. Morgan uses the mechanistic metaphor because he finds significant parallels between mechanical devices and the way managers traditionally think about their organizations.[1] In classical management theory, workers are seen as cogs in vast machines that function smoothly as long as their range of motion is clearly defined and their actions are lubricated with an adequate hourly wage.

Machines repeat straightforward, repetitive tasks, just as McDonald's workers have cooked billions of hamburgers, each one in exactly the same way. Machines have interchangeable parts that can be replaced when broken or worn out, just as a National Football League coach can insert a new player into the tight-end slot when the current starter is injured or begins to slow down. A new Chevy Tahoe comes with a thick operator's manual that specifies how the van should be driven, but the GM employee handbook is thicker and contains even more detailed instructions on how things are done within the company. As for the U.S. Navy, the fleet is an integral part of the country's war machine, and officers at every level are most comfortable when it runs like one.

Unity of command—an employee should receive orders from only one superior.

Scalar chain—the line of authority from superior to subordinate, which runs from top to bottom of the organization; this chain, which results from the unity-of-command principle, should be used as a channel for communication and decision making.

Division of work—management should aim to achieve a degree of specialization designed to achieve the goal of the organization in an efficient manner.

Authority and responsibility—attention should be paid to the right to give orders and to exact obedience; an appropriate balance between authority and responsibility should be achieved.

Discipline—obedience, application, energy, behavior, and outward marks of respect in accordance with agreed rules and customs.

Subordination of individual interest to general interest—through firmness, example, fair agreements, and constant supervision.

FIGURE OC–1 Selected Principles of Classical Management Theory
Excerpted from Gareth Morgan, "Organizations as Machines," in *Images of Organizations*

"Bad news, hon. I got replaced by an app."

The three theories in this section view classical management theory as outmoded and reject the idea that organization members are like replaceable parts. Each approach searches for ways of thinking about organizations other than as machines. The *cultural approach* looks for stories and shared meanings that are unique to a given organization. The *constitutive approach* believes communication itself is the essence of any organization. And the *critical approach* looks at organizations as political systems where conflict and power should be negotiated openly. Above all, the theorists who employ these approaches are committed to developing humane ways of talking about people and the organizational tasks they do.

CHAPTER 19

Objective — Interpretive

Socio-cultural tradition
Semiotic tradition

Cultural Approach to Organizations

of Clifford Geertz & Michael Pacanowsky

The late Princeton anthropologist Clifford Geertz wrote that "man is an animal suspended in webs of significance that he himself has spun."[1] He pictured culture as those webs. In order to travel across the strands toward the center of the web, an outsider must discover the common interpretations that hold the web together. Culture is shared meaning, shared understanding, shared sensemaking.

Geertz conducted field research in the islands of Indonesia and on the Moroccan highlands, rural settings remote from industrial activity. His best-known monograph is an in-depth symbolic analysis of the Balinese cockfight. Geertz never wrote a treatise on the bottom line, never tried to decipher the significance of the office Christmas party, and never met a payroll—a disqualifying sin in the eyes of many business professionals. Despite his silence on the topic of big business, Geertz' interpretive approach has proved useful in making sense of organizational activity.

In the field of communication, former University of Colorado professor Michael Pacanowsky has applied Geertz' cultural insights to organizational life. He says that if culture consists of webs of meaning that people have spun, and if spun webs imply the act of spinning, "then we need to concern ourselves not only with the structures of cultural webs, but with the process of their spinning as well."[2] That process is communication. It is communication that "creates and constitutes the taken-for-granted reality of the world."[3]

CULTURE AS A METAPHOR OF ORGANIZATIONAL LIFE

The use of culture as a root metaphor was undoubtedly stimulated by Western fascination with the economic success of Japanese corporations in the 1970s and 1980s. Back then, when American business leaders traveled to the Far East to study methods of production, they discovered that the superior quantity and quality of

Japan's industrial output had less to do with technology than with workers' shared cultural value of loyalty to each other and to their corporation. Organizations look radically different depending on how people in the host culture structure meaning. Communal face-saving in Japan is foreign to the class antagonism of Great Britain or the we're-number-one competitive mindset of the United States.

Today the term *corporate culture* means different things to different people. Some observers use the phrase to describe the surrounding environment that constrains a company's freedom of action. (U.S. workers would scoff at singing a corporate anthem at the start of their working day.) Others use the term to refer to a quality or property of the organization. (Acme Gizmo is a friendly place to work.) They speak of *culture* as synonymous with *image, character,* or *climate.* But Pacanowsky is committed to Geertz' symbolic approach and thus considers culture as more than a single variable in organizational research:

> Organizational culture is not just another piece of the puzzle; it is the puzzle. From our point of view, culture is not something an organization has; a culture is something an organization is.[4]

WHAT CULTURE IS; WHAT CULTURE IS NOT

Geertz admitted that the concept of culture as *systems of shared meaning* is somewhat vague and difficult to grasp. Though popular usage equates culture with concerts and art museums, he refused to use the word to signify *less primitive.* No modern anthropologist would fall into the trap of classifying people as high- or low-culture.

Culture
Webs of significance; systems of shared meaning.

Culture is not whole or undivided. Geertz pointed out that even close-knit societies have subcultures and countercultures within their boundaries. For example, employees in the sales and accounting departments of the same company may eye each other warily—the first group calling the accountants *number crunchers* and *bean counters,* the accountants in turn labeling members of the sales force *fast talkers* and *glad-handers.* Despite their differences, both groups may regard the blue-collar bowling night of the production workers as a strange ritual compared with their own weekend ritual of a round of golf.

For Pacanowsky, the web of organizational culture is the residue of employees' performance—"those very actions by which members constitute and reveal their culture to themselves and to others."[5] He notes that job performance may play only a minor role in the enactment of corporate culture.

> People do get the job done, true (though probably not with the singleminded task-orientation communication texts would have us believe); but people in organizations also gossip, joke, knife one another, initiate romantic involvements, cue new employees to ways of doing the least amount of work that still avoids hassles from a supervisor, talk sports, arrange picnics.[6]

Cultural performance
Actions by which members constitute and reveal their culture to themselves and others; an ensemble of texts.

Geertz called these cultural performances "an ensemble of texts . . . which the anthropologist strains to read over the shoulder of those to whom they properly belong."[7] The elusive nature of culture prompted Geertz to label its study a *soft science.* It is "not an experimental science in search of law, but an interpretive one in search of meaning."[8] The corporate observer is one part scientist, one part drama critic.

The fact that symbolic expression requires interpretation is nicely captured in a story about Pablo Picasso recorded by York University (Toronto) professor Gareth Morgan.[9] A man commissioned Picasso to paint a portrait of his wife. Startled by the nonrepresentational image on the canvas, the woman's husband complained, "It isn't how she really looks." When asked by the painter how she really looked, the man produced a photograph from his wallet. Picasso's comment: "Small, isn't she?"

THICK DESCRIPTION: WHAT ETHNOGRAPHERS DO

Geertz referred to himself as an *ethnographer,* one whose job is to sort out the symbolic meanings of people's actions within their culture. Just as geographers chart the physical territory, ethnographers map out social discourse. They do this "to discover who people think they are, what they think they are doing, and to what end they think they are doing it."[10] There's no shortcut for the months of participant observation required to collect an exhaustive account of interaction. Without that raw material, there would be nothing to interpret.

Ethnography
Mapping out social discourse; discovering who people within a culture think they are, what they think they are doing, and to what end they think they are doing it.

Geertz spent years in Indonesia and Morocco, developing his deep description of separate cultures. Pacanowsky initially invested nine months with W. L. Gore & Associates, best known for its Gore-Tex line of sports clothing and equipment. Like Geertz, he was completely open about his research goals, and during the last five months of his research he participated fully in problem-solving conferences at the company. Later, Pacanowsky spent additional time at the W. L. Gore plants in Delaware as a consultant. In order to become intimately familiar with an organization *as members experience it,* ethnographers must commit to the long haul. Pacanowsky did commit to the long haul of working full time at Gore, this despite his earlier caution against "going native." He had previously advised ethnographers to assume an attitude of "radical naïveté" that would make it possible for them to "experience organizational life as 'strange.'" This stance of wonder would help them get past taken-for-granted interpretations of what's going on and what it means to insiders. When Pacanowsky went to work for Gore, he no longer had that opportunity.[11]

The daily written accounts of intensive observation invariably fill the pages of many ethnographic notebooks. The visual image of these journals stacked on top of each other would be sufficient justification for Geertz to refer to ethnography as *thick description.* The term, however, describes the intertwined layers of common meaning that underlie what a particular people say and do. Thick descriptions are powerful reconstructions, not just detailed observations.[12] After Geertz popularized the concept, most ethnographers realized their task is to:

Thick description
A record of the intertwined layers of common meaning that underlie what a particular people say and do.

1. Accurately describe talk and actions and the context in which they occur.
2. Capture the thoughts, emotions, and web of social interactions.
3. Assign motivation, intention, or purpose to what people say and do.
4. Artfully write this up so readers feel they've experienced the events.
5. Interpret what happened; explain what it means within this culture.[13]

Thick description is tracing the many strands of a cultural web and tracking evolving meaning. No matter how high the stack of an ethnographer's notes, without interpretation, they would still be *thin* description.

Thick description starts with a state of bewilderment. *What the devil's going on?* Geertz asked himself as he waded into a new culture. The only way to reduce the puzzlement is to observe as if one were a stranger in a foreign land. This can be difficult for a manager who is already enmeshed in a specific corporate culture. He or she might overlook many of the signs that point to common interpretation. Worse, the manager might assume that office humor or the company grapevine has the same significance for people in this culture as it does for those in a previous place of employment. Geertz said it will always be different.

Behaviorists would probably consider employee trips to the office watercooler or coffee machine of little interest. If they did regard these breaks worth studying, they would tend to note the number of trips and length of stay for each worker. Ethnographers would be more interested in the significance this seemingly mundane activity had for these particular employees. Instead of a neat statistical summary, they'd record pages of dialogue while workers were standing around with a cup in their hands. Pacanowsky fears that a frequency count would only bleach human behavior of the very properties that interest him. Classifying performances across organizations would yield superficial generalizations at the cost of localized insight. He'd rather find out what makes a particular tribal culture unique.

Although Pacanowsky would pay attention to all cultural performances, he would be particularly sensitive to the imaginative language members used, the stories they told, and the nonverbal rites and rituals they practiced. Taken together, these three forms of communication provide helpful access to the unique shared meanings within an organization.

METAPHORS: TAKING LANGUAGE SERIOUSLY

When used by members throughout an organization (and not just management), *metaphors* can offer the ethnographer a starting place for accessing the shared meaning of a corporate culture. Pacanowsky records a number of prominent metaphors used at W. L. Gore & Associates, none more significant than the oft-heard reference within the company to Gore as a *lattice organization.*[14] If one tried to graph the lines of communication at Gore, the map would look like a lattice rather than the traditional pyramid-shaped organizational chart. The crosshatched lines would show the importance of one-on-one communication and reflect the fact that no person within the company needs permission to talk to anyone else. Easy access to others is facilitated by an average plant size of 150 employees and a variety of electronic media that encourage quick responses.

Metaphor
Clarifies what is unknown or confusing by equating it with an image that's more familiar or vivid.

This lack of hierarchical authority within the lattice organization is captured in the egalitarian title of *associate* given to every worker. People do have differential status at Gore, but it comes from technical expertise, a track record of good judgment, and evidence of follow-through that leads to accomplishment.

The company's stated objective (singular) is "to make money and have fun."[15] The founder, Bill Gore, was famous for popping into associates' offices and asking, "Did you make any money today? Did you have any fun today?" But work at Gore is not frivolous. The *waterline* operating principle makes it clear that associates should check with others before making significant decisions:

> Each of us will consult with appropriate Associates who will share the responsibility of taking any action that has the potential of serious harm to the reputation, success, or survival of the Enterprise. The analogy is that our Enterprise is like a

> ship that we are all in together. Boring holes above the waterline is not serious, but below the waterline, holes could sink us.[16]

When Kevin read about the emphasis Pacanowsky placed on metaphors, he analyzed their use among fellow computer-savvy student employees at Wheaton:

> As a student worker at ResNet, the technical support branch of our campus Internet service provider, I have become aware of our corporate culture. One thing I have noticed is we often talk about our department using the metaphor of a fortress wall. Computing Services makes decisions and institutes policy, and it's our responsibility to handle the waves of students with resulting problems. We talk about "stemming the flow" of students with problems and "manning the phones" or "manning the desk." We also talk about how we "take the blow" for the decisions of our superiors.

This realization later served Kevin and Wheaton students well when, after graduation, Kevin was hired as manager of the ResNet program. Desiring to change the fortress mentality that had permeated the organization, Kevin in effect "lowered the drawbridge" to give students easy access to computer help. He extended hours into the evening, established help desks in each of the dorms, and did away with the keypad locked door that had prevented face-to-face contact with frustrated users. Two years later, ResNet workers talked about themselves as guiding students on paths through a jungle—a more proactive metaphor that suggests the culture has changed.

Pacanowsky suggests that "fictional descriptions, by the very nature of their implicitness and impressionism can fully capture . . . both the bold outlines and the crucial nuances of cultural ethos."[17] Many TV critics believe the show *Mad Men* reliably reflects the culture of a 1960s New York advertising agency, not just in the retro style of clothing and cars, but in the dialogue. If so, the metaphors these men employ should reveal the shared meaning within their organizational culture.

In the very first episode of the series, Pete Campbell, a junior account executive, sucks up to Don Draper, creative director at the Sterling Cooper ad agency: "A man like you, I'd follow you into combat blindfolded and I wouldn't be the first. Am I right, buddy?" Don responds, "Let's take it a little slower. I don't want to wake up pregnant."[18] The obvious meaning is for Pete to back off, and Pete's muttered curse as Don walks away shows he gets the message. But there are overlapping layers of meaning within the *wake-up-pregnant* imagery that reflect the underlying culture that's Sterling Cooper.

Sexual allusions are present in almost every conversation among men at the agency, regardless of whether women are present. So is power. The self-described *mad men* are all highly competitive. Despite a surface backslapping camaraderie, in this ad game, it's every man for himself. Men at Sterling Cooper score by winning the multimillion dollar account or sleeping with a pretty associate. Losing is getting pregnant, which doesn't happen to men. And if it happens to you physically or metaphorically, you're on your own. So a guy has to be on guard lest he come to the office one morning and discover he's been screwed.

Can these multiple meanings really be teased out of a single metaphor heard only once? Probably not without other symbolic clues to collaborate the interpretation. Yet regular viewers of *Mad Men* who listen and watch with an ethnographer's mindset can look back on this first episode and realize that Draper's *wake-up-pregnant* metaphor is both a lens into the culture they've come to know and an artifact of it.

THE SYMBOLIC INTERPRETATION OF STORY

Stories that are told over and over provide a convenient window through which to view corporate webs of significance. Pacanowsky asks, "Has a good story been told that takes you to the heart of the matter?"[19] He focuses on the scriptlike qualities of narratives that portray an employee's part in the company play. Although workers have room to improvise, the anecdotes provide clues to what it means to perform a task in this particular theater. Stories capture memorable performances and convey the passion the actor felt at the time.

Pacanowsky suggests three types of narrative that dramatize organizational life. *Corporate stories* carry the ideology of management and reinforce company policy. Every McDonald's franchisee hears about the late Ray Kroc, who, when he was chairman of the board, picked up trash from the parking lot when he'd visit a store.

Corporate stories
Tales that carry management ideology and reinforce company policy.

Personal stories
Tales told by employees that put them in a favorable light.

Collegial stories
Positive or negative anecdotes about others in the organization; descriptions of how things "really work."

Personal stories are those that employees tell about themselves, often defining how they would like to be seen within the organization. If you've seen reruns of NBC's *The Office*, you've witnessed Dwight Schrute's interviews with the camera crew. During these interviews, he talks about his excellence as an employee and how he deserves the respect of others in the Dunder Mifflin paper company. These are Dwight's personal accounts.

Collegial stories are positive or negative anecdotes told about others in the organization. When the camera crew interviews Dwight's colleagues Jim and Pam, we hear stories of Dwight's eccentricity and lack of basic social awareness. These collegial stories describe Dwight as someone who is not to be taken seriously. Since these tales aren't usually sanctioned by management, collegial accounts convey how the organization "really works."

Stories at Dixie

Throughout most of my life, I've had access to some of the cultural lore of Dixie Communications, a medium-size corporation that operates a newspaper and a television station in a Southern city. Like so many other regional companies, Dixie has been taken over by an out-of-state corporation that has no local ties. The following three narratives are shorthand versions of stories heard again and again throughout the company.

> Although the original publisher has been dead for many years, old-timers fondly recall how he would spend Christmas Eve with the workers in the press room. Their account is invariably linked with reminders that he initiated health benefits and profit sharing prior to any union demand. (Corporate story)

> The current comptroller is the highest-ranking "local boy" in the corporation. He often tells the story about the first annual audit he performed long before computers were installed. Puzzled when he ran across a bill for 50 pounds of pigeon feed, he discovered that the company used homing pigeons to send in news copy and circulation orders from a town across the bay. The story usually concludes with an editorial comment about pigeons being more reliable than the new machines. His self-presentation reminds listeners that he has always been cost-conscious, yet it also aligns him with the human side of the "warm people versus cold machines" issue. (Personal story)

> Shortly after the takeover, a department head encouraged the new publisher to meet with his people for a few minutes at the end of the day. The new boss

> declined the invitation on the grounds of efficiency: "To be quite candid, I don't want to know about a woman's sick child or a man's vacation plans. That kind of information makes it harder to fire a person." Spoken in a cold, superior tone, the words *quite candid* are always part of the story. (Collegial story)

Both Geertz and Pacanowsky caution against any analysis that says, "This story means. . . ." Narratives contain a mosaic of significance and defy a simplistic, one-on-one translation of symbols. Yet taken as a whole, the three stories reveal an uneasiness with the new management. This interpretation is consistent with repeated metaphorical references to the old Dixie as *family* and the new Dixie as *a faceless computer*.

RITUAL: THIS IS THE WAY IT'S ALWAYS BEEN AND ALWAYS WILL BE

Geertz wrote about the Balinese rite of cockfighting because the contest represented more than a game. "It is only apparently cocks that are fighting there. Actually it is men." The cockfight is a dramatization of status. "Its function is interpretive: It is a Balinese reading of Balinese experience, a story they tell themselves about themselves."[20]

Ritual
Texts that articulate multiple aspects of cultural life, often marking rites of passage or life transitions.

Pacanowsky agrees with Geertz that some rituals (like the Balinese cockfight) are "texts" that articulate *multiple* aspects of cultural life.[21] These rituals are nearly sacred, and any attempt to change them meets with strong resistance. Although the emphasis on improvisation and novelty reduces the importance of ritual at Gore, organizational rites at more traditional companies weave together many threads of corporate culture.

More than a generation ago, workers in the classified advertising department at Dixie created an integrative rite that survives to the present. The department is staffed by more than 50 telephone sales representatives who work out of a large common room. At Dixie, these representatives not only take the "two lines/two days/two dollars" personal ads over the phone, they also initiate callbacks to find out if customers were successful and might want to sell other items. Despite the advent of eBay and other online sites for buying and selling, classified advertising at Dixie is a major profit center with low employee turnover. The department continues to have the *family atmosphere* of premerger Dixie. Most of the phone representatives are women under the age of 40. They regard Max, the male manager who has held his position for 35 years, as a *father confessor*—a warm, nonjudgmental person who has genuine concern for their lives. Whenever a female employee has a baby, Max visits her in the hospital and offers help to those at home preparing for her return. Women announce their pregnancy by taping a dime within a large picture frame on the outer wall of Max' office, inscribing their name and anticipated day of delivery. This rite of integration serves multiple functions for the women:

> At a time of potential anxiety, it is an occasion for public affirmation from the larger community.
>
> The rite is a point of contact between work and those outside Dixie. Employees often take pride in describing the ritual to customers and friends.
>
> Although the dime-on-the-wall practice originated with the workers, the authorized chronicle of decades of expected births proclaims a sense of permanence. It says, in effect: "The company doesn't consider motherhood a liability; your job will be here when you get back."

From the management's standpoint, the rite ensures there will be no surprises. Max has plenty of time to schedule the employee's maternity leave, arrange for another salesperson to cover her accounts, and anticipate stresses she might be encountering.

It is tempting to read economic significance into the fact that employees use dimes to symbolize this major change in their lives. But the women involved refer to the small size of the token rather than its monetary value. Geertz and Pacanowsky would caution that this is *their* story; we should listen to *their* interpretation.

CAN THE MANAGER BE AN AGENT OF CULTURAL CHANGE?

The popularity of the cultural metaphor when it was first introduced to the corporate world in the 1980s was undoubtedly due to business leaders' desire to shape interpretation within the organization. Symbols are the tools of management. Executives don't operate forklifts or produce widgets; they cast vision, state goals, process information, send memos, and engage in other symbolic behavior. If they believe culture is the key to worker commitment, productivity, and sales, the possibility of changing culture becomes a seductive idea. Creating favorable metaphors, planting organizational stories, and establishing rites would seem an ideal way to create a corporate myth that would serve managerial interests.

But once a corporate culture exists, can it be altered by a manager? Geertz regarded shared interpretations as naturally emerging from all members of a group rather than consciously engineered by leaders. In *The Office,* Jim, Pam, Stanley, and Phyllis all play a part in developing their corporate culture. And you'll notice that, despite his best efforts, manager Michael Scott can't alter it single-handedly. Managers may articulate a new vision in a fresh vocabulary, but it is the workers who smile, sigh, snicker, or scoff. For example, Martin Luther King's "I Have a Dream" speech, which will be discussed in Chapter 22, was powerful because he struck a chord that was already vibrating within millions of listeners.

Shared meanings are hard to dispel. Symbol watchers within a company quickly discount the words of management if they don't square with performance. But even if culture *could* be changed, there still remains the question of whether it *should* be. Symbolic anthropologists have traditionally adopted a nonintrusive style appropriate to examining fine crystal—look, admire, but don't touch. So managers

who regard themselves as agents of cultural change create bull-in-a-china-shop fears for ethnographers who have ethical concerns about how their corporate analyses might be used. University of Massachusetts management professor Linda Smircich notes that ethnographers would draw back in horror at the idea of using their data to extend a tribal priest's control over the population, yet most communication consultants are hired by top management to do just that.[22]

CRITIQUE: IS THE CULTURAL APPROACH USEFUL?

The cultural approach adopts and refines the qualitative research methodology of ethnography to gain a new understanding of a specific group of people. A crucial part of that understanding is a clarification of values within the culture under study. Today, however, there isn't the excitement about the cultural approach to organizations that there was when interpretive scholars introduced it in the 1980s. Perhaps that's because many researchers trained in organizational communication are hired as consultants by corporate managers who are looking for change. By now you understand that Geertz would regard the quest to alter culture as both inappropriate and virtually impossible. This purist position exposes him and his admirers within our discipline to criticism from corporate consultants who not only desire to understand organizational communication, but also want to influence it. That was certainly Kevin's ambition when he was hired to manage the ResNet technical support program at Wheaton.

If a thick description of the web of meanings within an organization can't be used to change the culture, how can the cost in time and money of an ethnographic study be justified? Better employee recruitment is one answer. Traditionally, companies stress their attractive features and downplay characteristics that potential hires would find disturbing. So it's only after the firm has spent about $15,000 to recruit, assess, orient, and train a new employee that the newcomer finds out if he or she is suited for the job. Early resignations are costly and leave everyone disgruntled.

Managers are learning that they can cut costs and avoid hassles by providing a realistic job preview right from the start.[23] Offering recruits a sensitive analysis of the culture they'd be entering gives potential hires the chance to make an informed decision as to whether they will fit within it or not. And for those who take the plunge, the shared knowledge of what means what within the organization will reduce mistakes and misunderstandings. W. C. Gore's subsequent hiring of Pacanowsky shows the high regard the founder placed on the theorist's thick description.

A different kind of objection comes from critical theorists who fault the cultural approach because interpretive scholars like Geertz and Pacanowsky refuse to evaluate the customs they portray. For example, if Pacanowsky were to discover that female associates at Gore hit a glass ceiling when they try to advance, these advocates insist he should *expose* and *deplore* this injustice rather than merely *describe* and *interpret* it for readers.[24] For researchers who take a cultural approach to organizational life, this criticism misses the point of their work. The purpose of ethnography is not to pass moral judgment or reform society. The goal of symbolic analysis is to create a better understanding of what it takes to function effectively within a culture.

Anthropologist Adam Kuper is critical of Geertz for his emphasis on interpretation rather than behavioral observation. Because if, as Geertz claimed, "we begin with our own interpretations of what our informants are up to or think they are up to and then systematize those,"[25] who's to say the meaning assigned by the ethnographer is right?[26] Kuper is afraid that the past experiences and biases of interpretive researchers will shape the conclusions they reach. But for Geertz, members within the culture are the ones who verify a thick description. Participant-observers need to check out their interpretation with the "natives" in their study. It's their culture. They should recognize the "truth" of the story told about them.[27] In organizational research, that means members affirming the ethnographer's construction of what's going on. *(Right. You've got it. That's what this means.)*

There might be another reason why interest in the cultural approach has waned in recent years. In Chapter 3, I cited *aesthetic appeal* as one of the criteria for a good interpretive theory. The force of an ethnographic analysis depends in large measure on the prose in which it's couched. In the *Times Literary Supplement* (U.K.), T. M. Luhrmann gives testimony to the compelling power of Geertz' writing: "Rarely has there been a social scientist who has also been so acute a writer; perhaps there has never been one so quotable."[28] Indeed, Geertz' interpretation of a Balinese cockfight reads like an engrossing novel that the reader can't put down. Though Pacanowsky writes well, it may not be until a perceptive ethnographer with Geertz' compelling way with words focuses on organizational life that the cultural approach to organizations will spark renewed interest.

QUESTIONS TO SHARPEN YOUR FOCUS

1. Based on the concept of organizational culture as a system of *shared meaning,* how would you describe the culture at your school to a prospective student?
2. Anthropologists say, "We don't know who discovered water, but we know it wasn't the fish." Does this adage suggest that it's foolish to ask members of a culture to verify or challenge an *ethnographer's interpretation?*
3. Think of your extended family as an *organizational culture.* What family *ritual* might you analyze to *interpret* the webs of significance you share for someone visiting your home?
4. What favorite *story* do you tell others about your most recent place of employment? Is it a *corporate, personal,* or *collegial* narrative?

SELF-QUIZ

For chapter self-quizzes, go to the book's Online Learning Center at *www.mhhe.com/griffin9e*

A SECOND LOOK

Recommended resource: Clifford Geertz, *The Interpretation of Cultures,* Basic Books, New York, 1973. (See especially "Thick Description: Toward an Interpretive Theory of Culture," pp. 3–30; and "Deep Play: Notes on the Balinese Cockfight," pp. 412–453.)

Culture as performance: Michael Pacanowsky and Nick O'Donnell-Trujillo, "Organizational Communication as Cultural Performance," *Communication Monographs,* Vol. 50, 1983, pp. 127–147.

Nonmanagerial orientation: Michael Pacanowsky and Nick O'Donnell-Trujillo "Communication and Organizational Cultures," *Western Journal of Speech Communicat[illegible]* Vol. 46, 1982, pp. 115–130.

Thick description: Joseph G. Ponterotto, "Brief Note on the Origins, Evolution, and Meaning of the Qualitative Research Concept 'Thick Description,'" *The Qualitative Report,* Vol. 11, 2006, pp. 538–549.

Cultural metaphor: Gareth Morgan, "Creating Social Reality: Organizations as Cultures," in *Images of Organization,* Sage, Newbury Park, CA, 1986, pp. 111–140.

Corporate ethnography: Michael Pacanowsky, "Communication in the Empowering Organization," in *Communication Yearbook 11,* James Anderson (ed.), Sage, Newbury Park, CA, 1988, pp. 356–379.

Corporate stories: Joanne Martin, Martha Feldman, Mary Jo Hatch, and Sim Sitkin, "The Uniqueness Paradox in Organizational Stories," *Administrative Science Quarterly,* Vol. 28, 1983, pp. 438–453.

Rites: Harrison Trice and Janice Beyer, "Studying Organizational Cultures Through Rites and Ceremonials," *Academy of Management Review,* Vol. 9, 1984, pp. 653–669.

Interpretive vs. objective approach: Linda L. Putnam, "The Interpretive Perspective: An Alternative to Functionalism," in *Communication and Organizations: An Interpretive Approach,* Linda L. Putnam and Michael Pacanowsky (eds.), Sage, Newbury Park, CA, 1982, pp. 31–54.

Brief autobiography: Clifford Geertz, "A Life of Learning" (ACLS Occasional Paper No. 45), American Council of Learned Societies, New York, 1999.

Webs of shared meaning in sports: Nick Trujillo, "Reflections on Communication and Sport: On Ethnography and Organizations," *Communication and Sport,* Vol. 1, 2013, pp. 68–75.

Fiction as scholarship: Michael Pacanowsky, "Slouching Towards Chicago," *Quarterly Journal of Speech,* Vol. 74, 1988, pp. 453–469.

Interpretive research: Bryan Taylor and Nick Trujillo, "Qualitative Research Methods," in *The New Handbook of Organizational Communication,* Fredric Jablin and Linda L. Putnam (eds.), Sage, Thousand Oaks, CA, 2001, pp. 161–194.

History and critique of Geertz: Adam Kuper, *Culture: The Anthropologists' Account,* Harvard University, Cambridge, MA, 1999, pp. 75–121.

For links to relavant websites and YouTube videos,
click on Links under Theory Resources at
www.afirstlook.com.

CHAPTER 20

Objective — Interpretive

Socio-cultural tradition

Communicative Constitution of Organizations

of Robert McPhee

Valve Corporation has achieved a reputation as one of the most innovative publishers in the video game industry. If you're a video gamer like me (Andrew), you've probably heard of Valve. It has produced *Portal,* a physics-based puzzle game so artistic that the Smithsonian American Art Museum showcased it for several months. Millions of players have battled online opponents in hit games like *Counter-Strike* and *Half-Life,* or purchased classic games from Valve's popular Steam download service. Valve's success has earned more than a reputation, with one industry analyst estimating Valve's worth at $2.5 billion.[1] By comparison, that's about a half billion higher than the value of Wendy's fast-food restaurants.[2]

Although Valve leads in the video game industry, it isn't clear who leads Valve. Among its 300 employees, the company insists that no one holds the title of manager, supervisor, boss, or head honcho. In fact, the company handbook even describes founder Gabe Newell this way: "Of all the people at this company who aren't your boss, Gabe is the MOST not your boss, if you get what we're saying."[3] Instead of a manager dictating priorities, all employees possess the freedom to initiate projects they believe will benefit the company. Although Valve believes such an environment unleashes employees' creative potential, it's unsettling to those who've spent a career working in traditional organizations. For this reason, the new employee handbook bluntly describes its purpose: "Mainly, it's about how not to freak out now that you're here."[4]

Robert McPhee and other *communicative constitution of organizations (CCO)* theorists believe that Valve's business practices arise from the daily interactions of the organization's members. Their conclusion isn't based on the unusual structure of the company. They insist *any* company is what it is because communication brings the organization into existence. In other words, like CMM theorists, they believe that persons-in-conversation co-construct their social worlds (see

Chapter 6)—and in this case, those worlds are organizations. They also agree with Pacanowsky (see Chapter 19) and Deetz (see Chapter 21) that an organization isn't a set of buildings, a stack of handbooks, or even a group of people with a common purpose. Although these are important ingredients, they believe only *communication* can bind them into an organization.

McPhee, a communication professor at Arizona State University, has devoted much of his career to understanding four types of communication—or *communication flows*—that constitute organizations. Before we consider McPhee's four flows and four principles that guide them, we'll take a closer look at what McPhee and other CCO theorists mean when they say that communication creates—or constitutes—an organization. McPhee believes that CCO theory can help us see order in Valve's chaos—or, rather, that any organization's chaos has an underlying order.

COMMUNICATION: THE ESSENCE OF AN ORGANIZATION

In the introduction to this section on organizational communication, we examined classical management theory's claim that organizations are like machines and workers are its cogs. McPhee thinks that's precisely the wrong metaphor. Employees are not a set of lifeless parts. Rather, people create an organization like General Motors, the American Red Cross, or the Internal Revenue Service through their actions—especially their communication. One CCO theorist defines *constitution* in five simple words: "Communication calls organization into being."[5]

Constitution
Communication that calls organization into being.

In trying to help us understand exactly how communication does this, McPhee acknowledges his intellectual debt to Karl Weick's *information systems approach.* According to Weick, organizations are like organisms—active beings who must continually process information to survive.[6] But the diet of information an organization has on its plate is often equivocal, meaning a given message has at least two equally possible interpretations. When faced with such equivocality, Weick encouraged organizations to engage in *sensemaking*—communication behavior designed to reduce ambiguity. His advice is summarized in his famous question, "How can I know what I think till I see what I say?"[7]

Sensemaking
Communication behavior that reduces ambiguity and equivocality.

To illustrate Weick's advice, imagine Valve employees gathered in a meeting room, trying to decide what video game to make next. They have the results of an extensive marketing survey in front of them, suggesting that 55 percent of respondents would like a new *Portal* sequel. Weick would be concerned if Valve jumped into designing a new game based on this information alone. He'd insist the information is equivocal because it raises several new questions: What about the other 45 percent? Is there a difference between male and female respondents? Teenagers and adults? How much profit did Valve make on the last *Portal* game? Would a new game flood the market with too much *Portal* and lead to boredom with the franchise? When employees discuss such questions, they're sensemaking—"squeezing" meaning out of ambiguous data.

McPhee goes a step further. He thinks communication doesn't just reduce ambiguity—it creates organization itself. But it's one thing to observe that communication creates organization; it's much harder to explain exactly *how* that happens. McPhee's answer to this big CCO question is four specific forms of communication, or *flows,* that accomplish this. He wouldn't be surprised if Valve's game-planning conversation revealed that they need to hire new employees (*membership negotiation),* change the relationships among current workers (*self-structuring*), alter the daily work schedule (*activity coordination*), or launch an ad campaign against a competing company (*institutional positioning*). Each of those possible conclusions represents one of the four flows, and McPhee thinks each flow literally creates the company as members talk. We'll examine each flow in more detail. But as you read, McPhee wouldn't want you to think of the flows as something an organization *does*. Rather, these four flows, functioning together, are what an organization *is*.

THE FOUR FLOWS OF CCO

The ancient Greek philosopher Heraclitus once said, "You cannot step twice into the same river, for other waters and yet others go ever flowing on."[8] CCO theorists believe organizations are like a river—always changing, always active, and sometimes violent. And although water constitutes a river, the mere presence of H_2O isn't enough. After all, no one would claim that Lake Michigan, the Pacific Ocean, or an Aquafina bottle is a river. Likewise, just because people are talking to each other doesn't mean they are an organization.

Flows
Circulating fields of messages that constitute organization.

To talk an organization into being, McPhee believes the communication must occur in four *flows*, or "circulating systems or fields of messages."[9] Specifically, these four flows concern who is a *member* of the organization, how these members *structure* their working relationships, how they *coordinate* their work, and how the organization *positions* itself with other people and organizations. It's worth noting that not all communication between organization members involves the four flows. Co-workers may swap stories about their weekends, share photos of the kids, and discuss the news, but the four flows don't appear in that kind of talk. What sets the four flows apart is that they are *necessary* for creating the organization itself. We can imagine a workplace where co-workers don't share kid photos, but McPhee thinks it's impossible to imagine a workplace that doesn't regularly address all of the four flows.

I will describe each of these flows as they occur at Valve but, probably like you, working at a multibillion-dollar video game company is outside the range of my experience. To connect the flows more directly to your life and mine, I'll also describe them in the context of campus Greek organizations (a.k.a. social fraternities and sororities). About 800 North American universities have social Greek life, with membership estimated at approximately 600,000 students—so chances are that if you aren't a member, you probably know someone who is.[10] Although a fraternity or sorority's purpose is much different than a company like Valve's, McPhee believes communication constitutes both.

Membership Negotiation: Joining and Learning the Ropes

All organizations regulate who is a member and who is not. If you've ever held a job, it's likely you've been through an interview process—but probably not like Valve's. Because Valve's unusual structure gives employees considerable power over the direction of the company, the company handbook remarks that "hiring is the single most important thing you will ever do at Valve. Any time you interview a potential hire, you need to ask yourself . . . if they're capable of literally running this company, because they will be."[11]

Although the details of Valve's intense interview process aren't public knowledge, Google is another tech company that carefully vets potential hires.

Google famously asks tough questions during interviews, such as, "Using only a four-minute hourglass and a seven-minute hourglass, measure exactly nine minutes—without the process taking longer than nine minutes."[12] McPhee would see such communication as one part of the *membership negotiation* flow. For Google and Valve, such questions constitute a rigorous, competitive, and intellectual workplace.

Membership negotiation Communication that regulates the extent to which a person is an organization member.

But Texas A&M University communication professor Kevin Barge reminds us that membership negotiation doesn't end after accepting a job offer. The next step of membership negotiation is *socialization,* or learning what it means to be a member of the organization. With David Schlueter (Baylor University), Barge asked people who had started jobs in the previous two years to recall memorable messages about adjusting to the new workplace. They discovered that messages addressed a variety of topics, including standards for professional behavior, office politics, and the importance of customer service. Strikingly, only about a quarter of participants received the memorable message during formal training, while 63 percent received the message during informal conversation.[13] For McPhee, this supports his claim that everyday conversations constitute an organization. For you, it suggests that occasional breakroom chats with colleagues will help you adjust to a new job.

Sororities and fraternities also engage in membership negotiation, although they do it differently than a company does. Maybe you've seen college women lined up outside sorority houses early in the semester, waiting to participate in recruitment (sometimes called rush). At most campuses, recruitment involves attending social events with current Greek members and viewing presentations and skits about each house. After each house meets privately to decide whom to invite, prospective members participate in secret rituals that formally admit them into the Greek organization. That secrecy hasn't prevented the attention of parents and law enforcement concerned about hazing. Many Greek organizations take hazing laws seriously and may dismiss members who violate hazing policies—another form of membership negotiation.

Self-Structuring: Figuring Out Who's Who in the Organization

My wife once worked as a business attorney in a small-town law firm. Part of her work involved drafting the documents that legally bring a business into being. Documents such as the company charter, bylaws, and constitution—a word with double meaning for CCO theorists—define what the organization is and how it operates. To McPhee, they're communication acts that birth an organization, and such communication *self-structures* the organization.

Self-structuring Communication that shapes the relationships among an organization's members.

After the organization's founding, self-structuring continues through the writing of procedures manuals, memos, and sometimes a chart that specifies the relationships among employees. Typically, the CEO is at the top of the chart along with the rest of upper management. Middle management lies further down the chart, and so on, until you get to clerks and call center employees at the bottom.

You won't find such a chart at a flat organization like Valve, but that doesn't mean the company doesn't engage in self-structuring. At any given time, Valve structures itself into *cabals,* or work teams assigned to accomplish a goal (such as developing new levels for a game or updating the Steam distribution website). When any employee has an idea, he or she can start a cabal and recruit others to join. Because this cabal structure is ever-changing, all desks have wheels, allowing cabals to form and re-form at any time. Each cabal collectively decides what each member will do, and a person's assignment "changes as requirements change, but the temporary structure provides a shared understanding of what to expect from each other."[14] Through talk, members gather around a task, initiate work, and solidify the cabal's structure. As Valve's employee handbook constitutes it: "Structure happens."[15]

Even in more traditional organizations, McPhee reminds us that the official chart isn't the final word on structure. In early seasons of NBC's *The Office,* a chart of the Dunder Mifflin Paper Company might have placed regional manager Michael Scott at the top and receptionist Pam Beesly near the bottom. Nevertheless, if you're familiar with the TV show that ran for nine seasons, you know that Michael's trust in Pam gave her influence over him that other employees lacked. Although *The Office* is fiction, I've often heard that the receptionist is one of the most powerful employees. He or she may have a lot of influence over the organization's resources and key decision makers, and that kind of informal structuring tends to trump the formal chart.

Greek organizations self-structure too, but face an additional challenge: they must constitute the organization's values and practices across dozens of geographically separated campuses. The U.S. military and megacorporations like Apple must also confront distance. How can workers align their activities when they're so far apart? CCO theorists François Cooren (University of Montreal) and Gail Fairhurst (University of Cincinnati) believe this is no small question. To answer it, they point out that we seek *closure,* or a sense of shared understanding that emerges in back-and-forth interaction.[16] Sensemaking doesn't happen until such closure occurs.

Closure
A sense of shared understanding that emerges in back-and-forth interaction.

In many Greek organizations, chapters communicate with local alumni about how to maintain the chapter's traditions, and consult documents about the organization's history—this is closure across *time.* Meanwhile, the organization's headquarters sets goals and establishes policies for all chapters—this is closure across *space.* Through these mediated interactions and shared texts, each chapter's local communication reflects, re-creates, and sometimes deviates from structure established at different times and places.

Activity Coordination: Getting the Job Done

McPhee believes all organizations have goals. Schools teach students, soup kitchens serve the hungry, political parties elect candidates, and Valve sells "award-winning games, leading-edge technologies, and a groundbreaking social entertainment platform."[17] Such a defined purpose separates an organization from a crowd of people. Most important to CCO theorists, members communicate to accomplish the organization's day-to-day work toward their goals—a flow McPhee terms *activity coordination.*

Activity coordination
Communication that accomplishes the organization's work toward goals.

The activity coordination flow presumes the existence of the self-structuring flow. It's hard to get work done unless members know who is doing what. But once people settle into their roles, they may need to adjust their work. A member may grow bored with a task or find that his or her skills aren't well suited to it. Or, members who enjoy their work may come down with the flu and ask someone to fill in for a shift or two. Mundane communication about such things is activity coordination in action.

Activity coordination becomes quite complex at any organization with more than a handful of employees. At most companies, departments as diverse as accounting, sales and marketing, shipping, quality control, production, and human resources must coordinate their activities to achieve the organization's mission. Although Valve lacks such clear departmental structure, the employee handbook has no ambiguity about Valve's core activity: "The core of the software-building process is engineering. As in, writing [computer] code."[18] They urge noncoders to become as familiar as they can with programming. At the same time, they encourage programmers to familiarize themselves with the "creative, legal, financial, even psychological" workers at the firm.[19] In contrast to the high degree of specialization found at most companies, Valve believes broad expertise streamlines activity coordination.

In some organizations, effective activity coordination can save lives. McPhee's Arizona State University colleague Sarah Tracy examined activity coordination among 911 operators, firefighters, and correctional officers—workers whose activity coordination frequently involves difficult, disgusting, and dangerous experiences. Her interviews and field observations revealed that workers frequently used humor to cope with their jobs. For example, 911 operators sometimes laughed together while replaying tapes of strange calls, and firefighters joked about "frequent flyers" who called the fire department for regular medical care.[20] Although such humor often had a dark tone, Tracy believes that "by joking about aberrant and shocking duties, our participants sustained the notion that they were . . . capable of doing the demanding work."[21]

Campus Greek organizations coordinate a variety of activities, too. Many members particularly value social activities, and thus the social coordinator is often one of the most influential members of the chapter. Although parties and formals are probably the most well-known Greek activities, fraternities and sororities also plan service events. I once served as a consultant for a prominent national sorority's membership satisfaction survey. Results indicated that philanthropic service was one of members' favorite parts of Greek life—even more than social events.[22] Overall, fraternities and sororities devote more than 3 million hours and $17 million per year to philanthropic aims.[23] When members communicate to arrange a reading event for underprivileged children or a fundraising drive to benefit the sick, they're engaging in worthwhile activity coordination. Such partnerships with local libraries, hospitals, and charities engage the next flow, as well.

Institutional Positioning: Dealing with Other People and Organizations

Greek houses aren't the only organizations interested in community service. Many for-profit businesses partner with philanthropies. St. Jude Children's Research Hospital, for example, lists dozens of corporate sponsors, ranging from AutoZone to Zynga.[24] According to Northwestern University communication professor Michelle Shumate, such corporate–nonprofit alliances possess value only if customers and investors perceive the corporation as socially responsible. For instance, although a nonprofit may have many corporate sponsors, most corporations make their charitable work memorable by partnering with a limited set of nonprofits.[25] This is one form of *institutional positioning,* or communication between an organization and external entities—other organizations and people.

Institutional positioning Communication between an organization and external entities.

No organization survives on its own. Even small organizations must interact with banks, insurance providers, labor unions, government regulators, and so

"I just think it undermines our organization's fiery rhetoric when you close your Internet postings with a smiley face."

forth. This includes navigating the legal environment—a big deal for many organizations. As an entertainment company whose software is easy to copy, some of Valve's institutional positioning has involved intellectual property lawsuits. In the company's early years, Valve published its software through Vivendi Entertainment. When Vivendi began distributing Valve's games in Internet cafés, Valve sued for copyright infringement. After three years of lawsuits and counter-lawsuits, the court ruled in Valve's favor.[26] Of course, such legal wrangling isn't Valve's only institutional positioning. Other examples include coordinating with Microsoft to release *Portal* 2 on the Xbox LIVE store—or, like any for-profit company, jockeying against competitors for the customer's dollar.

Greek organizations also compete with each other (for popularity and for members) and collaborate (for social events and service work). But their most fundamental institutional positioning is with universities and colleges. Most schools have an entire department dedicated to overseeing student organizations. Just before writing this section, I spent some time reviewing Texas Christian University's (TCU) regulations for the communication honor society Lambda Pi Eta—a set of rules applicable to social Greek groups as well. Many of these rules aim to manage legal risk (such as *all events must end by midnight* and *off-campus drivers must switch every two hours*). McPhee would see that as institutional positioning with lawyers and insurance providers. Chronic violation of the rules can lead to a different type of institutional positioning on the part of TCU—removal of the group from campus.

FOUR PRINCIPLES OF THE FOUR FLOWS

In summary, McPhee claims that communication constitutes organization through the four flows of membership negotiation, self-structuring, activity coordination, and institutional positioning. He would be disappointed if you thought of these flows as containers for different types of communication. After all, contained water doesn't flow, and over time it becomes stagnant. It's the intersection of the four flows, mixing and blending together, that constitutes organization. To help you understand how the four flows are separate yet function together, we'll take a look at four principles that direct the four flows.

1. All four flows are necessary for organization. On September 17, 2011, Occupy Wall Street protesters began camping out in New York's Zuccotti Park. Soon, the Occupy movement spread to cities throughout the United States and the world. After the initial wave of excitement, Occupy protesters tried to organize themselves more cohesively. Although many of them cared about income inequality, commentators noted that the movement lacked guiding principles and clear demands. Consequently, the protests drew all sorts of disgruntled folks. Competing bids for leadership created bitter rivalries that reduced the size and strength of the protests.[27] Although the social movement still exists as of this writing, it hasn't achieved the membership negotiation and self-structuring necessary for organization. Activity coordination (through meetings) and institutional positioning (against Wall Street) alone weren't enough.

2. Different flows happen in different places. At the start of spring, the minds of many sports fans turn to major league baseball. If you attend the opening game of your home team, you'll focus on the strength of the batters, the strategy of the pitchers, and the errors of the outfielders as each team strives to beat the other. That's institutional positioning, and there's plenty of it in the ballpark. However, you probably won't see the other flows taking place on the field. That's because space and time often separate the four flows. In other words, "contract negotiations for a baseball player don't occur too often in the dugout during a game."[28] Likewise, the general manager's office and the team locker room contain different flows than the baseball diamond.

3. The same message can address multiple flows. Note that McPhee says space *often* separates the flows. That's an important qualifier. He also observes that a single message can belong to more than one flow. For example, my department is currently hiring two new communication professors. Clearly, that's membership negotiation. But conversations about the hires have also led us to discuss the courses we offer in our department (activity coordination) and how those courses compare to other nearby communication programs (institutional positioning). CCO theorist Larry Browning (University of Texas) goes a step further than McPhee. For Browning, the intersection of flows in a single message isn't just a possibility, but the very essence of organizing itself.[29] In other words, if our hiring didn't involve the other flows, we might question whether we're really an organization.

4. Different flows address different audiences. Notre Dame versus USC. Alabama versus Auburn. Oklahoma versus Texas. Some students choose their college for a firsthand view of these classic football rivalries. Many of my students care passionately about TCU's historic rivalry with Baylor University. Those same students probably don't worry much about the workflow of Baylor's provost's office—or, for that matter, TCU's. Likewise, they're probably less interested in how TCU hires new professors (see the previous principle) than changes in graduation requirements. That's because different flows deal with different audiences. *Self-structuring* is of little interest to those outside an organization. *Membership negotiation* targets new members or those who may be leaving. *Activity coordination* addresses specific groups within an organization, and *institutional positioning* focuses on external organizations.[30]

DIVERTING THE FLOW: CRAFTING SOLUTIONS TO ORGANIZATIONAL PROBLEMS

At this point, you may think that McPhee's CCO theory *describes* organizations but doesn't tell us how to *change* them. After all, objective as well as interpretive scholars have critiqued Pacanowsky's cultural approach for that reason (see Chapter 19). Recall, however, that one goal of an interpretive theory is to foster new understanding of people, and describing an organization's four flows is a good place to start. Some CCO scholars are pragmatists who try to use such insights to fix organizational problems.

One such CCO scholar is Pamela Lutgen-Sandvik (North Dakota State University). Along with colleague Virginia McDermott, she used the four flows to examine *employee-abusive organizations*—places where "workers experience persistent emotional abuse and hostile communication they perceive as unfair, unjust, and unwanted" and consequently "suffer heightened fear, dread, and job insecurity."[31] She notes that in a school context, we'd call that bullying. It's just as destructive in the workplace.

These researchers examined a community women's center with a toxic work environment. Ironically, this safe haven for abused women was anything but for the center's employees. Much of the abuse arose from the head manager—the researchers gave her the pseudonym "Sue." Based on extensive interviews and ethnographic observation, Lutgen-Sandvik was convinced that each of the four flows constituted the center's abusive climate.

After working at the women's center for several years, Sue followed the founder as only the second head manager. Although she had no previous managerial history, she had plenty of negative experiences with other center workers. When those struggles led to firings, employees in charge of hiring began to ask questions designed to screen applicants who couldn't take the heat: "Tell me about a time when you had to deal with a controlling manager. How did you handle that situation?"[32] If hired, current employees soon told collegial stories (see Chapter 19) about Sue "standing over people as they cleaned out their desks, publicly screaming at employees, and humiliating staff in front of clients and co-workers."[33]

These alterations to the membership negotiation flow enabled Sue's abuse. So did the center's self-structuring. On paper, a board of directors controlled the center, but that board was reluctant to do anything about Sue. Rather than confronting her directly, they sent her to external training that often emphasized the importance of managerial control.[34] Ironically, this led Sue to develop even more authoritarian rules.

In the face of a hesitant board and an unsympathetic manager, workers remained silent about Sue's abuse of power in the regular course of activity coordination. As other managers focused on securing grant funds, employees performed the center's grunt work with clients in need. With employees being overworked, underpaid, and abused, it's not surprising the center struggled to retain workers.

Eventually, the board fired Sue as a first step to healing the center. But as CCO theorists, Lutgen-Sandvik and McDermott don't think solving a widespread organizational problem is as simple as removing one problem member. After all, shutting down a polluting factory is just a first step to cleaning up a river—it doesn't remove the contamination that's already in the flow. So in addition to firing Sue, the center increased communication between the board and staff by self-structuring a new liaison between them. They also introduced an evaluation system for the supervisor as part of regular activity coordination. And to attract the most qualified manager, they increased the salary to a more competitive level. Eventually, word got out that the organization's culture had changed, and some former employees even returned to the center. Lutgen-Sandvik credits these improvements to members changing the four flows.

CRITIQUE: IS CONSTITUTION REALLY SO SIMPLE?

For a communication scholar, what's not to like about a theory that claims communication is the essence of organization? Assuming that's not a rhetorical question, we might point out that organizations and communication are both incredibly complex. Trying to unite the two might just produce a big theoretical migraine. That's the genius of McPhee's approach—by identifying four clear flows, he's provided a degree of *relative simplicity* that few interpretive theories possess. But that simplicity doesn't appeal to everybody.

For decades, communication professor James Taylor (University of Montreal) led one of the world's most visible CCO research programs. Taylor shares McPhee's belief that communication constitutes organizations.[35] Despite this foundational agreement, Taylor suspects McPhee's view is too simplistic. He also thinks it starts from the wrong place. McPhee's theory takes a top-down approach to organizing—it's a bit like flying over a river and seeing the structure of its tributaries and inlets. It gives you the big picture, but you miss the messy details you'd see by putting on your boots and wading into the riverbank. That's the kind of approach Taylor prefers—from the ground up. And that ground is everyday conversation.

To Taylor, McPhee's theory isn't precise enough to explain how a chat at the watercooler can shape the structure of an organization. He places some of the blame on McPhee's vague definition of flow. Although the liquid analogy captures the fluid nature of organizing, Taylor notes that it's never clear precisely what the metaphor represents. He asks, "What exactly is a 'flow,' for example: a sequence of communication interactions or episodes? A pattern of activities? A history? And what are the properties of flow that explain the genesis of organization?"[36] If McPhee's theory can't answer these questions, then Taylor thinks it can't account for how communication constitutes organization.

Taylor provides his own description of constitution through a masterful yet dizzying appeal to linguists such as Chomsky, Greimas, Husserl, and Latour.[37] He argues that conversations organize when members engage in *co-orientation*, or communication "wherein two or more actors are entwined in relation to an object."[38] Such an object may be a financial report, new product idea, or contract negotiation. Over time, these conversations are the glue that binds organizations across time and space. If organizing occurs in such specific conversations, then McPhee's looking in the wrong place when he searches for higher-order communication patterns (like the four flows).

Co-orientation
Communication wherein two or more people focus on a common object.

So which is best—McPhee's top-down approach or Taylor's from-the-bottom-up? University of Oklahoma communication professor Ryan Bisel values both approaches while also believing they share a common fault. According to Bisel, Taylor assumes that co-orientation is a *sufficient condition* for organizing. That means the very presence of co-orientating conversations is enough to create an organization. Likewise, McPhee believes his four flows are such sufficient conditions. But Bisel thinks both are only *necessary conditions*. In other words, such communicative patterns mean that organization *can* occur, not that it *will* occur. He supports his claim with words that resonate with anyone who has worked in a team or seen an episode of *The Office:* "Empirical observations and anecdotal experiences indicate that poor workplace talk can lead to inefficiencies, errors, and an inability to interrelate heedfully."[39] Communication can disorganize, too.

Sufficient conditions Conditions under which something *will* occur.

Necessary conditions Conditions under which something *can* occur.

I don't find these debates discouraging. On the contrary, I think they're the mark of a relatively young theory that has energized a new generation of organizational communication scholars. Although they may disagree on the details, CCO theorists share a broad *community of agreement*—a community convinced that communication is the most important element binding any organization together. For all who take communication seriously, any brand of CCO is well worth considering.

QUESTIONS TO SHARPEN YOUR FOCUS

1. The phrase *communication constitutes organizations* comes out of the socio-cultural tradition of communication theory. How might a cybernetic scholar describe the essence of organizations? A critical scholar?
2. According to McPhee, the *four flows* constitute an organization. Using this definition, is a family an organization? A religious congregation? A group of close friends? Your communication theory course?
3. Your school is an organization. What memorable messages do you remember from your *membership negotiation?* Did you receive different messages from members versus nonmembers?
4. Some research investigates the challenges of organizations that function at a distance using communication technology. Which flow do you think is most difficult to sustain when workers can't meet face-to-face?

A SECOND LOOK

Recommended resource: Linda L. Putnam and Anne Maydan Nicotera (eds.), *Building Theories of Organization: The Constitutive Role of Communication,* Routledge, New York, NY, 2009.

Original statement: Robert D. McPhee and Pamela Zaug, "The Communicative Constitution of Organizations: A Framework for Explanation," *Electronic Journal of Communication,* Vol. 10, 2000, http://www.cios.org/EJCPUBLIC/010/1/01017.html.

Taylor's view of CCO: James R. Taylor and Elizabeth J. Van Every, *The Emergent Organization: Communication As Its Site and Surface,* Lawrence Erlbaum, Mahwah, NJ, 2000.

Membership negotiation and the millennial generation: Karen K. Myers and Kamyab Sadaghiani, "Millennials in the Workplace: A Communication Perspective on Millennials' Organizational Relationships and Performance," *Journal of Business and Psychology,* Vol. 25, 2010, pp. 225–238.

Institutional positioning with nonprofit organizations: Michelle Shumate and Amy O'Connor, "Corporate Reporting of Cross-Sector Alliances: The Portfolio of NGO Partners Communicated on Corporate Websites," *Communication Monographs,* Vol. 77, 2010, pp. 207–230.

Constitution and corporate scandals: Timothy Kuhn and Karen Lee Ashcraft, "Corporate Scandal and the Theory of the Firm: Formulating the Contributions of Organizational Communication Studies," *Management Communication Quarterly,* Vol. 17, 2003, pp. 20–57.

Discourse and organizations: Gail T. Fairhurst and Linda Putnam, "Organizations as Discursive Constructions," *Communication Theory,* Vol. 14, 2004, pp. 5–26.

Critique: Special Forum in *Management Communication Quarterly,* Vol. 24, 2010. See articles by Ryan Bisel, John A. A. Sillince, Graham Sewell, Mike Reed, Linda Putnam, and Anne Maydan Nicotera.

To access a chapter on Karl Weick's concept of sensemaking, click on Information Systems Approach in the Archive under Theory Resorses at *www.afirstlook.com.*

CHAPTER 21

Objective — Interpretive

Critical tradition
Phenomenological tradition

Critical Theory of Communication in Organizations

of Stanley Deetz

University of Colorado professor Stan Deetz seeks to unmask what he considers unjust and unwise communication practices within organizations. Deetz deplores the increasing overt and covert control that corporate managers exert in the name of doing "good business." But unlike many critical theorists, Deetz is not only explicit about what he's against, he's also clear about what he's for. He calls it "stakeholder participation." He believes that everyone who will be significantly affected by a corporate policy should have a voice in the decision-making process. His *critical theory of communication in organizations* presents the rationale for that obligation.

CORPORATE COLONIZATION AND CONTROL OF EVERYDAY LIFE

If you've never worked in a large corporation, you may be tempted to dismiss Deetz' theory as having little to do with your life. Big mistake. As Deetz points out, multinational corporations such as GM, AT&T, Apple, Time Warner, Disney, and Microsoft are the dominant force in society—more powerful than the church, state, or family in their ability to influence the lives of individuals. For example, over 90 percent of the mass media outlets—newspaper, broadcast, cable, telephone, and satellite—are owned by just a handful of corporations.[1] Deetz notes that hourly reports of the Dow-Jones Industrial Average underscore the absence of an equivalent index of quality in the arts, health care, or the environment. Even in a media account of blatant corporate greed or fraud, it would be naïve to assume that the story doesn't reflect a pro-business bias.

The corporate executive suite is the place where most decisions are made regarding the use of natural resources, development of new technologies, product availability, and working relations among people. Deetz says that corporations "control and colonize" modern life in ways that no government or public body since the feudal era ever thought possible.[2] Yet the fallout of corporate control is a sharp decrease in quality of life for the vast majority of citizens.

Corporate colonization
Encroachment of modern corporations into every area of life outside the workplace.

Within the lifetime of most of today's college students, the average American workweek has increased from 40 to 50 hours, and leisure time has declined by a corresponding 10 hours. Despite the fact that 85 percent of families with children now have mothers working outside the home, their real standard of living has *decreased* over the last two decades. The number of full-time workers whose income has fallen below the poverty line has doubled, yet compensation for chief executive officers (CEOs) has risen from 42 times to 354 times that of the average worker.[3] Deetz suggests that "we need to consider in depth what type of 'business' this is, who the moral claimants are, how privilege is organized, and what the possible democratic responses are."[4]

Deetz' theory of communication is *critical* in that he wants to reveal the easy assumption that "what's good for General Motors is good for the country" has a downside both for GM and the country. Specifically, he wants to examine communication practices in organizations that undermine fully representative decision making and thus reduce the quality, innovation, and fairness of business decisions.

INFORMATION OR COMMUNICATION: TRANSMISSION OR THE CREATION OF MEANING

Deetz begins his analysis by challenging the view that communication is the transmission of information. Even though a majority of human communication scholars now dismiss the familiar source → message → channel → receiver conception of communication, the conduit model is still taken for granted in organizations and in everyday life. There's an intuitive appeal in the idea that words refer to real things—that by using the right words we can express state-of-the-art knowledge. As Deetz notes, "Clearly, the public really wants to believe in an independent reality."[5] He warns, however, that as long as we accept the notion that communication is merely the transmission of information, we will continue to perpetuate corporate dominance over every aspect of our lives.

Information model
A view that communication is merely a conduit for the transmission of information about thereal-world.

Consider a company's annual report. The sanitized numbers present themselves as facts compiled and categorized according to "standard accounting procedures." But Deetz contends that each line item is *constitutive*—created by corporate decision makers who have the power to make their decisions stick. What seems to be value-free information is really meaning *in formation.* The end-of-the-year audit is not fact—it's artifact. All corporate information is an outcome of political processes that are usually undemocratic, with consequences that usually hurt democracy.

In place of the *information model* of messages, Deetz presents a *communication model* that regards language as the principal medium through which social reality is created and sustained. He states that "language does not represent things that already exist. In fact, language is a part of the production of the thing that we treat as being self-evident and natural within the society."[6] Humanists like I. A. Richards have long pointed out that meanings are in people, not in words (see Chapter 4). But Deetz moves even further away from a representational view of language when he raises the question, *Whose meanings are in people?* Once we accept that organizational forms are continually produced and reproduced through language, we'll understand that corporations produce not only goods and services, but also meaning.

Communication model
A view that language is the principal medium through which social reality is created and sustained.

People who adopt the lingo of big business may not be aware that they are putting corporate values into play. For example, the bottom line on a profit-and-loss statement is only that—the last line on the financial report. But a CEO's continual use of the term *bottom line* to justify all managerial decisions produces a perceived reality that shuts out nonfinancial considerations. When ordinary citizens begin to use this economic idiom to characterize the deciding or crucial factor in their own family decisions, they reinforce and expand the influence of corporate thinking in life without even realizing they are doing so.

Figure 21–1 contrasts Deetz' communication approach to organizational practices with an information approach that regards language as neutral and neutered. Like Pearce and Cronen (see Chapter 6), Deetz considers communication the ongoing social construction of meaning. But his critical theory differs from CMM in that he thinks the issue of power runs through all language and communication. He believes managerial control often takes precedence over representation of conflicting interests and long-term company and community health.

> The fundamental issue in my analysis is control and how different groups are represented in decision making. . . . Since industrialization, managers in American corporations have primarily operated from a philosophy of control.[7]

The upper level of Figure 21–1 represents corporate decision processes that systematically exclude the voices of people who are directly affected by the decisions. Deetz labels this practice *managerial control.* The bottom half of the figure pictures decision processes that invite open dialogue among all stakeholders. Deetz calls this practice *codetermination.* When coupled with the constitutive view of communication, codetermination represents the "collaborative collective constructions of self, other, and the world"[8] that Deetz believes are the product of participatory democracy.

Codetermination
Collaborative decision making; participatory democracy in the workplace.

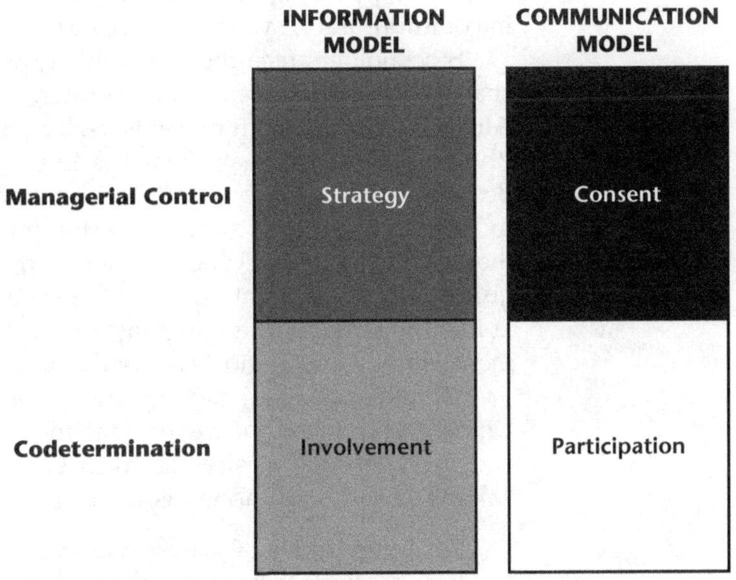

FIGURE 21–1 Two Approaches to Organizational Practice
Based on Deetz, *Transforming Communication, Transforming Business,* Chapter 7

The 2 × 2 nature of Figure 21–1 yields four different ways in which public decisions—including corporate ones—can be made: *strategy, consent, involvement,* and *participation.* Deetz' analysis of these four corporate practices provides the core of his critique of managerialism.

STRATEGY: OVERT MANAGERIAL MOVES TO EXTEND CONTROL

Deetz doesn't portray individual managers as scoundrels in his saga of corporate control. He makes it clear that managers are not the problem—the real culprit is *managerialism.* Deetz describes managerialism as discourse based on "a kind of systematic logic, a set of routine practices, and ideology" that values control above all else.[9] Stockholders want profits and workers desire freedom, but management craves control.

Whenever there's a corporate disaster or scandal, the public and media look for a scapegoat or "bad apple" who's responsible. Deetz thinks that's short-sighted because it diverts attention away from a failed managerial system based on control. He cites social psychologist Philip Zimbardo's book *The Lucifer Effect,* which suggests we'd do well to stop talking about a few bad apples and look at the consequences of what happens when you put good people in bad barrels.[10]

Managerialism
A systematic logic, set of routine practices, and ideology that values control over all other concerns.

No matter what their job, workers around the world often experience the same dictatorial style in the expressed and implied messages that come from the top:

"Because I'm the boss."
"Because I say so."
"If you don't like it, quit."
"It's my way or the highway."

Some employees do object by saying, in effect, "Take this job and shove it," but that doesn't increase representation. Choice is often limited to loyalty or exit—"love it or leave it." Without a voice, workers have no say in the decisions that affect them during the majority of their waking hours. Deetz argues that while control of this sort is disappearing in most enlightened corporations, new forms of control based in communication systems impede any real worker voice in structuring their work.

Stockholders face the same either/or dilemma. They can choose to hold their shares or sell them, but neither option offers a way to influence corporate policy. Although management presents itself as making decisions on behalf of stockholders (the owners), Deetz says that the interests of the two groups are often at odds. Because of stock options and "golden parachutes," top management has benefited more than any other group from the merger mania and cost-cutting strategies of the last two decades. Whereas long-term growth would help the average investor, quick profits and tight control of costs are the manager's ticket up the corporate ladder. Regardless of a company's product line or service, "control is the management product and is most clearly the one on which individual advancement rests."[11]

Initially, managers may regard efficiency as a means to the end of higher profits. Deetz is convinced, however, that the desire for control soon becomes a valued end in itself. That desire can even exceed the desire for corporate performance. Talking in terms of money is often more for control than for efficiency or profits.

> The control drive of managerialism seeks the medium of its extension, and money is it. . . . Everything that cannot be adequately translated into money is implicitly suppressed, and all competing rights of decisions regarding one's life are made marginal.[12]

Nowhere is this quest for control more apparent than in corporate aversion to public conflict. The managerial rule of thumb seems to be that conflict is to be "dealt with" rather than openly discussed. Managers are rewarded for "putting out fires," "running a tight ship," or "making things run smoothly." The impersonal nature of these metaphors suggests that executives should place responsibility to the company ahead of personal feelings or ethical concerns. In the corporate context, claims of "company policy" and "just doing my job" provide sufficient moral justification for suppressing almost any act of employee resistance or dissent.

Deetz argues there is little evidence that strategic control has beneficial effects beyond accelerating advancement on the managerial career path. He claims that most corporate successes (or failures) are the result of factors beyond managerial control.[13] Control does have distinct disadvantages, however. The cost is high, and workers resent the constant surveillance. Frequent references to "clearing out the deadwood" or "trimming the fat" create an understandable jumpiness among employees, and sometimes their fear is acted out in covert rebellion. Since dominance creates this kind of resistance, most modern managers prefer to maintain control through the voluntary consent of the worker rather than the strategic use of raw power.

CONSENT: UNWITTING ALLEGIANCE TO COVERT CONTROL

Deetz believes in capitalism, but he's convinced that corporations are unreasonable. "They expect more than a fair day's work for a fair day's pay; they want love, respect, and above all loyalty."[14] Even though the company gets the workers' most rested, alert, and chemical-free portion of the day, apparently that's not enough. Management insists that allegiance to the company should come before family, friends, church, and community. Through the process Deetz calls *consent*, most employees willingly give that loyalty without getting much in return. "Consent is the term I use to designate the variety of situations and processes in which someone actively, though unknowingly, accomplishes the interests of others in the faulty attempt to fulfill his or her own interests. The person is complicit in her or his own victimization."[15]

Consent
The process by which employees actively, though unknowingly, accomplish managerial interests in a faulty attempt to fulfill their own.

Lynn, a former student of mine, wrote an application log entry for Deetz' critical theory that poignantly captures the human cost of consent:

> My father was very loyal to his company in the interest of moving up the ladder for pay increases. When my brother and I were babies and toddlers, my family lived in four different places in three years because the company required that we move. Later on, my father spent much of his time traveling and lived in New York for over six months while the rest of us lived in Baltimore. During my high school years, he worked until about eight or nine o'clock in the evening even though it wasn't demanded of him. His entire department was often there because it was common practice to spend that much time getting the job done.
>
> I would love to see the ideal world where employees have a lot more power in their communication within a large company. I think that it would possibly save families like mine from growing up without a full-time father.
>
> I can see further implications. If employees, especially men, feel like they have more power in the workplace, they will be less likely to come home and feel the need to prove their power at home by demeaning their wives in many different ways. I think that if Deetz' proposals ever worked on a wide scale, our country would see a decrease in domestic violence.

How do companies manage to strike such an unfair bargain with their employees? It's tempting to point to the workaholism of Lynn's father as the core of the problem, but Deetz lays more of the blame on managerial control of workplace language, information, forms, symbols, rituals, and stories. Although these are the practices that Pacanowsky and other interpretive scholars treat as indicators of a given organizational culture (see Chapter 19), Deetz views them as attempts to produce and reproduce a culture that is sympathetic to managerial interests. As McPhee's CCO states, all corporations have their own sets of constitutive practices. The question Deetz asks is not *What do these mean?* Rather, it is *Whose meanings are these?*

Managerialism promotes workers' unwitting consent through a process of *systematically distorted communication.* Unlike strategic control, which is open and deliberate, systematically distorted communication operates under the radar. When this happens, expectations and norms within a group setting restrict what can be openly expressed or even thought. Deetz emphasizes that the workers deceive themselves because they believe they are interacting freely, while in reality only certain options are available. As an example, Deetz notes that arbitrary authority relations within an organization may be disguised as legitimate divisions of labor. That way any talk about power relations must assume the validity of the status quo, thus reproducing the organizational hierarchy rather than challenging it. Real interactive decisions can't be made in such a context.

Systematically distorted communication
Operating outside of employees' awareness, a form of discourse that restricts what can be said or even considered.

Systematically distorted communication requires suppression of potential conflict. This process, which Deetz calls *discursive closure,* occurs in a variety of ways. For example, certain groups of people within an organization may be classified as "disqualified" to speak on important issues. Arbitrary definitions can be labeled "natural" to avoid further discussion. The values that guided a manager's judgment call may be kept hidden so that it appears to be an objective decision (see Chapter 20). A group may discourage members from talking about certain subjects. Or the organization may allow the discussion of a topic such as gender-linked job classification or pay differences but discount its importance or quickly divert attention to other issues.

Discursive closure
Suppression of conflict without employees realizing that they are complicit in their own censorship.

Deetz suggests that the force of an organizational practice is strongest when no one even thinks about it. If someone were to question such a routine, employees would be hard-pressed to explain why it is standard operating procedure. The best response they could muster would be a nonanswer: "That's the way it's done around here." Practices that have this taken-for-granted quality are often equated with common sense. Without a clear understanding that communication produces rather than reflects reality (the right side of Figure 21–1), employees will unknowingly consent to the managerial mentality that wants to expand corporate control.

INVOLVEMENT: FREE EXPRESSION OF IDEAS, BUT NO VOICE

For anyone who has a stake in corporate decisions (all of us), shifting from managerial control at the top of Figure 21–1 to involvement at the bottom is a crucial move. In political terms, it represents a switch from autocracy to liberal democracy—from managerial decisions made behind closed doors to open discussions where all have the opportunity to express their opinions.

Involvement
Stakeholders' free expression of ideas that may, or may not, affect managerial decisions.

Employee *involvement* in corporate choices began with a suggestion box mounted on a wall. In some companies, this invitation for expression evolved over decades into open forums that look like early-American town meetings. At their best, these attempts at corporate democracy are based on a commitment to free speech and the value of an open marketplace of ideas (see Nilsen's ethic of significant choice, pp. 197–198).

Deetz claims that liberal eighteenth-century Jeffersonian democracy was based on three notions about communication: (1) freedom of speech guaranteed equitable participation in decision making; (2) persuasion and advocacy were the best ways to reach a good decision; and (3) autonomous individuals could then make up their own minds. Taken together, this meant truth would emerge from the free flow of information in an open marketplace of ideas. As long as people shared the same values, an information-transfer model of communication worked well.[16] But not in today's society. Freedom of speech doesn't mean the right to be in on the decision. Adversarial posturing doesn't lend itself to creative consensus. And consent conditions make autonomy rare.

Organizations in the twenty-first century must operate in a pluralistic and interdependent world. People have always been different, but it used to be that mountains and oceans made it possible to stick with your own kind. Today in business and government, that's almost impossible. You can't expect much empathy from a person raised in a different culture, who has had radically different experiences, and who holds a worldview that you might find disturbing. And isolation is no longer an option. As the worldwide economic meltdown in 2008, the 2010 BP Gulf oil spill, and bankrupt European economies in 2012 illustrate, whatever happens up the road or overseas will surely affect us all. Deetz is convinced that if Thomas Jefferson lived downwind or downstream from a factory hog farm, the Declaration of Independence he wrote would be a different document.[17] It might well have been a Declaraton of Interdependence.

As Deetz surveys present-day corporate communication practices, he concludes that "the right of expression appears more central than the right to be informed or to have an effect."[18] Through involvement in discussions of company policy, employees have a chance to air their grievances, state their desires, and recommend alternative ways of working. Many managers use these sessions as a way to give employees a chance to let off steam. But advocacy is not negotiation. If workers find out their ideas aren't represented in the final decision, they quickly become cynical about the process. And when consent is present, the right to freely express ideas is only the right to express the meanings belonging to someone else.

In national politics as well as corporate governance, meaningful democracy requires that people not only have a chance to discuss the issues, but also have a voice in the final outcome. Forums provide the opportunity for involvement, yet *voice* is not just having a say. It means expressing interests that are freely and openly formed, and then having those interests reflected in joint decisions. That's real participation. Deetz says it's only possible when all stakeholders realize that their communication creates reality rather than merely describing it.

PARTICIPATION: STAKEHOLDER DEMOCRACY IN ACTION

Deetz' theory of communication is critical, but not just negative. While he strongly criticizes the managerial strategy of increasing control over workers, engineering their consent, and granting them free expression without giving them a voice in decisions, he also believes that joint, open decisions in the workplace are possible. Deetz is convinced that "meaningful democratic participation creates better citizens and better social choices, and provides important economic benefits."[19] One of the goals of his theory is to reclaim the possibility of open negotiations of power. He calls it *stakeholder democracy.*

The first move Deetz makes is to expand the list of people who should have a say in how a corporation is run. Besides managers, he sees at least six groups of stakeholders with multiple needs and desires.[20]

Participation
Stakeholder democracy; the process by which all stakeholders in an organization negotiate power and openly reach collaborative decisions.

Investors seek security of principal and a decent return on their investment.

Workers seek a reasonable wage, safe working conditions, a chance to take pride in their labor, security of employment, and time for their families.

Consumers seek quality goods and services at a fair price.

Suppliers seek a stable demand for their resource with timely payment upon delivery.

Host communities seek payment for services provided, stable employment, environmental care, and the quality of family and public life enhanced rather than diminished.

Greater society and the world community seek environmental care, economic stability, overall civility, and fair treatment of all constituent groups (racial, ethnic, gender).

Deetz notes that some stakeholders have taken greater risks and made longer-term investments in a company than typical owners of stock or top-level managers.[21] He believes it's imperative that those who are affected by corporate decisions have a say in how such decisions are made. Of course, this stance runs counter to traditional notions of exclusive stockholder rights or managerial prerogatives, but Deetz says there's no legitimate basis for privileging one group of stakeholders over another. He reminds us that nature did not make corporations—we did. "The rights and responsibilities of people are not given in advance by nature or by a privileged, universal value structure, but are negotiated through interaction."[22]

As you scan the list of stakeholders and their interests, it's obvious that current corporate governance is not set up to address their social, financial, and ecological goals. In light of the widespread corporate greed and corruption that led to the financial meltdown and Great Recession we've been through, relying on managerial goodwill would seem a joke. Some would expect government to insert social values into the marketplace but, except for brief periods of time following a crisis, government policy is largely influenced by business leaders and lobbyists. Free-enterprise advocates suggest that the unseen hand of the market will sort things out, but that reduces all values to a matter of dollars and cents—and those not equitably.

Deetz offers his appraisal and previews his solution: Taken together, corporate "stewardship, government regulation, and markets offer weak mechanisms for value inclusion and virtually no support for communication processes that create win/win situations where multiple stakeholders can successfully pursue their mutual interests."[23] Rather than trying to leverage participatory governance from the outside, Deetz believes building stakeholder values into corporate decision-making practices is the route to go. In addition to his academic work, he acts as a consultant to companies' top management and their boards of directors, showing why it's in their long-term interest to initiate collaborative practices themselves.

POLITICALLY ATTENTIVE RELATIONAL CONSTRUCTIONISM (PARC)

Deetz has recently proposed an extension of his critical theory that describes six types of conflict that must be addressed in organizations. He calls it *politically attentive relational constructionism (PARC).*[24] He suggests it can also serve as a framework or metatheory within which to compare his theory with other organizational and/or critical theories. Although the four-word label to which PARC refers may strike you as daunting, when split into two-word pairs you can see that the phrase reflects the *communication model* and *codetermination* features of stakeholder participation shown in Figure 21–1.

PARC model
Politically attentive relational constructionism; a collaborative view of communication based in stakeholder conflict.

Relational Constructionism

Deetz maintains that most organizational theories are based on some form of social construction. That's certainly the case with Pacanowsky's cultural approach, which looks at cultural artifacts and seeks to interpret what they mean (see Chapter 19). It's also true with McPhee's version of CCO, which describes the four flows constituted by communication within an organization (see Chapter 20). Both theories focus on *what* has been created, not on *how* it was done. Since Deetz is just as concerned with the process of construction as he is with its end product, he uses the designation *relational* rather than the more common term *social.* He makes this switch to signal that he differs from those who think they're looking at an already etched-in-stone culture or, conversely, those who think they're writing a blank slate. "Relational constructionism asks us to return to explore the moments of co-constructions and the conditions making particular constructions possible rather than accept the productions as given."[25]

Deetz outlines nine conditions that must be met in order for diverse stakeholders to successfully negotiate their needs and interests:[26]

1. Stakeholders have divergent interests, not set positions.
2. Stakeholders possess roughly the same level of communication skill.
3. Authority relationships and power positions are set aside.
4. All stakeholders have an equal opportunity to express themselves.
5. Stakeholders' wants are openly investigated in order to determine their interests.
6. Participants transparently share information and how decisions are made.
7. Facts and knowledge claims are revisited to see how they were created.
8. Focus on outcomes and interests rather than bargaining on rival solutions.
9. Stakeholders jointly make decisions rather than just having "their say."

This batch of preconditions might seem impossible to meet, but those trained in the art of negotiation and conflict mediation are quite familiar with most of the requirements and are committed to using them for the benefit of all parties. It's not surprising that Deetz, director of peace and conflict studies at his university, finds them useful in his PARC model.

Politically Attentive

Deetz uses the term "political" to refer to the presence of power dynamics in relationships. He's convinced that the world is "fundamentally based on conflict and tension rather than consensus and order,"[27] so all communication is political and we should be frequently aware of that fact. Recall that one of Watzlawick's axioms in the *interactional view* is Communication = Content + Relationship, and that our relationship tells us how to classify or interpret the content (see Chapter 13). Deetz sees power as an ever-present part of our relationships—certainly so in our organizational lives. To be *politically attentive* means to honestly explore the power in play behind so-called neutral facts and taken-for-granted positions.

In corporations, for example, political awareness might lead us to examine specific "standard accounting practices" to uncover how they came to be—who benefited and who suffered loss by their adoption. Deetz isn't bothered that the world is political, but he thinks it's disingenuous and deceptive when managers pretend it isn't. An organization's stakeholders need to recover the conflict that was repressed so that all interests are on the table and openly discussed. Only in this way can fair and beneficial negotiations take place.

Deetz would have managers take the role of mediators rather than persuaders, manipulators, or dictators. They would coordinate the conflicting interests of all parties affected by corporate decisions. He understands that even those who are committed to open dialogue will feel insecure as they relinquish control. He suggests a good way for them to start is to "complicate" their perceptions of subordinates and other stakeholders by being around them, talking with them, and learning their hopes, dreams, fears, values, and needs. And when stakeholders come together to discuss corporate policy, managers should make sure all areas of conflict are considered. PARC suggests six that are almost always an issue.[28]

Inner life: What feelings are present and possible? What organizational practices are necessary for those feelings to surface?

Identity and recognition: Who are the people involved? Given their identities, what rights and responsibilities do they have?

Social order: What behaviors, actions, and ways of talking are considered appropriate? What norms and rules support these?

Truth: What do members think is true? How do they back up these claims? What are the processes for resolving different views?

Life narratives: How does the world work for them? What would a good and beautiful future look like?

Justice: What is fair? How should limited goods and services be distributed?

AVOIDING MELTDOWN—PUTTING THEORY INTO PRACTICE

Given entrenched managerial power and privilege in corporations, most economic observers are skeptical that the workplace participation Deetz advocates will become reality. But Deetz' recent work with the International Atomic Energy Agency (IAEA) might give naysayers cause for pause. The agency invited Deetz to join a working group of international experts, nuclear plant supervisors, and government regulators concerned with creating "cultures of safety" around the construction and operation of atomic generating sites. Although anything involving radiation is always a concern, fears of power-plant disasters skyrocketed after the 2011 Fukushima meltdown following an earthquake and subsequent tsunami. The chairman of the independent commission that investigated the accident made it clear this wasn't a natural disaster:

> What must be admitted—very painfully—is that this was a disaster "Made in Japan." Its fundamental causes are to be found in the ingrained conventions of Japanese culture: our reflexive obedience; our reluctance to question authority; our devotion to 'sticking with the program'; our groupism; and our insularity.[29]

Deetz would call this consent actively reproduced at work. The nuclear community was shocked the meltdown took place in a technologically sophisticated nation known for quality control and a highly skilled workforce. If this could happen in Japan, how much more risk will atomic energy pose in less developed countries such as Mexico, Poland, or Vietnam, where plans are quickly moving ahead?

Most members of IAEA admit that a check-list approach to safety isn't working and that nuclear engineers know little about the human side of organizational dynamics. This is why communication experts looking at the consent production and change process need to be involved. Deetz, of course, advocates bringing the workers into the process, with places for active participatory dialogue. (See a link to his presentation at the IAEA 2012 annual meeting in the Second Look bibliography.) Members of his working group realize that people welding pipe know things that people who aren't welding pipe don't know. So if welders are part of the decision-making process, the decision will be based on on better information.

Imagine Deetz on a video conference call with nuclear plant managers around the world.

> SUPERVISOR #1: I have a lot of trouble at these safety meetings getting people to pay attention, listen, or even care.
>
> SUPERVISOR #2: You know, I just don't let that happen. I get in their face and tell them to pay attention and listen.

DEETZ: Have you ever asked them why they're not paying attention—what there is about this that makes it seem unworthy of them? You might ask them what conversations about safety they'd want to turn off their cell phones to be part of.[30]

Deetz says you'll never know unless you ask and then treat their answers as valuable. You may find out that workers believe safety is just managerial lip service because what their boss really wants is the job done fast. Perhaps a lot of the crew thinks everything in the building of these plants is overengineered. They're pouring twice as much concrete as needed, so cutting a few corners doesn't seem dangerous. Or you might pick up a machismo swagger that sees caution as unmanly. Only when the discussion turns to the safety of one's family or the chance of radiation rendering a guy sterile does there seem to be a reason to turn off the cell phone.

Stan Deetz is not naïve. He knows atomic energy is not just an alternative way to boil water. Moving toward an industry culture of safety through stakeholder participation is a complex and difficult process, and there aren't enough regulators to look over the shoulder of every worker eight hours a day. So the goal is to reach a point where all stakeholders voluntarily do the right thing because they see it's in their own interest or the interests of those they love. But if Deetz is wrong—or managers ignore his advice—you might learn about it first on the evening news.

CRITIQUE: IS WORKPLACE DEMOCRACY JUST A DREAM?

Deetz' approach to corporate decision making is inherently attractive because it is built on values that many of us in the field of communication share. By reserving a seat at the decision-making table for every class of stakeholders, Deetz affirms the importance of democratic participation, fairness, equality, diversity, and cooperation.

Without question, Deetz' insistence on the constitutive nature of all communication can help us understand consent practices in the workplace. Yet his advocacy of stakeholder rights and participatory democracy isn't necessarily furthered by his constructionist view of communication. In fact, his reform agenda could be hindered. If, contrary to the U.S. Declaration of Independence, there are no self-evident truths on which to stand, everything is in play and it doesn't make much sense to assume we have a *right* to participate in decisions that affect us. And his pragmatic criteria that the reduction of systematically distorted communication leads to more creativity and better business and social decisions may not seem as important to many as a right of free speech.

Political realism may be another problem. As applied to corporate life, Deetz' theory is a critique of managerialism. Arizona State University communication professor Robert McPhee offers a somewhat tongue-in-cheek summary: "If we just didn't find it natural and right and unavoidable to hand power over to managers, everything would be very different and our problems would be solved."[31] Although a caricature, this capsule statement underscores the problematic nature of the stakeholder negotiations Deetz pictures and the incredible challenge of getting all parties to sit at the table as equals. But the increased number of problems like those faced in nuclear power plants may put the forces of a changing world on Deetz' side. The old system was built for the old world. We may need a new system.

Deetz admits that a positive alternative to managerialism is at times difficult to work out in conception and in practice.[32] Moving from the dark quadrant of consent to the clear quadrant of participation in Figure 21–1 is a quantum leap. The PARC model moves critical theory to a higher level of conceptual sophistication. As for stakeholder participation in practice, Deetz finds that businesses increasingly recognize they must work with others. He cites cases where resources are scarce—river basin governance, mineral extraction, environmental choices, as well as social and economic development. Stakeholders at the table often include governmental agencies, businesses, nongovernmental organizations, special-interest groups, and community members. Deetz reports that "critical theories work to increase equality by surfacing unnecessary and harmful control mechanisms, showing the importance of different forms of knowledge and values, and building interaction processes that make this greater equality meaningful and productive."[33]

Moving from the theory to the theorist, Deetz insists that critical scholars be "filled with care, thought, and good humor."[34] That third quality may surprise you for, like prophets, critical theorists have the reputation of being a rather grim bunch. But Deetz suggests that with good humor we can smile at our inconsistencies, contradictions, and bruised pride. We are to take the plight of the oppressed—but not ourselves—seriously. "The righteousness and pretense is gone, we must act without knowing for sure. The grand narratives are dead, but there is meaning and pleasure in the little ones. The pleasure embarrasses us but also gives us energy and a smile at ourselves."[35]

QUESTIONS TO SHARPEN YOUR FOCUS

1. Deetz contrasts *information models* that assume language *reflects* reality with *communication models* that assume reality emerges out of a *relationship* among self, others, language, and the world. What other theories already covered fit the communication model?
2. Managers use *strategy* and *consent* to maintain *control* over subordinates. According to Deetz, which practice is more effective? Why?
3. The *stakeholder model* requires *participation,* not just *involvement.* What is the difference between the two practices?
4. To what extent do you agree with the following statement: "Autocracy at work is the price we pay for *democracy* after hours"? Does it apply equally to work in the classroom?

CONVERSATIONS

View this segment online at www.mhhe.com.griffin9e or www.afirstlook.com.

In this eight-minute segment, critical theorist Stan Deetz offers a host of pithy opinions. Here's a sample. *On communication:* "The field for a long time argued that meanings were in people. I raise the opposite kind of question: Whose meanings are in people?" *On management:* "A lot of managers talk about thinking out of the box, but they don't understand . . . that you do not think out of the box by commanding the box." *On corporate assets:* "Their primary assets are not what investors gave them, but what employees gave them. . . . Their primary assets go down the elevator every night." And there are lots more. Watch and discover your favorites.

A SECOND LOOK

Recommended resource: Stanley Deetz, *Transforming Communication, Transforming Business: Building Responsive and Responsible Workplaces,* Hampton, Cresskill, NJ, 1995.

Critical foundation: Stanley Deetz, *Democracy in an Age of Corporate Colonization: Developments in Communication and the Politics of Everyday Life,* State University of New York, Albany, NY, 1992.

Critique of communication theory and practice: Stanley Deetz, "Critical Theory," in *Engaging Organizational Communication Theory: Multiple Perspectives,* S. May and Dennis Mumby (eds.), Sage, Thousand Oaks, CA, 2004, pp. 85–111.

Organizational politics: "Interests, Conflict, and Power: Organizations as Political Systems," in Gareth Morgan, *Images of Organization,* 2nd ed., Sage, Thousand Oaks, CA, 1997, pp. 153–213.

PARC model compared to McPhee's CCO: Stanley Deetz and Elizabeth K. Eger, "Developing a Metatheoretical Perspective for Organizational Communication Studies," in *The New Handbook of Organizational Communication: Advances in Theory, Research, and Methods,* 2nd ed., Fredrick Jablin and Linda L. Putnam (eds.), Sage, Thousand Oaks, CA, 2013.

PARC model compared to CMM: Stanley Deetz, "Power and the Possibility of Generative Community Dialogue," in *The Coordinated Management of Meaning: A Festschrift in Honor of W. Barnett Pearce,* Stephen Littlejohn (ed.), Fairleigh Dickinson, Madison, NJ, 2013.

PARC model compared to Habermas' theory of communicative action: Stanley Deetz, "Politically Attentive Relational Constructionism (PARC) and Making a Difference in a Pluralistic, Independent World," in *Distinctive Qualities in Communication Research,* Donal Carbaugh and Patrice M. Buzzanell (eds.), Routledge, New York, 2010, pp. 32–51.

Deetz' IAEA paper on creating a safe nuclear culture: http://gnssn.iaea.org/NSNI/SC/SCPoP/Papers prepared for meeting/Stanley Deetz_Being Transformative - How Hearts, Minds and Souls All Matter_Paper.pdf

Review and critique: Branislav Kovačić, "The Democracy and Organizational Communication Theories of Deetz, Mumby, and Associates," in *Watershed Research Traditions in Communication Theory,* Donald Cushman and Branislav Kovačić (eds.), State University of New York, Albany, NY, 1995, pp. 211–238.

To access scenes from feature films that illustrate the Critical Theory of Communication in Organizations, click on Suggested Movie Clips under Theory Resources at *www.afirstlook.com.*

Public Rhetoric

Aristotle defined rhetoric as "an ability, in each particular case, to see the available means of persuasion."[1] That designation centers attention on the intentional act of using words to have an effect. I use the term *public rhetoric* in this section to refer to a speaking context in which the orator has an opportunity to monitor and adjust to the response of his or her immediate audience.

For citizens of ancient Greece, knowing how to speak in public was part of their democratic responsibility. Later on, when Rome ruled the world, rhetorical ability was a survival skill in the rough-and-tumble politics of the forum. Rhetoricians have always had a special interest in judicial argument, legislative debate, political rallies, religious sermons, and speeches given at celebrations. In each setting, teachers and practitioners champion the art of rhetoric as a means of ensuring that speakers of truth are not at a disadvantage when trying to win the hearts and minds of an audience.

The Greeks and Romans distinguished five parts, or divisions, of the study of rhetoric:

1. *Invention*—discovery of convincing arguments
2. *Arrangement*—organization of material for best impact
3. *Style*—selection of compelling and appropriate language
4. *Delivery*—coordination of voice and gestures
5. *Memory*—mastery and rehearsal of content

With the possible exception of memory, these concerns of rhetoric require that a speaker first analyze and then adapt to a specific group of listeners. We can, of course, react to the idea of audience adaptation in two different ways. If we view speakers who adjust their message to fit a specific audience in a positive light, we'll praise their rhetorical sensitivity and flexibility. If we view them negatively, we'll condemn them for their pandering and lack of commitment to the truth. Rhetorical thought across history swings back and forth between these two conflicting poles. The words of most rhetoricians reflect the tension they feel between "telling it like it is" and telling it in such a way that the audience will listen.

Greek philosopher Plato regarded rhetoric as mostly flattery. Far from seeing it as an art, he described rhetoric as a *knack*—similar to the clever use of cosmetics. Both are attempts to make things seem better than they really are.[2] In spite of his scorn, Plato imagined an ideal rhetoric based on a speaker's understanding of listeners with different natures and dispositions.

Plato's ideal discourse was an elite form of dialogue meant for private, rather than public, consumption. This philosophic, one-on-one mode of communication is known as *dialectic* (a different meaning for the term than its use in Baxter and Montgomery's relational dialectics). Unlike typical oratory in Athens, where speakers addressed large audiences on civic issues, Plato's dialectic focused on exploring eternal Truths in an intimate setting.

Although Plato hoped that philosophic dialectic would supplant public rhetoric, his best student, Aristotle, rejuvenated public rhetoric as a serious academic subject. More than 2,000 years ago, Aristotle's *Rhetoric* systematically explored the topics

"I found the old format much more exciting."

of speaker, message, and audience. His ideas have stood the test of time and form a large portion of the advice presented in contemporary public speaking texts. But even though Aristotle defined rhetoric as the art of discovering all available means of persuasion, this conception doesn't solve the problem of how to get audiences to listen to hard truths.

Religious rhetors face the same paradox. In many ways the apostle Paul seemed to personify the lover of diverse souls that Plato had earlier described. In his first letter to the Corinthians, Paul reminds the people of Corinth that he made a conscious decision to let his message speak for itself: "My speech and my proclamation were not with plausible words of wisdom."[3] Yet further on in the same letter he outlines a conscious rhetorical strategy: "I have become all things to all people, that I might by all means save some."[4] Four centuries later, Augustine continued to justify the conscious use of rhetoric by the church. Why, he asked, should defenders of truth be long-winded, confusing, and boring, when the speech of liars was brief, clear, and persuasive?

The tension between the logic of a message and the appeal it has for an audience isn't easily resolved. British philosopher Francis Bacon sought to integrate the two concerns when he wrote that "the duty of rhetoric is to apply Reason to Imagination for the better moving of the will."[5]

The three rhetoricians I introduce in this section face the dilemma that rhetoricians have struggled with since Plato: "How do you move an audience without changing your message or losing your integrity?" As you read, see which theorist comes up with an answer that is most satisfying for you.

CHAPTER 22

Objective — Interpretive

Rhetorical tradition

The Rhetoric

of Aristotle

Aristotle was a student of Plato's in the golden age of Greek civilization, four centuries before the birth of Christ. He became a respected instructor at Plato's Academy but disagreed with his mentor over the place of public speaking in Athenian life.

Ancient Greece was known for its traveling speech teachers called Sophists. Particularly in Athens, those teachers trained aspiring lawyers and politicians to participate effectively in the courts and deliberative councils. In hindsight, they appear to have been innovative educators who offered a needed and wanted service.[1] But since their advice was underdeveloped theoretically, Plato scoffed at the Sophists' oratorical devices. His skepticism is mirrored today in the negative way people use the term *mere rhetoric* to label the speech of *tricky* lawyers, *mealy-mouthed* politicians, *spellbinding* preachers, and *fast-talking* salespeople.

Aristotle, like Plato, deplored the demagoguery of speakers using their skill to move an audience while showing a casual indifference to the truth. But unlike Plato, he saw the tools of rhetoric as a neutral means by which the orator could either accomplish noble ends or further fraud: ". . . by using these justly one would do the greatest good, and unjustly, the greatest harm."[2] Aristotle believed truth has a moral superiority that makes it more acceptable than falsehood. But unscrupulous opponents of the truth may fool a dull audience unless an ethical speaker uses all possible means of persuasion to counter the error. Speakers who neglect the art of rhetoric have only themselves to blame when their hearers choose falsehood. Success requires wisdom *and* eloquence.

Both the *Politics* and the *Ethics* of Aristotle are polished and well-organized books compared with the rough prose and arrangement of his text on rhetoric. The *Rhetoric* apparently consists of Aristotle's reworked lecture notes for his course at the academy. Despite the uneven nature of the writing, the *Rhetoric* is a searching study of audience psychology. Aristotle raised rhetoric to a science by systematically exploring the effects of the speaker, the speech, and the audience. He regarded the speaker's use of this knowledge as an art. Quite likely, the text your communication department uses for its public speaking classes is basically a contemporary recasting of the audience analysis provided by Aristotle more than two thousand years ago.

RHETORIC: MAKING PERSUASION PROBABLE

Rhetoric
Discovering all possible means of persuasion.

Aristotle saw the function of *rhetoric* as the discovery in each case of "the available means of persuasion." He never spelled out what he meant by persuasion, but his concern with noncoercive methods makes it clear that he ruled out force of law, torture, and war. His threefold classification of speech situations according to the nature of the audience shows that he had affairs of state in mind.

The first in Aristotle's classification is courtroom (forensic) speaking, which addresses judges who are trying to render a just decision about actions alleged to have taken place in the *past*. The closing arguments presented by the prosecution and defense in the trial of George Zimmerman for killing an unarmed Trayvon Martin are examples of judicial rhetoric centered on guilt or innocence. The second, ceremonial (epideictic) speaking, heaps praise or blame on another for the benefit of *present-day* audiences. For example, Rev. Al Sharpton's eulogy for Michael Jackson gave fans an opportunity to celebrate the life of the conflicted rock star. The third, political (deliberative) speaking, attempts to influence legislators or voters who decide *future* policy. The 2012 presidential debates gave Barack Obama and Mitt Romney a chance to sway undecided voters. These different temporal orientations could call for diverse rhetorical appeals.

Because his students were familiar with the question-and-answer style of Socratic dialogue, Aristotle classified rhetoric as a counterpart or an offshoot of dialectic. Dialectic is one-on-one discussion; rhetoric is one person addressing many. Dialectic is a search for truth; rhetoric tries to demonstrate truth that's already been found. Dialectic answers general philosophical questions; rhetoric addresses specific, practical ones. Dialectic deals with certainty; rhetoric deals with probability. Aristotle saw this last distinction as particularly important: rhetoric is the art of discovering ways to make truth seem more probable to an audience that isn't completely convinced.

RHETORICAL PROOF: *LOGOS, ETHOS, PATHOS*

Inartistic proofs
External evidence the speaker doesn't create.

According to Aristotle, the available means of persuasion can be artistic or inartistic. *Inartistic* or external proofs are those the speaker doesn't create. They would include testimonies of witnesses or documents such as letters and contracts. *Artistic* or internal proofs are those the speaker creates. There are three kinds of artistic proofs: logical (*logos*), ethical (*ethos*), and emotional (*pathos*). Logical proof comes from the line of argument in the speech, ethical proof is the way the speaker's character is revealed through the message, and emotional proof is the feeling the speech draws out of the hearers. Some form of *logos, ethos,* and *pathos* is present in every public presentation, but perhaps no other modern-day speech has brought all three appeals together as effectively as Martin Luther King Jr.'s "I Have a Dream," delivered in 1963 to civil rights marchers in Washington, DC. In the year 2000, American public address scholars selected King's "I Have a Dream" as the greatest speech of the twentieth century. We'll look at this artistic speech throughout the rest of the chapter to illustrate Aristotle's rhetorical theory.

Artistic proofs
Internal proofs that contain logical, ethical, or emotional appeals.

Case Study: "I Have a Dream"

At the end of August 1963, a quarter of a million people assembled at the Lincoln Memorial in a united march on Washington. The rally capped a long, hot summer of sit-ins protesting racial discrimination in the South. (The film

Mississippi Burning portrays one of the tragic racial conflicts of that year.) Two months before the march, President John F. Kennedy submitted a civil rights bill to Congress that would begin to rectify segregation and other racial injustices, but its passage was seriously in doubt. The organizers of the march hoped it would put pressure on Congress to outlaw segregation in the South, but they also wanted the demonstration to raise the national consciousness about economic exploitation of blacks around the country.

Martin Luther King shared the platform with a dozen civil rights leaders, each limited to a five-minute presentation. King's successful Montgomery bus boycott, freedom rides across the South, and solitary confinement in a Birmingham jail set him apart in the eyes of demonstrators and TV viewers. The last of the group to speak, King had a dual purpose. In the face of a Black Muslim call for violence, he urged blacks to continue their nonviolent struggle without hatred. He also implored white people to get involved in the quest for freedom and equality, to be part of a dream fulfilled rather than contribute to an unjust nightmare.

A few years after King's assassination, I experienced the impact his speech continued to have upon the African-American community. Teaching public address in a volunteer street academy, I read the speech out loud to illustrate matters of style. The students needed no written text. As I came to the last third of the speech, they recited the eloquent "I have a dream" portion word for word with great passion. When we finished, all of us were teary-eyed.

David Garrow, author of the Pulitzer Prize–winning biography of King, called the speech the "rhetorical achievement of a lifetime, the clarion call that conveyed the moral power of the movement's cause to the millions who watched the live national network coverage."[3] King shifted the burden of proof onto those who opposed racial equality. Aristotle's three rhetorical proofs can help us understand how King made the status quo of segregation an ugly option for the moral listener.

Logical Proof: Lines of Argument That Make Sense

Logos
Logical proof, which comes from the line of argument in a speech.

Aristotle focused on two forms of *logos*—the *enthymeme* and the *example.* He regarded the enthymeme as "the strongest of the proofs."[4] An enthymeme is merely an incomplete version of a formal deductive syllogism. To illustrate, logicians might create the following syllogism out of one of King's lines of reasoning:

Major or general premise: *All people are created equal.*
Minor or specific premise: *I am a person.*
Conclusion: *I am equal to other people.*

Typical enthymemes, however, leave out a premise that is already accepted by the audience. *All people are created equal. . . . I am equal to other people.* In terms of style, the enthymeme is more artistic than a stilted syllogistic argument. But as University of Wisconsin rhetorician Lloyd Bitzer notes, Aristotle had a greater reason for advising the speaker to suppress the statement of a premise the listeners already believe.

> Because they are jointly produced by the audience, enthymemes intuitively unite speaker and audience and provide the strongest possible proof. . . . The audience itself helps construct the proof by which it is persuaded.[5]

Most rhetorical analysis looks for enthymemes embedded in one or two lines of text. In the case of "I Have a Dream," the whole speech is one giant enthymeme.

Enthymeme
An incomplete version of a formal deductive syllogism that is created by leaving out a premise already accepted by the audience or by leaving an obvious conclusion unstated.

If the logic of the speech were to be expressed as a syllogism, the reasoning would be as follows:

> Major premise: *God will reward nonviolence.*
> Minor premise: *We are pursuing our dream nonviolently.*
> Conclusion: *God will grant us our dream.*

King used the first two-thirds of the speech to establish the validity of the minor premise. White listeners are reminded that blacks have been "battered by the storms of persecution and staggered by winds of police brutality." They have "come fresh from narrow jail cells" and are "veterans of creative suffering." Blacks are urged to meet "physical force with soul force," not to allow "creative protest to degenerate into physical violence," and never to "satisfy our thirst for freedom by drinking from the cup of bitterness and hatred." The movement is to continue to be nonviolent.

King used the last third of the speech to establish his conclusion; he painted the dream in vivid color. It included King's hope that his four children would not be "judged by the color of their skin, but by the content of their character." He pictured an Alabama where "little black boys and black girls will be able to join hands with little white boys and white girls as sisters and brothers." And in a swirling climax, he shared a vision of all God's children singing, "Free at last, free at last. Thank God Almighty, we are free at last." But he never articulated the major premise. He didn't need to.

King and his audience were already committed to the truth of the major premise—that God would reward their commitment to nonviolence. Aristotle stressed that audience analysis is crucial to the effective use of the enthymeme. The centrality of the church in American black history, the religious roots of the civil rights protest, and the crowd's frequent response of "My Lord" suggest that King knew his audience well. He never stated what to them was obvious, and this strengthened rather than weakened his logical appeal.

The enthymeme uses deductive logic—moving from global principle to specific truth. Arguing by example uses inductive reasoning—drawing a final conclusion from specific cases. Since King mentioned few examples of discrimination, it might appear that he failed to use all possible means of logical persuasion. But pictures of snarling police dogs, electric cattle prods used on peaceful demonstrators, and signs over drinking fountains stating "Whites only" appeared nightly on TV news. As with the missing major premise of the enthymeme, King's audience supplied its own vivid images.

Ethical Proof: Perceived Source Credibility

According to Aristotle, it's not enough for a speech to contain plausible argument. The speaker must *seem* credible as well. Many audience impressions are formed before the speaker even begins. As poet Ralph Waldo Emerson cautioned more than a century ago, "Use what language you will, you can never say anything but what you are."[6] Some who watched Martin Luther King on television undoubtedly tuned him out because he was black. But surprisingly, Aristotle said little about a speaker's background or reputation. He was more interested in audience perceptions that are shaped by what the speaker does or doesn't say. In the *Rhetoric* he identified three qualities that build high source credibility—*intelligence, character,* and *goodwill.*

1. Perceived Intelligence. The quality of intelligence has more to do with practical wisdom (phronesis) and shared values than it does with training at

"Trust me, at this point it's the only way we can boost your numbers on likability."

Plato's Academy. Audiences judge intelligence by the overlap between their beliefs and the speaker's ideas. ("My idea of an agreeable speaker is one who agrees with me.") King quoted the Bible, the United States Constitution, the patriotic hymn "My Country, 'Tis of Thee," Shakespeare's *King Lear,* and the Negro spiritual "We Shall Overcome." With the exception of violent terrorists and racial bigots, it's hard to imagine anyone with whom he didn't establish strong value identification.

2. Virtuous Character. Character has to do with the speaker's image as a good and honest person. Even though he and other blacks were victims of "unspeakable horrors of police brutality," King warned against a "distrust of all white people" and against "drinking from the cup of bitterness and hatred." It would be difficult to maintain an image of the speaker as an evil racist while he was being charitable toward his enemies and optimistic about the future.

3. Goodwill. Goodwill is a positive judgment of the speaker's intention toward the audience. Aristotle thought it possible for an orator to possess extraordinary intelligence and sterling character yet still not have the listeners' best interest at heart. King was obviously not trying to reach "the vicious racists" of Alabama, but no one was given reason to think he bore them ill will. His dream included "black men and white men, Jews and Gentiles, Protestants and Catholics."

Ethos
Perceived credibility, which comes from the speaker's intelligence, character, and goodwill toward the audience, as these personal characteristics are revealed through the message.

Although Aristotle's comments on *ethos* were stated in a few brief sentences, no other portion of his *Rhetoric* has received such close scientific scrutiny. The results of sophisticated testing of audience attitudes show that his three-factor theory of source credibility stands up remarkably well.[7] Listeners definitely think in terms of competence (intelligence), trustworthiness (character), and care (goodwill). As Martin Luther King spoke in front of the Lincoln Memorial, most listeners perceived him as strong in all three.

Emotional Proof: Striking a Responsive Chord

Recent scholarship suggests that Aristotle was quite skeptical about the emotion-laden public oratory typical of his era.[8] He preferred the reason-based discussion characteristic of relatively small councils and executive deliberative bodies. Yet he understood that public rhetoric, if practiced ethically, benefits society. Thus, Aristotle set forth a theory of *pathos.* He offered it not to take advantage of an audience's destructive emotions, but as a corrective measure that could help a speaker craft emotional appeals that inspire reasoned civic decision making. To this end, he cataloged a series of opposite feelings, then explained the conditions under which each mood is experienced, and finally described how the speaker can get an audience to feel that way. Aristotle scholar and translator George Kennedy claims that this analysis of pathos is "the earliest systematic discussion of human psychology."[9] If Aristotle's advice sounds familiar, it may be a sign that human nature hasn't changed much in the last 2,300 years.

Pathos
Emotional proof, which comes from the feelings the speech draws out of those who hear it.

Anger versus Mildness. Aristotle's discussion of anger was an early version of Freud's frustration–aggression hypothesis. People feel angry when they are thwarted in their attempt to fulfill a need. Remind them of interpersonal slights, and they'll become irate. Show them that the offender is sorry, deserves praise, or has great power, and the audience will calm down.

Love or Friendship versus Hatred. Consistent with present-day research on attraction, Aristotle considered similarity the key to mutual warmth. The speaker should point out common goals, experiences, attitudes, and desires. In the absence of these positive forces, a common enemy can be used to create solidarity.

Fear versus Confidence. Fear comes from a mental image of potential disaster. The speaker should paint a vivid word picture of the tragedy, showing that its occurrence is probable. Confidence can be built up by describing the danger as remote.

Indignation versus Pity. We all have a built-in sense of fairness. As the producers of *60 Minutes* prove weekly, it's easy to arouse a sense of injustice by describing an arbitrary use of power upon those who are helpless.

Admiration versus Envy. People admire moral virtue, power, wealth, and beauty. By demonstrating that an individual has acquired life's goods through hard work rather than mere luck, admiration will increase.

THE FIVE CANONS OF RHETORIC

Although the organization of Aristotle's *Rhetoric* is somewhat puzzling, scholars and practitioners synthesize his words into four distinct standards for measuring the quality of a speaker: the construction of an argument (invention), ordering of material (arrangement), selection of language (style), and techniques of delivery. Later writers add memory to the list of skills the accomplished speaker must master. As previewed in the introduction to this section on public rhetoric, the

Canons of rhetoric
The principle divisions of the art of persuasion established by ancient rhetoricians—invention, arrangement, style, delivery, and memory.

five canons of rhetoric have set the agenda of public address instruction for more than 2,000 years. Aristotle's advice strikes most students of public speaking as surprisingly up-to-date.

Invention
A speaker's "hunt" for arguments that will be effective in a particular speech.

Invention. To generate effective enthymemes and examples, the speaker draws on both specialized knowledge about the subject and general lines of reasoning common to all kinds of speeches. Imagining the mind as a storehouse of wisdom or an informational landscape, Aristotle called these stock arguments *topoi,* a Greek term that can be translated as "topics" or "places." As Cornell University literature professor Lane Cooper explained, "In these special regions the orator hunts for arguments as a hunter hunts for game."[10] When King argued, "We refuse to believe that there are insufficient funds in the great vaults of opportunity of this nation," he marshaled the specific American topic or premise that the United States is a land of opportunity. When he contended that "many of our white brothers, as evidenced by their presence here today, have come to realize that their destiny is tied up with our destiny," he established a causal connection that draws from Aristotle's general topics of cause/effect and motive.

Arrangement. According to Aristotle, you should avoid complicated schemes of organization. "There are two parts to a speech; for it is necessary first to state the subject and then to demonstrate it."[11] The introduction should capture attention, establish your credibility, and make clear the purpose of the speech. The conclusion should remind listeners what you've said and leave them feeling good about you and your ideas. Like public address teachers today, Aristotle decried starting with jokes that have nothing to do with the topic, insisting on three-point outlines, and waiting until the end of the speech to reveal the main point.

Style. Aristotle's treatment of style in the *Rhetoric* focuses on metaphor. He believed that "to learn easily is naturally pleasant to all people" and that "metaphor most brings about learning."[12] Furthermore, he taught that "metaphor especially has clarity and sweetness and strangeness."[13] But for Aristotle, metaphors were more than aids for comprehension or aesthetic appreciation. Metaphors help an audience visualize—a "bringing-before-the-eyes" process that energizes listeners and moves them to action.[14] King was a master of metaphor:

> The Negro lives on a *lonely island* of poverty in the midst of a *vast ocean* of material prosperity.
>
> To rise from the *dark and desolate valleys* of segregation to the *sunlit path* of racial justice.

King's use of metaphor was not restricted to images drawn from nature. Perhaps his most convincing imagery was an extended analogy picturing the march on Washington as people of color going to the federal bank to cash a check written by the Founding Fathers. America had defaulted on the promissory note and had sent back the check marked "insufficient funds." But the marchers refused to believe that the bank of justice was bankrupt, that the vaults of opportunity were empty. These persuasive images gathered listeners' knowledge of racial discrimination into a powerful flood of reason:

> Let justice roll down like waters
> and righteousness like a mighty stream.[15]

Delivery. Audiences reject delivery that seems planned or staged. Naturalness is persuasive; artifice just the opposite. Any form of presentation that calls attention to itself takes away from the speaker's proofs.

Memory. Aristotle's students needed no reminder that good speakers are able to draw upon a collection of ideas and phrases stored in the mind. Still, Roman teachers of rhetoric found it necessary to stress the importance of memory. In our present age of word processing and teleprompters, memory seems to be a lost art. Yet the stirring I-have-a-dream litany at the end of King's speech departed from his prepared text and effectively pulled together lines he had used before. Unlike King and many Athenian orators, most of us aren't speaking in public every day. For us, the modern equivalent of memory is rehearsal.

ETHICAL REFLECTION: ARISTOTLE'S GOLDEN MEAN

Aristotle's *Rhetoric* is the first known systematic treatise on audience analysis and adaptation. His work therefore begs the same question discussed in the introduction to this section on public rhetoric: *Is it ethical to alter a message to make it more acceptable for a particular audience?*

The way I've phrased the question reflects a Western bias for linking morality with behavior. Does an act produce benefit or harm? Is it right or wrong to do a certain deed? Aristotle, however, spoke of ethics in terms of character rather than conduct, inward disposition instead of outward behavior. He took the Greek admiration for moderation and elevated it to a theory of virtue.

When Barry Goldwater was selected as the Republican Party's nominee for president in 1964, he boldly stated, "Extremism in the defense of liberty is no vice . . . moderation in the pursuit of justice is not virtue."[16] Aristotle would have strongly disagreed. He assumed virtue stands between the two vices.[17] Aristotle saw wisdom in the person who avoids excess on either side. Moderation is best; virtue develops habits that seek to walk an intermediate path. This middle way is known as the *golden mean.* That's because out of the four cardinal virtues—courage, justice, temperance, and practical wisdom—temperance is the one that explains the three others.

Golden mean
The virtue of moderation; the virtuous person develops habits that avoid extremes.

As for audience adaptation, Aristotle would have counseled against the practice of telling people only what they want to hear, pandering to the crowd, or "wimping out" by not stating what we really think. He would be equally against a disregard of audience sensitivities, riding roughshod over listeners' beliefs, or adopting a take-no-prisoners, lay-waste-the-town rhetorical belligerence. The golden mean would lie in winsome straight talk, gentle assertiveness, and adaptation.

Whether the issue is truth-telling, self-disclosure, or risk-taking when making decisions, Aristotle's golden mean suggests other middle-way communication practices:

Extreme	Golden Mean	Extreme
Lies	Truthful statements	Brutal honesty
Secrecy	Transparency	Soul-baring
Cowardice	Courage	Recklessness

The golden mean will often prove to be the best way to persuade others. But for Aristotle, that was not the ethical issue. Aristotle advocated the middle way because it is the well-worn path taken by virtuous people.

CRITIQUE: STANDING THE TEST OF TIME

For many teachers of public speaking, criticizing Aristotle's *Rhetoric* is like doubting Einstein's theory of relativity or belittling Shakespeare's *King Lear.* Yet the Greek philosopher often seems less clear than he urged his students to be. Scholars are puzzled by Aristotle's failure to define the exact meaning of *enthymeme,* his confusing system of classifying metaphor according to type, and the blurred distinctions he made between deliberative (political) and epideictic (ceremonial) speaking. At the beginning of the *Rhetoric,* Aristotle promised a systematic study of *logos, ethos,* and *pathos,* but he failed to follow that three-part plan. Instead, it appears that he grouped the material in a speech-audience-speaker order. Even those who claim there's a conceptual unity to Aristotle's theory admit the book is "an editorial jumble."[18] We must remember, however, that Aristotle's *Rhetoric* consists of lecture notes rather than a treatise prepared for the public. To reconstruct Aristotle's meaning, scholars must consult his other writings on philosophy, politics, ethics, drama, and biology. Such detective work is inherently imprecise.

Some present-day critics are bothered by the *Rhetoric's* view of the audience as passive. Speakers in Aristotle's world seem to be able to accomplish any goal as long as they prepare their speeches with careful thought and accurate audience analysis. Other critics wish Aristotle had considered a fourth component of rhetoric—the situation. Any analysis of King's address apart from the context of the march on Washington would certainly be incomplete.

Referring to Aristotle's manuscript in a rare moment of sincere appreciation, French skeptic Voltaire declared what many communication teachers would echo today: "I do not believe there is a single refinement of the art that escapes him."[19] Despite the shortcomings and perplexities of this work, it remains a foundational text of our discipline—a starting point for social scientists and rhetoricians alike.

QUESTIONS TO SHARPEN YOUR FOCUS

1. For most people today, the term *rhetoric* has unfavorable associations. What synonym or phrase captures what Aristotle meant yet doesn't carry a negative connotation?
2. What *enthymemes* have advocates on each side of the abortion issue employed in their public *deliberative rhetoric?*
3. Aristotle divided *ethos* into issues of *intelligence, character,* and *goodwill.* Which quality is most important to you when you hear a campaign address, sermon, or other public speech?
4. Most scholars who define themselves as rhetoricians identify with the humanities rather than the sciences. Can you support the claim that Aristotle took a *scientific approach to rhetoric?*

SELF-QUIZ

www.mhhe.com/griffin9e

A SECOND LOOK

Recommended resource: Aristotle, *On Rhetoric: A Theory of Civil Discourse,* George A. Kennedy (ed. and trans.), Oxford University, New York, 1991.

Key scholarship: Richard Leo Enos and Lois Peters Agnew (eds.), *Landmark Essays on Aristotelian Rhetoric,* Lawrence Erlbaum, Mahwah, NJ, 1998.

Rhetoric as art: George A. Kennedy, "Philosophical Rhetoric," in *Classical Rhetoric,* University of North Carolina, Chapel Hill, NC, 1980, pp. 41–85.

Rhetoric as science: James L. Golden, Goodwin F. Berquist, and William E. Coleman, *The Rhetoric of Western Thought,* Kendall/Hunt, Dubuque, IA, 1976, pp. 25–39.

Twenty-first-century interpretation: Alan Gross and Arthur Walzer (eds.), *Rereading Aristotle's Rhetoric,* Southern Illinois University, Carbondale, IL, 2000.

Enthymeme: Lloyd F. Bitzer, "Aristotle's Enthymeme Revisited," *Quarterly Journal of Speech,* Vol. 45, 1959, pp. 399–409; also in Enos and Agnew, pp. 179–191.

Metaphor: Sara Newman, "Aristotle's Notion of 'Bringing-Before-the-Eyes': Its Contributions to Aristotelian and Contemporary Conceptualizations of Metaphor, Style, and Audience," *Rhetorica,* Vol. 20, 2002, pp. 1–23.

Measuring ethos: James McCroskey and Jason Teven, "Goodwill: A Reexamination of the Construct and Its Measurement," *Communication Monographs,* Vol. 66, 1999, pp. 90–103.

Ethos and oral morality: Charles Marsh, "Aristotelian Ethos and the New Orality: Implications for Media Literacy and Media Ethics," *Journal of Mass Media Ethics,* Vol. 21, 2006, pp. 338–352.

Rhetoric and ethics: Eugene Garver, *Aristotle's Rhetoric: An Art of Character,* University of Chicago, Chicago, IL, 1994.

History of rhetoric: Thomas Conley, *Rhetoric in the European Tradition,* Longman, New York, 1990.

Analysis of King's speech: Alexandra Alvarez, "Martin Luther King's 'I Have a Dream,'" *Journal of Black Studies,* Vol. 18, 1988, pp. 337–357.

March on Washington: David J. Garrow, *Bearing the Cross,* William Morrow, New York, 1986, pp. 231–286.

For a twentieth century theory of rhetoric, click on
I. A. Richards' Meaning of Meaning in
Archive under Theory Resources at
www.afirstlook.com.

CHAPTER 23

Objective — Interpretive

Rhetorical tradition

Dramatism

of Kenneth Burke

Kenneth Burke was a twentieth-century rhetorical critic. He carefully analyzed the language that speakers and authors used so he could discern the motivation behind their message. He considered clusters of words as dances of attitudes. According to Burke, the critic's job is to figure out *why* a writer or speaker selected the words that were choreographed into the message. The critic's task is ultimately one of assessing motives.

Burke coined the umbrella term *dramatism* to describe both his rhetorical theory and his research methodology because the two were tightly bound together. He defined dramatism as "a technique of analysis of language and thought as basically modes of action rather than as means of conveying information."[1] Note that like Barnett Pearce in CMM and Stan Deetz in his critical theory of communication, Burke rejected the commonly held notion that communication is primarily a process of message transmission. (See Chapters 6 and 21.) He insisted instead that anything freely said for a reason is a rhetorical act—an actor choosing to perform a dramatic action for a purpose.[2]

Dramatism
A technique of analysis of language and thought as basically modes of action rather than as means of conveying information.

Until his death in 1993 at the age of 96, Burke picked his way through the human "motivational jungle" by using the tools of philosophy, literature, psychology, economics, linguistics, sociology, and communication. He spent his young adult years in Greenwich Village, a New York bohemian community that included E. E. Cummings and Edna St. Vincent Millay. Like many intellectuals during the Depression of the 1930s, Burke flirted with communism but was disillusioned by Stalin's intolerance and brutality. Although he never earned a college degree, he taught for 15 years at Bennington College in Vermont and filled visiting lectureships at Harvard, Princeton, Northwestern, and the University of Chicago. Burke's writing shows an intellectual breadth and depth that leads admirers to refer to him as a Renaissance man. He called himself a "gypsy scholar" and responded to questions about his field of interest by asking, "What am I but a word man?"[3]

As Burke viewed the human scene, life is not *like* a drama; life *is* drama. Almost every public utterance speaks to a moral conflict where something has gone wrong or might soon go awry. The late Harry Chapin (who happened to be Burke's grandson) captured some of the tragedy and comedy of everyday life by putting words to music in *story songs.* My personal favorite is "Cat's in the

Cradle," the timeless tale of a father too busy to spend time with his son. Any male who hears the song realizes that he has a part in the drama rather than the role of passive listener.

The latest Taylor Swift lyrics or any other "somebody-done-somebody-wrong" country song make it clear that a critic's skills could be helpful in understanding human motivation. But it wasn't until 1952 that University of Illinois rhetorician Marie Hochmuth Nichols alerted the field of communication to the promises of Burke's dramatistic methodology.[4] Since that time, thousands of communication scholars have used his dramatistic tools to gain a deeper understanding of public discourse and other forms of symbolic action. In this chapter I introduce four key features of his theory that focus on how language works.

An example is Bill Clinton's speech at the 2012 Democratic National Convention, which both Republicans and Democrats regarded as the most effective political speech of the presidential campaign. What motivated Clinton? Did he truly admire President Obama? Was he trying to build political capital to help his wife, Hillary, run for office in 2016? Or was he working to reestablish personal credibility lost during the impeachment trial in his second term as president? Burke claimed that dramatistic critics could determine what drove Clinton from the words he chose. Burke's devotees would claim his methodology would be equally effective in uncovering the motivation of Occupy Wall Street demonstrators based on the protest signs they waved.

THE DRAMATISTIC PENTAD: A LENS FOR INTERPRETING VERBAL ACTION

Burke's *dramatistic pentad* is his best-known method to figure out the motive behind a message. This five-pronged tool provides a way for the critic to dig beneath surface impressions in order to identify the sometimes complex motives of a speaker or writer. As Burke says, it's a shorthand way the rhetorical critic can "talk about their talk about" in a meaningful way.

> In a well-rounded statement about motives, you must have some word that names the act (names what took place in thought or deed), and another that names the scene (the background of the act, the situation in which it occurred); also you must indicate what person or kind of person (agent) performed the act, what means or instruments he used (agency), and the purpose.[5]

Dramatistic pentad
A tool critics can use to discern the motives of a speaker or writer by labeling five key elements of the human drama: act, scene, agent, agency, and purpose.

By suggesting that the critic must specifically name the *act, scene, agent, agency,* and *purpose* of the speech or publication, Burke's advice seems deceptively similar to the questions that journalism students are taught to answer in the lead paragraph of their story: Who (agent)? What (act)? Where and when (scene)? How (agency)? Why (purpose)? But most reporters claim they are reporting the facts. Critics know they are interpreting the drama.

God-term. Although Burke was an advocate of creativity, he believed the critic's choice of labels for the five categories should be constrained by the language the speaker actually selects. He recommended beginning with a content analysis that identifies key terms on the basis of their frequency and intensity of use. For example, in his celebrated "I Have a Dream" speech, Martin Luther King Jr. used the word *freedom* 20 times, each time with passion.[6] So freedom is King's *god-term,* and that word names the *purpose* of the civil rights movement. Once critics discover this key term, they should avoid dictionary definitions as a way

God-term
The word a speaker uses to which all other positive words are subservient.

of determining its exact meaning. A speaker's god-term is best understood by other words that cluster around it—known by the company it keeps. In King's speech, multiple references to *dream* and *justice* in the same context add depth and breadth to the meaning of freedom.

Devil-term
The term that sums up all that a speaker regards as bad, wrong, or evil.

Devil-term. In like fashion, the critic should seek a *devil-term* that sums up all that a speaker regards as bad, wrong, or evil. For example, in his nationally broadcast address to a joint session of Congress following the attacks of 9/11, President George W. Bush used the word *terror* or *terrorist* 34 times.[7] It was in that speech that the president declared a "War on Terror," and more than a decade later this terminology continues to shape much of the country's human rights policy. Al-Qaeda *agents* are labeled as *terrorists* and therefore don't receive the legal protections granted to suspected criminals.

The five elements of the pentad usually refer to the act described *within* the speech rather than the act of *giving* the speech. Just for fun, however, we could turn the tables on Burke and do a content analysis of Burke's own rhetoric—"Burking Burke," we might call it. As I read through the theorist's extensive writing, I find he repeatedly comes down hard on laboratory experiments, cause-and-effect claims, empiricism, behaviorism, and almost everything else associated with the research performed by objective scholars. For Burke, *science* is a devil-term. In Figure 23–1 we can see how Burke takes language seriously when he asks readers to contrast his pentad with a parallel five-point scheme constructed from a scientific perspective. Both sets of words point to the same five issues, but the terms used reflect vastly different ways of viewing the world. The dramatistic pentad on the top assumes a world of intentional action, whereas the scientific terms on the bottom describe motion without intention or purpose.

Philosophical assumptions. More than any other theorist featured in this text, Burke drew hundreds of connections between his theoretical ideas and a wide sweep of literature, history, politics, sociology, philosophy, and religion. As for a pentadic analysis, he claimed that each of the five terms has a linguistic affinity with a different school of philosophy. When a message foregrounds one of the five terms at the expense of the other four, the critic can assume that knowingly or unconsciously, the speaker shares the language and assumptions of a corresponding philosophy:[8]

Act. A critic's label for the act illustrates what was done. Multiple acts form the plot of the drama. A speech that features dramatic verbs demonstrates a commitment to *realism.*

Scene. Public speaking that emphasizes setting and circumstance, downplays free will, and reflects an attitude of situational *determinism.*

Agent. Some messages are filled with references to self, mind, spirit, and personal responsibility. This focus on character and the actor as instigator is consistent with philosophical *idealism.*

Dramatistic pentad	Act	Scene	Agent	Agency	Purpose
Scientific observation	Response	Situation	Subject	Stimulus	Target

FIGURE 23–1 Dramatistic Terms as Opposed to the Language of Science

Agency. A long description of methods or technique reflects a "get-the-job-done" approach that springs from the speaker's mindset of *pragmatism.*

Purpose. An extended discussion of purpose within the message shows a strong desire on the part of the speaker for unity or ultimate meaning in life, which are common concerns of *mysticism.*

Ratio. After the critic has labeled the act, scene, agent, agency, and purpose of the message, the next step is to discern the relative importance that the speaker or writer gives to each of these five categories. Burke does this by looking at the *ratio* or the relationship between any two of the pentadic terms.[9] For example, if a speaker places equal stress on both sides of the act–agent ratio when telling a woman's story, we could conclude that what she did is consistent with her character. Conversely, if an author goes to great length to describe the circumstances under which he performed a harmful act, the scene–act ratio suggests he was compelled to do the dirty deed. In effect, he's saying, *Due to circumstances beyond my control, I could do no other.* There are ten possible pair combinations. By identifying the most prominent or prevailing ratio of pentadic terms within a message, the critic can determine which element of the drama provides the best clue to the motives of the speaker or author.

Ratio
The relative importance of any two terms of the pentad as determined by their relationship.

LANGUAGE AS THE GENESIS OF GUILT

Burke regarded human beings as symbol-using animals and was obviously in love with language. He examined words, defined words, played with words, and made up his own words. But Burke also regarded our creation of language as the source of our downfall. That's because language introduced the negative—*no, not, nothing, never,* and prefixes such as *un-, dis-,* and *non-* that negate the meaning of other words.[10] Even our definitions of words are dependent on the negative. As Burke said, "You can go on forever saying what a thing is not."[11]

There are no negatives in nature; things just are. But man-made language gives us the capacity to create rules and standards for behavior that Burke called the "thou shalt nots" of life.[12] These *shoulds* and *oughts* inevitably produce guilt in us when we fail to live up to their moral imperatives. Burke uses *guilt* as his catchall term to cover every form of tension, anxiety, embarrassment, shame, disgust, and other noxious feelings he believed inherent in human symbol-using activity. Burke's *Definition of Man* below is a discouraging counterpoint to the optimism of Carl Rogers outlined in the introduction to the Relationship Development section on page 94. Like most writers of an earlier generation, Burke used the word *man* to designate both men and women. Given his record of using words to startle and stretch his readers, if he were writing today, I wonder if he might recast his definition in exclusively feminine symbols. But in order to remain faithful to what he wrote, I won't alter his gender-loaded references.

Guilt
Burke's catchall term to cover every form of tension, anxiety, embarrassment, shame, disgust, and other noxious feelings intrinsic to the human condition.

Man is
the symbol-using inventor of the negative
separated from his natural condition by instruments
of his own making
goaded by the spirit of hierarchy
and rotten with perfection.[13]

Burke started out by acknowledging our animal nature, but like Mead (see Chapter 5), he emphasized the uniquely human ability to create, use, and abuse language. The rest of his definition makes it clear that the capacity to manipulate symbols is not an unmixed blessing. The remaining lines suggest three linguistic causes for the sense of inner pollution.

By writing "inventor of the negative," Burke reiterated that it's only through man-made language that the possibility of choice comes into being. In a world without human beings, there are no negative commands, no prohibitions. It's only when humans come into the world and begin to act symbolically that the possibility of *No! Don't do it!* arrives.

The phrase "separated from his natural condition by instruments of his own making" bounces off the traditional description of humans as *tool-using animals*. Here again, Burke suggested that our inventions—language and all the tools developed with language—cause us grief. Murphy's Law states that anything that can go wrong will.[14] When it comes to relations among people, Burke would say Murphy was an optimist. That's because language is morally loaded.

Burke wrote extensively about hierarchies, bureaucracies, and other ordered systems that rank how well people observe society's negative rules. He was convinced that no matter how high you climb on the performance ladder, you'll always feel a strong sense of embarrassment for not having achieved perfection. A perfect 10 on the ladder of esteem, privilege, or power is exceedingly rare, and if ever achieved, fleeting. The guilt-inducing high priests of the hierarchy are the professional symbol users of society—teachers, lawyers, journalists, artists, and advertisers.

Perspective by incongruity
Calling attention to a truth by linking two dissonant or discrepant terms.

The final phrase, "rotten with perfection," is an example of what Burke called *perspective by incongruity*.[15] The device calls attention to a truth by linking two incongruous words. In his description of human nature, Burke uses this technique to suggest that our seemingly admirable drive to do things perfectly can hurt us and others in the process. Thus our greatest strength is also our greatest weakness. Both our successes and our failures heighten our desire to find someone on whom we can dump our load of guilt.

THE GUILT–REDEMPTION CYCLE: A UNIVERSAL MOTIVE FOR RHETORIC

Whatever private purpose a speaker or writer has, Burke believed that getting rid of guilt is the ultimate motive for public rhetoric. He saw the quest for redemption as the basic plot of the human drama, even if the rhetor is unaware of its force. Rhetoric is the public search for a perfect scapegoat.

Those who have rejected or never had a religious commitment may be impatient with Burke's use of theological terms. Surprisingly, he made no claim to be a man of faith, nor did he ask his readers to believe in God. Regardless of whether you accept the Christian doctrine of human sin, purification through the death of Jesus, and divine redemption, Burke claimed that the "purely social terminology of human relations cannot do better than to hover about that accurate and succinct theological formula."[16] He regarded theology as a field that has fine-tuned its use of language, and he urged the social critic to look for secular equivalents of the major religious themes of guilt, purification, and redemption. That's because he regarded almost every rhetorical act as part of a continual pattern of redemption through victimage.

Burke said that the speaker or author has two possible ways of offloading guilt. The first option is to purge guilt through self-blame. Described theologically as *mortification,* this route requires confession of sin and a request for forgiveness.[17] As demonstrated by sports stars Lance Armstrong, Sammy Sosa, and Manti Te'o in 2013, those who are obvious candidates find it excruciatingly difficult to admit publicly that they are the cause of their own grief. Since it's much easier for people to blame their problems on someone else—the second option—Burke suggested we look for signs of *victimage* in every rhetorical act.[18] He was sure we would find them.

Mortification
Confession of guilt and request for forgiveness.

Victimage is the process of designating an external enemy as the source of all ills. The list of possibilities is limited only by our imagination—Eastern liberals, Tea Party fanatics, al-Qaeda, the Colombian drug cartel, Wall Street bankers, socialists, blacks, Jews, Muslims, gays, chauvinistic males, the police, religious fundamentalists, billionaire capitalists, illegal immigrants. For Americans, the massively callous act of terrorism on 9/11 made Osama bin Laden seem like the personification of evil and the obvious candidate for a scapegoat. Perfect guilt requires a perfect victim. God-terms are only as powerful as the devil-terms they oppose. That seems to be why President Obama believed that bin Laden's death would assuage some of the guilt Americans were feeling during the country's Great Recession. In turn, many right-wing Republicans saw Obama as the perfect scapegoat to blame for all that had happened and all they feared.

Victimization
The process of naming an external enemy as the source of all personal or public ills; scapegoating.

Burke was not an advocate of redemption through victimization, but he said he couldn't ignore the historical pattern of people uniting against a common enemy ("congregation through segregation"[19]). His most famous rhetorical analysis was of Hitler's *Mein Kampf,* a book that blamed Jews for all of Germany's problems.[20] This symbolic victimage was followed by extermination in death camps.

IDENTIFICATION: WITHOUT IT, THERE IS NO PERSUASION

How can a public speaker convince an audience to embrace his or her viewpoint and enter into the guilt–redemption cycle? Although he was a great admirer of Aristotle's *Rhetoric,* Burke was less concerned with enthymeme and example than he was with a speaker's overall ability to identify with the audience.

> The key term for the "old rhetoric" was *persuasion* and its stress upon deliberative design. The key term for the "new rhetoric" is *identification* and this may include partially unconscious factors in its appeal.[21]

Identification is the common ground that exists between speaker and audience. Burke used the word *substance* to describe a person's physical characteristics, talents, occupation, friends, experiences, personality, beliefs, and attitudes. The more overlap between the substance of the speaker and the substance of the listener, the greater the identification. Behavioral scientists have used the term *homophily* to describe perceived similarity between speaker and listener,[22] but again, Burke preferred religious language rather than scientific jargon. Borrowing from Martin Luther's description of what takes place at the communion table, Burke said identification is *consubstantiality.*[23] This religious term calls to mind the oft-quoted Old Testament passage where Ruth pledges solidarity with her mother-in-law, Naomi: "For where you go I will go, and where you lodge I will

"My fellow victims. . ."

Identification
The common ground between speaker and audience; overlap of physical characteristics, talents, occupation, friends, experiences, personality, beliefs, and attitudes; consubstantiation.

lodge; your people shall be my people, and your God my God."[24] That's identification. It's also part of Ruth and Naomi's story that we'll revisit in Chapter 24, Walter Fisher's narrative paradigm.

One of the most common ways for an orator to identify with an audience is to lash out at whatever or whomever people fear. ("My friend is one who hates what I hate.") But audiences sense a joining of interests through style as much as through content. Burke said that the effective communicator can show consubstantiality by giving signs in language and delivery that his or her properties are the same as theirs. The style of a typical street preacher probably turns off cosmopolitan New Yorkers more than does the content of the message. The mood and manner of revival-style preaching signals a deep division between the evangelist and urbane listeners. To the extent that the speaker could alter the delivery to match the hearers' sophisticated style, they'd think the speaker was "talking sense."

Burke said that identification works both ways. Audience adaptation not only gives the evangelist a chance to sway the audience, it also helps the preacher fit into the cultural mainstream. But identification in either direction will never be complete. If nothing else, our tennis elbow or clogged sinuses constantly remind us that each of us is separate from the rest of the human race. But without some kind of division in the first place, there would be no need for identification. And without identification, there is no persuasion.

A RHETORICAL CRITIQUE USING DRAMATISTIC INSIGHT

Many rhetorical critics in communication have adopted Burke's techniques of literary criticism to inform their understanding of specific public address events. I asked Ken Chase, a colleague at Wheaton, and Glen McClish at San Diego State University to perform a Burkean analysis of Malcolm X's famous speech "The Ballot or the Bullet."[25] The brief critique that follows is the result of their combined insight.

Malcolm X, "The Ballot or the Bullet"

Often paired with Martin Luther King Jr., Malcolm X was one of the most influential civil rights speakers of the 1960s. Malcolm's rhetoric, though, was more militant and angry, and for many African Americans, more realistic than the idealism of King's "I Have a Dream." Malcolm delivered his famous speech "The Ballot or the Bullet" in April 1964, only 11 months before his assassination.

By viewing public rhetoric as an attempt to build a particular social order, Kenneth Burke helped reveal the power of "The Ballot or the Bullet." Malcolm's address portrays America as a nation that promises full equality, dignity, and freedom for all its citizens, yet African Americans have never received their birthright. Epitomizing his commitment to Black Nationalism, Malcolm urged his brothers and sisters to start their own businesses and elect their own leaders. At the same time he attacked white politicians who impede civil rights. The audience at the Corey Methodist Church in Cleveland, Ohio, interrupted Malcolm X with applause and laughter more than 150 times during the lengthy oration.

Malcolm asserted that the struggle for civil rights is not only the work of his fellow Black Muslims, but is shared by all concerned African Americans. By strategically aligning himself with Christian ministers like King and Congressman Adam Clayton Powell, he minimized the alienation his Islamic faith could potentially create. He emphasized the shared heritage of all African Americans: "Our mothers and fathers invested sweat and blood. Three hundred and ten years we worked in this country without a dime in return. . . ." In this way, Malcolm created a strong sense of *identification* as he coaxed his audience to share his social purpose and his means of achieving it.

The title of the speech, "The Ballot or the Bullet," refers to the means, or *agency,* by which the *agents*—African Americans—can *act* as citizens to accomplish the *purpose* of equality, dignity, and freedom. Malcolm strategically placed his audience within the larger context of American history and the international struggle for human rights. It is this *scene* that motivates the militant message that African Americans will proclaim—"We've got to fight until we overcome."

Malcolm's emphasis on the means to achieve his purpose ("by whatever means necessary") results in a high agency–purpose ratio—an indicator of his pragmatic motivation. The ballot enforces civil rights legislation; the bullet defends blacks from white violence. The bullet also warns white society that equality must not be delayed: "Give it to us now. Don't wait for next year. Give it to us yesterday, and that's not fast enough."

Malcolm criticized his brothers and sisters for failing to show the courage, knowledge, and maturity necessary to reap the full benefits of citizenship. It is the white man, however, who has enslaved, lynched, and oppressed the Africans living on American soil, and it is he who must bear the brunt of collective *guilt.* Through *victimage,* the white man and his society become the *scapegoat* that must be sacrificed for the *redemption* of blacks. Within the drama of African-American life, "Black Nationalism" serves as the *god-term* that embodies the spirit of the movement. Conversely, "white man" is the *devil-term* that epitomizes all who oppose equality, dignity, and freedom for all.

CRITIQUE: EVALUATING THE CRITIC'S ANALYSIS

Kenneth Burke was perhaps the foremost rhetorician of the twentieth century. Burke wrote about rhetoric; other rhetoricians write about Burke. Universities offer entire courses on Burkean analysis. On two occasions the National Communication Association featured the man and his ideas at its national convention. The Kenneth Burke Society holds conferences and competitions that give his followers the opportunity to discuss and delight over his wide-ranging thoughts. *KB Journal* exists solely to explain, clarify, and critique Burke's ideas. He obviously had something to say.

The problem for the beginning student is that he said it in such a roundabout way. Burke was closely tied to symbolic interactionism (see Chapter 5), and complexity seems to be characteristic of much of the writing within that tradition. Even advocates like Nichols have felt compelled to explain why Burke was frequently confusing and sometimes obscure: "In part the difficulty arises from the numerous vocabularies he employs. His words in isolation are usually simple enough, but he often uses them in new contexts."[26] Clarity is compromised further by Burke's tendency to flood his text with literary allusions. Unless a student is prepared to grapple with Coleridge's "The Rime of the Ancient Mariner," Augustine's *Confessions,* and Freud's *The Psychopathology of Everyday Life*—all on the same page—Burke's mental leaps and breadth of scholarship will prove more frustrating than informative.

Yet Burke enthusiasts insist that the process of discovery is half the fun. Like a choice enthymeme, Burke's writing invites active reader participation as he surrounds an idea. And no matter what aspect of rhetoric that idea addresses, the reader will never again be able to dismiss words as "mere rhetoric." Burke has done us all a favor by celebrating the life-giving quality of language.

Without question, the dramatistic pentad is the feature of Burke's writing that has gained the most approval. Many rhetorical critics use this tool to pinpoint a speaker's motivation and the way the speech serves that need or desire.

Burke's concept of rhetoric as identification was also a major advance in a field of knowledge that many scholars had thought complete. Rather than opposing Aristotle's definition, he gave it a contemporary luster by showing that common ground is the foundation of emotional appeal. Communication scientists can't test Burke's claim that unconscious identification produces behavior and attitude change, but they can confirm that perceived similarity facilitates persuasion.

Of all Burke's motivational principles, his strategies of redemption are the most controversial. Perhaps that's because his "secular religion" takes God too seriously for those who don't believe, yet not seriously enough for those who do. Both camps have trouble with Burke's unsubstantiated assumption that guilt is the primary human emotion that underlies all symbolic action. There's no doubt that Malcolm X's "The Ballot or the Bullet" exploited a guilt–scapegoat linkage, but whether the same drama is played out in every public address or essay is another matter.

As for me, I appreciate Burke's commitment to an ethical stance that refuses to let desirable ends justify unfair means. He urged speakers not to make a victim out of someone else in order to become unified with the audience. True believers in dramatistic theory and practice maintain that it's unwise to talk about communication without some understanding of Burke. The inclusion of this chapter is my response to their claim.

QUESTIONS TO SHARPEN YOUR FOCUS

1. Apply the *dramatistic pentad* to the typical nonverbal rhetoric of a Friday night party on campus. Which of the five elements of the pentad would you stress to capture the meaning of that human drama?

2. Despite the fact that Burke is a *rhetorical critic* who describes himself as a "word man," he's convinced that the creation of *language* began the downfall of the human race. Why?
3. Burke claims that all rhetoric ultimately *expiates guilt through victimage.* If he's right, is it the guilt of the speaker, the listener, or the victim that is being purged?
4. Burke says that without *identification,* there is no persuasion. A number of the theories already covered deal with ideas or principles akin to identification. Can you name five?

A SECOND LOOK

Recommended resource: Sonja Foss, Karen Foss, and Robert Trapp, *Contemporary Perspectives on Rhetoric,* 3rd ed., Waveland, Prospect Heights, IL, 2002, pp. 187–232.

Dramatism: Kenneth Burke, "Dramatism," in *The International Encyclopedia of the Social Sciences,* Vol. 7, David L. Sills (ed.), Macmillan, New York, 1968, pp. 445–451.

Summary of key concepts: Edward Appel, *Language, Life, Literature, Rhetoric and Composition as Dramatic Action: A Burkean Primer,* Oar Press, Leola, PA, 2012, pp. 265–271.

Key scholarship: Barry Brummet (ed.), *Landmark Essays on Kenneth Burke,* Hermagoras, Davis, CA, 1993.

Identification: Kenneth Burke, *A Rhetoric of Motives,* University of California, Berkeley, 1969, pp. 20–46.

Dramatistic pentad: Kenneth Burke, *A Grammar of Motives,* University of California, Berkeley, 1969, pp. xv–xxiii.

Guilt–redemption cycle: Kenneth Burke, "On Human Behavior Considered 'Dramatistically,'" in *Permanence and Change,* Bobbs-Merrill, Indianapolis, IN, 1965, pp. 274–294.

Human nature: Kenneth Burke, "Definition of Man," in *Language as Symbolic Action,* University of California, Berkeley, 1966, pp. 3–24.

Burkean analysis of King's "I Have a Dream": David Bobbitt, *The Rhetoric of Redemption: Kenneth Burke's Redemption Drama and Martin Luther King Jr.'s "I Have a Dream" Speech,* Rowman & Littlefield, Lanham, MD, 2004.

Dramatism within a larger context: Charles Edgley, "The Dramaturgical Genre," in *Handbook of Symbolic Interactionism,* Larry Reynolds and Nancy Herman-Kinney (eds.), AltaMira, Walnut Creek, CA, 2003, pp. 141–172.

Limits of dramatism: James W. Chesebro, "Extensions of the Burkean System," *Quarterly Journal of Speech,* Vol. 78, 1992, pp. 356–368.

Explication and critique of guilt–redemption cycle: Kristy Maddux, "Finding Comedy in Theology: A Hopeful Supplement to Kenneth Burke's Logology," *Philosophy and Rhetoric,* Vol. 39, 2006, pp. 208–232.

Feminist critique: Celeste Michelle Condit, "Post-Burke: Transcending the Substance of Dramatism," *Quarterly Journal of Speech,* Vol. 78, 1992, pp. 349–355; also in Brummet, pp. 3–18.

CHAPTER 24

Objective — Interpretive

Rhetorical tradition

Narrative Paradigm

of Walter Fisher

People are storytelling animals. This simple assertion is Walter Fisher's answer to the philosophical question *What is the essence of human nature?*

Many of the theorists discussed in preceding chapters offer different answers to this key question of human existence. For example, Thibaut and Kelley's social exchange theory operates on the premise that humans are rational creatures. Berger's uncertainty reduction theory assumes that people are basically curious. More pertinent for students of communication, Mead's symbolic interactionism insists that our ability to use symbols is what makes us uniquely human. (See Chapters 8, 9, and 5.)

Fisher doesn't argue against any of these ideas, but he thinks that human communication reveals something more basic than rationality, curiosity, or even symbol-using capacity. He is convinced that we are narrative beings who "experience and comprehend life as a series of ongoing narratives, as conflicts, characters, beginnings, middles, and ends."[1] If this is true, then all forms of human communication that appeal to our reason need to be seen fundamentally as stories.[2]

Walter Fisher is a professor emeritus at the University of Southern California's Annenberg School of Communication. Throughout his professional life he has been uncomfortable with the prevailing view that rhetoric is only a matter of evidence, facts, arguments, reason, and logic that has its highest expression in courts of law, legislatures, and other deliberative bodies. In 1978, he introduced the concept of *good reasons,* which led to his proposal of the narrative paradigm in 1984.[3] He proposed that offering good reasons has more to do with telling a compelling story than it does with piling up evidence or constructing a tight argument.

Fisher soon became convinced that all forms of communication that appeal to our reason are best viewed as stories shaped by history, culture, and character. When we hear the word *story,* most of us tend to think of novels, plays, movies, TV sitcoms, and yarns told sitting around a campfire. Some of us also call to mind accounts of our past—tales we tell to others in which we are the central character. But with the exception of jokes, *Hi, How are you?* greetings, and other forms of *phatic communication,* Fisher regards almost *all* types of communication as story. Obviously, he sees differences in form between a Robert Frost poem, a *Harry Potter* book, or a performance of *As You Like It* on the one hand, and a philosophical essay, historical report, political debate, theological discussion, or

Phatic communication Communication aimed at maintaining relationships rather than passing along information or saying something new.

scientific treatise on the other. But if we want to know whether we should believe the "truth" each of these genres proclaims, Fisher maintains that all of them can and should be viewed as narrative. He uses the term *narrative paradigm* to highlight his belief that there is no communication of ideas that is purely descriptive or didactic.

TELLING A COMPELLING STORY

Most religious traditions are passed on from generation to generation through the retelling of stories. The faithful are urged to "tell the old, old story" to encourage believers and convince those in doubt. American writer Frederick Buechner takes a fresh approach to passing on religious story. His book *Peculiar Treasures* retells the twelfth-century B.C. biblical story of Ruth's devotion to Naomi, her mother-in-law, in twenty-first-century style.[4] Buechner's account of true friendship provides a vehicle for examining Fisher's narrative paradigm in the rest of this chapter. The story begins after the death of Naomi's husband and two sons:

> Ruth was a Moabite girl who married into a family of Israelite transplants living in Moab because there was a famine going on at home. When her young husband died, her mother-in-law, Naomi, decided to pull up stakes and head back for Israel where she belonged. The famine was over by then, and there was no longer anything to hold her where she was, her own husband having died about the same time that Ruth's had. She advised Ruth to stay put right there in Moab and to try to snag herself another man from among her own people.
>
> She was a strong-willed old party, and when Ruth said she wanted to go to Israel with her, she tried to talk her out of it. Even if by some gynecological fluke she managed to produce another son for Ruth to marry, she said, by the time he was old enough, Ruth would be ready for the geriatric ward. But Ruth had a mind of her own too, besides which they'd been through a lot together what with one thing and another, and home to her was wherever Naomi was. "Where you go, I go, and where you live, I live," Ruth told her, "and if your God is Yahweh, then my God is Yahweh too" (*Ruth 2:10–17*). So Naomi gave in, and when the two of them pulled in to Bethlehem, Naomi's home town, there was a brass band to meet them at the station.
>
> Ruth had a spring in her step and a fascinating Moabite accent, and it wasn't long before she caught the eye of a well-heeled farmer named Boaz. He was a little long in the tooth, but he still knew a pretty girl when he saw one, and before long, in a fatherly kind of way, he took her under his wing. He told the hired hands not to give her any trouble. He helped her in the fields. He had her over for a meal. And when she asked him one day in her disarming Moabite way why he was being so nice to her, he said he'd heard how good she'd been to Naomi, who happened to be a distant cousin of his, and as far as he was concerned, she deserved nothing but the best.
>
> Naomi was nobody's fool and saw which way the wind was blowing long before Ruth did. She was dead-set on Ruth's making a good catch for herself, and since it was obvious she'd already hooked old Boaz whether she realized it or not, all she had to do was find the right way to reel him in. Naomi gave her instructions. As soon as Boaz had a good supper under his belt and had polished off a nightcap or two, he'd go to the barn and hit the sack. Around midnight, she said, Ruth should slip out to the barn and hit the sack too. If Boaz's feet just happened to be uncovered somehow, and if she just happened to be close enough to keep

them warm, that probably wouldn't be the worst thing in the world either (*Ruth 3:1–5*). But she wasn't to go too far. Back in Jericho, Boaz's mother, Rahab, had had a rather seamy reputation for going too far professionally, and anything that reminded him of that might scare him off permanently.

Ruth followed her mother-in-law's advice to the letter, and it worked like a charm. Boaz was so overwhelmed that she'd pay attention to an old crock like him when there were so many young bucks running around in tight-fitting jeans that he fell for her hook, line and sinker, and after a few legal matters were taken care of, made her his lawful wedded wife.

They had a son named Obed after a while, and Naomi came to take care of him and stayed on for the rest of her life. Then in time Obed had a son of his own named Jesse, and Jesse in turn had seven sons, the seventh of whom was named David and ended up as the greatest king Israel ever had. With Ruth for his great-grandmother and Naomi for his grandfather's nurse, it was hardly a wonder.[5]

NARRATION AND PARADIGM: DEFINING THE TERMS

Fisher defines *narration* as "symbolic actions—words and/or deeds—that have sequence and meaning for those who live, create, or interpret them."[6] Ruth's life and Buechner's account of it clearly qualify as narrative. But Fisher's definition is broad and is especially notable for what it doesn't exclude. On the basis of his further elaboration,[7] I offer this expanded paraphrase of his definition:

> Narration is communication rooted in time and space. It covers every aspect of our lives and the lives of others in regard to character, motive, and action. The term also refers to every verbal or nonverbal bid for a person to believe or act in a certain way. Even when a message seems abstract—devoid of imagery—it is narration because it is embedded in the speaker's ongoing story that has a beginning, middle, and end, and it invites listeners to interpret its meaning and assess its value for their own lives.

Narration
Symbolic actions—words and/or deeds—that have sequence and meaning for those who live, create, or interpret them.

Under this expanded definition, Ruth's *my God is Yahweh* statement is as much a story of love and trust as it is a declaration of belief. Framed in the context of King David's genealogy, it is also an early episode in the *Greatest Story Ever Told*. Those who identify with the human love, trust, loyalty, and commitment described in the narrative can't help but feel the solidarity of an extended family of faith.

Fisher uses the term *paradigm* to refer to a *conceptual framework*—a widely shared perceptual filter. Perception is not so much a matter of the physics of sight and sound as it is one of interpretation. Meaning isn't inherent in events; it's attached at the workbench of the mind. A paradigm is a universal model that calls for people to view events through a common interpretive lens.

Paradigm
A conceptual framework; a universal model that calls for people to view events through a common interpretive lens.

In *The Structure of Scientific Revolutions*, Thomas Kuhn argues that an accepted paradigm is the mark of a mature science.[8] Responding to this challenge, communication scientists in the 1970s sought to discover a universal model that would explain communication behavior. Fisher's narrative paradigm is an interpretive counterpart to their efforts. Fisher offers a way to understand all communication and to direct rhetorical inquiry. He doesn't regard the narrative paradigm as a specific rhetoric. Rather, he sees it as "the foundation on which a complete rhetoric needs to be built. This structure would provide a comprehensive explanation of the creation, composition, adaptation, presentation, and reception of symbolic messages."[9]

PARADIGM SHIFT: FROM A RATIONAL-WORLD PARADIGM TO A NARRATIVE ONE

Fisher begins his book *Human Communication as Narration* with a reference to the opening line of the Gospel of John: "In the beginning was the word (*logos*)." He notes that the Greek word *logos* originally included story, reason, rationale, conception, discourse, thought—all forms of human communication. Imagination and thought were not yet distinct. So the story of Naomi and Ruth was *logos*.

According to Fisher, the writings of Plato and Aristotle reflect the early evolution from a generic to a specific use of *logos*—from story to statement. *Logos* had already begun to refer only to philosophical discourse, a lofty enterprise that relegated imagination, poetry, and other aesthetic concerns to second-class status. Rhetoric fell somewhere between *logos* and *mythos*. As opposed to the abstract discourse of philosophy, it was practical speech—the secular combination of pure logic on the one hand and emotional stories that stir up passions on the other. The Greek citizen concerned with truth alone should steer clear of rhetoric and consult an expert on wisdom—the philosopher.

Fisher says that 2,000 years later the scientific revolution dethroned the philosopher–king. In the last few centuries, the only knowledge that seems to be worth knowing in academia is that which can be spotted in the physical world. The person who wants to understand the way things are needs to check with a doctor, a scientist, an engineer, or another technical expert. Despite the elevation of technology and the demotion of philosophy, both modes of decision making are similar in their elitist tendencies to "place that which is not *formally* logical or which is not characterized by *expertise* within a somehow subhuman framework of behavior."[10] Fisher sees philosophical and technical discussion as scholars' standard approach to knowledge. He calls this mindset the *rational-world paradigm*. Hirokawa and Gouran's functional perspective on group decision making is a perfect example (see Chapter 17).

Fisher lists five assumptions of the prevailing rational-world paradigm. See if they match what you've been taught all along in school.[11]

Rational-world paradigm
A scientific or philosophical approach to knowledge that assumes people are logical, making decisions on the basis of evidence and lines of argument.

1. People are essentially rational.
2. We make decisions on the basis of arguments.
3. The type of speaking situation (legal, scientific, legislative) determines the course of our argument.
4. Rationality is determined by how much we know and how well we argue.
5. The world is a set of logical puzzles that we can solve through rational analysis.

Viewed through the rational-world paradigm, the story of Ruth is suspect. Ruth ignores Naomi's argument, which is based on uncontestable biological facts of life. Nor does Ruth offer any compelling rationale for leaving Moab or for worshiping Yahweh. Once they are back in Israel, Naomi's scheme for Ruth to "reel in" Boaz has nothing to do with logic and everything to do with emotional bonds. Other than the Old Testament passage, the author offers no evidence that Naomi and Ruth are historical characters, that any kind of god exists, or that a book about friendship, kinship, and romance deserves a place in the Old Testament canon. Thus, from a rational-world perspective, the story makes little sense.

Fisher is convinced that the assumptions of the rational-world paradigm are too limited. He calls for a new conceptual framework (a paradigm shift) in order to better understand human communication. His *narrative paradigm* is built on five assumptions similar in form to the rational-world paradigm, but quite different in content.[12]

1. People are essentially storytellers.
2. We make decisions on the basis of good reasons, which vary depending on the communication situation, media, and genre (philosophical, technical, rhetorical, or artistic).
3. History, biography, culture, and character determine what we consider good reasons.
4. Narrative rationality is determined by the coherence and fidelity of our stories.
5. The world is a set of stories from which we choose, and thus constantly re-create, our lives.

Narrative paradigm
A theoretical framework that views narrative as the basis of all human communication.

Viewing human beings as storytellers who reason in various ways is a major conceptual shift. For example, in a logical system, values are emotional nonsense. From the narrative perspective, however, values are the stuff of stories. Working from a strictly logical standpoint, aesthetic proof is irrelevant, but within a narrative framework, style and beauty play a pivotal role in determining whether we get into a story. Perhaps the biggest shift in thinking has to do with who is qualified to assess the quality of communication. Whereas the rational-world model holds that only experts are capable of presenting or discerning sound arguments, the narrative paradigm maintains that, armed with a bit of common sense, almost any of us can see the point of a good story and judge its merits as the basis for belief and action. No one taught us how to do this. It's an inherent awareness that's honed by life experience. Fisher would say that each of us will make a judgment about Buechner's account of Ruth (or any story) based upon *narrative rationality.*

NARRATIVE RATIONALITY: COHERENCE AND FIDELITY

Narrative rationality
A way to evaluate the worth of stories based on the twin standards of narrative coherence and narrative fidelity.

According to Fisher, not all stories are equally good. Even though there's no guarantee that people won't adopt a bad story, he thinks everybody applies the same standards of *narrative rationality* to whatever stories they hear: "The operative principle of narrative rationality is identification rather than deliberation."[13] Will we accept a cross-cultural tale of a young widow's total commitment to her mother-in-law and of Naomi's enthusiastic efforts to help Ruth remarry and have children by another man? Fisher believes that our answer depends on whether Buechner's account meets the twin tests of *narrative coherence* and *narrative fidelity.* Together they are measures of a story's truthfulness and humanity.

Narrative Coherence: Does the Story Hang Together?

Narrative coherence has to do with how probable the story sounds to the hearer. Does the narrative *hang together?* Do the people and events it portrays seem to be of one piece? Are they part of an organic whole or are there obvious contradictions among them? Do the characters act consistently?

"I know what you're thinking, but let me offer a competing narrative."

Narrative coherence Internal consistency with characters acting in a reliable fashion; the story hangs together.

Buechner's version of Ruth and Naomi's relationship translates an ancient tale of interpersonal commitment into a contemporary setting. To the extent that his modern-day references to a brass band at the station, polishing off a nightcap, and young bucks running around in tight-fitting jeans consistently portray the present, the story has structural integrity. Fisher regards the internal consistency of a narrative as similar to lines of argument in a rational-world paradigm. In that sense, his narrative paradigm doesn't discount or replace logic. Instead, Fisher lists the test of reason as one, but only one, of the factors that affect narrative coherence.

Stories hang together when we're convinced that the narrator hasn't left out important details, fudged the facts, or ignored other plausible interpretations. Although the TV series *Lost* and the re-imagined *Battlestar Galactica* garnered critical acclaim throughout their runs, their final episodes were roundly panned by fans and critics because they didn't meet those criteria. At the end, both shows lacked narrative coherence.

We often judge the coherence of a narrative by comparing it with other stories we've heard that deal with the same theme. How does Buechner's account of feminine wiles used to move an older man toward marriage without going "too far" stack up against the blatant seduction scenes in the TV series *House of Lies* or the typical daytime soap opera? To the extent that Ruth's ploy seems more believable, we'll credit Buechner's biblical update with coherence.

For Fisher, the ultimate test of narrative coherence is whether we can count on the characters to act in a reliable manner. We are suspicious of accounts where characters behave uncharacteristically. We tend to trust stories of people who show continuity of thought, motive, and action. Whether you regard Buechner's Naomi as a wise matchmaker or an overcontrolling mother-in-law, her consistent concern that Ruth find a man to marry is a thread that gives the fabric of the story a tight weave.

Narrative Fidelity: Does the Story Ring True and Humane?

Narrative fidelity is the quality of a story that causes the words to strike a responsive chord in the life of the listener. A story has fidelity when it rings true with the hearers' experiences—it squares with the stories they might tell about themselves.[14]

Have we, like Boaz, done special favors for a person we found especially attractive? Like Naomi, have we stretched the rules of decorum to help make a match? Or, like Ruth, have we ever experienced a bond with a relative that goes beyond obligation to family? To the extent that the details of this 3,000-year-old story portray the world we live in today, the narrative has fidelity.

Narrative fidelity
Congruence between values embedded in a message and what listeners regard as truthful and humane; the story strikes a responsive chord.

Fisher's book *Human Communication as Narration* has the subtitle *Toward a Philosophy of Reason, Value, and Action.* He believes a story has fidelity when it provides good reasons to guide our future actions. When we buy into a story, we buy into the type of character we should be. Thus, values are what set the narrative paradigm's logic of good reasons apart from the rational-world paradigm's mere logic of reasons.

The *logic of good reasons* centers on five value-related issues. Fisher says we are concerned with (1) the values embedded in the message, (2) the relevance of those values to decisions made, (3) the consequence of adhering to those values, (4) the overlap with the worldview of the audience, and (5) conformity with what the audience members believe is "an ideal basis for conduct."[15] The last two concerns—congruity with the listeners' values and the actions they think best—form the basis of Fisher's contention that people tend to prefer accounts that fit with what they view as truthful and humane. But what specific values guide audiences as they gauge a story's truth or fidelity? Fisher suggests there is an *ideal audience* or permanent public that identifies the humane values a good story embodies:

> It appears that there is a permanent public, an actual community existing over time, that believes in the values of truth, the good, beauty, health, wisdom, courage, temperance, justice, harmony, order, communion, friendship, and oneness with the Cosmos—as variously as those values may be defined or practiced in "real" life.[16]

Ideal audience
An actual community existing over time that believes in the values of truth, the good, beauty, health, wisdom, courage, temperance, justice, harmony, order, communion, friendship, and oneness with the cosmos.

Fisher admits that other communities are possible—ones based on greed or power, for example. But he maintains that when people are confronted by "the better part of themselves," these less-idealistic value systems won't be "entirely coherent or true to their whole lives, or to the life that they would most like to live."[17] Fisher believes, then, that the humane virtues of the ideal audience shape our logic of good reasons. They help us pick which stories are reliable and trustworthy. If we are convinced that this audience of good people would scoff at Boaz' protection of Ruth or squirm in discomfort at her midnight visit to the barn, Buechner's version of the biblical narrative will lack fidelity. But inasmuch as we think that these ideal auditors would applaud Ruth's rarified devotion to Naomi—while appreciating the older woman's down-to-earth approach to courtship—Buechner's words will have the ring of truthfulness and humanity.

According to Fisher, when we judge a story to have fidelity, we are not merely affirming shared values. We are ultimately opening ourselves to the possibility that those values will influence our beliefs and actions. For example, many engaged couples for whom the love of Ruth rings true have adopted her words to Naomi as a model for their wedding vows:

> I will go wherever you go and live wherever you live.
> Your people will be my people, and your God will be my God.[18]

I have employed the age-old story of Ruth to illustrate features of the narrative paradigm. In like manner, most of my students—like Chris below—pick a book or a film to demonstrate their application of Fisher's theory.

> Beginning with *The Lion, The Witch, and the Wardrobe* in *The Chronicles of Narnia,* C. S. Lewis presents a coherent set of stories. While the characters, places, and events may not be "of this world"—the rational world we live in—Lewis has constructed a set of relationships and rules so consistent that it makes the fictional world seem plausible. The stories also have fidelity because Lewis skillfully creates parallels to our common human reality. The characters relate directly to people in my life (including me). For instance, I can identify with "doubting" Susan as she grows out of her childlike faith. Yet I long for the innocent passion of Lucy and the nobleness of Peter.

A good story is a powerful means of persuasion. Fisher would remind us, however, that almost *all* communication is narrative, and that we evaluate it on that basis. This chapter and all the others in this book are story. According to his narrative paradigm, you can (and will) judge whether they hang together and ring true to the values held by the people who make up your ideal audience.

CRITIQUE: DOES FISHER'S STORY HAVE COHERENCE AND FIDELITY?

Fisher's narrative paradigm offers a fresh reworking of Aristotelian analysis, which has dominated rhetorical thinking in the field of communication. His approach is strongly democratic—people usually don't need specialized training or expertise to figure out if a story holds together or offers good reasons for believing it to be true. There's still a place for experts to provide information and explanation in specialized fields, but when it comes to evaluating coherence and fidelity, people with ordinary common sense are competent rhetorical critics.

In *Human Communication as Narration,* Fisher applies the principles of narrative coherence and narrative fidelity to analyze various types of communication. He explains why a sometimes illogical President Ronald Reagan was aptly known as "The Great Communicator." He examines the false values of Willy Loman that lead to his downfall in *Death of a Salesman.* And he explores the consequences of adopting the rival philosophies embedded in the stories of two Greek thinkers—Socrates and Callicles. According to Fisher, the fact that the narrative paradigm can be applied to this wide range of communication genres provides strong evidence for its acceptance. And unlike a value-neutral scientific or rational-world approach, Fisher's narrative paradigm is clear about the motives, actions, and outcomes that make a story good.

Of course, Fisher's theory is itself a story, and as you might expect, not everyone accepts his tale. For example, many critics charge that he is overly optimistic when, similar to Aristotle, he argues that people have a natural tendency to prefer the true and the just. Challenging Fisher's upbeat view of human nature, rhetorical critic Barbara Warnick at the University of Pittsburgh calls attention to the great communicative power of evil or wrongheaded stories such as Hitler's *Mein Kampf.* Fisher declares that Hitler's opus "must be judged a bad story,"[19] but as Warnick notes, it "struck a chord in an alienated, disunited, and despairing people."[20] Hitler's success in scapegoating the Jews ranks as one of history's most notorious acts of rhetoric, yet in its time and place it achieved both coherence and fidelity. Fisher thinks Warnick is confusing Hitler's *effective* discourse with the *good* discourse people tend to prefer. But he grants that evil can overwhelm that tendency and thinks that's all the more reason to identify and promote the humane values described by the narrative paradigm.

William Kirkwood at East Tennessee State University claims there is another problem with the logic of good reasons. Kirkwood says a standard of narrative rationality implies that good stories cannot and perhaps should not go beyond what people already believe and value. He charges that the logic of good reasons encourages writers and speakers to adjust their ideas to people rather than people to their ideas, and thus denies the "rhetoric of possibility," the chance to be swayed by that which is unfamiliar or radically different.[21]

University of Rhode Island communication professor Kevin McClure agrees with Kirkwood, and argues that Fisher's understanding of probability and fidelity are too tightly linked with normative concepts of rationality. He reminds us that Fisher wrote that "the operative principle of narrative rationality is identification."[22] If Fisher would concentrate on Kenneth Burke's understanding of identification as "an aesthetic and poetic experience, and thus a relational experience or encounter with the symbolic rather than an encounter with rational argument," McClure believes the narrative paradigm could easily explain how improbable stories that "lack a sense of fidelity are accepted and acted on."[23]

Fisher thinks these critiques are ridiculous. He explicitly states that people have the capacity to "formulate and adopt new stories that better account for their lives or the mystery of life itself."[24] In a somewhat wry fashion, Fisher credits his detractors for demonstrating the wisdom of the narrative paradigm:

> I want to thank my critics, for they cannot but substantiate the soundness of my position. They do this in two ways: whatever line of attack they may take, they end up criticizing either the coherence or fidelity of my position, or both. And whatever objections they may make, the foundation for their objections will be a rival story, which, of course, they assume to be coherent and which has fidelity.[25]

Is most communication story, and do we judge every message we hear on the basis of whether it hangs together and rings true with our values? If you take Fisher's ideas seriously, you won't need me or a trained rhetorician to give you the final word. Like everyone else, you can spot the difference between a good story and a bad one.

QUESTIONS TO SHARPEN YOUR FOCUS

1. Using Fisher's definition of *narration,* can you think of any types of communication other than jokes or phatic communication that don't fit within the *narrative paradigm?*
2. Fisher claims that the *rational-world paradigm* dominates Western education. Can you list college courses you've taken that adopt the assumptions of this conceptual framework?
3. What is the difference between *narrative coherence* and *narrative fidelity?*
4. You apply a *logic of good reasons* to the stories you hear. What are the *values* undergirding Buechner's story of Ruth? Which one do you most admire? What *values* do you hold that cause you to ultimately accept or reject his narrative?

A SECOND LOOK

Recommended resource: Walter R. Fisher, *Human Communication as Narration: Toward a Philosophy of Reason, Value, and Action,* University of South Carolina, Columbia, 1987.

Original statement: Walter R. Fisher, "Narration as a Human Communication Paradigm: The Case of Public Moral Argument," *Communication Monographs,* Vol. 51, 1984, pp. 1–22.

Storytelling and narrativity in communication research: Journal of Communication, Vol. 35, No. 4, 1985, entire issue.

Scientific communication as story: Walter R. Fisher, "Narration, Knowledge, and the Possibility of Wisdom," in *Rethinking Knowledge: Reflections Across the Disciplines,* Robert F. Goodman and Walter R. Fisher (eds.), State University of New York, Albany, 1995, pp. 169–197.

Narrative ethics: Walter R. Fisher, "The Ethic(s) of Argument and Practical Wisdom," in *Argument at Century's End,* Thomas Hollihan (ed.), National Communication Association, Annandale, VA, 1999, pp. 1–15.

Telling the old story in a new way: Frederick Buechner, *Peculiar Treasures,* Harper & Row, New York, 1979.

Coherent life stories: Dan McAdams, "The Problem of Narrative Coherence," *Journal of Constructivist Psychology,* Vol. 19, 2006, pp. 109–125.

Ethics as story: Richard Johannesen, "A Rational World Ethic Versus a Narrative Ethic for Political Communication," in *Ethics in Human Communication,* 6th ed., Waveland, Prospect Heights, IL, 2008, pp. 254–262.

Empirical measure of believability: Robert Yale, "Measuring Narrative Believability: Development and Validation of the Narrative Believability Scale (NBS-12)," *Journal of Communication,* Vol. 63, 2013, pp. 578–599.

Critique: Barbara Warnick, "The Narrative Paradigm: Another Story," *Quarterly Journal of Speech,* Vol. 73, 1987, pp. 172–182.

Critique: Robert Rowland, "On Limiting the Narrative Paradigm: Three Case Studies," *Communication Monographs,* Vol. 56, 1989, pp. 39–54.

Response to critics: Walter R. Fisher, "Clarifying the Narrative Paradigm," *Communication Monographs,* Vol. 56, 1989, pp. 55–58.

Suggested revision: Kevin McClure, "Resurrecting the Narrative Paradigm: Identification and the Case of Young Earth Creationism," *Rhetoric Society Quarterly,* Vol. 39, 2009, pp. 189–211.

Are you convinced you can detect when a story is false?
Click on Interpersonal Deception Theory in
Archive under Theory Resources at
www.afirstlook.com.

Mass Communication

DIVISION FOUR

Mass Communication

Media and Culture

Students who begin to learn about the relationship between media and culture quickly run across multiple references to *postmodernism*. While most of us understand that this term refers to many elements of contemporary Western society, we may be hard-pressed to explain the specific values or practices that distinguish a postmodern culture from others. Since media expression is at the heart of postmodernism, I'll illustrate six of its defining features.[1]

1. Postmodern *describes a period of time when the promise of modernism no longer seems justified.* The modernistic ideologies that postmodernism rejects include the Industrial Revolution, nationalistic imperialism, the rationality of the Enlightenment, faith in science, and any sense that the world is on an upward trajectory. In his essay "On Nihilism," Jean Baudrillard, a leading French postmodernist, claims that he and his colleagues are neither optimistic nor pessimistic. Yet the absence of meaning he describes strikes most readers as devoid of hope.

> I have the impression with postmodernism that there is an attempt to rediscover a certain pleasure in the irony of things. Right now one can tumble into total hopelessness—all the definitions, everything, it's all been done. What can one do? What can one become? And postmodernity is the attempt . . . to reach a point where one can live with what is left. It is more a survival amongst the remnants than anything else.[2]

2. *We have become tools of our tools.* Canadian Marshall McLuhan surveyed the history of media technology and observed that *we shape our tools and they in turn shape us.* According to McLuhan, when we continually use a communication technology, it alters our symbolic environment—the socially constructed, sensory world of meanings that shapes our perceptions, experiences, attitudes, and behavior. If we concentrate on analyzing the content of media messages or strive to resist their impact, we miss the fact that the medium itself is the "message" that shapes us.

3. *In a postmodern world, any claim of truth or moral certainty is suspect.* In his book *The Postmodern Condition*, Baudrillard's countryman Jean-François Lyotard was the first to popularize the use of the term *postmodern* to describe our culture. "Simplifying to the extreme," wrote Lyotard, "I define *postmodern* as incredulity towards metanarratives."[3] He was referring specifically to any systems of thought that claimed to be true for all people, such as Marxism, Freudianism, or Christianity. But the relativity of knowledge applies to any assertion of truth. In postmodern thinking, there are no facts, only interpretations. We can't know anything for certain. (As you ponder this idea, you might wonder how certain we can be that we can't know anything for certain.) In the world of art, postmodernism ignores universal principles of aesthetic beauty. There are no standard rules for creating a painting, sculpture, movie, or concerto.

4. *Images become more important than what they represent.* Postmodernists are convinced that recurrent media images take on a *hyperreality*—they are more real than reality. Our mental pictures of the perfect body, house, meal, vacation, and sexual relationship have been created through exposure to constantly

recycled media depictions that have no basis in fact—but it is these images that shape our expectations. As Baudrillard suggested, "It's not TV as a mirror of society but just the reverse: *it's society as the mirror of television.*"[4] For postmodernists, the issue is not whether media distort reality. In today's world, media have become reality—the only one we have.

5. *With a media assist, we can mix and match diverse styles and tastes to create a unique identity.* Lyotard regarded this kind of eclecticism as the norm for postmodern culture. "One listens to reggae, watches a Western, eats McDonald's food for lunch and local cuisine for dinner, wears Paris perfume in Tokyo and 'retro' clothes in Hong Kong; knowledge is a matter for TV games."[5] The possibilities of identity construction are endless in an urban setting with thousands of cable channels and high-speed Internet to provide infinite variety. Postmodernism is an age of individualism rather than one of community.

6. *Postmodernism can also be seen as a new kind of economic order—a consumer society based on multinational capitalism.* In a postmodern society, information rather than production is the key to profits. Money is especially important in a consumer society because *people are what they consume.*

Operating from a neo-Marxist perspective, Duke University literature professor Fredric Jameson is a high-profile postmodernist who takes this economic view. He sees in our current era "the emergence of a new type of social life and a new economic order,"6 specifically a late stage of capitalism. He is not surprised to see the erosion of the old distinction between high culture and so-called popular culture. In the absence of aesthetic standards, profits become the measure of whether art is good or bad. Thus, media conglomerates such as Disney and Time Warner cannot help but work in the interest of those who already have financial control.

The theorists featured in this section don't identify themselves as postmodernists, but their analysis of media and culture certainly places them in that camp. Their highly interpretive methodological approach is in sharp contrast with the empirical approach that marks the scientific media theorists featured in the section following this one.

CHAPTER 25

Objective ● Interpretive

Socio-cultural tradition

Media Ecology

of Marshall McLuhan

Rachael Dretzin, an award-winning documentary filmmaker and journalist, began her 2010 PBS documentary, *Digital Nation*,[1] with a personal observation:

> So it really hit me one night not that long ago. I was in the kitchen and I was cooking dinner, chopping vegetables—and my husband was in the next room on his laptop and across the table from my husband was my oldest son—who was also on a laptop doing his homework—and my younger kids had picked up my iPhone and were playing a game on it or something and it just hit me. We're all in the same house but we're also in *other* worlds—and it just kind of snuck up on us. I didn't see it coming.

The heart of Dretzin's insight is the fact that her entire home *environment* had changed dramatically due to electronic media—a change she'd never noticed until that one evening chopping vegetables.

Dretzin's realization highlights what media ecologists study. You're probably familiar with the word *ecology* because it comes up in discussions about global warming, recycling garbage, and saving rain forests. Ecologists study the environment, how people interact with it, and the way these interactions result in change. *Media* ecologists study *media* environments. They seek to understand how people interact with media and how those interactions shape our culture and our daily experiences. If Marshall McLuhan could have heard Dretzin's comment, he would have probably smiled knowingly. At the same time McLuhan claimed to understand the changes media bring, he also confidently theorized about why most of us are oblivious to those changes.

In the 1960s, Marshall McLuhan was an English professor at the University of Toronto. He burst onto the public scene by asking questions about the relationship between media and culture. His book *Understanding Media* was a surprise hit that generated both admiration and dissension. His theory suggests that media should be understood ecologically. Changes in technology alter the *symbolic environment*—the socially constructed, sensory world of meanings that in turn shapes our perceptions, experiences, attitudes, and behavior.

Symbolic environment
The socially constructed, sensory world of meanings.

THE MEDIUM IS THE MESSAGE

McLuhan's theory of media ecology is best captured in his famous aphorism "The medium is the message." This pithy statement is meant to upset our expectations. We're accustomed to thinking that people change because of the messages they consume. The whole field of persuasion revolves around message content (see Chapter 15). We think of media as mere channels of message delivery that play a minor role in effecting change.

When McLuhan said, "the medium is the message," he wanted us to see that media—regardless of content—reshape human experience and exert far more change in our world than the sum total of the messages they contain. He made this point forcefully in a famous interview with *Playboy* magazine in 1969: "The content or message of any particular medium has about as much importance as the stenciling on the casing of an atomic bomb."[2]

Media
Generic term for all human-invented technology that extends the range, speed, or channels of communication.

Medium
A specific type of media; for example, a book, newspaper, radio, television, telephone, film, website, or email.

McLuhan loved using metaphors to explain theoretical concepts. He was convinced that when we consider the cultural influence of *media,* we are usually misled by the illusion of *content.* One metaphor that he used to make this point was particularly colorful. He wrote, "For the 'content' of a medium is like the juicy piece of meat carried by the burglar to distract the watchdog of the mind."[3] We focus on the content and overlook the *medium*—even though content doesn't exist outside of the way it's mediated. *Moby Dick* is a book. *Moby Dick* is a movie. *Moby Dick* is an oral tale. These are different stories. For this reason, we shouldn't complain that a movie is not like the book, because a movie can never be like a book. A movie can only be a movie.

Whether a TV show is about killer whales, current events, crime scene investigations, the next American pop star, or *The Real Housewives of New Jersey,* the message is always television. It is the distinct experience of TV that alters the symbolic environment. From the perspective of media ecology, the Clydesdale ad discussed in Chapter 2 is important not for its content but because it offered a shared media experience that captured the time and attention of millions of people. It also triggered nearly 3 million visits to YouTube to watch the ad again.[4] Media ecologists might point out that neither Glenn nor Marty even mentioned these features in their analysis.

After reading about McLuhan's theory, John had no problem recognizing the message of a medium. In his application log, he wrote:

> Instant messaging is a recent fad as society moves deeper into the digital age. I don't regard IM as necessary for exchanging information. Emails and phone calls can take care of that. For me, instant messages are a sign of affection; they are "flirtatious." I've got a crush on Ashley, and when I see that I have an instant message from her, I can't help but smile—this even before I read the message. Overshadowed by a media form that signifies intimacy and fondness, the content seems irrelevant. The medium is the message.

THE CHALLENGE OF MEDIA ECOLOGY

Media ecology
The study of different personal and social environments created by the use of different communication technologies.

Any understanding of social and cultural change is impossible without a knowledge of the way media work as environments.[5] But evaluating the *ecology of media* is a difficult enterprise because all environments are inherently intangible and interrelated. An environment is not a thing to identify; rather, it is the intricate association of many things. By definition, these things are part of the background. They are everything and no thing. McLuhan noted that "their ground rules, pervasive structure, and overall patterns elude easy perception."[6]

Invisibility of Environments

McLuhan was fond of quoting the mantra of anthropologists: "We don't know who discovered water, but we're pretty sure it wasn't the fish." In the same way, we have trouble recognizing "the way media work as environments" because we are so immersed in them.

McLuhan's theory of media differs from the traditional warnings against technological advances. The tales of *Frankenstein, Blade Runner, Jurassic Park,* and *The Matrix* posit technology gone awry and turning on its maker. These fantastical threats prove terribly obvious. As long as our technologies are not chasing after us, we are supposedly safe from the consequences of our creations.

According to McLuhan, it's not technological abnormality that demands our attention, since it's hard *not* to notice the new and different. Instead, we need to focus on our everyday experience of *technology.* A medium shapes us because we partake of it over and over until it becomes an extension of ourselves. Because every medium emphasizes different senses and encourages different habits, engaging a medium day after day conditions the senses to take in some stimuli and not register others. A medium that emphasizes the ear over the eye alters the ratios of sense perception. Like a blind man who begins to develop a heightened sense of hearing, society is shaped in accordance with the dominant medium of the day.

Technology
According to McLuhan, human inventions that enhance communication.

It's the ordinariness of media that makes them invisible. When a new medium enters society, there's a period of time in which we're aware of its novelty. It's only when it fades into the background of our lives that we're truly subjected to its patterns—that is, its environmental influence. In the same way that a girl growing up in California may unconsciously absorb a West Coast attitude, a boy growing up in our electronic age may unconsciously absorb a digital attitude. Rachael Dretzin noted that the media changes that had transformed her family's home environment had "snuck up" on them.

Complexity of Environments

If you surveyed the landscape of media research, you'd discover plenty of material devoted to the effects of content. You'd also discover numerous studies focusing instead on specific media such as television, computers, and iPhones, as well as applications like Facebook and Twitter. In contrast, research on media ecology is rather sparse because it takes up the challenge of trying to understand the interplay between all of these things in a culture that changes at blazing speed.

McLuhan believed it took a special ability to stand back from the action and take in the big picture. Dretzin realized what was going on inside her home only when she was able to assume the role of a sideline observer preparing dinner. One way McLuhan tried to gain a broader perspective was by stepping outside the moment and considering all of human history. He found it helpful to trace the major ecological shifts in media over thousands of years. That grand historical perspective is the foundation of McLuhan's theory.

A MEDIA ANALYSIS OF HUMAN HISTORY

McLuhan was critical of social observers who analyzed the Western world but bypassed the effects of symbolic environments, be they oral, print, or electronic. He specifically accused modern scholars of being "ostrichlike" in refusing to acknowledge the revolutionary impact of electronic media on the sensory experience of contemporary society.

As Figure 25–1 shows, McLuhan divided all human history into four periods, or epochs—a tribal age, a literate age, a print age, and an electronic age. According to McLuhan, the crucial inventions that changed life on this planet were the

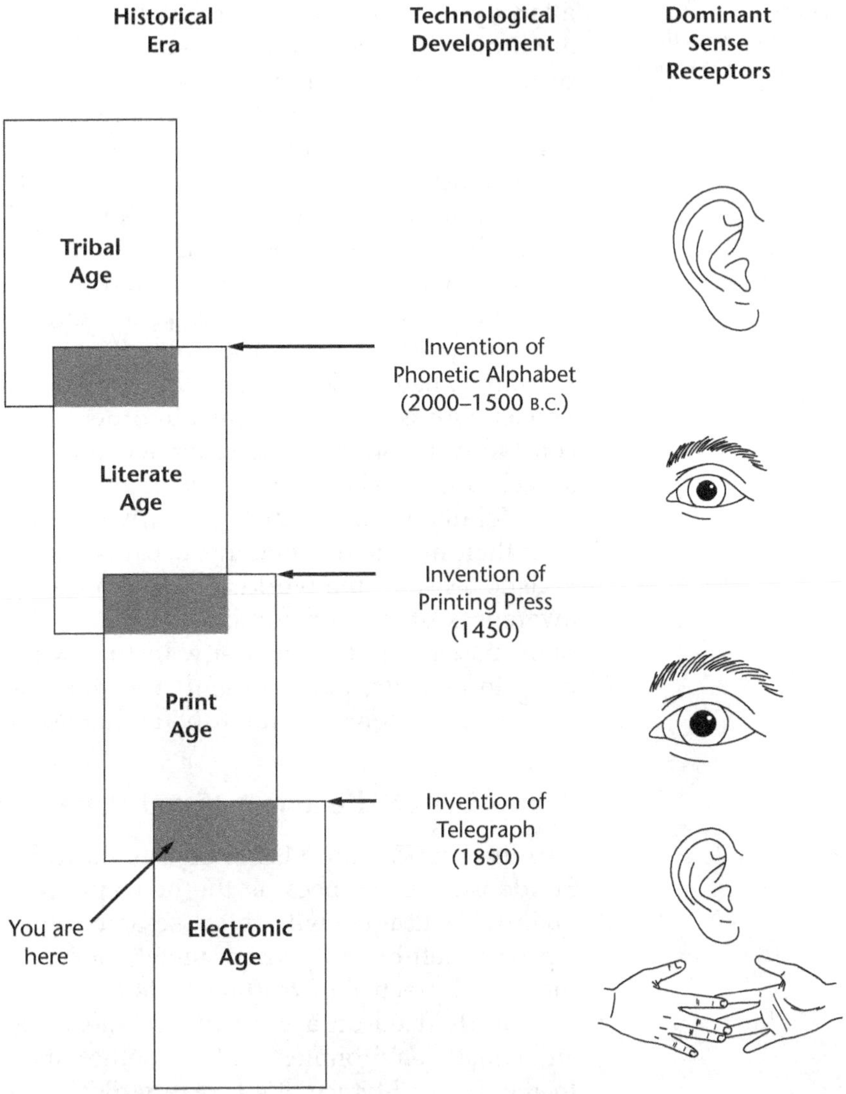

FIGURE 25–1 Marshall McLuhan's Media Map of History

phonetic alphabet, the printing press, and the telegraph. In each case the world was wrenched from one era into the next because of new developments in media technology. Those of us born in the twentieth century are living through one of those turbulent transitions—from the tail end of the *print* age to the very beginning of the *electronic* age. McLuhan believed the transitions (shaded in gray in Figure 25–1) took 300 to 400 years to complete. While you might think you're living in the electronic age right now, you're not there yet. The full transition will take another two centuries.

1. The Tribal Age: An Acoustic Place in History

According to McLuhan, the tribal village was an acoustic place where the senses of hearing, touch, taste, and smell were developed far beyond the ability to visualize. In untamed settings, hearing is more valuable than seeing because it

Tribal age
An acoustic era; a time of community because the ear is the dominant sense organ.

allows you to be more immediately aware of your surroundings. With sight, we are limited to direction and distance. We can only sense what is clearly in front of us. If a preying animal is behind us or hidden by a tree, we are hopelessly unaware without a sensitivity to sound or smell. Hearing and smelling provide a sense of that which we cannot see, a crucial ability in the tribal age.

The omnidirectional quality of sound also enhances community. The spoken word is primarily a communal experience. To tell a secret, we must whisper or speak directly in someone's ear or make sure no one else is listening. The sense of sound works against privatization. Listening to someone speak in a group is a unifying act. Everyone hears at the same time.

The spoken word is also immediate and alive. It exists only at the moment it is heard. There is no sense of the word as something that is fixed or objectified. Spoken words lack materiality. In order to keep an idea or an event alive, it must constantly be shared and reiterated and passed down. The ethereal quality of speech doesn't allow for detached analysis. In a tribal age, hearing is believing.

McLuhan claimed that "primitive" people led richer and more complex lives than their literate descendants because the ear, unlike the eye, encourages a more holistic sense of the world. There is a deeper feeling of community and greater awareness of the surrounding existence. The acoustic environment also fosters more passion and spontaneity. In that world of surround sound, everything is more immediate, more present, and more actual.

Then someone invented the alphabet.

2. The Age of Literacy: A Visual Point of View

Turning sounds into visible objects radically altered the symbolic environment. Suddenly, the eye became the heir apparent. Hearing diminished in value and quality. To disagree with this assessment merely illustrates McLuhan's belief that a private, left-brain "point of view" becomes possible in a world that encourages the visual practice of reading texts.

Words fixed on a page detach meaning from the immediacy of context. In an acoustic environment, taking something out of context is nearly impossible. In the age of literacy, it's a reality. Both writer and reader are always separate from the text. Words are no longer alive and immediate. They can be read and reread. They can be thoroughly analyzed. Hearing no longer becomes trustworthy. "Seeing it in writing" becomes proof that it's true.

Literary age
A visual era; a time of private detachment because the eye is the dominant sense organ.

Literacy also jarred people out of collective tribal involvement into "civilized" private detachment. Reading words, instead of hearing them, transforms group members into individuals. Even though the words may be the same, the act of reading a text is an individual one. It requires singular focus. A tribe no longer needs to come together to get information. Proximity becomes less important.

McLuhan also claimed that the phonetic alphabet established the line as the organizing principle in life. In writing, letter follows letter in a connected, orderly line. Logic is modeled on that step-by-step linear progression. According to McLuhan, when literate people say, "I don't follow you," they mean, "I don't think you are logical." He alleged that the invention of the alphabet fostered the sudden emergence of mathematics, science, and philosophy in ancient Greece. He cited the political upheaval in colonial Africa as twentieth-century evidence that literacy triggers an ear-to-eye switch that isolates the reader. When oppressed people learned to read, they became independent thinkers.

3. The Print Age: Prototype of the Industrial Revolution

If the phonetic alphabet made visual dependence possible, the printing press made it widespread. In *The Gutenberg Galaxy,* McLuhan argued that the most important aspect of movable type was its ability to reproduce the same text over and over again, and a press run of 100,000 copies of *Understanding Media* suggests he was right. Because the print revolution demonstrated mass production of identical products, McLuhan called it the forerunner of the industrial revolution.

Print age
A visual era; mass-produced books usher in the industrial revolution and nationalism, yet individuals are isolated.

He saw other unintended side effects of Gutenberg's invention. The homogenization of fluid regional tongues into a fixed national language was followed closely by the rise of nationalism. Concurring with this new sense of unification was a countering sense of separation and aloneness.

> Printing, a ditto device, confirmed and extended the new visual stress. It created the portable book, which men could read in privacy and in isolation from others.[7]

Many libraries have the words "The truth will set you free" carved in stone above the main entrance.[8] From McLuhan's perspective, libraries provide readers with the freedom to be alienated from others and from the immediacy of their surroundings.

4. The Electronic Age: The Rise of the Global Village

With the tap-tap-tap of the telegraph, the power of the printed word lost its bearings. Of course, Samuel Morse's invention was only the first of the new electronic media devices that would make the corner Radio Shack seem, to previous generations, like a magic shop.

Electronic age
An era of instant communication; a return to the global village with all-at-once sound and touch.

Telegraph Radio Telephone
Film projector Phonograph TV
Photocopier Tape recorder Answering machine
VCR Computer CD
Cell phone Fax Video game
Internet DVD MP3 Smart phone Tablet

McLuhan insisted that electronic media are retribalizing the human race. Instant communication has returned us to a pre-alphabetic oral tradition where sound and touch are more important than sight. We've gone "back to the future" to become a village unlike any other previous village. We're now a *global village.*

Global village
A worldwide electronic community where everyone knows everyone's business and all are somewhat testy.

Electronic media bring us in touch with everyone, everywhere, instantaneously. Whereas the book extended the eye, electronic circuitry extends the central nervous system.[9] Constant contact with the world becomes a daily reality. All-at-once-ness is our state of being. Closed human systems no longer exist. The rumble of empty stomachs in Bangladesh and of roadside bombs in Baghdad vibrate in the living rooms of Boston. For us, the first postliterate generation, privacy is either a luxury or a curse of the past. The planet is like a general store where nosy people keep track of everyone else's business—a 12-way party line or a "Dear Abby" column writ large. "The new tribalism is one where everyone's buiness is everyone else's and where we all are somewhat testy."[10] Citizens of the world are back in acoustic space.

Linear logic is useless in the electronic society McLuhan described. Acoustic people no longer inquire, "Do you see my point?" Instead we ask, "How does that grab you?" What we feel is more important than what we think.

5. The Digital Age? Rewiring the Global Village

When *Wired,* a magazine on digital culture, was launched in 1992, the editors declared Marshall McLuhan the magazine's "patron saint." There was a sense that another revolution was looming, and many returned to the words of McLuhan for guidance. However, digital technology doesn't pull the plug on the electronic age, because, quite frankly, it still needs its power source. The *digital age* is wholly electronic.

With that said, there's no doubt that the introduction of digital technology is altering the electronic environment. The mass age of electronic media is

"You see, Dad, Professor McLuhan says the environment that man creates becomes his medium for defining his role in it. The invention of type created linear, or sequential, thought, separating thought from action. Now, with TV and folk singing, thought and action are closer and social involvement is greater. We again live in a village. Get it?"

Digital age
A possible fifth era of specialized electronic tribes contentious over diverse beliefs and values.

becoming increasingly personalized. Instead of one unified electronic tribe, we have a growing number of digital tribes forming around the most specialized ideas, beliefs, values, interests, and fetishes. Instead of mass consciousness, which McLuhan viewed rather favorably, we have the emergence of a tribal warfare mentality. Despite the contentious nature of this tribalization of differences, many see benefit in the resulting decentralization of power and control.

Were he alive today (he died in 1980), McLuhan undoubtedly would have spotted other ways that digital media are altering our present environment. And he would probably speculate on whether the electronic environment is the destiny of humankind, or if there's another media force waiting to upset the ecology of the previous century.

ETHICAL REFLECTION: POSTMAN'S FAUSTIAN BARGAIN

McLuhan's probes stimulated others to ponder whether specific media environments were beneficial or destructive for those immersed in them. Neil Postman founded the media ecology program at New York University and was regarded by many as McLuhan's heir apparent. Like McLuhan, Postman believed that the forms of media regulate and even dictate what kind of content the form of a given medium can carry.[11] For example, smoke signals implicitly discourage philosophical argument.

> Puffs of smoke are insufficiently complex to express ideas on the nature of existence and even if they were not, a Cherokee philosopher would run short of either wood or blankets long before he reached his second axiom. You cannot use smoke to do philosophy. Its form excludes the content.[12]

But unlike McLuhan, Postman believed that the primary task of media ecology is to make moral judgments. "To be quite honest about it," he once proclaimed, "I don't see any point in studying media unless one does so within a moral or ethical context."[13]

According to Postman, a new technology always presents us with a *Faustian bargain*—a potential deal with the devil. As Postman was fond of saying, "Technology giveth and technology taketh away. . . . A new technology sometimes creates more than it destroys. Sometimes, it destroys more than it creates. But it is never one-sided."[14] His media ecology approach asks, *What are the moral implications of this bargain? Are the consequences more humanistic or antihumanistic? Do we, as a society, gain more than we lose, or do we lose more than we gain?*

Faustian bargain
A deal with the devil; selling your soul for temporary earthly gain.

As for television, Postman argued that society lost more than it gained. He believed whatever advantages TV offers are more than offset by the fact that it has led to the loss of serious public discourse. Television changes the form of information "from discursive to nondiscursive, from propositional to presentational, from rationalistic to emotive."[15] He explicated this argument in his popular book *Amusing Ourselves to Death,* which argues that TV has transformed our culture into one that is focused too heavily on entertainment.

Postman died in 2003, just before social media exploded in American culture. Had he been here to witness this change, he could have easily cast his analysis in terms of the *Faustian bargain.* Social media offers unprecedented opportunities to maintain electronic connections with family and friends. At the same time, relying on virtual interaction may sabotage the kind of intimacy that only comes by being in the physical presence of others. Have we gained more than we've lost?

Like McLuhan, Postman preferred questions to answers, so it is fitting that his legacy be defined by three questions he urged us to ask about any new technology:

1. What is the problem to which this technology is a solution?
2. Whose problem is it, actually?
3. If there is a legitimate problem to be solved, what other problems will be created by my using this technology?

Postman certainly considered these questions when he thought about the coming age of computer technology. He questioned if we were yielding too easily to the "authority" of computation and the values of efficiency and quantification. He pondered whether the quest for technological progress was becoming increasingly more important than being humane. He wondered if information was an acceptable substitute for wisdom. While Postman was primarily concerned with the ecology of television, his work set a precedent for considering the moral consequences of all symbolic environments.

CRITIQUE: HOW COULD HE BE RIGHT? BUT WHAT IF HE WAS?

McLuhan likened himself to "Louis Pasteur telling doctors that their greatest enemy is quite invisible, and quite unrecognized by them."[16] Of course, the major difference is that Pasteur was a scientist who ultimately gave tangible evidence for his germ theory. The problem with McLuhan's theory is that it suggests objectivity without scientific evidence. In other words, he used the subjective approach to make objective claims.

McLuhan faced harsh criticism from the scholarly community. He was one of the first academic superstars of the TV era, so perhaps his enormous popularity gave added impetus to critics' scorn for his methods and message. The pages of *McLuhan: Hot & Cool* and *McLuhan: Pro & Con* denounce his ideas and the way he expressed them:

> [McLuhan] prefers to rape our attention rather than seduce our understanding.[17]

> He has looted all culture from cave painting to *Mad* magazine for fragments to shore up his system against ruin.[18]

> The style . . . is a viscous fog through which loom stumbling metaphors.[19]

George Gordon, then chairman of the department of communication at Fordham University, labeled McLuhan's work "McLuhanacy" and dismissed it as worthless. Gordon stated, "Not one bit of sustained and replicated scientific evidence, inductive or deductive, has to date justified any one of McLuhan's most famous slogans, metaphors, or dicta."[20] Indeed, it is hard to know how one could prove that the phonetic alphabet created Greek philosophy, that the printing press fostered nationalism, or that television is a tactile medium.

It is also hard to say he was wrong, because it's difficult to be certain what he said. As a writer, McLuhan often abandoned the linearity and order that he claimed were the legacy of print technology. As a speaker, he was superb at crafting memorable phrases and 10-second sound bites, but his truths were enigmatic and seldom woven into a comprehensive system. He preferred to offer theoretical punch lines for people to accept or reject at face value.

A different attack on McLuhan comes from those who lament that he merely *explored* rather than publicly *deplored* the effects of electronic media on public morals. His biographers agree that he held a deep faith in God as represented by the Roman Catholic Church; he was well read in theology and attended Mass almost every day. Yet he believed that as a professor, he should keep his personal beliefs private.[21] In a letter to anthropologist Edward Hall, he wrote, "I deliberately keep Christianity out of these discussions lest perception be diverted from structural processes by doctrinal sectarian passions."[22] But as a comment he made during a radio interview reveals, his scholarship informed his faith and his faith informed his scholarship. "In Jesus Christ, there is no distance or separation between the medium and the message: it is the one case where we can say that the medium and the message are fully one and the same."[23]

For those who regard falsifiability as a mark of a good theory, McLuhan's leaps of faith make it difficult to take his ideas seriously. However, history is littered with theories that were ahead of their time and couldn't immediately be tested. Journalist Tom Wolfe reverses the question: "What if he's right? Suppose he is what he sounds like, the most important thinker since Newton, Darwin, Freud, Einstein and Pavlov?"[24]

You might wonder how Wolfe could say McLuhan sounds like such an important thinker when so many others have nothing but derisive comments to offer. One answer to that question revolves around McLuhan's habit of "explaining" things that people already know to be true. He used his perspective to shed light on all sorts of cultural phenomena that, while easy to observe, are no less bewildering. These include the rise in drug abuse, shortened attention spans, decline in standardized test scores, popularity of rock music and tattoos, and the success and failure of specific political candidates. It's difficult to deny the intuitive appeal of many of McLuhan's explanations, even if that appeal is accompanied by a healthy dose of skepticism.

McLuhan's historical analysis has heightened awareness of the possible cultural effects of new media technologies. Other scholars have been more tempered in their statements and more rigorous in their documentation, but none has raised media consciousness to the level achieved by McLuhan with his catchy statements and dramatic metaphors.

The late economist Kenneth Boulding, who headed the Institute of Behavioral Sciences at the University of Colorado, captured both the pro and con reactions to McLuhan by using a metaphor of his own: "It is perhaps typical of very creative minds that they hit very large nails not quite on the head."[25]

QUESTIONS TO SHARPEN YOUR FOCUS

1. What would McLuhan say about the impact of the Internet on the *global village?* Consider the fact that civic, political, and religious participation are declining in America.[26] Has *electronic technology* increased social connectedness?
2. How are portable media devices such as smart phones, iPads, and handheld video games altering the *media environment?* How are these devices shaping sensibilities?
3. Beyond changes in content, what are the differences in experiencing a book and its translations into film or television?
4. Can you conceive of any way that McLuhan's idea of *media ecology* could be proved false?

SELF-QUIZ

www.mhhe.com/griffin9e

A SECOND LOOK

Recommended resource: Marshall McLuhan, "*Playboy* Interview: A Candid Conversation with the High Priest of Popcult and Metaphysician of Media," March 1969, p. 53ff. Reprinted in *Essential McLuhan,* Eric McLuhan and Frank Zingrone (eds.), BasicBooks, New York, 1995, pp. 233–269.

McLuhan primer: Marshall McLuhan and Quentin Fiore, *The Medium Is the Massage,* Gingko, Corte Madera, CA, 2005.

Impact of print media: Marshall McLuhan, *The Gutenberg Galaxy,* University of Toronto, Toronto, 1962.

Impact of electronic media: Marshall McLuhan, *Understanding Media,* McGraw-Hill, New York, 1964.

Impact of digital media à la McLuhan: Paul Levinson, *Digital McLuhan: A Guide to the Information Millennium,* Routledge, London, 1999.

Early vs. late McLuhan: Bruce E. Gronbeck, "McLuhan as Rhetorical Theorist," *Journal of Communication,* Vol. 31, 1981, pp. 117–128.

Intellectual roots: Harold Innis, *The Bias of Communication,* University of Toronto, Toronto, 1964.

Methodology: Paul Levinson, "McLuhan and Rationality," *Journal of Communication,* Vol. 31, 1981, pp. 179–188.

Scientific claims: Marshall McLuhan and Eric McLuhan, *Laws of Media: The New Science,* University of Toronto, Toronto, 1988.

Recent scholarship: Eric McLuhan and Marshall McLuhan, *Theories of Communication,* Peter Lang, New York, 2010.

Rethinking McLuhan through critical theory: Paul Grosswiler, *Method Is the Message,* Black Rose, Montreal, 1998.

Postmodern connections: Gary Genosko, "McLuhan's Legacy of Indiscipline," in *Undisciplined Theory,* Sage, London, 1998, pp. 154–182.

Brief interpretive biography: Douglas Coupland, *Extraordinary Canadians: Marshall McLuhan,* Penguin, Viking Canada, 2010.

Legacy of McLuhan: Lance Strate and Edward Wachtel (eds.), *The Legacy of McLuhan,* Hampton, Cresskill, NJ, 2005, Chapters 1–4.

Neil Postman's ethical view of new media: Neil Postman, *Amusing Ourselves to Death: Public Discourse in the Age of Show Business,* Viking, NY, 1985; Neil Postman, *Technopoly: The Surrender of Culture to Technology,* Knopf, New York, 1992.

Critique: Gerald Stearn (ed.), *McLuhan: Hot & Cool,* Dial, New York, 1967.

Do we respond to people and digital media in the same way?
Click on The Media Equation in Archive
under Theory Resources at
www.afirstlook.com.

CHAPTER 26

Objective — Interpretive

Semiotic tradition

Semiotics

of Roland Barthes

French literary critic and semiologist Roland Barthes (rhymes with "smart") wrote that for him, semiotics was not a cause, a science, a discipline, a school, a movement, nor presumably even a theory. "It is," he claimed, "an adventure."[1] The goal of semiotics is interpreting both verbal and nonverbal *signs*. The verbal side of the field is called *linguistics*. Barthes, however, was mainly interested in the nonverbal side—multifaceted visual signs just waiting to be read. Barthes held the chair of literary semiology at the College of France when he was struck and killed by a laundry truck in 1980. In his highly regarded book *Mythologies*, Barthes sought to decipher the cultural meaning of a wide variety of visual signs—from sweat on the faces of actors in the film *Julius Caesar* to a magazine photograph of a young African soldier saluting the French flag.

Unlike most intellectuals, Barthes frequently wrote for the popular press and occasionally appeared on television to comment on the foibles of the French middle class. His academic colleagues found his statements witty, disturbing, flashy, overstated, or profound—but never dull. He obviously made them think. With the exception of Aristotle, the four-volume *International Encyclopedia of Communication* refers to Barthes more than to any other theorist in this book.[2]

Semiology (or semiotics, as it is better known in America) is concerned with *anything that can stand for something else*. Italian semiologist and novelist Umberto Eco has a clever way of expressing that focus. Semiotics, he says, is "the discipline studying everything which can be used in order to lie, because if something cannot be used to tell a lie, conversely it cannot be used to tell the truth; it cannot, in fact, be used to tell at all."[3] Barthes was interested in signs that are seemingly straightforward but that subtly communicate ideological or connotative meaning and perpetuate the dominant values of society. As such, they are deceptive.

Semiotics (semiology) The study of the social production of meaning from sign systems; the analysis of anything that can stand for something else.

Barthes was a mercurial thinker who changed his mind about the way signs work more than once over the course of his career. Yet most current practitioners of semiotics follow the basic analytical concepts of his original theory. His approach provides great insight into the use of signs, particularly those channeled through the mass media.

WRESTLING WITH SIGNS

Myth
The connotative meaning that signs carry wherever they go; myth makes what is cultural seem natural.

Barthes initially described his semiotic theory as an explanation of *myth*. He later substituted the term *connotation* to label the ideological baggage that signs carry wherever they go, and most students of Barthes' work regard connotation as a better word choice to convey his true concern.

Barthes' theory of connotative meaning won't make sense to us, however, unless we first understand the way he viewed the structure of signs. His thinking was strongly influenced by the work of Swiss linguist Ferdinand de Saussure, who coined the term *semiology* and advocated its study.[4] To illustrate Barthes' core principles I'll feature portions of his essay on professional wrestling entertainment.

1. A Sign Is the Combination of Its Signifier and Signified

The distinction between signifier and signified can be seen in Barthes' graphic description of the body of a French wrestler who was selected by the promoter because he typified the repulsive slob:

> As soon as the adversaries are in the ring, the public is overwhelmed with the obviousness of the roles. As in the theatre, each physical type expresses to excess the part which has been assigned to the contestant. Thauvin, a fifty-year-old with an obese and sagging body . . . displays in his flesh the characters of baseness. . . . The physique of the wrestlers therefore constitutes a basic sign, which like a seed contains the whole fight.[5]

According to Barthes, the image of the wrestler's physique is the *signifier*. The concept of baseness is the *signified*. The combination of the two—the villainous body—is the *sign*.

Sign
The inseparable combination of the signifier and the signified.

This way of defining a sign differs from our customary use of the word. We would probably say the wrestler's body *is a sign* of his baseness—or whatever else comes to mind. But Barthes considered the wrestler's body just *part* of the overall sign; it's the signifier. The other part is the concept of hideous baseness. The signifier isn't a sign of the signified. Rather, they work together in an inseparable bond to form a unified sign.

Signifier
The physical form of the sign as we perceive it through our senses; an image.

Barthes' description of a sign as the correlation between the signifier and the signified came directly from Saussure. The Swiss linguist visualized a sign as a piece of paper with writing on both sides—the signifier on one side, the signified on the other. If you cut off part of one side, an equal amount of the other side automatically goes with it.

Using a similar metaphor, I see signs as coins. For example, the image of a country's president is stamped on the "heads" side of a gold coin—the signifier. It's only on the flip side of the coin that we see its value in the United States of America is $1—the signified. The signifier and the signified can't be separated. They are combined in our reference to that monetary sign as a U.S. gold dollar.

Signified
The meaning we associate with the sign.

Is there any logical connection between the image of the signifier and the content of the signified? Saussure insisted the relationship is arbitrary—one of correlation rather than cause and effect. Barthes wasn't so sure. He was willing to grant the claim of Saussure that words have no inherent meaning. For example, there is nothing about the word *referee* that makes it stand for the third party in the ring who is inept at making Thauvin follow the rules. But nonverbal signifiers seem to have a natural affinity with their signifieds. Barthes noted that Thauvin's body was so repugnant that it provoked nausea. He classified the relationship between signifiers and signifieds as "quasi-arbitrary." After all, Thauvin really did strike the crowd as vileness personified.

2. A Sign Does Not Stand on Its Own: It Is Part of a System

Barthes entitled his essay "The World of Wrestling" because, like all other semiotic systems, wrestling creates its own separate world of interrelated signs:

> Each moment in wrestling is therefore like an algebra which instantaneously unveils the relationship between a cause and its represented effect. Wrestling fans certainly experience a kind of intellectual pleasure in *seeing* the moral mechanism function so perfectly. . . . A wrestler can irritate or disgust, he never disappoints, for he always accomplishes completely, by a progressive solidification of signs, what the public expects of him.[6]

Barthes noted that the grapplers' roles are tightly drawn. There is little room for innovation; the men in the ring work within a closed system of signs. By responding to the unwavering expectation of the crowd, the wrestlers are as much spectators as the fans who cheer or jeer on cue.

Wrestling is just one of many semiotic systems. Barthes also explored the cultural meaning of designer clothes, French cooking, automobiles, Japanese gift giving, household furniture, urban layout, and public displays of sexuality. He attempted to define and classify the features common to all semiotic systems. This kind of structural analysis is called *taxonomy,* and Barthes' book *Elements of Semiology* is a "veritable frenzy of classifications."[7] Barthes later admitted that his taxonomy "risked being tedious," but the project strengthened his conviction that all semiotic systems function the same way, despite their apparent diversity.

Barthes believed that the significant semiotic systems of a culture lock in the status quo. The mythology that surrounds a society's crucial signs displays the world as it is today—however chaotic and unjust—as *natural, inevitable,* and *eternal.* The function of myth is to bless the mess. We now turn to Barthes' theory of connotation, or myth, which suggests how a seemingly neutral or inanimate sign can accomplish so much.

THE YELLOW RIBBON TRANSFORMATION: FROM FORGIVENESS TO PRIDE

According to Barthes, not all semiological systems are mythic. Not every sign carries ideological baggage. How is it that one sign can remain emotionally neutral while other signs acquire powerful inflections or connotations that suck people into a specific worldview? Barthes contended that a mythic or connotative system is a *second-order semiological system*—built off a preexisting sign system. The sign of the first system becomes the signifier of the second. A concrete example will help us understand Barthes' explanation.

In an *American Journal of Semiotics* article, Donald and Virginia Fry of Emerson College examined the widespread American practice of displaying yellow ribbons during the 1980 Iranian hostage crisis,[8] which began with the storming of the U.S. embassy vividly portrayed in the Academy Award–winning film *Argo*. They traced the transformation of this straightforward yellow symbol into an ideological sign. Americans' lavish display of yellow ribbons during Operation Desert Storm in 1991 and the occupation of Iraq that began in 2003 adds a new twist to the Frys' analysis. I'll update their yellow ribbon example to illustrate Barthes' semiotic theory.

"Tie a Yellow Ribbon Round the Ole Oak Tree" was the best-selling pop song of 1972 in the United States.[9] Sung by Tony Orlando and Dawn, the lyrics express the thoughts of a convict in prison who is writing to the woman he loves. After three years in jail, the man is about to be released and will travel home by bus. Fearing her possible rejection, he devises a plan that will give her a way to signal her intentions without the potential embarrassment of a face-to-face confrontation.

Since he'll be able to see the huge oak planted in front of her house when the bus passes through town, he asks her to use the tree as a message board. If she still loves him, wants him back, and can overlook the past, she should tie a yellow ribbon around the trunk of the tree. He will know that all is forgiven and join her in rebuilding a life together. But if this bright sign of reconciliation isn't there, he'll stay on the bus, accept the blame for a failed relationship, and try to get on with his life without her.

The yellow ribbon is obviously a sign of acceptance, but one not casually offered. There's a taint on the relationship, hurts to be healed. Donald and Virginia Fry labeled the original meaning of the yellow ribbon in the song as "forgiveness of a stigma."

Yellow ribbons in 1991 continued to carry a "we want you back" message when U.S. armed forces fought in Operation Desert Storm. Whether tied to trees, worn in hair, or pinned to lapels, yellow ribbons still proclaimed, "Welcome home." But there was no longer any sense of shameful acts to be forgiven or disgrace to be overcome. Vietnam was ancient history and America was the leader of the "new world order." Hail the conquering heroes.

The mood surrounding the yellow ribbon had become one of triumph, pride, and even arrogance. After all, hadn't we intercepted Scud missiles in the air, guided "smart bombs" into air-conditioning shafts, and "kicked Saddam Hussein's butt across the desert"? People were swept up in a tide of "yellow fever." More than 90 percent of U.S. citizens approved of America's actions in the Persian Gulf. The simple yellow ribbon of personal reconciliation now served as a blatant sign of nationalism.

The yellow-ribbon sign functioned the same way for about three years after the 2003 U.S. invasion of Iraq, which was the centerpiece of America's "War on Terror." Millions of citizens displayed yellow-ribbon decals and magnets on their cars and trucks that urged all to "Support Our Troops." The ribbon called up feelings of national pride and memories of the shock-and-awe attack on Baghdad that had squashed immediate resistance; Saddam Hussein had been driven from office, his statue toppled; democracy was being established; and President George W. Bush had dramatically landed a fighter jet on an aircraft carrier proclaiming "Mission Accomplished." The yellow ribbon continued to signify that the soldiers' return would be joyous, but its message held no sense of shame. What had originally signified forgiveness of a stigma now symbolized pride in victory.

THE MAKING OF MYTH: STRIPPING THE SIGN OF ITS HISTORY

According to Barthes' theory, the shift from "forgiveness of stigma" to "pride in victory" followed a typical semiotic pattern. Figure 26–1 shows how it's done.

Barthes claimed that every ideological sign is the result of two interconnected sign systems. The first system represented by the smaller coins is strictly descriptive—the signifier image and the signified concept combining to produce a denotative sign. The three elements of the sign system based on the "Tie a Yellow Ribbon . . ." lyrics are marked with Arabic numerals on the three images of the smaller coins. The three segments of the connotative system are marked with Roman numerals on the images of the larger coins. Note that the sign of the first system does double duty as the signifier of the Iraqi war connotative system. According to Barthes, this lateral shift, or connotative sidestep, is the key to transforming a neutral sign into an ideological tool. Follow his thinking step-by-step through the diagram.

Denotative sign system
A descriptive sign without ideological content.

The signifier (1) of the *denotative sign system* is the image of a yellow ribbon that forms in the mind of the person who hears the 1972 song. The content of the signified (2) includes the stigma that comes from the conviction of a crime, a term in jail, the prisoner's willingness to take responsibility for the three-year separation, and the explosive release of tension when the Greyhound passengers cheer

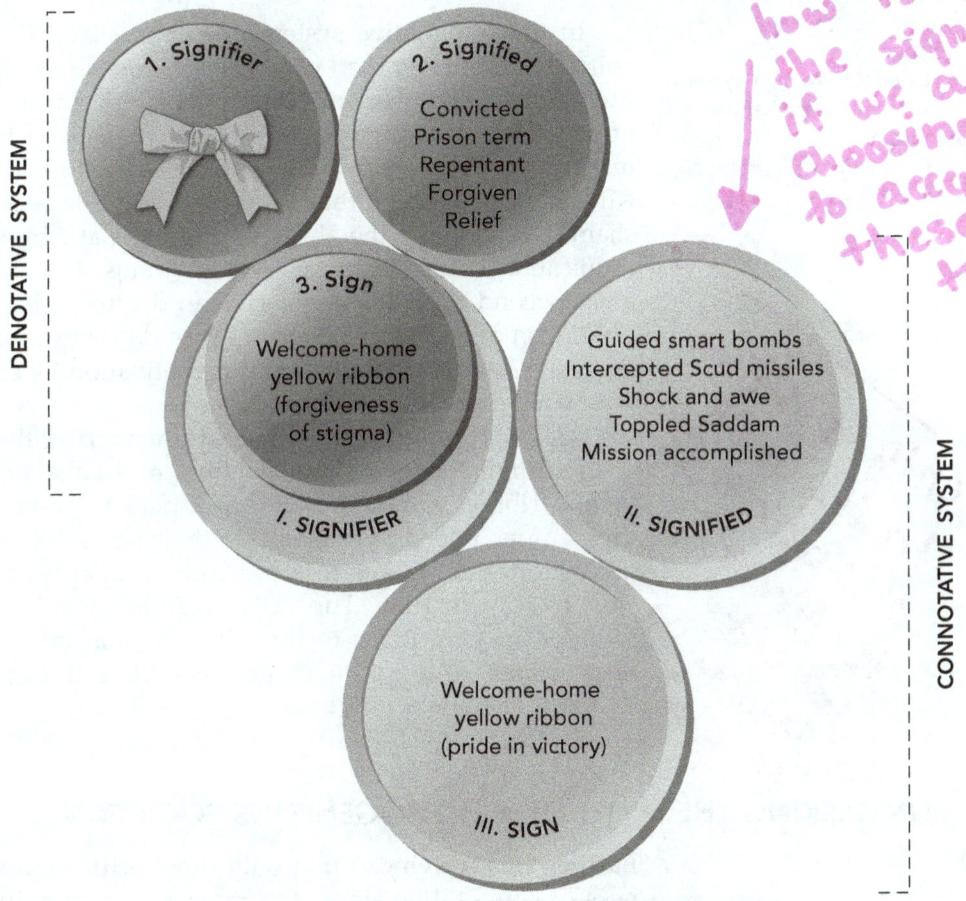

FIGURE 26–1 Connotation as a Second-Order Semiotic System
Based on Barthes, "Myth Today"

at the sight of the oak tree awash in yellow ribbons. The corresponding denotative sign (3) is "forgiveness of a stigma." For those who heard the song on the radio, the yellow-ribbon sign spoke for itself. It was a sign rich in regret and relief.

Current usage takes over the sign of the denotative system and makes it the signifier (I) of a secondary (connotative) system. The "welcome-home" yellow ribbon is paired with the mythic content of a signified (II) that shouts to the world, "Our technology can beat up your technology." But as the symbol of the yellow ribbon is expropriated to support the myth of American nationalism, the sign loses its historical grounding.

As a mere signifier of the *connotative sign system,* the yellow ribbon is no longer rooted in the details of the song. It ceases to stand for three years of hard time in prison, repentance, wrongdoing, or forgiveness that gains meaning because there is so much to be forgiven. Now in the service of the mythic semiotic system, the yellow ribbon becomes empty and timeless, a form without substance. But according to Barthes, the meaning of the original denotative sign is not completely lost:

> The essential point in all this is that the form does not suppress the meaning, it only impoverishes it, it puts it at a distance. . . . One believes that the meaning is going to die, but it is a death with reprieve; the meaning loses its value, but keeps its life, from which . . . the myth will draw its nourishment.[10]

Connotative sign system
A mythic sign that has lost its historical referent; form without substance.

In the connotative system, the generalized image of a yellow ribbon is now paired with the signified content of victory in the Iraqi wars as seen on television. But since the signifier can't call up a historical or cultural past, the mythic sign (III) of which it is a part carries the "crust of falsity."[11] For example, there was no sense of American culpability in supplying arms to Saddam Hussein until he invaded Kuwait, no confession that a post-war plan for peace hadn't been prepared, and no shame for allowing the abuse of prisoners at Abu Ghraib. And since mythic communication is unable to imagine anything alien, novel, or other, the sign sweeps away second thoughts about civilian deaths in Baghdad. The transformed yellow ribbon is now a lofty sign that allows no room for nagging doubts that love of oil may have been our country's prime motivation for championing the United Nations' "humanitarian" intervention.

As a semiologist who relished uncovering the ideological subtext in apparently straightforward signs, Barthes might also note that the support-our-troops yellow ribbon is not merely an appeal to write encouraging letters, pray for their safety, and praise them for their service when they come home. In effect, the exhortation makes it unpatriotic to openly criticize George W. Bush's decision to invade Iraq. The juxtaposition of yellow ribbons with Bush-Cheney bumper stickers prior to the 2004 election, as well as the conservative stance of websites selling the magnets, makes it clear that these are not neutral denotative signs.

UNMASKING THE MYTH OF A HOMOGENEOUS SOCIETY

Barthes was convinced that only those with semiotic savvy can spot the hollowness of connotative signs. For most Americans, the yellow ribbon will continue to elicit an unreflective "we're number one" feeling of national pride. Of course, it goes without saying that people will love their country. But that's precisely the problem with mythic signs. They *go without saying.* They don't explain, they don't defend, and they certainly don't raise questions. So it's up to the semiologist to expose or deconstruct the mythic system.

Deconstruction
The process of unmasking contradictions within a text; debunking.

Throughout his life, Roland Barthes deciphered and labeled the *ideologies* foisted upon naïve consumers of images. Although the starting-point signifiers varied, Barthes concluded that society's connotative spin always ends up the same. *Mythic signs reinforce the dominant values of their culture.* For example, the wrestling match we examined earlier seems at first glance to be no more than a harmless Saturday night diversion. Under Barthes' watchful eye, however, it was the site of dangerous mythmaking. He explained that the honorable wrestler's eventual triumph over the rule-breaking villain signifies a make-believe ideology of pure "justice." The "good guys win" simplicity of the spectacle provides false comfort for an audience that lives in a world of dubious morality and inherent inequality.

Ideology
Knowledge presented as common sense or natural, especially when its social construction is ignored or suppressed.

According to Barthes, ideological signs enlist support for the status quo by transforming history into nature—pretending that current conditions are the natural order of things. As with the ribbons and the wrestling match, everything that is personal, conditional, cultural, and temporal disappears. We are left with

a sign that makes the world seem inevitable and eternal. Barthes' analysis calls to mind the final words of the "Gloria Patri," a choral response that many Christians sing in worship:

> As it was in the beginning,
> Is now and ever shall be,
> World without end. Amen. Amen.

For believers, singing these words about anything or anyone but God would be unthinkable. Barthes wouldn't grant even that exception. All his semiotic efforts were directed at unmasking what he considered the heresy of those who controlled the images of society—the naturalizing of history.

THE SEMIOTICS OF MASS COMMUNICATION: "I'D LIKE TO BE LIKE MIKE"

Like wrestlers and ribbons, most semiotic signs gain cultural prominence when broadcast through the electronic and print media. Because signs—as well as issues of power and dominance—are integral to mass communication, Barthes' semiotic analysis has become a seminal media theory. As Kyong Kim, author of a book on semiotics, concludes:

> Information delivered by mass media is no longer information. It is a commodity saturated by fantasized themes. Mass audiences are nothing more than consumers of such commodities. One should not forget that, unlike nature, the media's reality is always political. The mass signification arising in response to signs pouring from the mass media is not a natural process. Rather it is an artificial effect calculated and induced by the mass media to achieve something else.[12]

The advertisements that make commercial television so profitable also create layers of connotation that reaffirm the status quo. During the 1998 NBA playoffs, one of the most frequently aired spots featured Chicago Bulls' superstar Michael Jordan slam-dunking the basketball over a variety of helpless defenders. He then gulps down Gatorade while a host of celebrity and everyday admirers croon his praises. The most memorable of these adoring fans is a preschool African American boy, who stares up in awe at the towering Jordan. "Sometimes I dream," we hear him sing, "that he is me." He *really* wants to be like Mike.

Obviously, the commercial is designed to sell Gatorade by linking it to the virtually unlimited achievement of basketball's greatest player. To partake of this liquid is to reach for the stars. In that sense, the little boy, rather than MJ himself, becomes the spot's crucial sign. Within this denotative system, the youngster's rapt gaze is the signifier, and his dream of becoming a famous athlete is the signified. The resultant denotative sign—a look of yearning—has the potential to move cartons of Gatorade off the shelf. But as the signifier of a secondary connotative system, it has greater cultural impact.

At the connotative level, the original "look of yearning" suggests a new second-order signified—a more general kind of dreaming about one's future in which the ad's audience is invited to participate. Viewers are encouraged to wish for careers and goals that are virtually unattainable, even in the best of circumstances. The CEO of Microsoft, the conductor of the New York Philharmonic, Hollywood's greatest star, the president of the United States, and the world's leading AIDS researcher constitute the lofty heights surveyed by the gaze that the connotative shift implies.

With its attractive visuals, uplifting soundtrack, and good-natured humor, the commercial functions as a glorification of *unfulfilled desire*, the very essence of its second-order sign. This is America, after all, so think big, aim high, and don't be satisfied with anything but the top. Do what it takes—and purchase what is required—to be the very best. Ideologically speaking, it is this kind of naturalized longing that enslaves the average citizen and fuels the capitalist system. Although the commercial evokes a warm, fuzzy reaction from the viewer, it surreptitiously enforces our fundamental cultural myths about unlimited possibilities for success, myths that—according to Barthes—maintain the dominance of those who hold the reins of commerce and power.

Furthermore, Barthes would no doubt seek to expose the semiotic sleight of hand that subtly drains the second-order connotative system of the historical reality implicit in the original sign. At this denotative level, the African American boy's fixation with MJ is necessarily embedded in a long history of racial injustice and economic hardship. Michael Jordan's accomplishments, as well as the dream of his pint-sized fan, exist in a world in which African Americans must strive particularly hard to succeed. As the documentary *Hoop Dreams* brilliantly portrays, the desire-filled faces of the kids who populate the rough basketball courts of urban America also reflect the poverty, substance abuse, shattered families, and harsh, big-city surroundings that constantly threaten to engulf them. Nonetheless, the yearning connoted by the second-order system generated by the commercial is utterly stripped of this rather grim social reality. The boy, his life, and his dream are deftly co-opted by the system. Or so Barthes would argue.

Katherine, a student who read the semiotic analysis above, was inspired to look for another connotative sign system involving Michael Jordan and his admirers.

> Michael Jordan played most of his games (especially his slam dunks) with his mouth hanging wide and his tongue wagging. This came to signify talent, expectation of greatness, and pride. Jordan wannabes across the country picked up this little quirk. For them, keeping their mouth open signifies Michael Jordan and, therefore, being cool, talented, and better than everyone else. The image of superiority, however, is not derived from any comparable history of success or talent of their own; it's based on myth.

She could have added that since his retirement from the Bulls in 1999, some less talented NBA players have adopted the Jordanesque tongue wag to signal great skill when sinking even a routine shot.

SEMIOTICS GOES TO THE MOVIES

More than 100 years ago, when Ferdinand de Saussure was describing a *sign* as the combination of the *signifier* and *signified*, American philosopher Charles Sanders Peirce (pronounced "purse") was independently developing his own model of how signs work. Similar to Barthes, but unlike Saussure whose concern was with spoken and written words, Peirce included nonverbal signs in his semiotic theorizing right from the start. He classified signs by type based on their relationship to what they represent.

Symbolic signs bear no resemblance to the objects to which they refer. The association is arbitrary and must be learned within the culture as a matter of convention. Examples: almost all words; mathematical symbols; the meaning of a red light on a traffic signal; a yellow ribbon.

Iconic signs have a perceived resemblance with the objects they portray. They look, sound, taste, smell, or feel similar to their referents. Examples: cartoon art; metaphors; onomatopoeic words like *slush* or *ring;* shadows; a wrestler's ignoble body.

Indexical signs are directly connected with their referents spatially, temporally, or by cause and effect. Like an index finger, they point to the object, action, or idea to which they refer. Examples: smoke as a sign of fire; fever as a sign of illness; a wind sock as a sign of the direction and speed of the wind; a wrinkled brow as a sign of confusion.

Cinesemiotics, a branch of semiotics that informs filmmaking, draws upon Peirce's distinctions among signs.[13] Symbolic signs are usually quite obvious—religious films that use the sign of the cross; courtroom dramas that show the scales of justice; adventure thrillers that quickly train audiences to associate a particular musical score with impending disaster. (Zombie movies, anyone?)

Directors known for realism draw upon signs that index, but film them sparingly. They foreground natural scenes and actions rather than scripted images. Their aim is for the film to reveal the world as it is rather than for what it signifies. They believe that indexical connections should be captured rather than created or contrived. That way the movie evokes reality instead of an imaginary world. The film classic *Bicycle Thieves* exemplifies the use of indexical signs.

Expressionistic directors use iconic signs to create a fantasy world of their own choosing. When artfully done, the choices they make present an interpretation of life that's difficult for viewers to resist. The film *Avatar* did this well. Not many viewers left the theater convinced that the need for minerals justified displacing or dispatching human beings.

CRITIQUE: DO MYTHIC SIGNS ALWAYS REAFFIRM THE STATUS QUO?

Roland Barthes' semiotics fulfills five of the criteria of a good interpretive theory (see Chapter 3) exceedingly well. His qualitative analyses of middle-class values and practices are fascinating and well-written. As readers of his essays, we chuckle with new understanding at how consumers of mediated images are taken in, and only belatedly realize that Barthes was describing us. More than most interpretive scholars, Barthes intended that this new realization would inoculate us against being sucked into thinking that life should not, and could not, be altered. He wanted to change the world.

When it comes to the good-theory standard of a community of agreement, however, semiotics doesn't quite deliver. Barthes spoke and wrote for wide audiences, so he can't be accused of presenting his ideas only to true believers. But are connotative systems always ideological, and do they inevitably uphold the values of the dominant class? Many who study the theory are dubious. For them, Barthes' monolithic Marxist approach to mythmaking borders on being a conspiracy theory. These critics are unwilling to accept the idea that all representation is a capitalistic plot, or that familiar visual signs can't be used to promote resistance to dominant cultural values.

Perhaps there are significant semiotic systems that suggest divergent perspectives or support alternative voices. University of Pennsylvania political scientist Anne Norton expands Barthes' semiotic approach to account for other possibilities. For example, she argues that Madonna's MTV persona signifies an autonomous, independent sexuality that inspires young girls to control—rather than be controlled by—their environment.[14] In the same vein, UCLA media scholar Douglas Kellner suggests that Madonna's provocative outfits and unabashed eroticism may seem at first glance to reinforce traditionally patriarchal views of women, but her onstage character refigures her body as "the means to her wealth" and recasts her sexuality as "a form of feminine power."[15]

Or consider Lauren's faithful application of Barthes' theory to her own self-presentation. Does the semiotic shift she describes below reinforce the dominant values of our society?

> My senior year in high school, I thought classmates with a lanyard hanging out of their pocket were very cool. In this denotative sign system, the signifier was the lanyard itself. To me, it signified that the guy or gal had a set of car keys and rich parents. Or perhaps the lanyard advertised acceptance at a great college or deep attachment to a successful sports team. Any of these things meant the person was popular.
>
> Here at Wheaton I've decided to sport a lanyard from Honey Rock, where I counseled last summer. For me the signifier of the secondary connotative sign system is the cool lanyard of status, which was the sign of the denotative system. The signified is higher self-esteem and popularity. I realize that in this connotative system the sign has lost its history. I don't have a car or a record of great achievement, so I just attach the lanyard to my wallet. But I feel the epitome of cool when I see my shadow with the prestigious loop swinging as I walk from my apartment to campus.

Whether or not we accept Barthes' claim that all connotative signs reinforce dominant values, his semiotic approach to imagery remains a core theoretical perspective for a wide variety of communication scholars, particularly those who emphasize media and culture. For example, cultural studies guru Stuart Hall builds directly on Barthes' analysis of myth to establish his critique of the "hegemonic" effects of mass communication.[16] Hall's innovative analysis, though, deserves a chapter all its own.

QUESTIONS TO SHARPEN YOUR FOCUS

1. What are the *signifier* and *signified* of an engagement ring? Can you think of a way that this sign has already been *stripped of history?*
2. Why did Barthes think it was crucial to *unmask* or *deconstruct* the original *denotation* of a sign?
3. Identify two or more distinct *nonverbal signifiers* from different reality TV shows that have basically the same *signified*—"You're out of here."
4. "It's not over 'til the fat lady sings": what are the *denotative signifier, signified,* and *sign* to which this statement originally referred? When spoken about a baseball game, what *connotative shift* has altered the meaning of the original sign?

A SECOND LOOK

Recommended resource: Roland Barthes, *Mythologies,* Annette Lavers (trans.), Hill and Wang, New York, 1972, especially "The World of Wrestling" and "Myth Today," pp. 15–25, 109–159.

Barthes' structuralism: Annette Lavers, *Roland Barthes: Structuralism and After,* Harvard University, Cambridge, MA, 1982.

Essays on semiotics: Roland Barthes, *The Semiotic Challenge,* Richard Howard (trans.), Hill and Wang, New York, 1988.

Saussure on signs: Ferdinand de Saussure, *A Course in General Linguistics,* McGraw-Hill, New York, 1966.

Introduction to semiotics: Daniel Chandler, *Semiotics: The Basics,* 2nd ed., Routledge, London, 2002.

Intermediate semiotics: Kyong Kim, *Caged in Our Own Signs: A Book About Semiotics,* Ablex, Norwood, NJ, 1996.

Applied semiotics: Wendy Leeds-Hurwitz, *Semiotics and Communication: Signs, Codes, Cultures,* Lawrence Erlbaum, Hillsdale, NJ, 1993.

Yellow ribbon in a second-order semiotic system: Donald Fry and Virginia Fry, "Continuing the Conversation Regarding Myth and Culture: An Alternative Reading of Barthes," *American Journal of Semiotics,* Vol. 6, No. 2/3, 1989, pp. 183–197.

Autobiography: Roland Barthes by Roland Barthes, Richard Howard (trans)., Hill and Wang, New York, 1977.

Barthes' critique of his own theory: Roland Barthes, "Inaugural Lecture, College de France," in *A Barthes Reader,* Susan Sontag (ed.), Hill and Wang, New York, 1982, pp. 457–478.

Barthes' Semiotics is a theory about connotation. To access a theory on denotation, click on General Semantics in Archive under Theory Resources at *www.afirstlook.com.*

CHAPTER 27

Objective — Interpretive

Critical tradition

Cultural Studies
of Stuart Hall

Stuart Hall was a Jamaican-born emeritus professor of sociology at the Open University in the U.K. He died in February of 2014. In previous pages you read about the ideas of the Frankfurt School sociologists, Stanley Deetz, and Roland Barthes (see Chapters 4, 21, and 26). Hall joins this group of critical scholars who attack "mainstream" communication research that is empirical, quantitative, and narrowly focused on discovering cause-and-effect relationships. In particular, Hall doubted social scientists' ability to find useful answers to important questions about media influence. He rejected the "body counts" of survey research, which are "consistently translating matters that have to do with signification, meaning, language, and symbolization into crude behavioral indicators." For Hall, the question is not what percentage of Americans now favor Obamacare—a law that provides affordable insurance for 32 million previously uninsured U.S. citizens. Rather, the critical issue is how the media swayed public opinion after the law passed, so that only 42 percent of the nation favored the law just before the Fall 2013 website registration fiasco put the program in jeopardy.[1]

CULTURAL STUDIES VERSUS MEDIA STUDIES: AN IDEOLOGICAL DIFFERENCE

Hall believed the mass media maintain the dominance of those already in positions of power. Broadcast and print outlets serve the Warren Buffetts, Michael Bloombergs, and Bill Gateses of this world. Conversely, the media exploit the poor and powerless. Hall charged that the field of communication continues to be "stubbornly sociologically innocent." He was "deeply suspicious of and hostile to empirical work that has no ideas because that simply means that it does not know the ideas it has."[2] Noncritical researchers represent their work as pure science with no presuppositions, but every media theory by its very nature has ideological content. Hall defined *ideologies* as "the mental frameworks—the languages, the concepts, categories, imagery of thought, and the representation—which different classes and social groups deploy in order to make sense of, define, figure out and render intelligible the way society works."[3] Most of us are unaware of our ideologies and the tremendous impact they can have on our lives.

Ideology
The mental frameworks different classes and social groups deploy in order to make sense of the way society works.

As for mainstream mass communication research in the United States, Hall believed that it serves the myth of *democratic pluralism*—the pretense that society is held together by common norms, including equal opportunity, respect for diversity, one person–one vote, individual rights, and rule of law. The usual finding that media messages have little effect celebrates the political claim that democracy works. Such research claims that the American dream has been empirically verified, and science beckons developing countries to become "fully paid-up members of the consensus club."

Democratic pluralism
The myth that society is held together by common norms such as equal opportunity, respect for diversity, one person–one vote, individual rights, and rule of law.

Hall believed that typical research on individual voting behavior, brand loyalty, or response to dramatic violence fails to uncover the struggle for power that the media mask. He thought it was a mistake to treat communication as a separate academic discipline (a view that may or may not endear him to your instructor). Academic isolation tends to separate messages from the culture they inhabit:

> All the repetition and incantation of the sanitized term *information,* with its cleansing cybernetic properties, cannot wash away or obliterate the fundamentally dirty, semiotic, semantic, discursive character of the media in their cultural dimensions.[4]

Therefore, Hall referred to his work as *cultural studies* rather than *media studies,* and in the 1970s he directed the Center for Contemporary Cultural Studies (CCCS) at the University of Birmingham in the U.K. Under Hall, the staff and graduate students at CCCS sought to articulate their perceptions of the cultural struggle between the haves and the have-nots. Hall used the term *articulate* in the dual sense of *speaking out* on oppression and *linking* that subjugation with the communication media because they provide the terrain where meaning is shaped. He said he didn't seek to be a "ventriloquist" for the masses, but he did desire to "win some space" where their voices can be heard.[5] The effort to jar people loose from their entrenched power positions often requires harsh words, but a "cozy chat among consenting scholars" won't dissolve the ideology that is the glue binding together most communication study.

Articulate
The process of speaking out on oppression and linking that subjugation with media representations; the work of cultural studies.

Since one of Hall's stated aims was to unmask the power imbalances within society, he said the cultural studies approach is valid if it "deconstructs" the current structure of a media research establishment that fails to deal with ideology. Just as Deetz wants to give a meaningful voice to stakeholders affected by corporate decisions (see Chapter 21), Hall wanted to liberate people from an unknowing acquiescence to the dominant ideology of the culture. Obviously, *critical theory* and *cultural studies* are close relatives. However, Hall placed less emphasis on rationality and more emphasis on resistance. As far as he was concerned, the truth of cultural studies is established by its ability to raise our consciousness of the media's role in preserving the status quo.

Cultural studies
A neo-Marxist critique that sets forth the position that mass media manufacture consent for dominant ideologies.

Hall was suspicious of any cultural analysis that ignores power relationships. That's because he believed the purpose of theory and research is to empower people who live on the margins of society, people who have little say in the direction of their lives and who are scrambling to survive. He took the epitaph on Karl Marx' tombstone as a mission statement for cultural studies: "The philosophers have only *interpreted* the world in various ways; the point, however is to *change* it."

HEGEMONY: MARXISM WITHOUT GUARANTEES

Stuart Hall owed an intellectual debt to Karl Marx. Of course, for many students in the West, the word *Marxist* conjures up images of failed Communist states, repressive dictators, and the Tiananmen Square massacre. Marxism, however, is at root a theory of economics and power. At the risk of oversimplifying, the Marxist golden rule suggests that *he who has the gold, rules.* Because workers lack capital or the means of production, they must sell their labor to live. Therefore, in a capitalistic society, people who own the means of production gain more wealth by extracting labor from workers, who get no extra benefit from the wealth created by their work. So the rich get richer and the poor get poorer. Great wealth comes to the privileged few who did little to create it. According to Marx, as the gap between the managerial class and the working class grows ever larger, desperate workers will overthrow the owners and create a classless society.

Although Hall was strongly influenced by Marxist thought, he didn't subscribe to the hard-line brand of *economic determinism* that sees all economic, political, and social relationships as ultimately based on money. He thought that would be an oversimplification. As a Jamaican person of color who immigrated to England as a young adult, Hall found that his physical appearance was often as important as his economic class in the way people reacted to him. Nor was he convinced that the masses will inevitably revolt against those who control the means of production in a capitalistic society. Instead, he adopted a Marxism without guarantees. He realized that his theory was not pure, but he preferred to be "right but not rigorous" than "rigorous but wrong."[6]

Economic determinism
The belief that human behavior and relationships are ultimately caused by differences in financial resources and the disparity in power that those gaps create.

Hall drew upon Italian political theorist Antonio Gramsci's concept of *hegemony* to explain why the revolution Marx predicted hasn't occurred in any industrial society.[7] On the international scene, *hegemony* usually refers to the preponderant influence or domination of one nation over another. The word is little used by Americans, perhaps because it describes how many countries see the United States. In a specific cultural context, Hall employed the term to describe the subtle sway of society's *haves* over its *have-nots.* He emphasized that media hegemony is not a conscious plot, it's not overtly coercive, and its effects are not total. The broadcast and print media present a variety of ideas, but then they tend to prop up the status quo by privileging the already-accepted interpretation of reality. The result is that the role of mass media turns out to be *production of consent* rather than a *reflection of consensus* that already exists.

Hegemony
The subtle sway of society's haves over its have-nots.

Recall that Stan Deetz uses the term *consent* to describe how workers unwittingly accomplish the desires of management in the faulty attempt to fulfill their own interests. They are complicit in their own victimization (see Chapter 21). In the same way, Hall believed that the consent-making function of the mass media is to convince readers and viewers that they share the same interests as those who hold the reins of power. Because the media's hegemonic influence has been relatively successful, it's played an important role in maintaining worker unrest at the level of moaning and groaning rather than escalating into revolutionary fervor.

MAKING MEANING THROUGH DISCOURSE

In his book *Representation,* Hall stated that the primary function of discourse is to *make meaning.* Many students of communication would agree that words and other signs contain no intrinsic meaning. A catchy way of stating this reality is "Words don't mean; people mean." But Hall asked us to push further and ask, *Where do people get their meanings?* After all, humans don't come equipped with ready-made meanings, either. Hall's answer was that they learn what signs mean through discourse—through communication and culture.

> Primarily, culture is concerned with the production and exchange of meanings—"the giving and taking of meaning"—between the members of a society or group. To say that two people belong to the same culture is to say that they interpret the world in roughly the same ways and can express themselves, their thoughts and feelings about the world in ways that will be understood by each other.[8]

To illustrate that meaning comes through discourse, Hall asked his readers how they know that a red light means *stop* and a green light means *go*. The answer is that someone, many years ago, told them so. The process is the same when we consider signs such as a picture of a cigarette covered by a circle slash, the golden arches, or the word *terrorist*. But it is not enough to simply recognize that meaning is created in discourse. We must also examine the *sources* of that discourse, especially the originators or "speakers" of it.

Discourse
Frameworks of interpretation.

Hall was struck by French philosopher Michel Foucault's extensive study of mental illness, sexuality, and criminality in different historical eras. Foucault concentrated on what people were saying, what people were *not* saying, and *who* got to say it. As you might suspect, he discovered that throughout history, not everyone in society had an equal voice or power. That's certainly true in America today. Undoubtedly, CNN founder Ted Turner has more discursive power than I have. But, due to the fact that I'm an author of a college textbook, I'm aware that I have more power to frame meaning than do many of the students who read it.

In terms of mental illness, Foucault found that the definition of what constitutes insanity and what to do about it have changed dramatically over time.[9] People with power drew arbitrary lines between the normal and the abnormal, and these distinctions became *discursive formations* that had real, physical effects on those deemed to belong to each group.[10] Over time, these unquestioned and seemingly natural ways of interpreting the world became ideologies, which then perpetuated themselves through further discourse. The right to make meaning can literally be the power to make others crazy.

Discursive formation
The process by which unquestioned and seemingly natural ways of interpreting the world become ideologies.

CORPORATE CONTROL OF MASS COMMUNICATION

Hall worked to move the study of communication away from the compartmentalized areas reflected in the organization of this text: relationship development, influence, media effects, and so on. He believed we should be studying the unifying *atmosphere* in which they all occur and from which they emanate—human culture. Consistent with Marxist theory, he also insisted that communication scholarship should examine power relations and social structures. For Hall, stripping the study of communication away from the cultural context in which it is found and ignoring the realities of unequal power distribution in society have weakened our field and made it less theoretically relevant.

Scholars who follow Hall's lead wish to place the academic spotlight directly on the ways media representations of culture reproduce social inequalities and keep the average person more or less powerless to do anything but operate within a corporatized, commodified world. At least within the United States, the vast majority of information we receive is produced and distributed by corporations. If your family-room television is tuned to CNN, and the table beneath it holds a copy of *Sports Illustrated (SI)*, your home is a virtual advertisement for a

"What about business—which branch is that?"

media conglomerate. Time Warner owns *SI*, CNN, and most likely the cable company that brings the signal to your house. And if you switch channels to HBO to watch a flick produced by the largest Hollywood studio, you'll get a double dose of meanings produced and sponsored by Time Warner.

As long as subscription rates don't go up, what difference does monopoly ownership make? Hall would answer that corporate control of such influential information sources prevents many stories from being told. Consider the plight of the vast majority of the people in Africa. Except for your knowledge of the scourge of HIV/AIDS across the continent and news of pirates hijacking ships off the coast of Somalia, that may be hard for you to do. For example, there's almost no reporting of decades of genocide in Sudan. It's not the subject of a television drama and it rarely makes the evening news. On the few occasions when the atrocities are mentioned, they are paired with the issue of who will control the country's oil reserves. That linkage squares with Hall's belief that news comes with a spin reflecting the interests of Western multinational corporations. A growing economy and rising stock prices are good news. A labor strike for higher wages is bad news. The ultimate issue for cultural studies is not *what* information is presented but *whose* information it is.

CULTURAL FACTORS THAT AFFECT THE SELECTION OF NEWS

Hall saw corporate clout as only one reason broadcast and print journalism support the *status quo*. Consistent with his brand of Marxism without guarantees, he believed a number of cultural factors also influence the selection of news that furthers the interests of those who already have money and power. While Hall was articulating his theory at CCCS in Great Britain, an extensive study of national news organizations in the United States gave credence to his cultural studies approach.

Over an eight-year period, Herbert Gans of Northwestern University's Medill School of Journalism conducted a content analysis of newscasts at CBS and NBC along with the coverage of two news magazines—*Newsweek* and *Time.* He spent additional months observing and talking with reporters and editors in the newsrooms of these organization.[11] Gans discovered multiple values, procedures, and publishing realities that ensure their stories favor people who already have power, fame, and fortune. These same factors help explain why media consumers saw and heard mostly negative news about Obamacare after it became law.

Ethnocentrism. Like reporters in other nations, American journalists value their own country over others. They don't want the United States to look bad. So even though infant mortality in America is higher than in 33 other countries,[12] claims that Americans receive the best medical care are seldom challenged. The exorbitant cost of health care in the United States isn't ignored, but it's often framed as the price of getting expert medical attention, a benefit assumed not to be available in the managed care systems of Canada, England, or Russia. As a result, the need for health care reform is downplayed.

Source of news. The bulk of broadcast and print news comes from those who already have power. Government officials, corporate CEOs, trade associations, and Washington think tanks issue frequent press releases and hold news conferences. Given the time pressure of deadlines and management's insistence on cutting costs, a reporter is more likely to draw upon these resources than go into the field to discover the plight or opinion of a "nobody." Powerful and well-heeled business, medical, and political pressure groups have lobbied against Obamacare, but those who can't get, or can't afford, medical insurance have less chance to get their story across to reporters on a regular basis.

Objectivity. Most journalists have a strong commitment to report the news without bias—objective reporting of facts without taking sides. The desire to be fair is reinforced by editors and lawyers who fear the flak that comes from groups who perceive media bias. This effort to be impartial, however, often leads to "on the one hand . . . on the other" type reporting. That leaves the impression that the truth value of all ideas is equal. One argument floated by opponents of Obamacare is the claim that even before the law went into effect, more doctors were refusing to accept new Medicare patients. Therefore, the reform won't work. Yet the Department of Health and Human Services reports a four-year trend showing a 35 percent increase in physicians accepting Medicare.[13] A detached, balanced approach suggests that both claims have equal validity, so there's no impetus for either camp to abandon the status quo.

Individualism. Americans value individual effort. Part of the American myth is the "rugged individual" who is a "self-made" man or woman. News stories are usually framed around a single person. *Time* magazine regularly features a single face on its weekly cover. With the exception of major criminals and their victims, almost all people covered in the news are powerful, wealthy people. (How many people living in poverty can you name?) Doctors who discover new diseases or invent new medical procedures are heroes. None of these models are depicted as relying on the government for help—even if they received it in the form of tax breaks or grants. It's therefore not surprising that the news reported would run counter to the idea of the rich giving up some of their wealth to fund medical services for the poor. The idea that the government would violate our "God-given freedom" by requiring us to do so comes across as even more outrageous.

Democratic process. Gans found that reporters are committed to democracy. They believe that Americans will more often elect better representatives if they honor the "public's right to know" and reveal the conflict and corruptions most people don't see. But journalists frame every election or dispute in terms of who won and who lost rather than on the basis of the sometimes complex issues. Even the label "Obamacare" was coined by opponents of the original "Affordable Care Act" who wanted to personalize the fight. When the press latched onto the term, the issue ceased to be expanding health care versus saving money. It was treated as President Obama versus his many critics, a frame that locked people into fixed positions.

In post-recession Great Britain, Hall believed that a whole list of changes hurting the working poor, people of color, and immigrants have been furthered by the way these people are represented (or not represented) through the media. These negative outcomes include massive layoffs; wage freezes; pension cuts; support for the vulnerable whittled away; college students building lifelong debt; the closing of libraries, parks, and museums; and a distinct decline in the quality of life for all but the wealthy. The list looks quite familiar on this side of the Atlantic as well.[14]

EXTREME MAKEOVER: THE IDEOLOGICAL WORK OF REALITY TV

Not all of the media's ideological work is accomplished through the presentation of news. Luke Winslow, a business communication lecturer at the University of Texas at Austin, claims that the representation of ordinary people on reality TV "offers its viewer more explicit 'guidelines for living' than other television genres."[15] Specifically, he analyzes *Extreme Makeover: Home Edition* to show how it reinforces the myth of the American Dream.

From 2003 to 2012, the Sunday-night show featured the fairytale story of a down-and-out family living in a decrepit house and then having it transformed into a dream home in seven days, at no cost to them.[16] But as Winslow notes, the weekly feel-good program didn't "become ABC's top-rated series and the winner of back-to-back Emmy awards because it is concerned with concrete and drywall."[17] The real focus is on a deserving family that has suffered misfortune and on their restoration to a perfect life.

Although the show spotlights a different family each week, they have much in common. The producers intentionally sought out all-American families whose moral character, love for each other, and demonstrated care for others make it clear that they are worthy recipients. In the first segment of the show we meet the family and hear their story. Through his questions and comments, host Ty Pennington assures his team that these are good folks who play by the rules. In the second segment we learn that, through no fault of their own, the family has fallen on hard times made much worse by the dump they live in. Whether victims of heinous crime, survivors of a natural disaster, or those who suffer from medical problems that insurance companies refuse to cover, they've all hit rock bottom. The combination of their moral goodness and tragic circumstances convinces Ty and his viewers that these are *deserving people*—truly worthy of being chosen to get an extreme makeover or a brand new home.

The rest of the show chronicles the ingenuity and commitment of the designers, contractors, and volunteers as they frantically race against time. We learn to appreciate ABC and other major corporations that donate materials and services to make this extreme makeover possible. Meanwhile, the family has been sent away for an all-expenses-paid week of vacation. At the end of the show they are brought back in a stretch limousine to see their new home, but their view is intentionally blocked by a bus. Then Ty and the whole crew yell to the driver, "Move that bus!" When they can see their new home, family members are blown away by the total transformation. Amid tears of joy they tell Ty that it's unbelievable, miraculous, an answer to prayer. As for television viewers, their belief that good things happen to good people is reinforced and reaffirmed. All's right with the world.[18]

Perhaps you've already anticipated Winslow's cultural critique of the show. He believes the real work done in *Extreme Makeover* is on the audience rather than the house. Each episode is a mini morality play that suggests wealth goes only to those who deserve it. These good people deserved a decent house and they got it. The system works. Winslow cites Stuart Hall when he summarizes the message that's enacted every week:

> The result is a reduced and simplified ideology regarding the connection between morality and economics: who should be poor and who should not, and, more importantly, frameworks of thinking about how the social world works, what the viewers' place is in it, and what they ought to do. We not only learn who deserves to be rich, and who deserves to be poor, but also how each should be treated.[19]

Winslow's critique is typical of scholarship done under the banner of Hall's cultural studies. As he explains, "Ultimately, a primary goal of ideological scholarship is to bring comfort to the afflicted and [to] afflict the comfortable by questioning taken-for-granted assumptions, giving voice to the voiceless, and bringing in those on the margins of society."[20]

Although many intellectuals dismiss the study of popular culture as frivolous, Hall sees it as a key site where the struggle for power between the haves and the have-nots takes place. "That's why 'popular culture' matters," he writes. "Otherwise, to tell you the truth, I don't give a damn about it."[21]

AN OBSTINATE AUDIENCE

The fact that the media present a preferred interpretation of human events is no reason to assume that the audience will correctly "take in" the offered ideology. Hall held out the possibility that the powerless may be obstinate, resist the dominant ideology, and translate the message in a way that's more congenial to their own interests. He outlined three decoding options:

1. *Operating inside the dominant code.* The media produce the message; the masses consume it. The *audience reading* coincides with the *preferred reading.*
2. *Applying a negotiable code.* The audience assimilates the leading ideology in general but opposes its application in specific cases.
3. *Substituting an oppositional code.* The audience sees through the establishment bias in the media presentation and mounts an organized effort to demythologize the news.

With all the channels of mass communication in the unwitting service of the dominant ideology, Hall had trouble believing that the powerless can change the system. He called this his "pessimism of the intellect."[22] Yet he was determined to do everything he could to expose and alter the media's structuring of reality. He referred to this as his "optimism of the will." Hall had genuine respect for the ability of people to resist the dominant code. He didn't regard the masses as cultural dupes who are easily manipulated by those who control the media, but he was unable to predict when and where resistance will spring up.

Of all the programs on American television, the satires of Jon Stewart on *The Daily Show* and Stephen Colbert on *The Colbert Report* seem to offer the most effective challenge to the dominant political ideology. Both programs mock the pretentious statements of people in power and ridicule the positions of television commentators. Stewart's and Colbert's humor are highly popular, so network heads and advertisers don't have the option of canceling or censoring their shows. And surprisingly, not only is *The Daily Show* rated, "the most trusted source for political news on television," but viewers who only watch Stewart have proved to be better informed on domestic and international affairs than viewers who only get their news from Fox News, CNN, or MSNBC.[23]

Despite Stewart's and Colbert's withering parodies of those in power, two University of Illinois professors suggest that both shows may actually support the hegemony their stars skewer with their wit. James Anderson (Urbana–Champaign campus) and Amie Kincaid (Springfield campus) point out the paradox of satire used by Stewart and Colbert.[24] In order to lampoon an idea or practice, the satirists have to make sure the audience knows what they're knocking. Their very exposure and reiteration of the dominant ideology may make it more acceptable. And some in the audience may miss the satire and think Stewart or Colbert are advocating the position they voice. At the very least, talking about an idea or practice increases the chance that viewers will recall it in the future.

Anderson and Kincaid also point out that after getting their laughs, both comedians fail to offer a better way of thinking or acting. Without naming a viable alternative, the dominant ideology will have no rival and seem to be natural. All of this suggests that hegemony is never total, but effective resistance is never easy.

Hall cited one small victory by activists in the organized struggle to establish that black is beautiful. By insisting on the term *black* rather than *Negro* or *colored*, people of African heritage began to give dignity in the 1970s to what was once a racial slur. Jesse Jackson's call for an African American identity is a continuing effort to control the use of symbols. This is not a matter of "mere" semantics, as some would charge. Although there is nothing inherently positive or negative in any of these racial designations, the connotative difference is important because the effects are real. The ideological fight is a struggle to capture language. Hall saw those on the margins of society doing semantic battle on a media playing field that will never be quite level. In her cultural studies application log, Sharon depicts a clear winner in the linguistic struggle within the abortion debate:

> The media seems to favor those with "pro-choice" beliefs. I wish copywriters would even the debate by referring to the other side as "pro-life" rather than "anti-abortion." This would be a sign that pro-life groups are seen as reasonable, positive people. Up to this point, they haven't been able to make that label stick in the public arena. The media gives an ideological spin by the use of connotative language.

ETHICAL REFLECTION: WEST'S PROPHETIC PRAGMATISM

Cornel West is a pragmatist philosopher and a professor at Union Theological Seminary. Like well-known American pragmatist John Dewey (see Chapter 17), West regards pragmatism as "a mode of cultural critical action that focuses on the ways and means by which human beings have, do, and can overcome obstacles, dispose predicaments, and settle problematic situations."[25] The moral obstacle West wants to overcome is the institutional oppression of "the disadvantaged, degraded, and dejected" people who struggle on the margins of society.[26] They face racism, sexual discrimination, and economic injustice. West agrees with the analysis of Christian realist Reinhold Niebuhr, who deplored the inhuman treatment of workers in Henry Ford's auto factory.[27] Both men said that these evils exist not just because of ignorance or apathy—they are the result of pervasive human sin.

West is also sympathetic to a Marxist critique of capitalism,[28] but his own brand of pragmatism is deeply rooted in the narratives of the Scriptures:

> I have dubbed it "prophetic" in that it harks back to the Jewish and Christian tradition of prophets who brought urgent and compassionate critique to bear on the evils of their day. The mark of the prophet is to speak the truth in love with courage—come what may.[29]

For example, Hebrew prophets like Amos demanded social justice for the powerless; Jesus' parable of the Good Samaritan reminds believers that they are responsible to help those who are hurting, whoever and wherever they are.[30]

Claire Alexander is the editor of a special edition of *Cultural Studies* exploring "Stuart Hall and Race." She describes attending the "Race Matters" conference at Princeton University held in honor of Cornel West and attended by a who's who of black intellectuals. Following the first panel discussion, the chair invited questions and comments. The first person who came to the microphone simply introduced himself, "Stuart Hall, the Open University." The packed room exploded in applause. When Alexander later mentioned to West that she'd never seen a person get this kind of response just by saying his or her name, he explained: "The thing you have to understand, Claire, is that we all grew up reading Stuart. We wouldn't be here without him. We all stand on his shoulders."[31]

CRITIQUE: YOUR JUDGMENT WILL DEPEND ON YOUR IDEOLOGY

In his early work, Marshall McLuhan was highly critical of television. Hall accused McLuhan of being co-opted by the media establishment in his later years. He characterized McLuhan's final position as one of "lying back and letting the media roll over him; he celebrated the very things he had most bitterly attacked."[32] No one has ever accused Stuart Hall of selling out to the dominant ideology of Western society. Many communication scholars, however, question the wisdom of performing scholarship under an ideological banner.

Do such explicit value commitments inevitably compromise the integrity of research? Former surgeon general C. Everett Koop lamented that pro-choice researchers always conclude that abortion does no psychological harm to the mother, whereas pro-life psychologists invariably discover that abortion leaves long-term emotional scars. In like manner, the findings of the economically conservative American Enterprise Institute in Washington, DC, differ greatly from the conclusions reached at the Center for Contemporary Cultural Studies under the direction of Hall. Ever since Copernicus thought the unthinkable, that the earth is not the center of the universe, truth has prospered by investigating what *is*, separately from what we think it *ought* to be. Hall seemed to blur that distinction.

Although Hall is recognized as a founding figure of cultural studies, there are those who work within this fast-growing field who are critical of his leadership. While appreciating his advocacy for ethnic minorities and the poor, many women decried his relative silence on their plight as equal victims of the hegemony he railed against. Hall belatedly became an advocate for women and acquiesced to their demand for shared power at the Birmingham Center. But his now-famous description of the feminist entry into British cultural studies shows that for him the necessary change was painful and messy: "As the thief in the night, it broke in; interrupted, made an unseemly noise, seized the time, crapped on the table of cultural studies."[33]

The most often heard criticism of Hall's work is that he didn't offer specific remedies for the problems he identified. While it's true that he had no grand action agenda for defusing the media's influence on behalf of the powerful elite, he worked hard to expose racism that's reinforced by press reporting. For example, Hall served as a key member of a commission that issued an influential report in 2000 on the future of a multiethnic Britain. The following excerpt is a sample of Hall's impact on the commission's call for a change in the way ethnic groups are represented in the media.

> A study by the *Guardian* of its own coverage of Islam in a particular period in 1999 found that the adjective "Islamic" was joined with "militants" 16 times, "extremists" 15 times, "fundamentalism" eight times and "terrorism" six times; in the same period the adjective "Christian" was joined, in so far as it appeared at all, to positive words and notions or to neutral ones such as tradition or belief.[34]

Hall's most positive contribution to mass communication study is his constant reminder that it's futile to talk about meaning without considering power at the same time. Cliff Christians, former director of the Institute for Communications Research at the University of Illinois and a leading writer in the field of media ethics, agrees with Hall that the existence of an idealistic communication situation where no power circulates is a myth. Christians is lavish in his praise of Hall's essay "Ideology and Communication Theory," which I've listed as a Second Look resource: "His essay, like the Taj Mahal, is an artistic masterpiece inviting a pilgrimage."[35]

Stuart Hall has attracted tremendous interest and a large following. Samuel Becker, former chair of the communication studies department at the University of Iowa, described himself as a besieged empiricist and noted the irony of Hall's attack. Hall knocked the dominant ideology of communication studies, yet he "may himself be the most dominant or influential figure in communication studies today."[36]

QUESTIONS TO SHARPEN YOUR FOCUS

1. *Hegemony* is not a household word in the United States. How would you explain what the term means to your roommate? Can you think of a metaphor or an analogy that would clarify this critical concept?
2. What is the nature of Hall's complaint about *American media scholarship?*

3. Hall said that the *media encode the dominant ideology of our culture.* If you don't agree with his thesis, what *evidence* could he have mustered that would convince you he's right? What evidence would you provide to counter his argument?
4. In what way is Roland Barthes' *semiotic* perspective (see Chapter 26) similar to Hall's cultural studies? How do they differ?

A SECOND LOOK

Recommended resource: Stuart Hall, "Introduction" and "The Work of Representation," in *Representation: Cultural Representations and Signifying Practices,* Stuart Hall (ed.), Sage, London, 1997, pp. 1–64.

Intellectual biography: Helen Davis, *Understanding Stuart Hall,* Sage, Thousand Oaks, CA, 2004.

Anthology of theory and practice: Rhonda Hammer and Douglas Kellner (eds.), *Media/Cultural Studies,* Peter Lang, New York, NY, 2009.

Hall's critique of the dominant communication paradigm: Stuart Hall, "Ideology and Communication Theory," in *Rethinking Communication Theory: Vol. 1,* Brenda Dervin, Lawrence Grossberg, Barbara O'Keefe, and Ellen Wartella (eds.), Sage, Newbury Park, CA, 1989, pp. 40–52. (See also multiple reactions following.)

Hegemony, ideology, Marxism, and postmodernism: Journal of Communication Inquiry, Vol. 10, No. 2, 1986. The entire issue addresses Stuart Hall's cultural studies.

Marxist interpretations: Samuel Becker, "Marxist Approaches to Media Studies: The British Experience," *Critical Studies in Mass Communication,* Vol. 1, 1984, pp. 66–80.

Race and ethnicity: Cultural Studies, Vol. 23, No. 4, 2009. The entire issue addresses Stuart Hall and race.

Historical perspective: Stuart Hall, "Cultural Studies and Its Theoretical Legacies," in *Cultural Studies,* Lawrence Grossberg, Cary Nelson, and Paula Treichler (eds.), Routledge, New York, 1992, pp. 277–294.

Autobiographical account of work at CCCS: Stuart Hall, "Stuart Hall Interview—2 June 2011," *Cultural Studies,* Vol. 27, 2013, pp. 757–777; available at http://www.tandfonline.com/doi/abs/10.1080/09502386.2013.773674?af=R#.Ui36lMasiSo, accessed September 9, 2013.

Ideology in reality TV: Luke Winslow, "Comforting the Comfortable: *Extreme Makeover: Home Edition's* Ideological Conquest," *Critical Studies in Mass Communication,* Vol. 27, 2010, pp. 267–290.

Appreciative retrospective: Paul Gilroy, Lawrence Grossberg, and Angela McRobbie (eds.), *Without Guarantees: In Honour of Stuart Hall,* Verso, London, 2000.

Critical retrospective: Chris Rojek, *Stuart Hall,* Polity, Cambridge, 2003.

Critique from quantitative perspective: Justin Lewis, "What Counts in Cultural Studies?" *Media, Culture & Society,* Vol. 19, 1997, pp. 83–97.

Critique from qualitative perspective: Patrick Murphy, "Media Cultural Studies' Uncomfortable Embrace of Ethnography," *Journal of Communication Inquiry,* Vol. 23, 1999, pp. 205–221.

To learn more about your book's authors, click on Em Griffin, Andrew Ledbetter, or Glenn Sparks on the Home Page of *www.afirstlook.com.*

Media Effects

In 1940, before the era of television, a team of researchers from Columbia University, headed by Paul Lazarsfeld, descended on Erie County, Ohio, an area that had reflected national voting patterns in every twentieth-century presidential election. By surveying people once a month from June to November, the interviewers sought to determine how the press and radio affected the people's choice for the upcoming presidential election.[1]

Contrary to the then-accepted *magic-bullet* model of direct media influence, the researchers found little evidence that voters were swayed by what they read or heard. Political conversions were rare. The media seemed merely to reinforce the decisions of those who had already made up their minds.

Lazarsfeld attributed the lack of media effect to *selective exposure* (see Chapter 16). Republicans avoided articles and programs that were favorable to President Franklin Roosevelt; Democrats bypassed news stories and features sympathetic to Republican Wendell Willkie. The principle of selective exposure didn't always test out in the laboratory, where people's attention was virtually guaranteed, but in a free marketplace of ideas it accounted for the limited, short-term effects of mass communication.

The Erie County results forced media analysts to recognize that friends and family affect the impact of media messages. They concluded that print and electronic media influence masses of people only through an indirect *two-step flow of communication.* The first stage is the direct transmission of information to a small group of people who stay well informed. In the second stage, those opinion leaders pass on and interpret the messages to others in face-to-face discussion.

The two-step flow theory surfaced at a time of rapid scientific advancement in the fields of medicine and agriculture. The model accurately described the diffusion of innovation among American doctors and farmers in the 1950s, but the present era of saturation television and Internet news has made alterations necessary. The first step of the *revised two-step theory* of media influence is the transmission of information to a mass audience. The second step is validation of the message by people the viewer respects.[2]

By the 1970s, empirical studies on viewer response to television had reestablished belief in a *powerful-effects* model of media influence, and the explanatory links between the two were becoming clear. The possible connection between violence on the screen and subsequent viewer aggression was of particular interest to media theorists, and remains an important research focus today.

In the 1980s and 1990s, theorists continued to study how media content affects behavior, but expanded their focus to include thoughts and feelings. Dolf Zillmann, professor emeritus at the University of Alabama, used his *excitation transfer theory* to highlight the role of physiological arousal when we react to media.[3] According to the theory, emotional reactions like fear, anger, joy, and lust all generate heightened arousal that takes a while to dissipate after media exposure. The leftover excitation can amplify any mood we feel afterward. If a man becomes angry at his wife, the arousal he experiences from watching televised aggression can fuel his anger and lead to domestic violence. But Zillmann says that arousal from an erotic bedroom scene or a protagonist's joyful triumph can cause the same effect.

Excitation transfer can account for violent acts performed immediately after TV viewing. But Stanford psychologist Albert Bandura's *social learning theory* takes the findings a step further and predicts that the use of force modeled on television today may erupt in antisocial behavior years later.[4] Although Bandura's theory can explain imitation in many contexts, most students of his work apply it specifically to the vicarious learning of aggression through television.

Social learning theory postulates three necessary stages in the causal link between television and the actual physical harm we might inflict on another some time in the future. The three-step process is attention, retention, and motivation. Video violence grabs our *attention* because it's simple, distinctive, prevalent, useful, and depicted positively. If you doubt that last quality, remember that television draws in viewers by placing attractive people in front of the camera. There are very few overweight bodies or pimply faces on TV. When the winsome star roughs up a few hoods to rescue the lovely young woman, aggression is given a positive cast.

Without any risk to ourselves, watching media violence can expand our repertoire of behavioral options far beyond what we'd discover on our own through trial-and-error learning. For example, we see a knife fighter holding a switchblade at an inclined angle of 45 degrees and that he jabs up rather than lunging down. This kind of street smarts is mentally filed away as a visual image. But Bandura says *retention* is strongest when we also encode vicarious learning into words: *Hold the pistol with both hands. Don't jerk the trigger; squeeze it. Aim six inches low to compensate for recoil.*

Without sufficient *motivation,* we may never imitate the violence we saw and remember. But years later we may be convinced that we won't go to jail for shooting a prowler lurking in our backyard or that we might gain status by punching out a jerk who is hassling a friend. If so, what we learned earlier and stored in our memory bank is now at our disposal.

Communication scholars are playing catch-up trying to document the effects of the rapid changes brought by new media technology. We need to be patient before a strong consensus forms about some of the effects. A few researchers blame Facebook content for increasing feelings of depression,[5] while others find no such relationship.[6] Still others tout the social network's benefits for keeping us closely connected to friends.[7] Theorists are busy attempting to scope out the conditions that might explain these divergent findings.

CHAPTER 28

Objective — Interpretive

Socio-psychological tradition

Uses and Gratifications

of Elihu Katz

Paul and Alex are college sophomores who have roomed together since freshman year. At the end of their first year, Paul notices that Alex is spending more and more time playing *Call of Duty: Modern Warfare*, an online game in which many players join together in a common mission. During their second year, the gaming gets even more intense. Paul becomes concerned that his roommate's game playing is draining time from his studies and ruining his social life.

Thinking about Alex, Paul remembers what he heard in his media class about the case of Lien Wen-cheng. The 27-year-old Taiwanese man died of exhaustion in 2002 after playing a video game for 32 straight hours.[1] And in 2005 in South Korea, a man died after playing a game for 50 consecutive hours. Authorities said the man had hardly eaten during his game playing and hadn't slept.[2] While Paul knows that these deaths happened in Asian countries where addiction to video games has been a greater problem than in the United States,[3] he wonders if he should try to have a serious talk with Alex about his game playing. He feels especially motivated to talk with Alex after reading about Chris Staniforth, the 20-year-old British man who died in 2011 after playing *Halo* on his Xbox. Staniforth sat for 12 hours straight while playing the game and developed a blood clot in his leg that eventually hit his heart and killed him.[4]

Whether or not you spend time playing video games like Alex does, you do make daily choices to consume different types of media. In the late 1950s, when communication scholar Elihu Katz began his work on uses and gratifications theory (commonly referred to as *uses & grats*), no one was playing video games on campus. But newspapers, magazines, radio, and movies were well established, and 80 percent of American households had a TV. There were plenty of media to choose from.

Katz thought studying all of those media choices was so important that it could save the entire field of communication.[5] He made his argument about saving the field in response to another communication scholar, Bernard Berelson, who had just published an influential essay arguing that the future of communication research was bleak.[6] Berelson based his case on the study of the persuasive power of radio during the 1940 presidential campaign[7]—research described in the introduction to this section. The study showed that media didn't do anything to change people's attitudes. Berelson reasoned that if media weren't persuasive, the field of communication research would simply wither away.

Katz, who is now a professor emeritus of both sociology and communication at The Hebrew University of Jerusalem, introduced a different logic. In order to prevent the disintegration of the field, he suggested that scholars change the question used to generate their research. Instead of asking, "What do media do to people?" Katz flipped the question around to ask, "What do people do with media?"[8] In retrospect, the field of communication was hardly on its deathbed. Berelson's perspective was overly pessimistic and, by focusing only on media effects, it was overly narrow as well. Though Katz' theory didn't "save" the discipline, it was still valuable because it encouraged scholars to think about mass communication in a different way. As it turns out, uses & grats has endured for more than 50 years and still inspires cutting-edge research.

The theory attempts to make sense of the fact that people consume a dizzying array of media messages for all sorts of reasons, and that the effect of a given message is unlikely to be the same for everyone. The driving mechanism of the theory is need gratification. By understanding the particular needs of media consumers, the reasons for media consumption become clear. Particular media effects, or lack of effects, can also be clarified. For example, radio listeners in 1940 may have been so loyal to their political party that they had little need to listen to the opposing party's campaign ads. If they didn't attend to the ads, the ads couldn't have any effect. Let's look more closely at the five key assumptions that underlie uses & grats.

PEOPLE USE MEDIA FOR THEIR OWN PARTICULAR PURPOSES

The theory's fundamental assumption was revolutionary at the time Katz proposed it: *The study of how media affect people must take account of the fact that people deliberately use media for particular purposes.* Prior to this proposal, scholars thought that audiences were passive targets waiting to be hit by a magic bullet (the media message) that would affect everyone in the same way. In uses & grats, audiences are seen as anything but passive. They decide which media they want to use and what effects they want the media to have.

Consider an example: When Game 6 of the 2010 NHL Stanley Cup Finals was on TV, I (Glenn) wanted to watch it in hopes of seeing the Chicago Blackhawks become hockey champions. I wasn't a big fan of the sport, but after talking with Em, a hockey aficionado, I got sucked into the series. When I sat down to watch I was already prepared to celebrate. My wife, Cheri, who would ordinarily choose to watch *anything* instead of hockey, decided that the clacking of hockey sticks was exactly what she needed to prevent her from stumbling upon the depressing CNN videos of oil gushing into the Gulf of Mexico from the exploded BP oil well. So we decided to watch the game together—each for very different reasons and with very different effects. For me, watching the game resulted in happiness as I basked in the Blackhawks' victory. For her, the game provided a boring, but safe, distraction from unpleasant news she wanted to avoid. According to uses & grats, audiences are strong; they play a pivotal role in determining how any influence of media will play out. When Cheri and I each decided to watch that hockey game for different reasons, we behaved in a way that was consistent with the theory.

Fast-forward to 2013 with the Blackhawks again trying to win the Stanley Cup in Game 6 but trailing the Boston Bruins 2 to 1 with just 76 seconds left in the game. When the Hawks scored two goals in 17 seconds to win the championship, I was once again basking in their success. But this time around, Cheri wasn't viewing just to hear the clack of hockey sticks. She had become a fan and her excitement for the Blackhawks matched mine. This illustrates an underlying premise of uses and gratifications theory: reasons to consume media—even the same type of media—can change over time.

In the history of media theory, uses & grats is known for its deliberate shift away from the notion that powerful media messages have uniform effects on large audiences (passive receivers). Instead, the theory emphasizes the personal media choices consumers make to fulfill different purposes at different times. The *uniform-effects model* does not easily account for Paul's and Alex' very different behavior surrounding video games. But uses & grats assumes that the two roommates make deliberate choices that result in different patterns of media use and different effects. The uniform-effects view of media evokes the image of a parent who force-feeds the kids with a prepared formula that's guaranteed to have the same effect on each child. Uses & grats rejects that image and replaces it with one of adults in a cafeteria deciding what to eat based on individual yearnings at particular times. You might compare Alex' obsession with playing video games to someone craving the same food for every meal.

Uniform-effects model
The view that exposure to a media message affects everyone in the audience in the same way; often referred to as the "magic-bullet" or "hypodermic-needle" model of mass communication.

PEOPLE SEEK TO GRATIFY NEEDS

Just as people eat in order to satisfy certain cravings, uses & grats assumes people have needs that they seek to gratify through media use.[9] Note the close connection between the concepts of *media use* and *gratification from media.* The deliberate choices people make in using media are presumably based on the gratifications they seek from those media. Thus, *uses* and *gratifications* are inextricably linked. By taking this position, Katz was swimming against the tide of media theory at the time. In 1974, he wrote an essay with Jay Blumler and Michael Gurevitch, two scholars often considered co-creators of the theory. The essay states:

> In the mass communication process much initiative in linking need gratification and media choice lies with the audience member. This places a strong limitation on theorizing about any form of straight-line effect of media content on attitudes and behavior.[10]

A *straight-line effect of media* is a specific effect on behavior that is predicted from media content alone, with little consideration of the differences in people who consume that content. A theory predicting this sort of effect might guess that *both* Cheri and I would have become excited watching the Blackhawks win the Stanley Cup in 2010. But Katz thought the key to understanding media depended upon which need(s) a person was trying to satisfy when selecting a media message. One reason that hockey game affected Cheri and I differently is that we were watching the game to satisfy different needs.

Straight-line effect of media
A specific effect on behavior that is predicted from media content alone, with little consideration of the differences in people who consume that content.

MEDIA COMPETE FOR YOUR ATTENTION AND TIME

One of Paul's concerns as he watches Alex spend so much time playing video games is that gaming is ruining Alex' social life. From Paul's perspective, the technology that permits Alex to interact with other gamers online is competing with opportunities to interact with peers on campus. The uses & grats approach directly acknowledges the competition. Not only do media compete with each other for your time, they compete with other activities that don't involve media exposure.

While Paul evaluates Alex' situation as unhealthy, uses & grats first attempts to understand exactly what needs motivate Alex' use of video games. Why does he choose to spend his time gaming instead of socializing with Paul and the other guys who live in the dorm? Some of the more recent attempts to understand these sorts of choices might provide an answer. Uses & grats researchers have discovered that some people experience high levels of anxiety when they think about talking face-to-face; they don't enjoy these sorts of interactions or find them rewarding.[11] Meeting in person just doesn't gratify their needs. In contrast, extroverts express a clear preference for one-on-one conversations over spending time with media.[12]

The notion that media compete for attention and time is only an initial step in understanding the choices people eventually make. The more interesting question is *why* some people choose to watch TV while others decide to play a video game or read a book, and still others decide to have coffee with a friend. On any given day, the number of ways we can choose to spend our time is nearly limitless. According to uses & grats, we won't understand the media choices we make unless we first recognize the underlying needs that motivate our behavior. Paul's well-intentioned concern might cause him to overlook the needs Alex has that are gratified by playing video games. Helping Alex get a good grasp of the reasons he plays may be the key to helping him alter his behavior.

MEDIA AFFECT DIFFERENT PEOPLE DIFFERENTLY

One of the core concepts of uses and gratifications theory is that the same media message doesn't necessarily affect everyone the same way. That's because media audiences are made up of people who are not identical to each other. In terms of media effects, the differences matter.

My own studies on the effects of frightening media have confirmed this central tenet of uses & grats. Assuming that Hollywood makes so many scary movies because of the popularity of the genre, journalists often ask me, "Why do people enjoy watching scary movies?" My first response to this question is always the same and echoes the fundamental point of uses & grats: Not everyone *does* enjoy scary movies. Some people systematically avoid them and can suffer for days if they become emotionally upset from what they see in a film.

As it turns out, few people voluntarily expose themselves to scary movies in order to experience fear. Fear is a negative emotion and, in general, people want to avoid it. However, some people are willing to tolerate fear in order to ooh and aah at high-tech special effects they can't see anywhere else. Others are willing to endure fear to experience a sense of mastery over something threatening—much like the effect of riding a roller coaster. Still others might actually enjoy the adrenaline rush that accompanies a scary movie and the intense relief that comes when the film is over.[13] Current research seeks to understand the factors that lead some individuals to shun frightening entertainment and others to seek it out. Media effects scholarship lends strong support to the uses & grats claim that media affect different people differently.

PEOPLE CAN ACCURATELY REPORT THEIR MEDIA USE AND MOTIVATION

If uses & grats was to have any future as a theory, researchers had to find a way to uncover the media that people consumed and the reasons they consumed it. For these purposes, the most obvious way to collect data involved asking people directly and recording their answers. There is now a long tradition in mass communication research that asks people to report the amount of time they devote to different kinds of media. The early research on uses & grats can take a good deal of the credit for starting that practice.[14]

The controversial aspect of this measurement strategy is whether or not people are truly capable of discerning the reasons for their media consumption. It may be easy for us to report the reason why we watch a local weather forecast, but it might be more difficult to know exactly why we're so willing to kill a few hours each day playing a game like *Angry Birds* on our smart phones.

If Paul were to ask Alex why he spends so much time playing video games, Alex might simply say, "Because I like it." Scholars attempting to arrive at the best scientific explanation for Alex' behavior might question that response. Is it possible, for example, that Alex is playing the games to avoid having to talk with others face-to-face? If so, would he necessarily be aware of that motivation? While some scholars have attempted to show that we can trust people's reports of the reasons for their media consumption,[15] this assumption of the theory continues to be debated. Sometimes assumptions turn out to be wrong.

A TYPOLOGY OF USES AND GRATIFICATIONS

What are the reasons people give for their media consumption? For the last 50 years, uses & grats researchers have compiled various lists of the motives people report. These studies are designed to construct a *typology* of the major reasons why people voluntarily expose themselves to different media. A typology is simply a classification scheme that attempts to sort a large number of specific instances into a more manageable set of categories.

One of the most comprehensive typologies of media uses and gratifications was proposed by communication scholar Alan Rubin in 1981.[16] Rubin claims that his typology of eight motivations can account for most explanations people give for why they watch television. Notice that each category describes both a reason for TV *use* as well as a potential *gratification* experienced from that use.

1. **Passing time.** Consider the waiting room at the doctor's office. The primary reason for watching TV is to simply pass the time until you're called in for your appointment.
2. **Companionship.** When sports fans get together to watch the big game, some fans are there primarily for the chance to get together with friends. Watching the game is secondary.
3. **Escape.** Instead of focusing on that anxiety-causing term paper due in two weeks, a college student might just turn on the tube to escape the pressure.
4. **Enjoyment.** Many report that the main reason they watch a TV show is that they find the whole experience enjoyable. This might be the most basic motivation to consume any media.

5. **Social interaction.** TV viewing provides a basis for connecting to others. If I make sure to watch the most recent episode of a series like *Game of Thrones,* I may find that I have more opportunities to start a conversation with someone else who saw the same show.
6. **Relaxation.** After working all day, many people report that they find watching TV to be relaxing. Today, many households have at least one bedroom with a TV set. People sometimes report that watching TV relaxes them so much that they have difficulty falling asleep any other way.
7. **Information.** News junkies report that watching TV is all about keeping up with the latest information of the day. If they don't get to watch TV for several days, they report feeling uncomfortable about the information they know they've missed.
8. **Excitement.** Sometimes media consumers are after an intense sense of excitement. This could be one reason why media violence is a staple of TV entertainment. Conflict and violence generate a sense of excitement that few other dramatic devices can match.

Typology
A classification scheme that attempts to sort a large number of specific instances into a more manageable set of categories.

When you look at Rubin's eight categories, it's easy to see that the examples filed under any one label don't have to be identical. While some people look for violence to gratify their need for excitement, others, like Alex, look for a competitive online game. Still others might seek out a movie with erotic content in order to provide a sense of sexual excitement. Excitement can be subdivided into sexual excitement, competitive excitement, and excitement that arises from a suspenseful story line. But if each of Rubin's eight categories were subdivided into three more, the resulting typology of 24 categories would seem unwieldy and inelegant. Remember that relative simplicity is a valuable asset for objective theories.

Rubin claims that his typology captures *most* of the explanations people give for their media consumption. There may well be others. When Bradley Greenberg studied uses and gratifications among British children back in 1974, he discovered that many kids reported they watched TV simply because they had developed a *habit* of doing so that was difficult to break.[17] Rubin discussed habitual viewing under the "passing time" category. If he were doing his research today, he'd find habitual texting or Facebook use as common activities. Of course, kids aren't the only ones who cite habit as the main reason they use media. In "Television

Addiction Is No Mere Metaphor," a 2002 *Scientific American* cover story, communication researchers Robert Kubey and Mihaly Csikszentmihalyi present hard evidence of TV's habit-forming nature.[18] Maintaining that habit feels good. Breaking it is agony. Paul may realize that if he asks Alex to simply stop playing video games, his roommate will balk at the request. Alex may have developed a habitual behavior that is no longer volitional.

PARASOCIAL RELATIONSHIPS: USING MEDIA TO HAVE A FANTASY FRIEND

Using media to gratify a habitual urge may not be the only motivation to consider as an additional category for Rubin's typology. Years ago, actor Robert Young played the lead role in the hit TV series *Marcus Welby, M.D.* As the ideal physician who combined kindness with authority and expertise, he attracted millions of weekly viewers who were curious about how Dr. Welby would solve the next medical mystery. As the popularity of the series grew, something strange started to happen—the actor began receiving personal letters from viewers asking him for medical advice. In fact, according to one researcher who wrote a book on the "psychology of fame and celebrity," Robert Young received more than 250,000 such letters during the first five years of the program.[19] Why did so many viewers come to believe that a Hollywood actor with no medical credentials was a good source of medical advice?

The answer to that intriguing question is now best understood in terms of what researchers refer to as the *parasocial relationship.* According to Rubin, a parasocial relationship is basically a sense of friendship or emotional attachment that develops between TV viewers and media personalities. This relationship can be measured by asking viewers some basic questions about their involvement with popular characters. Rubin says these relationships are experienced in different ways, including ". . . seeking guidance from a media persona, seeing media personalities as friends, imagining being part of a favorite program's social world, and desiring to meet media performers."[20] While Rubin doesn't suggest that desire for a parasocial relationship might count as another category in his typology, it certainly seems to be a candidate.

Parasocial relationship
A sense of friendship or emotional attachment that develops between TV viewers and media personalities.

Knowing which media consumers will form parasocial relationships can help researchers predict how media will affect different viewers in different ways. An illustration is found in the surprising aftermath of an episode of the old TV series *Happy Days.*[21] Shortly after the episode where "The Fonz" applied for a library card was broadcast, library card applications around the country increased 500 percent. By applying uses & grats, a researcher might hypothesize that viewers who were more deeply involved in a parasocial relationship with The Fonz would be the ones most likely to apply for a card.

In the same way that uses & grats could be used to analyze TV viewing, it also holds potential for studying social media. For example, the theory could be applied to make sense of the huge number of people who felt the urge to share their grief online after the death of Cory Monteith in July 2013. Monteith, a star on the TV show *Glee,* died suddenly and tragically from a lethal mix of heroin and alcohol. Weeks later, tribute pages with thousands of followers continued to percolate with activity. In fact, Monteith's followers on Twitter increased by over a half million *after* he was gone.[22] Who would start subscribing to the Twitter feed of a dead person? A uses & grats theorist might suggest that signing up for the Twitter feed is a way of expressing a deep parasocial involvement with Monteith.

Although fans who feel attached to celebrities aren't able to express their grief by going to the funeral and hugging grieving family members, they *are* able to use social media to show they care. Following the Twitter feed of the deceased may serve the same function as paying respects at the funeral home to the family members of a personal acquaintance. In both cases, the expression shows appropriate concern.

In his review of some of the current directions of research on uses & grats, Rubin notes several studies that utilize the existence of parasocial relationships to predict differential effects of media content on viewers.[23] For example, after basketball star Magic Johnson announced in 1991 that he had tested positive for HIV, one study compared college students who may have had a parasocial relationship with Johnson to those who said they had only heard of him. News reports of Johnson's disease affected the two groups differently. Those who may have had a parasocial relationship said they were more concerned about HIV among heterosexuals and expressed an intention to reduce risky sexual behavior. Students who had only heard of Magic Johnson weren't affected by the news reports in the same way.[24]

CRITIQUE: HEAVY ON DESCRIPTION AND LIGHT ON PREDICTION?

In Chapter 3 you read that a good objective theory explains the past and present and predicts the future. These two criteria are called the "twin objectives of scientific knowledge." One criticism of uses & grats is that its major contribution is a *descriptive* typology of media uses and gratifications. For some, the emphasis on description rather than *explanation* and *prediction* is one of the theory's weak spots. This criticism might be countered by pointing out that studies such as the one on reactions to reports of Magic Johnson's contracting HIV offer more than just description; they enable researchers to predict which media will affect consumers in particular ways, and they offer an explanation for the data observed.

Jiyeon So, a communication professor at the University of Georgia, recently published an article that tackles the "description–prediction" critique head-on.[25] She notes that uses and gratifications theory was never intended to be merely descriptive; it was originally designed to offer specific predictions about media effects. But for whatever reason, the research on uses & grats has emphasized description. She goes on to explain that the theory can be used to predict different media effects by first understanding why people are consuming a particular media message. If her article helps set a new course for uses & grats research, the standard critique about prediction should fade away.

How well does uses & grats measure up against the other criteria mentioned in Chapter 3: *relative simplicity, testability, practical utility,* and *quantitative research?* There's nothing overly complex about the theory. The propositions that people use media to gratify particular needs and that those needs can be succinctly described using eight categories have the ring of *relative simplicity.* On the other hand, scholars continue to question the extent to which people can accurately report the reasons for their media use.[26] If they can't, the theory's *testability* is jeopardized. While people may be able to report with reasonable accuracy *what* media they consume, who is to say *why* they consume it? Depth psychologists from Freud to present-day therapists would suggest that the average media user is probably in one of the *worst* positions to explain his or her choices. There may also be a logical contradiction between the habit motive for consuming media and the theory's notion that media choices are conscious and deliberate. To the extent that Alex plays video games out of a deeply ingrained habit, he may not reflect on how he spends his time before he sits down to play. If so, his failure to reflect creates a problem for testing a theory that takes such reflection for granted.

To their credit, uses & grats scholars don't just dig in and defend the theory. They've tried to respond to critics by making changes. Instead of staying with the simple assertion that media audiences are uniformly active and making conscious choices, Rubin modified uses & grats by claiming that activity is actually a variable in the theory.[27] Though some consumers exemplify the highly active audience member described in early versions of the theory, others consume media passively, out of habit, or with little conscious deliberation. Still others fall somewhere in between—or even at different points of the continuum at different times or in different situations. When Alex returns from class and unthinkingly slumps into his chair to play *Call of Duty*, he's on the passive end of the continuum. When he makes arrangements with his friends to meet online to play the game together, he's much more active.

As a student of communication theory and an expert in your own personal media consumption, you may be in the best position to evaluate the *practical utility* of uses & grats. What implications does the theory have for you? At the very least, you might think of uses & grats as raising your own personal consciousness about the media you consume and the reasons you consume it. By reflecting on your media use, you could come to a new realization of your needs and how you choose to gratify them. And this self-awareness can lead to more satisfying choices in the long run. If Alex realizes his game playing is based on a habitual urge that's threatening his health, he might be more inclined to take the advice of a concerned friend like Paul and seek help to curtail his habit.

Katz' notion in the 1950s that the theory of uses and gratifications could save the entire field of communication turned out to be an extreme exaggeration. Perhaps that was his way of getting scholars to pay attention to a new idea. A view that emphasizes what people do with media instead of what media do to people seemed like a strange theoretical twist. But despite the fact that Katz may have initially overplayed his hand, the theory has fared well. Uses & grats has generated a large body of *quantitative research*. It's also poised to serve as one of the main theories guiding media research well into the twenty-first century.

QUESTIONS TO SHARPEN YOUR FOCUS

1. To what extent can we give an *accurate report* of the media content we consume? Are we always aware of the reasons we choose the media we do? Why or why not?
2. Consider Facebook and other *social networking sites*. Have you heard others express reasons for using Facebook that aren't reflected in the typology proposed by Alan Rubin?
3. Do you think many people have *parasocial relationships* with media characters? Were the people who wrote letters to Robert Young seeking medical advice genuinely confused about whether he was an actor or a doctor?
4. Think of a specific example of how two individuals might use *media content* to gratify different needs. How will those individuals experience very different *media effects?*

A SECOND LOOK

Recommended resource: Elihu Katz, Jay G. Blumler, and Michael Gurevitch, "Utilization of Mass Communication by the Individual," in *The Uses of Mass Communications: Current Perspectives on Gratifications Research,* Jay G. Blumler and Elihu Katz (eds.), Sage, Beverly Hills, CA, 1974, pp. 19–32.

Current update and overview: Alan M. Rubin, "Uses-And-Gratifications Perspective on Media Effects," in *Media Effects: Advances in Theory and Research,* 3rd ed., Jennings Bryant and Mary Beth Oliver (eds.), Lawrence Erlbaum, New York, 2009, pp. 165–184.

Parasocial relationships: Alan M. Rubin and Mary M. Step, "Impact of Motivation, Attraction, and Parasocial Interaction on Talk Radio Listening," *Journal of Broadcasting & Electronic Media,* Vol. 44, 2000, pp. 635–654.

Using media as a substitute for face-to-face relationships: Will Miller and Glenn Sparks, *Refrigerator Rights: Creating Connections and Restoring Relationships,* Perigree, New York, 2002.

Validity of self-reports in uses & grats research: Jack M. McLeod and Lee B. Becker, "Testing the Validity of Gratification Measures Through Political Effects Analysis," in *The Uses of Mass Communications,* pp. 137–164.

Related theory: Dolf Zillmann, "Mood Management: Using Entertainment to Full Advantage," *Communication, Social Cognition, and Affect,* Lewis Donohew, Howard E. Sypher, and E. Tory Higgins (eds.), Lawrence Erlbaum, Hillsdale, NJ, 1988.

Gender differences in media use: Silvia Knobloch-Westerwick, "Gender Differences in Selective Media Use for Mood Management and Mood Adjustment," *Journal of Broadcasting & Electronic Media,* Vol. 51, 2007, pp. 73–92.

New media: Isolde Anderson, "The Uses and Gratifications of Online Care Pages: A Study of CaringBridge," *Health Communication,* Vol. 26, 2011, pp. 546–559.

Policy implications: Harold Mendelsohn, "Some Policy Implications of the Uses and Gratifications Paradigm," in *The Uses of Mass Communications,* pp. 303–318.

Comprehensive critique: Philip Elliott, "Uses and Gratifications Research: A Critique and a Sociological Alternative," in *The Uses of Mass Communications,* pp. 249–268.

Uses & grats is a theory describing needs and interests.
For another theory of motivation, click on Hierarchy of Needs
in Archive under Theory Resources at
www.afirstlook.com.

CHAPTER 29

Objective — Interpretive

Socio-psychological tradition
Socio-cultural tradition

Cultivation Theory

of George Gerbner

What are the odds that you'll be involved in some kind of violent act within the next seven days? 1 out of 10? 1 out of 100? 1 out of 1,000? 1 out of 10,000?

According to Hungarian-born George Gerbner, the answer you give may have more to do with how much TV you watch than with the actual risk you face in the week to come. Gerbner, who died in 2005, was dean emeritus of the Annenberg School for Communication at the University of Pennsylvania and founder of the Cultural Environment Movement. He claimed that because TV contains so much violence, people who spend the most time in front of the tube develop an exaggerated belief in a *mean and scary world.* The violence they see on the screen can cultivate a social paranoia that counters notions of trustworthy people or safe surroundings.

Like Marshall McLuhan, Gerbner regarded television as the dominant force in shaping modern society. But unlike McLuhan, who viewed the medium as the message, Gerbner was convinced that TV's power comes from the symbolic content of the real-life drama shown hour after hour, week after week. At its root, television is society's institutional storyteller, and a society's stories give "a coherent picture of what exists, what is important, what is related to what, and what is right."[1]

Until the advent of broadcast media, the two acceptable storytellers outside the home were schools and faith communities. Today, the TV set is a key member of the household, with virtually unlimited access to every person in the family. Television dominates the environment of symbols, telling most of the stories, most of the time. Gerbner claimed that people now watch television as they might attend church, "except that most people watch television more religiously."[2]

What do they see in their daily devotions? According to Gerbner, violence is one of the major staples of the TV world. He wrote that violence "is the simplest and cheapest dramatic means to demonstrate who wins in the game of life and the rules by which the game is played."[3] Those who are immersed in the world of TV drama learn these "facts of life" better than occasional viewers do.

Most people who decry violence on television are worried that it affects receptive young viewers by encouraging aggressive *behavior.* Gerbner was more concerned that it affects viewers' *beliefs* about the world around them and the *feelings* connected to those beliefs. If viewers come to believe that the world around them is filled with crime, they're also likely to feel scared about the prospect of engaging in that crime-filled world. Gerbner thought that watching television violence might result in viewers wanting to own guard dogs, double-bolt locks, and home security systems. He was concerned that television violence convinces viewers that it is indeed "a jungle out there."

Gerbner's general expertise in the field of communication was widely acknowledged. He served as editor of the *Journal of Communication,* and for almost two decades he spearheaded an extensive research program that monitored the level of violence on television, classified people according to how much TV they watch, and compiled measures of how viewers perceive the world around them. He was especially interested in how viewers' consumption of TV violence increased their perceptions of risk for crime, and most of his research sought to gather support for that idea.

But cultivation theory isn't limited to TV violence. Other scholars have used it to theorize about how TV affects perceptions about the health risks of smoking, the popularity of various political positions, and appropriate gender roles. The ways that TV might affect views of social reality are probably too many to count. Partly because of Gerbner's credentials and partly because of the intuitive appeal of the theory itself, his cultivation explanation of his research findings remains one of the most popular and controversial theories of mass communication.

Gerbner introduced the theory of cultivation as part of his "cultural indicators" paradigm. As you'll recall from Fisher's *narrative paradigm* (see Chapter 24), a paradigm is a conceptual framework that calls for people to view events through a common interpretive lens. You might think of Gerbner's framework as a three-pronged plug leading to a TV set, with each of the prongs uniquely equipped to tell us something different about the world of TV.[4] Each of the three prongs is associated with a particular type of analysis that Gerbner considers a critical component in understanding the effects of television on its viewers.

INSTITUTIONAL PROCESS ANALYSIS—THE FIRST PRONG

The first prong of the plug represents scholars' concern for the reasons why media produce the messages they do. Gerbner labeled the research addressing this concern *institutional process analysis.* Scholars who do this type of research penetrate behind the scenes of media organizations in an effort to understand what policies or practices might be lurking there. For example, Gerbner believed that one reason there is so much violence on TV is that Hollywood is mainly concerned with how to export its product globally for maximum profit at minimum cost. Since violence is cheap to produce and speaks in a language that is universally understood, studios adopt policies that call for their shows to include lots of violent content.

Institutional process analysis
Scholarship that penetrates behind the scenes of media organizations in an effort to understand what policies or practices might be lurking there.

It would be difficult for a scholar to discover institutional policy without conducting in-depth interviews with media producers, accountants, and studio executives. When scholars conduct these sorts of interviews, they are engaging in institutional process analysis. Gerbner was fond of promoting his own views about the inner workings of Hollywood, but it isn't always clear whether those views were based on systematic scholarship. Cultivation theory is far better known for the concerns represented by the second and third prongs of the plug.

MESSAGE SYSTEM ANALYSIS—THE SECOND PRONG

If TV cultivates perceptions of social reality among viewers, it becomes essential to know exactly what messages TV transmits. The only way to know for sure is to undertake careful, systematic study of TV content—*message system analysis.* For Gerbner, that involved employing the method of quantitative *content analysis,* which resulted in numerical reports of exactly what the world of television contained.

Message system analysis Scholarship that involves careful, systematic study of TV content, usually employing content analysis as a research method.

While Gerbner designed most of his content analyses to reveal how much violence was on TV and how that violence was depicted, this method can be used to focus on any type of TV content. For example, scholars who thought that TV cultivated perceptions about smoking behavior and appropriate gender roles used content analysis to document the prevalence of smoking and the different roles played by males and females in prime time. Other researchers have examined depictions of marriage and work, attitudes about science, depictions of the paranormal, treatment of various political views, and ways environmental issues are handled. Before one can examine how certain messages might affect perceptions of social reality, however, it's important to know exactly what those messages contain.

An Index of Violence

As the opening paragraphs of the chapter reveal, Gerbner devoted most of his research to studying the cultivating impact of media violence. His content analysis was designed to uncover exactly how violence was depicted on TV. Of course, that required Gerbner to clearly specify what he meant by violence. He defined *dramatic violence* as "the overt expression of physical force (with or without a weapon, against self or others) compelling action against one's will on pain of being hurt and/or killed or threatened to be so victimized as part of the plot."[5]

Dramatic violence The overt expression or serious threat of physical force as part of the plot.

The definition rules out verbal abuse, idle threats, and pie-in-the-face slapstick. But it includes the physical abuse presented in a cartoon format. When the coyote pursuing the roadrunner is flattened by a steamroller or the *Mighty Morphin Power Rangers* crush their enemies, Gerbner would label the scene violent. He also counted auto crashes and natural disasters. From an artistic point of view, these events are no accident. The screenwriter inserted the trauma for dramatic effect. Characters die or are maimed just as effectively as if they'd taken a bullet in the chest.

For more than two decades, Gerbner's team of researchers randomly selected a week during the fall season and videotaped every prime-time (8 to 11 p.m.) network show. They also recorded programming for children on Saturday and Sunday (8 a.m. to 2 p.m.). After counting up the incidents that fit their description, they gauged the overall level of violence with a formula that included the ratio of programs that scripted violence, the rate of violence in those programs, and the percentage of characters involved in physical harm and killing. They found that the annual index was both remarkably stable and alarmingly high.

Equal Violence, Unequal Risk

One indisputable fact to emerge from Gerbner's analysis is that the cumulative portrayal of violence varies little from year to year. More than half of prime-time programs contain actual bodily harm or threatened violence. *The Big Bang Theory* and *Two and a Half Men* are not typical. Dramas that include violence average five traumatic incidents per viewing hour. Almost all the weekend children's shows major in mayhem. They average 20 cases an hour. By the time the typical TV viewer graduates from high school, he or she has observed 13,000 violent deaths.

On any given week, two-thirds of the major characters are caught up in some kind of violence. Heroes are just as involved as villains, yet there is great inequality as to the age, race, and gender of those on the receiving end of physical force. Old people and children are harmed at a much greater rate than are young or middle-aged adults. In the pecking order of "victimage," African Americans and Hispanics are killed or beaten more than their Caucasian counterparts. Gerbner noted that it's risky to be "other than clearly white." It's also dangerous to be female. The opening lady-in-distress scene is a favorite dramatic device to galvanize the hero into action. And finally, blue-collar workers "get it in the neck" more often than do white-collar executives.

The symbolic vulnerability of minority-group members is striking, given their gross underrepresentation in TV drama. Gerbner's analysis of the world of television recorded that 50 percent of the characters are white, middle-class males, and women are outnumbered by men 3 to 1. Although one-third of our society is made up of children and teenagers, they appear as only 10 percent of the characters on prime-time shows. Two-thirds of the United States labor force have blue-collar or service jobs, yet that group constitutes a mere 10 percent of the players on television. African Americans and Hispanics are only occasional figures, but the elderly are by far the most excluded minority. Less than 3 percent of the dramatic roles are filled by actors over the age of 65. If insurance companies kept actuarial tables on the life expectancy of television characters, they'd discover that the chance of a poor, elderly black woman's avoiding harm for the entire hour is almost nil.

"You do lovely needlepoint, grandma, but . . ."

In sum, Gerbner's content analyses reveal that people on the margins of American society are put in symbolic double jeopardy. Their existence is understated, but at the same time their vulnerability to violence is overplayed. When written into the script, they are often made visible in order to be victims. Not surprisingly, these are the very people who exhibit the most fear of violence when the TV set is turned off.

CULTIVATION ANALYSIS—THE THIRD PRONG

Most devotees of cultivation theory subscribe to the notion that *message system analysis* is a prerequisite to the third prong of the plug: *cultivation analysis.* It's important to recognize the difference between the two. Message system analysis deals with the content of TV; cultivation analysis deals with how TV's content might affect viewers—particularly the viewers who spend lots of time glued to the tube.

It might be helpful to think of cultivation analysis as the prong that carries the most electrical current in the theory. This is the part of the paradigm where most of the action takes place. Gerbner's research associates, Michael Morgan, James Shanahan, and Nancy Signorielli, offer a clear definition of *cultivation:*

> The concept of "cultivation" thus refers to the independent contribution television viewing makes to audience members' conceptions of social reality. Television viewing cultivates ways of seeing the world—those who spend more time "living" in the world of television are more likely to see the "real world" in terms of the images, values, portrayals and ideologies that emerge through the lens of television.[6]

After watching an episode of *Law & Order: Special Victims Unit,* Em's student Jeremy found the idea of cultivation perfectly plausible when it comes to watching media violence and developing a fear of real-world crime. His description of the episode and his conclusion about cultivation are worth noting:

Cultivation analysis
Research designed to find support for the notion that those who spend more time watching TV are more likely to see the "real world" through TV's lens.

> In the episode, a child found the dead bodies of both his nanny and his mom. His nanny was killed by someone she met online and his mom was killed by his dad a few days later because she was having an affair and wanted to leave him. At the end of the episode, a detective and the wife of another detective were in a car accident. Of the nine central characters in the episode, three were victims of violent crime and two were perpetrators of violent crime. Two of the four remaining characters were involved in the car crash, so only two people made it out of the episode unscathed. I can see how heavy viewers of such shows would get the idea that the world is mean and scary.

CULTIVATION WORKS LIKE A MAGNETIC OR GRAVITATIONAL FIELD

If Gerbner is right that heavy TV watching influences viewers' beliefs about the world, how can we understand exactly how this happens? It's tempting to think of cultivation as a linear *push* process, where TV content influences viewers much like the cue ball on a billiard table pushes the other balls to new locations upon impact. But cultivation researchers aren't fond of that metaphor. Michael Morgan and his co-authors point out that the cultivation process is much more like the *pull* of a gravitational field.[7]

As a researcher who majors in media effects and has published research on media cultivation,[8] I (Glenn) like to extend the metaphor of gravity to magnetism. Imagine a table of billiard balls that are made of metal, with the cue ball (representing TV) possessing powerful magnetic properties. Regardless of where the other balls (representing individual viewers) are positioned on the table, they will be affected by the magnetic pull of the cue ball and tend to move closer to it. Depending on the initial position of the balls on the table, they won't all move toward the magnetic cue ball at the same angle and at the same speed—but they will all be susceptible to the pull of the magnet to some degree. In the same way, although the magnitude of TV's influence is not the same for every viewer, all are affected by it.

While metaphors like the magnetic cue ball can shed light on a theoretical process like cultivation, some scholars see them as limited in terms of explaining what's really going on. L. J. Shrum, a professor of marketing at the University of Texas at San Antonio, offers insight into the "black box" of the mind so we can better understand how watching TV affects judgments of the world around us. Shrum relies on the *accessibility principle* in explaining TV's cultivating impact.[9] This principle states that when people make judgments about the world around them, they rely on the smallest bits of information that come to mind most quickly—the information that is most accessible.

Accessibility principle
When people make judgments about the world around them, they rely on the smallest bits of information that come to mind most quickly.

For those who consume lots of TV, the most accessible information for making judgments is more likely to come from TV shows than anywhere else. Heavy TV viewing keeps messages from the screen at the top of the mind's vast bin of information. If you're a heavy TV viewer and someone asks you about your odds of being involved in a violent act, the most accessible information about crime that you will use to construct your answer could come from your steady diet of *CSI*.

Gerbner seemed content to leave scholars like Shrum with the task of explaining exactly how the cultivation process works. In the meantime, he was busy spinning out more specific propositions to test. The two main propositions that guided his thinking about cultivation were *mainstreaming* and *resonance.*

MAINSTREAMING: BLURRING, BLENDING, AND BENDING OF ATTITUDES

Mainstreaming is Gerbner's term to describe the process of "blurring, blending, and bending" that those with heavy viewing habits undergo. He thought that through constant exposure to the same images and labels, heavy viewers develop a commonality of outlook that doesn't happen with radio. Radio stations segment the audience to the point where programming for left-handed truck drivers who bowl on Friday nights is a distinct possibility. But instead of *narrowcasting* their programs, TV producers *broadcast* in that they seek to "attract the largest possible audience by celebrating the moderation of the mainstream."[10] Television homogenizes its audience so that those with heavy viewing habits share the same orientations, perspectives, and meanings with each other.

Mainstreaming
The blurring, blending, and bending process by which heavy TV viewers from disparate groups develop a common outlook through constant exposure to the same images and labels.

Think of the metaphor of the metal billiard balls scattered on the pool table and visualize the magnetic cue ball in the center. Despite the fact that the individual metal balls are located in many different positions on the table, each one is drawn closer to the magnetic cue ball and, in the process, all of the balls become closer to each other—assuming positions on the table that are more alike than before the magnet had its effect. In a similar way, as TV mainstreams people, it pulls those who might initially be different from each other into a common perception of reality that resembles the TV world. We needn't ask how close this common perception of the way the world works is to the mainstream of culture. According to Gerbner, the "television answer" *is* the mainstream.

Gerbner illustrated the mainstreaming effect by showing how heavy TV viewers blur economic and political distinctions. TV glorifies the middle class, and those with heavy viewing habits assume that label, no matter what their income. But those with light viewing habits who have blue-collar jobs accurately describe themselves as working-class people.

In like fashion, those with heavy viewing habits label themselves political *moderates.* Most characters in TV dramas frown on political extremism—right or left. This nonextremist ethic is apparently picked up by the constant viewer. It's only from the ranks of sporadic TV users that Gerbner found people who actually label themselves *liberal* or *conservative.*

Social scientists have come to expect political differences between rich and poor, blacks and whites, Catholics and Protestants, city dwellers and farmers. Those distinctions still emerge when sporadic television viewers respond to the survey. But Gerbner reported that traditional differences diminish among those with heavy viewing habits. It's as if the light from the TV set washes out any sharp features that would set them apart.

Even though those with heavy viewing habits call themselves moderates, Gerbner and his associates studying cultural indicators noted that their positions on social issues are decidedly conservative. Heavy viewers consistently voice opinions in favor of lower taxes, more police protection, and stronger national defense. They are against big government, free speech, the Equal Rights Amendment, abortion, open-housing legislation, and affirmative action. The *mainstream* is not *middle of the road.* The magnetic cue ball isn't sitting in the middle of the table—it's distinctly skewed to the right.

RESONANCE: THE TV WORLD LOOKS LIKE MY WORLD, SO IT MUST BE TRUE

To understand the resonance process, consider again the billiard metaphor. The balls closest to the magnetic cue ball are like TV viewers whose real-world environment is very much like the world of TV. They might be viewers who live in the inner city and are accustomed to violent attacks, police chases, and losing friends to violent crime. The balls farthest away from the cue ball are like viewers who live in a world that doesn't resemble TV at all. Which of the balls on the table are most affected by the magnetic cue ball? If you remember how magnets behave and you have a clear image of the billiard table, the answer is clear: the closest balls are the ones that will be most affected. In fact, if they are extremely close to the cue ball, they will be pulled in quickly and end up firmly attached. Although Gerbner didn't use this metaphor, I think he would have seen it as illustrative of the *resonance* process. He thought the cultivating power of TV's messages would be especially strong over viewers who perceived that the world depicted on TV was a world very much like their own. He thought of these viewers as ones who get a "double dose" of the same message.[11]

Resonance
The condition that exists when viewers' real-life environment is like the world of TV; these viewers are especially susceptible to TV's cultivating power.

For three years Em was a volunteer advocate in a low-income housing project. Although he felt relatively safe walking through the project, police and social workers told stories of shootings and stabbings. Even peace-loving residents were no strangers to violence. Em can't recall ever entering an apartment where the TV was turned off. Gerbner would expect that the daily diet of symbolic savagery would reinforce people's experience of doorstep violence, making life even more frightening. The hesitation of most tenants to venture outside their apartments is consistent with his resonance assumption.

RESEARCH ON CULTIVATION ANALYSIS

Cultivation takes time. Gerbner viewed the process as one that unfolds gradually through the steady accumulation of TV's messages. Consequently, he shunned the experimental method many researchers used to study the effects of TV violence on aggressive behavior. According to Gerbner, these experiments couldn't possibly detect the sort of changes he sought to document. Change due to cultivation takes place over months and years; most experiments measure change that takes place over 30 or 60 minutes. That's why the strategy for performing *cultivation analysis* relies on surveys instead of experiments.

Gerbner's basic prediction was that heavy TV viewers would be more likely than light viewers to see the social world as resembling the world depicted on TV. The strategy for testing this notion was simple. Survey respondents were asked two types of questions: one type focused on reports of TV exposure so that Gerbner could distinguish between heavy and light viewers; the second focused on perceptions of social reality that he thought media might cultivate. Once measured, the responses could be correlated to find out if heavy viewers perceive the world as a scarier place than light viewers do.

Heavy viewers
TV viewers who report that they watch at least four hours per day; television types.

Based on the data from survey questionnaires on TV viewing, most of Gerbner's work established a self-report of two hours a day as the upper limit of light viewing. He labeled *heavy viewers* as those who watch four hours or more. He also referred to the heavy viewer as the *television type,* a more benign term than *couch potato* with its allusion to either a steady diet of television and potato chips or a vegetable with many eyes. There are more heavy viewers than light viewers, but each group makes up about one-fourth of the general population. People whose viewing habits are in the two- to four-hour midrange make up the other half, but Gerbner wanted to compare people with distinctly different patterns of television exposure.

THE MAJOR FINDINGS OF CULTIVATION ANALYSIS

Cultivation differential
The difference in the percentage giving the "television answer" within comparable groups of light and heavy TV viewers.

Believing that violence is the backbone of TV drama and knowing that people differ in how much TV they watch, Gerbner sought to discover the *cultivation differential.* That's his term for "the difference in the percent giving the 'television answer' within comparable groups of light and heavy viewers."[12] He referred to *cultivation differential* rather than *media effects* because the latter term implies a comparison between *before*-TV exposure and *after*-TV exposure. Gerbner believed there is no before-television condition. Television enters people's lives in infancy. His surveys have revealed some provocative findings:

1. *Positive correlation between TV viewing and fear of criminal victimization.* In most of the surveys Gerbner conducted, the results reveal a small but statistically significant relationship between TV consumption and fear about becoming the victim of a crime. The question at the start of the chapter is illustrative:

Those with light viewing habits predict their weekly odds of being a victim are 1 out of 100; those with heavy viewing habits fear the risk to be 1 out of 10. Actual crime statistics indicate that 1 out of 10,000 is more realistic. Not surprisingly, more women than men are afraid of dark streets. But for both sexes, the fear of victimization correlates with time spent in front of the tube. People with heavy viewing habits tend to overestimate criminal activity, believing it to be 10 times worse than it really is. In actuality, muggers on the street pose less bodily threat to pedestrians than does injury from cars.

Because so many cultivation studies have been published, it is possible to compute an overall average effect based on the correlations from all the individual surveys. Such a study is called a *meta-analysis*. One meta-analysis estimated the average correlation over 82 different studies to be consistently small, but positive ($r = +0.09$)—indicating that as TV viewing increases, there is a tendency for fear of victimization to increase as well.[13] Since correlations can range from 0.0 to 1.0, a value of 0.09 is certainly on the small side. But in most of the studies, the correlation was large enough to conclude that the relationship was not just a chance finding. TV viewing is definitely related to fear of criminal victimization.

Meta-analysis
A statistical procedure that blends the results of multiple empirical and independent research studies exploring the same relationship between two variables (e.g., TV viewing and fear of violence).

2. *Perceived activity of police.* People with heavy viewing habits believe that 5 percent of society is involved in law enforcement. Their video world is populated with police officers, judges, and government agents. People with light viewing habits estimate a more realistic 1 percent. Gerbner's television type assumes that cops draw their guns almost every day, which isn't true.
3. *General mistrust of people.* Those with heavy viewing habits are suspicious of other people's motives. They subscribe to statements that warn people to expect the worst:

"Most people are just looking out for themselves."

"In dealing with others, you can't be too careful."

"Do unto others before they do unto you."

Mean world syndrome
The cynical mindset of general mistrust of others subscribed to by heavy TV viewers.

Gerbner called this cynical mindset the *mean world syndrome*. The evidence suggests that the minds of heavy TV viewers are fertile ground for sowing thoughts of danger.

CRITIQUE: HOW STRONG IS THE EVIDENCE IN FAVOR OF THE THEORY?

For most observers, Gerbner's claim that the dramatic content of television creates a fearful climate makes sense. How could the habitual viewer watch so much violence without it having a lasting effect? Yet over the last 30 years, communication journals have been filled with the sometimes bitter charges and countercharges of critics and supporters. Opponents have challenged Gerbner's definition of violence, the programs he selected for content analysis, his decision to lump together all types of dramatic programs (action, soap operas, sitcoms, and so on), his assumption that there is always a consistent television answer, his nonrandom methods of selecting respondents, his simple hours-per-day standard of categorizing viewers as *light* or *heavy*, his multiple-choice technique of measuring their perceived risk of being mugged, his statistical method of analyzing the data, and his interpretation of correlational data.

Perhaps the most daunting issue to haunt cultivation research is how to clearly establish the causal claim that heavy TV viewing leads a person to perceive the world as mean and scary. Because cultivation researchers shun the experimental method in favor of the survey, they are stuck with a method that is incapable of establishing clear evidence of causality. Critics are quick to point out that the correlation between TV viewing and fear of criminal victimization can be interpreted plausibly in more than one way. The correlation could indicate, as Gerbner contended, that TV viewing cultivates or causes fear of crime. But it could make just as much sense to interpret the relationship the other way—fear of crime causes people to watch more TV. After all, most TV shows depict a just world in which the bad guys get caught in the end. Perhaps those most afraid of crime are the ones most motivated to tune in to TV to become assured that justice will ultimately triumph.

With correlational data, the only way to distinguish what causes what is to collect data from the same people on more than one occasion over a longer period of time. *Longitudinal studies* like these can help determine which of the two variables comes before the other. Unfortunately, longitudinal research typically takes many months or years to complete. Scholars who live by the adage "publish or perish" are not usually attracted to projects that require them to wait around that long to collect data. As a result, cultivation studies of this type are virtually nonexistent. This state of affairs causes some critics to give cultivation theory low marks on the criterion of *testability* that you read about in Chapter 3.

Another possibility is that the relationship between TV viewing and fear of crime is like the relationship between a runny nose and a sore throat. Neither one causes the other—they are both caused by something else. Just as the cold virus is a common cause of runny noses *and* sore throats, some critics suggest that the neighborhoods people live in could be the common cause of TV viewing *and* fear of crime.[14] People who live in high-crime areas may fear crime for good reason. They also tend to stay inside to avoid victimization. While indoors, they pass the time by watching TV. In contrast, people who live in low-crime areas don't fear crime as much and so they tend to go outside more frequently, which leads to less TV consumption. If researchers ignore where people live—and most cultivation researchers do—they might miss the role played by this variable or others that weren't included in their questionnaires.

Scholars have another reservation about the evidence: cultivation effects tend to be statistically small. Imagine an entire pie that represents all the fear of crime that is measured in a cultivation questionnaire. The amount of the pie that researchers can attribute to watching TV might be just a single bite. On the other hand, champions of the theory point out that tiny statistical effects can be crucial. Consider the fact that a 1 percent swing in voting patterns in 3 of the last 14 presidential elections would have resulted in a different person being elected (Kennedy–Nixon in 1960; Nixon–Humphrey in 1968; Bush–Gore in 2000). Or reflect on the fact that a change in the average temperature of just a single degree could have catastrophic consequences for our planet.

Issues of statistical size aside, Gerbner's defenders would emphasize the *importance* of the issue at hand. Fear of violence is a paralyzing emotion. As Gerbner repeatedly pointed out, worry can make people prisoners in their own homes, change the way they vote, affect how they feel about themselves, and dramatically lower their quality of life. Even if the effect of TV viewing on these factors is relatively small, the consequences at stake make TV's message one that we should be concerned about.

But what is TV's message? When Gerbner formulated his theory decades ago, there were only three major networks. The vast offerings of today's cable and satellite menu were unimaginable. Critics contend that Gerbner's original assumption that TV viewers are constantly exposed to the same images and labels is no longer true. While there may not yet be a channel for left-handed truck drivers who bowl on Friday nights, the TV environment seems to be moving in that direction. The choices between such channels as the Food Network, the Golf Channel, and C-SPAN permit a level of viewing selectivity that cultivation theory doesn't acknowledge. If the theory is to continue to exert influence, many critics maintain that it will have to adapt to the new media environment.

Compared to most of the other theories in this text, the "critique" section of cultivation theory is much longer. Does this mean it's a bad theory? Not necessarily. Consider the fact that cultivation theory has generated research for almost a half-century. Theories that have been around that long sustain more attacks than ones recently hatched. It's also important to keep in mind that amid all the criticism, few theories in the area of mass communication have generated as many studies. In addition to its tremendous contribution to research, the theory has influenced at least three generations of scholars to think about media in a particular way. Most theorists would love to have even a fraction of the recognition that cultivation theory has managed to garner.

As for Gerbner, in 1996 he founded the Cultural Environment Movement, a coalition of organizations and social activists who believe it's vitally important who gets to tell the stories within a culture, and whose stories don't get told. They are committed to changing the stories that American television tells and are convinced this will happen only when the public wrests control of the airwaves from media conglomerates. Gerbner underscored the movement's agenda with repeated references to a line from Scottish patriot Andrew Fletcher:

> "If a man were permitted to make all the ballads, he need not care who should make the laws of a nation."[15]

QUESTIONS TO SHARPEN YOUR FOCUS

1. How would you change Gerbner's definition of *dramatic violence* so that his index of TV violence would measure what you think is important?
2. What types of people are underrepresented in television drama? What types of people are overrepresented? Who are the victims of symbolic violence on the screen?
3. How do your *political* and *social values* differ from, or coincide with, the *mainstream* attitudes of Gerbner's *television type?*
4. The *meta-analysis* finding of a +0.09 relationship between TV exposure and worldview can be seen as *significant, small,* and/or *important.* How do these interpretations differ? Which impresses you most?

A SECOND LOOK

Recommended resource: Michael Morgan, James Shanahan, and Nancy Signorielli, "Growing Up with Television," in *Media Effects: Advances in Theory & Research,* 3rd ed., Jennings Bryant and Mary Beth Oliver (eds.), Routledge, New York, 2009, pp. 34–49.

Primary sources: Michael Morgan (ed.), *Against the Mainstream: The Selected Works of George Gerbner,* Peter Lang, New York, 2002.

Violence index: George Gerbner, Larry Gross, Marilyn Jackson-Beeck, Suzanne Jeffries-Fox, and Nancy Signorielli, "Cultural Indicators: Violence Profile No. 9," *Journal of Communication,* Vol. 28, No. 3, 1978, pp. 176–207.

Violence update: Amir Hetsroni, "Four Decades of Violent Content on Prime-Time Network Programming: A Longitudinal Meta-Analytic Review," *Journal of Communication,* Vol. 57, No. 4, 2007, pp. 759–784.

Introduction to key concepts: George Gerbner, "Cultivation Analysis: An Overview," *Mass Communication & Society,* Vol. 1, 1998, pp. 175–194.

Profile of Gerbner: Scott Stossel, "The Man Who Counts the Killings," *Atlantic,* May 1997, pp. 86–104.

Mainstreaming and resonance: George Gerbner, Larry Gross, Michael Morgan, and Nancy Signorielli, "The 'Mainstreaming' of America: Violence Profile No. 11," *Journal of Communication,* Vol. 30, No. 3, 1980, pp. 10–29.

Mainstreaming and resonance research: L. J. Shrum and Valerie D. Bischak, "Mainstreaming, Resonance, and Impersonal Impact: Testing Moderators of the Cultivation Effect for Estimates of Crime Risk," *Human Communication Research,* Vol. 27, 2001, pp. 187–215.

Research review and meta-analysis: Michael Morgan and James Shanahan, "Two Decades of Cultivation Research: An Appraisal and a Meta-Analysis," in *Communication Yearbook 20,* Brant Burleson (ed.), Sage, Thousand Oaks, CA, 1997, pp. 1–45.

Television news violence: Daniel Romer, Kathleen Hall Jamieson, and Sean Aday, "Television News and the Cultivation of Fear of Crime," *Journal of Communication,* Vol. 53, 2003, pp. 88–104.

Computer game violence: Dmitri Williams, "Virtual Cultivation: Online Worlds, Offline Perceptions," *Journal of Communication,* Vol. 56, 2006, pp. 69–87.

Causality with correlation data: Constanze Rossmann and Hans-Bernd Brosius, "The Problem of Causality in Cultivation Research," *Communications,* Vol. 29, 2004, pp. 379–397.

How Cultivation Works: L. J. Shrum, Jaehoon Lee, James Burroughs, and Aric Rindfleisch, "An Online Process Model of Second-Order Cultivation Effects: How Television Cultivates Materialism and Its Consequences for Life Satisfaction," *Human Communication Research,* Vol. 37, No. 1, 2011, pp. 34–57.

Critique: Dolf Zillmann and Jacob Wakshlag, "Fear of Victimization and the Appeal of Crime Drama," in *Selective Exposure to Communication,* Dolf Zillmann and Jennings Bryant (eds.), Lawrence Erlbaum, Hillsdale, NJ, 1985, pp. 141–156.

To access a chapter that predicts when and how viewers will imitate TV violence, click on Social Learning Theory in Archive under Theory Resources at *www.afirstlook.com.*

CHAPTER 30

Objective — Interpretive

Socio-psychological tradition

Agenda-Setting Theory

of Maxwell McCombs & Donald Shaw

For some unexplained reason, in June 1972, five unknown men broke into the Democratic National Committee headquarters looking for undetermined information. It was the sort of local crime story that rated two paragraphs on page 17 of *The Washington Post.* Yet editor Ben Bradlee and reporters Bob Woodward and Carl Bernstein gave the story repeatedly high visibility even though the public initially seemed to regard the incident as trivial.

President Nixon dismissed the break-in as a "third-rate burglary," but over the following year Americans showed an increasing public awareness of Watergate's significance. Half the country became familiar with the word *Watergate* over the summer of 1972. By April 1973, that figure had risen to 90 percent. When television began gavel-to-gavel coverage of the Senate hearings on the matter a year after the break-in, virtually every adult in the United States knew what Watergate was about. Six months after the hearings President Nixon still protested, "I am not a crook." But by the spring of 1974, he was forced from office because the majority of citizens and their representatives had decided that he was.

THE ORIGINAL AGENDA: NOT WHAT TO *THINK,* BUT WHAT TO THINK *ABOUT*

Journalism professors Maxwell McCombs and Donald Shaw regard Watergate as a perfect example of the agenda-setting function of the mass media. They were not surprised that the Watergate issue caught fire after months on the front page of *The Washington Post.* McCombs and Shaw believe that the "mass media have the ability to transfer the salience of items on their news agendas to the public agenda."[1] They aren't suggesting that broadcast and print personnel make a deliberate attempt to influence listener, viewer, or reader opinion on the issues. Most reporters in the free world have a deserved reputation for independence and fairness. But McCombs and Shaw say that we look to news professionals for cues on where to focus our attention. "*We* judge as important what the *media* judge as important."[2]

Although McCombs and Shaw first referred to the agenda-setting function of the media in 1972, the idea that people desire media assistance in determining political reality had already been voiced by a number of current events analysts. In an attempt to explain how the United States had been drawn into World War I, Pulitzer Prize–winning author Walter Lippmann claimed that the media act as a mediator between "the world outside and the pictures in our heads."[3] McCombs and Shaw also quote University of Wisconsin political scientist Bernard Cohen's observation concerning the specific function the media serve: "The press may not be successful much of the time in telling people what to think, but it is stunningly successful in telling its readers what to think about."[4]

Agenda-setting hypothesis
The mass media have the ability to transfer the salience of issues on their news agenda to the public agenda.

Starting with the Kennedy–Nixon contest in 1960, political analyst Theodore White wrote the definitive account of four presidential elections. Independent of McCombs and Shaw, and in opposition to then-current wisdom that mass communication had limited effects upon its audience, White came to the conclusion that the media shaped those election campaigns:

> The power of the press in America is a primordial one. It sets the agenda of public discussion; and this sweeping political power is unrestrained by any law. It determines what people will talk and think about—an authority that in other nations is reserved for tyrants, priests, parties and mandarins.[5]

A THEORY WHOSE TIME HAD COME

McCombs and Shaw's agenda-setting theory found an appreciative audience among mass communication researchers. The prevailing selective-exposure hypothesis claimed that people would attend only to news and views that didn't threaten their established beliefs. The media were seen as merely stroking preexistent attitudes. After two decades of downplaying the influence of newspapers, magazines, radio, and television, the field was disenchanted with this limited-effects approach. Agenda-setting theory boasted two attractive features: it reaffirmed the power of the press while maintaining that individuals were free to choose.

McCombs and Shaw's agenda-setting theory represents a back-to-the-basics approach to mass communication research. Like the initial Erie County voting studies,[6] the focus is on election campaigns. The hypothesis predicts a cause-and-effect relationship between media content and voter perception. Although later work explores the conditions under which media priorities are most influential, the theory rises or falls on its ability to show a match between the media's agenda and the public's agenda later on. McCombs and Shaw supported their main hypothesis with results from surveys they took while working together at the University of North Carolina at Chapel Hill.[7] (McCombs is now at the University of Texas.) Their analysis of the 1968 race for president between Richard Nixon and Hubert Humphrey set the pattern for later agenda-setting research. The study provides an opportunity to examine in detail the type of quantitative survey research that Stuart Hall and other critical theorists so strongly oppose.

MEDIA AGENDA AND PUBLIC AGENDA: A CLOSE MATCH

McCombs and Shaw's first task was to measure the *media agenda.* They determined that Chapel Hill residents relied on a mix of nine print and broadcast sources for political news—two Raleigh papers, two Durham papers, *Time, Newsweek,* the out-of-state edition of *The New York Times,* and the CBS and NBC evening news.

Media agenda
The pattern of news coverage across major print and broadcast media as measured by the prominence and length of stories.

They established *position* and *length* of story as the two main criteria of prominence. For newspapers, the front-page headline story, a three-column story on an inside page, and the lead editorial were all counted as evidence of significant focus on an issue. For news magazines, the requirement was an opening story in the news section or any political issue to which the editors devoted a full column. Prominence in the television news format was defined by placement as one of the first three news items or any discussion that lasted more than 45 seconds.

Because the agenda-setting hypothesis refers to substantive issues, the researchers discarded news items about campaign strategy, position in the polls, and the personalities of the candidates. The remaining stories were then sorted into 15 subject categories, which were later boiled down into 5 major issues. A composite index of media prominence revealed the following order of importance: foreign policy, law and order, fiscal policy, public welfare, and civil rights.

In order to measure the *public's agenda,* McCombs and Shaw asked Chapel Hill voters to outline what each one considered the key issue of the campaign, regardless of what the candidates might be saying. People who were already committed to a candidate were dropped from the pool of respondents. The researchers assigned the specific answers to the same broad categories used for media analysis. They then compared the aggregate data from undecided voters with the composite description of media content. The rank of the five issues on both lists was nearly identical.

Public agenda
The most important public issues as measured by public opinion surveys.

WHAT CAUSES WHAT?

McCombs and Shaw believe that the hypothesized agenda-setting function of the media is responsible for the almost perfect correlation they found between the media and public ordering of priorities:

Media Agenda → Voters' Agenda

But as critics of cultivation theory remind us, correlation is not causation. It's possible that newspaper and television coverage simply reflects public concerns that already exist:

Voters' Agenda → Media Agenda

The results of the Chapel Hill study could be interpreted as providing support for the notion that the media are just as market-driven in their news coverage as they are in programming entertainment. By themselves, McCombs and Shaw's findings were impressive, but equivocal. A true test of the agenda-setting hypothesis must be able to show that public priorities lag behind the media agenda. I'll briefly describe two research studies that provide evidence that the media agenda is, in fact, the *cause,* while the public agenda is its somewhat delayed *effect.*

Critics have suggested that *both* the media agenda and the public agenda merely reflect current events as they unfold; it's just that news professionals become aware of what's happening sooner than the rest of us do. To examine that possibility, communication researcher Ray Funkhouser, now retired from Pennsylvania State University, undertook an extensive *historical* review of stories in news magazines from 1960 to 1970.[8] He charted the rise and fall of media attention on issues and compared these trends with annual Gallup poll responses to a question about "the most important problem facing America." Funkhouser's results make it clear that the twin agendas aren't mere reflections of reality. For example, the number of American troops in Vietnam increased until 1968, but news coverage peaked two years before that. The same was true of urban violence and campus unrest. Press interest cooled down while cities and colleges were still heating up. It appears that Walter Lippmann was right—the actual environment and the pictures in our mind are two different worlds.

This historical study provides strong support for McCombs and Shaw's basic agenda-setting hypothesis. But it took a tightly controlled *experiment* run by Yale researchers to establish a cause-and-effect chain of influence from the media agenda to the public agenda.[9] Political scientists Shanto Iyengar, Mark Peters, and Donald Kinder spliced previously aired news features into tapes of current network newscasts. For four days straight, three groups of New Haven residents came together to watch the evening news and fill out a questionnaire about their own concerns. Each group saw a different version—one version contained a daily story on environmental pollution, another had a daily feature on national defense, and a third offered a daily dose of news about economic inflation. Viewers who saw the media agendas that focused on pollution and defense elevated those issues on their own lists of concerns—definite confirmation of a cause-and-effect relationship between the media agenda and the public agenda. (As it turned out, inflation was already an important topic for most participants, so there wasn't any room for that issue to move up on the third group's agenda.)

WHO IS MOST AFFECTED BY THE MEDIA AGENDA?

Even in their original Chapel Hill study, McCombs and Shaw understood that "people are not automatons waiting to be programmed by the news media."[10] They suspected that some viewers might be more resistant to the media's political priorities than others—that's why they filtered out the responses of voters who were already committed to a candidate. In follow-up studies, McCombs and Shaw turned to the *uses and gratifications* approach, which suggests that viewers are selective in the kinds of TV programs they watch (see Chapter 28). The theorists sought to discover exactly what kind of person is most susceptible to the media agenda. They concluded that people who have a willingness to let the media shape their thinking have a high *need for orientation.* Others refer to it as an *index of curiosity.*

Index of curiosity
A measure of the extent to which individuals' need for orientation motivates them to let the media shape their views.

Need for orientation arises from high *relevance* and *uncertainty.* For example, because I'm a dog and cat owner, any story about cruelty to animals always catches my attention (high relevance). However, I don't really know the extent to which medical advances require experimentation on live animals (high uncertainty). According to McCombs and Shaw, this combination would make me a likely candidate to be influenced by media stories about vivisection. If the news editors of *Time* and ABC think it's important, I probably will too.

FRAMING: TRANSFERRING THE SALIENCE OF ATTRIBUTES

Until the 1990s, almost every article about the theory included a reiteration of the agenda-setting mantra—*the media aren't very successful in telling us what to think, but they are stunningly successful in telling us what to think about.* In other words, the media make some issues more *salient.* We pay greater attention to those issues and regard them as more important. By the mid-1990s, however, McCombs was saying that the media do more than that. They do, in fact, influence the way we think. The specific process he cites is one that many media scholars discuss—*framing.*

James Tankard, one of the leading writers on mass communication theory, defines a media frame as "the central organizing idea for news content that supplies a context and suggests what the issue is through the use of *selection, emphasis, exclusion,* and *elaboration.*"[11] The final four nouns in that sentence suggest that the media not only set the agenda for what issues, events, or candidates are most important, they also transfer the salience of specific attributes belonging to those potential objects of interest. My own "final four" experience may help explain the distinction.

I'm writing this section while visiting relatives in St. Petersburg, Florida. The *St. Petersburg Times* is filled with stories about the finals of the NCAA men's basketball tournament that starts here tomorrow. The field of 64 teams has now been narrowed to 4, and it's hard to imagine anything the newspaper or television stations could do to make this Final Four event more prominent for local residents. No one seems to talk about anything else.

What is it about the Final Four extravaganza that captures people's attention? For some it's the high quality of basketball play they expect to see. For others it's a rooting interest for a particular team. But beyond these inherent characteristics of a basketball tournament, there are many other potential features of the event that might come to mind:

Gambling—there's more money bet on this game than on the Super Bowl.

Party scene—a guy leans out the window and yells, "This is where it's at."

Local economy—this is the weekend that could keep Florida green.

Exploitation of players—how many of these guys will ever graduate?

Beach forecast—it will be sunny and warm both today and tomorrow.

"Your royal command has been obeyed, Highness. Every town crier in the land is crying: 'Old King Cole is a merry ole soul.' Before nightfall we'll have them all believing it."

Cartoon by Ed Frascino. Reprinted by permission.

The morning paper carried separate stories on each of these features, but coverage on benefits to the local economy and the gambling angle were front-page features that ran five times as long as the brief article on player exploitation buried inside.

We see, therefore, that there are two levels of agenda setting. The first level, according to McCombs, is the transfer of salience of an *attitude object* in the mass media's pictures of the world to a prominent place among the pictures in our head. The Final Four becomes important to us. This is the agenda-setting function that survey researchers have traditionally studied.

Framing
The selection of a restricted number of thematically related attributes for inclusion on the media agenda when a particular object or issue is discussed.

The second level of agenda setting is the transfer of salience of a dominant set of *attributes* that the media associate with an attitude object to the specific features of the image projected on the walls of our minds.[12] Now when I think of the Final Four, I imagine money changing hands for a variety of reasons. I don't think about GPAs or diplomas. According to McCombs, the agenda setting of attributes mirrors the process of framing that Robert Entman describes in his article clarifying the concept:

> To frame is to select some aspects of a perceived reality and make them more salient in a communication text, in such a way as to promote a particular problem definition, causal interpretation, moral evaluation and/or treatment recommendation for the item described.[13]

NOT JUST WHAT TO THINK ABOUT, BUT HOW TO THINK ABOUT IT

Is there evidence that the process of framing as defined by agenda-setting theorists actually alters the pictures in the minds of people when they read the newspaper or tune in to broadcast news? Does the media's construction of an agenda with a cluster of related attributes create a coherent image in the minds of subscribers, listeners, and viewers? McCombs cites national election studies in Spain, Japan, and Mexico that show this is how framing works.[14] I also find compelling evidence in another framing study conducted by Salma Ghanem for her doctoral dissertation under McCombs' supervision at the University of Texas.[15]

Ghanem, now dean of communication at Central Michigan University, analyzed the changing percentage of Texans who ranked crime as the most important problem facing the country between 1992 and 1995. The figure rose steadily from 2 percent of respondents in 1992 to 37 percent in 1994, and then dipped down to a still high 21 percent a year later. Ironically, even as public concern about crime was on the rise the first two years, the actual frequency and severity of unlawful acts were going down. On the basis of many first-level agenda-setting studies like the Chapel Hill research, Ghanem assumed that the increased salience of crime was driven by media that featured crime stories prominently and often. She found a high correlation (+0.70) between the amount of media coverage and the depth of public concern.

Ghanem was more interested in tracking the transfer of salience of specific crime attributes—the second level of agenda setting. Of the dozen or so media frames for stories about crime, two bundles of attributes were strongly linked to the public's increasing alarm. The most powerful frame was one that cast crime as something that could happen to anyone. The stories noted that the robbery took place in broad daylight, or the shooting was random and without provocation.

The second frame was where the crime took place. Out-of-state problems were of casual interest, but when a reported felony occurred locally or in the state of Texas, concern rose quickly. Note that both frames were features of news stories that shrank the psychological distance between the crimes they described and the average citizens who read or heard about them. Many concluded, "I could be next." The high correlations (+0.78, +0.73) between these media frames and the subsequent public concern suggest that attribute frames make compelling arguments for the choices people make after exposure to the news.

Framing is not an option. Reporters inevitably frame a story with the personal attributes of public figures they select to describe. For example, the media continually reported on the "youthful vigor" of John F. Kennedy while he was alive but made no mention of his extramarital affairs, which were well known to the White House press corps. The 1988 presidential race was all but over after *Time* framed the contest between George H. W. Bush and Michael Dukakis as "the Nice Man vs. the Ice Man." In 1996 Republican spin doctors fought an uphill battle positioning their candidate once media stories focused on Bob Dole's lack of passion—"Dead Man Walking" was the quip of commentator Mark Shields. And the press picked up on George W. Bush's claim to be a "compassionate conservative" in the 2000 presidential election, whereas Senator John Kerry, his opponent in 2004, was repeatedly described as "flip-flopping" on the issues. In all of these cases it's easy to spot the affective tone of the attribute.

For the last decade, researchers seeking to determine the public's agenda during an election campaign have asked potential voters, "Suppose one of your friends has been away a long time and knows nothing about the candidates. . . . What would you tell your friend about __________?" They take note of each attribute mentioned and later sort them into content categories such as experience, competence, personality, and morality. They then code each attribute as positive, neutral, or negative. Summing all of these affective aspects of attributes gives researchers a reliable measure of voters' attitudes toward the candidate. In most studies, the voters' agenda mirrors the media's agenda in substance and in tone, and also predicts the outcome of the election.[16]

McCombs and Shaw no longer subscribe to Bernard Cohen's classic remark about the media's limited agenda-setting role. They now headline their work with a revised and expanded version that describes agenda setting as a much more powerful media function:

> The media may not only tell us what to think about, they also may tell us how and what to think about it, and perhaps even what to do about it.[17]

BEYOND OPINION: THE BEHAVIORAL EFFECT OF THE MEDIA'S AGENDA

Most of the research studies on agenda setting have measured the effect of media agendas on public *opinion*. But some intriguing findings suggest that media priorities also affect people's *behavior*. Craig Trumbo, a professor of journalism and technical communication at Colorado State University, monitored the headlines for stories about the flu virus in 32 different newspapers between 2002 and 2008.[18] He also had access to the regular flu reports issued by the Centers for Disease Control and Prevention. Those reports showed the number of visits to doctors for flu-like symptoms as well as the actual number of cases of the flu. It would certainly make sense that with more actual flu cases, doctor visits would increase and journalists would be more likely to cover the story. But Trumbo found that even when he took account of the actual flu cases, there was still an agenda-setting effect. The amount of media coverage on the flu during one week predicted the number of doctor visits the next week. There was no evidence of a reverse effect. Patient visits to the doctor for flu symptoms didn't predict later media coverage about the virus. Trumbo's study provides evidence that the agenda-setting effect extends to behavior.

Nowhere is the behavioral effect of the media agenda more apparent than in the business of professional sports. In his book *The Ultimate Assist,* John Fortunato explores the commercial partnership between network television's agenda and the National Basketball Association's (NBA).[19] Television dramatically raised the salience of the sport (the first level of agenda setting) by scheduling games in prime-time viewing slots. It also put basketball's best attributes forward (the second level of agenda setting) by selecting the teams with the premier competitors to play in those games and focusing on those players. During the peak years of Michael Jordan's basketball career, it was "all Michael, all the time."

Television shaped an attractive picture of the NBA in viewers' minds through a series of off-court frames. Interviews with select players and coaches, color commentary, graphics, and instant replays of players' spectacular moves all created a positive image of the NBA. As for the rape accusation against L.A. Lakers superstar Kobe Bryant, and later his feud with teammate Shaquille O'Neal that split the team, the media cooperated in downplaying those attributes that tarnish the NBA's image. As McCombs and other researchers have discovered by analyzing multiple presidential elections, it's the cumulative effect of long-term attribute salience that can alter attitudes and behavior.[20]

This 30-year effort to shape the public agenda has not only had a spectacular effect on fan behavior, it has also altered the face of popular culture. From 1970 to 2000, the number of NBA teams and the number of games doubled. The number of fans going to games quadrupled. But the astronomical difference is in the money. In 1970, television provided $10 million in revenue to the NBA. In 2000, the payout was $2 billion, and in 2012 it was $5 billion—no small change. McCombs' comment: "Agenda setting the theory can also be agenda setting the business plan."[21]

WHO SETS THE AGENDA FOR THE AGENDA SETTERS?

News doesn't select itself. So who sets the agenda for the agenda setters? One view regards a handful of news editors as the guardians, or "gatekeepers," of political dialogue. Nothing gets put on the political agenda without the concurrence of a few select people—the operations chiefs of the Associated Press, *The New York Times, The Washington Post, Time, Newsweek,* ABC, NBC, CBS, CNN, Fox, and MSNBC. Although there is no evidence to support right-wing conservative charges that the editors are part of a liberal, eastern-establishment conspiracy, when one of them features an issue, the rest of the nation's media tend to pick up the story.

An alternative view regards candidates and office holders themselves as the ultimate source of issue salience. George H. W. Bush put the tax issue on the table with his famous statement "Read my lips: no new taxes." But he was unable to get the issue off the table when he broke that pledge. He also tried to dismiss the economic recession as a "mild technical adjustment." The press and the populace decided it was major.

Current thinking on news selection focuses on the crucial role of public relations professionals working for government agencies, corporations, and interest groups. Even prestigious newspapers with large investigative staffs such as *The Washington Post* and *The New York Times* get more than half of what they print straight from press releases and press conferences.[22]

Interest aggregations Clusters of people who demand center stage for their one overriding concern; pressure groups.

Interest aggregations are becoming increasingly adept at creating news that must be reported. This term refers to clusters of people who demand center stage for their one overriding concern, whatever it might be—anti-abortion, antiwar, anti-communism, antipollution, anti-immigration, anti-same-sex-marriage. As the examples indicate, these groups usually rally around a specific action that they oppose. They stage demonstrations, marches, and other media events so that television and the press will be forced to cover their issue. The prominence of the Tea Party's campaign against government spending and taxes is a striking example. The media seem to pay attention to those who grab it.

On rare occasions, news events are so compelling that editors have no choice but to feature them for extended periods of time. The month-long Florida recount in 2000 to determine whether George W. Bush or Al Gore would be president was one such case. And, of course, the 9/11 terrorist attack totally dominated U.S. print and broadcast news, pushing almost every other story off the front page and television screen for the rest of the year. Stories like these clearly reveal what McCombs has referred to recently as *intermedia* agenda setting. Editors at most newspapers are influenced to some extent by what other news outlets are covering. When many news sources continue to feature the same story, it's tough for an editor to ignore the trend. There's more than one answer to the question of who sets the agenda for the agenda setters. The gatekeepers, interest aggregations, and the media themselves all play a role.[23]

WILL NEW MEDIA STILL SHAPE THE AGENDA, OPINIONS, AND BEHAVIOR?

Ironically, the power of agenda setting that McCombs and Shaw describe may be on the wane. In a creative experiment, University of Illinois researchers Scott Althaus and David Tewksbury predicted that traditional print media would be more effective than new electronic media in setting a reader's agenda.[24] They reasoned that people who are reading a newspaper know that editors consider a long, front-page article under a banner headline more important than a short story buried on an inside page. Not only are these comparative cues absent on the computer screen, but online readers can click on links to similar stories and never see accounts of events that paper readers see as they thumb through the pages.

Althaus and Tewksbury recruited students to spend 30 to 60 minutes a day for 5 days reading either a print version or an online version of *The New York Times* under controlled conditions. For both groups it was their only exposure to news that week. On the sixth day, the researchers tested recognition and recall of the week's stories and assessed which problems facing the country students personally regarded as most important. Not only did those who read the traditional paper remember more content, they also selected a higher percentage of international issues as more important to them, thus aligning closer to the prioritized agenda of the *Times'* editors. The researchers concluded that "by providing users with more content choices and control over exposure, new technologies may allow people to create personalized information environments that shut them off from larger flows of public information in a society."[25] Abby's application log illustrates this point.

> I confess to being an online newsreader who only clicks on links that interest me. I easily bypass information and headlines on my computer that I couldn't avoid when reading a print version of the news. This caught up with me in my class in American politics. Our assignment was to stay informed about worldwide current

> events by reading *The New York Times.* I chose to read the paper online—to my detriment. I found myself clicking on stories of personal interest and didn't even notice headlines on other issues. My weekly quiz grades let me know that my study agenda didn't match the media agenda.

McCombs wouldn't be surprised that Abby chose to get news online rather than through newspapers or news broadcasts. In a study reported in 2007, he and Renita Coleman, a colleague at the University of Texas, found that most of the younger generation (18 to 34) relied on the Internet for news, middle-aged viewers (35 to 54) tended to favor TV, and older readers (55+) preferred newspapers. The correlation between the media agenda and the younger generation was somewhat lower than for boomers or the older generation, but at 0.70, it was still high. These results are consistent with a 2013 study by Adam Shehata and Jesper Strömbäck, media professors at Mid Sweden University. While these researchers discovered that the size of the agenda-setting effect is shrinking as people rely more on a variety of online news outlets, it certainly hasn't vanished.[26] McCombs thinks that's because "most Internet news sources are subsidiaries of traditional news media, and there is a high degree of redundancy in the media agendas even on diverse media."[27] He does note, however, that young adults are also learning what's important from late-night comedians like Jon Stewart on *The Daily Show.* It's not yet clear if the news they parody parallels the agenda of other media outlets.

ETHICAL REFLECTION: CHRISTIANS' COMMUNITARIAN ETHICS

Clifford Christians is the former director of the Institute of Communications Research at the University of Illinois at Urbana–Champaign and the lead author of *Good News: Social Ethics and the Press.*[28] Although he values free speech, he doesn't share the near-absolute devotion to the First Amendment that seems to be the sole ethical commitment of many journalists. Christians rejects reporters' and editors' insistence on an absolute right of free expression that is based on the individualistic rationalism of John Locke and other Enlightenment thinkers. In our age of ethical relativism where *continue the conversation* is the best that philosophy has to offer,[29] Christians believes that discovering the truth is still possible if we are willing to examine the nature of our humanity. The human nature he perceives is, at root, personhood in community.[30]

Christians agrees with Martin Buber that the relation is the cradle of life. ("In the beginning is the relation."[31]) He is convinced, therefore, that mutuality is the essence of humanness. People are most fully human as "persons-in-relation" who live simultaneously for others and for themselves.

> A moral community demonstrates more than mere interdependence; it is characterized by mutuality, a will-to-community, a genuine concern for the other apart from immediate self-interest. . . . An act is morally right when compelled by the intention to maintain the community of persons; it is wrong if driven by self-centeredness.[32]

Communitarian ethics
A moral responsibility to promote community, mutuality, and persons-in-relation who live simultaneously for others and for themselves.

Christians understands that a commitment to mutuality would significantly alter media culture and mission. His *communitarian ethics* establish civic transformation rather than objective information as the primary goal of the press. Reporters' aim would thus become a revitalized citizenship shaped by community norms—morally literate and active participants, not just readers and audiences provided with data.[33] Editors, publishers, and owners—the gatekeepers of the media agenda—would be held to the same standard. Christians insists that media criticism must be willing to reestablish the idea of moral right and wrong. Selfish practices aimed at splintering community are not merely misguided; they are evil.[34]

Christians' communitarian ethics are based on the Christian tradition of *agape love*—an unconditional love for others because they were created in the image of God. He believes journalists have a social responsibility to promote the sacredness of life by respecting human dignity, truthtelling, and doing no harm to innocents.[35] With an emphasis on establishing communal bonds, alienated people on the margins of society receive special attention from communitarians. Christians ultimately judges journalists on the basis of how well they use the media's power to champion the goal of social justice. For example, Christians asks:

Agape love
An unconditional love for others because they were created in the image of God.

> Is the press a voice for the unemployed, food-stamp recipients, Appalachian miners, the urban poor, Hispanics in rural shacks, the elderly, women discriminated against in hiring and promotion, ethnic minorities with no future in North America's downsizing economy?[36]

If the media sets that kind of agenda and features attributes that promote community, he believes they are fulfilling their communitarian responsibility.

CRITIQUE: ARE THE EFFECTS TOO LIMITED, THE SCOPE TOO WIDE?

When McCombs and Shaw first proposed the agenda-setting hypothesis, they saw it as a sharp break from the limited-effects model that had held sway in media research since Paul Lazarsfeld introduced the concept of *selective exposure* (see the introduction to Media Effects). Although not reverting to the old magic-bullet conception of media influence, McCombs and Shaw ascribed to broadcast and print journalism the significant power to set the public's political priorities. As years of careful research have shown, however, agenda setting doesn't always work. Perhaps the best that could be said until the mid-1990s was that the media agenda affects the salience of some issues for some people some of the time. So in 1994, McCombs suggested that "agenda setting is a theory of limited media effects."[37] That would be quite a comedown from its original promise.

The new dimension of framing reasserts a powerful media-effects model. As Ohio State University journalism professor Gerald Kosicki states,

> Media "gatekeepers" do not merely keep watch over information, shuffling it here and there. Instead, they engage in active construction of the messages, emphasizing certain aspects of an issue and not others.[38]

But Kosicki questions whether framing is even a legitimate topic of study under an agenda-setting banner. He sees nothing in McCombs and Shaw's original model that anticipates the importance of interpretive frames.

As McCombs is fond of pointing out, the evidence is there. In the lead article of a 1977 book that he and Shaw edited, they clearly previewed the current "New Frontiers" of agendas of attributes and framing:

> Agenda setting as a concept is not limited to the correspondence between salience of topics for the media and the audience. We can also consider the saliency of various attributes of these objects (topics, issues, persons or whatever) reported in the media. To what extent is our view of an object shaped or influenced by the picture sketched in the media, especially by those attributes which the media deem newsworthy?[39]

McCombs' definition of framing appears to be quite specific: "Framing is the selection of a restricted number of thematically related attributes for inclusion on the media agenda when a particular object is discussed."[40] In contrast, the popularity of framing as an *interpretive* construct in media studies has resulted in diverse and ambiguous meanings. The way Stuart Hall and other critical theorists use the term is so elastic that the word seems to refer to anything they don't like. Thus, I regard a narrow view of framing as a distinct advantage for empirically based media-effects research.

As for the six criteria for evaluating a social science theory, agenda setting fares well. It *predicts* that the public's agenda for the salience of attitude objects and key attributes will follow the media's lead, and it *explains* why some people are more susceptible to media influence than others. Those predictions are *testable* by using content analysis to establish the media agenda, surveys to determine public opinion, and *quantitative* statistical tests to determine the overlap. More than 400 empirical studies have supported and refined the theory. Even with the theorists' added concern for the affective tone of attributes, their theory remains relatively simple. And as for *practical utility,* agenda setting tells journalists, advertisers, political operatives, and media scholars not only what to look for, but how they might alter the pictures in the heads of those who read, view, or listen to the news.

QUESTIONS TO SHARPEN YOUR FOCUS

1. If the media aren't telling you what to think, why is their ability to tell you *what to think about* so important?
2. What *type of person* under what *type of circumstances* is most susceptible to the media's *agenda-setting function?*
3. Sarah Palin is one of the most controversial public figures in America. What *dominant set of attributes* could you use to *frame* her visit to a children's hospital to make her look good? How could you make her look bad?
4. Is there a recent issue that *news reporters and commentators* are now talking about daily that you and the people you know don't care about? Do you think you'll still be unconcerned two months from now?

CONVERSATIONS

View this segment online at www.mhhe.com/griffin9e or www.afirstlook.com.

In our conversation, Max McCombs discusses the process of framing and how this concept has changed the scope of his theory. He also answers questions posed by my students: How many issues can a person focus on at one time? If he ran the classic Chapel Hill study today, would he use CNN as a media outlet that sets the public agenda? Do TV entertainment shows have an agenda-setting function? I wanted to know how he saw potential media bias. Are all news stories delivered with a spin? Does he see anything sinister about intentionally framing a story? Is there a liberal bias in the national media? I think you'll be surprised by his direct responses.

A SECOND LOOK

Recommended resource: Maxwell McCombs and Amy Reynolds, "How the News Shapes our Civic Agenda," in *Media Effects: Advances in Theory and Research,* Jennings Bryant and Dolf Zillmann (eds.), Routledge, New York, 2009, pp. 1–16.

Comprehensive summary of theory and research: Maxwell McCombs, *Setting the Agenda,* Polity, Cambridge, UK, 2004.

Historical development: Maxwell McCombs and Tamara Bell, "The Agenda-Setting Role of Mass Communication," in *An Integrated Approach to Communication Theory and Research,* Michael Salwen and Donald Stacks (eds.), Lawrence Erlbaum, Hillsdale, NJ, 1996, pp. 93–110.

Five stages of agenda-setting research and development: Maxwell McCombs, "A Look at Agenda-Setting: Past, Present and Future," *Journalism Studies,* Vol. 6, 2005, pp. 543–557.

Prototype election study: Maxwell McCombs and Donald Shaw, "The Agenda-Setting Function of the Mass Media," *Public Opinion Quarterly,* Vol. 36, 1972, pp. 176–187.

Framing: Maxwell McCombs and Salma Ghanem, "The Convergence of Agenda Setting and Framing," in *Framing Public Life,* Stephen Reese, Oscar Gandy Jr., and August Grant (eds.), Lawrence Erlbaum, Mahwah, NJ, 2001, pp. 67–81.

Relationship among agenda setting, framing, and priming: Dietram Scheufele and David Tewksbury, "Framing, Agenda Setting, and Priming: The Evolution of Three Media Effects Models," *Journal of Communication,* Vol. 57, 2007, pp. 9–20.

Bundles of attributes: Maxwell McCombs, "New Frontiers in Agenda Setting: Agendas of Attributes and Frames," *Mass Comm Review,* Vol. 24, 1997, pp. 4–24.

Anthology of earlier agenda-setting research: Maxwell McCombs, Donald Shaw, and David Weaver, *Communication and Democracy: Exploring the Intellectual Frontiers in Agenda-Setting Theory,* Lawrence Erlbaum, Mahwah, NJ, 1997.

Israeli election study: Meital Balmas and Tamir Sheafer, "Candidate Image in Election Campaigns: Attribute Agenda Setting, Affective Priming, and Voting Intentions," *International Journal of Public Opinion Research,* Vol. 22, 2010, pp. 204–229.

Focus on the theorist: William Davie and T. Michael Maher, "Maxwell McCombs: Agenda-Setting Explorer," *Journal of Broadcasting and Electronic Media,* Vol. 50, 2006, pp. 358–364.

Critique: Gerald Kosicki, "Problems and Opportunities in Agenda-Setting Research," *Journal of Communication,* Vol. 43, No. 2, 1993, pp. 100–127.

For a theory that explains the role of media in shaping public opinion, click on Spiral of Silence in Archive under Theory Resources in *www.afirstlook.com.*

Cultural Context

DIVISION FIVE

Cultural Context

Intercultural Communication

When we think of *culture,* most of us picture a place—the South American culture of Brazil, the Middle Eastern culture of Saudi Arabia, or the Far Eastern culture of Japan. But Gerry Philipsen, a professor of communication at the University of Washington who specializes in intercultural communication, says that culture is not basically geographical. Nor is it essentially political or a matter of race. Philipsen describes *culture* as "a socially constructed and historically transmitted pattern of symbols, meanings, premises, and rules."[1] At root, culture is a code.

Ethnographers study the speech and nonverbal communication of people in order to crack that code. We've already looked at Mead's reliance on participant observation (see Chapter 5) and Geertz' use of thick description (see Chapter 19) to unravel the complex web of meanings that people share within a society or culture. In like manner, Philipsen spent multiple years conducting two ethnographic studies. The first study revealed what it was like to "speak like a man" in a multiethnic, blue-collar Chicago neighborhood he called "Teamsterville." He discovered that men used talk primarily to show solidarity with friends who were part of the neighborhood.[2] The second study identified the communication patterns of a large group of people dispersed around the United States whom he dubbed the "Nacirema" (*American* spelled backward). He regarded the live audience for the television talk show *Donahue*—a forerunner of *Oprah*—as typical members of the Nacirema culture. He and Donal Carbaugh (University of Massachusetts) found that any appeal to a universal standard of ethical conduct was considered by members of that culture to be an infringement of their right to be an individual.[3]

Philipsen selected these two American subcultures for study in part because he saw their communication practices as so different from one another. Is there a way he could have measured the extent of their discrepancy—or for that matter, the cultural variability of any two countries across the globe? From a study of multinational corporations in more than 50 countries, Dutch researcher Geert Hofstede concluded that there are four crucial dimensions on which to compare cultures.[4]

1. *Power distance*—the extent to which the less powerful members of society accept that power is distributed unequally (Americans—low; Japanese—medium)
2. *Masculinity*—clearly defined gender roles, with male values of success, money, and possessions dominant in society (Americans—high; Japanese—extremely high)
3. *Uncertainty avoidance*—the extent to which people feel threatened by ambiguity and create beliefs and institutions to try to avoid it (Americans—low; Japanese—extremely high)
4. *Individualism*—people look out for themselves and their immediate families as opposed to identifying with a larger group that is responsible for taking care of them in exchange for group loyalty (Americans—extremely high; Japanese—low)

Many researchers agree that Hofstede's distinction between individualism and collectivism is the crucial dimension of cultural variability. The *we-centered* focus of Teamsterville sets it apart from individualistic American society in general, and from the extremely *I-centered* preoccupation of the Nacirema subculture in particular. Cultural anthropologist Edward Hall was the first to label the communication style of collectivistic cultures as *high-context* and the style of individualistic cultures as *low-context.* The designation divides groups of people on the basis of how they interpret messages.

> A high-context communication or message is one in which most of the information is either in the physical context or internalized in the person, while very little is in the coded, explicit part of the message. A low-context communication is just the opposite, i.e., the mass of information is vested in the explicit code.[5]

Hall contrasted American and Japanese cultures to illustrate the differences between collectivistic societies that have a message-*context* orientation and individualistic societies that rely more on message *content.*[6]

Americans believe in straight talk. Assertiveness is saying what you mean; honesty is meaning what you say. Both are highly prized. Perhaps the highest art form of explicit communication is the legal contract. A U.S. lawyer's dream is to prepare a verbal document that allows no room for interpretation. Hall said that Japanese communication is more subtle. Bluntness is regarded as rude; patience and indirection are the marks of a civilized person. What is said is less important than how it is said and who did the saying. Meaning is embedded in the setting and the nonverbal code. In Japan, the highest form of communication competency is empathy—the ability to sense what others are thinking and feeling without their having to spell it out for you.

Co-author Glenn Sparks experienced these distinctions when he—a typically low-context American—worked with high-context Africans in Ethiopia.

> When I was in Ethiopia, I worked daily with various folks at the university. I came to learn that about half the time, a lunch appointment, a promise to have a key for a room at a certain time, or a commitment to make copies of a reading for the class just didn't pan out. But all of these commitments were made with kindness and politeness. Ethiopians were much more attuned to the overall tenor of an interaction than they were to the actual words that were said.[7]

Glenn is a quick study. By reminding himself of the crucial contextual issue that Hall identified, he was able to reduce his frustration. Hopefully, in turn, his Ethiopian hosts gave him a "visitor's pass" for misinterpreting what they had "said."

CHAPTER 31

Objective — Interpretive

Socio-psychological tradition

Communication Accommodation Theory

of Howard Giles

I was born, raised, and educated in the Great Lakes region of the United States. During my sophomore year of college, my folks moved from the south side of Chicago to the Deep South, a region where the style of speech was foreign to my ear. When speaking with other college students I met there over summer vacation, I noticed that I started to talk slower, pause longer, maintain less eye contact, and drop the final *g* off of words ending with *-ing* ("Nice *talkin'* with you"). Although I didn't adopt a southern drawl, I definitely adjusted my style of speaking to better match that of those I met. As an outsider, I wanted to fit in.

Although I couldn't lose my Chicago twang, one of the guys I met commented on my go-along-to-get-along effort. "You're beginnin' to talk just like us," he said. His smile suggested appreciation rather than scorn. Not so my older sister when I drove her from San Antonio, Texas, to Anniston, Alabama, the following Christmas. "You sound ridiculous," was her disdainful reaction when she heard me talk to people in restaurants and motels along the way.

In 1973, Welsh social psychologist Howard Giles suggested that my experience was typical. Now a professor of communication at the University of California, Santa Barbara, Giles claimed that when two people from different ethnic or cultural groups interact, they tend to accommodate each other in the way they speak in order to gain the other's approval.[1] He specifically focused on the nonverbal adjustments of speech rate, accent, and pauses. Based on the principle that we tend to like others who strike us as similar, Giles claimed that speech accommodation is a frequently used strategy to gain the appreciation of people who are from different groups or cultures. This process of seeking approval by meshing with another's style of speaking is at the core of what he then labeled *speech accommodation theory.*

A SIMPLE NOTION BECOMES A COMPREHENSIVE COMMUNICATION THEORY

Giles and his colleagues launched an extensive program of lab and field research to answer the questions that the practice of speech accommodation raises. For example:

Are there times we don't adjust our speech style to match that of others?

If so, what is our motive for not accommodating?

How do groups with which we identify affect our accommodation choices?

Is accommodation always conscious?

Do others accurately perceive our intent when we shift our speech style?

To what extent do we adjust *what* we say as well as the *way* we say it?

What are the social consequences if we overaccommodate?

Because the answers to these questions led Giles to communication issues that go far beyond the narrow issue of accent mobility, pauses, and pronunciation, the scope of the theory expanded dramatically. In 1987, Giles changed the name of the theory to *communication accommodation theory (CAT)* and offered it as "a theory of intercultural communication that actually attends to communication."[2]

The early research of Giles and his colleagues centered on interethnic communication, often between two bilingual groups in the same country. In the last two decades, however, CAT researchers have also shown consistent interest in exploring *communication accommodation* in an intergenerational context. They broadly define *young* communicators as those who are teenagers up to adults in their 40s or even 50s. They define *old* or *elderly* communicators as those who are 65 and over.[3] To what extent do members of these two groups adjust their communication when talking to someone of the other generation?

Accommodation
The constant movement toward or away from others by changing your communicative behavior.

Since the vast majority of this book's readers fall within that younger classification, I'll use intergenerational communication to illustrate the main predictions of the theory. That way you'll have a personal stake in understanding the theory's claims. So will I. In the spirit of full disclosure, you should know that for the past 11 years I've qualified as a member of the elder group. Of course, this means that every time I walk into a college classroom it becomes a potential laboratory to explore intergenerational communication. I also have a lot of experience in the other direction. For years, my centenarian mother-in-law lived with us until she passed away.

COMMUNICATION ACCOMMODATION STRATEGIES

Throughout the theory's extensive development, Giles has consistently contrasted two strategic forms of communication that diverse people use when they interact—*convergence* and *divergence.* He sees both types of behavior as accommodation because they each involve constant movement toward or away from others through a change in communicative behavior.

Convergence

Convergence is a strategy by which you adapt your communication behavior in such a way as to become more similar to another person. As we've already seen, one way to do this is to adjust your speaking style to approximate that of your

Convergence
A strategy of adapting your communication behavior in such a way as to become more similar to another person.

conversational partner. If you're talking with an octogenarian man who speaks in short phrases delivered in a gravelly voice, you could abandon smoothly flowing sentences in favor of brief, raspy responses. You wouldn't try to mimic his voice, but you'd try to get closer to its sound and cadence. If the elderly man desires to converge toward your speaking style, he might need to speak with more energy, display greater facial expression, and increase vocal variety.

Another way you could converge toward the elderly gentleman would be to talk in a way that would make it easier for him to grasp what you're saying. If you notice that he's hard of hearing, convergence would involve speaking one notch louder, while clearly enunciating consonants. Or if he seems to have trouble tracking with abstract ideas, you could aid his comprehension by using examples to illustrate what you're saying. For his part, he might help you interpret what he's saying by not assuming you know the political background of the Korean War or singer Pat Boone's biggest hits.

An additional way to bridge the generation gap can be through *discourse management*—the sensitive selection of topics to discuss. Giles and Angie Williams (Cardiff University, Wales) elicited college students' retrospective accounts of both satisfying and frustrating intergenerational conversations. They found that young people greatly appreciated the elderly when they discerned what stories the students wanted to hear. For example, one girl wrote, "She just talked about the history of the team and all that she knew. . . . I stayed and listened to her stories, which were fascinating."[4] They also appreciated elders who sensed when not to pry: "I'm glad she didn't ask anything about Bekki and my relationship. . . . I would have felt awkward."[5]

As Brittany's application log describes, some parties converge to facilitate communication. When they do, mutual appreciation is often a byproduct.

> Some family members on my father's side are deaf. Some of my family members who can hear know how to sign and some of those who can't hear are able to read lips. I've learned to sign a bit so I can communicate more effectively with those who can't hear. I also slow my speech down and try to enunciate my words more clearly so they can more easily understand what I'm saying. They've told me that they appreciate my willingness to reach out to them. In the same way, I appreciate their convergence when they sign slower and also lip words so that I can catch what they're saying.

Divergence

Divergence
A communication strategy of accentuating the differences between you and another person.

Divergence is a communication strategy of accentuating the differences between you and another person. In interethnic encounters, you might insist on using a language or dialect with which the other is uncomfortable. In terms of speech style, you could diverge by employing a thicker accent, adopting a rate of speaking distinct from that used by the other person, or speaking in either a monotone or with exaggerated animation. Linguistically, divergence could be signaled by a deliberate substitution of words. Giles offers an example where a young speaker flippantly says to an elderly man, "Okay, mate, let's get it together at my place around 3:30 tomorrow." The disdainful elder might reply, "Fine, young man, we'll meet again at 15:30, at your house tomorrow."[6] All of these communication moves are examples of counter-accommodation—direct ways of maximizing the differences between two speakers.

"Hey, Gramps, is 'deathbed' one word or two?"

During intergenerational encounters, CAT researchers have found that divergence is the norm and convergence the exception, especially when the two aren't members of the same family. Young people typically characterize the elderly as *closed-minded, out of touch, angry, complaining,* and *negatively stereotyping youth.*[7] The elderly often increase the social distance through the process of *self-handicapping*—a defensive, face-saving strategy that uses age as a reason for not performing well. For example, University of Arizona communication professor Jake Harwood and two colleagues discovered that many of the ways the elderly talk continually remind younger listeners that their grandparents are old.[8]

Self-handicapping
For the elderly, a face-saving strategy that invokes age as a reason for not performing well.

1. Talk about age: *You're so young. I turn 70 next December.*
2. Talk about health: *They warned of blood clots with my hip replacement surgery.*
3. Don't understand the world today: *Are Facebook and texting the same?*
4. Patronizing: *You kids today don't know the meaning of hard work.*
5. Painful self-disclosure: *I cried when she said that to me. It still hurts.*
6. Difficulty hearing: *Please speak up and try not to mumble.*
7. Mental confusion: *I can't think of the word. What were we talking about?*

These features consistently make the speakers' age salient (or noticeable) to the listener, and all seven leave a negative impression. They might as well tattoo GZR on their forehead.

Giles and his colleagues describe two other strategies similar to divergence that are a bit more subtle. *Maintenance* is the strategy of persisting in your original communication style regardless of the communication behavior of the other. Giles offers a college student's recollections of a dissatisfying conversation with a senior citizen as a description of maintenance: "He did most of the talking and did not really seem to care about what I said. . . . He appeared to be so closed minded and unreceptive to new ideas."[9] Conversely, an older person is likely to feel woefully underaccommodated if she shares a fear or frustration and then only hears a quick, "I know exactly how you feel," before the younger person changes the topic.[10]

Maintenance
Persisting in your original communication style regardless of the communication behavior of the other; similar to divergence.

The other strategy that's similar to divergence is *overaccommodation,* which may be well-intended, but has the effect of making the recipient feel worse. Giles describes overaccommodation as "demeaning or patronizing talk . . . when excessive concern is paid to vocal clarity or [amplification], message simplification, or repetition"[11] Often characterized as "baby talk," this way of speaking can frustrate the elderly, thus leading to a perception that they are irritable or grumpy. Alternatively, frequent overaccommodation from caregivers can not only make the recipient feel less competent, it can actually talk them into becoming less competent (see Chapter 5).

Overaccommodation
Demeaning or patronizing talk; excessive concern paid to vocal clarity or amplification, message simplification, or repetition; similar to divergence.

If overaccommodating communication is often counterproductive and sometimes harmful, why do younger folks talk that way? For that matter, other than sheer obstinacy, why would old or young people opt for any kind of divergent strategy rather than one that's convergent? The next section shows that the motivation for these contrasting behaviors is tied to people's concern for their identity.

DIFFERENT MOTIVATIONS FOR CONVERGENCE AND DIVERGENCE

As the first page of this chapter indicates, CAT theorists have always regarded *desire for social approval* as the main motivation for convergence. You meet a person different from you and you'd like him or her to think well of you, respect you, or find you attractive. As one of the theorems of *uncertainty reduction theory* states, there's a positive relationship between similarity and attraction (see Chapter 9). So you identify with the other person by adjusting what you say and the way you say it in order to appear more similar. As long as you're both acting as unique individuals who are shaping their own personal identities and relationships, representing convergence as a two-step, cause-and-effect relationship seems justified:

Desire for approval (personal identity) → Convergence → Positive response

There are two problems, however. First, this motivational sequence can't explain why we frequently communicate in a divergent way, and second, the causal chain doesn't take into account the fact that we often act as a representative of a group. Giles and other CAT theorists draw upon *social identity theory,* the work of Henri Tajfel (University of Bristol, UK) and John Turner (Australian National University) to solve that problem.[12]

Social Identity Theory

Social identity
Group memberships and social categories that we use to define who we are.

Tajfel and Turner suggested that we often communicate not as individual actors, but as representatives of groups that help define who we are. Our *social identity* is based upon our intergroup behavior. As Jake Harwood puts it, "We are not random individuals wandering the planet with no connections to others, and our connections to others cannot be understood purely as a function of individual phenomena."[13] Our group memberships—whether formal associations or allegiances only in our minds—can greatly affect our communication.

As a case in point, if you click on "Em Griffin" at the bottom of the home page of *www.afirstlook.com,* you'll find that I identify with groups of communication professors, conflict mediators, people of faith, pilots, an extended Griffin family, and those who work for economic justice in the developing world. By accident of birth, I also have at least four other group identifications: I'm an older, white, American male. According to Tajfel and Turner, whenever any of these associations comes to mind in talking with others, my motivation will be to reinforce and defend my ties to those groups. After all, they make up my social identity. And when these groups are salient at the start of an interaction with someone different, CAT claims that my communication will diverge away from my partner's speech rather than converge toward it.

Tajfel and Turner pictured a motivational continuum with *personal identity* on one end of the scale and *social identity* at the other pole. As long as both parties consider themselves and their conversational partner to be unencumbered, autonomous individuals acting for themselves, the theorists believed the *desire for approval → convergence → positive response* sequence is what takes place. But if one (or both) of the interactants regards self or other as a representative of a group of people, Tajfel and Turner said that their communication will likely become divergent because of their need to emphasize their distinctiveness. So when group identity is salient, the two-step, cause-and-effect sequence is quite different:

Need for distinctiveness (social identity) → Divergence → Negative response

Giles and his colleagues believe that this alternative sequence occurs quite frequently. They hold out the possibility that a person could seek approval and distinctiveness within the same conversation when their personal and social identities are both salient. For example, consider an interracial friendship where buddies never lose sight of their ethnicity. Or think of a loving marriage in which both husband and wife are keenly aware of their gender roles. Your first look at communication accommodation theory will come into focus more easily, however, if we stick with Tajfel and Turner's either/or conception of one of the two motivations holding sway in a given interaction. To the extent that their theory is accurate, how can we predict whether concerns for personal identity or social identity will kick in? According to Giles there's no hard-and-fast rule. But a person's *initial orientation* is a somewhat reliable predictor.

Initial Orientation

Initial orientation is the predisposition a person has toward focusing on either individual identity or group identity. Predicting which route a person will take is difficult, but the additive presence of five factors increases the odds that a

Initial orientation
Communicators' predisposition to focus on either their individual identity or group identity during a conversation.

communicator will see the conversation as an intergroup encounter. I'll continue to illustrate these factors by referring to intergenerational communication.

1. **Collectivistic cultural context.** As noted in the introduction to the intercultural communication section, the distinction between collectivistic and individualistic cultures is probably the crucial dimension of cultural variability. The *we-centered* focus of collectivism emphasizes similarity and mutual concern within the culture—definitely oriented toward social identity. Their communication toward out-group members is often divergent. The *I-centered* focus of individualistic cultures valorizes the individual actor—definitely oriented toward individual identity. As for intergenerational relationships, despite the cultural value of respect for elders shared among East Asian cultures, there's strong evidence that Pacific Rim young people and their Western counterparts both regard the elderly as a group apart.[14] Age transcends ethnic culture.

2. **Distressing history of interaction.** If previous interactions were uncomfortable, competitive, or hostile, both interactants will tend to ascribe that outcome to the other person's social identity. *(Men are like that. The poor are lazy. Presbyterians are God's frozen people.)* If the previous time together was positive, the result is often ascribed to the individual rather than to a group or class to which he or she belongs. *(By the end I felt good knowing that not all older people hate the younger generation. . . . Every other elder I've talked to has made me fear or want to avoid getting old.)*[15]

3. **Stereotypes.** The more specific and negative the images people have of an out-group, the more likely they are to think of the other in terms of social identity and then resort to divergent communication. This is a big factor in intergenerational communication. The young tend to stereotype the elderly as *irritable, nagging, grouchy, verbose,* and *addled.*[16] Conversely, the elderly stereotype "youth today" as *spoiled,* an accusation often introduced with the phrase, *Why, when I was your age. . . .* These rigid group stereotypes make convergent communication across generations a rare and difficult achievement.

Norms
Expectations about behavior that members of a community feel should (or should not) occur in particular situations.

4. **Norms for treatment of groups.** Norms can be defined as "expectations about behavior that members of a community feel should (or should not) occur in particular situations."[17] These expectations can affect whether a member of one group regards a person from another group as an individual or as "one of them." The oft-stated rule to "respect your elders" suggests that the elderly are a group of people who deserve high regard because they've stayed alive, rather than because they have individual worth. The result of that group norm may be young adults showing deference to an elderly person, but *biting their tongue* and *not talking back,* a process that could build resentment toward a group they may join someday.

5. **High group-solidarity / high group-dependence.** Picture Lucile, a 70-year-old widow living in a small retirement village where residents rely on each other for social, emotional, and even physical well-being. As the organizer of a successful food co-op, she's at the nexus of communication and has a higher status among her neighbors than she's ever had before. When a young county health department official questions the co-op's food handling practices, Lucile goes to talk with him in what she regards as an us-against-them encounter. Giles would predict that she would have an initial intergroup orientation because of her strong identification with the group and her high dependence on it for relational warmth and a sense of worth.[18]

No single factor determines a person's initial orientation, but if all five factors line up in the direction of public identity, it's almost certain that a communicator will approach a conversation with an intergroup mindset. That seems to be the case in most intergenerational interactions. Giles would note, however, that a person may change orientations during a conversation.

RECIPIENT EVALUATION OF CONVERGENCE AND DIVERGENCE

Let's start with the bottom line. After 35 years of multiple revisions, restatements, and research studies, Giles and his colleagues continue to believe what he wrote about accommodation in his first major article—that listeners regard convergence as positive and divergence as negative. Specifically, converging speakers are viewed as more competent, attractive, warm, and cooperative.[19] On the other hand, "divergence is often seen by its recipients as insulting, impolite, or downright hostile."[20] But CAT researchers are quick to remind us that accommodation is in the eyes and ears of the beholder. What's ultimately important is not how the communicator converged or diverged, but how the other *perceived* the communicator's behavior.

Objective Versus Subjective Accommodation

Early in his research, Giles realized that there was a disconnect between the communication behavior that he and other neutral researchers observed and what participants heard and saw. He described the gap as the difference between *objective* and *subjective* accommodation. For example, a speaker's accent, rate, pitch, and length of pauses could actually be shifting toward a conversational partner's style of speaking, but the partner might regard it as divergent. In light of this discrepancy, Giles says it's recipients' subjective evaluation that really matters, because that's what will shape their response.

Speakers who desire to seek approval by converging with the other's way of speaking may also misperceive what that style really is. From an objective point of view, what strikes them as the other group's preferred style of communication may woefully miss the mark. For example, a granddad might try to identify with his grandkids by using phrases like *right on, really hep,* or *that's square,* not realizing that these phrases were more typical of teenagers in the late 1960s than of teens today. Giles notes that "one does not converge toward (or diverge from) the *actual* speech of the recipient, but toward (or from) one's *stereotype* about the recipient's speech."[21]

Attribution Theory

Attribution
The perceptual process by which we observe what people do and then try to figure out their intent or disposition.

Our response to others' communication hinges not only on the behavior we perceive, but also on the intention or motive we ascribe to them for speaking that way. Giles draws from *attribution theory* to cast light on how we'll interpret our conversational partners' convergent or divergent behavior. In two different versions of attribution theory, social psychologists Fritz Heider (University of Kansas) and Harold Kelley (UCLA) suggested that we attribute an internal disposition to the behavior we see another enact.[22] As amateur psychologists, our default assumption is that *people who do things like that are like that.* Yet three mitigating factors may come into play: (1) the other's ability, (2) external constraints, and (3) the effort expended.

Suppose you're talking with an elderly man who continually asks you to repeat what you've said. If you know that his hearing is good (high ability) and the room is quiet (no external constraints), yet he's not paying much attention (low effort), you'll attribute his divergent behavior to lack of respect for you. You'll be more understanding if you know he's hard of hearing (low ability). But as one research study shows, you'll still be irritated by his lack of consideration if he freely chooses not to wear a hearing aid (low effort).[23] What if you know he's almost deaf (low ability), the room is noisy (environmental constraint), and he's wearing a hearing aid and still struggling to catch your words (high effort)? You'll probably appreciate the fact that he cares about what you're saying and wants to understand, even if you find the conversation tiring or uncomfortable.

Overall, listeners who interpret convergence as a speaker's desire to break down cultural barriers react quite favorably.[24] That response is at the core of CAT. But because there's a societal constraint or norm that those with less power (workers, patients, students, immigrants) ought to accommodate to the communication practices of those with higher status (bosses, doctors, professors, citizens), upward convergers don't get as much credit as when status is relatively equal. Still, this moderate reaction is much more favorable than the response toward a low-power person who adopts a divergent strategy. As a case in point, consider the anger of many Anglo Americans toward Latino immigrants who "refuse" to become bilingual.

There are benefits and costs to both convergent and divergent strategies. CAT research continues to document the positive interpersonal relationship development that can result from appropriate convergence. The practice also facilitates better comprehension and understanding. But these gains come at the potential risk of offending other in-group members, just as my sister was disgusted by my attempt to talk like a "down-home" southerner. They may feel that converging toward an out-group is diverging from them. And, of course, the one who accommodates may also feel a sense of inauthenticity.

The interpersonal tension created by divergence or maintenance can certainly block the formation of intergroup or intercultural relationships and understanding. But the upside for the communicator is the reaffirmed social identity and solidarity that comes from enacting a divergent strategy. In that sense, divergence is an accommodation strategy just as much as convergence is, but it's accommodation to the in-group rather than members of the out-group.

APPLYING CAT TO POLICE OFFICER–CITIZEN INTERACTION

My extensive discussion of intergenerational communication may have given you the idea that the scope of communication accommodation theory is limited to conversations between the young and the elderly. Not so. CAT can be applied to any intercultural or intergroup situation where the differences between people are apparent and significant. Since Giles is a retired chaplain and reserve lieutenant in the Santa Barbara Police Department, he's found it helpful to apply CAT to the interaction between police officers and citizens during routine traffic stops.

At one time or another, most of us have been pulled over by a police officer for a possible driving infraction. Giles describes these encounters as "potentially negatively valenced, emotionally charged interactions" in which our group membership may be particularly salient and the uncertainty of the outcome can cause great anxiety.[25] If you've been stopped by a cop, you know the feeling. What you might not realize is that the event is also fraught with danger for the officer—as one top FBI official remarks, "Every stop can be potentially fatal." Statistics back up that claim, with police officer deaths rising by 25 percent from 2010 to 2011.[26] Police officers are trained to stay on guard throughout the process, a mindset that could affect the quality of communication in the police–citizen interaction.

Tensions in this already stressful interaction may escalate when the issue of race comes into play. For example, civil rights advocates suggest that cops often treat blacks more harshly than whites. The goal of one CAT study was "to move beyond casual assumptions to systematically investigate the extent to which the race of interactants might influence the nature of police–civilian communication."[27]

Giles was part of a team of researchers that viewed 313 randomly selected video recordings from police cars during traffic stops in Cincinnati, Ohio. The research team analyzed the verbal and nonverbal interaction of officer and driver in each encounter to determine the extent of convergence or divergence. For officers, approachability, listening to the driver's explanation, and showing respect were the marks of accommodation. Indifference, dismissive behavior, and an air of superiority were scored as non-accommodative. Drivers who were courteous, apologetic, pleasant, and who showed respect were rated as accommodating. Drivers who were belligerent were regarded as non-accommodating.

Based on communication accommodation theory, the Cincinnati study predicted that interracial interactions would be less accommodating than those where the officer and driver were of the same race. Researchers anticipated this outcome because a mixed-race interaction in this high-pressure context would make each party's ethnic-group identity significant for them during the encounter. With that mind-set, they would no longer act as independent agents; they would see themselves as representatives of their race and speak in a way that accentuates their differences.

The videotapes confirmed the accommodation prediction for the police. When the cop and driver were the same race, the officer's communication was viewed by objective judges as convergent. When the cop was white and the driver was black, or the cop was black and the driver was white, the officer's communication was judged as divergent. But the videotape evidence did not support the prediction of similar adjustments in the drivers' communication. Although Giles still suggests that "accommodating civilians may be less susceptible to harsh penalties and reprimands from officers,"[28] that's not a guaranteed prescription for avoiding a ticket if a cop pulls you over.

CRITIQUE: ENORMOUS SCOPE AT THE COST OF CLARITY

From a modest beginning as a narrowly conceived theory of social psychology, communication accommodation theory has morphed into a communication theory of enormous scope. Giles' adoption of *social identity theory of group behavior* and *attribution theory,* which are essential to CAT's explanation of accommodation, demonstrates that Giles' theory hasn't abandoned its social psych roots. It's appropriate, therefore, to evaluate CAT by using the six criteria for good social science theories presented at the start of the book.

1. Explanation of data. CAT not only describes communication behavior, it explains why it happens. The dual theoretical engines of *desire for approval* and *need to maintain a distinctive social identity* are compelling reasons for two very different communication strategies. Further, Giles and his colleagues offer multiple factors to clarify which motivation will kick in at any given time.

2. Prediction of the future. Giles doesn't shy away from forecasting what will happen in specific situations. As the scope of the theory has expanded, he's found it necessary to alter or qualify many of these predictions, but CAT places its bets ahead of time. As a communication scholar who was first trained in experimental methodology, I find this put-up-or-shut-up approach appealing. I also appreciate Giles' movement toward qualitative methods as he attempts to predict how recipients will interpret accommodating behavior.

3. Relative simplicity. CAT is an extraordinarily complex theory presented in multiple versions that are sometimes offered simultaneously. As Cindy Gallois (University of Queensland, Australia), Tania Ogay (University of Fribourg, Switzerland), and Giles admit in a summary chapter, CAT's "structure and the underlying terminology are not always represented consistently in texts and propositions."[29] Even the meaning of *accommodation* within the theory is slippery. Sometimes the term seems to be synonymous with convergence (as opposed to divergence), while other times it's used to refer to any adjustment of communication behavior. Gallois, Ogay, and Giles take on the challenge of "explaining the increased propositional complexity in terms of a parsimonious and unique set of integrative principles."[30] The end result of this attempt to simplify is not for the faint of heart. In fairness, the authors could respond, "Intercultural communication is devilishly complicated. Let's not pretend it isn't."

4. Testable hypotheses. The complexity problem also spills over into the possibility of being able to demonstrate that the theory is false. In 1998, Gallois and Giles wrote:

> CAT has become very complex, so that the theory as a whole probably cannot be tested at one time. This means that researchers using CAT must develop mini-theories to suit the contexts in which they work, while at the same time keeping the whole of the theory in mind.[31]

Looking back over four decades of theory development, Giles and his colleagues admit that it's not clear what "the whole of the theory" actually is.[32] If they aren't sure, it's hard for others to know. *Falsifiable* it isn't.

5. Quantitative research. Many alterations and additions to Giles' original theory have been made in response to field research that shows that communication accommodation is more complicated than originally thought. Studies using surveys and interviews are the norm; experiments are rare. As illustrated by the Cincinnati traffic-stop study, the frequency of responses is tabulated, but figuring out what the behavior means depends on how the people themselves interpret their own actions. Many scholars appreciate this mix of quantitative and qualitative methodology, but it's surprising to find it in a theory rooted in social psychology.

6. Practical utility. As Giles noted in a recent review of the published research, researchers have used CAT to understand communication in many important contexts—the family, the doctor's office, the classroom, the workplace, and many more.[33] Clearly, the theory provides practical insight into many situations where people from different groups or cultures come into contact.

QUESTIONS TO SHARPEN YOUR FOCUS

1. Can you think of a time when you found another's *divergence* in *speech style* delightful or another's *convergence* distressing?
2. To what extent is it possible to interact with another person and not have *age, gender, race, nationality, sexual orientation, religious commitment,* or *political ideology* be *salient* when you know that one or more of these differs from your own?
3. In what way might you *overaccommodate* to the *stereotypical image* you hold of opposite-sex communication behavior?
4. As you read about the actions and reactions of young people cited from *intergenerational research,* with which strategies and responses do you identify? Which do you believe are uncharacteristic of you?

CONVERSATIONS

View this segment online at www.mhhe.com/griffin9e or www.afirstlook.com.

In his interview with Andrew, Howie Giles doesn't just explain how his interest in different accents led to the development of CAT—he acts those accents out. Giles also provides advice informed by CAT: first to Andrew about moving from the northern United States to the South, and then to students who might be pulled over by a cop. You might consider how his advice compares with what other intercultural communication theories might say. To conclude the interview, Andrew asks Giles whether his knowledge of CAT makes him communicate strategically rather than authentically. As a communication theory student, you'll probably empathize with his candid response.

A SECOND LOOK

Recommended resource: Howard Giles and Tania Ogay, "Communication Accommodation Theory," in *Explaining Communication: Contemporary Theories and Exemplars,* Bryan B. Whaley and Wendy Samter (eds.), Lawrence Erlbaum, Mahwah, NJ, 2007, pp. 293–310.

Original statement of speech accommodation theory: Howard Giles, "Accent Mobility: A Model and Some Data," *Anthropological Linguistics,* Vol. 15, 1973, pp. 87–109.

SAT expanded and renamed CAT: Howard Giles, Anthony Mulac, James Bradac, and Patricia Johnson, "Speech Accommodation Theory: The First Decade and Beyond," in *Communication Yearbook 10,* Margaret L. McLaughlin (ed.), Sage, Newbury Park, CA, 1987, pp. 13–48.

Propositional synthesis: Cindy Gallois, Tania Ogay, and Howard Giles, "Communication Accommodation Theory: A Look Back and a Look Ahead," in *Theorizing About Intercultural Communication,* William Gudykunst (ed.), Sage, Thousand Oaks, CA, 2005, pp. 121–148.

Social identity theory: Henri Tajfel and John C. Turner, "The Social Identity Theory of Intergroup Behavior," in *The Psychology of Intergroup Relations,* L. Worchel and W. Austin (eds.), Nelson Hall, Chicago, IL, 1986, pp. 7–24.

Importance of social identity: Jake Harwood, "Communication as Social Identity," in *Communication as . . . Perspectives on Theory,* Gregory Shepherd, Jeffrey St. John, and Ted Striphas (eds.), Sage, Thousand Oaks, CA, 2006, pp. 84–90.

Intergenerational communication between grandparents and grandchildren: Karen Anderson, Jake Harwood, and Mary Lee Hummert, "The Grandparent–Grandchild Relationship: Implications for Models of Intergenerational Communication," *Human Communication Research,* Vol. 31, 2005, pp. 268–294.

Accommodation in multiracial/ethnic families: Jordan Soliz, Allison R. Thorson, and Christine E. Rittenour, "Communicative Correlates of Satisfaction, Family Identity, and Group Salience in Multiracial/Ethnic Families," *Journal of Marriage and Family,* Vol. 71, 2009, pp. 819–832.

Accommodation in the workplace: Robert M. McCann and Howard Giles, "Communication With People of Different Ages in the Workplace: Thai and American Data," *Human Communication Research,* Vol. 32, 2006, pp. 74–108.

Police–citizen interaction and simplified propositions: Howard Giles, Michael Willemyns, Cindy Gallois, and M. C. Anderson, "Accommodating a New Frontier: The Context of Law Enforcement," in *Social Communication,* Klaus Fiedler (ed.), Psychology Press, New York, 2007, pp. 129–162.

Application to law enforcement: Howard Giles, Charles W. Choi, Travis L. Dixon, "Police–Civilian Encounters," in *The Dynamics of Intergroup Communication,* Howard Giles, Scott A. Reid, and Jake Harwood (eds.), Peter Lang, New York, 2010, pp. 65–75.

To access a different theory of intercultural communication,
click on Anxiety/Uncertainty Management Theory
in Archive under Theory Resources at
www.afirstlook.com.

CHAPTER 32

Objective — Interpretive

Socio-psychological tradition

Face-Negotiation Theory

of Stella Ting-Toomey

For the past two decades I've served as a volunteer mediator at a metropolitan center for conflict resolution. My role as a mediator is to help people in conflict reach a voluntary agreement that satisfies both sides. I'm neither a judge nor a counselor, and I work hard not to make moral judgments about who's right and who's wrong. As a mediator, I'm a neutral third party whose sole job is to facilitate the process of negotiation. That doesn't mean it's easy.

Most disputants come to the center in a last-ditch effort to avoid the cost and intimidation of a day in court. The service is free, and we do everything possible to take the threat out of the proceedings. But after failing or refusing to work out their differences on their own, people walk in the door feeling various degrees of anger, hurt, fear, confusion, and shame. On the one hand, they hope that the mediation will help resolve their dispute. On the other hand, they doubt that talk around a table will soften hard feelings and change responses that seem to be set in stone.

The professional staff at the center instructs volunteers in a model of negotiation that maximizes the chance of people's reaching a mutually acceptable agreement. From the first day of training, the staff insists that "the mediator controls the process, not the outcome." Figure 32–1 lists some of the techniques that mediators use to ensure progress without suggesting the shape of the solution. Used artfully, the techniques work well. The majority of the negotiations end in freely signed and mutually kept agreements.

This model of negotiation doesn't work equally well for everyone, however. Although the center serves a multiethnic urban area, my colleagues and I have noticed that the number of people of Asian origin seeking conflict mediation is disproportionately small. On rare occasions when Japanese, Vietnamese, Chinese, or Koreans come to the office, they're more embarrassed than angry. If they do reach agreement, they seem more relieved that the conversation is over than pleased with the solution.

Stella Ting-Toomey's face-negotiation theory helps explain cultural differences in responses to conflict. A communication professor at California State University, Fullerton, Ting-Toomey assumes that people of every culture are always negotiating *face*. The term is a metaphor for our public self-image, the way we want others to see us and treat us. *Facework* refers to "specific verbal and nonverbal messages that help to maintain and restore face loss, and to uphold and

Face
The projected image of one's self in a relational situation.

Assure impartiality: "Since neither of you has met me before, I have no stake in what you decide."

Guarantee confidentiality: "What you say today is strictly between us. I'll rip up my notes before you go."

Display disputant equality: "Nate, thanks for not interrupting while Beth was telling her story. Now it's your turn. What do you want to tell me?"

Avoid "why" questions: Harmful—"Why did you do that?" Helpful—"What would you like to see happen?"

Acknowledge emotions while defusing their force: "I can understand that you were bothered when you found the bike was broken."

Summarize frequently: "I'd like to tell you what I've heard you say. If I don't get it right, fill me in."

Hold individual private conferences: "I wanted to meet privately with you to see if there's anything you want to tell me in confidence that you didn't feel you could say with Beth in the room."

Reframe issues of "right" and "wrong" into interests: "Beth, I'm not sure I understand. Tell me, how will Nate's going to jail give you what you need?"

Brainstorm: "Let's see how many different solutions you can think of that might solve the problem. Just throw out any ideas you have and we'll sort through them later."

Perform a reality check: "Have you checked to see if the bike can be put back in mint condition?"

Consider the alternative: "What are you going to do if you don't reach an agreement today?"

Move toward agreement: "You've already agreed on a number of important issues. I'm going to begin to write them down."

FIGURE 32–1 Selected Techniques of Third-Party Mediation

Facework
Specific verbal and nonverbal messages that help to maintain and restore face loss, and to uphold and honor face gain.

honor face gain."[1] Our identity can always be called into question, and the anxiety and uncertainty churned up by conflict make us especially vulnerable. Face-negotiation theory postulates that the facework of people from individualistic cultures like the United States or Germany will be strikingly different from the facework of people from collectivistic cultures like Japan or China. Ting-Toomey's face-negotiation theory suggests that face maintenance is the crucial intervening variable that ties culture to people's ways of handling conflict. In the following sections of this chapter, I'll unpack the meaning of the four concepts that are linked together in the causal chain:

Type of Culture → Type of Self-Construal → Type of Face Maintenance → Type of Conflict Management

COLLECTIVISTIC AND INDIVIDUALISTIC CULTURES

Ting-Toomey bases her face-negotiation theory on the distinction between *collectivism* and *individualism.* The most extensive differentiation between the two types of cultures has been made by University of Illinois emeritus psychology professor Harry Triandis. He says that the three important distinctions between collectivistic and individualistic cultures are the different ways members perceive *self, goals,* and *duty.*[2]

Consider a man named Em. Collectivistic Em might think of himself as a father, Christian, and teacher. Individualistic Em would probably define himself simply as Em, independent of any group affiliation. Collectivistic Em wouldn't go against group goals, but his individualistic counterpart would naturally pursue personal interests. Collectivistic Em would have been socialized to enjoy duty that requires sacrifice in the service of others; individualistic Em would employ the minimax principle to determine a course of action that he would see as enjoyable and personally rewarding (see Chapter 8).

More than two-thirds of the world's people are born into collectivistic cultures, while less than one-third of the population lives in individualistic cultures.[3] To help you draw a clearer mental picture of the distinctions, I'll follow the lead of cross-cultural researchers who cite Japan and the United States as classic examples of collectivistic and individualistic cultures, respectively. Note that it would be equally appropriate to use most countries in Asia, Africa, the Middle East, or Latin America to represent a collectivistic perspective. I could also insert Australia, Germany, Switzerland, or one of the Scandinavian societies as the model of an individualistic approach. It is Ting-Toomey's grouping of national cultures within the collectivistic and individualistic categories that separates her theory of conflict management from a mere listing of national characteristics.

Collectivistic culture
Wherein people identify with a larger group that is responsible for providing care in exchange for group loyalty; *we*-identity; a high-context culture.

Triandis says that the Japanese value collective needs and goals over individual needs and goals. They assume that in the long run, each individual decision affects everyone in the group. Therefore, a person's behavior is controlled by the norms of the group. This *we*-identity of the Japanese is quite foreign to the *I*-identity of the American who values individual needs and goals over group needs and goals. The American's behavior is governed by the personal rules of a freewheeling self that is concerned with individual rights rather than group responsibilities. Marching to a different drummer is the rule in the United States, not the exception.

Triandis claims that the strong in-group identity of the Japanese people leads them to perceive others in us–them categories. It is more important for the Japanese to identify an outsider's background and group affiliation than the person's attitudes or feelings—not because they don't care about their guest, but because unique individual differences seem less important than group-based information. People raised in the United States show a different curiosity. They are filled with questions about the interior life of visitors from other cultures. What do they think? What do they feel? What do they plan to do? Americans assume that every person is unique, and they reduce uncertainty by asking questions to the point of cross-examination.

Individualistic culture
Wherein people look out for themselves and their immediate families; *I*-identity; a low-context culture.

With this understanding of the differences between collectivistic and individualistic cultures in mind, read through the description of mediation techniques in Figure 32–1. Taken as a whole, the list provides a reliable window to the values that guide this type of conflict resolution. Participants who come to the conflict center are treated as responsible individuals who can make up their own minds about what they want. The mediator encourages antagonists to deal directly with their differences and keeps the conversation focused on the possibility of a final agreement. While the mediator is careful never to pressure clients to reach an accord, the climate of immediacy suggests this is their best chance to put the whole mess behind them in an acceptable way and get on with their lives. The mediator works hard to make sure that the individual rights of both parties are respected.

Whether or not disputants reach an agreement, the mediation approach outlined in Figure 32–1 offers a safe place where no one need feel embarrassed—at least no one from an individualistic American culture. As it turns out, the open discussion of conflict, the encouragement to voice specific needs and interests, and the explicit language used to document any agreement all make the process quite uncomfortable for people raised in a high-context culture. No wonder potential clients from collectivistic cultures often stay away or leave dissatisfied.

SELF-CONSTRUAL: VARIED SELF-IMAGES WITHIN A CULTURE

People aren't cultural clones, however. Just as cultures vary along a scale anchored by individualistic or collectivistic orientations, so, too, do their members. Ting-Toomey emphasizes that people *within* a culture differ on the relative emphasis they place on individual self-sufficiency or group solidarity. She uses the terms *independent* and *interdependent self* to refer to "the degree to which people conceive of themselves as relatively autonomous from, or connected to, others."[4] Psychologists Hazel Markus and Shinobu Kitayama call this dimension *self-construal,* or the more familiar term *self-image.*[5]

The independent self values *I*-identity and is more self-face oriented, so this concept of self is prevalent within individualistic cultures like the United States. Yet due to the ethnic diversity of American society, there are people raised in the United States who are highly interdependent. The interdependent self values *we*-identity and emphasizes relational connectedness, and is therefore closely aligned with collectivism. But again, it would be dangerous to stereotype all members of a collectivist society as having the same self-construal. Culture is an overall framework for face concern, but individuals within a culture have different images of self as well as varied views on the degree to which they give others face or restore their own face in conflict situations.

Self-construal
Self-image; the degree to which people conceive of themselves as relatively autonomous from, or connected to, others.

The relational reality of self-image differences within two cultures is represented in the following diagram. Each circle (●) stands for the self-construal of a person raised in a collectivistic society that socializes its members to be interdependent and includes everyone in face concerns. Each triangle (▲) stands for the self-construal of a person raised in an individualistic culture that stresses independence and self-reliance. The cultures are obviously different. But the overlap shows that an American might have a self-image more interdependent than that of a person raised in Japan with a relatively high independent self-construal.

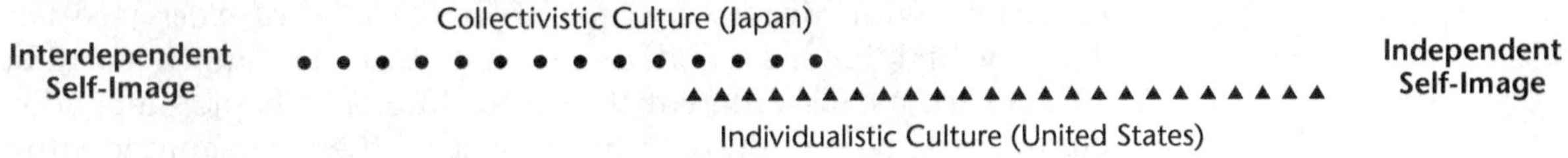

As you will see in the following sections, Ting-Toomey built her theory on the foundational idea that people from collectivistic/high-context cultures are noticeably different in the way they manage face and conflict situations than people from individualistic/low-context cultures. In dozens of scholarly articles she has defended that basic conviction. Yet more recently, Ting-Toomey and colleague John Oetzel at the University of Waikato in New Zealand have discovered that "self-construal is a better predictor of conflict styles than ethnic/cultural background."[6] You can now see why face-negotiation theory is "in progress," and Ting-Toomey writes that "more theorizing effort is needed to 'decategorize' the colossal concepts of 'individualism' and 'collectivism' . . . into finer *culture-level,* explanatory-categories."[7]

Ting-Toomey and Oetzel identify people's self-construal by asking them to respond to surveys about real or imagined conflict situations. Strong agreement with the first two of the following four statements indicates an *independent* self-image. Endorsing the last two shows an *interdependent* self-image.[8]

"It was important for me to be able to act as a free and independent person."

"I tried not to depend on others."

"I sacrificed my self-interest for the benefit of our relationship."

"I was sensitive to the wishes of the other person."

The distinction between collectivistic and individualistic cultures is still important because culture has a strong effect on an individual's self-construal. But that sense of individual identity is one step closer to the person's preferred style of dealing with conflict, so it predicts dispute behavior better than generalized culture does.

THE MULTIPLE FACES OF FACE

Although popular Western wisdom regards *face* as an Asian preoccupation, Ting-Toomey and other relational researchers find it to be a universal concern. That's because face is an extension of self-concept: a vulnerable, identity-based resource. As Ting-Toomey notes, most of us blush. It's a telltale sign that we feel awkward, embarrassed, ashamed, or proud—all face-related issues.[9] In their well-developed theory of politeness, Penelope Brown and Stephen Levinson (Max Planck Institute for Psycholinguistics, the Netherlands) define face as "the public self-image that every member of society wants to claim for himself/herself."[10] Many Western writers regard face as an almost tangible good that can rise or fall like soybean futures on the commodity exchange at the Board of Trade. Taiwanese writer Lin Yutang called face "a psychological image that can be granted and lost and fought for and presented as a gift."[11] The term includes the patrician concern for dignity, honor, and status. It also covers the effect of trash talk after a slam dunk on the basketball court—"in your face!" Ting-Toomey simply refers to face as "the projected image of one's self in a relational situation."[12]

Although an overall view of face as public self-image is straightforward and consistent with Mead's concept of the *generalized other* (see Chapter 5), Ting-Toomey highlights several issues that turn face into a multifaceted object of study. Face means different things to different people, depending first on their culture, and second on how they construe their personal identities.

The question *Whose face are you trying to save?* may seem ridiculous to most Americans or members of other individualistic cultures. The answer is obvious: *mine.* Yet Ting-Toomey reminds us that in over two-thirds of the world, face concerns focus on the other person. Even in the midst of conflict, people in these collectivistic cultures pay more attention to maintaining the face of the other party than they do to preserving their own. Their answer to the *face-concern* question would honestly be an altruistic *yours.*

Face concern
Regard for self-face, other-face, or mutual-face.

But self-face and other-face concerns don't exhaust the possibilities. Ting-Toomey describes a third orientation in which there's equal concern for both parties' images, as well as the public image of their relationship. She calls this a *mutual-face* concern, and people who have it would answer the *Whose face . . . ?* question with *ours.*

JoLynda applied the concept of mutual-face concern to what she learned about a desert nomadic culture:

> A Bedouin tradition that exemplifies concern for honor and mutual-face is one of raiding. In order to properly raid a village you had to raid it early in the morning in order to give the villagers all day to recover the animals. It gave the other tribe a chance to show their strength and save face by regaining what livestock they may have lost. Also, if an enemy asked for hospitality, you were required to treat him as the guest of honor for three days. If he had not left by that time you were allowed to do what you wanted to him. It would be his fault. The only reason an enemy would ask for hospitality is if he were injured or weak. You would then be in charge of healing him and giving him a fair chance in a fight.

Self-concerned *face-restoration* is the facework strategy used to stake out a unique place in life, preserve autonomy, and defend against loss of personal freedom. Not surprisingly, face-restoration is the typical face strategy across individualistic cultures. *Face-giving* out of concern for others is the facework strategy used to defend and support another person's need for inclusion. It means taking care not to embarrass or humiliate the other in public. Face-giving is the characteristic face strategy across collectivistic cultures.

Face-restoration
The self-concerned facework strategy used to preserve autonomy and defend against loss of personal freedom.

Face-giving
The other-concerned facework strategy used to defend and support another person's need for inclusion.

Of course, collectivism and individualism aren't all-or-nothing categories. The difference between other-face and self-face concerns is not absolute. Just as relational dialectics insists that everyone wants connection *and* autonomy in a close relationship (see Chapter 11), so, too, all people desire affiliation and autonomy within their particular society. People raised in Japan or other Asian countries do have personal wants and needs; Americans and northern Europeans still desire to be part of a larger group. The cultural difference is always a matter of degree.

Yet when push comes to shove, most people from a collectivistic culture tend to privilege other-face or mutual-face over self-face. In like manner, people raised in an individualistic culture are normally more concerned with self-face than with other-face.

PREDICTABLE STYLES OF CONFLICT MANAGEMENT

Based on the work of M. Afzalur Rahim, professor of management at Western Kentucky University, Ting-Toomey initially identified five distinct responses to situations where there is an incompatibility of needs, interests, or goals. The five styles are *avoiding (withdrawing), obliging (giving in), compromising (negotiating), dominating (competing),* and *integrating (problem solving).*[13] Most Western writers refer to the same five styles of conflict, although they often use the labels that are in parentheses.[14]

Avoiding
Responding to conflict by withdrawing from open discussion.

Obliging
Accommodating or giving in to the wishes of another in a conflict situation.

Compromising
Conflict management by negotiating or bargaining; seeking a middle way.

Suppose, for example, that you are the leader of a group of students working together on a class research project. Your instructor will assign the same grade to all of you based on the quality of the group's work, and that project evaluation will count for two-thirds of your final grade in the course. As often happens in such cases, one member of the group has just brought in a shoddy piece of work, and you have only three days to go until the project is due. You don't know this group member well, but you do know that it will take 72 hours of round-the-clock effort to fix this part of the project. What mode of conflict management will you adopt?

"We realize it's a win-win, Jenkins—we're trying to figure out a way to make it a win-lose."

Dominating
Competing to win when people's interests conflict.

Integrating
Problem solving through open discussion; collaborating for a win–win resolution of conflict.

Emotional expression
Managing conflict by disclosure or venting of feelings.

Passive aggressive
Making indirect accusations, showing resentment, procrastination, and other behaviors aimed at thwarting another's resolution of conflict.

Avoiding: "I would avoid discussing my differences with the group member."

Obliging: "I would give in to the wishes of the group member."

Compromising: "I would use give-and-take so that a compromise could be made."

Dominating: "I would be firm in pursuing my side of the issue."

Integrating: "I would exchange accurate information with the group member to solve the problem together."

These five styles of conflict management have been discussed and researched so often that they almost seem chiseled in stone. Yet Ting-Toomey and Oetzel remind us that these styles have surfaced in work situations in Western countries. Using an ethnically diverse sample, they have identified three additional styles of conflict management that American, individualistic-based scholarship has missed. The styles are *emotional expression, passive aggressive,* and *third-party help.*[15] In the student-project example, these styles might be expressed in the following ways:

Emotional expression: "Whatever my 'gut' and my 'heart' tell me, I would let these feelings show."

Passive aggressive: "Without actually accusing anyone of being lazy, I'd try to make him or her feel guilty."

Third-party help: "I would enlist the professor to aid us in solving the conflict."

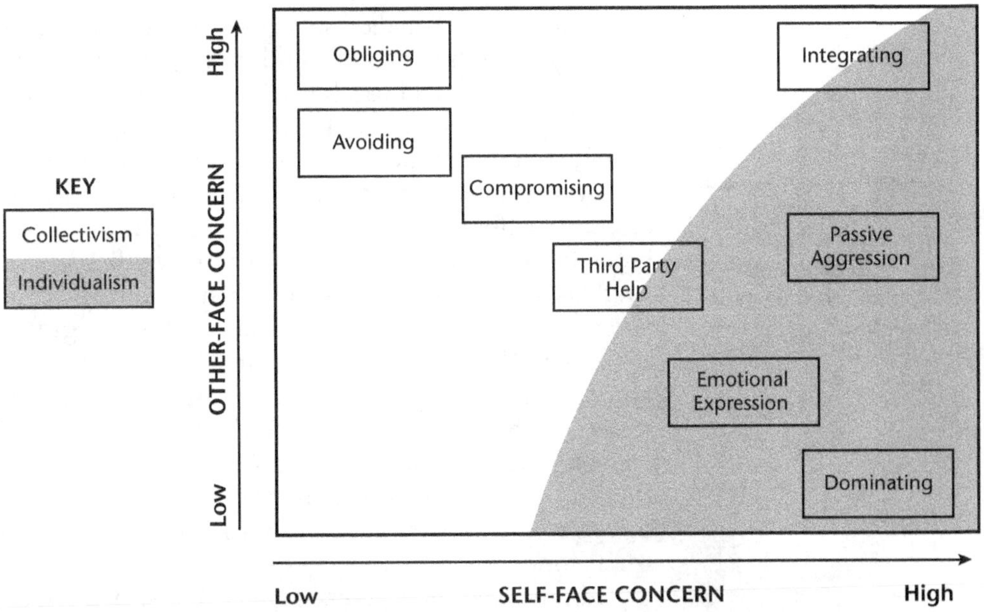

FIGURE 32–2 A Cultural Map of Eight Conflict-Management Styles
Based on Stella Ting-Toomey and John Oetzel, *Managing Intercultural Conflict Effectively*

Figure 32–2 charts Ting-Toomey and Oetzel's map of conflict styles, arranged according to their culture-related face concern. The chart plots self-face concern on the horizontal axis and other-face concern on the vertical axis. For example, obliging is the behavior of choice for people who are concerned for another's public image, but not their own. Conversely, dominating is the act of someone who is concerned with his or her own face repair but doesn't care about promoting or honoring another's reputation. The smaller, shaded area on the right side depicts individualistic cultures that usually spawn conflict styles of emotional expression, passive aggression, and attempts to dominate. The larger, clear area on the left side reflects collectivistic cultures where obliging, avoiding, compromising, third-party help, and integrating are more the norm. Several explanations are in order.

You might be surprised to see *avoiding* rating almost as high as *obliging* on concern for the other person's face. Isn't withdrawing showing a casual disregard for the issue or your conversational partner? Ting-Toomey would disagree:

> It should be noted that in U.S. conflict management literature, obliging and avoiding conflict styles often take on a Western slant of being negatively disengaged (i.e., "placating" or "flight") from the conflict scene. However, collectivists do not perceive obliging and avoiding conflict styles as negative. These two styles are typically employed to maintain mutual-face interests and relational network interests.[16]

Ting-Toomey would also point out that *third-party help* as practiced in a collectivistic culture is quite different from the interest-based mediation I described at the start of the chapter. In these societies, parties in conflict voluntarily go to someone they greatly admire who has a good relationship with both of them. In order to "give face" to this wise elder or high-status person, they may be willing to follow his or her advice and in the process honor each other's image as well.[17] Perhaps that's why third-party help is sought out by conflicting parties in collectivistic cultures, but the vast majority of Western-style mediations are court-ordered. Most people with an independent self-construal think first of getting a lawyer.

Third-party help
A method of conflict management in which disputing parties seek the aid of a mediator, arbitrator, or respected neutral party to help them resolve their differences.

Of course, the entire figure assumes that people from a given culture construe their self-image consistent with the collectivistic or individualistic nature of their society. In one multiethnic study, Ting-Toomey and Oetzel identified some people whose self-image embraced both interdependence and independence. The researchers now believe that these "biconstrual" individuals possess a wider repertoire of behavioral options to use in different conflict situations.[18] Face-negotiation theory predicts that regardless of his or her culture of origin, "the biconstrual type is associated positively with compromising/integrating conflict style."[19]

Given that an integrating, or win–win, style of conflict resolution is extolled among theorists and practitioners in the West, why does the cultural map place it across the border in the land of collectivists?[20] Ting-Toomey suggests that collectivists who adopt this interpersonal style focus on relational-level collaboration, whereas individualists concentrate on solving the task in a way that brings closure.[21] "Problem solving," the alternative label, has a distinctly impersonal tone.

Figure 32–2 is a freeze-frame snapshot of what people in different cultures report they do, and, according to face-negotiation theory, why they do it. Yet as summarized near the start of the chapter, the theory lays out a multiple-stage *process* that captures the dynamics of response to conflict, and shows where the crucial matter of face concern fits in that flow. Using basically the same information that informed the map just discussed, Figure 32–3 depicts the comparative flow of the

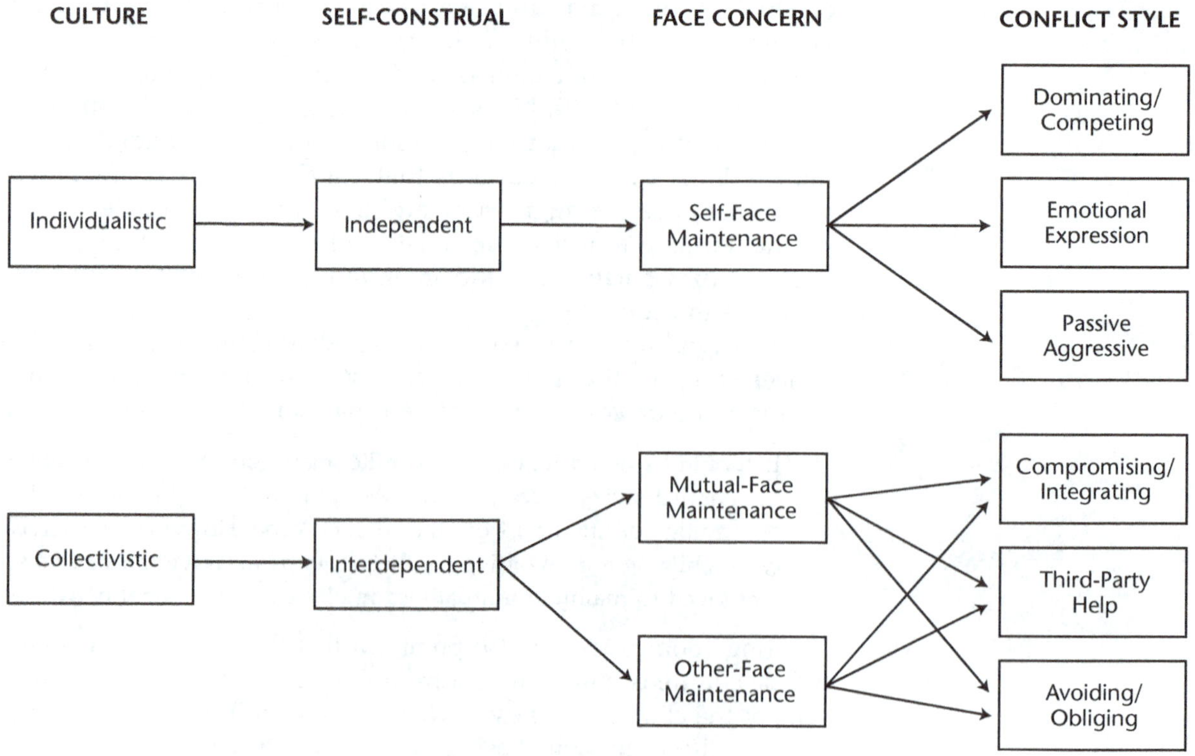

FIGURE 32–3 Face-Negotiation Model
Based on Ting-Toomey's hypotheses in "The Matrix of Face: An Updated Face-Negotiation Theory"

parallel processes for people with different face concerns. It incorporates most of the 24 propositions that form the backbone of Stella Ting-Toomey's theory.

COMPLICATING FACTORS: POWER DISTANCE AND PERCEIVED THREATS

Figure 32-3 and the discussion that led up to it seem to indicate that the individualism–collectivism variable is the sole factor that shapes cross-cultural differences in managing conflict. Ting-Toomey suggests, however, that power distance complicates the situation. *Power distance* refers to "the way a culture deals with status differences and social hierarchies."[22] Large power-distance cultures tend to accept unequal power as natural; small power-distance cultures value equality and regard most differences based on status as unjust.

Power distance
The way a culture deals with status differences and social hierarchies; the degree to which low-power members accept unequal power as natural.

Individualistic values and small power distance usually go together. That mix is exemplified in the Scandinavian countries, Ireland, and Israel, where concern for personal freedom and equality are paramount. The United States, Canada, Great Britain, Germany, and Australia tend to share that concern, although their power distance isn't as small.

Collectivistic values and the acceptance of large power distance is common in Central and South America, Asia, and Africa. In these cultures, the sense of obligation to others and acceptance of inequality go hand-in-hand. Those who have little power hope that those who have much will act in a benevolent way.

But there are exceptions to these two clusters of cultural values. Ting-Toomey reports that Costa Rica is a country that combines small power distance with collectivistic values, as do feminist subcultures and the Kibbutz movement in Israel. Conversely, Italy and France are individualistic countries where great differences in power are accepted if they are earned. The United States and Great Britain share some of this status-through-achievement appreciation. If all of this seems somewhat confusing, that's because it's not simple in practice. The collectivism–individualism distinction becomes more complicated when power distance is taken into consideration. Ting-Toomey says that power-distance values affect responses to conflict, but she doesn't offer specific predictions in the latest version of the theory.[23]

Ting-Toomey also says that specific face *threats* can affect your face concern and the type of facework you do. She lists seven additive factors that increase the level of threat you perceive. The more . . .

a. central the violated-facework rule is in your culture
b. cultural difference causes mistrust between you
c. important the topic under dispute is to you
d. power the other has over you
e. harm that will be done when the threat is carried out
f. you view the other as responsible for initiating the conflict
g. you regard the other as an out-group member

. . . the more severe the threat to your face will seem. When a threat looms large, almost everyone uses a face-defending strategy. Those raised in individualistic cultures usually turn aggressive; collectivists typically opt for avoidance.[24]

APPLICATION: COMPETENT INTERCULTURAL FACEWORK

Ting-Toomey's ultimate goal for her theory goes beyond merely identifying the ways people in different cultures negotiate face or handle conflict. She believes that cultural *knowledge, mindfulness,* and facework *interaction skill* are the three requirements for effectively communicating across cultures. Imagine that you are a Japanese student in a U.S. college. As the appointed leader of the class research project, you feel it is your uncomfortable duty to talk with the unproductive American member of the group. How might you achieve competent intercultural facework?

Knowledge is the most important dimension of facework competence. It's hard to be culturally sensitive unless you have some idea of the ways you might differ from your classmate. Ting-Toomey's theory offers basic insights into collectivistic and individualistic cultures, self-construals, face concerns, and conflict styles, all of which could help you understand the American student's perspective, and vice versa. If you've read this chapter carefully, this knowledge will stand you in good stead.

Mindfulness shows a recognition that things are not always what they seem. It's a conscious choice to seek multiple perspectives on the same event. Perhaps the other's inferior work is not due to laziness but is the best he or she can do in this situation. The student might have a learning disability, an emotional problem, a lack of clarity about the assignment, or a desire to merely pass the course. Of course, your initiation of a conversation to discuss the project is also open to multiple interpretations. Ting-Toomey writes:

> Mindfulness means being particularly aware of our own assumptions, viewpoints, and ethnocentric tendencies in entering any unfamiliar situation. *Simultaneously,* mindfulness means paying attention to the perspectives and interpretive lenses of dissimilar others in viewing an intercultural episode.[25]

Mindfulness
Recognizing that things are not always what they seem, and therefore seeking multiple perspectives in conflict situations.

When you are mindful, you mentally switch off automatic pilot and process the situation and conversation through the central route of the mind, as ELM suggests (see Chapter 15). But you are also freed up to empathize with the other student and approach the discussion with a fresh or creative mindset. The result might be a novel solution that takes advantage of your different ways of thinking.

Interaction skill is your ability to communicate appropriately, effectively, and adaptively in a given situation. Perhaps you are studying communication to gain that type of competence. Hopefully your department offers a course in interpersonal or intercultural communication that includes structured exercises, role plays, or simulations. Without hands-on learning and feedback from others on how you're doing, it's hard to improve.

CRITIQUE: PASSING THE TEST WITH A GOOD GRADE

Most cross-cultural researchers analyze different cultures from a highly interpretive perspective. Ting-Toomey and her co-researcher, John Oetzel, are different because they are committed to an objective social science research agenda that looks for measurable commonalities across cultures. They then link these transcultural similarities (individualism or collectivism) to subsequent behavioral outcomes—in this case, response to others in conflict situations. In the course of this chapter you've seen that face-negotiation theory uses the concept of face concern to explain, predict, and ultimately advise. The theory's value therefore rests on the extent to which it can be tested, and whether it can withstand that close scrutiny. Like all objective social science theories, it ultimately has to meet the "put-up-or-shut-up" test.

In 2003, Oetzel and Ting-Toomey conducted a four-nation survey to test the core of the theory.[26] More than 700 students from collectivistic cultures (China and Japan) and individualistic cultures (United States and Germany) responded to scales that reliably measure self-construal. The students then recounted a specific case of conflict with someone from their country and filled out scales that tapped into the face concern they felt and the way they acted in that situation. The test was simplified in that mutual-face wasn't factored in and the researchers measured only the three primary conflict styles—*dominating, integrating,* and *avoiding.*

Figure 32–4 shows the links that were examined. All of the solid lines represent significant relationships among variables that were validated by the data. The results were sufficiently strong that they couldn't be explained away as mere chance findings. The two dotted lines represent predicted relationships that didn't materialize. Despite these two failures, I regard the overwhelmingly positive results as clear support for the theory.

The findings regarding face concern were especially impressive. In earlier critiques of the theory I had questioned whether knowing a person's face concern would actually improve the model's prediction of conflict behavior. Note that the lines running directly from the individualistic–collectivistic (I–C) cultures at the beginning of the process to the three conflict styles at the end represent a way to find out if cutting out face concern would create a model that fit the data better. It did not. The results showed the *culture → self-construal → face concern → conflict style* paths provided a better prediction of what people reported than did the *culture → conflict style* direct route. In fact, when people scored high in *self-face* ("I was concerned with protecting my self-image"), they always took a *dominating* stance ("I insisted my position be accepted during the conflict").

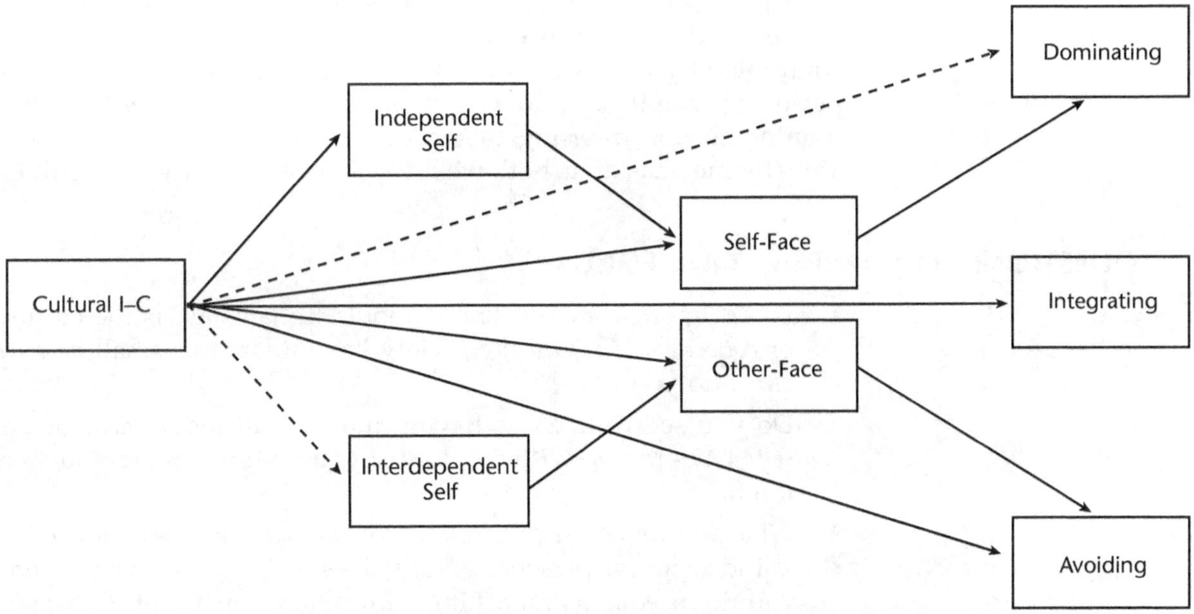

FIGURE 32–4 A Four-Culture Test of Face-Negotiation Theory

Based on Oetzel and Ting-Toomey, "Face Concerns in Interpersonal Conflict: A Cross-Cultural Empirical Test of Face-Negotiation Theory"

Yet Oetzel and Ting-Toomey's procedures and findings still provide some cause for pause. As a mediator who highly values the goal of integrating, collaborating, and a win–win outcome, I'm bothered by the questions that supposedly assessed this conflict-resolution behavior. The survey items used referred to "meeting the other person halfway," proposing a "middle ground," and "'give and take' so that a compromise could be made." These items would seem to be a great way to assess *compromising,* but they don't measure what I and other mediators mean by *integrating.* Nor do I believe they do justice to what Ting-Toomey describes as behavior springing from high other-face *and* high self-face concerns. The following statements would more accurately assess integration: "We worked together to find a solution we could both be proud of" or "I sought to reach an agreement that met both of our needs and preserved our relationship."

Finally, the researchers report that "both individualistic and collectivistic samples had more independence and self-face tendencies than interdependence and other-face tendencies."[27] They suggest that college students in a collectivistic culture may be more competitive (or selfish?) than the rest of the population. This admission that the "individualistic–collectivistic" distinction may not explain everyone's behavior equally well resonates strongly with Gerry Philipsen's critique (see Chapter 33). Ting-Toomey uses the term *culture* to refer to groups that live in different places. Philipsen objects: "I do not . . . speak of being a 'member of' a culture, but rather speak of someone who 'uses,' 'deploys,' or 'experiences' a particular cultural code."[28] Ting-Toomey's recent writing shows signs of responding to this objection. She's investigating how "Asian/Caucasians" negotiate their identity as members of *both* individualistic and collectivistic cultures.[29] Her tentative solution focuses heavily on "complex lived experience"—understanding how people navigate the many cultural and situational factors that shape their identities. While this explanation adds insight, it also increases the theory's complexity and makes it more difficult to offer clear predictions.

I'm impressed by the ambitious research program that Ting-Toomey has headed, and I also admire her willingness to adjust face-negotiation theory when confronted by unanticipated results. To create and test a theory that's later supported by empirical evidence obviously creates face within the research community. So does revising the theory when parts of it are disconfirmed. Stella Ting-Toomey has done both well. I look forward to the next edition of her theory.

QUESTIONS TO SHARPEN YOUR FOCUS

1. Based upon what you know about Afghanistan, is the culture *individualistic* or *collectivistic?* Does the society have a large or small *power distance?* What clues do you have?
2. Do you see yourself as having more of an *independent* or an *interdependent self?* Does this go with the flow of your culture, or are you swimming against the tide?
3. What *face concern* (*self-face, other-face, mutual-face*) does your religious faith, political ideology, or personal set of values embrace? To what extent is the *facework* you do in your relationships with others consistent with that face concern?
4. What *style of conflict management* would you use with the group member who did poor work? Do you think that your response is based on your culture, self-construal, gender, or status? What other factors affect your decision?

CONVERSATIONS

View this segment online at www.mhhe.com/griffin9e or www.afirstlook.com.

While talking with Stella Ting-Toomey, I raise the embarrassing possibility that our students may be bored while watching our discussion. If so, both she and I have some serious facework to do. Ting-Toomey shows how she, a child of a collectivistic culture, might give face to students. She then role-plays how I, the product of an individualistic culture, might save face. Later in the conversation I ask if she's bothered that self-construal has turned out to be a better predictor of conflict style than cultural origin—a potentially face-threatening question. You then get to see Ting-Toomey's real-life facework.

A SECOND LOOK

Recommended resource: Stella Ting-Toomey, "The Matrix of Face: An Updated Face-Negotiation Theory," in *Theorizing About Intercultural Communication,* William Gudykunst (ed.), Sage, Thousand Oaks, CA, 2005, pp. 71–92.

Original theory: Stella Ting-Toomey, "Intercultural Conflict Styles: A Face-Negotiation Theory," in *Theories in Intercultural Communication,* Young Yun Kim and William Gudykunst (eds.), Sage, Newbury Park, CA, 1988, pp. 213–235.

Progression of the theory: Stella Ting-Toomey and Atsuko Kurogi, "Facework Competence in Intercultural Conflict: An Updated Face-Negotiation Theory," *International Journal of Intercultural Relations,* Vol. 22, 1998, pp. 187–225.

Literature review: Stella Ting-Toomey and John Oetzel, "Cross-Cultural Face Concerns and Conflict Styles," in *Handbook of International and Intercultural Communication,* 2nd ed., William Gudykunst and Bella Mody (eds.), Sage, Thousand Oaks, CA, 2002, pp. 143–163.

Comprehensive treatment of face: Stella Ting-Toomey (ed.), *The Challenge of Facework,* State University of New York, Albany, 1994.

Collectivistic/individualistic culture: Harry C. Triandis, *Individualism & Collectivism,* Westview, Boulder, CO, 1995.

Theory into practice: Stella Ting-Toomey, "Translating Conflict Face-Negotiation Theory into Practice," in *Handbook of Intercultural Training,* 3rd ed., Dan Landis, Jane Bennett, and Milton Bennett (eds.), Sage, Thousand Oaks, CA, 2004, pp. 217–248.

Conflict in intercultural communication: Stella Ting-Toomey and John Oetzel, *Managing Intercultural Conflict Effectively,* Sage, Thousand Oaks, CA, 2001.

Face-negotiation in the context of other theories of conflict: Stella Ting-Toomey and Jiro Takai, "Explaining Intercultural Conflict: Promising Approaches and Directions," in *The SAGE Handbook of Conflict Communication: Integrating Theory, Research, and Practice,* John G. Oetzel and Stella Ting-Toomey (eds.), Sage, Thousand Oaks, CA, 2006, pp. 691–723.

A personal account of face: Stella Ting-Toomey, "An Intercultural Journey: The Four Seasons," in *Working at the Interface of Cultures: Eighteen Lives in Social Science,* Michael Bond (ed.), Routledge, New York, 1997, pp. 202–215.

Test and critique of the theory: John Oetzel and Stella Ting-Toomey, "Face Concerns in Interpersonal Conflict: A Cross-Cultural Empirical Test of the Face-Negotiation Theory," *Communication Research,* Vol. 36, 2003, pp. 599–624.

CHAPTER 33

Objective — Interpretive

Socio-cultural tradition

Speech Codes Theory

of Gerry Philipsen

After three years on the staff of a youth organization, I resigned to pursue full-time graduate work in communication at Northwestern University. Gerry Philipsen was one of my classmates. When I finished my Ph.D. course work, the labor market was tight; I felt fortunate to receive an offer to teach at Wheaton College. A while later I heard Gerry was doing youth work on the south side of Chicago. I remember thinking that while my career was progressing, Gerry's was going backward. How wrong I was. As articles in the *Quarterly Journal of Speech* soon made evident, Gerry Philipsen was doing ethnography.[1]

While at Northwestern, Philipsen read an article by University of Virginia anthropologist and linguist Dell Hymes, "The Ethnography of Speaking." Hymes called for a "close to the ground" study of the great variety of communication practices around the world.[2] Philipsen decided to start in the Chicago community where he worked, a place he dubbed "Teamsterville," since driving a truck was the typical job for men in the community. For three years Philipsen talked to kids on street corners, women on front porches, men in corner bars, and everyone at the settlement house where he worked so that he would be able to describe the speech code of Teamsterville residents. By *speech code*, Philipsen means "a historically enacted, socially constructed system of terms, meanings, premises, and rules pertaining to communicative conduct."[3]

Ethnography
The work of a naturalist who watches, listens, and records communicative conduct in its natural setting in order to understand a culture's complex web of meanings.

Even though the people of Teamsterville spoke English, Philipsen noted that their whole pattern of speaking was radically different from the speech code he knew and heard practiced within his own family of origin, by his friends at school, and across many talk shows on radio and TV. The stark contrast motivated him to conduct a second, multiyear ethnographic study, which began while he was teaching communication at the University of California, Santa Barbara, and continued when he moved on to the University of Washington. Although most of his "cultural informants" were from Santa Barbara or Seattle, the speech code community from which they were drawn was not confined to the West Coast of the United States. He labeled them the "Nacirema" (*American* spelled backward), because their way of using language was intelligible to, and practiced by, a majority of Americans. Typical Nacirema speech is a "generalized U.S. conversation that is carried out at the public level (on televised talk shows) and at the interpersonal level in face-to-face interaction."[4] For Philipsen, me, and many reading this text, "Nacirema are us."

Philipsen defines the Nacirema culture by speech practices rather than geographical boundaries or ethnic background. It's a style of speaking about self, relationships, and communication itself that emerged for Philipsen as he spent hundreds of hours listening to tapes of dinner-table conversations, life stories, and ethnographic interviews. Just as cultural markers emerge gradually for the ethnographer, so the defining features of the Nacirema code will become more clear as you read the rest of the chapter. But for starters, one characteristic feature of that speech code is a preoccupation with metacommunication—their talk about talk.[5]

Speech code
A historically enacted, socially constructed system of terms, meanings, premises, and rules pertaining to communicative conduct.

As Philipsen intended, the Teamsterville and Nacirema ethnographic studies provided rich comparative data on two distinct cultures. But he also wanted to go beyond mere description of interesting local practices. His ultimate goal was to develop a general theory that would capture the relationship between communication and culture. Such a theory would guide cultural researchers and practitioners in knowing what to look for and would offer clues on how to interpret the way people speak.

Based on the suggestion of Hymes, Philipsen first referred to his emerging theory as the *ethnography of communication.* He has found, however, that many people can't get past the idea of ethnography as simply a research method, so now that his theory has moved from description to explanation, Philipsen labels his work *speech codes theory.* Specifically, the theory seeks to answer questions about the existence of speech codes, their substance, the way they can be discovered, and their force upon people within a culture.

Philipsen outlines the core of speech codes theory in the following six general propositions. He is hopeful, however, that their presentation can be intertwined with the story of his fieldwork and the contributions of other scholars that stimulated the conceptual development of the theory. I've tried to capture that narrative mix within the limited space of this chapter.

THE DISTINCTIVENESS OF SPEECH CODES

> *Proposition 1:* Wherever there is a distinctive culture, there is to be found a distinctive speech code.

Philipsen describes an ethnographer of speaking as "a naturalist who watches, listens, and records communicative conduct in its natural setting."[6] When he entered the working-class, ethnic world of Teamsterville, Philipsen found patterns of speech that were strange to his ears. After many months in the community, he was less struck by the pronunciation and grammar that was characteristic of then Chicago mayor Richard J. Daley than he was by the practice of "infusing a concern with place into every conversation."[7] He realized that Teamsterville residents say little until they've confirmed the nationality, ethnicity, social status, and place of residence of the person with whom they're speaking. Most conversations start (and end) with the question *Where are you from and what's your nationality?*

Philipsen gradually found out that discussion of "place" is related to the issue of whether a person is from "the neighborhood." This concern isn't merely a matter of physical location. Whether or not a person turns out to be from "around here" is a matter of cultural solidarity. Unlike *Mister Rogers' Neighborhood,* Teamsterville does not welcome diversity. As Philipsen heard when he first entered a corner tavern, "We don't want no yahoos around here."

While Philipsen discovered that Teamsterville conversation is laced with assurances of common place among those in the neighborhood, he found that speech among the Nacirema is a way to express and celebrate psychological uniqueness. Dinnertime is a speech event where all family members are encouraged to have their say. Everyone has "something to contribute," and each person's ideas are treated as "uniquely valuable."

In Teamsterville, children are "to be seen, not heard." Among the Nacirema, however, it would be wrong to try to keep a child quiet at the dinner table. Communication is the route by which kids develop "a positive self-image," a way to "feel good about themselves." Through speech, family members "can manifest their equality and demonstrate that they pay little heed to differences in status—practices and beliefs that would puzzle and offend a proper Teamsterviller."[8]

Philipsen was raised in a largely Nacirema speech community, but until his research in Teamsterville, he hadn't thought of his family's communication as a particular cultural practice. Its taken-for-granted quality illustrates the saying that's common among ethnographers: "We don't know who discovered water, but we're pretty sure it wasn't the fish."

THE MULTIPLICITY OF SPEECH CODES

Proposition 2: In any given speech community, multiple speech codes are deployed.

Philipsen later added this proposition to the five he first stated in 1997.[9] He did so because he and his students now observe times when people recognize and are affected by other codes or employ dual codes at the same time. In his Teamsterville ethnography, Philipsen stressed the unified nature of their neighborhood speech patterns. Yet he noticed that the men gauge their relative worth by comparing their style of talk with that of residents in other city neighborhoods. They respect, yet resent, middle-class northside residents who speak Standard English. On the other hand, they are reassured by their perceived ability to speak better than those whom they refer to as lower-class "Hillbillies, Mexicans, and Africans." Any attempt a man makes to "improve" his speech is regarded as an act of disloyalty that alienates him from his friends. Thus, the men define their way of speaking by contrasting it with other codes.

The awareness of another speech code is equally strong among the Nacirema. Their repeated references to the importance of "a good talk" or "meaningful dialogue" distinguish speech that they value from "mere talk," or what today is parodied as "blah, blah, blah." As Philipsen notes, the Nacirema characterized "their present way of speaking ('really communicating') by reference to another way of speaking and another communicative conduct that they had now discarded."[10]

Dell Hymes suggested that there may be more than one code operating within a speech community.[11] Some doctors, lawyers, clergy, and teachers have been socialized to follow a professional code of language use in public, but recognize and use different rules of speech when talking with others in a locker room, kitchen, or garage. In his book *The Presentation of Self in Everyday Life,* pioneer ethnographer Erving Goffman referred to this code-switching as *backstage behavior* and documented the discrepancies in restaurants, schools, and mental institutions.[12]

THE SUBSTANCE OF SPEECH CODES

> *Proposition 3:* A speech code involves a culturally distinctive psychology, sociology, and rhetoric.

With this proposition, Philipsen takes a step back from the cultural relativism that characterizes most ethnographers. He continues to maintain that every culture has its own unique speech code; there's no danger we'll mistake a Nacirema discussion of personal worth with Teamsterville talk of neighborhood solidarity. But this third proposition asserts that whatever the culture, the speech code reveals structures of self, society, and strategic action.

Psychology. According to Philipsen, every speech code contains the notion of what it means to be a person within that speech community—the nature of the self. The Teamsterville code defines people as a bundle of social roles. In the Nacirema code, however, the individual is conceptualized as unique—someone whose essence is defined from the inside out.

Sociology. Philipsen writes that "a speech code provides a system of answers about what linkages between self and others can properly be sought, and what symbolic resources can properly and efficaciously be employed in seeking those linkages."[13] According to the unwritten code of Teamsterville, speech is not a valued resource for dealing with people of lower status—wives, children, or persons from outside the neighborhood who are lower on the social hierarchy. Nor is speech a resource for encounters with bosses, city officials, or other higher-status outsiders. In cases where the latter kind of contact is necessary, a man draws on his personal connections with a highly placed intermediary who will state his case. Speech is reserved for symmetrical relationships with people matched in age, gender, ethnicity, occupational status, and neighborhood location. Words flow freely with friends.

Rhetoric Both the discovery of truth and a persuasive appeal.

Honor A code that grants worth to an individual on the basis of adherence to community values.

Dignity The worth an individual has by virtue of being a human being.

Rhetoric. Philipsen uses the term *rhetoric* in the double sense of *discovery of truth* and *persuasive appeal.* Both concepts come together in the way Teamsterville men talk about women. To raise doubts about the personal hygiene or sexual purity of a man's wife, mother, or sister is to attack his honor. *Honor* is a code that grants worth to an individual on the basis of adherence to community values. The language of the streets in Teamsterville makes it clear that a man's social identity is strongly affected by the women he's related to by blood or marriage. "If she is sexually permissive, talks too much, or lacks in personal appearance, any of these directly reflects on the man and thus, in turn, directly affects his honor."[14] In contrast, Philipsen discovered that a verbalized code of dignity holds sway among the Nacirema. *Dignity* refers to the worth that an individual has by virtue of being a human being. Within a code of dignity, personal experience is given a moral weight greater than logical argument or appeal to authority. Communication is a resource to establish an individual's uniqueness.[15]

THE INTERPRETATION OF SPEECH CODES

Proposition 4: The significance of speaking depends on the speech codes used by speakers and listeners to create and interpret their communication.

Proposition 4 can be seen as a speech code extension of I. A. Richards' maxim that words don't mean; people mean (see Chapter 4). If we want to understand the significance of a prominent speech practice within a culture, we must listen to the way people talk about it and respond to it. It's their practice; they decide what it means.

No speech practice is more important among the Nacirema than the way they use the term *communication.* Philipsen and Tamar Katriel (University of Haifa, Israel) have shown that the Nacirema use this key word as a shorthand way of referring to *close, open, supportive speech.*[16] These three dimensions set communication apart from speech that the Nacirema dismiss as *mere communication, small talk,* or *normal chitchat.*

Close relationships contrast with *distant* affiliations, where others are "kept at arm's length."

Open relationships, in which parties listen and demonstrate a willingness to change, are distinct from routine associations, where people are stagnant.

Supportive relationships, in which people are totally "for" the other person, stand in opposition to *neutral* interactions, where positive response is conditional.

You may have noticed my not-so-subtle switch from a description of *communication* to a discussion of *relationships.* Philipsen and Katriel say that Nacirema speakers use the two words almost interchangeably. In Burkean terms (see Chapter 23), when not qualified by the adjective *casual, communication* and *relationship* are "god-terms" of the Nacirema. References to *self* have the same sacred status.

Although the people of Teamsterville know and occasionally use the word *communication,* it holds none of the potency that it has for the Nacirema. To the contrary, for a Teamsterville male involved in a relationship with someone of higher or lower status, communicating is considered an unmanly thing to do. Philipsen first discovered this part of the Teamsterville speech code through his work with youth at the community center. He ruefully recalls, "When I spoke to unruly Teamsterville boys in order to discipline them I was judged by them to be unmanly because, in such circumstances, I spoke."[17] The guys "naturally" expected this older male to use power or physical force to bring them in line. They were confused when Philipsen, consistent with his Nacirema speech code, sat down with them to "talk things out." The only explanation that made sense to them was that their youth leader was gay. Not until much later did their conclusion get back to him.

THE SITE OF SPEECH CODES

Proposition 5: The terms, rules, and premises of a speech code are inextricably woven into speaking itself.

How can we spot the speech code of a given culture—our own or anyone else's? The basic answer is to listen for the traces of culture woven into everyday

Cathy
by Cathy Guisewite
SUPER BOWL XXVII
YAK YAK YAK YAK YAK YAK YAK YAK YAK YAK YAK YAK YAK
YAK YAK
SHH!
THE PROBLEM WITH WATCHING SPORTS WITH MEN IS THAT I NEVER KNOW WHEN IT'S OK TO TALK.
ME NEITHER.
IT SEEMS RUDE TO TALK DURING THE GAME, BUT THERE ARE PARTS OF THE GAME WHEN MEN TALK ALL THE TIME.
THEY DON'T EVEN TALK ABOUT THE GAME!
I KNOW. THERE ARE PARTS OF THE GAME WHERE NON-GAME TALK IS ACCEPTABLE AND PARTS WHERE ONLY GAME-RELATED TALK IS ACCEPTABLE.
AND PARTS WHERE NO ONE IS SUPPOSED TO SAY A PEEP.
HOW ARE WE SUPPOSED TO KNOW WHICH PARTS ARE WHICH?
THEY DON'T WANT US TO KNOW. THEY HAVE A SECRET CODE.
THEY HAVE A SECRET CODE AS A DEFENSE AGAINST US GETTING TOO CLOSE.
THEY WANT US CLOSE, BUT THEY DON'T WANT US THAT CLOSE!
THEY WANT US, BUT THEY DON'T WANT TO WANT US... THEY NEED US, BUT THEY DON'T WANT TO NEED US... THEY NEED TO WANT US, BUT THEY DON'T WANT TO NEED TO WANT US!
WE MUST UNDERSTAND AND REACH OUT TO THEM!
IF YOU SPENT FIVE MINUTES LEARNING SOMETHING ABOUT FOOTBALL INSTEAD OF FIVE HOURS PSYCHOANALYZING US, YOU'D KNOW WHEN IT WAS OK TO TALK!
SHH! NO TALKING ALLOWED DURING THE COMMERCIALS!
WHY DID WE INVITE THEM?
THEY BROUGHT THE FOOD.

talk. Especially be on the lookout for words or phrases about communication behavior—the metacommunication that Watzlawick's *interactional view* deems so important (see Chapter 13). This process of discovery takes time and a person with patience who is willing to listen and watch without preconceived notions. Michelle's application log suggests that, with a little help from her friend, she was a quick learner.

> I see speech code differences when I visit my friend's extended family in rural Michigan. Sometimes I express an opinion or ask a question and am reproached by my friend with, "We don't talk about that." At the dinner table, the adults talk and consider it disrespectful for the kids to try to join the conversation, especially when they don't know much about the topic or they ask questions. The code violation isn't expressed, but I notice looks pass or short answers given. There's an unwritten list of topics to talk about—the farm, people in town, other relatives, motorcycles, and topics where it's assumed everyone agrees, like conservative politics. It would be strange for someone to bring up the economy in China or something that isn't perceived as directly affecting the family. When I try to adapt, I fit in better and enjoy getting to know people from a different background.

Philipsen is not a fan of assuming a culture is *either* individualistic *or* collectivistic. He believes speech communities are more nuanced than that simple classification and their subtleties will be missed or blotted out by dichotomous labels.

Philipsen also focuses on highly structured cultural forms that often display the cultural significance of symbols and meanings, premises, and rules that might not be accessible through normal conversation. For example, *social dramas* are public confrontations in which one party invokes a moral rule to challenge the conduct of another. The response from the person criticized offers a way of testing and validating the legitimacy of the "rules of life" that are embedded in a particular speech code.

Philipsen analyzed Mayor Daley's reply in the city council to charges of nepotism—in this case the appointment of his best friend's son to a political position.[18] By all accounts, Daley went ballistic. Most reporters regarded the speech as an irrational diatribe, yet his appeal to place, honor, and traditional gender roles resonated with the values of Teamsterville. When Philipsen asked people in the neighborhood if it was right for Daley to favor his friends, they responded, "Who should he appoint, his enemies?"

Totemizing rituals offer another window to a culture's speech code. They involve a careful performance of a structured sequence of actions that pays homage to a sacred object. Philipsen and Katriel spotted a *communication ritual* among the Nacirema that honors the sacred trinity of self, communication, and relationships.[19] Known as "a good talk," the topic is often a variation on the theme of how to be a unique, independent *self* yet still receive validation from close others. The purpose of the ritual is not problem solving per se. Instead, people come together to express their individuality, affirm each other's identity, and experience intimacy.

Totemizing ritual
A careful performance of a structured sequence of actions that pays homage to a sacred object.

The communication ritual follows a typical sequence:

1. Initiation—a friend voices a need to work through an interpersonal problem.
2. Acknowledgment—the confidant validates the importance of the issue by a willingness to "sit down and talk."

3. Negotiation—the friend self-discloses, the confidant listens in an empathic and nonjudgmental way, the friend in turn shows openness to feedback and change.
4. Reaffirmation—both the friend and the confidant try to minimize different views, and they reiterate appreciation and commitment to each other.

By performing the communication ritual correctly, both parties celebrate the central tenet of the Nacirema code: "Whatever the problem, communication is the answer."

THE FORCE OF SPEECH CODES IN DISCUSSIONS

> *Proposition 6:* The artful use of a shared speech code is a sufficient condition for predicting, explaining, and controlling the form of discourse about the intelligibility, prudence, and morality of communication conduct.

Does the knowledge of people's speech codes in a given situation help an observer or a participant *predict* or *control* what others will say and how they'll interpret what is said? Philipsen thinks it does. It's important, however, to understand clearly what Philipsen is *not* saying.

Let's assume that Philipsen is again working with youth in Teamsterville and now knows the code of when a man should speak. Proposition 6 does not claim he should or could keep an unruly kid in line with a smack on the head. Speech codes theory deals with only one type of human behavior—speech acts. Nor does it claim that fathers in Nacirema homes will always encourage their kids to talk at the dinner table. Even when people give voice to a speech code, they still have the power, and sometimes the desire, to resist it. Perhaps the father had a bad day and wants some peace and quiet. Proposition 6 does suggest, however, that by a thoughtful use of shared speech codes, participants can guide metacommunication—the talk about talk. This is no small matter.

The dad-at-the-dinner-table example can help us see how prediction and control might work. Suppose a Nacirema father growls at his kids to finish their dinner without saying another word. Inasmuch as we understand the speech code of the family, we can confidently predict that his children will say that his demand is unfair, and his wife will object to his verbal behavior. As for artful control, she could choose to pursue the matter in private so that her husband wouldn't lose face in front of the children. She might also tie her objection to shared values: "If you don't communicate with our kids, they're going to grow up bitter and end up not liking you." In this way she would tap into issues that her husband would recognize as legitimate and would set the moral agenda for the rest of the discussion about the way he talks with the kids.

The dinner-table example I've sketched is based on an actual incident discussed by Philipsen.[20] He uses it to demonstrate the rhetorical force of appealing to shared speech codes. While the scope of Proposition 6 is limited to metacommunication, talk about the clarity, appropriateness, and ethics of a person's communication is an important feature of everyday life. In the vernacular of the Nacirema, "It's a big deal." For people who study communication, it's even bigger.

PERFORMANCE ETHNOGRAPHY

In an extension and critique of the style of ethnography that Philipsen conducts, some researchers have stopped talking about *doing* ethnography in favor of *performing* ethnography. Much like Philipsen, Dwight Conquergood, a former Northwestern University performance ethnographer, spent several years with teenagers in the "Little Beirut" district of Chicago. Conquergood lived in a multiethnic tenement and performed participant observation among local street gangs. *Performance ethnography* is more than a research tool; it is grounded in several theoretical principles.

The first principle is that performance is both the *subject* and the *method* of performance ethnography. All social interactions are performance because, as Philipsen notes, speech not only reflects but also alters the world. Thus, Conquergood viewed the daily conversations of gang members who were hangin' on the street corner as performances. Of particular interest to Conquergood were rituals, festivals, spectacles, dramas, games, and other metaperformances. The ritualistic handshakes and elaborate graffiti enacted by the gangs are examples of metaperformance because the gang members themselves recognized the actions as symbolic. Neither fiction nor farce, metaperformances are reminders that life consists of "performances about performances about performances."[21]

Performance ethnography
A research methodology committed to performance as both the subject and method of research, to researchers' work being performance, and to reports of fieldwork being actable.

These researchers also consider their work performative. Fieldwork is performance because it involves suspension of disbelief on the part of both the participant observer and the host culture. In the act of embodied learning, researchers recognize that they are doing ethnography *with* rather than *of* a people group—they are co-performers. Conquergood didn't merely observe the greetings of gang members on the street; he greeted them.

In reporting their fieldwork, performance ethnographers are no less concerned about performance. They consider the thick descriptions traditionally produced to be a bit thin. By taking speech acts out of dialogues and dialogues out of context, published ethnographies smooth all the voices of the field "into the expository prose of more or less interchangeable 'informants.'"[22] Thus, the goal of performance ethnographies is to produce actable ethnographies. As Conquergood wrote, "What makes good theatre makes more sensitive and politically committed anthropological writing."[23]

Conquergood performed his ethnographies through public reading and even acting the part of a gang member. This kind of performance enables the ethnographer to recognize the limitations of, and uncover the cultural bias in, his or her written work. For those participating as audience members, performance presents complex characters and situations eliciting understanding that's responsive rather than passive.

Performance ethnography almost always takes place among marginalized groups. The theoretical rationale underlying this fact is that oppressed people are not passive but create and sustain their culture and dignity. In the face of daily humiliations, they create "subtle, complex, and amazingly nuanced performances that subversively key the events and critique the hierarchy of power."[24] Conquergood was committed to chronicling the performances of the oppressed in order to give them a voice in the larger society.

CRITIQUE: DIFFERENT SPEECH CODES IN COMMUNICATION THEORY

A favorite grad school professor of mine was fond of saying, "You know you're in the wrong place on an issue if you aren't getting well roasted from all sides." By this "golden mean" standard, Gerry Philipsen is on the right academic path.

Most interpretive scholars applaud Philipsen's commitment to long-term participant observation and his perceptive interpretations, but they are critical of his efforts to generalize across cultures. Granted, he doesn't reduce cultural variation to a single issue such as an individualistic–collectivistic dichotomy. Philipsen's critics recoil, however, when he talks about explanation, prediction, and control—the traditional goals of science. Any theory that adopts these aims, no matter how limited its scope, strikes them as reductionist.

Theorists who operate from a feminist, critical, or cultural studies perspective (see Chapters 35–36, 21, and 27, respectively) charge that Philipsen is silent and perhaps naïve about power relationships. His description of the Nacirema speech code fails to unmask patterns of domination, and he doesn't speak out against male hegemony in Teamsterville. In response, Philipsen says the practice of ethnography that he recommends gives voice to the people who are observed. He offers this advice to critical scholars:

1. Look and listen for the variety and particularity in what people do; it is not all, or only, power that energizes human action.
2. Look at and listen to the concrete details of what people say before you interpret their conduct, even with those people whom you have been taught to think of as the usual suspects.
3. Try to learn what words and other symbols mean to those who use them, because sometimes such open inquiry will surprise you.[25]

If power is an issue—as it was in Mayor Daley's city council speech—Philipsen believes it will be evident in the way people speak. If it's not an issue, the ethnographer shouldn't make it one.

Stella Ting-Toomey's face-negotiation theory suggests that Philipsen's interpretive approach is needlessly drawn out and almost guarantees that the person crossing cultural boundaries will experience culture shock.[26] It can take years to do the sort of ethnography that's central to speech codes theory. Without some sort of cultural map as a guide, the sojourner will likely be overwhelmed with new impressions, many of them ultimately leading nowhere. And once the analysis is complete, the inquirer only has a handle on the communication patterns and meanings of, for example, men in a corner bar or students in a particular school—local knowledge not transferable to other communities.

Ting-Toomey offers a tool kit of cultural variables for strangers to use, headed by the value dimensions of collectivism–independence and small power differences–large power differences already validated by social scientists. Unlike ethnographic interpretations, these two sliding-scale issues provide security and predictability early in intercultural encounters and can be used to compare national cultures, not just local knowledge. But Philipsen remains skeptical of this cultural cookie-cutter approach. He believes *a priori* labeling causes those trying to understand another culture to ignore perceptions that don't square with preconceived ideas or to miss nuances that are unique to a given speech community.[27] As for the theory's scope of coverage, researchers trained in speech codes theory and methodologies have published ethnographies conducted in Colombia, Finland, Germany, Israel, Mexico, Spain, as well as in the United States and other countries.

Philipsen does offer a reminder, however, that the scope of his theory is limited to communication behavior. Those of us immersed in the Nacirema speech code may quickly affirm that good communication is the most important thing to create and nurture successful relationships. But Philipsen cautions that "carefulness in making and keeping romantic and marital vows, self-sacrifice in consideration of the other's well-being . . . or fidelity to a partner" may be as important or more important than self-disclosure or other forms of speech we might favor.[28] I appreciate his interpretation. To me it sounds right.

QUESTIONS TO SHARPEN YOUR FOCUS

1. Most of *speech codes theory* is concerned with *cross-cultural* rather than *intercultural* communication. What is the difference? Which incidents described in the chapter are examples of intercultural encounters?
2. Which *propositions* of the theory suggest a *scientific* approach to the study of speech codes?
3. Many scholars still think of Philipsen's work as the *ethnography of communication*. Why do you (or don't you) think *speech codes theory* is a better name?
4. Philipsen says that the *Nacirema* way of talking is the prevailing *speech code* in the United States. What *research* cited in this chapter supports his claim?

CONVERSATIONS

View this segment online at www.mhhe.com/griffin9e or www.afirstlook.com.

My conversation with Gerry Philipsen is an exploration of contrasts. Philipsen highlights differences in cultures by listing topics that a Sioux interpersonal communication textbook would cover as opposed to the typical Nacirema text, which emphasizes self-disclosure. He then distinguishes between the ethnography of communication and his theory of speech codes. Philipsen goes on to suggest why the potential of using a culture's speech code to explain, predict, and even control people's behavior isn't at odds with the interpretive approach of ethnography. Finally, he discusses the fine line he draws between learning to understand and appreciate how other people see the world and still embrace his own ethical standards.

A SECOND LOOK

Recommended resource: Gerry Philipsen, "Speech Codes Theory: Traces of Culture in Interpersonal Communication," in *Engaging Theories of Interpersonal Communication,* Leslie A. Baxter and Dawn O. Braithwaite (eds.) Sage, Thousand Oaks, CA, 2008, pp. 269–280.

Systematic statement and Teamsterville/Nacirema ethnographies: Gerry Philipsen, *Speaking Culturally: Explorations in Social Communication,* State University of New York, Albany, 1992.

Revision and update: Gerry Philipsen, Lisa M. Coutu, and Patricia Covarrubias, "Speech Codes Theory: Restatement, Revisions, and Response to Criticisms," in *Theorizing About Intercultural Communication,* William Gudykunst (ed.), Sage, Thousand Oaks, CA, 2005, pp. 55–68.

The 2008 NCA Carroll C. Arnold distinguished lecture: Gerry Philipsen, "Coming to Terms with Cultures," Allyn & Bacon, Boston, MA, 2010.

Review of scholarship on culture and communication: Gerry Philipsen, "Cultural Communication," in *Handbook of International and Intercultural Communication,* 2nd ed., William Gudykunst and Bella Mody (eds.), Sage, Thousand Oaks, CA, 2002, pp. 51–67.

How to understand a culture: Gerry Philipsen, "Some Thoughts on How to Approach Finding One's Feet in Unfamiliar Cultural Terrain," *Communication Monographs,* Vol. 77, 2010, pp.160–168.

Original call for ethnography of communication: Dell Hymes, "The Ethnography of Speaking," in *Anthropology and Human Behavior,* T. Gladwin and W. C. Sturtevant (eds.), Anthropological Society of Washington, Washington, DC, 1962, pp. 13–53.

Differences among interpretive and social sciences approaches to culture: Stella Ting-Toomey, "Applying Dimensional Values in Understanding Intercultural Communication," *Communication Monographs,* Vol. 77, 2010, pp. 169–180.

Performance ethnography: Dwight Conquergood, "Homeboys and Hoods: Gang Communication and Cultural Space," in *Group Communication in Context,* Lawrence Frey (ed.), Lawrence Erlbaum, Hillsdale, NJ, 1994, pp. 23–55.

Critique: John Stewart, "Developing Communication Theories," in *Developing Communication Theories,* Gerry Philipsen and Terrance Albrecht (eds.), State University of New York, Albany, 1997, pp. 183–186.

For a theory that claims the emotional meaning of language is constant across cultures, click on Mediational Theory of Meaning in Archive under Theory Resources at *www.afirstlook.com.*

Gender and Communication

Most of us believe that women and men interact differently. When we think about the differences (and most of us think about them a lot), we usually draw on the rich data of our lives to construct our own minitheories of masculine–feminine communication.

For example, I remember sitting from 9 a.m. to 4 p.m. in a large room at the federal courthouse with a hundred other prospective jurors. We entered as strangers, but by midmorning the women were sitting in clusters of three to seven, engrossed in lively discussions. All the men sat by themselves. I thought about that stark difference as I went to my interpersonal communication class. Reviewing the class list, I realized that 70 percent of the students who took the course as an elective were female. Conversely, two-thirds of those who opted for my persuasion course were male. On the basis of this limited personal experience, I jumped to the conclusion that women talk more than men do and that their communication goal is connection rather than influence.

But stereotyping is a risky business. The distinction between women's focus on intimacy and men's concern for power has held up well under scrutiny by communication researchers. But most studies of gender differences show that women actually talk *less* than men do in mixed groups.

Linguist Robin Lakoff of the University of California, Berkeley, was one of the first scholars who attempted to classify regularities of women's speech that differentiate "women-talk" from "men-talk."[1] Lakoff claimed that women's conversation is marked by tentativeness and submission. Unfortunately, this conclusion and others were based mainly on her personal reflection and anecdotal evidence—much like my courthouse and classroom theorizing. Almost four decades of systematic research offers at least three cautions.

1. There are more similarities among men and women than there are differences. After conducting a meta-analysis of hundreds of research studies that reported gender differences on topics such as talk time, self-disclosure, and styles of conflict management, University of Wisconsin–Milwaukee communication professor Kathryn Dindia found that the differences were actually quite small. She parodies the popular belief that men and women come from two different planets in the way she summarizes her findings: "Men are from North Dakota, Women are from South Dakota."[2] (Can you really see a difference?) If I tell you that Pat talks fast, uses big words, and holds eye contact, your chances of guessing whether Pat is male or female are just slightly better than 50/50.[3]

2. Greater variability of communication style exists among women and among men than between the two groups. Scores on the *Sex-Role Inventory,* developed by former Cornell University psychologist Sandra Lipsitz Bem, illustrate this within-group diversity.[4] Bem asks people to rate themselves on a series of gender-related descriptions—many related to speech. A person who marks *soft-spoken, eager to soothe hurt feelings,* and *does not use harsh language* ranks high in femininity. A person who marks *assertive, defends own beliefs,* and *willing to take a stand* ranks high in masculinity. As you might expect, males tend to fit masculine sex roles and females tend to fit feminine sex roles, but the scores from a group of people of the same sex are typically all over the map. Sometimes individuals—male or

"How is it gendered?"

female—score high on both scales. Bem regards this combination as the best of both worlds and refers to people with blended identities as *androgynous.* Obviously, gender-related speech isn't an either/or proposition.

3. Sex is a fact; gender is an idea.[5] Within the literature of the field, the sex-related terms *male* and *female* are typically used to categorize people biologically, as they do at the Olympics—by chromosomes and genitalia. On the other hand, the terms *men* and *women* or *masculine* and *feminine* are usually employed to describe an idea that's been learned from and reinforced by others. When we forget that our concept of gender is a human construction, we fall into the trap of thinking that there is a real-in-nature category called *masculine*—an early Clint Eastwood archetype who smokes Marlboros, doesn't eat quiche, won't cry, and lives by the code that *a man's got to do what a man's got to do.* Sex is a given, but we negotiate, or work out, our concept of gender with others throughout our lives.

CHAPTER 34

Objective — Interpretive

Semiotic tradition
Socio-cultural tradition

Genderlect Styles

of Deborah Tannen

"Male–female conversation is cross-cultural communication."[1] This simple statement is the basic premise of Deborah Tannen's *You Just Don't Understand,* a book that seeks to explain why men and women often talk past each other.

Tannen is a linguistics professor at Georgetown University, and her research specialty is conversational style—not what people say but the way they say it. In her first book on conversational style she offers a microanalysis of six friends talking together during a two-and-a-half-hour Thanksgiving dinner.[2] Tannen introduces this sociolinguistic study with a quote from E. M. Forster's novel *A Passage to India:* "A pause in the wrong place, an intonation misunderstood, and a whole conversation went awry."[3] Forster's novel illustrates how people of goodwill from different cultures can grossly misunderstand each other's intentions.

Tannen is convinced that similar miscommunication occurs all the time between women and men. The effect may be more insidious, however, because the parties usually don't realize that they are in a cross-cultural encounter. At least when we cross a geographical border we anticipate the need to bridge a communication gap. In conversing with members of the opposite sex, Tannen notes, our failure to acknowledge different conversational styles can get us in big trouble. Most men and women don't grasp that "talking through their problems" with each other will only make things worse if it's their divergent ways of talking that are causing the trouble in the first place.

Tannen's writing is filled with imagery that underscores the mutually alien nature of male and female conversation styles. When she compared the style of boys and girls who were in second grade, she felt she was looking at the discourse of "two different species." For example, two girls could sit comfortably face-to-face and carry on a serious conversation about people they knew. But when boys were asked to talk about "something serious," they were restless, never looked at each other, jumped from topic to topic, and talked about games and competition. These stylistic differences showed up in older kids as well. Tannen notes that "moving from the sixth-grade boys to the girls of the same age is like moving to another planet."[4] There is no evidence that we grow out of these differences as we grow up. She describes adult men and women as speaking "different words from different worlds," and even when they use the same terms, they are "tuned to different frequencies."

Tannen's cross-cultural approach to gender differences departs from much of feminist scholarship that claims conversations between men and women reflect men's efforts to dominate women. She assumes that male and female conversational styles are equally valid: "We try to talk to each other honestly, but it seems at times that we are speaking different languages—or at least different genderlects."[5] Although the word *genderlect* is not original with Tannen, the term nicely captures her belief that masculine and feminine styles of discourse are best viewed as two distinct cultural dialects rather than as inferior or superior ways of speaking.

Genderlect
A term suggesting that masculine and feminine styles of discourse are best viewed as two distinct cultural dialects.

Tannen realizes that categorizing people and their communication according to gender is offensive to many women and men. None of us like to be told, "Oh, you're talking just like a (wo)man." Each of us regards himself or herself as a unique individual. But at the risk of reinforcing a simplistic reductionism that claims biology is destiny, Tannen insists there *are* gender differences in the ways we speak.

> Despite these dangers, I am joining the growing dialogue on gender and language because the risk of ignoring differences is greater than the danger of naming them.[6]

WOMEN'S DESIRE FOR CONNECTION VS. MEN'S DESIRE FOR STATUS

Tannen says that, more than anything else, women seek human *connection*, whereas men are concerned mainly with *status*. While women are focused on cultivating a sense that they're *in touch*, men are working hard to preserve their *independence* as they jockey for position on a hierarchy of competitive accomplishment. When they're together, women's longing for *intimacy* threatens men's desire for freedom and sidetracks the masculine quest to be *one up* in all relationships.

Tannen does believe that some men are open to intimacy, just as some women have a concern for power. You'll recall that Baxter and Montgomery's relational dialectics assumes that all people feel a tension between connection and autonomy in their relationships (see Chapter 11). Tannen agrees that many men and women would like to have intimacy *and* independence in every situation if they could, but she doesn't think it's possible. As a result, these differences in priority tend to give men and women differing views of the same situation.

> Girls and women feel it is crucial that they be liked by their peers, a form of involvement that focuses on symmetrical connection. Boys and men feel it is crucial that they be respected by their peers, a form of involvement that focuses on asymmetrical status.[7]

RAPPORT TALK VS. REPORT TALK

Why is Tannen so certain that women focus on connection while men focus on status? Her answer is that she listens to men and women talk. Just as an ethnographer pores over the words of native informants to discover what has meaning within their society, so Tannen scrutinizes the conversation of representative speakers from the feminine culture and the masculine culture to determine their core values. She offers numerous examples of the divergent styles she observes in everyday communication. These linguistic differences give her confidence that the connection–status distinction structures every verbal contact between women and men.

Julia Wood, communication professor at the University of North Carolina and co-author of standpoint theory (Chapter 35), thinks that Tannen's observations have merit and that the connection–status distinction is evident even in childhood. In her book *Gendered Lives,*[8] Wood draws upon research with children[9] to highlight the different rules[10] that girls and boys learn as they grow up. Understanding those rules provides insight for some of the key differences that Tannen believes characterize the genderlect styles at the root of much of the miscommunication between men and women. Three of the key rules boys learn are:

1. Communicate to assert your ideas, opinions, and identity.
2. Use talk to solve problems or develop a strategy.
3. Speak in a way that attracts attention to yourself.

In contrast to these rules, girls learn to:

1. Use communication to create and maintain relationships.
2. Involve others in conversations and respond to their ideas.
3. Show sensitivity to others and to relationships.

Consider the following types of talk. Each of these speech forms shows that women value *rapport* talk, while men value *report* talk.

1. Private Speaking vs. Public Speaking

Folk wisdom suggests that women talk more than men. Tannen cites a version of an old joke that has a wife complaining to her husband, "For the past 10 years you've never told me what you're thinking." Her husband caustically replies, "I didn't want to interrupt you." Tannen grants the validity of the wordy-woman–mute-male stereotype as it applies to a couple alone. She finds that women talk more than men do in private conversations, and she endorses Alice Walker's notion that a woman falls in love with a man because she sees in him "a giant ear."[11] In *The Female Brain,* Louann Brizendine, clinical professor of psychiatry at the University of California, San Francisco, provides hard data that bolsters Tannen's position. According to Brizendine, women speak an average of 20,000 words per day. Men speak about 7,000.[12] But according to Tannen, that huge disparity is built up mainly in private conversations. In the public arena, men vie for ascendancy and speak much more than women do.

Rapport talk
The typical conversational style of women, which seeks to establish connection with others.

I (Glenn) believe that if Tannen studied the talk of professors at faculty meetings, she'd gather a wealth of data to support her claim that men are more likely to engage in report rather than rapport talk. Tannen says men use talk as a weapon. The function of the long explanations they employ is to command attention, convey information, and insist on agreement. In my 30-plus years of attending faculty meetings, I've witnessed countless examples of men who hold the floor with their talk in order to win a point or badger colleagues into reluctant agreement. It's not surprising that faculty members who bristle the most at male monologues are women. In most cases, they're more concerned with building faculty rapport by seeking input from others. My perception of this difference between male and female faculty members conforms well to the conversational rules summarized by Julia Wood. Girls learn to involve others in conversations, while boys learn to use communication to assert their own ideas and draw attention to themselves.

Report talk
The typical monologic style of men, which seeks to command attention, convey information, and win arguments.

2. Telling a Story

Along with theorists Clifford Geertz, Michael Pacanowsky, and Walter Fisher (see Chapters 19 and 24), Tannen recognizes that the stories people tell reveal a great deal about their hopes, needs, and values. Consistent with men's focus on status, Tannen notes that men tell more stories than women do—especially jokes. Telling jokes is a masculine way to negotiate status. Men's humorous stories have a *can-you-top-this?* flavor that holds attention and elevates the storyteller above his audience.

When men aren't trying to be funny, they tell stories in which they are heroes, often acting alone to overcome great obstacles. On the other hand, women tend to express their desire for community by telling stories about others. On rarer occasions when a woman is a character in her own narrative, she usually describes herself as doing something foolish rather than acting in a clever manner. This downplaying of self puts her on the same level with her hearers, thus strengthening her network of support.

3. Listening

A woman listening to a story or an explanation tends to hold eye contact, offer head nods, and react with *yeah, uh-huh, mmmn, right,* or other responses that indicate *I'm listening* or *I'm with you.* For a man concerned with status, that overt style of active listening means *I agree with you,* so he avoids putting himself in a submissive, or *one-down,* stance. Women, of course, conclude that men aren't listening, which is not necessarily true.

When a woman who is listening starts to speak before the other person is finished, she usually does so to add a word of agreement, to show support, or to finish a sentence with what she thinks the speaker will say. Tannen labels this *cooperative overlap.* She says that from a woman's perspective, cooperative overlap is a sign of rapport rather than a competitive ploy to control the conversation. She also recognizes that men don't see it that way. Men regard any interruption as a power move to take control of the conversation, because in their world that's how it's done. Those who win the conversational game can take a don't-talk-while-I'm-interrupting-you stance and make it stick. Tannen concludes that these different styles of conversation management are the source of continuing irritation in cross-gender talk. "Whereas women's cooperative overlaps frequently annoy men by seeming to co-opt their topic, men frequently annoy women by usurping or switching the topic."[13]

Cooperative overlap
A supportive interruption often meant to show agreement and solidarity with the speaker.

4. Asking Questions

Tannen thinks that men and women also annoy each other with their different ways of asking questions—or of *not* asking them. When we were first married, my wife Cheri and I set out on a trip from Chicago to Muskegon, Michigan, to visit friends. I glanced at a map before the trip—today's GPS was the stuff of science fiction back then—and noted that I needed to take I-94. About an hour into the trip, Cheri encouraged me to stop and ask for directions because the road we were on didn't seem familiar to her. Knowing that we were on I-94, I confidently declined her request. But when I saw signs for Milwaukee, Wisconsin, I was finally persuaded to stop at a gas station. To my horror, I discovered that I-94 went up *both sides* of Lake Michigan. I was driving up the wrong side.

Cheri and I can laugh now about our late arrival in Muskegon, but when she tells the story, she always emphasizes my stubborn refusal to stop and ask for directions.

According to Tannen, men don't ask for that kind of help. Every admission of ignorance whittles away at the image of self-sufficiency that is so important to a man. "If self-respect is bought at the cost of a few extra minutes of travel time, it is well worth the price," she explains.[14] In my case, I gained no self-respect at a cost of several hours of travel time. But I'm still not fond of asking others for directions.

Women ask questions to establish a connection with others. Even a five-minute stop at a gas station to check the best route can create a sense of community, however brief. Tannen notes that when women state their opinions, they often tag them with a question at the end of the sentence: "That was a good movie, *don't you think?*" *Tag questions* soften the sting of potential disagreement that might drive people apart. They are also invitations to participate in open, friendly dialogue. But to men, they make the speaker seem wishy-washy.

Tag question
A short question at the end of a declarative statement, often used by women to soften the sting of potential disagreement or invite open, friendly dialogue.

Ever since *You Just Don't Understand* was published, Tannen has entertained questions during television interviews, radio call-in shows, and discussions following lectures. Women almost always seek more information or offer their own experiences that validate her insights. That's now true for men as well. But when the book was riding high on best-seller lists, men would often pose questions that seemed designed to bring her down from her high horse or to establish their own expertise. Even though she understands that public face is crucial to men, she identifies with the words of a wife in a short story: "I'd have been upset about making the mistake—but not about people *knowing*. That part's not a big deal to me." Her husband replied, "Oh, is it ever a big deal to me."[15]

5. Conflict

After his divorce, Rob Reiner decided to direct the film *When Harry Met Sally*, a humorous depiction of the relationship between a man (Billy Crystal) and a woman (Meg Ryan). Nora Ephron wrote the script and, after interviewing Reiner, used him as the inspiration for Harry's character. The film became a classic after its release in 1989, and is listed among Bravo's "100 Funniest Movies." Reiner's divorce provided the grist for an argument between Harry and Sally, in which Harry blows up at their friends Jess and Marie and then storms out of the room. After making an excuse for his behavior, Sally goes to him to try to calm him down.

HARRY: I know, I know, I shouldn't have done it.

SALLY: Harry, you're going to have to try and find a way of not expressing every feeling that you have every moment that you have them.

HARRY: Oh, really?

SALLY: Yes, there are times and places for things.

HARRY: Well the next time you're giving a lecture series on social graces, would you let me know, 'cause I'll sign up.

SALLY: Hey. You don't have to take your anger out on me.

HARRY: Oh, I think I'm entitled to throw a little anger your way. Especially when I'm being told how to live my life by Miss Hospital Corners.

SALLY: What's that supposed to mean?

HARRY: I mean, nothing bothers you. You never get upset about anything.

This scene illustrates Tannen's description of much male–female strife. Since they see life as a contest, many men are more comfortable with conflict and are therefore less likely to hold themselves in check. By trying to placate Harry and excuse his anger toward their friends, Sally responds in what Tannen believes is an equally typical fashion. "To most women, conflict is a threat to connection—to be avoided at all costs."[16]

The dialogue illustrates another feature of conflict between men and women. As often happens, Sally's attempt to avert a similar outburst in the future sparks new conflict with Harry. Tannen says men have an early warning system that's geared to detect signs that they are being told what to do. Harry bristles at the thought that Sally is trying to limit his autonomy, so her efforts backfire.

6. Nonverbal Communication

Curiously, Tannen doesn't extend the connection–status distinction to the ways in which men and women communicate nonverbally. Susan Pease Gadoua, a licensed marriage counselor with a column in *Psychology Today* magazine, finds it difficult to analyze the way men and women talk to each other without including the nonverbal component. Based on her years of experience helping married couples, she's learned to anticipate a common scenario when she sees a man and a woman trying to get over a serious fight or navigate a rift in their relationship.

> Each partner has a different way of wanting to resolve the problem: women want to talk things out and perhaps make love later (when they feel more connected); men want to connect by making love and (maybe) talking later.[17]

Gadoua recalls one husband who told her that all of his marital problems would be solved if only he and his wife could go away for a whole weekend and dedicate the entire time to sex. His wife saw this solution as a superficial gesture that wouldn't solve anything. Deborah Tannen might see it as a way for the husband to score in a never-ending game of who's on top. The husband's solution seems like a classic acting out of one of the early rules that boys learn at play—communicate to assert your identity. The wife's solution reflects one of the rules girls learn—connect through conversation. Sadly, Gadoua observes that when women want to connect and men want to have sex, it's often the case that neither activity takes place.

MEN AND WOMEN GROW UP IN DIFFERENT SPEECH COMMUNITIES

Do men and women really live in different worlds? Tannen cites dialogue from Anne Tyler's *The Accidental Tourist,* Ingmar Bergman's *Scenes from a Marriage,* Alice Walker's *The Temple of My Familiar,* Erica Jong's *Fear of Flying,* and Jules Feiffer's *Grown Ups* to support her claim that the different ways women and men talk reflect their separate cultures. If these fictional examples depict an accurate view of the separate worlds of real men and women, it makes sense to find out how and when these worlds formed.

When Tannen witnessed dramatic differences in conversational style between second-grade boys and girls, she concluded that the origins of speaking in genderlect must be traced back to early childhood. Is it plausible to suggest that boys and girls as young as 7 are already segregated and using conversation styles that will follow them into adult life? Many linguists and communication scholars believe the answer to that question is yes. They refer to the segregated groups to which boys and girls belong as *speech communities*.[18]

Julia Wood summarized the concept of a *speech community* this way: "[A] speech community exists when people share understandings about goals of communication, strategies for enacting those goals, and ways of interpreting communication."[19] Tannen's conclusion that the second-grade boys and girls she observed were "two different species" certainly matches up with the idea that they were from distinct speech communities. But these communities don't appear out of thin air. To get insight into their origins, we need to look back to the preschool years.

Speech community
A community of people who share understandings about goals of communication, strategies for enacting those goals, and ways of interpreting communication.

Louise Cherry Wilkinson, professor of education, psychology, and communication sciences at Syracuse University, suggests that separate speech communities begin with the conversations young boys and girls have with their mothers. She reached this conclusion when she studied the interactions between moms and kids during a free-play session. She recruited mothers with a 2-year-old daughter or son to take part, giving no instructions as to what they should talk about. Along with her colleague Michael Lewis, Wilkinson transcribed the interactions that took place and trained coders to analyze the words that were used. The coders didn't know whether they were coding interactions between a mother and daughter or a mother and son.[20]

Wilkinson and Lewis discovered that mothers of girls talked more, asked more questions, used longer sentences, and were more likely to verbally acknowledge their daughters' comments than mothers of boys. Mothers of boys were more likely to use directives—telling their sons what to do—than mothers of girls. Wilkinson and Lewis speculated that these sorts of differences could set early expectations in males and females about what type of conversation is most appropriate for them. The findings suggest that the differences Tannen sees between adult male and female speech have their roots in the early socialization of children.

"NOW YOU'RE BEGINNING TO UNDERSTAND"

What if Tannen is right and all conversation between men and women is best understood as cross-cultural communication? Does that mean genderlect can be taught, like French, Swahili, or any other foreign language? Tannen offers a qualified yes. She regards sensitivity training as an effort to teach men how to speak in a feminine voice, while assertiveness training is an effort to teach women how to speak in a masculine voice. But she's aware of our ethnocentric tendency to think it's the other person who needs fixing, so she expresses only guarded hope that men and women will alter their linguistic styles.

Tannen has much more confidence in the benefits of multicultural understanding. She believes that understanding each other's style, and the motives behind it, is the first step in overcoming destructive responses.

> The answer is for both men and women to try to take each other on their own terms rather than applying the standards of one group to the behavior of the other. . . . Understanding style differences for what they are takes the sting out of them.[21]

"And do you, Deborah Tannen, think they know what they're talking about?"

Tannen suggests that one way to measure whether we are gaining cross-gender insight is a drop in the frequency of the oft-heard lament *You just don't understand.* I can personally testify to the validity of this standard. While I certainly make no claim to have arrived at a complete understanding of Cheri or her conversational style, I've only heard her say, "You just don't understand," in the early stages of our 38 years together. She'd say the same about me. It's difficult for a marriage to survive and thrive without partners gaining insight into each other's conversational style.

ETHICAL REFLECTION: GILLIGAN'S DIFFERENT VOICE

For more than 30 years, Carol Gilligan was a professor of education in the Harvard Graduate School of Education. Her book *In a Different Voice* presents a theory of moral development claiming that women tend to think and speak in an ethical voice different from that of men.[22] Gilligan's view of gender differences parallels Deborah Tannen's analysis of men as wanting independence and women as desiring human connection. Gilligan is convinced that most men seek autonomy and think of moral maturity in terms of *justice.* She's equally certain that women desire to be linked with others and that they regard their ultimate ethical responsibility as one of *care.*

On the basis of the quantity and quality of feminine relationships, Gilligan contrasts *women who care* with *men who are fair*. Individual rights, equality before the law, fair play, a square deal—all these masculine ethical goals can be pursued without intimate ties to others. Justice is impersonal. But women's moral judgment is more contextual, more immersed in the details of relationships and narratives.[23] Sensitivity to others, loyalty, self-sacrifice, and peacemaking all reflect interpersonal involvement.

Gilligan's work arose in response to the theory of moral development of her Harvard colleague Lawrence Kohlberg, who identified increasing levels of ethical maturity by analyzing responses to hypothetical moral dilemmas.[24] According to his justice-based scoring system, the average young adult female was a full stage behind her male counterpart. Women were rated as less morally mature than men because they were less concerned about abstract concepts like justice, truth, and freedom. Instead, they based their ethical decisions on considerations of compassion, loyalty, and a strong sense of responsibility to prevent pain and alleviate suffering. Their moral reasoning was more likely to reflect Buber's call for genuine I–Thou relationships than Kant's categorical imperative (see Chapters 6 and 7).

Gilligan is comfortable with the idea that men and women speak in different ethical voices. But she's disturbed that when women don't follow the normative path laid out by men, "the conclusion has generally been that something is wrong with women."[25] She points out "the unfair paradox that the very traits that have traditionally defined the 'goodness' of women are those that mark them as deficient in moral development."[26]

Although Gilligan's theory is more descriptive than prescriptive, the underlying assumption is that the way things *are* reflects the way things *ought to be.* Most ethical theorists are bothered by the idea of a double standard—justice from some, care from others. Traditional moral philosophy has never suggested different ethics for different groups. Yet readers of both sexes report that Gilligan's theory resonates with their personal experience.

CRITIQUE: IS TANNEN SOFT ON RESEARCH—AND MEN?

Is male–female conversation really cross-cultural communication? Tannen suggests we use the *aha factor* to test the validity of her two-culture hypothesis:

Aha factor
A subjective standard ascribing validity to an idea when it resonates with one's personal experience.

> If my interpretation is correct, then readers, on hearing my explanation, will exclaim within their heads, "Aha!" Something they have intuitively sensed will be made explicit. . . . When the subject of analysis is human interaction—a process that we engage in, all our lives—each reader can measure interpretation against her/his own experience.[27]

If we agree to this subjective standard of validity, Tannen easily makes her case. For example, in the book *You Just Don't Understand,* she describes how women who verbally share problems with men are often frustrated by the masculine tendency to offer solutions. According to Tannen, women don't want advice; they're looking for the gift of understanding. When Em first read her book, he had the kind of *aha* reaction that Tannen says validates her theory. He says, "I realized that her words described me. Anytime my wife, Jean, tells me about a problem she's facing, I either turn coldly analytic or dive in and try to fix things for the woman I love. I now know that Jean would rather have me just listen or voice some version of *I feel your pain.*"

Brittany's application log suggests that she's convinced. Perhaps her masculine upbringing explains why she experienced the *aha factor* even before she read about Tannen's theory.

> From ages 4 to 11, I was raised by my single father. During this developmental time in my life, I conversed mainly with Dad, and therefore adopted the kind of *report talk* that Tannen characterizes as primarily male. Whenever we had conflict, we dealt with it right away. Most of my friends were boys and I had difficulties making connections with girls my age. After my dad eventually remarried and I had a stepmother to talk with, I began to develop friendships with girls in high school. During a conversation one of them said, "You always try to think of a solution rather than just listen." I understand now that I picked up this communication trait from my dad. Whenever we faced conflict in our home, we immediately addressed it and figured out how we should deal with it. As I have developed more relationships with women I feel my genderlect style has moved towards *rapport talk,* which Tannen categorizes as primarily female. Sometimes though, I'll have a conversation with a close guy friend back home who will say, "You are the only girl who I've ever been able to talk with like this."

Apparently, Tannen's analysis of common misunderstandings between men and women has struck a responsive chord in a million other readers. *You Just Don't Understand* was on the best-seller list for most of the 1990s. And in that decade it was rated by hundreds of mental health professionals as the best of 1,000 self-help books.[28] But does a chorus of *ahas* mean that she is right? Astrologer and psychic Jeane Dixon might have made 10 predictions, and if only one came true, that's the prophecy people remembered and lauded her for. They forgot that the other nine turned out to be wrong. According to many social scientists, Tannen's "proof" may be like that.

Perhaps using selective data is the only way to support a reductionist claim that women are one way and men are another. Tannen's theme of intimacy versus independence echoes one of the dialectics Leslie Baxter and Barbara Montgomery observe in Chapter 11. However, Tannen suggests none of the flux, internal contradiction, or ongoing complexity of human existence that relational dialectics describes. Tannen's women are programmed within their gendered culture to embrace connection and deny any desire for autonomy. Her men seek autonomy but avoid connection. Neither group feels any sense of internal contradiction. Saying it's so may eventually make it so—self-fulfilling prophecy is a powerful force. But as stated in the introduction to this section, most gender researchers spot more diversity *within* each gender than *between* them.

Adrianne Kunkel (University of Kansas) and Brant Burleson (Purdue University) directly challenged the different-cultures perspective that is at the heart of Tannen's genderlect theory. According to Tannen's two-culture worldview, verbal support should be highly desired in the world of women but of little value in the competitive world of men. Kunkel and Burleson's empirical research doesn't bear out Tannen's claim. They said while it's true that women often *do* it better, both sexes place an equally high value on comforting communication:

> Both men and women view highly person-centered comforting messages as most sensitive and effective; both see messages low in person-centeredness as relatively insensitive and ineffective. . . . Both sexes view comforting skills as important in the context of various personal relationships and as substantially more important than instrumentally focused communication skills.[29]

On the basis of this shared meaning, Kunkel and Burleson rejected the different-cultures perspective. They believed it was a myth that had lost its narrative force. Men and women do understand.

A very different critique comes from feminist scholars. For example, German linguist Senta Troemel-Ploetz accuses Tannen of having written a dishonest book that ignores issues of male dominance, control, power, sexism, discrimination, sexual harassment, and verbal insults. "If you leave out power," she says, "you do not understand talk."[30] The two genderlects are anything but equal. "Men are used to dominating women; they do it especially in conversations. . . . Women are trained to please; they have to please also in conversations."[31]

Contrary to Tannen's thesis that mutual understanding will bridge the culture gap between the sexes, Troemel-Ploetz believes that "men understand quite well what women want but they give only when it suits them. In many situations they refuse to give and *women cannot make them give.*"[32] She thinks it's ridiculous to assume that men will give up power voluntarily. To prove her point, she suggests doing a follow-up study on men who read Tannen's best seller. Noting that many women readers of *You Just Don't Understand* give the book to their husbands to peruse, Troemel-Ploetz states that if Tannen's theory is true, a follow-up study should show that these men are now putting down their papers at the breakfast table and talking empathetically with their wives. She doesn't think it will happen.

QUESTIONS TO SHARPEN YOUR FOCUS

1. Apart from the topics of nonverbal communication, conflict, questions, listening, storytelling, and public vs. private speaking, can you come up with your own examples of how *rapport talk* is different from *report talk?*
2. What are the practical implications for you if talk with members of the opposite sex is, indeed, *cross-cultural communication?*
3. What might be the most effective ways for men and women to gain insight into how their *conversational styles* affect their relationships?
4. Tannen's *aha factor* is similar to Carl Rogers' standard of basing our knowledge on personal experience (see Chapter 4). What are the dangers of relying solely on the aha factor?

SELF-QUIZ

www.mhhe.com/griffin9e

A SECOND LOOK

Recommended resource: Deborah Tannen, *You Just Don't Understand,* Ballantine, New York, 1990.

Conversational style: Deborah Tannen, *That's Not What I Meant!* William Morrow, New York, 1986.

Linguistic microanalysis of conversation: Deborah Tannen, *Conversational Style: Analyzing Talk Among Friends,* Ablex, Norwood, NJ, 1984.

Gender differences in children's talk: Deborah Tannen, "Gender Differences in Topical Coherence: Creating Involvement in Best Friends' Talk," *Discourse Processes,* Vol. 13, 1990, pp. 73–90.

Discourse analysis: Deborah Tannen, *Gender and Discourse,* Oxford University, Oxford, UK, 1994/96.

Gendered language in the workplace: Deborah Tannen, *Talking from 9 to 5: Women and Men at Work—Language, Sex, and Power,* Avon, New York, 1994.

Gendered language in the family: Deborah Tannen, *I Only Say This Because I Love You: Talking in Families,* Ballantine, New York, 2002.

Support of two-culture hypothesis: Anthony Mulac, James Bradac, and Pamela Gibbons, "Empirical Support for the Gender-as-Culture Hypothesis: An Intercultural Analysis of Male/Female Language Differences," *Human Communication Research,* Vol. 27, 2001, pp. 121–152.

Communication scholars' dialogue on two-culture hypothesis: "Reflections on the Different Cultures Hypothesis: A Scholars' Symposium," Sandra Metts (ed.), *Personal Relationships,* Vol. 4, 1997, pp. 201–253.

Critique of two-culture hypothesis: Adrianne Kunkel and Brant Burleson, "Social Support and the Emotional Lives of Men and Women: An Assessment of the Different Cultures Perspective," in *Sex Differences and Similarities in Communication,* Daniel Canary and Kathryn Dindia (eds.), Lawrence Erlbaum, Mahwah, NJ, 1998, pp. 101–125.

Critique centering on power discrepancy: Senta Troemel-Ploetz, "Review Essay: Selling the Apolitical," *Discourse and Society,* Vol. 2, 1991, pp. 489–502.

For a chapter on Carol Gilligan's theory, click on Different Voice in Archive under Theory Resources in *www.afirstlook.com.*

CHAPTER 35

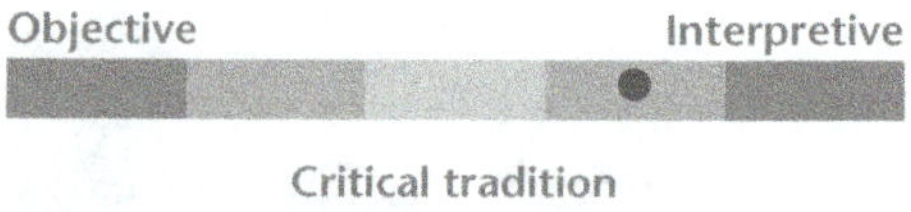

Standpoint Theory

of Sandra Harding & Julia T. Wood

As you've seen throughout the book, many communication theories raise questions about knowledge. For example,

How does a person develop a concept of self?

What's the best way to reduce uncertainty about someone you've just met?

Does the "bottom line" in an annual report reflect corporate reality?

How can we find out whether television has a powerful effect?

Are men and women from different cultures?

If you're interested in communication, you'll want to find the answers. ("Inquiring minds want to know.") Standpoint theorists Sandra Harding and Julia Wood claim that one of the best ways to discover how the world works is to start the inquiry from the standpoint of women and other groups on the margins of society.

Standpoint
A place from which to critically view the world around us.

A *standpoint* is a place from which to view the world around us. Whatever our vantage point, its location tends to focus our attention on some features of the natural and social landscape while obscuring others. Synonyms for *standpoint* include *viewpoint, perspective, outlook,* and *position.* Note that each of these words suggests a specific location in time and space where observation takes place, while also referring to values or attitudes. Sandra Harding and Julia Wood think the connection is no accident. As standpoint theorists, they claim that "the social groups within which we are located powerfully shape what we experience and know as well as how we understand and communicate with ourselves, others, and the world."[1] Our standpoint affects our worldview.

Harding is a philosopher of science who holds joint appointments in women's studies, education, and philosophy at the University of California, Los Angeles. To illustrate the effect of standpoint, she asks us to imagine looking into a pond and seeing a stick that appears to be bent.[2] But is it really? If we walk around to a different location, the stick seems to be straight—which it actually is. Physicists have developed a theory of light refraction that explains why this visual distortion occurs. In like manner, a variety of standpoint theorists from different disciplines suggest that we can use the inequalities of gender, race, class, and sexual orientation to observe how different locations within the social hierarchy tend to generate distinctive accounts of nature and social relationships.

All of them concentrate on the relationship between power and knowledge. Specifically, Harding claims that "when people speak from the opposite sides of power relations, the perspective from the lives of the less powerful can provide a more objective view than the perspective from the lives of the more powerful."[3] Her main focus is the standpoint of women who are marginalized.

Just as Harding is recognized as the philosopher who has most advanced the standpoint theory of knowledge among feminist scholars,[4] Julia Wood, a professor of communication at the University of North Carolina at Chapel Hill, has championed and consistently applied standpoint logic within the field of communication. She regards all perspectives as partial, but she insists that some standpoints are "more partial than others since different locations within social hierarchies affect what is likely to be seen."[5] For communication researchers, taking women's location seriously means heeding Wood's call to choose research topics that are responsive to women's concerns:

> Abiding concern with oppression leads many feminist scholars to criticize some of the topics that dominate research on relationships. When four women are battered to death by intimate partners every day in North America, study of how abusive relationships are created and sustained seems more compelling than research on heterosexual college students' romances. Is it more significant to study friendships among economically comfortable adolescents or social practices that normalize sexual harassment and rape?[6]

As a male researcher who has studied romance and friendship on a private college campus, I am compelled to explore the logic of Harding and Wood's standpoint agenda. But their standpoint epistemology raises other questions. Do all women share a common standpoint? Why do Harding and Wood believe a feminist standpoint is more objective or less partial than other starting points for inquiry? Would grounding future research in the lives of women compel me to regard every report of feminine experience as equally true? Should we disregard what men have to say? The rest of this chapter will explore these issues and other questions raised by standpoint theory. The answers to these questions will make more sense if we understand the varied intellectual resources standpoint theorists have drawn upon to inform their analyses.

A FEMINIST STANDPOINT ROOTED IN PHILOSOPHIES

In 1807, German philosopher Georg Hegel analyzed the master–slave relationship to show that what people "know" about themselves, others, and society depends on which group they are in.[7] For example, those in captivity have a decidedly different perspective on the meaning of chains, laws, childbirth, and punishment than do their captors who participate in the same "reality." But since masters are backed by the established structure of their society, it is they who have the power to make their view of the world stick. They are the ones who write the history books.

Following Hegel's lead, Karl Marx and Friedrich Engels referred to the *proletarian standpoint*. They suggested that the impoverished poor who provide sweat equity are society's *ideal knowers*, as long as they understand the class struggle in which they are involved.[8] Harding notes that standpoint theory "was a project 'straining at the bit' to emerge from feminist social theorists who were familiar with Marxian epistemology."[9] By substituting *women* for *proletariat*, and *gender discrimination* for *class struggle,* early feminist standpoint theorists had a ready-made framework for advocating women's way of knowing.

As opposed to the economic determinism of Marx, George Herbert Mead claimed that culture "gets into individuals" through communication (see Chapter 5). Drawing on this key principle of symbolic interactionism, Wood maintains that gender is a cultural construction rather than a biological characteristic. "More than a variable, gender is a system of meanings that sculpts individuals' standpoints by positioning most males and females in disparate material, social and symbolic circumstances."[10]

Strains of postmodernism also weave throughout standpoint theory. When Jean-François Lyotard announced an "incredulity toward metanarratives," he included Enlightenment rationality and Western science.[11] Since many feminists regard these two enterprises as dominated by men who refuse to acknowledge their male-centered bias, they embrace a postmodern critique. In reciprocal fashion, postmodernists applaud the standpoint emphasis on knowledge as locally situated, though they push the idea to the point where there is no basis for favoring one perspective over another. As we will see, Harding and Wood reject that kind of absolute relativism.

Harding and Wood have drawn upon these somewhat conflicting intellectual traditions without letting any one of them dictate the shape or substance of their standpoint approach. The resulting theory might seem a bewildering crosshatch of ideas were it not for their repeated emphasis on starting all scholarly inquiry from the lives of women and others who are marginalized. In order to honor this central tenet of standpoint theory and to illustrate the way of knowing that Harding and Wood propose, I've excerpted events and dialogue from Kathryn Stockett's best-selling novel *The Help.*[12] The story was also portrayed in the 2011 movie of the same name that garnered an Oscar nomination for best picture of the year. The title refers to the term that Southern white families used for the African American women who cooked their meals, cleaned their homes, and served as nursemaids to raise their children.

THE HELP: STORIES FROM THE LIVES OF MARGINALIZED WOMEN

The setting for *The Help* is early 1960s Jackson, Mississippi, before Congress overturned Jim Crow laws that guaranteed racial segregation. Of the three women who narrate the tale, Skeeter is the one who hails from a family of privilege. She's a young white college grad who double majored in English and journalism and now longs for a career as a serious writer. But she can only find a part-time job ghostwriting a weekly "Miss Myrna" advice column in a local newspaper. Skeeter describes her reaction to a typical question from a reader:

> "Dear Miss Myrna," I read, "how do I remove the rings from my fat slovenly husband's shirt collar when he is such a pig and . . . sweats like one too. . . ."
>
> Wonderful. A column on cleaning and relationships. Two things I know absolutely nothing about. [13]

In desperation, Skeeter seeks help from Aibileen, the black maid working for one of Skeeter's friends. Aibileen, the second narrator, has decades of experience serving white families—cleaning their homes, cooking their meals, raising their kids. She is warm, wise, and sought out by other maids in her church who believe her prayers have special power. High on her prayer list is Mae Mobley, her 17th child, the 3-year-old daughter of her current employer.

> Soon as I walk in her nursery, Mae Mobley smile at me, reach out her fat little arms.
>
> "You already up, Baby Girl? Why didn't you holler for me?"
>
> She laugh, dance a little happy jig waiting on me to get her out. I give her a good hug. I reckon she don't get too many good hugs like this after I go home. Ever so often, I come to work and find her bawling in her crib. Miss Leefolt busy on the sewing machine rolling her eyes like it's a stray cat stuck in the screen door. . . . You see her in the Jitney 14 grocery, you never think she go and leave her baby crying in her crib like that. But the help always know.[14]

Those last five words capture the essence of standpoint theory. The looked-down-upon members of society have a clearer vantage point than those with status and power. If you want to know how things work, start your research with the lives of those on the margins. In *The Help*, that means listening to the stories of dirt-poor, African American women.

Listening to Aibileen, Skeeter catches a glimpse of Mississippi life that she's never seen. She's convinced that firsthand accounts of anonymous Southern maids' experiences with their white "families" would make a fascinating book. After much hesitation, and despite the danger, Aibileen agrees to tell her story. She also recruits her best friend Minny to take part in the project.

Minny, the third narrator, is "perhaps the sassiest woman in Mississippi. She can cook like nobody's business, but she can't mind her own tongue, so she's lost yet another job."[15] After reading about Minny, Skeeter's New York editor calls her "every Southern white woman's nightmare. I adore her."[16] Octavia Spencer won an Academy Award for best supporting actress as the outspoken Minny. I'll continue to cite passages from *The Help* that reinforce the principles of Harding and Wood's feminist standpoint theory.

I'm well aware of the irony of a white male professor (me) using a novel authored by a white woman (Stockett) who has created a white fictional character (Skeeter) who represents the lives of African American maids. Biracial communication professor Rachael Griffin at Southern Illinois University questions whether any of these three privileged Caucasian characters could possibly get it right—a fair critique.[17] But since my reason for using the film is to illustrate how diverse standpoints provide differing degrees of objectivity, I believe the power discrepancies that *The Help* portrays will help you better grasp the theory.

WOMEN AS A MARGINALIZED GROUP

Standpoint theorists see important differences between men and women. Wood uses the relational dialectic of autonomy–connectedness as a case in point (see Chapter 11): "While all humans seem to seek both autonomy and connectedness, the relative amount of each that is preferred appears to differ rather consistently between genders."[18] Men tend to want more autonomy; women tend to want more connection. This difference is evident in each group's communication. The masculine community uses speech to accomplish tasks, assert self, and gain power. The feminine community uses speech to build relationships, include others, and show responsiveness.[19]

Wood does not attribute gender differences to biology, maternal instinct, or women's intuition. To the extent that women are distinct from men, she sees the difference largely as a result of cultural expectations and the treatment that each group receives from the other. For example, otherness in Minny is engendered through segregation rules crafted by white men before she was born. "Negroes and whites are not allowed to share water fountains, movie houses, public restrooms, ballparks, phone booths, circus shows."[20] That's during the day. At night with her husband it's worse.

> Leroy screamed at me all night, threw the sugar bowl upside my head, threw my clothes out on the porch. I mean, when he's drinking the Thunderbird, it's one thing, but . . . oh. The shame is so heavy I think it might pull me to the floor. Leroy, he wasn't on the Thunderbird this time. This time he beat me stone-cold sober. . . . He was just beating me for the pure pleasure of it.[21]

What Minny describes also reflects the power discrepancies that Harding and Wood say are found in all societies: "A culture is not experienced identically by all members. Cultures are hierarchically ordered so that different groups within them offer dissimilar power, opportunities, and experiences to members."[22] Along these lines, feminist standpoint theorists suggest that women are underadvantaged and, thus, men are overadvantaged—a gender difference that makes a huge difference.

Harding and Wood are quick to warn against thinking of women as a monolithic group. They point out that not all women share the same standpoint, nor for that matter do all men. Besides the issue of gender, Harding stresses economic condition, race, and sexual orientation as additional cultural identities that can either draw people to the center of society or push them out to the fringes. Thus, an intersection of minority positions creates a highly looked-down-upon location in the social hierarchy. Impoverished African American lesbian women are almost always marginalized. On the other hand, positions of high status and power are overwhelmingly "manned" by wealthy, white, heterosexual males.

Even more than Harding, Wood is troubled by the tendency of some feminists to talk as if there were an "essence of women," then to "valorize" that quality. She believes that Carol Gilligan makes this mistake by claiming that women, as opposed to men, speak in an ethical voice of care (see Chapter 34). For Wood, biology is not destiny. She fears that "championing any singular model of womanhood creates a mold into which not all women may comfortably fit."[23] Yet as an unapologetic feminist committed to the equal value of all human life, Wood understands that a sense of solidarity is politically necessary if women are to effectively critique an androcentric world.

This awareness of feminine solidarity can be seen in Skeeter's growing realization after her book revealing the experiences of Mississippi maids was published. "Wasn't that the point of the book? For women to realize, *We are just two people. Not that much separates us. Not nearly as much as I'd thought.*"[24]

Standpoint theorists emphasize the importance of social location because they are convinced that people at the top of the societal hierarchy are the ones privileged to define what it means to be female, male, or anything else in a given culture. This power is starkly portrayed in *The Help* when Aibileen overhears the pronouncement of Hilly—the wife of a Mississippi legislator—who wants to physically ensure colored maids know their place:

> "All these houses they're building without maid's quarters? It's just plain dangerous. Everybody knows they carry different kinds of diseases than we do. . . .

"Actually, Lou, I think it was more than just my being in the right place at the right time. I think it was my being the right race, the right religion, the right sex, the right socioeconomic group, having the right accent, the right clothes, going to the right schools . . ."

> That's exactly why I've designed the Home Help Sanitation Initiative," Miss Hilly say. "As a disease preventive measure. . . . A bill that requires every white home to have a separate bathroom for the colored help. I've even notified the surgeon general of Mississippi to see if he'll endorse the idea."[25]

KNOWLEDGE FROM NOWHERE VERSUS LOCAL KNOWLEDGE

Why is standpoint so important? Because, Harding argues, "the social group that gets the chance to define the important problematics, concepts, assumptions, and hypotheses in a field will end up leaving its social fingerprints on the picture of the world that emerges from the results of that field's research process."[26] Imagine how different a book entitled *Maids* by Hilly would be from one of the same title written from the standpoint of Aibileen or Minny. The texts would surely differ in starting point, method, and conclusion.

Harding's insistence on *local knowledge* contrasts sharply with the claim of traditional Western science that it can discover "Truth" that is value-free and accessible to any objective observer. In her book *Whose Science? Whose Knowledge?* Harding refers to empiricism's claims of disembodied truths as "views from nowhere." Feminist writer Donna Haraway calls such pronouncements the *God trick,* which Harding describes as "speaking authoritatively about everything in the world from no particular location or human perspective at all."[27] As for the notion of value-free science, Harding characterizes the claim as promoting

Local knowledge
Knowledge situated in time, place, experience, and relative power, as opposed to knowledge from nowhere that's supposedly value-free.

"a fast gun for hire" and chides detached scientists that "it cannot be value-free to describe such social events as poverty, misery, torture, or cruelty in a value-free way."[28] Even Galileo's democratic ideal of interchangeable knowers is open to question. His statement *Anyone can see through my telescope* has been interpreted by empirical scientists as dismissing concern for any relationship between the knower and the known.

Harding and other standpoint theorists insist there is no possibility of an unbiased perspective that is disinterested, impartial, value-free, or detached from a particular historical situation. The physical and the social sciences are always situated in time and place. She writes that "each person can achieve only a partial view of reality from the perspective of his or her own position in the social hierarchy."[29] Unlike postmodernists, however, she is unwilling to abandon the search for reality. She simply thinks that the search for it should begin from the lives of those in the underclass.

Neither Harding nor Wood claims that the standpoint of women or any other marginalized group gives them a clear view of the way things are. *Situated knowledge*—the only kind there is—will always be partial. Standpoint theorists do maintain, however, that "the perspectives of subordinate groups are more complete and thus, better than those of privileged groups in a society."[30] They recognize that this is a controversial claim. U.S. Supreme Court Justice Sonia Sotomayor voiced the same idea in a 2001 lecture on law and multicultural diversity: "I would hope that a wise Latina woman with the richness of her experiences would more often than not reach a better conclusion than a white male who hasn't lived that life."[31] That one remark was the stated reason why many white male congressmen voted against her confirmation to the U.S. Supreme Court in 2009.

STRONG OBJECTIVITY: LESS PARTIAL VIEWS FROM THE STANDPOINT OF WOMEN

Harding uses the term *strong objectivity* to refer to the strategy of starting research from the lives of women and other marginalized groups whose concerns and experience are usually ignored.[32] Her choice of label not only suggests the wisdom of taking all perspectives into account but also suggests that knowledge generated from the standpoint of dominant groups offers, by contrast, only a *weak* objectivity. To illustrate this claim, she speaks directly of the oppositional standpoints of slaves and their masters a century ago: "It is absurd to imagine that U.S. slaveowners' views of Africans' and African Americans' lives could outweigh in impartiality, disinterestedness, impersonality, and objectivity their slaves' view of their own and slaveowners' lives."[33]

Why should the standpoints of women and other marginalized groups be less partial, less distorted, or less false than the perspectives of men who are in dominant positions? Wood offers two explanations: "First, people with subordinate status have greater motivation to understand the perspective of more powerful groups than vice versa."[34] Even if the meek don't inherit the earth, they have a special interest in figuring out what makes it turn. Taking the role of the other is a survival skill for those who have little control over their own lives. Lacking this motivation, those who wield power seem to have less reason to wonder how the "other half" views the world.

Wood's second reason for favoring the standpoint of groups that are constantly put down is that they have little reason to defend the status quo. Not so for those who have power. She asserts that "groups that are advantaged by the prevailing system have a vested interest in not perceiving social inequities that benefit them at the expense of others."[35]

Robbie, a student in my class, expressed a new realization of the link between a standpoint of privilege and the tunnel vision that may go with it.

> This is a hard theory to write on. I am an upper-middle-class white male and this theory deals with the marginalized and underappreciated, particularly women. I struggled to think of any way the theory related to me. But then I got it. My standpoint made it difficult for me to apply the theory. I was born into the dominant culture and have been taught to maintain the status quo. Our opinion is the "right" one because it follows the "rules" (rules that we wrote, by the way). Admittedly, my standpoint is probably one of the least objective of all, and what's worse, I have been taught to think that it is objective.

Robbie's words are unusual coming from a privileged white man with much to lose if the status quo is shattered. Most of his contemporaries would resist grappling with the theory. For those with money, status, and power, ignorance of perspectives on the margin is bliss, so it's folly to be wise. Robbie's new insight is perhaps a testimony to the power of feminist standpoint theory to change the world one mind at a time. Yet Harding wouldn't want Robbie or us to automatically accept the testimony of African American maids as coming from a more objective standpoint. She insists it's the "objective perspective *from women's lives*" that provides a preferred starting place from which to generate research projects, hypotheses, and interpretations.[36] And even that starting point doesn't guarantee *strong objectivity.*

Strong objectivity
The strategy of starting research from the lives of women and other marginalized groups, which upon critical reflection and resistance provides them with a less false view of reality.

Harding and Wood emphasize that a woman's location on the margin of society is a necessary, but not sufficient, condition to attain a feminist standpoint. It is only through critical reflection on unjust power relations and working to resist this oppression that a feminist standpoint is formed. A feminist standpoint is an *achievement* rather than a piece of territory automatically inherited by virtue of being a woman.[37] Within *The Help,* Aibileen, Minny, and the other maids who told their stories to Skeeter qualify on both counts. By the end of the novel, so does Skeeter. She writes:

> the responsibility of the project lays on my shoulders and I see it in their hard-working, lined faces, how much the maids want this book to be published. They are scared, looking at the back door every ten minutes, afraid they'll get caught talking to me. Afraid they'll be beaten like Louvenia's grandson, or, hell, bludgeoned in their front yard like Medgar Evers. The risk they're taking is proof they want this to get printed and they want it bad.[38]

THEORY TO PRACTICE: COMMUNICATION RESEARCH BASED ON WOMEN'S LIVES

If we want to see a model of communication research that starts from the lives of women, a good place to begin is Julia Wood's in-depth study of caregiving in the United States. Consistent with standpoint theory's insistence that all knowledge is situated in a time and place, the first chapter of Wood's *Who Cares? Women, Care, and Culture* describes her own situation as a white, heterosexual, professional woman who for nine years took on the consuming responsibility of caring for her infirm parents until they died. Her experience squared with her subsequent research findings:

> First, it seems that caring can be healthy and enriching when it is informed, freely chosen, and practiced within a context that recognizes and values caring and those who do it. On the other hand, existing studies also suggest that caring can be quite damaging to caregivers if they are unaware of dangers to their identities, if they have unrealistic expectations of themselves, and/or if caring occurs within contexts that fail to recognize its importance and value.[39]

Wood discovered that gendered communication practices reflect and reinforce our societal expectation that caregiving is women's work. After rejecting his daughter's proposal to hire a part-time nurse, her father mused, "It's funny, Julia. I used to wish I had sons, but now I'm glad I have daughters, because I couldn't ask a son to take this kind of time away from his own work just to take care of me."[40] She heard similar messages that devalued caregiving from male colleagues at her university. While praising Wood for her sacrifice, they reassured a fellow professor that he had taken the proper action by placing his mother in a nursing home: "Well, she surely understood that as busy as you are with your work you couldn't be expected to take on that responsibility."[41]

Wood says these comments reveal the opposing, gender-based privileges and restraints in our society. As illustrated in the book/film *One True Thing,* women are given the freedom to make caregiving a priority but are denied the right to put their work first and still be a "good woman." Men are given the freedom to make their work a priority but are deprived of the right to focus on caregiving and still be a "good man."

Wood suggests that a standpoint approach is practical to the extent that it generates an effective critique of unjust practices. She believes that "our culture itself must be reformed in ways that dissociate caring from its historical affiliations with women and private relationships and redefine it as a centrally important and integral part of our collective public life."[42] Perhaps a proposal in President Clinton's 1999 State of the Union address was a first step. He endorsed a $1,000 tax write-off for families taking care of an incapacitated relative in their homes. A male network news commentator dismissed the idea as "more symbolic than significant." The female cohost chided that the symbolic recognition of worth was *quite* significant. She shared Wood's standpoint.

THE STANDPOINT OF BLACK FEMINIST THOUGHT

Consistent with the description of maids' experience in *The Help,* Patricia Hill Collins, an African American sociologist at the University of Maryland, claims that the patterns of "intersecting oppressions" that black women in the United States have experienced puts them in a different marginalized place in society than is occupied by either white women or black men. "Countless numbers of Black women have ridden buses to their white 'families' where they not only cooked, cleaned, and executed other domestic duties, but where they also nurtured their 'other' children, shrewdly offered guidance to their employers, and frequently became honorary members of their white 'families.'"[43] She refers to this social location as that of an "outsider within," a status that provides a privileged view of white society, yet one in which a black woman will never belong. She agrees with other black feminists that "we have to see clearly that we are a unique group set undeniably apart because of race and sex with a unique set of challenges."[44] That different social location means that black women's way of knowing is different from Harding and Wood's standpoint epistemology.

I'll use Collins' words from her book *Black Feminist Thought* to describe the four ways she says black women collectively validate what they know:[45]

1. *Lived experience as a criterion of meaning.* For most African American women, individuals who have lived through the experience about which they claim to be experts are more believable and credible than those who have merely read or thought about such experiences.
2. *The use of dialogue in assessing knowledge claims.* For ideas to be tested and validated, everyone in the group must participate. To refuse to join in, especially if one really disagrees with what has been said, is seen as "cheating."
3. *The ethic of caring.* Emotion indicates that a speaker believes in the validity of an argument. The sound of what is being said is as important as the words themselves, in what is, in a sense, a dialogue of reason and emotion.
4. *The ethic of personal accountability.* Assessments of an individual's knowledge claims simultaneously evaluate an individual's character, values, and ethics.

Collins doesn't claim that a black feminist standpoint epistemology provides African American women with the best view of how the social world works. She rejects an additive model of oppression that would claim that poor, black, lesbian women are more oppressed than any other marginalized group. But when the same ideas are validated through black feminist thought and from the standpoints of other oppressed groups as well, those ideas become the least partial, most "objective" truths available.

ETHICAL REFLECTION: BENHABIB'S INTERACTIVE UNIVERSALISM

Seyla Benhabib has undertaken a formidable task. Recall that Enlightenment thinkers such as Kant, Locke, and Habermas believed "that reason is a natural disposition of the human mind, which when governed by proper education can discover certain truths."[46] Benhabib, who is a professor of political science and philosophy at Yale University, wants to maintain that a universal ethical standard is a viable possibility. But she also feels the force of three major attacks on Enlightenment rationality in general, and Habermas' discourse ethics in particular (see pages 225–226). Thus, she sets out to "defend the tradition of universalism in the face of this triple-pronged critique by engaging the claims of feminism, communitarianism, and postmodernism."[47] At the same time, she wants to learn from these theories and incorporate their insights into her interactive universalism. I'll discuss these charges in reverse order.

Postmodern critique. Recall that in his widely discussed 1984 treatise *The Postmodern Condition,* Jean-François Lyotard declares that there are no longer any *grand narratives* on which to base a universal version of truth.[48] Postmodernists dismiss any *a priori* assumptions, or givens, that attempt to legitimate the moral ideals of the Enlightenment and Western liberal democracy. They are suspicious of consensus and Habermas' attempt to legislate rationality. Benhabib sums up the postmodern critique: "Transcendental guarantees of truth are dead . . . there is only the endless struggle of local narratives vying with one another for legitimization."[49] She appreciates the postmodern insistence that a moral point of view is an accomplishment rather than a discovery, but she is not "content with singing the swan-song of normative thinking in general."[50] Benhabib holds out the possibility that instead of reaching a consensus on how everyone *should act*, interacting individuals can align themselves with a *common good*.

Communitarian critique. If there is one commitment that draws communitarians and postmodernists together, it is the "critique of Western rationality as seen from the perspective of the margins, from the standpoint of what and whom it excludes, suppresses, delegitimatizes, renders mad, imbecilic or childish."[51] Benhabib realizes the danger of pressing a global moral template onto a local situation. If we regard people as disembodied moral agents devoid of history, relationships, or obligations, we'll be unable to deal with the messiness of real-life contexts. To avoid this error, Benhabib insists that any panhuman ethic be achieved through interaction with collective concrete others—ordinary people who live in community—rather than imposed on them by a rational elite.

Feminist critique. Carol Gilligan, Deborah Tannen, Sandra Harding, Julia Wood, and Cheris Kramarae (see Chapter 36) all agree that women's experiences and the way they talk about them are different from men's. But, typical of rationalistic approaches, Habermas virtually ignores gender distinctions. His conception of discourse ethics speaks to issues of political and economic justice in the masculine-dominated public sphere. Think about the activities to which women have historically been confined—rearing children, housekeeping, satisfying the emotional and sexual needs of the male, tending to the sick and the elderly. Habermas relegates these actions to a private sphere where norms of freedom, equality, and reciprocity don't seem to apply.[52] Because of its emphasis on open dialogue in which no topics are regarded as trivial, interactive universalism would avoid privatizing women's experiences.

Despite these three critiques, Benhabib believes that a new breed of universal ethic is possible. "Such a universalism would be interactive not legislative, cognizant of gender differences, not gender blind, contextually sensitive and not situation indifferent."[53] It would be a moral framework that values the diversity of human beliefs without thinking that every difference is ethically significant.[54] Perhaps it would include a commitment to help all people survive and thrive.

CRITIQUE: DO STANDPOINTS ON THE MARGINS GIVE A LESS FALSE VIEW?

Standpoint theory was originally developed to better appreciate the value of women's perspective. But other marginalized groups see the theory as offering a rationale for privileging their experience and giving traction to their voice. For example, Patricia Collins combines multiple standpoints of gender, ethnicity, class, and sexuality to fashion a powerful critique of mainstream society's version of the way things are. The problem is that the more specific we become about the standpoints from which people communicate, the more dubious becomes the claim of group solidarity that's at the heart of the theory. Julia Wood says the concept of women as a single group is politically useful to bring about needed reform, but is this core idea a reality or just a fiction?

Feminist scholars such as Susan Hekman and Nancy Hirschmann are concerned that Harding's version of standpoint theory underestimates the role of language in expressing one's sense of self and view of the world.[55] As theorists throughout this book have maintained, people's communication choices are never neutral or value-free, so people can't separate their standpoint from the language they use to describe it. The words they choose are inevitably influenced by their cultural and societal filters. This critique of standpoint theory doesn't negate the importance of situated knowledge, but it complicates our reception of anyone's take on reality, whether it comes from the center or the margins of the social fabric. In fact, voices from the edge might be particularly difficult to express, since linguistic conventions traditionally are controlled by the privileged. This point is developed in the context of *muted group theory* in the next chapter.

Finally, other critics dismiss the concept of *strong objectivity* as contradictory.[56] Harding and Wood propose that the oppressed are less biased or more impartial than the privileged. Yet they argue that standpoints are relative and can't be evaluated by any absolute criteria. This appears to bring universal standards of judgment back into play. Thus, on the matter of transcendental truths, the theory seems to want to have it both ways.

Despite these difficulties, I find the logic of standpoint theory appealing. If all knowledge is tainted by the social location of the knower, then we would do well to start our search for truth from the perspective of people who are most sensitive to inequities of power. They will have the least to lose if findings challenge the status quo. Wood acknowledges that we may have trouble figuring out which social groups are more marginalized than others. As a white, professional woman, is Wood lower on the social hierarchy than her African American male colleague who has attained the same faculty rank at the university? Standpoint theory doesn't say, but it clearly suggests that we should question much of the received wisdom that comes from a male-dominated, Western European research establishment and replace it when a *strong objectivity* provides a more complete picture of the world. (Pay close attention to the experiences of people like Aibileen and Minny.) The idea energizes Idaho State University rhetorician Lynn Worsham and others who believe that minority standpoints can be a partial corrective to the biased knowledge that now passes for truth:

> In what I consider, in all sincerity, to be a heroic and marvelous conception, Harding turns the tables on philosophy and the sciences and constructs a sort of feminist alchemy in which the idea of standpoint, revamped by postmodern philosophy, becomes the philosophers' stone capable of transforming the West's base materials into resources for producing a more "generally useful account of the world."[57]

QUESTIONS TO SHARPEN YOUR FOCUS

1. What is common to the standpoints of *women, African Americans, the poor,* and *homosexuals* that may provide them with a *less false view* of the way society works?
2. How could we test the claim that *strong objectivity from women's lives* provides a more accurate view of the world than knowledge generated by a predominantly male research establishment?

3. Andrew, Glenn, and I are privileged white males who decided which theories would be covered in this book. Suppose we were disadvantaged African American women. What theories might we drop and which might we keep? Why might this be a ridiculous question?
4. *Standpoint epistemology* draws on insights from *Marxism, symbolic interactionism,* and *postmodernism.* Based on what you've read in this chapter, which of these intellectual influences do you see as strongest? Why?

A SECOND LOOK

Recommended resource: Julia T. Wood, *Communication Theories in Action,* 3rd ed., Wadsworth, Belmont, CA, 2004, pp. 212–220.

Comprehensive statement: Sandra Harding, *Whose Science? Whose Knowledge? Thinking from Women's Lives,* Cornell University Press, Ithaca, NY, 1991.

Diverse forms of standpoint theory: Sandra Harding (ed.), *The Feminist Standpoint Theory Reader: Intellectual and Political Controversies,* Routledge, New York, 2004.

Explanation and defense of strong objectivity: Sandra Harding, "Rethinking Standpoint Epistemology: What Is 'Strong Objectivity'?" in *The Feminist Standpoint Theory Reader,* pp. 127–140.

Reconstruction of scientific objectivity: Sandra Harding, *Is Science Multicultural? Postcolonialisms, Feminisms and Epistemologies,* Indiana University, Bloomington, 1998.

Standpoint critique of science: Sandra Harding, *Science and Social Inequality: Feminist and Postcolonial Issues,* University of Illinois, Urbana, 2006, pp. 80–97.

Avoiding essentialism: Julia T. Wood, "Gender and Moral Voice: Moving from Woman's Nature to Standpoint Epistemology," *Women's Studies in Communication,* Vol. 15, 1993, pp. 1–24.

Women and care: Julia T. Wood, *Who Cares? Women, Care, and Culture,* Southern Illinois University Press, Carbondale, 1994.

Standpoint of women in communication discipline: Lynn O'Brien Hallstein (ed.), *Women's Studies in Communication,* Vol. 23, Spring 2000 (special issue on standpoint theories).

Black feminist thought: Patricia Hill Collins, *Black Feminist Thought: Knowledge, Consciousness, and the Politics of Empowerment,* 2nd ed., Routledge, New York, 2000.

Collins' stand on standpoint theory: Patricia Hill Collins, *Fighting Words: Black Women and the Search for Justice,* University of Minnesota, Minneapolis, 1998, pp. 201–228.

Comparing two feminist theories: Julia T. Wood, "Feminist Standpoint Theory and Muted Group Theory: Commonalities and Divergences," *Women and Language,* Vol. 28, 2005, pp. 61–64.

Interactive universalism: Seyla Benhabib, *Situating the Self: Gender, Community and Postmodernism in Contemporary Ethics,* Routledge, New York, 1992.

Feminist critiques: Susan Hekman, "Truth and Method: Feminist Standpoint Theory Revisited" in *The Feminist Standpoint Theory Reader,* pp. 225–241; Lynn Worsham, "Romancing the Stones: My Movie Date with Sandra Harding," *Journal of Advanced Composition,* Vol. 15, 1995, pp. 565–571.

CHAPTER 36

Objective — Interpretive

Critical tradition
Phenomenological tradition

Muted Group Theory

of Cheris Kramarae

Cheris Kramarae maintains that language is literally a *man*-made construction.

> The language of a particular culture does not serve all its speakers equally, for not all speakers contribute in an equal fashion to its formulation. Women (and members of other subordinate groups) are not as free or as able as men are to say what they wish, when and where they wish, because the words and the norms for their use have been formulated by the dominant group, men.[1]

According to Kramarae and other feminist theorists, women's words are discounted in our society; women's thoughts are devalued. When women try to overcome this inequity, the masculine control of communication places them at a tremendous disadvantage. Man-made language "aids in defining, depreciating and excluding women."[2] Women are thus a muted group.

For many years Kramarae was a professor of speech communication and sociology at the University of Illinois. She has also served as a dean for the International Women's University in Germany and is now a visiting professor at the Center for the Study of Women in Society at the University of Oregon. She began her research career in 1974 when she conducted a systematic study of the way women were portrayed in cartoons.[3] She found that women were notable mostly by their absence. A quick survey of the cartoon art we've used in this book will show that little has changed since Kramarae's study. Less than half of the 52 cartoons contain female characters, and only 14 of these women speak. All but two of the cartoonists are men.

Kramarae discovered that women in cartoons were usually depicted as emotional, apologetic, or just plain wishy-washy. Compared with the simple, forceful statements voiced by cartoon males, the words assigned to female characters were vague, flowery, and peppered with adjectives like *nice* and *pretty*. Kramarae noted at the time that women who don't appreciate this form of comic put-down are often accused by men of having no sense of humor or simply told to "lighten up." According to Kramarae, this type of male dominance is just one of the many ways that women are rendered inarticulate in our society. For the last 40 years Kramarae has been a leader in the effort to explain and alter the muted status of women and other marginalized groups.

MUTED GROUPS: BLACK HOLES IN SOMEONE ELSE'S UNIVERSE

The idea of women as a *muted group* was first proposed by Oxford University social anthropologist Edwin Ardener. In his monograph "Belief and the Problem of Women," Ardener noted the strange tendency of many ethnographers to claim to have "cracked the code" of a culture without ever making any direct reference to the half of society made up of women. Field researchers often justify this omission by reporting the difficulty of using women as cultural informants. Females "giggle when young, snort when old, reject the question, laugh at the topic," and generally make life difficult for scholars trained in the scientific (masculine) method of inquiry.[4] Ardener acknowledged the challenge, but he also reminded his colleagues how suspicious they'd be of an anthropologist who wrote about the men of a tribe on the sole basis of talking to the women.

Ardener initially assumed that inattention to women's experience was a problem of gender unique to social anthropology. But along with his Oxford co-worker and wife Shirley Ardener, he began to realize that mutedness is due to the lack of power that besets any group occupying the low end of the totem pole. Mutedness doesn't mean that low-power groups are completely silent.[5] The issue is whether people can say what they want to say when and where they want to say it. Muted groups must change their language when communicating in the public domain, and thus cannot fully share their true thoughts.[6] As a result, they are often overlooked, muffled, and rendered invisible—"mere black holes in someone else's universe."[7]

Muted group
People belonging to low-power groups who must change their language when communicating publicly, thus, their ideas are often overlooked; e.g., women.

Cheris Kramarae believes that men's dominant power position in society limits women's access to communication in public spaces. Her extension of the Ardeners' initial concept offers insight into why women are muted and what can be done to loosen men's lock on public modes of communication. Kramarae argues that the ever-prevalent *public–private* distinction in language is a convenient way to exaggerate gender differences and pose separate sexual spheres of activity. This is, of course, a pitfall into which Deborah Tannen virtually leaps (see Chapter 34). Within the logic of a two-sphere assumption, women speak often in the home—a "small world" of interpersonal communication. But their words appear less often in the "large world" of significant public debate—a place where the words of men resonate.

Elizabeth, who is now a grad student at Purdue University preparing to become a professor of critical rhetoric, describes how men's public discourse shapes the meaning of one of her favorite activities:

> I am a passionate knitter. In the dominant communication code, knitting is associated with domestic women. I cannot count the number of times when men have made jokes or comments about me preparing to be a good wife, or looking for a husband, while I am knitting. But I knit because I enjoy it. I love working with my hands and knitting makes a good change from schoolwork. My choice to knit has nothing to do with finding a husband or preparing to be a housewife. Still, even though knitting is an activity that is primarily engaged in by women, it is men who define its meaning.

Kramarae wonders what it would be like if there were a word that pointed to the *connection* of public and private communication. If there were such a word in everyone's speaking vocabulary, its use would establish the idea that both spheres have equal worth and that similarities between women and men are more important than their differences. Since there is no such word in our lexicon, I think of this textbook as a *public* mode of communication. I am male, as are the other two authors of this book. I realize that in the process of trying to present muted group theory with integrity, I may unconsciously put a masculine spin on Kramarae's ideas and the perceptions of women. In an effort to minimize this bias, I will quote extensively from Kramarae and other feminist scholars. Kramarae is just one of many communication professionals who seek to unmask the systematic silencing of a feminine *voice.* I'll also draw freely on the words and experiences of other women to illustrate the communication double bind that Kramarae says is a feminine fact of life. This reliance on personal narrative is consistent with a feminist research agenda that takes women's experiences seriously.

THE MASCULINE POWER TO NAME EXPERIENCE

Kramarae starts with the assumption that "women perceive the world differently from men because of women's and men's different experience and activities rooted in the division of labor."[8] Kramarae rejects Freud's simplistic notion that "anatomy is destiny." She is certain, however, that power discrepancies between the sexes ensure that women will view the world in a way different from men. While women vary in many ways, in most cultures, if not all, women's talk is subject to male control and censorship. French existentialist Simone de Beauvoir underscored this common feminine experience when she declared, "'I am woman': on this truth must be based all further discussion."[9]

The problem facing women, according to Kramarae, is that further discussions about how the world works never take place on a level playing field. "Because of their political dominance, the men's system of perception is dominant, impeding the free expression of the women's alternative models of the world."[10]

Note that my phrase *level playing field* is a metaphor drawn from competitive team sports—historically, an experience familiar to more men than women. This is precisely Kramarae's point. As possessors of the public mode of expression, men frame the discussion. If a man wants to contest the point about a tilted playing field, he can argue in the familiar idiom of sports. But a woman who takes issue with the metaphor of competition has to contest it with stereotypically masculine linguistic terms.

Mead's symbolic interactionist perspective asserts that the extent of knowing is the extent of naming (see Chapter 5). If this is true, whoever has the ability to make names stick possesses an awesome power. Kramarae notes that men's control of the dominant mode of expression has produced a vast stock of derogatory, gender-specific terms to refer to women's talking—*catty, bitchy, shrill, cackling, gossipy, chitchat, sharp-tongued,* and so forth. There is no corresponding vocabulary to disparage men's conversation.

In case you think this lexical bias is limited to descriptions of speech, consider the variety of terms in the English language to describe sexually promiscuous individuals. By one count, there are 22 gender-related words to label men who are sexually loose—*playboy, stud, rake, gigolo, player, Don Juan, lothario, womanizer,* and so on. There are more than 200 words that label sexually loose women—*slut, whore, hooker, prostitute, trollop, mistress, harlot, Jezebel, hussy, concubine, streetwalker, strumpet, easy lay,* and the like.[11] Since most surveys of sexual activity show that more men than women have multiple sexual partners, there's no doubt that the inordinate number of terms describing women serves the interests of men.

Under the socio-cultural tradition in Chapter 4, we introduced the Sapir-Whorf hypothesis, which claims that language shapes our perception of reality. Kramarae suggests that women are often silenced by not having a publicly recognized vocabulary through which to express their experience. She says that "words constantly ignored may eventually come to be unspoken and perhaps even unthought."[12] After a while, muted women may even come to doubt the validity of their experience and the legitimacy of their feelings.

MEN AS THE GATEKEEPERS OF COMMUNICATION

Gatekeepers
Editors and other arbiters of culture who determine which books, essays, poems, plays, film scripts, etc. will appear in the mass media.

Even if the public mode of expression contained a rich vocabulary to describe feminine experience, women would still be muted if *their* modes of expression were ignored or ridiculed. Indeed, Kramarae describes a "good-ole-boys" cultural establishment of gatekeepers that virtually excludes women's art, poetry, plays, film scripts, public address, and scholarly essays from society's mass media. She notes that women were locked out of the publishing business for 500 years. It wasn't until the 1970s and the establishment of women's presses in the Western world that women could exercise ongoing influence through the print medium. The electronic age provides women with additional opportunities to publish on blogs and wikis. Of course, most people look for information through search engines such as Google—and the vast majority of technology companies are led by men. Overall, Kramarae sees traditional mainstream mass media as *malestream expression.*

Long before Edwin Ardener noted women's absence in anthropological research, Virginia Woolf protested women's nonplace in recorded history. The British novelist detected an incongruity between the way men characterize women in fiction and how women concurrently appear in history books. "Imaginatively she is of the highest importance; practically she is completely insignificant. She pervades poetry from cover to cover; she is all but absent from history."[13]

Feminist writer Dorothy Smith claims that women's absence from history is a result of closed-circuit masculine scholarship.

> Men attend to and treat as significant only what men say. The circle of men whose writing and talk was significant to each other extends backwards in time as far as our records reach. What men were doing was relevant to men, was written by men about men for men. Men listened and listen to what one another said.[14]

As an example of men's control of the public record, Cheris Kramarae cites the facts surrounding her change of name. When she was married in Ohio, the law required her to take the name of her husband. So at the direction of the state, she became *Cheris Rae Kramer.* Later, when it became legal for her to choose her own name, she reordered the sounds and spelling to Cheris Kramarae. Many people questioned Kramarae about whether her name change was either loving or wise. Yet no one asked her husband why he kept *his* name. Kramarae points out that both the law and the conventions of proper etiquette have served men well.

SPEAKING WOMEN'S TRUTH IN MEN'S TALK: THE PROBLEM OF TRANSLATION

Assuming masculine dominance of public communication to be a current reality, Kramarae concludes that "in order to participate in society women must transform their own models in terms of the received male system of expression."[15]

Like speaking a second language, this translation process requires constant effort and usually leaves a woman wondering whether she's said it "just right." One woman writer said men can "tell it straight." Women have to "tell it slant."[16]

Think back again to Mead's symbolic interactionism (see Chapter 5). His theory describes *minding* as an automatic pause before we speak in order to consider how those who are listening might respond. These periods of hesitation grow longer when we feel linguistically impoverished. According to Kramarae, women have to choose their words carefully in a public forum. "What women want to say and can say best cannot be said easily because the language template is not of their own making."[17]

I have gained a new appreciation of the difficulty women face in translating their experiences into man-made language by discussing Kramarae's ideas with three female friends. Marsha, Kathy, and Susan have consciously sought and achieved positions of leadership in professions where women are rarely seen or heard.

Marsha is a litigation attorney who was the first female president of the Hillsborough County Bar Association (Florida) and was chair of a branch of the Federal Reserve Board. Marsha attributes her success to a conscious shifting of gears when she addresses the law.

> I've learned to talk like a man. I consciously lower my voice, speak more slowly, think bigger, and use sports analogies. I care about my appearance, but a woman who is too attractive or too homely has a problem. A man can be drop-dead gorgeous or ugly as sin and get along OK. I've been told that I'm the most feared and respected attorney in the firm, but that's not the person I live with day by day. After work I go home and make reindeer pins out of dog biscuits with my daughters.

Kathy is an ordained minister who works with high school students and young adults. She is the best speaker I've ever heard in a public address class. Working in an organization that traditionally excludes women from up-front speaking roles, Kathy is recognized as a star communicator. Like Marsha, she feels women have little margin for error when they speak in public.

> Women have to work both sides to pull it off. I let my appearance and delivery say feminine—jewelry, lipstick, warm soft voice. But I plan my content to appeal to men as well. I can't get away with just winging it. I prepare carefully, know my script, use lots of imagery from the world of guys. Girls learn to be interested in whatever men want to talk about, but men aren't used to listening to the things that interest women. I rarely refer to cooking or movies that might be dismissed as "chick flicks."

Susan is the academic dean of a professional school within a university. When her former college closed, Susan orchestrated the transfer of her entire program and faculty to another university. She's received the Professional of the Year award in her field. When she first attended her national deans' association, only 8 out of 50 members were women.

> I was very silent. I hated being there. If you didn't communicate by the men's rules you were invisible. The star performers were male and they came on strong. But no one was listening; everyone was preparing their own response. The meeting oozed one-upmanship. At the reception it was all "Hail fellow well met." You wouldn't dare say, "Look, I'm having this rough situation I'm dealing with. Have you ever faced this problem?" It was only when some of the women got together for coffee or went shopping that I could be open about my experiences.

"The committee on women's rights will now come to order."

Reproduced by permission of Punch Ltd., www.punch.co.uk

Although their status and abilities clearly show that Marsha, Kathy, and Susan are remarkable individuals, their experience as women in male hierarchical structures supports muted group theory. Kramarae says that "men have structured a value system and a language that reflects that value system. Women have had to work through the system organized by men."[18] For women with less skill and self-confidence than Marsha, Kathy, or Susan, that prospect can be daunting.

SPEAKING OUT IN PRIVATE: NETWORKING WITH WOMEN

Susan's relief at the chance to talk freely with other female deans illustrates a central tenet of muted group theory. Kramarae states that "females are likely to find ways to express themselves outside the dominant public modes of expression used by males in both their verbal conventions and their nonverbal behavior."[19]

Kramarae lists a variety of back-channel routes that women use to discuss their experiences—diaries, journals, letters, oral histories, folklore, gossip, chants, art, graffiti, poetry, songs, nonverbal parodies, gynecological handbooks passed between women for centuries, and a "mass of 'noncanonized' writers whose richness and diversity we are only just beginning to comprehend."[20] She labels these outlets the female "sub-version" that runs beneath the surface of male orthodoxy.

Today, Pinterest posts may be the latest version of these back channels. Although the popular, visually oriented social media site is available to men, so far they've shown little interest in it.[21] That wouldn't surprise Kramarae—she notes that men are often oblivious to the shared meanings women communicate through alternative channels. In fact, Kramarae is convinced that "males have more difficulty than females in understanding what members of the other gender mean."[22] She doesn't ascribe men's bewilderment to biological differences between the sexes or to women's attempts to conceal their experience. Rather, she suggests that when men don't have a clue about what women want, think, or feel, it's because they haven't made the effort to find out.

When British author Dale Spender was editor of *Women's Studies International Quarterly*, she offered a further interpretation of men's ignorance. She proposed that many men realize that a commitment to listen to women would necessarily involve a renunciation of their privileged position. "The crucial issue here is that if women cease to be muted, men cease to be so dominant and to some males this may seem unfair because it represents a loss of rights."[23] A man can dodge that equalizing bullet by claiming, "I'll never understand women."

ENRICHING THE LEXICON: A FEMINIST DICTIONARY

Like other forms of critical theory, feminist theory is not content to merely point out asymmetries in power. The ultimate goal of muted group theory is to change the man-made linguistic system that keeps women "in their place." According to Kramarae, reform includes challenging dictionaries that "ignore the words and definitions created by women and which also include many sexist definitions and examples."[24] Traditional dictionaries pose as authoritative guides to proper language use, but, because of their reliance on male literary sources, lexicographers systematically exclude words coined by women.

Kramarae and Paula Treichler have compiled a feminist dictionary that offers definitions for women's words that don't appear in *Merriam-Webster's Collegiate Dictionary* and presents alternative feminine readings of words that do. The dictionary "places *women* at the center and rethinks language from that crucially different perspective."[25] Kramarae and Treichler don't claim that all women use words the same way, nor do they believe women constitute a single, unified group. But they include women's definitions of approximately 2,500 words in order to illustrate women's linguistic creativity and to help empower women to change their muted status. Figure 36–1 provides a sample of brief entries and acknowledges their origin.

SEXUAL HARASSMENT: COINING A TERM TO LABEL EXPERIENCE

Perhaps more than any other single entry in the Kramarae and Treichler dictionary, the inclusion of *sexual harassment* illustrates a major achievement of feminist communication scholarship—encoding women's experience into the received language of society. Although stories of unwanted sexual attention on the job are legion, women haven't always had a common term to label what has been an ongoing fact of feminine life.

Sexual harassment
An unwanted imposition of sexual requirements in the context of a relationship of unequal power.

In 1992, the *Journal of Applied Communication Research* published 30 stories of communication students and professionals who had been sexually embarrassed, humiliated, or traumatized by a person who was in a position of academic power. All but 2 of the 30 accounts came from women. As Kramarae notes, "Sexual harassment is rampant but not random."[26] One woman wrote this account of her attempt to talk to a senior professor who had made an unsolicited sexual advance:

> I was at a disadvantage in our "open talk," because I approached it as a chance to clarify feelings while he used it as an occasion to reinterpret and redefine what was happening in ways that suited his purposes. I told him I didn't feel right "being so friendly" with him. He replied that I was over-reacting and, further, that my small-town southern upbringing was showing. . . . I told him I was concerned that he wasn't being objective about my work, but was praising it because he wanted to be "friends" with me; he twisted this, explaining he was judging my work fairly, BUT that being "friends" did increase his interest in helping me professionally. No matter what I said, he had a response that defined my feelings as inappropriate.[27]

Appearance: A woman's appearance is her work uniform. . . . A woman's concern with her appearance is not a result of brainwashing; it is a reaction to necessity. (A Redstockings Sister)

Cuckold: The husband of an unfaithful wife. The wife of an unfaithful husband is just called a wife. (Cheris Kramarae)

Depression: A psychiatric label that . . . hides the social fact of the housewife's loneliness, low self-esteem, and work dissatisfaction. (Ann Oakley)

Doll: A toy playmate given to, or made by children. Some adult males continue their childhood by labeling adult female companions "dolls." (Cheris Kramarae)

Family man: Refers to a man who shows more concern with members of the family than is normal. There is no label *family woman,* since that would be heard as redundancy. (Cheris Kramarae)

Feminist: "I myself have never been able to find out precisely what feminism is: I only know that people call me a feminist whenever I express sentiments that differentiate me from a doormat." (Rebecca West)

Gossip: A way of talking between women in their roles as women, intimate in style, personal and domestic in topic and setting; a female cultural event which springs from and perpetuates the restrictions of the female role, but also gives the comfort of validation. (Deborah Jones)

Guilt: The emotion that stops women from doing what they may need to do to take care of themselves as opposed to everyone else. (Mary Ellen Shanesey)

Herstory: The human story as told by women and about women. . . . (Anne Forfreedom)

Ms.: A form of address being adopted by women who want to be recognized as individuals rather than being identified by their relationship with a man. (Midge Lennert and Norma Wilson)

One of the boys: Means NOT one of the girls. (Cheris Kramarae)

Parenthood: A condition which often brings dramatic changes to new mothers — "loss of job, income, and status; severing of networks and social contacts; and adjustments to being a 'housewife.' Most new fathers do not report similar social dislocations." (Lorna McKee and Margaret O'Brien)

Pornography: Pornography is the theory and rape is the practice. (Andrea Dworkin)

Sexual harassment: Refers to the unwanted imposition of sexual requirements in the context of a relationship of unequal power. (Catharine MacKinnon)

Silence: Is not golden. "There is no agony like bearing an untold story inside you." (Zora Neale Hurston) "In a world where language and naming are power, silence is oppressive, is violence." (Adrienne Rich)

FIGURE 36–1 Excerpts from Kramarae and Treichler's Feminist Dictionary
Kramarae and Treichler, *A Feminist Dictionary: Amazons, Bluestockings and Crones*

Muted group theory can explain this woman's sense of confusion and lack of power. Her story is as much about a struggle for language as it is a struggle over sexual conduct. As long as the professor can define his actions as "being friendly," the female student's feelings are discounted—even by herself. Had she been equipped with the linguistic tool of "sexual harassment," she could have validated her feelings and labeled the professor's advances as both inappropriate and illegal.

Date rape
Unwanted sexual activity with an acquaintance, friend, or romantic partner.

Communication professor Ann Burnett (North Dakota State University) identifies similar confusion and powerlessness regarding *date rape*—an acute form of sexual harassment often directed at college women. Although students possess a relatively clear understanding of stranger rape, they have difficulty even defining date rape. That confusion is only heightened by *rape myths* common on campuses. ("All guys expect sex on a first date." "Women who dress a certain way are just asking for it.") Burnett notes that although universities offer programs addressing drug and alcohol abuse, few similar programs exist regarding date rape. There's further uncertainty when a woman tries to say no, because men and women often don't agree on what constitutes sexual consent. After a date rape, the lack of clarity makes the victim feel confused and uncertain about what she's experienced. Talking about the incident with friends doesn't always help: "After the rape occurs, both women and male acquaintances blame the victim for not being more 'sensible.' This vicious circle mutes women by making them feel badly for not 'doing enough' to protect themselves, but sadly, the ambiguity arises, what is 'enough'?"[28] This uncertainty favors men—and mutes women—before, during, and after date rape.

According to Kramarae, when *sexual harassment* was first used in a court case in the late 1970s, it was the only legal term defined by women. Although *date rape* and *rape culture* are beginning to enter our cultural vocabulary, research like Burnett's indicates that many men don't understand what women mean by these terms. For muted group theory, the struggle to contest man-made language continues.

CO-CULTURAL THEORY: HOW MUTED GROUPS TALK TO DOMINANT GROUPS

Kramarae acknowledges that women aren't the only muted group. Western Michigan University professor Mark Orbe agrees. His *co-cultural theory* extends Kramarae's work to understand *how* members of any muted group cope with their status when communicating with dominant groups. From interviews with "people of color, women, gay/lesbian/bisexuals, and those from a lower socioeconomic status," he discovered that the way members of muted groups communicate with the dominant culture depends on their *preferred outcome,* or goal, for the interaction.[29] Specifically, Orbe found three common goals.

Preferred outcome
A co-culture's goal for interaction with the dominant group.

One goal is *assimilation,* or blending in with the dominant group. When British author Joanne Rowling wrote her first fantasy novel for kids, her publisher insisted on printing the book using initials rather than her first name, fearing boys wouldn't read a story written by a woman.[30] This is not an isolated incident. Throughout literary history, many women have suppressed their feminine identity to satisfy the demands of a gatekeeper. In the end, the author of *Harry Potter* became one of the wealthiest women in the world. In other cases, such a go-along-to-get-along approach may be unsatisfying if the dominant group simply ignores the unique identity of the muted group.

Assimilation
Blending in with the dominant group.

A second option is *separation,* or minimizing any contact with the dominant group. For more than a century this has been the approach of the Amish in the northeastern United States. Their technologically simple lifestyle includes only limited contact with the world beyond their community.

Separation
Minimizing contact with the dominant group.

A third approach is *accommodation,* or trying to persuade the dominant culture to "change the rules so that they incorporate the life experiences" of muted groups.[31] In U.S. history, the movements for women's suffrage, African American civil rights, and same-sex marriage are all examples of the accommodation approach.

Accommodation
Persuading the dominant group to incorporate the experiences of the co-cultural group.

On college campuses, Orbe's research has identified first-generation college students as a muted group.[32] First-generation students encounter an unfamiliar world of syllabi, fraternities, sports, dorms, and, of course, complex theories and ideas. It's an especially rough transition for students whose relatives can't fully understand the experience. Some family members might express skepticism in the value of "book learning." In addition, many first-generation students come from a position of lower socioeconomic status than their peers. To manage their constant feeling of difference, some students *assimilate* by avoiding topics that would reveal their family's educational background. Other students *accommodate* by sharing their first-generation status with a few people they can trust. Orbe found that first-generation students especially benefit when they find trusted mentors who provide academic advice and emotional support. Of course, *separation* is another option. Statistics gathered by the U.S. Department of Education reveal many first-generation students do just that—they are more than twice as likely to drop out as students whose parents attended college.[33]

Orbe's theory has yielded insights into several co-cultural groups, ranging from ethnic minorities to physically disabled workers.[34] As an interpretive theory, co-cultural theory does not prescribe which of the three goals is most effective. Rather, the theory recognizes that the best choice depends on the unique circumstances of the co-culture.

CRITIQUE: DO MEN MEAN TO MUTE?

In 2005, a group of scholars met at George Mason University to celebrate muted group theory's insight into how people use language to shape power relations. Convention speakers from two continents addressed the theory's relevance not only for women, but also for any group at the margins of society. The convention reflected the theory's broad *community of agreement,* and their words, later published in a special issue of the journal *Women and Language,* revealed their dedication to *understanding people, clarifying values,* and *reforming society.*[35] Muted group theory stands up well to these criteria for good critical scholarship (see Chapter 3).

Feminist scholars insist that "the key communication activities of women's experiences—their rituals, vocabularies, metaphors, and stories—are an important part of the data for study."[36] In this chapter I've presented the words of 30 women who give voice to the mutedness they've experienced because they aren't men. I could have easily cited hundreds more. It strikes me that ignoring or discounting women's testimony would be the ultimate confirmation of Kramarae's muted group thesis.

Readers might be uncomfortable with muted group theory's characterization of men as oppressors and women as the oppressed. Kramarae addresses this issue:

> Some people using the theory have boxed oppression within discrete, binary categories, e.g., women/men; AfricanAmericans/EuroAmericans. A focus only on the categories of women and men, or white and non-white, for example, is simplistic and ignores other forms of struggle. . . .[37]

Kramarae acknowledges that oppression is more complex than identification with any one group. Yet she also states that "fixing names to the ones we call 'oppressors' may be necessary in order to have clear discussions" about oppressive power differences.[38] How can we name an oppressive group without speaking in terms of demographic categories? The theory's lack of clarity regarding this thorny question may frustrate activists looking for practical answers.

The question of men's motives is also problematic. Tannen criticizes feminist scholars like Kramarae for assuming that men are trying to control women. Tannen acknowledges that differences in male and female communication styles sometimes lead to imbalances of power, but, unlike Kramarae, she is willing to assume that the problems are caused primarily by men's and women's "different styles." Tannen cautions that "bad feelings and imputation of bad motives or bad character can come about when there was no intention to dominate."[39]

Kramarae thinks Tannen's apology for men's abuse of power is too simple. She notes that men often ignore or ridicule women's statements about the problems of being heard in a male-dominated society. Rather than blaming *style differences,* Kramarae points to the many ways that our political, educational, religious, legal, and media systems support gender, race, and class hierarchies. Your response to muted group theory may well depend on whether you are a beneficiary or a victim of these systems.

For men and women who are willing to hear what Kramarae has to say, the consciousness-raising fostered by muted group theory can prod them to quit using words in a way that preserves inequities of power. The term *sexual harassment* is just one example of how women's words can be levered into the public lexicon and give voice to women's collective experience. Phrases like *glass ceiling* and *date rape* weren't even around when Kramarae and Treichler compiled their feminist dictionary in 1985, but now these terms are available to label social and professional injustices that women face. Cheris Kramarae's insights and declarations of women as a group muted by men have helped shake up traditional patterns of communication between the sexes.

QUESTIONS TO SHARPEN YOUR FOCUS

1. What words do you use with your same-sex friends that you don't use with members of the opposite sex? Does this usage support Kramarae's hypothesis of *male control of the public mode of expression?*
2. In a journal article about *dictionary bias,* Kramarae wrote the sentence "I *vaginated* on that for a while."[40] Can you explain her wordplay in light of the principles of muted group theory? How does the meaning of the sentence change when you replace her provocative term with alternative verbs?
3. Given a definition of *sexual harassment* as "unwanted imposition of sexual requirements in the context of a *relationship of unequal power,*" can you think of a time you harassed or were harassed in this way by someone?
4. Do you tend to agree more with Tannen's genderlect perspective or Kramarae's muted group theory? To what extent is your choice influenced by the fact that you are a *male* or a *female?*

CONVERSATIONS

In my conversation with Cheris Kramarae, she suggests that the creation of university departments of women's studies is an encouraging sign that women aren't doomed to remain muted. When I asked if there should also be a "men's studies" program, her unexpected response not only made me laugh but also underscored the rationale for her theory. Describing her *Encyclopedia of Women's Experience* entry on *witches,* she gives a fascinating account of how the meaning of that word has changed to women's disadvantage. I conclude the interview by asking Kramarae to look back on our conversation to see if I had said or done something that constrained what she said. See if you agree with her assessment.

View this segment online at www.mhhe.com/griffin9e or www.afirstlook.com.

A SECOND LOOK

Recommended resource: "Cheris Kramarae," in *Feminist Rhetorical Theories,* Karen A. Foss, Sonja K. Foss, and Cindy L. Griffin, Sage, Thousand Oaks, CA, 1999, pp. 38–68.

Comprehensive statement: Cheris Kramarae, *Women and Men Speaking,* Newbury House, Rowley, MA, 1981, pp. v–ix, 1–63.

Original concept of mutedness: Edwin Ardener, "Belief and the Problem of Women" and "The 'Problem' Revisited," in *Perceiving Women,* Shirley Ardener (ed.), Malaby, London, 1975, pp. 1–27.

Kramarae's reflection on her theory: Cheris Kramarae, "Muted Group Theory and Communication: Asking Dangerous Questions," *Women and Language,* Vol. 22, 2005, pp. 55 61.

Dictionary of women's words: Cheris Kramarae and Paula Treichler, *A Feminist Dictionary: Amazons, Bluestockings and Crones,* 2nd ed., Pandora, London, 1992.

Worldwide feminist scholarship: Cheris Kramarae and Dale Spender (eds.), *Routledge International Encyclopedia of Women: Global Women's Issues and Knowledge* (4 vol.), Routledge, New York, 2000.

Sexual harassment: Julia T. Wood (ed.), "Special Section—'Telling Our Stories': Sexual Harassment in the Communication Discipline," *Journal of Applied Communication Research,* Vol. 20, 1992, pp. 349–418.

Date rape and muting: Ann Burnett, Jody L. Mattern, Liliana L. Herakova, David H. Kahl Jr., Cloy Tobola, and Susan E. Bornsen, "Communicating/Muting Date Rape: A Co-Cultural Theoretical Analysis of Communication Factors Related to Rape Culture on a College Campus," *Journal of Applied Communication Research,* Vol. 37, 2009, pp. 465–485.

Alternative interpretations of gender differences in discourse: Candace West, Michelle M. Lazar, and Cheris Kramarae, "Gender in Discourse," in *Discourse as Social Interaction,* Vol. 2, Teun van Dijk (ed.), Sage, Thousand Oaks, CA, 1997, pp. 119–143.

Foundational statement of co-cultural theory: Mark P. Orbe, "From the Standpoint(s) of Traditionally Muted Groups: Explicating a Co-Cultural Communication Theoretical Model," *Communication Theory,* Vol. 8, 1998, pp. 1–26.

Recent application of co-cultural theory to the college experience: Cerise L. Glenn and Dante L. Johnson, "'What They See as Acceptable:' A Co-Cultural Theoretical Analysis of Black Male Students at a Predominantly White Institution," *Howard Journal of Communications,* Vol. 23, 2012, pp. 351–368.

Critique: Celia J. Wall and Pat Gannon-Leary, "A Sentence Made by Men: Muted Group Theory Revisited," *European Journal of Women's Studies,* Vol. 6, 1999, pp. 21–29.

To discover scenes from feature films that illustrate Muted Group Theory, click on Suggested Movie Clips under Theory Resources at *www.afirstlook.com.*

Integration

DIVISION SIX

Integration

Integration

By the end of the term, most students have decided which type of theory they favor—objective or interpretive. If you've made your choice, consider four distinct ways you can respond to classmates, instructors, or others who don't share your preference.

1. **Reject inferior scholarship.** Objective as well as interpretive scholars who take this position believe it's ridiculous to say the other side has something to offer. For example, University of Kentucky communication professors Robert Bostrom and Lewis Donohew who search for objective truth launch a blistering attack against theorists like Barnett Pearce, Roland Barthes, Paul Watzlawick, and Stuart Hall. They claim the interpretive approach represents "an intellectual nihilism" that leads to "theoretical anarchy and the substitution of pseudo-explanation for scientific explanation."[1] Hall in turn is "deeply suspicious and hostile" to the work of behavioral scientists who focus solely on outward behavior while "consistently translating matters of signification, meaning, language, and symbolization into crude behavioral indicators."[2] You could follow their lead by criticizing the views of misguided others.

2. **Respect differences.** Princeton University philosophical pragmatist Richard Rorty comes down equally hard on objective and interpretive theorists when either group claims that only their approach has value. He admits, however, that there *are* irreconcilable differences between the two camps. Both groups are self-sealing language communities that don't—and really can't—talk to each other. The questions posed in one approach have no answers in the other approach. For this reason, Rorty says the debates between the sciences and humanities about human nature, knowledge, and methodology are "not issues to be resolved, only . . . differences to be lived with."[3]

Clinical psychology is a discipline in which this response is common. The behavioral, humanist, and psychoanalytic schools of counseling differ in starting point, method, and conclusion. Most counselors choose to be trained in one approach and then stick to it in their practice. Yet they respect any form of therapy that helps a hurting person get better. Similarly, you could respect any approach that helps people communicate more effectively.

3. **Explore the other side.** We tend to like what's familiar and not really know what we're missing. You may favor an objective approach because of your interest in interpersonal communication, a field where most theory and research is crafted from a social science perspective. But you might find that taking a course in the qualitative methods of conducting ethnography, discourse analysis, and focus groups could attach faces and feelings to the people behind your statistics. In like manner, if public speaking, debate, and rhetorical criticism are your passion, you might be pleasantly surprised to find that a controlled experiment described in a research design course could confirm or cast doubt on your hunches about what sways an audience.

If you pursue an advanced degree in communication, there's no doubt you'll be asked to narrow your focus. But starting your studies or career track with a narrow focus could cause you to miss out on a variety of ideas and possibilities.

Exploring the best of the social sciences and humanities can be enjoyable now and reap unexpected rewards in the future. There will be time to specialize later.

4. Cooperate with colleagues. Cultivation theorist George Gerbner pictures a symbiotic relationship between two worldviews, whereby scientists and artists help each other fulfill a promise that can't be reached by either approach alone.[4] When dealing with communication theory, what would a collaborative relationship between objective and interpretive communication majors look like?

Studying together for exams in courses that investigate both approaches could be a first step. Collaborating on a research project with someone who holds a different worldview is another possibility. Perhaps a creative student in film studies could shoot and edit a video on binge drinking across campus. Another student trained in empirical research could perform a before-and-after study of alcohol consumption of students who watched the video. Or a social scientist among you could test one of the theories in this book, while an interpretive scholar concentrates on its implications and applied practice. However you might work together, rhetorician Marie Hochmuth Nichols insists that the sciences and humanities need each other: "The humanities without science are blind, but science without the humanities may be vicious."[5]

Reject. Respect. Explore. Cooperate. Which response do you choose?

"You realize I'm taking an enormous personal as well as professional risk just being seen with you."

© Michael Maslin/The New Yorker Collection/www.cartoonbank.com

CHAPTER 37

Common Threads in Comm Theories

The first four chapters in this book laid the groundwork for understanding the relationship among the wide range of theories you would study. Chapter 1 presented a working definition of both *theory* and *communication.* Chapter 2 introduced the objective–interpretive distinction, and Chapter 3 outlined separate lists of six criteria for evaluating these two types of theories. Chapter 4 mapped out seven distinct traditions of theory within our discipline. Hopefully these integrative tools have helped you compare and contrast the theories throughout the course.

In this final chapter, I present another approach to identifying similarities and differences among the theories, which wouldn't have made sense before you read about them. I identify 10 recurring principles that in one form or another appear in multiple theories. I refer to these as *threads* because each strand weaves in and out of theories that might otherwise seem unrelated.

These threads represent key concepts in other communication courses so they may be quite familiar. In order to qualify as a thread in the tapestry of communication theory, I've decided that the principle or concept must be a significant feature of at least six different theories covered in the text. The feature could be the engine that drives a theory, a common characteristic of messages, a variable that's related to the process of communication, or the outcome of an interaction.

Each thread is introduced with a shorthand label followed by a summary statement set in boldface. I first illustrate the principle with an exemplar theory that's clearly entwined with that thread, and then describe how other theorists employ this key idea, which is sometimes at odds with how it's used in the exemplar. That's the *contrast* of this compare-and-contrast integration. Consistent with the critique sections that close each theory chapter of the text, I end each thread discussion with a cause-for-pause reservation that those who warmly embrace the thread might ponder.

Unraveling these threads isn't intended to exhaust all possibilities—nor to be exhausting. I cite every theory covered in the book at least once, but never more than twice. With one exception, I limit the number of theories tied into a thread to three or four. You or your instructor can think of multiple examples for each thread that I don't mention.

Students tell me that working through the threads helps them make new connections between the theories, and also serves as a comprehensive course review. I hope it does both of these for you.

1. MOTIVATION

Communication is motivated by our basic social need for affiliation, achievement, and control, as well as our strong desire to reduce our uncertainty and anxiety.

Social exchange theory holds that relationships develop based upon the perceived benefits and costs of interaction. Recall that in *social penetration theory*, Altman and Taylor adopt the principle of social exchange to predict when people will become more vulnerable in their depth and breadth of self-disclosure (Ch. 8). The greater the probable outcome (benefits minus costs), the more transparent a person will be. Of course, potential rewards and costs are in the eye of the beholder. As Katz' *uses and gratifications* maintains, people act to gratify their felt needs, but those needs vary from person to person (Ch. 28). It follows, therefore, that the rewards and costs that satisfy those needs can be quite diverse. Despite this range of potential motives, almost every theory you've read about in the book invokes at least one of the five motives named in the thread. I've selected five different theories to illustrate the strong pull that these five different needs exert.

Motivation
Needs and desires that drive or draw us to think, feel, and act as we do.

Need for affiliation. *Social penetration theory* is based on a strong human need for affiliation, which is satisfied through mutual self-disclosure (Ch. 8).

Need for achievement. Hirokawa and Gouran's *functional perspective on group decision making* assumes that people in problem-solving groups want to achieve a high-quality solution. Any comment that doesn't analyze the problem, set goals, identify alternatives, or evaluate the relative merits of each option is considered a distraction that disrupts the group's effort to achieve their goal (Ch. 17).

Need for control. Hall's *cultural studies* is based on a broad Marxist interpretation of history that claims money is power. Society's haves exercise hegemonic control over the have-nots in an effort to maintain the status quo. Corporately controlled media shape the dominant discourse of the day that frames the interpretation of events. (Ch. 27).

Need to reduce uncertainty. Berger's *uncertainty reduction theory* suggests that the motive for most communication is to gain knowledge and create understanding in order to increase our ability to predict how future interaction with others will go (Ch. 9). Our desire to reduce uncertainty is especially high when we know we'll meet again, the other has something we want, or the person is acting in a weird way.

Need to reduce anxiety. Burke's "Definition of Man" suggests that the language of perfection makes us all feel guilty that we aren't better than we are. Guilt is his catchall term to cover every form of anxiety, tension, embarrassment, shame, and disgust intrinsic to the human condition. *Dramatism* claims the only way to get rid of this noxious feeling is through mortification or victimage (Ch. 23).

Cause for pause: If it's true that all of my communication—including this book—is undertaken solely to meet my own personal needs and interests, then it strikes me that I am a totally selfish person. I don't doubt that my desire for affiliation, achievement, and control shapes much of my conversation, as does my desire to reduce my levels of doubt and fear. But there are times when I could (and should) say no to the pull of these needs out of concern for others or a sense of ethical responsibility. To the extent that any theory of motivation suggests I have no choice, I choose to be skeptical.

2. SELF-IMAGE

Communication affects and is affected by our sense of identity, which is strongly shaped within the context of our culture.

Mead's ***symbolic interactionism*** claims that our concept of self is formed through communication (Ch. 5). By taking the role of the other and seeing how we look to them, we develop our sense of identity. In turn, this looking-glass self shapes how we think and act within the community. According to Aronson and Cooper's revisions of *cognitive dissonance theory,* dissonance negatively impacts our self-image until we find a way to dissipate this distressing feeling (Ch. 16).

Self-image
Identity; a mental picture of who I see myself to be, which is greatly influenced by the way others respond to me.

Ting-Toomey's *face-negotiation theory* defines face as our public self-image (Ch. 32). She says that people raised in individualistic cultures tend to have an *I-identity* and are concerned with saving face. People born into collectivistic cultures almost always have a *we-identity* and are mainly concerned with giving face to others.

Cause for pause: Accepted wisdom in our discipline suggests that most of us have been put down by others and need to find ways to boost our self-esteem. As a counterpoint to this concern, social psychologists have identified a fundamental attribution error—a basic perceptual bias we consistently show.[1] When we have success, we interpret it as the result of our hard work and ability, but when others have that same success, we tend to think of them as lucky. Conversely, when others fail, we consider it their own fault, but when we fail, we blame others or curse the fickle finger of fate. As a corrective to this biased perception, perhaps we should consider giving others the benefit of the doubt while holding ourselves to a more rigorous standard of accountability.

3. CREDIBILITY

Our verbal and nonverbal messages are validated or discounted by others' perception of our competence and character.

More than 2,000 years ago, ***The Rhetoric*** of Aristotle used the term ethical proof (ethos) to describe the credibility of a speaker, which affects the probability that the speech will be persuasive. Aristotle defined *ethos* as a combination of the speaker's perceived intelligence or competence, character or trustworthiness, and goodwill toward the audience (Ch. 22). Since credibility is in the eye of the beholder, audience perceptions of the speaker's ability, virtue, and concern for their well-being can change while he or she is speaking.

Credibility
The intelligence, character, and goodwill that audience members perceive in a message source.

In election studies based on recent versions of McCombs and Shaw's *agenda-setting theory,* researchers not only monitor the frequency of candidate attributes mentioned by the media, but also note the affective tone of these references. The way the media frame a public figure's competence, personality, and morality clearly affects voters' perception of a candidate's credibility and therefore has a major effect on the election (Ch. 30).

Harding and Wood's *standpoint theory* recognizes that women, racial minorities, and others on the margins of society have low credibility in the eyes of those with higher status. The irony of this negative judgment is that the powerless occupy a position that affords them a less false view of social reality than is available to the overprivileged who look down on them (Ch. 35).

Cause for pause: The theories cited in this thread regard perceived credibility as a valuable asset in the communication process. But our focus on the source of a message may cause us to lose sight of the intrinsic value of what's being said. Before embracing the speaker's point of view, we might ask ourselves, "Would I think this was such a good idea if it were presented by someone less attractive, sexy, or popular?" We might also ask, "Just because an idea is voiced by a creep I can't stand, does that mean it's totally wrong and without merit?"

4. EXPECTATION

What we expect to hear or see will affect our perception, interpretation, and response during an interaction.

Burgoon's ***expectancy violations theory*** defines expectation as what we anticipate will happen rather than what we might desire (Ch. 7). In interpersonal encounters, our expectations are shaped by the cultural and situational context; communicator characteristics such as age, gender, appearance, personality, and style of speaking; and the nature of our relationship. When our expectations are violated, we react either positively or negatively depending on the violation valence and the communicator's reward valence. And according to Burgoon's subsequent *interaction adaptation theory,* we change our interaction position as a result of our expectations.

Expectation
In human interaction, our anticipation of how others will act or react toward us.

Expectation is integral to other interpersonal theories as well. Berger's *uncertainty reduction theory* states that the expectation of future interaction increases our motivation to reduce uncertainty (Ch. 9). This prediction is echoed in Walther's *social information processing theory.* According to his *hyperpersonal perspective* extension of SIP, anticipation of future interaction coupled with an exaggerated sense of similarity results in a self-fulfilling prophecy. The person who is perceived through CMC to be wonderful starts acting that way (Ch. 10).

Theories introduced in the media effects section classify expectation as a crucial variable. Gerbner's *cultivation theory* maintains that a steady diet of symbolic violence on television creates an exaggerated fear that the viewer will be physically threatened, mugged, raped, or killed. This expectation causes heavy viewers to have a general mistrust of others, which leads them to urge more restrictions and the use of force against those whom they fear (Ch. 29).

Cause for pause: Perceptions are interpretations of sensory experiences occurring in the present. Expectations are projections of our perceptions into the future—we anticipate a repeat performance. The two concepts are easy to confuse and tricky to measure. Since we can never know for sure what another person experiences, theories that appeal to the concept of expectation may sound more definitive than they really are.

5. AUDIENCE ADAPTATION

By mindfully creating a person-centered message specific to the situation, we increase the possibility of achieving our communication goals.

Sherif's ***social judgment theory*** predicts that those who want to influence others should try to figure out their latitudes of acceptance, rejection, and noncommitment on a particular issue. Based on this audience analysis, the persuader can craft a message that falls at the edge of a person's latitude of acceptance—an adaptation that offers the best chance of desired attitude change (Ch. 14). Petty and Cacioppo's *elaboration likelihood model* suggests the persuader first assess

Audience adaptation
The strategic creation or adjustment of a message in light of the audience characteristics and specific setting.

whether the target audience is ready and able to think through issue-relevant arguments that support the advocate's position. If not, the persuader can still achieve a temporary change of attitude by focusing attention on peripheral cues (Ch. 15).

Burke's *dramatism* is concerned with the speaker's ability to successfully identify with the audience. Without identification there is no persuasion. To the extent that the speaker can establish common ground by demonstrating a similar background, personality, speaking style, and belief and value system, the speech will be successful (Ch. 23).

In an intercultural setting, Giles' *communication accommodation theory* focuses on parties' adjustment of their speech styles. CAT regards convergence of speaking styles as a natural outcome of wanting to be accepted by the other, usually drawing a positive response. Divergence—accentuating differences through manner of speech—occurs when the communicator is concerned with maintaining his or her distinctive group identity (Ch. 31). As each theory in this thread would predict, divergence induces a negative response from the other person.

Cause for pause: All of these theories suggest that for maximum effectiveness, we should consciously adapt our message to the attitudes, actions, or abilities of the audience. Makes sense. There is, however, a danger that in doing so we'll lose the authenticity of our message or the integrity of our own beliefs. Adjusting becomes pandering when we say whatever others want to hear. Raymond Bauer's article "The Obstinate Audience" suggests an intriguing third possibility—that audience adaptation ends up changing the speaker more than the speaker changing the audience.[2] If so, the counterattitudinal advocacy studies of Festinger's *cognitive dissonance theory* might explain this surprising prediction (Ch. 16).

6. SOCIAL CONSTRUCTION

Persons-in-conversation co-construct their own social realities and are simultaneously shaped by the worlds they create.

This statement of social construction is taken directly from Pearce and Cronen's ***coordinated management of meaning*** (Ch. 6). They see themselves as curious participants in a pluralistic world as opposed to social scientists who they describe as detached observers trying to discover singular Truth. Because CMM claims that people jointly create the social worlds in which they live, the theorists urge us to ask, "What are we doing? What are we making together? How can we make better social worlds?"

Social construction
The communal creation of the social world in which we live.

McPhee's *communicative constitution of organizations* clearly indicates that an organization is what it is because communication has brought it into existence—a particular type of social construction. It's hard to imagine a workplace without four flows of ongoing talk about membership negotiation, self-structuring, activity coordination, and institutional positioning (Ch. 20).

Watzlawick's *interactional view* sees every family as playing a one-of-a-kind game with homemade rules that create the family's own reality—one that's often destructive. He regards the function of therapy as helping members frame an alternative social reality in which they can survive, and perhaps even thrive (Ch. 13).

McLuhan's *media ecology* describes a more subtle construction process, summarized in his statement that we shape our tools and they in turn shape us (Ch. 25). McLuhan claimed that television and other communication inventions change the sensory environment in which we live. In this mass age, the medium is the message, and also the massage.

Cause for pause: The range of theories just cited shows that the idea of social construction is well established in the field of communication. But is there a foundational reality that language can describe, however poorly? As I asked at the end of the chapter on *CMM*, are you willing to give up the notion of a Truth you can count on for a linguistically created social reality that has no existence apart from how it's talked about?

7. SHARED MEANING

Our communication is successful to the extent that we share a common interpretation of the signs we use.

Shared meaning
People's common interpretation or mutual understanding of what a verbal or nonverbal message signifies.

Geertz and Pacanowsky's ***cultural approach to organizations*** describes culture as webs of significance—systems of shared meaning. In light of this definition, Geertz said we should concern ourselves not only with the structures of cultural webs, but also with the process of their spinning—communication. Applying Geertz' ideas to organizations, Pacanowsky focuses on the collective interpretation of stories, metaphors, and rituals (Ch. 19). Philipsen defines a *speech code* as a historically enacted, socially constructed system of terms, meanings, premises, and rules pertaining to communicative conduct (Ch. 33). He champions ethnography—participant observation within the community—as the way to determine what a speech code means to those who use it.

On the other hand, the road to common understanding is sometimes devious. Barthes' *semiotics* regards the mass media as powerful ideological tools

"You'll have to phrase it another way. They have no word for 'fetch.'"

that frame interpretation of events for the benefit of the haves over the have-nots. The media take a denotative sign and use it as a signifier to be paired with a different signified. The result is a new connotative sign that looks like the original sign but has lost its historical meaning (Ch. 26). Its effect is to affirm the status quo.

Cause for pause: The idea that it's people rather than words that *mean* suggests that texts don't interpret themselves. If that's true, shared interpretation is an accomplishment of the audience rather than of the clarity of the message. Pushed to an extreme, however, the meaning-in-persons idea implies that what is said or written is wide open for any interpretation, no matter what the communicator intended. As an author, I'm uneasy about this notion. I take words and images seriously and try to choose them carefully. When I write about a theory, my aim is to create a mutual understanding that's consistent with what I had in mind. To the extent that this takes place, I see communication as successful. Of course, you're then free to respond as you choose.

8. NARRATIVE

We respond favorably to stories and dramatic imagery with which we can identify.

Fisher's ***narrative paradigm*** claims that people are essentially storytellers. We experience life as a series of ongoing narratives—as conflicts, characters, beginnings, middles, and ends (Ch. 24). Almost all communication is story that we judge by its narrative coherence and narrative fidelity. We continually ponder, does that story hang together? Does it ring true? Bormann's *symbolic convergence theory* can't predict when a story or other dramatizing message will catch fire among group members. But when it does, the resultant fantasy chain shows that it not only rings true, but also creates a symbolic explosion. When a group's fantasies are shared this way, the result is symbolic convergence—a common group consciousness and often a greater cohesiveness (Ch. 18).

Narrative
Story; words and deeds that have sequence and meaning for those who live, create, or interpret them.

Gerbner's *cultivation theory* says that television has become the dominant force in our society because it tells most of the stories, most of the time. Because the stories that TV runs are filled with symbolic violence, the world it creates for heavy viewers is a mean and scary place. These stories gradually cultivate fear by slowly changing viewers' perception of their social environment (Ch. 29).

Tannen observes that the disparity between men's and women's *genderlect styles* can be seen in how they tell a story. As the heroes of their own stories, men try to elevate their status. By telling stories about others, or downplaying their role in their narratives, women seek connection (Ch. 34).

Cause for pause: I believe stories are both fascinating and powerful. Throughout the book I've used extended examples to make theories come alive. But as Warnick reminds us in her commentary on the *narrative paradigm,* there are bad stories that can effectively lead people astray or destroy them. Unless we filter narratives through the values of justice, goodness, and integrity that Fisher and the National Communication Association Credo for Ethical Communication advocate, we could embrace a lie or perpetuate error. Well-told tales are inherently attractive, but they might not all be good.

9. CONFLICT

Unjust communication stifles needed conflict; healthy communication can make conflict productive.

Deetz' ***critical theory of communication in organizations*** describes managerial efforts to suppress conflict through discursive closure rather than address legitimate disagreements through open discussion (Ch. 21). He believes that corporations and their stakeholders would be well served by more conflict rather than less when decisions are made. The managerial quest for greater control counters any attempt to establish democracy in the workplace. Opportunities for employees to voice complaints are a chance to let off steam but rarely lead to meaningful participation in the decisions that affect their lives.

Theories of face-to-face interaction also deal with the use of power to quell conflict rather than work through differences. The *double bind* that Watzlawick describes in his *interactional view* is a classic case of the dominant person in a complementary relationship insisting that the low-power person act as if the relationship were symmetrical (Ch. 13).

Conflict
The struggle between people who are contesting over scarce resources or who perceive that they have incompatible values and goals.

Some theories suggest that conflict must be headed off by proactively talking about the potential problem. A core principle of Petronio's *communication privacy management theory* warns that when co-owners of private information don't effectively negotiate and follow mutually held privacy rules, boundary turbulence is the likely result (Ch. 12).

Cause for pause: As a mediator, I try to facilitate straight talk between parties in conflict. Confronting the problem but not the person is a well-accepted principle of conflict resolution in the West. But, in her *face-negotiation theory,* Ting-Toomey warns that a free and open discussion of conflicting needs and interests within a collectivistic society is counterproductive (Ch. 32). In societies where giving face to others is the cultural norm, straight talk creates great embarrassment. Those of us from Western individualistic cultures need to appreciate and employ subtlety when we're together with people from the East.

10. DIALOGUE

Dialogue is transparent conversation that often creates unanticipated relational outcomes due to parties' profound respect for disparate voices.

Drawing upon Bakhtin's conception of dialogue, Baxter's second generation of ***relational dialectics*** describes dialogue as an aesthetic accomplishment that produces fleeting moments of unity through a profound respect for disparate voices (Ch. 11). Baxter stresses that dialogue doesn't bring resolution to the contradictions that parties experience in close relationships. But dialogue and relationship rituals that honor multiple voices provide assurance that living within changing tensions can be exhilarating—never boring.

Dialogue
Transparent conversation that often creates unanticipated relational outcomes due to parties' profound respect for disparate voices.

In their *coordinated management of meaning,* Pearce and Cronen adopt Buber's view of dialogue, which is more optimistic than Bakhtin's. The theorists agree that dialogue can't be produced on demand, but they think we can experience it if we seek and prepare for it. Buber said dialogue takes place only in I–Thou relationships where we regard our partner as the very one we are. We stand our own ground yet are profoundly open to the other. Pearce believed that dialogic communication is learnable, teachable, and contagious (Ch. 6).

In *muted group theory,* Kramarae suggests that it's difficult for women to participate as equal partners in a dialogue while speaking in a man-made language in which the rules for use are frequently controlled by men. Because women are often muted in the public sphere, they've developed back-channel routes to openly share their experiences with other women (Ch. 36).

Cause for pause: In the communication discipline, *dialogue* is a term that's often used and highly favored, yet advocates have a tough time describing what it is or how to achieve it. The boldfaced statement at the beginning of the thread is my best effort to put the concept into words, but I'm not sure I've captured the essence of what many theorists mean when they use the term.

In practice, dialogue is also exceedingly rare. Whatever criteria we use, probably less than 1 in 1,000 conversations would qualify as dialogue. That suggests a full-blown theory of relational communication must also take into account legitimate authority, jealousies, boredom, insecurities, interruptions, distractions, time pressures, headaches, and all the other "complications" that make everyday communication less than ideal.

UNRAVELING THE THREADS

At this point the 10 threads may be tangled together in your mind like pieces of string intertwined in a drawer. If so, Figure 37–1 helps unravel the threads. The labeled threads are stretched out vertically and crosshatched with the theories featured in the text. Each black dot is like a knot showing a theory tied into a specific thread. I've identified only some of the possible intersections. Whether with classmates, your instructor, or on your own, I encourage you to identify other knots. Adding dots on the chart is like finishing a crossword puzzle or putting numbers into a sudoku matrix.

The sense of discovery that comes from figuring out where to place additional knots can be quite satisfying, and it has practical benefits as well. It's a great way to study for a final exam, and any insights you gain now will serve you well in future courses. So if you've studied 15 to 20 theories over the term, try to identify at least one additional knot for each thread. If your instructor assigned all of the theories, see if you can tie in two more theories per thread. By working

through this integrative exercise, you'll increase your odds of remembering the practical advice a theory offers when you find yourself in a crucial communication situation. That's been our hope all along—that you'll use the thoughts of the theorists you've studied to enrich your life and the lives of those around you.

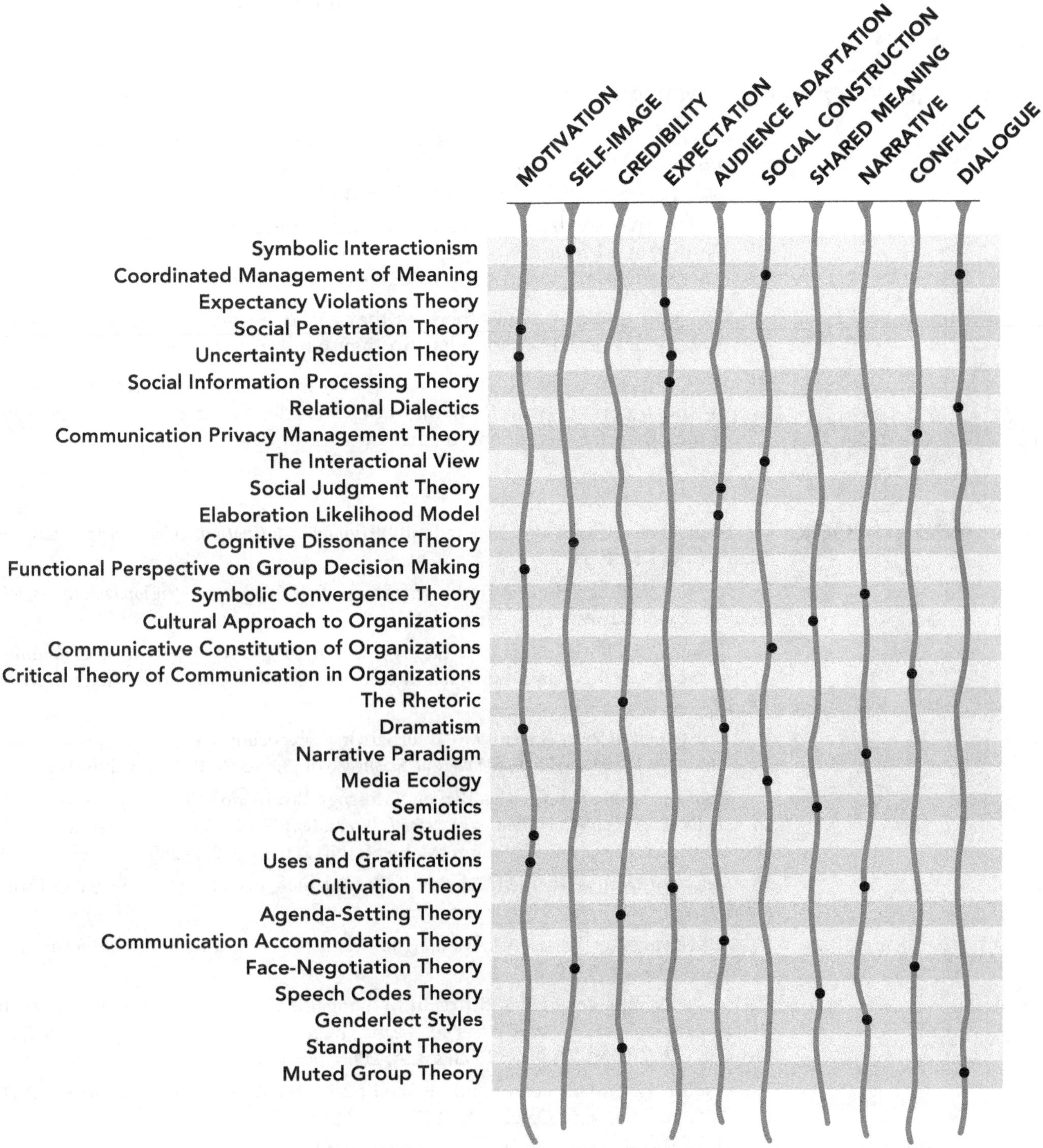

FIGURE 37–1 Common Threads That Run Through Communication Theories

The field is wide open for new ideas. There's no reason you have to stop with a first look at communication theory or settle for a secondhand glance. You've probably been mulling over an idea not suggested in these pages. Perhaps that notion could be developed and become the focus of a new chapter in a revised edition of this book. Choose the theoretical perspective or communication context that fascinates you, and switch from casual observation to an intensive gaze. Keep looking.

QUESTIONS TO SHARPEN YOUR FOCUS

1. Which *thread* most intrigues you? Are the theories it connects *objective* or *interpretive?* What *communication principle* that you've learned or discovered isn't represented in this chapter? Why do you think it's missing?
2. Which five theories presented in this book are your personal favorites? Do they tend to line up with a *thread* or *principle,* come out of a single *scholarly tradition,* or address a particular *communication context?*
3. Can you think of a few theories that could be tied into at least five of the threads discussed? If so, what do they have in common?
4. What questions do you have about communication that weren't addressed by the theories covered in this book? Under what *communication contexts* would theories that speak to these issues fit best?

A SECOND LOOK

Motivation: David C. McClelland, *Human Motivation,* Cambridge University, Cambridge, UK, 1988.

Self-image: Bruce Bracken (ed.), *Handbook of Self-Concept: Developmental, Social, and Clinical Considerations,* Wiley, New York, 1995.

Credibility: Charles Self, "Credibility," in *An Integrated Approach to Communication Theory and Research,* Michael Salwen and Don Stacks (eds.), Lawrence Erlbaum, Mahwah, NJ, 1996, pp. 421–441.

Expectation: Robert Rosenthal, "Interpersonal Expectancy Effects: A 30-Year Perspective," *Current Directions in Psychological Science,* Vol. 3, No. 6, 1994, pp. 176–179.

Audience adaptation: Charles Berger, "Message Production Skill in Social Interaction," in *Handbook of Communication and Social Interaction Skills,* John O. Greene and Brant Burleson (eds.), Lawrence Erlbaum, Mahwah, NJ, 2003, pp. 257–289.

Social construction: Kenneth Gergen, *An Invitation to Social Construction,* Sage, Thousand Oaks, CA, 1999.

Shared meaning: Steve Duck, *Meaningful Relationships: Talking, Sense, and Relating,* Sage, Thousand Oaks, CA, 1994.

Narrative: Eric Peterson and Kristin M. Langellier, "Communication as Storytelling," in *Communication as . . . Perspectives on Theory,* Gregory Shepherd, Jeffrey St. John, and Ted Striphas (eds.), Sage, Thousand Oaks, CA, 2006, pp. 123–131.

Conflict: W. Barnett Pearce and Stephen Littlejohn, *Moral Conflict: When Social Worlds Collide,* Sage, Thousand Oaks, CA, 1997.

Dialogue: Rob Anderson, Leslie A. Baxter, and Kenneth Cissna (eds.), *Dialogue: Theorizing Difference in Communication Studies,* Sage, Thousand Oaks, CA, 2003.

APPENDIX A

Abstracts of Theories

What follows are brief summaries of the 32 theories featured in the book. There's potential danger, of course, in trying to capture the gist of a theory in a few cryptic lines, but we didn't craft the abstracts to convey new concepts. Instead, these capsule statements are designed to jog your memory of ideas already considered. The abstracts are arranged in the same order as the theories appear in the text. At the end of each summary, we've labeled the communication theory tradition or traditions that undergird each theorist's thought. We hope you'll find the summaries as well as their intellectual roots helpful.

Interpersonal Communication

Mead's symbolic interactionism: Humans act toward people, things, and events on the basis of the meanings they assign to them. Once people define a situation as real, it has very real consequences. Without language there would be no thought, no sense of self, and no socializing presence of society within the individual. (Socio-cultural tradition)

Pearce and Cronen's coordinated management of meaning: Persons-in-conversation co-construct their own social realities and are shaped by the worlds they create. Communication is a two-sided process of making and managing meaning and coordinating our actions. What we say matters because we get what we make. If we get the pattern right, the best possible things will happen. (Socio-cultural and phenomenological traditions)

Burgoon's expectancy violations theory: Violating another person's interpersonal expectations can be a superior strategy to conformity. When the meaning of a violation is ambiguous, communicators with a high reward valence can enhance their attractiveness, credibility, and persuasiveness by doing the unexpected. When the violation valence or reward valence is negative, they should act in a socially appropriate way. (Socio-psychological tradition)

Altman and Taylor's social penetration theory: Interpersonal closeness proceeds in a gradual and orderly fashion from superficial to intimate levels of exchange as a function of anticipated present and future outcomes. Lasting intimacy requires continual and mutual vulnerability through breadth and depth of self-disclosure. (Socio-psychological tradition)

Berger's uncertainty reduction theory: When people meet, their primary concern is to reduce uncertainty about each other and their relationship. As verbal output, nonverbal warmth, self-disclosure, similarity, and shared communication networks increase, uncertainty decreases—and vice versa. Information seeking and reciprocity are positively correlated with uncertainty. (Socio-psychological tradition)

Walther's social information processing theory: Based solely on the information available via computer-mediated communication (CMC), parties who meet online

Reproduced by permission of Punch Ltd., www.punch.co.uk

can develop relationships that are just as close as those formed face-to-face—though it takes longer. Because online senders select, receivers magnify, channels promote, and feedback enhances favorable impressions, CMC may create hyperpersonal relationships. (Socio-psychological tradition)

Baxter and Montgomery's relational dialectics: Social life is a dynamic knot of contradictions, a ceaseless interplay between contradictory or opposing tendencies such as integration–separation, stability–change, and expression–nonexpression. Quality relationships are constituted through dialogue, which is an aesthetic accomplishment that produces fleeting moments of unity through a profound respect for the disparate voices. (Phenomenological tradition)

Petronio's communication privacy management theory: People believe they own and have a right to control their private information; they do so by using personal privacy rules. When others are told, they become co-owners of the information. If co-owners don't effectively negotiate mutually agreeable privacy rules about telling third parties, boundary turbulence is the likely result. (Socio-cultural and cybernetic traditions)

Watzlawick's interactional view: Relationships within a family system are interconnected and highly resistant to change. Communication among members has a content component and a relationship component that centers on issues of control. The system can be transformed only when members receive outside help to reframe their metacommunication. (Cybernetic tradition)

Sherif's social judgment theory: The larger the discrepancy between a speaker's position and a listener's point of view, the greater the change in attitude—as long as the message doesn't fall within the hearer's latitude of rejection. High ego-involvement usually indicates a wide latitude of rejection. Messages that fall there may have a boomerang effect. (Socio-psychological tradition)

Petty and Cacioppo's elaboration likelihood model: Message elaboration is the central route of persuasion that produces major positive attitude change. It occurs when unbiased listeners are motivated and able to scrutinize arguments they consider strong. Message-irrelevant factors hold sway on the peripheral path, a more common route that produces fragile shifts in attitude. (Socio-psychological tradition)

Festinger's cognitive dissonance theory: Cognitive dissonance is an aversive drive that causes people to (1) avoid opposing viewpoints, (2) seek reassurance after making a tough decision, and (3) change private beliefs to match public behavior when there is minimal justification for an action. Self-consistency, a sense of personal responsibility, or self-affirmation can explain dissonance reduction. (Socio-psychological tradition)

Group and Public Communication

Hirokawa and Gouran's functional perspective on group decision making: Groups make high-quality decisions when members fulfill four requisite functions: (1) problem analysis, (2) goal setting, (3) identification of alternatives, and (4) evaluation of positive and negative consequences. Most group communication disrupts progress toward accomplishing these functional tasks, but counteractive communication can bring people back to rational inquiry. (Socio-psychological and cybernetic traditions)

Bormann's symbolic convergence theory: Dramatizing messages are group members' expressed interpretations of events other than those in the here-and-now. Message content becomes a group fantasy theme when it spontaneously chains out among members. The sharing of group fantasies creates symbolic convergence—group consciousness and often cohesiveness. Fantasy theme analysis across groups can reveal a rhetorical vision. (Rhetorical and socio-psychological traditions)

Geertz and Pacanowsky's cultural approach to organizations: Humans are animals suspended in webs of significance that they themselves have spun. An organization doesn't have a culture, it is a culture—a unique system of shared meanings. A nonintrusive ethnographic approach interprets stories, rites, and other symbolism to make sense of corporate culture. (Socio-cultural tradition)

McPhee's communicative constitution of organizations: Communication calls organization into being. Such constitutive communication is patterned into four flows: membership negotiation, self-structuring, activity coordination, and institutional positioning. All four flows are necessary for organization to occur, although time and space often separate where each flow appears. (Socio-cultural tradition)

Deetz' critical theory of communication in organizations: The naïve notion that communication is merely the transmission of information perpetuates managerialism, discursive closure, and the corporate colonization of everyday life. Language is the principal medium through which social reality is produced and reproduced. Managers can further a company's health and democratic values by coordinating stakeholder participation in corporate decisions. (Critical and phenomenological traditions)

Aristotle's rhetoric: Rhetoric is the art of discovering all available means of persuasion. A speaker supports the probability of a message by logical, ethical, and emotional proofs. Accurate audience analysis results in effective invention, arrangement, style, delivery, and, presumably, memory. (Rhetorical tradition)

Burke's dramatism: Life is drama. The dramatistic pentad of act, scene, agent, agency, and purpose is the critic's tool for discovering a speaker's motives. The ultimate motive of rhetoric is the purging of guilt. Without audience identification with the speaker, there is no persuasion. (Rhetorical and semiotic traditions)

Fisher's narrative paradigm: People are storytelling animals; almost all forms of human communication are fundamentally narrative. Listeners judge a story by whether it hangs together and rings true with the values of an ideal audience. Thus, narrative rationality is a matter of coherence and fidelity. (Rhetorical tradition)

Mass Communication

McLuhan's media ecology: The media must be understood ecologically. Changes in communication technology alter the symbolic environment—the socially constructed, sensory world of meanings. We shaped our tools—the phonetic alphabet, printing press, and telegraph—and they in turn have shaped our perceptions, experiences, attitudes, and behavior. Thus, the medium is the message. (Sociocultural tradition)

Barthes' semiotics: The significant visual sign systems of a culture affirm the status quo by suggesting that the world as it is today is natural, inevitable, and eternal. Mythmakers do this by co-opting neutral denotative signs to become signifiers without historical grounding in second-order connotative semiotic systems. (Semiotic tradition)

Hall's cultural studies: The mass media function to maintain the ideology of those who already have power. Corporately controlled media provide the dominant discourse of the day that frames interpretation of events. Critics should seek not only to interpret culture, but to change it. Media audiences do have the capacity to resist hegemony. (Critical tradition)

Katz' uses and gratifications: The media-effects tradition focuses on what media do to people. Uses & grats focuses on what people do with media. Media consumption is a deliberate choice designed to satisfy particular needs. Media don't have uniform effects on the audience; effects vary according to the individual reasons for media use. (Socio-psychological tradition)

Gerbner's cultivation theory: Television has become society's storyteller. Heavy television viewers see a vast quantity of dramatic violence, which cultivates an exaggerated belief in a mean and scary world. Mainstreaming and resonance are two of the processes that create a homogeneous and fearful populace. (Sociocultural and socio-psychological traditions)

McCombs and Shaw's agenda-setting theory: The media tell us (1) what to think about and (2) how to think about it. The first process (agenda setting) transfers the salience of items on their news agenda to our agenda. The second process (framing) transfers the salience of selected attributes to prominence among the pictures in our heads. (Socio-psychological tradition)

Cultural Context

Giles' communication accommodation theory: People in intercultural encounters who see themselves as unique individuals will adjust their speech style and content to mesh with others whose approval they seek. People who want to reinforce a strong group identification will interact with those outside the group in a way that accentuates their differences. (Socio-psychological tradition)

Ting-Toomey's face-negotiation theory: People who have an interdependent self-image in a collectivistic culture are concerned with giving other-face or mutual-face, so they adopt a conflict style of avoiding or integrating. People who have an independent self-image in an individualistic culture are concerned with protecting self-face, so they adopt a conflict style of dominating. (Socio-cultural and socio-psychological traditions)

Philipsen's speech codes theory: Through ethnography of communication, we know all cultures have multiple speech codes that involve a distinctive psychology, sociology, and rhetoric. The meaning of a speech code is determined by speakers and listeners, and is woven into speech itself. Artful use of the code can explain, predict, and control talk about talk. (Socio-cultural tradition)

Tannen's genderlect styles: Male–female conversation is cross-cultural communication. Masculine and feminine styles of discourse are best viewed as two distinct cultural dialects rather than as inferior or superior ways of speaking. Men's report talk focuses on status and independence; women's rapport talk seeks human connection. (Semiotic and socio-cultural traditions)

Harding and Wood's standpoint theory: Different locations within the social hierarchy affect what is seen. The standpoints of marginalized people provide less false views of the world than do the privileged perspectives of the powerful. Strong objectivity requires that scientific research start from the lives of women, the poor, gays and lesbians, and racial minorities. (Critical tradition)

Kramarae's muted group theory: Man-made language aids in defining, depreciating, and excluding women. Because men have primarily shaped language, women frequently struggle to make their voices heard in the public sphere. As women cease to be muted, men will no longer maintain their position of dominance in society. (Critical and phenomenological traditions)

APPENDIX C

NCA Credo for Ethical Communication

Questions of right and wrong arise whenever people communicate. Ethical communication is fundamental to responsible thinking, decision making, and the development of relationships and communities within and across contexts, cultures, channels, and media. Moreover, ethical communication enhances human worth and dignity by fostering truthfulness, fairness, responsibility, personal integrity, and respect for self and others. We believe that unethical communication threatens the quality of all communication and consequently the well-being of individuals and the society in which we live. Therefore, we, the members of the National Communication Association, endorse and are committed to practicing the following principles of ethical communication.

We advocate truthfulness, accuracy, honesty, and reason as essential to the integrity of communication.

We endorse freedom of expression, diversity of perspective, and tolerance of dissent to achieve the informed and responsible decision making fundamental to a civil society.

We strive to understand and respect other communicators before evaluating and responding to their messages.

We promote access to communication resources and opportunities as necessary to fulfill human potential and contribute to the well-being of families, communities, and society.

We promote communication climates of caring and mutual understanding that respect the unique needs and characteristics of individual communicators.

We condemn communication that degrades individuals and humanity through distortion, intimidation, coercion, and violence and through the expression of intolerance and hatred.

We are committed to the courageous expression of personal convictions in pursuit of fairness and justice.

We advocate sharing information, opinions, and feelings when facing significant choices while also respecting privacy and confidentiality.

We accept responsibility for the short- and long-term consequences of our own communication and expect the same of others.

CALVIN AND HOBBES
by WATTERSON
WHENEVER I NEED TO DO SOME SERIOUS THINKING, I GO FOR A WALK IN THE WOODS.
THERE ARE ALWAYS A MILLION DISTRACTIONS OUT HERE.
I DON'T BELIEVE IN ETHICS ANY MORE.
AS FAR AS I'M CONCERNED, THE ENDS JUSTIFY THE MEANS.
GET WHAT YOU CAN WHILE THE GETTING'S GOOD – THAT'S WHAT I SAY! MIGHT MAKES RIGHT! THE WINNERS WRITE THE HISTORY BOOKS!
IT'S A DOG-EAT-DOG WORLD, SO I'LL DO WHATEVER I HAVE TO, AND LET OTHERS ARGUE ABOUT WHETHER IT'S "RIGHT" OR NOT.
HEYY!
SHOVE!
WHY'D YOU DO THAT?!?
YOU WERE IN MY WAY. NOW YOU'RE NOT. THE ENDS JUSTIFY THE MEANS.
I DIDN'T MEAN FOR EVERYONE, YOU DOLT! JUST ME!
AHH...
WATTERSON 2-28

CREDITS AND ACKNOWLEDGMENTS

Chapter 4

Page 48: "NCA Credo for Ethical Communication" reprinted by permission of National Communication Association, Washington, DC, www.natcom.org.

Interpersonal Messages

Page 52: Em Griffin, "Game Metaphors" from *Making Friends (& Making Them Count)*, pp. 12–18. Copyright © 1987 Em Griffin. Used by permission of InterVarsity Press, P.O. Box 1400, Downers Grove, IL 60515, www.ivpress.com.

Chapter 5

Page 55: Jane Wagner, *The Search For Signs of Intelligent Life in the Universe*, pp. 15, 18. Copyright © 1986 by Jane Wagner Inc. Reprinted by permission of HarperCollins Publishers.

Chapter 6

Page 68: W. Barnett Pearce and Kimberly A. Pearce, "Transcendent Storytelling: Abilities for Systemic Practitioners and Their Clients," *Human Systems: The Journal of Systemic Consultation & Management*, Vol. 9, 1998, pp. 178–179. Used by permission of the KCC Foundation and the Leeds Family Therapy.

Page 69 (Fig 6–2): LUUUUTT Model from CMM Institute for Personal and Social Evolution, www.cmminstitute.net. © 2014 CMM Institute. All rights reserved. Used by permission.

Chapter 7

Page 83: W. H. Auden, "Prologue: The Birth of Architecture." Copyright © 1965 by W. H. Auden; *Collected Poems* by W. H. Auden. Used by permission of Random House, an imprint of the Random House Publishing Group, a division of Random House LLC; copyright © 1962 by W. H. Auden, renewed. Reprinted by permission of Curtis Brown, Ltd.

Chapter 9

Pages 108, 110–111: Axioms from Charles Berger and Richard Calabrese, "Some Explorations in Initial Interaction and Beyond: Toward a Developmental Theory of Interpersonal Communication," *Human Communication Research*, Vol. 1, 1975, pp. 99–112. © 2013 International Communication Association. Reproduced by permission of Wiley Inc.

Page 112 (Fig 9–1): Theorems of Uncertainty Reduction Theory adapted from Charles Berger and Richard Calabrese, "Some Explorations in Initial Interaction and Beyond: Toward a Developmental Theory of Interpersonal Communication," *Human Communication Research*, Vol. 1, 1975, p. 100. © 2013 International Communication Association. Reproduced by permission of Wiley Inc.

Chapter 11

Pages 137, 140–142, 144–146: Gurinder Chadha, Guljit Bindra, and Paul Mayeda Berges, *Bend It Like Beckham*, 2002, Kintop Pictures. Used by permission.

Page 147: Gurinder Chadha, director and co-writer of *Bend It Like Beckham* in *FLM Magazine*, 2003. Courtesy of Landmark Theatres / FLM Magazine.

Chapter 13

Page 170 (Fig 13–2): Adapted from Edna Rogers and Richard Farace, Matrix of Transactional Types, "Analysis of Relational Communication in Dyads: New Measurement Procedures," *Human Communication Research*, © 1975, Vol. 1, p. 233. Reprinted and adapted by permission of Blackwell Publishing, http://onlinelibrary.wiley.com/doi/10.1111/j.1468-2958.1975.tb00270.x/abstract

Chapter 14

Page 184 (Fig. 14–2): Adapted from Stephen Bochner and Chester Insko, "Communicator Discrepancy, Source Credibility, and Opinion Change," *Journal of Personality and Social Psychology*, Vol. 4(6), 1966, pp. 614–622. Copyright © 1966 by the American Psychological Association. Adapted with permission. The use of APA information does not imply endorsement by APA.

Chapter 15

Page 190 (Fig. 15–1): Adapted from Richard E. Petty and John T. Cacioppo, "The Elaboration Likelihood Model of Persuasion," *Advances in Experimental Social Psychology*, Leonard Berkowitz (ed.), Academic Press, Orlando, Vol. 19, 1986, p. 126. Reprinted with permission from Elsevier.

Chapter 16

Page 201: "Smoke! Smoke! Smoke! (That Cigarette)," words and music by Merle Travis and Tex Williams © 1947 (Renewed) Unichappell Music Inc., Elvis Presley Music, Inc. and Merle's Girls Music. All rights on behalf of itself and Elvis Presley Music, Inc. administered by Unichappell Music, Inc. All rights for Merle's Girls Music administered by Warner-Tamerlane Publishing Corp. All rights reserved. Used by permission of Alfred Music Publishing Co., Inc.

Page 203: Quoted from "I Will Not Pass Gas," from the American Legacy Foundation and the Advertising Council. Reprinted by permission.

Chapter 22

Pages 286–287, 289: Martin Luther King Jr., "I Have a Dream" speech, delivered 1963 to civil rights marchers in Washington, DC. Reprinted by arrangement with The Heirs to the Estate of Martin Luther King Jr., c/o Writers House as agent for the proprietor New York, NY. Copyright 1963 Dr. Martin Luther King Jr.; copyright renewed 1991 Coretta Scott King.

Chapter 24

Page 305: Frederick Buechner, *Peculiar Treasures: A Biblical Who's Who*, pp. 166–168. Copyright © 1979 by Frederick Buechner. Reprinted by permission of HarperCollins Publishers.

Chapter 29

Page 366: Reproduced by permission of Punch Ltd., www.punch.co.uk.

Chapter 30

Page 379: Cartoon from the *Saturday Review of Literature,* 1970. © Ed Frascino. Reprinted by permission.

Chapter 34

Pages 432, 433, 435–438: Deborah Tannen, *You Just Don't Understand: Men and Women in Conversation,* pp. 16, 42, 62, 72, 108, 120–122, 150, 212, 259, 279, 298. Ballantine, 1990. Copyright © 1990 by Deborah Tannen. Reprinted by permission of HarperCollins Publishers, and by Virago, an imprint of Little, Brown Book Group Ltd.

Chapter 35

Pages 446–449: Kathryn Stockett, *The Help,* copyright © 2009 by Kathryn Stockett. Used by permission of G. P. Putnam's Sons, a division of Penguin Group (USA) Inc. and by Penguin Books Ltd.

Chapter 36

Page 462: Reproduced by permission of Punch Ltd., www.punch.co.uk.

Pages 462–464: Cheris Kramarae and Paula Treichler, with assistance from Ann Russo, *The Feminist Dictionary* 2e, Pandora Press Routledge & Kegan Paul plc, London 1992. Used by permission of the authors.

Appendix A

Page A–2: Reproduced by permission of Punch Ltd., www.punch.co.uk.

Appendix C

Page A–8: "NCA Credo for Ethical Communication" reprinted by permission of National Communication Association, Washington, DC, www.natcom.org.

APPENDIX B

Feature Films That Illustrate Communication Theories

(With a strong assist from our cinematic colleagues and friends Russ Proctor, Ron Adler, and Darin Garard)

Interpersonal Messages

The Miracle Worker (general)
Pygmalion / My Fair Lady (symbolic interactionism)
Nell (symbolic interactionism)
American Teen (symbolic interactionism)
*Precious** (symbolic interactionism)
Black Like Me (symbolic interactionism)
The Color Purple (symbolic interactionism)
Mask (symbolic interactionism)
The Perks of Being a Wallflower (symbolic interactionism)
Stand and Deliver (symbolic interactionism)
She's All That (symbolic interactionism)
Lars and the Real Girl (CMM)
Pay It Forward (CMM)
Chocolat (CMM)
Don Juan DeMarco (CMM)
Life Is Beautiful (CMM)
Anger Management (CMM)
*Atonement** (expectancy violations)
*The Intouchables** (expectancy violations)
*Almost Famous** (expectancy violations)
How to Lose a Guy in 10 Days (expectancy violations)
*Crash** [2004] (expectancy violations)
Ferris Bueller's Day Off (expectancy violations)
The Sting (expectancy violations)

Relationship Development

*Good Will Hunting** (general)
Annie Hall (general)
Guess Who's Coming to Dinner (general)
*Brothers McMullen** (general)
*Bridget Jones's Diary** (general)
The Perks of Being a Wallflower (social penetration)
Before Sunrise / Before Sunset** (social penetration)
Get Low (social penetration)
Shrek (social penetration)
*Coming Home** (social penetration)
Waitress (social penetration)
*The Breakfast Club** (social penetration)
Driving Miss Daisy (uncertainty reduction)
My Big Fat Greek Wedding (uncertainty reduction)
*Witness** (uncertainty reduction)
*Knocked Up** (uncertainty reduction)
Down in the Delta (uncertainty reduction)
*Sideways** (uncertainty reduction)
The Chosen [1982] (uncertainty reduction)
The Social Network (SIP)
*Trust** (SIP)
Catfish (SIP)
American Teen (SIP)
You've Got Mail (SIP)
Sleepless in Seattle (SIP)

*Asterisk indicates movie is rated R.

Relationship Maintenance

Breaking Away (general)
(500) Days of Summer (relational dialectics)
*Children of a Lesser God** (relational dialectics)
*Cyrus** (relational dialectics)
*Knocked Up** (relational dialectics)
Bend It Like Beckham (relational dialectics)
Like Crazy (relational dialectics)
*The Story of Us** (relational dialectics)
Whale Rider (relational dialectics)
Brave (relational dialectics)
*Dead Man Walking** (CPM)
I've Loved You So Long (CPM)
Blue Jasmine (CPM)
*The Darjeeling Limited** (CPM)
*Trust** (CPM)
*Rachel Getting Married** (interactional view)
*Silver Linings Playbook** (interactional view)
*Little Miss Sunshine** (interactional view)
City Island (interactional view)
*Soul Food** (interactional view)
*Ordinary People** (interactional view)
Pieces of April (interactional view)
*Parenthood** (interactional view)
What's Eating Gilbert Grape (interactional view)
*When a Man Loves a Woman** (interactional view)
*One True Thing** (interactional view)

Influence

Norma Rae (general)
*Dead Man Walking** (social judgment)
The Great Debaters (social judgment)
A Civil Action (social judgment)
Hotel Rwanda (social judgment)
*Schindler's List** (social judgment)
An Inconvenient Truth (ELM)
12 Angry Men (ELM)
*My Cousin Vinny** (ELM)
*Up in the Air** (cognitive dissonance)
Swing Kids (cognitive dissonance)
*Thank You for Smoking** (cognitive dissonance)
10 Things I Hate About You (cognitive dissonance)
Casablanca (cognitive dissonance)

Group Communication
O Brother, Where Art Thou? (general)
Fantastic Mr. Fox (general)
Stagecoach [1939] (general)
Argo (functional perspective)
Apollo 13 (functional perspective)
Flight of the Phoenix (functional perspective)
Poseidon [2006] (functional perspective)
*Alien** (functional perspective)
*The 40-Year-Old Virgin** (symbolic convergence)
*The Breakfast Club** (symbolic convergence)
Dead Poets Society (symbolic convergence)
Paper Clips (symbolic convergence)

Organizational Communication
*Office Space** (general)
Moneyball (cultural approach)
Gung Ho (cultural approach)
Morning Glory (cultural approach)
Outsourced (cultural approach)
Friday Night Lights (cultural approach)
For Love or Money (cultural approach)
*Good Morning, Vietnam** (cultural approach)
Up the Down Staircase (cultural approach)
*The Firm** (cultural approach)
*A Few Good Men** (cultural approach)
The Social Network (CCO)
*Erin Brockovich** (critical theory)
The Devil Wears Prada (critical theory)
The Corporation (critical theory)
*North Country** (critical theory)
*Roger & Me** (critical theory)
*The Insider** (critical theory)
*Silkwood** (critical theory)

Public Rhetoric
*The King's Speech** (general)
Clarence Darrow (general)
Inherit the Wind (general)
Judgment at Nuremberg (general)
Lincoln (rhetoric)
The Great Debaters (rhetoric)
The Apostle (rhetoric)
*My Cousin Vinny** (rhetoric)
*The Verdict** (rhetoric)
*Amistad** (rhetoric)
*Nixon** (dramatism)
Malcolm X (dramatism)
Julius Caesar (dramatism)
Snow Falling on Cedars (dramatism)
*The Widow of St. Pierre** (dramatism)
*Stories We Tell** (narrative paradigm)
Lars and the Real Girl (narrative paradigm)
*Smoke** (narrative paradigm)
Big Fish (narrative paradigm)
Forrest Gump (narrative paradigm)

Media and Culture
*Blade Runner** (media ecology)
*Network** (media ecology)
*Broadcast News** (media ecology)
*Medium Cool** (media ecology)
Being There (media ecology)
*Amarcord** (semiotics)
The Manchurian Candidate [1962] (semiotics)
Stardust Memories (semiotics)
*The Seventh Seal** (semiotics)
The Year of Living Dangerously (cultural studies)
The Hunger Games (cultural studies)
*Bamboozled** (cultural studies)
Good Night and Good Luck (cultural studies)
Lee Daniels' The Butler (cultural studies)
*Blood Diamond** (cultural studies)
*Fahrenheit 9/11** (cultural studies)

Media Effects
*Network** (general)
The Candidate (general)
*Nurse Betty** (uses & grats)
Avalon (cultivation)
Being There (cultivation)
All the President's Men (agenda-setting)
*Wag the Dog** (agenda-setting)
Absence of Malice (agenda-setting)
Quiz Show (agenda-setting)

Intercultural Communication
A Passage to India (general)
*Do the Right Thing** (general)
*Tsotsi** (general)
Beasts of the Southern Wild (CAT)
Lone Star (general)
*Crash** [2004] (CAT)
Redhook Summer (CAT)
The Right Stuff (CAT)
Zelig (CAT)
*Win Win** (face-negotiation)
*The Joy Luck Club** (face-negotiation)
42 (face-negotiation)
Iron and Silk (face-negotiation)
Easy A (face-negotiation)
Antz (face-negotiation)
Gung Ho (face-negotiation)
Shall We Dance? [1997] (face-negotiation)
*Gran Torino** (speech codes)
Dances with Wolves (speech codes)
Kramer vs. Kramer (speech codes)
Hoop Dreams (speech codes)
Billy Elliot (speech codes)
Mean Girls (speech codes)
Clueless (speech codes)
*Working Girl** (speech codes)

Gender and Communication
*When Harry Met Sally** (genderlect styles)
The Break-Up (genderlect styles)
Sleepless in Seattle (genderlect styles)
*Diner** (genderlect styles)
Steel Magnolias (genderlect styles)
The Help (standpoint)
*Slumdog Millionaire** (standpoint)
*12 Years a Slave** (standpoint)
The Cider House Rules (standpoint)
*Waiting to Exhale** (standpoint)
*White Man's Burden** (standpoint)
*North Country** (muted group)
The Little Mermaid (muted group)
Fried Green Tomatoes (muted group)
*Maria Full of Grace** (muted group)
*Zero Dark Thirty** (muted group)
Tootsie (muted group)
Legally Blonde (muted group)

ENDNOTES

Chapter 1: Launching Your Study of Communication Theory

1 Judee Burgoon, "Expectancy Violations Theory," in *Conversations with Communication Theorists*, 2.0, McGraw-Hill, 2006. (DVD) Band 2; also available at http://www.afirstlook.com/edition_7/theory_resources/view_by_type, accessed January 23, 2013.
2 Ernest Bormann, *Communication Theory*, Sheffield, Salem, WI, 1989, p. 25.
3 Burgoon, *Conversations*. . . .
4 Fred Casmir, *Building Communication Theories: A Socio/Cultural Approach*, Lawrence Erlbaum, Hillsdale, NJ, 1994, p. 27.
5 Sir Karl Popper, *The Logic of Scientific Discovery*, Hutchinson, London, 1959, p. 59.
6 See "General Semantics of Alfred Korzybski" in the Theory List at www.afirstlook.com.
7 Frank E. X. Dance, "The Concept of Communication," *Journal of Communication*, Vol. 20, 1970, pp. 201–210.
8 Dance, p. 210.
9 Jennifer Daryl Slack, "Communication as Articulation," in *Communication as . . . Perspectives on Theory*, Gregory Shepherd, Jeffrey St. John, and Ted Striphas (eds.), Sage, Thousand Oaks, CA, 2006, p. 223.
10 Robert T. Craig, "Communication as a Practice," in *Communication as . . . Perspectives on Theory*, p. 39.
11 For further discussion of Blumer and this statement, see Chapter 5.
12 Wendell Johnson, *People in Quandaries*, Harper, New York, 1946, p. 26.
13 Celeste Condit, "Communication as Relationality," in *Communication as . . . Perspectives on Theory*, p. 3.
14 Frank E. X. Dance, "Toward a Theory of Human Communication," in *Human Communication Theory: Original Essays*, Holt, Rinehart, and Winston, 1967, p. 289.

Chapter 2: Talk About Theory

1 http://www.nfl.com/videos/nfl-super-bowl-commercials/0ap2000000134659/Brotherhood, accessed September 12, 2013.
2 Ken Wheaton, "Super Bowl Ad Review: The Good, the Bad, the Clydesdales," *Advertising Age*, February 4, 2013, p. 20.
3 http://www.gazette.net/article/20130204/NEWS/130209706/-1/ravens-nope-x2014-clydesdales-eke-out-super-bowl-victory&template=gazette, accessed February 11, 2013.
4 Tony Schwartz, *The Responsive Chord*, Doubleday, New York, 1973, pp. 1–40.
5 C. G. Jung, *The Archetypes and the Collective Unconscious*, 2nd ed., Princeton University, Princeton, NJ, 1981.
6 Michael Osborn, "The Evolution of the Archetypal Sea in Rhetoric and Poetic," *Quarterly Journal of Speech*, Vol. 63, 1977, pp. 347–363.
7 James A. Anderson, *Communication Theory: Epistemological Foundations*, Guilford, New York, 1996, p. 27.
8 Anderson, p. 120.
9 Philosophers call this a question of *ontology*—the study of existence.
10 William Henley, "Invictus," in *The Columbia Anthology of British Poetry*, Carl Woodring and James Shapiro (eds.), Columbia University, New York, 1995, p. 685.
11 Anderson, p. 133.
12 C. S. Lewis, *The Abolition of Man*, Macmillan, New York, 1944, p. 309.
13 Philosophers call this a question of *axiology*—the study of ethical criteria.
14 George C. Homans, *The Nature of Social Science*, Harcourt, New York, 1967, p. 4.
15 William Melody and Robin Mansell, "The Debate over Critical vs. Administrative Research: Circularity or Challenge," *Journal of Communication*, Vol. 33, No. 3, 1983, p. 112.
16 Stan Deetz, "Fundamental Issues in Communication Studies," unpublished paper distributed to students enrolled in his communication theory class.
17 Robert Ivie, "The Social Relevance of Rhetorical Scholarship," *Quarterly Journal of Speech*, Vol. 81, No. 2, 1995, p. 138a.

Chapter 3: Weighing the Words

1 Abraham Kaplan, *The Conduct of Inquiry*, Chandler, San Francisco, CA, 1964, p. 295.
2 James McCroskey, "Validity of the PRCA as an Index of Communication Apprehension," *Communication Monographs*, Vol. 45, 1978, pp. 192–203.
3 Walter Mischel, "Personality Dispositions Revisited and Revised: A View After Three Decades," in *Handbook of Personality: Theory and Research*, Lawrence Pervin (ed.), Guilford, New York, NY, 1990, pp. 111–134.
4 Francis Hylighen, "Occam's Razor," *Principia Cybernetica Web*, http://pespmc1.vub.ac.be/OCCAMRAZ.html, accessed September 16, 2013.
5 http://www.brainyquote.com/quotes/authors/a/albert_einstein.html, accessed September 16, 2013.
6 Karl Popper, *Conjectures and Refutations: The Growth of Scientific Knowledge*, Harper & Row, New York, 1965, pp. 36–37.
7 David Hume, *An Enquiry Concerning Human Understanding*, Tom L. Deauchamp (ed.), Oxford University, London, 1999, p. 211.
8 Donn Byrne, "An Overview (and Underview) of Research and Theory within the Attraction Paradigm," *Journal of Social and Personal Relationships*, Vol. 14, 1997, pp. 417–431.
9 See Chapter 29: "Cultivation Theory of George Gerbner."
10 Eric Rothenbuhler, "Communication as Ritual," in *Communication as . . . Perspectives on Theory*, Gregory Shepherd, Jeffrey St. John, and Ted Striphas (eds.), Sage, Thousand Oaks, CA, 2006, p. 19.
11 Klaus Krippendorff, "The Ethics of Constructing Communication," in *Rethinking Communication, Vol. 1: Paradigm Issues*, Brenda Dervin, Lawrence Grossberg, Barbara J. O'Keefe, and Ellen Wartella (eds.), Sage, Newbury Park, CA, 1989, p. 88.
12 William H. Melody and Robin Mansell, "The Debate over Critical vs. Administrative Research: Circularity or Challenge," *Journal of Communication*, Vol. 33, No. 3, 1983, p. 103.
13 Ernest G. Bormann, *Communication Theory*, Sheffield, Salem, WI, 1989, p. 214.
14 Krippendorff, "The Ethics of Constructing Communication," p. 83.
15 Barbara Warnick, "Left in Context: What Is the Critic's Role?" *Quarterly Journal of Speech*, Vol. 78, 1992, pp. 232–237.

16 Edwin Black, "Gettysburg and Silence," *Quarterly Journal of Speech*, Vol. 80, 1994, pp. 21–36.
17 David Zarefsky, "Approaching Lincoln's Second Inaugural Address," in *The Practice of Rhetorical Criticism*, 2nd ed., James R. Andrews (ed.), Longman, New York, 1990, p. 69.
18 John Stewart, "A Postmodern Look at Traditional Communication Postulates," *Western Journal of Speech Communication*, Vol. 55, 1991, p. 374.
19 Kenneth Gergen, *Toward Transformation in Social Knowledge*, Springer-Verlag, New York, 1982, p. 109.
20 Norman K. Denzin and Yvonna S. Lincoln, "Introduction: The Discipline and Practice of Qualitative Research," in *Handbook of Qualitative Research*, 2nd ed., Norman K. Denzin and Yvonna S. Lincoln (eds.), Sage, Thousand Oaks, CA, p. 3.
21 http://rescomp.stanford.edu/~cheshire/EinsteinQuotes.html, accessed September 16, 2013.
22 David J. Garrow, *Bearing the Cross*, William Morrow, New York, 1986, pp. 231–286.
23 Clifford Geertz, "Thick Description: Toward an Interpretive Theory of Culture," in *The Interpretation of Cultures*, Basic Books, New York, 1973, p. 5.
24 Bernie Miklasz, "A perfect union: Stan The Man and St. Louis," *St. Louis Post-Dispatch*, January 20, 2013, http://www.stltoday.com/sports/columns/bernie-miklasz/a-perfect-union-stan-the-man-and-st-louis/article_1f42f8b6-a9da-530f-9492-2a767479bd19.html, accessed January 27, 2013.
25 Isabel Briggs Myers, *Introduction to Type*, Consulting Psychologists, Palo Alto, CA, p. 5.
26 Gregory Bateson, *Mind and Nature: A Necessary Unity*, Bantam, New York, 1979, p. 242.
27 Marie Hochmuth Nichols, *Rhetoric and Criticism*, Louisiana State University, Baton Rouge, LA, 1963, p. 18.

Chapter 4: Mapping the Territory

1 Robert T. Craig, "Communication Theory as a Field," *Communication Theory*, Vol. 9, 1999, p. 122.
2 Robert T. Craig, "Communication as a Practical Discipline," in *Rethinking Communication, Vol. 1: Paradigm Issues*, Brenda Dervin, Lawrence Grossberg, Barbara J. O'Keefe, and Ellen Wartella (eds.), Sage, Newbury Park, CA, 1989, pp. 97–122.
3 Craig, "Communication Theory as a Field," p. 120.
4 Ibid., p. 130.
5 The identification and titles of the seven traditions are taken from Craig (see note 3). I have altered his order of presentation to match the conceptual plan of Figure 4–1. The boldfaced definitions of communication within each tradition are a paraphrase of, and consistent with, Craig's conception. The selection of a particular research study for each tradition was my decision and reflects the features of the tradition I chose to emphasize.
6 Em Griffin and Glenn G. Sparks, "Friends Forever: A Longitudinal Exploration of Intimacy in Same-Sex Friends and Platonic Pairs," *Journal of Social and Personal Relationships*, Vol. 7, 1990, pp. 29–46.
7 Harold H. Kelley, Ellen Berscheid, Andrew Christensen, John Harvey, Ted Huston, George Levinger, Evie McClintock, Letitia Anne Peplau, and Donald Peterson, *Close Relationships*, W. H. Freeman, New York, 1983, p. 38.
8 Andrew M. Ledbetter, Em Griffin, and Glenn G. Sparks, "Forecasting 'Friends Forever': A Longitudinal Investigation of Sustained Closeness between Best Friends," *Personal Relationships*, Vol. 14, 2007, pp. 343–350.
9 Norbert Wiener, *The Human Use of Human Beings*, Avon, New York, 1967, p. 23.
10 Malcolm Parks, *Personal Relationships and Personal Networks*, Lawrence Erlbaum, Mahwah, NJ, 2007, pp. 87–96.
11 Cicero, *De Oratore*, E. W. Sutton and H. Rackham (trans.), Harvard University, Cambridge, MA, 1942, p. 25.
12 Aristotle, *On Rhetoric: A Theory of Civic Discourse*, 2nd ed., George A. Kennedy (trans.), Oxford University Press, New York, 2007, 2.4.2.
13 Ibid., 2.4.26.
14 Bill Withers, "Lean on Me," 1972.
15 Eugene Garver, *Aristotle's Rhetoric: An Art of Character*, University of Chicago, Chicago, IL, 1994, pp. 104–138.
16 Em Griffin, *Making Friends (and Making Them Count)*, InterVarsity Press, Downers Grove, IL, 1987.
17 Michael Monsour, "Meanings of Intimacy in Cross- and Same-Sex Friendships," *Journal of Social and Personal Relationships*, Vol. 9, 1992, pp. 277–295.
18 Paul Kay and Willet Kempton, "What Is the Sapir–Whorf Hypothesis?" *American Anthropologist*, Vol. 86, 1984, pp. 65–79.
19 Edward Sapir, "The Status of Linguistics as a Science," in *Selected Writings*, David Mandelbaum (ed.), University of California, Berkeley, CA, 1951 (1929), p. 160.
20 James Carey, *Communication as Culture*, Unwin Hyman, Boston, MA, 1989, p. 23.
21 For an extended discussion of the socio-cultural concept, see Chapter 6: "Coordinated Management of Meaning of W. Barnett Pearce & Vernon Cronen."
22 Patricia M. Sias, Renee Heath, Tara Perry, Deborah Silva, and Bryan Fix, "Narratives of Workplace Friendship Deterioration," *Journal of Social and Personal Relationships*, Vol. 21, 2004, pp. 323–324.
23 Ibid., p. 337.
24 Kathy Werking, "Cross-Sex Friendship Research as Ideological Practice," *Handbook of Personal Relationships*, 2nd ed., Steve Duck (ed.), John Wiley & Sons, New York, 1997, pp. 391–410.
25 Ibid., p. 397.
26 Ibid.
27 Carl Rogers, "This Is Me," in *On Becoming a Person*, Houghton Mifflin, Boston, MA, 1961, p. 24.
28 William K. Rawlins, *The Compass of Friendship: Narratives, Identities, and Dialogues*, Sage, Thousand Oaks, CA, 2009, p. 72.
29 Ibid., pp. 94–95.
30 Ibid., p. 95.
31 *Ibid.*, p. 72.
32 Robert T. Craig and Heidi L. Muller (eds.), *Theorizing Communication: Readings Across Traditions*, Sage, Thousand Oaks, CA, 2007, p. 499.
33 Richard L. Johannesen, "Communication Ethics: Centrality, Trends, and Controversies," in *Communication Yearbook 25*, William B. Gudykunst (ed.), Lawrence Erlbaum, Mahwah, NJ, 2001, pp. 201–235.
34 "NCA Credo for Ethical Communication," National Communication Association, Washington, DC, http://www.natcom.org/uploadedFiles/About_NCA/Leadership_and_Governance/Public_Policy_Platform/PDF-Policy-Platform-NCA_Credo_for_Ethical_Communication.pdf, accessed September 16, 2013.
35 Philosophers refer to these three approaches as (1) teleological ethics, (2) deontological ethics, and (3) virtue ethics.
36 Rawlins, pp. 175–184.

Interpersonal Messages

1 An earlier version of these game metaphors appeared in Em Griffin, *Making Friends*, InterVarsity Press, Downers Grove, IL, 1987, pp. 12–18.

Chapter 5: Symbolic Interactionism

1 George Herbert Mead, *Mind, Self, and Society*, University of Chicago, Chicago, IL, [1934] 1962.
2 The three premises are found in Herbert Blumer, *Symbolic Interactionism*, Prentice-Hall, Englewood Cliffs, NJ, 1969, p. 2. I've paraphrased the principles for stylistic consistency and to avoid gender-specific language.
3 Gil Musolf, "The Chicago School," in Larry T. Reynolds and Nancy J. Herman-Kinney (eds.), *Handbook of Symbolic Interactionism*, AltaMira, Walnut Creek, CA, 2003, p. 93.
4 Jane Wagner, *The Search for Signs of Intelligent Life in the Universe*, Harper Perennial, New York, 1990, pp. 15, 18.
5 Musolf, pp. 97–98.
6 For a fascinating account of a gorilla that developed these symbolic associations with the word *kitten*, see Francine Patterson, *Koko's Kitten*, Scholastic, New York, 1985. Mead wouldn't have been troubled by the existence of an animal that can communicate hundreds of symbols in American Sign Language. He regarded the symbol-using difference between humans and other primates as one of great magnitude—a quantitative rather than a qualitative distinction.
7 Peter M. Hall, "Structuring Symbolic Interaction: Communication and Power" in *Communication Yearbook 4*, Dan Nimmo (ed.), Transaction, New Brunswick, NJ, 1980, p. 50.
8 Jodi O'Brien, *The Production of Reality*, 5th ed., Pine Forge, Thousand Oaks, CA, 2011, p. 54.
9 Douglas Hofstadter, "Changes in Default Words and Images Engendered by Rising Consciousness," in *The Production of Reality*, 3rd ed., Jodi O'Brien and Peter Kollock (eds.), Pine Forge, Thousand Oaks, CA, 2001, p. 158.
10 Mead, p. 43.
11 Peter Kollock and Jodi O'Brien (eds.), *The Production of Reality*, 2nd ed., Pine Forge, Thousand Oaks, CA, 1994, p. 63.
12 Kingsley Davis, "Final Note on a Case of Extreme Isolation," in *The Production of Reality*, 5th ed., pp. 75–80.
13 Oliver Sacks, *Seeing Voices: A Journey Into the World of the Deaf*, Vintage, New York, 2000.
14 Harper Lee, *To Kill a Mockingbird*, Warner, New York, 1982, p. 282.
15 Ralph Waldo Emerson, "Astraea," *The Works of Ralph Waldo Emerson*, Vol. III, Nottingham Society, Philadelphia, PA, n.d., p. 121.
16 David Lundgren, "Social Feedback and Self-Appraisals: Current Status of the Mead-Cooley Hypothesis," *Symbolic Interaction*, Vol. 27, 2004, p. 267.
17 Gregory Shepherd, "Transcendence," in *Communication as . . . Perspectives on Theory*, Gregory Shepherd, Jeffrey St. John, and Ted Striphas (eds.), Sage, Thousand Oaks, CA, 2006, p. 24.
18 Andrew Weigert and Viktor Gecas, "Self," in *Handbook of Symbolic Interactionism*, p. 267.
19 George Herbert Mead, "The Social Self," *Journal of Philosophy, Psychology and Scientific Methods*, Vol. 10, 1913, p. 375.
20 Mead, *Mind, Self, and Society*, p. 174.
21 Thomas Scheff, "A Theory of Genius," in *The Production of Reality*, 5th ed., Jodi O'Brien (ed.), Pine Forge, Thousand Oaks, CA, 2011, p. 137.
22 Shanyang Zhao, "The Digital Self: Through the Looking Glass of Telepresent Others," *Symbolic Interaction*, Vol. 28, 2005, pp. 387–405.
23 Kollock and O'Brien, 2nd ed., p. 63.
24 Michael Katovich and David Mains, "Society," in *Handbook of Symbolic Interactionism*, p. 292.
25 William Shakespeare, *As You Like It*, Act II, Scene VII, line 139, in *The Riverside Shakespeare*, G. Blakemore Evans (ed.), Houghton Mifflin, Boston, MA, 1974, p. 381.
26 Erving Goffman, *The Presentation of Self in Everyday Life*, Doubleday Anchor, Garden City, NY, 1959.
27 Ibid., p. 56.
28 Joan P. Emerson, "Behavior in Private Places: Sustaining Definitions of Reality in Gynecological Examinations," in *The Production of Reality*, 4th ed., pp. 201–214.
29 Jean Mizer, "Cipher in the Snow," *Today's Education*, Vol. 53, November 1964, pp. 8–10.
30 George Bernard Shaw, "Pygmalion," *Selected Plays*, Dodd, Mead, New York, 1948, p. 270.
31 Saul Alinsky, *Reveille for Radicals*, Vintage, New York, 1969 (1946), pp. 77–78.
32 Ronald Arnett, "Emmanuel Levinas: Priority of the Other," in *Ethical Communication: Moral Stances in Human Dialogue I*, Clifford Christians and John Merrill (eds.), University of Missouri, Columbia, MO, 2009, p. 203.
33 Quoted in James H. Olthius, "Face-to Face: Ethical Asymmetry or the Symmetry of Mutuality," in *Knowing the Other-wise*, James H. Olthuis (ed.), Fordham, New York, 1997, p. 139.
34 Arnett, p. 205.
35 Ibid., p. 200.
36 Sheldon Stryker, "From Mead to a Structural Symbolic Interactionism and Beyond," *Annual Review of Sociology*, Vol. 34, 2008, p. 18.
37 Ibid., p. 16.
38 Lundgren, p. 267.
39 Randall Collins, "Toward a Neo-Meadian Sociology of Mind," *Symbolic Interaction*, Vol. 12, 1989, p. 1.

Chapter 6: Coordinated Management of Meaning (CMM)

1 Kimberly Pearce, *Compassionate Communicating Because Moments Matter: Poetry, Prose, and Practices*, Lulu, 2012, p. 33.
2 W. Barnett Pearce, *Interpersonal Communication: Making Social Worlds*, HarperCollins, New York, 1994, p 366.
3 Ibid, p. 19.
4 W. Barnett Pearce, "'Listening for the Wisdom in the Public's Whining' or 'Working to Construct Patterns of Public Communication,'" unpublished manuscript.
5 W. Barnett Pearce and Kimberly A. Pearce, "Transcendent Storytelling: Abilities for Systemic Practitioners and Their Clients," *Human Systems: The Journal of Systemic Consultation & Management*, Vol. 9, 1998, pp. 178–179.
6 W. Barnett Pearce, *Interpersonal Communication*, p. 75.
7 W. Barnett Pearce, "A Sailing Guide for Social Constructionists," in *Social Approaches to Human Communication*, Wendy Leeds-Hurwitz (ed.), Guilford, New York, 1995, pp. 88–113.
8 W. Barnett Pearce, *Making Social Worlds: A Communication Perspective*, Blackwell, Malden, MA, 2007, pp. 210–213.
9 Kimberly Pearce, *Compassionate Communicating*, p. 55.
10 Ibid., p. 56.
11 W. Barnett Pearce, "Glossary," *Human Systems: The Journal of Systemic Consultation & Management*, Vol. 15, 2004, p. 9.
12 Vernon Cronen and W. Barnett Pearce, "Logical Force in Interpersonal Communication: A New Concept of the 'Necessity' in Social Behavior," *Communication*, Vol. 6, 1981, pp. 5–67.
13 Vernon Cronen, W. Barnett Pearce, and Lonna Snavely, "A Theory of Rule-Structure and Types of Episodes and a Study of Perceived Enmeshment in Undesired Repetitive Patterns ('URPs')," in *Communication Yearbook 3*, Dan Nimmo (ed.), Transaction Books, New Brunswick, NJ, 1979, pp. 225–240.
14 W. Barnett Pearce, Stephen W. Littlejohn, and Alison Alexander, "The Quixotic Quest for Civility: Patterns of

Interaction Between the New Christian Right and Secular Humanists," in *Secularization and Fundamentalism Reconsidered,* Jeffrey K. Hadden and Anson Shupe (eds.), Paragon, New York, 1989, pp. 152–177.

15 W. Barnett Pearce, *Communication and the Human Condition,* Southern Illinois University, Carbondale, IL, 1989, pp. 32–33.

16 Kimberly Pearce, *Compassionate Communicating,* p. 33.

17 W. Barnett Pearce, "At Home in the Universe with Miracles and Horizons: Reflections on Personal and Social Evolution," in *The Coordinated Management of Meaning: A Festschrift in Honor of W. Barnett Pearce,* Stephen Littlejohn (ed.), Fairleigh Dickinson University, Madison, NJ, 2013, p. 26.

18 Kimberly Pearce, *Compassionate Communicating,* p. 40.

19 Digest of Educational Statistics, http://nces.ed.gov/programs/digest/d11/ta; accessed December 19, 2011.

20 W. Barnett Pearce, "At Home in the Universe," p. 39.

21 Ibid, p. 43; Kimberly Pearce, *Compassionate Communicating,* p. 3.

22 Kimberly Pearce, p. 10.

23 Kimberly Pearce, pp. 3, 46, 70–71.

24 W. Barnett Pearce, "The Theory and Practice of Transforming Communication," lecture presented to the Hugh Downs School of Human Communication, Arizona State University, Tempe, AZ, April 16, 2008.

25 Tina Fey, *Bossypants,* Little, Brown & Co., New York, NY, 2011, p. 84.

26 W. Barnett Pearce, *Interpersonal Communication,* p. 366.

27 W. Barnett Pearce and Kimberly A. Pearce, "Combining Passions and Abilities: Toward Dialogic Virtuosity," *Southern Communication Journal,* Vol. 65, 2000, p. 172.

28 Kimberly Pearce, "On the Significance of 'The 7th Miracle' for Personal and Social Evolution," in *Festschrift,* p. 26.

29 W. Barnett Pearce and Stephen W. Littlejohn, *Moral Conflict: When Social Worlds Collide,* Sage, Thousand Oaks, CA, 1997, p. 37.

30 Martin Buber, *I and Thou,* 2nd ed., R. G. Smith (trans.), Scribner's, New York, 1958, pp. 60, 69.

31 Martin Buber, *Between Man and Man,* Macmillan, New York, 1965, p. 204.

32 Ronald Arnett, *Communication and Community,* Southern Illinois University, Carbondale, IL, 1986, p. 37.

33 Robert T. Craig and Heidi L. Muller, "Concluding Remarks," in *Theorizing Communication: Readings Across Traditions,* Robert T. Craig and Heidi L. Muller (eds.), Sage, Thousand Oaks, CA, 2007, pp. 499–500.

34 http://publicdialogue.org; http://www.cmminstitute.net

35 W. Barnett Pearce, "At Home in the Universe," p. 36.

36 J. Kevin Barge and W. Barnett Pearce, "A Reconnaissance of CMM Research," *Human Systems,* Vol. 15, 2004, pp. 13–32.

37 J. Kevin Barge, "Articulating CMM as a Practical Theory," *Human Systems,* Vol. 15, 2004, pp. 193–204.

38 Gabrielle Parker, "CMM: Reports from Users," p. 43, http://www.pearceassociates.com/essays/reports_from_users.pdf, accessed March 7, 2013.

39 Kimberly Pearce, *Compassionate Communicating,* pp. 30–45.

Chapter 7: Expectancy Violations Theory

1 Judee K. Burgoon, "A Communication Model of Personal Space Violations: Explication and an Initial Test," *Human Communication Research,* Vol. 4, 1978, pp. 129–142.

2 Ibid., p. 130.

3 Edward T. Hall, *The Hidden Dimension,* Doubleday, Garden City, NY, 1966, p. 1.

4 W. H. Auden, "Prologue: The Birth of Architecture," in *About the House,* Random House, New York, 1966, p. 14.

5 Judee K. Burgoon and Jerold Hale, "Nonverbal Expectancy Violations: Model Elaboration and Application to Immediacy Behaviors," *Communication Monographs,* Vol. 55, 1988, p. 58.

6 *Random House Webster's Electronic Dictionary and Thesaurus,* College Edition, WordPerfect, Orem, UT, 1994.

7 Judee K. Burgoon, "Cross-Cultural and Intercultural Applications of Expectancy Violations Theory," in *Intercultural Communication Theory,* Richard Wiseman (ed.), Sage, Thousand Oaks, CA, 1995, pp. 194–214.

8 Judee K. Burgoon and Joseph Walther, "Nonverbal Expectancies and the Evaluative Consequences of Violations," *Human Communication Research,* Vol. 17, 1990, p. 236.

9 Edward Hall, "A System of Notation of Proxemic Behavior," *American Anthropologist,* Vol. 41, 1963, pp. 1003–1026.

10 Cited in Judee K. Burgoon, Valerie Manusov, Paul Mineo, and Jerold Hale, "Effects of Gaze on Hiring, Credibility, Attraction, and Relational Message Interpretation," *Journal of Nonverbal Behavior,* Vol. 9, 1985, p. 133.

11 Douglas Kelley and Judee K. Burgoon, "Understanding Marital Satisfaction and Couple Type as Functions of Relational Expectations," *Human Communication Research,* Vol. 18, 1991, pp. 40–69.

12 Beth A. LePoire and Judee K. Burgoon, "Two Contrasting Explanations of Involvement Violations: Expectancy Violations Theory Versus Discrepancy Arousal Theory," *Human Communication Research,* Vol. 20, 1994, pp. 560–591.

13 Graham Chapman, John Cleese, Terry Gilliam, Eric Idle, Terry Jones, and Michael Palin, *The Complete Monty Python's Flying Circus: All the Words,* Volume One, Pantheon, New York, 1989, p. 40.

14 Judee K. Burgoon, "Nonverbal Violations of Expectations," in *Nonverbal Interaction,* John Wiemann and Randall P. Harrison (eds.), Sage, Beverly Hills, CA, 1983, p. 101.

15 Paul A. Mongeau, Colleen Carey, and Mary Lynn Williams, "First Date Initiation and Enactment: An Expectancy Violation Approach," in *Differences and Similarities in Communication,* Daniel J. Canary and Kathryn Dindia (eds.), Lawrence Erlbaum, Mahwah, NJ, 1998, pp. 413–426.

16 Judee K. Burgoon, Lesa Stern, and Leesa Dillman, *Interpersonal Adaptation: Dyadic Interaction Patterns,* Cambridge University, Cambridge, UK, 1995.

17 For Em Griffin's treatment of Abraham Maslow's hierarchy of needs, go to *www.afirstlook.com* and click on Theory List.

18 Burgoon, "Cross-Cultural and Intercultural Applications," p. 209.

19 Peter A. Andersen, Laura K. Guerrero, David B. Buller, and Peter F. Jorgensen, "An Empirical Comparison of Three Theories of Nonverbal Immediacy Exchange," *Human Communication Research,* Vol. 24, 1998, pp. 501–535.

20 Immanuel Kant, "On a Supposed Right to Lie from Altruistic Motives," in *Critique of Practical Reason and Other Writings in Moral Philosophy,* Lewis White Beck (trans. and ed.), University of Chicago, Chicago, IL, 1964, p. 346.

21 Immanuel Kant, *Groundwork of the Metaphysics of Morals,* H. J. Paton (trans.), Harper Torchbooks, New York, 1964, p. 88.

Relationship Development

1 Harold H. Kelley, Ellen Berscheid, Andrew Christensen, John Harvey, Ted Huston, George Levinger, Evie McClintock, Letitia Anne Peplau, and Donald Peterson, *Close Relationships,* W. H. Freeman, New York, 1983, p. 38.

2 Keith Davis and Michael Todd, "Friendship and Love Relationships" in *Advances in Descriptive Psychology*, Vol. 2, Keith Davis (ed.), JAI, Greenwich, CT, 1982, pp. 79–122.
3 Carl Rogers, "The Necessary and Sufficient Conditions of Therapeutic Personality Change," *Journal of Consulting Psychology*, Vol. 21, 1957, pp. 95–103.
4 Carl Rogers, "This Is Me," in *On Becoming a Person*, Houghton Mifflin, Boston, MA, 1961, p. 16.
5 Carl Rogers, "The Characteristics of a Helping Relationship," in *On Becoming a Person*, p. 52.
6 See Ron Adler and Russell Proctor II, *Looking Out/Looking In*, 13th ed., Wadsworth, Belmont, CA, 2011; and John Stewart, *Bridges Not Walls*, 11th ed., McGraw-Hill, New York, 2011.
7 Gary S. Becker, *The Economic Approach to Human Behavior*, University of Chicago, Chicago, IL, 1976.
8 http://www.eharmony.com/why, accessed March 12, 2013.

Chapter 8: Social Penetration Theory

1 Dalmas Taylor and Irwin Altman, "Communication in Interpersonal Relationships: Social Penetration Processes," in *Interpersonal Processes: New Directions in Communication Research*, Michael Roloff and Gerald Miller (eds.), Sage, Newbury Park, CA, 1987, p. 259.
2 C. Arthur VanLear, "The Formation of Social Relationships: A Longitudinal Study of Social Penetration," *Human Communication Research, Vol. 13, 1987*, pp. 299–322.
3 Harold H. Kelley and John W. Thibaut, *Interpersonal Relationships*, John Wiley & Sons, New York, 1978.
4 John Stuart Mill, *A System of Logic*, J. W. Parker, London, 1843, Book VI, Chapter XII.
5 J. M. Rist, *Epicurus: An Introduction*, Cambridge University, Cambridge, England, 1972, p. 124.
6 Epicurus, "Leading Doctrines, 8," cited in R. D. Hicks, *Stoic and Epicurean*, Charles Scribner's Sons, New York, 1910, p. 183.
7 Ayn Rand, *The Fountainhead*, Signet, New York, 1971, p. x.
8 Irwin Altman, Anne Vinsel, and Barbara Brown, "Dialectical Conceptions in Social Psychology: An Application to Social Penetration and Privacy Regulation," in *Advances in Experimental Social Psychology*, Vol. 14, Leonard Berkowitz (ed.), Academic Press, New York, 1981, p. 139.
9 Irwin Altman, "Toward a Transactional Perspective: A Personal Journey," in *Human Behavior and Environment: Advances in Theory and Research, Volume 13: Environment and Behavior Studies*, Irwin Altman and Kathleen Christensen (eds.), Plenum, New York, 1990, pp. 225–255.
10 Anne Vinsel, Barbara B. Brown, Irwin Altman, and Carolyn Foss, "Privacy Regulation, Territorial Displays, and Effectiveness of Individual Functioning," *Journal of Personality and Social Psychology*, Vol. 39, 1980, pp. 1104–1115.
11 Ibid, p. 1114.
12 Julia T. Wood, "Ethics, Justice, and the 'Private Sphere,'" *Women's Studies in Communication*, Vol. 21, 1998, p. 145.
13 Paul H. Wright, "Self-Referent Motivation and the Intrinsic Quality of Friendship," *Journal of Social and Personal Relationships*, Vol. 1, 1984, pp. 115–130.
14 Richard Conville, *Relational Transitions: The Evolution of Personal Relationships*, Praeger, New York, 1991, pp. 19–40.
15 John 15:13, *The New American Bible*, J. P. Kennedy & Sons, New York, 1970.

Chapter 9: Uncertainty Reduction Theory

1 Charles R. Berger, "Uncertainty and Information Exchange in Developing Relationships," in *Handbook of Personal Relationships*, Steve Duck (ed.), Wiley, New York, 1988, p. 244.
2 Charles R. Berger and Richard Calabrese, "Some Explorations in Initial Interaction and Beyond: Toward a Developmental Theory of Interpersonal Communication," *Human Communication Research*, Vol. 1, 1975, p. 100.
3 Charles R. Berger, "Beyond Initial Interaction: Uncertainty, Understanding, and the Development of Interpersonal Relationships," in *Language and Social Psychology*, H. Giles and R. St. Clair (eds.), Basil Blackwell, Oxford, UK, 1979, pp. 122–144.
4 Charles R. Berger and William B. Gudykunst, "Uncertainty and Communication," in *Progress in Communication Sciences*, Vol. X, Brenda Dervin and Melvin Voigt (eds.), Ablex, Norwood, NJ, 1991, p. 23.
5 For an excellent introduction to attribution theory, see Kelly Shaver, *An Introduction to Attribution Processes*, Lawrence Erlbaum, Hillsdale, NJ, 1983. Heider's theory is also described in the first two editions of this text (1991, 1994); click on Theory List at *www.afirstlook.com*.
6 Berger and Calabrese, pp. 99–112.
7 Joseph Cappella, "Mutual Influence in Expressive Behavior: Adult–Adult and Infant–Adult Dyadic Interaction," *Psychological Bulletin*, Vol. 89, 1981, pp. 101–132.
8 Berger and Gudykunst, p. 25.
9 Malcolm Parks and Mara Adelman, "Communication Networks and the Development of Romantic Relationships: An Extension of Uncertainty Reduction Theory," *Human Communication Research*, Vol. 10, 1983, pp. 55–79.
10 Ellen Berscheid and Elaine Walster, *Interpersonal Attraction*, 2nd ed., Addison-Wesley, Reading, MA, 1978, pp. 61–89.
11 Charles R. Berger, *Planning Strategic Interaction*, Lawrence Erlbaum, Mahwah, NJ, 1997, p. 17.
12 Charles R. Berger, "Goals, Plans, and Mutual Understanding in Relationships," in *Individuals in Relationships*, Steve Duck (ed.), Sage, Newbury Park, CA, 1993, p. 34.
13 Charles R. Berger, "Message Production Under Uncertainty," in *Developing Communication Theories*, Gerry Philipsen and Terrance Albrecht (eds.), State University of New York, Albany, NY, 1997, p. 39.
14 Charles R. Berger, "Producing Messages Under Uncertainty," in *Message Production: Advances in Communication Theory*, John O. Greene (ed.), Lawrence Erlbaum, Mahwah, NJ, 1997, p. 222.
15 Personal correspondence from Charles Berger to Em Griffin.
16 Artemio Ramirez Jr., Joseph B. Walther, Judee K. Burgoon, and Michael Sunnafrank, "Information-Seeking Strategies, Uncertainty, and Computer-Mediated Communication: Toward a Conceptual Model," *Human Communication Research*, Vol. 28, 2002, p. 220.
17 Berger, "Message Production Under Uncertainty," p. 39.
18 Charles R. Berger, "Inscrutable Goals, Uncertain Plans, and the Production of Communicative Action," in *Communication and Social Influence Processes*, Charles R. Berger and Michael Burgoon (eds.), Michigan State University, East Lansing, MI, 1995, p. 17.
19 Berger, *Planning Strategic Interaction*, pp. 132–135.
20 Proverbs 15:22, New Revised Standard Version of the Bible.
21 Leanne K. Knobloch and Denise H. Solomon, "Measuring the Sources and Content of Relational Uncertainty," *Communication Studies*, Vol. 50, 1999, pp. 261–278.
22 Denise H. Solomon and Leanne K. Knobloch, "A Model of Relational Turbulence: The Role of Intimacy, Relational Uncertainty, and Interference from Partners in Appraisals of Irritations," *Journal of Social and Personal Relationships*, Vol. 21, 2004, pp. 795–816.

23 Leanne K. Knobloch and Jennifer A. Theiss, "An Actor-Partner Interdependence Model of Relational Turbulence: Cognitions and Emotions," *Journal of Social and Personal Relationships*, Vol. 27, 2010, pp. 596–597.
24 Leanne K. Knobloch and Amy L. Delaney, "Themes of Relational Uncertainty and Interference from Partners in Depression," *Health Communication*, 2012, pp. 1–16.
25 Leanne K. Knobloch and Jennifer A. Theiss, "Experiences of U.S. Military Couples During the Post-Deployment Transition: Applying the Relational Turbulence Model," *Journal of Social and Personal Relationships*, Vol. 29, 2012, pp. 423–450.
26 Leanne K. Knobloch and Denise H. Solomon, "Information Seeking Beyond Initial Interaction: Negotiating Relational Uncertainty Within Close Relationships," *Human Communication Research*, Vol. 28, 2002, pp. 243–257.
27 Charles R. Berger, "Communicating Under Uncertainty," in *Interpersonal Processes: New Directions in Communication Research*, Michael Roloff and Gerald Miller (eds.), Sage, Newbury Park, CA, 1987, p. 40.
28 Kathy Kellermann and Rodney Reynolds, "When Ignorance Is Bliss: The Role of Motivation to Reduce Uncertainty in Uncertainty Reduction Theory," *Human Communication Research*, Vol. 17, 1990, p. 7.
29 Ibid., p. 71.
30 Michael Sunnafrank, "Predicted Outcome Value During Initial Interaction: A Reformulation of Uncertainty Reduction Theory," *Human Communication Research*, Vol. 13, 1986, pp. 3–33.
31 Walid A. Afifi and Judith L. Weiner, "Toward a Theory of Motivated Information Management," *Communication Theory*, Vol. 14, 2004, pp. 167–190.
32 Charles R. Berger, "Communication Theories and Other Curios," *Communication Monographs*, Vol. 58, 1991, p. 102.
33 Berger, "Communicating Under Uncertainty," p. 58.

Chapter 10: Social Information Processing Theory

1 *The Social Network*, Columbia Pictures, 2010.
2 Mary Madden and Kathryn Zickuhr, "65% of Online Adults Use Social Networking Sites," *Pew Internet & American Life Project*, 2011, http://pewinternet.org/Reports/2011/Social-Networking-Sites.aspx, accessed September 23, 2013.
3 Keith Hampton, Lauren S. Goulet, Cameron Marlow, and Lee Rainie, "Why Most Facebook Users Get More Than They Give," *Pew Internet & American Life Project*, 2012, http://pewinternet.org/Reports/2012/Facebook-users.aspx, accessed September 23, 2013.
4 John Short, Ederyn Williams, and Bruce Christie, *The Social Psychology of Telecommunications*, John Wiley, London, 1976.
5 Richard Daft, Robert Lengel, and Linda K. Trevino, "Message Equivocality, Media Selection, and Manager Performance: Implications for Information Systems," *MIS Quarterly*, Vol. 11, 1987, pp. 355–365.
6 Lee Sproull and Sara Kiesler, "Reducing Social Context Cues: Electronic Mail in Organizational Communication," *Managerial Science*, Vol. 32, 1986, pp. 1492–1512.
7 Mary J. Culnan and M. Lynne Markus, "Information Technologies," in *Handbook of Organizational Communication*, Fredric Jablin, Linda L. Putnam, Karlene H. Roberts, and Lyman Porter (eds.), Sage, Newbury Park, CA, 1987, pp. 420–443.
8 Joseph B. Walther, "Interpersonal Effects in Computer-Mediated Interaction: A Relational Perspective," *Communication Research*, Vol. 19, 1992, pp. 52–90.
9 The fluid dynamics analogy was suggested by University of Washington communication professor Malcolm Parks at the National Communication Association meeting at Miami Beach, November 2003, on the occasion of Walther receiving the 2002 Woolbert Award.
10 "U.S. Teen Mobile Report: Calling Yesterday, Texting Today, Using Apps Tomorrow," *Nielsenwire*, 2010, http://blog.nielsen.com/nielsenwire/online_mobile/u-s-teen-mobile-report-calling-yesterday-texting-today-using-apps-tomorrow/, accessed September 23, 2013.
11 Judy B. Litoff and David C. Smith, "'Will He Get My Letter?' Popular Portrayals of Mail and Morale During World War II," *Journal of Popular Culture*, Vol. 23, 1990, pp. 21–43.
12 Joseph B. Walther, Tracy Loh, and Laura Granka, "The Interchange of Verbal and Nonverbal Cues in Computer-Mediated and Face-to-Face Affinity," *Journal of Language and Social Psychology*, Vol. 24, 2005, pp. 36–65.
13 For a brief synthesis of the impact of nonverbal cues, see Judee K. Burgoon and Gregory D. Hoobler, "Nonverbal Signals," in *Handbook of Interpersonal Communication*, 3rd ed., Mark L. Knapp and John A. Daly (eds.), Sage, Thousand Oaks, CA, 2002, pp. 240–299.
14 Joseph B. Walther, "Relational Aspects of Computer-Mediated Communication: Experimental Observations Over Time," *Organization Science*, Vol. 6, 1995, pp. 186–202; Joseph B. Walther, "Time Effects in Computer-Mediated Groups: Past, Present, and Future," in *Distributed Work*, Pamela J. Hinds and Sara Kiesler (eds.), MIT, Cambridge, MA, 2002, pp. 235–257.
15 Jon Swartz, "Time Spent on Facebook, Twitter, YouTube Grows," *USA Today* online, August, 1, 2010, http://www.usatoday.com/tech/news/2010-08-02-networking02_ST_N.htm, accessed September 23, 2013.
16 Walther, "Time Effects," p. 248.
17 Andrew M. Ledbetter, "Chronemic Cues and Sex Differences in Relational E-mail: Perceiving Immediacy and Supportive Message Quality," *Social Science Computer Review*, Vol. 26, 2008, pp. 466–482.
18 Joseph B. Walther and Lisa C. Tidwell, "Computer-Mediated Communication: Interpersonal Interaction On-Line," in *Making Connections: Readings in Relational Communication*, 2 ed., Kathleen M. Galvin and Pamela J. Cooper (eds.), Roxbury, Los Angeles, 2000, p. 326.
19 "New Global Poll Suggests Wide Enthusiasm for Online Dating," *BBC World Service Press*, February 13, 2010, http://www.bbc.co.uk/pressoffice/pressreleases/stories/2010/02_february/13/poll.shtml, accessed September 23, 2013.
20 Joseph Walther, "Symposium on Relationships and the Internet: Interview 1 with Joseph Walther," *Oxford Internet Institute*, December 10, 2011, http://webcast.oii.ox.ac.uk/?view=Webcast&ID=20111210_412, accessed September 23, 2013.
21 Jeff Hancock, "Symposium on Relationships and the Internet: Interview 3 with Jeff Hancock," *Oxford Internet Institute*, December 10, 2011, http://webcast.oii.ox.ac.uk/?view=Webcast&ID=20111210_414, accessed September 23, 2013. The original research report is by Catalina L. Toma, Jeffrey T. Hancock, and Nicole B. Ellison, "Separating Fact from Fiction: Deceptive Self-Presentation in Online Dating Profiles," *Personality and Social Psychology Bulletin*, Vol. 34, 2008, pp. 1023–1036.
22 Joseph B. Walther, "Computer-Mediated Communication: Impersonal, Interpersonal, and Hyperpersonal Interaction," *Communication Research*, Vol. 23, 1996, p. 26.

23 Joseph B. Walther, "Language and Communication Technology: An Introduction to the Special Issue," *Journal of Language and Social Psychology,* Vol. 23, 2004, p. 393.

24 Elaine Hoter, Miri Shonfeld, and Asmaa Ganayim, "Information and Communication Technology (ICT) in the Service of Multiculturalism," *The International Review of Research in Open and Distance Learning,* Vol. 10, 2009, p. 9, http://www.irrodl.org/index.php/irrodl/article/view/601/1207, accessed September 23, 2013.

25 Roger Austin, "ICT and Citizenship in Northern Ireland: A Critique of Experience Since the 1998 Good Friday Agreement," in *Young Citizens in the Digital Age: Political Engagement, Young People and New Media,* Brian D. Loader (ed.), Routledge, New York, NY, 2007, pp. 143–157.

26 Joseph B. Walther, "Computer-Mediated Communication and Virtual Groups: Applications to Interethnic Conflict," *Journal of Applied Communication Research,* Vol. 37, 2009, pp. 225–238.

27 Joseph B. Walther, Brandon Van Der Heide, Sang-Yeon Kim, David Westerman, and Stephanie T. Tong, "The Role of Friends' Appearance and Behavior on Evaluations of Individuals on Facebook: Are We Known by the Company We Keep?" *Human Communication Research,* Vol. 34, 2008, p. 32.

28 David K. Westerman, Brandon Van Der Heide, Katherine A. Klein, and Joseph B. Walther, "How Do People Really Seek Information About Others? Information Seeking Across Internet and Traditional Communication Channels," *Journal of Computer-Mediated Communication,* Vol. 13, 2008, p. 763.

29 Walther, Van Der Heide, Kim, Westerman, and Tong, p. 32.

30 Ibid.

31 Joseph B. Walther, Brandon Van Der Heide, Lauren M. Hamel, and Hillary C. Shulman, "Self-Generated Versus Other-Generated Statements and Impressions in Computer-Mediated Communication: A Test of Warranting Theory Using Facebook," *Communication Research,* Vol. 36, 2009, pp. 229–253.

32 Harmeet Sawhney, "Strategies for Increasing the Conceptual Yield of New Technologies Research," *Communication Monographs,* Vol. 74, 2007, pp. 395–401.

33 Tom Postmes and Nancy Baym, "Intergroup Dimensions of the Internet," in *Intergroup Communication: Multiple Perspectives,* Jake Harwood and Howard Giles (eds.), Peter Lang, New York, NY, 2005, pp. 213–238.

34 Joseph B. Walther, "Theories, Boundaries, and All of the Above," in *Journal of Computer-Mediated Communication,* Vol. 14, 2009, p. 750.

35 Joseph B. Walther, "Theories of Computer-Mediated Communication and Interpersonal Relations," in *The Handbook of Interpersonal Communication,* 4th ed., Mark L. Knapp and John A. Daly (eds.), Sage, Thousand Oaks, CA, 2011, p. 460.

36 L. Crystal Jiang, Natalie N. Bazarova, and Jeffrey T. Hancock, "The Disclosure–Intimacy Link in Computer-Mediated Communication: An Attributional Extension of the Hyperpersonal Model," *Human Communication Research,* Vol. 37, 2011, pp. 58–77. See also Joseph B. Walther et al., "The Effect of Feedback on Identity Shift in Computer-Mediated Communication," *Media Psychology,* Vol. 14, 2011, pp. 1–26.

37 Jeffrey T. Hancock and Catalina L. Toma, "Putting Your Best Face Forward: The Accuracy of Online Dating Photographs," *Journal of Communication,* Vol. 59, 2009, pp. 367–386.

38 Walther, Van Der Heide, Hamel, and Shulman, p. 248.

39 Walther, "Computer-Mediated Communication and Virtual Groups," p. 227.

Relationship Maintenance

1 John Stewart, "Interpersonal Communication: Contact Between Persons," *Bridges Not Walls,* 5th ed., John Stewart (ed.), McGraw-Hill, New York, 1990, pp. 13–30.

2 Daniel Canary and Laura Stafford, "Maintaining Relationships through Strategic and Routine Interaction," in *Communication and Relational Maintenance,* Daniel Canary and Laura Stafford (eds.), Academic Press, San Diego, CA, 1994, pp. 3–22.

3 Laura Stafford and Daniel Canary, "Maintenance Strategies and Romantic Relationship Type, Gender and Relational Characteristics," *Journal of Social and Personal Relationships,* Vol. 8, 1991, p. 224.

4 Ibid., pp. 217–242.

5 Andrew M. Ledbetter, "Family Communication Patterns and Relational Maintenance Behavior: Direct and Mediated Associations with Friendship Closeness," *Human Communication Research,* Vol. 35, 2009, pp. 130–147; Scott A. Myers and Natica P. Glover, "Emerging Adults' Use of Relational Maintenance Behaviors with Their Parents," *Communication Research Reports,* Vol. 24, 2007, pp. 257–264.

6 Margaret S. Clark and Judson Mills, "Interpersonal Attraction in Exchange and Communal Relationships," *Journal of Personality and Social Psychology,* Vol. 37, 1979, pp. 12–24.

7 Andrew M. Ledbetter, Heather M. Stassen-Ferrara, and Megan M. Down, "Comparing Equity and Self-Expansion Theory Approaches to Relational Maintenance," *Personal Relationships,* Vol. 20, 2013, pp. 38–51.

Chapter 11: Relational Dialectics

1 Leslie A. Baxter, "Interpersonal Communication as Dialogue: A Response to the 'Social Approaches' Forum," *Communication Theory,* Vol. 2, 1992, p. 330.

2 Ibid., p. 335.

3 Leslie A. Baxter and Barbara Montgomery, *Relating: Dialogues and Dialectics,* Guilford, New York, 1996, p. 3.

4 Baxter and Montgomery, p. 8.

5 Leslie A. Baxter, "A Dialectical Perspective on Communication Strategies in Relationship Development," in *A Handbook of Personal Relationships,* Steve Duck (ed.), John Wiley & Sons, New York, 1988, p. 258.

6 Baxter and Montgomery, p. 43.

7 Leslie A. Baxter, "Relationships as Dialogues," *Personal Relationships,* Vol. 11, 2004, p. 14.

8 Baxter, "A Dialectical Perspective," p. 259.

9 Irwin Altman, Anne Vinsel, and Barbara Brown, "Dialectic Conceptions in Social Psychology: An Application to Social Penetration and Privacy Regulation," in *Advances in Experimental Social Psychology,* Vol. 14, Leonard Berkowitz (ed.), Academic Press, New York, 1981, pp. 107–160.

10 Leslie A. Baxter, *Voicing Relationships: A Dialogical Perspective,* Sage, Thousand Oaks, CA, 2011, p. 5.

11 Baxter, "Relationships as Dialogues," p. 3.

12 Leslie A. Baxter and Lee West, "Couple Perceptions of Their Similarities and Differences: A Dialectical Perspective," *Journal of Social and Personal Relationships,* Vol. 20, 2003, pp. 491–514.

13 Baxter, *Voicing,* p. 2.

14 Mikhail Bakhtin, *Four Essays by M. M. Bakhtin,* M. Holquist (ed.), C. Emerson and M. Holquist (trans.), University of Texas, Austin, TX, 1981, p. 272.

15 Baxter, "Relationships as Dialogues," p. 11.

16 Ibid., p. 12.

17 Ibid., p. 13.

18 Leslie A. Baxter and Dawn O. Braithwaite, "Performing Marriage: The Marriage Renewal Ritual as Cultural Performance," *Southern Communication Journal,* Vol. 67, 2002, pp. 94–109.
19 Mikhail Bakhtin, *Problems of Dostoevsky's Poetics,* C. Emerson (ed. & trans.), University of Minnesota, Minneapolis, MN, 1984, pp. 122–126.
20 G. Morson and C. Emerson, *Mikhail Bakhtin: Creation of a Prosaics,* Stanford University, Palo Alto, CA, 1990, p. 443.
21 Leslie A. Baxter and Carma Byland, "Social Influence in Close Relationships," in *Perspectives on Persuasion, Social Influence, and Compliance Gaining,* John Seiter and Robert Gass (eds.), Pearson, Boston, MA, 2004, pp. 317–336.
22 *FLM Magazine,* Landmark Theatres, 2003.
23 Sissela Bok, *Lying: Moral Choice in Public and Private Life,* Vintage, New York, 1979, p. 48.
24 Ibid., p. 32.
25 Ibid., p. 263.
26 Leslie A. Baxter and Barbara Montgomery, "Rethinking Communication in Personal Relationships from a Dialectical Perspective," in *Handbook of Personal Relationships,* 2nd ed., Steve Duck (ed.), John Wiley & Sons, New York, p. 326.
27 Baxter, "Relationships as Dialogues," p. 17.
28 Baxter, "A Tale of Two Voices," *Journal of Family Communication,* Vol. 4, 2004, p. 189; Baxter, *Voicing,* p. 122.
29 Barbara Montgomery, "Relationship Maintenance Versus Relationship Change: A Dialectical Dilemma," *Journal of Social and Personal Relationships,* Vol. 10, 1993, p. 221.

Chapter 12: Communication Privacy Management Theory

1 Sandra Petronio, "Brief Status Report on Communication Privacy Management Theory," *Journal of Family Communication,* Vol. 13, 2013, pp. 6–14.
2 The rules are paraphrased and abridged from Ashley Duggan and Sandra Petronio, "When Your Child Is in Crisis: Navigating Medical Needs with Issues of Privacy Management," in *Parent and Children Communicating with Society,* Thomas J. Socha (ed.), Routledge, New York, 2009, p. 122; and Sandra Petronio and Jennifer Reierson, "Regulating the Privacy of Confidentiality: Grasping the Complexities through Communication Privacy Management Theory," in *Uncertainty, Information Management, and Disclosure Decisions: Theories and Applications,* Tamara D. Afifi and Walid A. Afifi (eds.), Routledge, New York, 2009, pp. 366–367.
3 Sandra Petronio, *Boundaries of Privacy: Dialectics of Discourse,* State University of New York, Albany, NY, 2002, p. 6.
4 Mary Claire Morr Serewicz and Sandra Petronio, "Communication Privacy Management Theory," in *Explaining Communication: Contemporary Theories and Exemplars,* Bryan Whaley and Wendy Samter (eds.), Lawrence Erlbaum, Mahwah, NJ, 2007, p. 258.
5 Dawn O. Braithwaite, "'Just How Much Did That Wheelchair Cost?' Management of Privacy Boundaries by Persons with Disabilities," *Western Journal of Speech Communication,* Vol. 55, 1991, pp. 258, 266.
6 Serewicz and Petronio, p. 258.
7 Sandra Petronio, Heidi Reeder, Michael Hecht, and Teresa Mon't Ros-Mendoza, "Disclosure of Sexual Abuse by Children and Adolescents," *Journal of Applied Communication Research,* Vol. 24, 1996, pp. 181–199; Sandra Petronio, Lisa Flores, and Michael Hecht, *Western Journal of Communication,* Vol. 61, 1997, pp. 101–113.
8 Maureen Kenny and Adriana McEachern, "Racial, Ethnic, and Cultural Factors of Childhood Sexual Abuse: A Selected Review of the Literature," *Clinical Psychology Review,* Vol. 20, 2000, pp. 905–922.
9 Kathryn Dindia and Mike Allen, "Sex Differences in Self-Disclosure: A Meta-Analysis," *Psychological Bulletin,* Vol. 112, 1992, pp. 106–128.
10 Petronio, Flores, et al., p. 101.
11 Petronio, Reeder, et al., p. 188.
12 Ibid., p. 191.
13 Petronio and Reierson, p. 368.
14 Paige Toller and Chad McBride, "Enacting Privacy Rules and Protecting Disclosure Recipients: Parents' Communication with Children Following the Death of a Family Member," *Journal of Family Communication,* Vol. 13, 2013, pp. 32–45.
15 Petronio and Reierson, pp. 373–374.
16 Duggan and Petronio, p. 124.
17 Kathryn Greene, Valerian Derlega, Gust Yep, and Sandra Petronio, *Privacy and Disclosure of HIV in Interpersonal Relationships: A Sourcebook for Researchers and Practitioners,* Lawrence Erlbaum, Mahwah, NJ, 2003, pp. 36–83.
18 Mark Leary and Lisa Schreindorfer, "The Stigmatization of HIV and AIDS: Rubbing Salt in the Wound," in *HIV and Social Interaction,* Valerian Derlega and Anita Barbee (eds.), Sage, Thousand Oaks, CA, 1998, pp. 18–19.
19 Petronio and Reierson, pp. 366–367.
20 Petronio, *Boundaries of Privacy,* pp. 177–190.
21 Sandra Petronio, Jack Sargent, Laura Andea, Peggy Reganis, and David Cichocki, "Family and Friends as Healthcare Advocates: Dilemmas of Confidentiality and Privacy," *Journal of Social and Personal Relationships,* Vol. 21, 2004, pp. 33–52.
22 Ibid., p. 49.
23 Frederick Platt and Geoffrey Gordon, *Field Guide to the Difficult Patient Interview,* Lippincott Williams and Wilkins, Philadelphia, PA, 1999, p. 176.
24 Petronio, Sargent, et al., p. 43.
25 Sandra Petronio, "The Moral Imperative of Privacy Management," handout at the "Negotiating Moralities in Personal Relationships" preconference, National Communication Association Annual Convention, November 2009, Chicago.
26 Sandra Petronio, "Road to Developing Communication Privacy Management Theory: Narrative in Process, Please Stand By," *Journal of Family Communication,* Vol. 4, 2004, p. 200.
27 Duggan and Petronio, p. 124.
28 Petronio, "Brief Status Report," p. 6.
29 Petronio, *Boundaries of Privacy,* pp. 178–182.
30 Petronio, "Road to Developing," p. 193.
31 Petronio, "Brief Status Report," p. 12.

Chapter 13: The Interactional View

1 Codruta Porcar and Cristian Hainic, "The Interactive Dimension of Communication: The Pragmatics of the Palo Alto Group," *Journal for Communication and Culture,* Vol. 1, No. 2, 2011, pp. 4–19.
2 Paul Watzlawick, Janet Beavin, and Don Jackson, *Pragmatics of Human Communication,* W. W. Norton, New York, 1967, pp. 19–32.
3 Alan Watts, *The Book,* Pantheon, New York, 1966, p. 65. For other examples of Watts' use of the life-as-a-game metaphor, see Alan Watts, "The Game of Black-and-White," in *The Book,* pp. 22–46; and Alan Watts, "The Counter Game," in *Psychology East & West,* Ballantine, New York, 1969, pp. 144–185.

4 Paul Watzlawick, "The Construction of Clinical 'Realities,'" in *The Evolution of Psychotherapy: The Second Conference*, Jeffrey Zeig (ed.), Brunner/Mazel, New York, 1992, p. 64.
5 Watzlawick, Beavin, and Jackson, *Pragmatics of Communication*, pp. 48–71. The authors list an additional axiom stating that human beings communicate both digitally and analogically. They are referring to the difference between verbal and nonverbal communication. Since the verbal/nonverbal distinction is covered in the first two axioms and most readers find the digital/analogical labels confusing, I've chosen not to present this axiom.
6 Paul Watzlawick, *The Language of Change*, W. W. Norton, New York, 1978, p. 11.
7 Watzlawick, Beavin, and Jackson, *Pragmatics of Human Communication*, p. 54.
8 L. Edna Rogers, "Relational Communication Theory: An Interactional Family Theory," in *Engaging Theories in Family Communication: Multiple Perspectives*, Dawn O. Braithwaite and Leslie A. Baxter (eds.), Sage, Thousand Oaks, CA, 2006, p. 119.
9 Watzlawick, Beavin, and Jackson, p. 99.
10 L. Edna Rogers and Frank E. Millar III, "Domineeringness and Dominance: A Transactional View," *Human Communication Research*, Vol. 5, 1979, pp. 238–245.
11 Paul Watzlawick, John H. Weakland, and Richard Fisch, *Change*, W. W. Norton, New York, 1974, p. 95.
12 Watzlawick, *Language of Change*, p. 122.
13 Watzlawick, "The Construction of Clinical 'Realities,'" p. 61.
14 Janet Beavin Bavelas, "Research into the Pragmatics of Human Communication," *Journal of Strategic and Systemic Therapies*, Vol. 11, No. 2, 1992, pp. 15–29.

Influence

1 Irving Janis and Leon Mann, "Effectiveness of Emotional Roleplaying in Modifying Smoking Habits and Attitudes," *Journal of Experiential Research in Personality*, Vol. 1, 1965, pp. 84–90.
2 An earlier version of this description appeared in Em Griffin, "Role Play," in *The Mind Changers*, Tyndale House, Carol Stream, IL, 1976, pp. 79–94.
3 Gerald R. Miller and Michael Burgoon, *New Techniques of Persuasion*, Harper and Row, New York, 1973, p. 57.

Chapter 14: Social Judgment Theory

1 Carolyn Sherif, Muzafer Sherif, and Roger Nebergall, *Attitude and Attitude Change: The Social Judgment–Involvement Approach*, W. B. Saunders, Philadelphia, PA, 1965, p. 222.
2 *Lincoln*, DreamWorks, 2012.
3 Sherif, Sherif, and Nebergall, p. 225.
4 Ibid., p. 214.
5 Stephen Bochner and Chester Insko, "Communicator Discrepancy, Source Credibility and Opinion Change," *Journal of Personality and Social Psychology*, Vol. 4, 1966, pp. 614–621.
6 Sandi Smith, Charles Atkin, Dennis Martell, Rebecca Allen, and Larry Hembroff, "A Social Judgment Theory Approach to Conducting Formative Research in a Social Norms Campaign," *Communication Theory*, Vol. 16, 2006, pp. 141–152.

Chapter 15: Elaboration Likelihood Model

1 Richard E. Petty and John T. Cacioppo, *Communication and Persuasion: Central and Peripheral Routes to Attitude Change*, Springer-Verlag, New York, 1986, p. 7.
2 Richard E. Petty and John T. Cacioppo, *Attitudes and Persuasion: Classic and Contemporary Approaches*, Wm. C. Brown, Dubuque, IA, 1981, p. 256.
3 Robert B. Cialdini, *Influence: Science and Practice*, 4th ed., Allyn and Bacon, Needham Heights, MA, 2001.
4 Richard E. Petty and Duane Wegener, "The Elaboration Likelihood Model: Current Status and Controversies," in *Dual Process Theories in Social Psychology*, Shelly Chaiken and Yaacov Trope (eds.), Guilford, New York, 1999, pp. 44–48.
5 John T. Cacioppo et al., "Dispositional Differences in Cognitive Motivation: The Life and Times of Individuals Varying in Need for Cognition," *Psychological Bulletin*, Vol. 119, 1996, pp. 197–253.
6 Richard E. Petty and John T. Cacioppo, "The Elaboration Likelihood Model of Persuasion," in *Advances in Experimental Social Psychology*, Vol. 19, Leonard Berkowitz (ed.), Academic Press, Orlando, FL, 1986, p. 129.
7 Louis Penner and Barbara Fritzsche, "Magic Johnson and Reactions to People with AIDS: A Natural Experiment," *Journal of Applied Social Psychology*, Vol. 23, 1993, pp. 1035–1050.
8 Ibid., p. 1048.
9 Michael Hawthorne, "Madigan: Video Busts Band's Bus in Dumping," *Chicago Tribune*, August 25, 2004, sec. 1, p. 1.
10 Petty and Wegener, pp. 51–52.
11 Duane Wegener and Richard E. Petty, "Understanding Effects of Mood Through the Elaboration Likelihood and Flexible Correction Models," in *Theories of Mood and Cognition: A User's Guidebook*, L. L. Martin and G. L. Clore (eds.), Lawrence Erlbaum, Mahwah, NJ, 2001, pp. 177–210.
12 Thomas R. Nilsen, *Ethics of Speech Communication*, Bobbs-Merrill, Indianapolis, IN, 1966, p. 38.
13 Ibid., p. 35.
14 John Milton, *Areopagitica*, John Hales (ed.), with introduction and notes, 3rd ed., revised, Clarendon, Oxford, UK, 1882.
15 John Stuart Mill, *On Liberty*, Gateway, Chicago, IL, 1955.
16 Søren Kierkegaard, *Philosophical Fragments*, Princeton University, Princeton, NJ, pp. 17–28.
17 Em Griffin, *The Mind Changers*, Tyndale, Carol Stream, IL, 1976, pp. 27–41; Em Griffin, *Getting Together*, InterVarsity Press, Downers Grove, IL, 1982, pp. 159–167.
18 Paul Mongeau and James Stiff, "Specifying Causal Relationships in the Elaboration Likelihood Model," *Communication Theory*, Vol. 3, 1993, pp. 67–68.
19 In a personal communication with Richard Petty on March 13, 2013, he pointed out that "the ELM is about a myriad of persuasion variables indicating when and why they work." His position is that ELM never intended to focus on defining strong and weak arguments, nor does it focus on defining high and low credibility or any other message variable.

Chapter 16: Cognitive Dissonance Theory

1 Aesop, "The Fox and the Grapes," in *Aesop, Five Centuries of Illustrated Fables*, Metropolitan Museum of Art, New York, 1964, p. 12.
2 Leon Festinger, *A Theory of Cognitive Dissonance*, Stanford University, Stanford, CA, 1957, p. 4.
3 "Smoke! Smoke! Smoke! (That Cigarette)," Merle Travis, performed by Tex Williams, Capitol Records, 1947.
4 Leon Festinger, "Social Communication and Cognition: A Very Preliminary and Highly Tentative Draft," in *Cognitive Dissonance: Progress on a Pivotal Theory in Social Psychology*, Eddie Harmon-Jones and Judson Mills (eds.), American Psychological Association, Washington, DC, 1999, p. 361.
5 Festinger, *A Theory of Cognitive Dissonance*, pp. 5–6.

6 Ibid., pp. 84–97.

7 Dave D'Alessio and Mike Allen, "Selective Exposure and Dissonance After Decisions," *Psychological Reports,* Vol. 91, 2002, pp. 527–532.

8 Elizabeth Fernandez, "Smoking in Movies Increases in 2011, Reverses Five Years of Progress," University of California, San Francisco, http://www.ucsf.edu/news/2012/09/12812/smoking-movies-increases-2011-reverses-five-years-progress, accessed December 31, 2012. The story reports on Stanton A. Glantz, Anne Iaccopucci, Kori Titus, and Jonathan R. Polansky, "Smoking in Top-Grossing US Movies, 2011," *Preventing Chronic Disease,* Vol. 9, http://www.cdc.gov/pcd/issues/2012/pdf/12_0170.pdf, accessed December 31, 2012.

9 http://multivu.prnewswire.com/mnr/adcouncil/25956/, accessed June 7, 2013. For the text of the entire poem, see http://usmellfunneh.deviantart.com/art/A-stinky-poem-135349319, accessed June 7, 2013.

10 Dieter Frey, "Recent Research on Selective Exposure to Information," in *Advances in Experimental Social Psychology: Vol. 19,* Leonard Berkowitz (ed.), Academic Press, Orlando, FL, 1986, pp. 41–80.

11 Festinger, *A Theory of Cognitive Dissonance,* pp. 32–47.

12 Alan DeSantis and Susan E. Morgan, "Sometimes a Cigar [Magazine] Is More Than Just a Cigar [Magazine]: Pro-Smoking Arguments in *Cigar Aficionado,* 1992–2000," *Health Communication,* Vol. 15, 2003, p. 460.

13 Festinger, *A Theory of Cognitive Dissonance,* p. 95.

14 Leon Festinger and James Carlsmith, "Cognitive Consequences of Forced Compliance," *Journal of Abnormal and Social Psychology,* Vol. 58, 1959, pp. 203–210.

15 CPI Inflation Calculator, United States Bureau of Labor Statistics, http://data.bls.gov/cgi-bin/cpicalc.pl, accessed December 31, 2012.

16 "Barack Obama Quits Smoking After 30 Years," *The Telegraph,* February 9, 2011, http://www.telegraph.co.uk/news/worldnews/barackobama/8314049/Barack-Obama-quits-smoking-after-30-years.html, accessed December 31, 2012.

17 Amie Parnes, "Obama's Reason to Stop Smoking: His Daughters," *The Hill,* August 22, 2012, http://thehill.com/blogs/blog-briefing-room/news/244859-obamas-reason-to-stop-smoking-his-daughters, accessed December 31, 2012.

18 Elliot Aronson, "The Theory of Cognitive Dissonance: A Current Perspective," in *Advances in Experimental Social Psychology, Vol. 4,* Leonard Berkowitz (ed.), Academic Press, New York, 1969, p. 27.

19 Ibid., pp. 26–27.

20 Joel Cooper, "Unwanted Consequences and the Self: In Search of the Motivation for Dissonance Reduction," in *Cognitive Dissonance,* Harmon-Jones and Mills (eds.), p. 153.

21 Ibid., p. 151.

22 Richard Heslin and Michael Amo, "Detailed Test of the Reinforcement–Dissonance Controversy in the Counterattitudinal Advocacy Situation," *Journal of Personality and Social Psychology,* Vol. 23, 1972, pp. 234–242.

23 Anne E. Kornblut, "But Will They Love Him Tomorrow?" *The New York Times,* Nation, March 19, 2006, sec. 4, p. 1.

24 Jeff Stone and Joel Cooper, "A Self-Standards Model of Cognitive Dissonance," *Journal of Experimental Social Psychology,* Vol. 37, 2001, p. 231.

25 R. B. Zajonc, "Leon Festinger (1919–1989)," *American Psychologist,* Vol. 45, 1990, p. 661.

26 Daryl Bem, "Self-Perception: An Alternative Interpretation of Cognitive Dissonance Phenomena," *Psychological Review,* Vol. 74, 1947, pp. 183–200.

Group Communication

1 *Report of the Presidential Commission on the Space Shuttle* Challenger *Disaster* (5 vols.), Government Printing Office, Washington, DC, p. 1414.

2 Irving Janis, *Victims of Groupthink,* Houghton Mifflin, Boston, MA, 1972, p. 9.

3 Irving Janis, *Crucial Decisions: Leadership in Policymaking and Crisis Management,* Free Press, New York, 1989, p. 60.

4 Robert F. Bales, *Interaction Process Analysis,* Addison-Wesley, Reading, MA, 1950; Robert F. Bales, *Personality and Interpersonal Behavior,* Holt, Rinehart, & Winston, New York, 1970.

5 Won-Woo Park, "A Review of Research on Groupthink," *Journal of Behavioral Decision Making,* Vol. 3, 1990, pp. 229–245.

Chapter 17: Functional Perspective on Group Decision Making

1 Some scholars also question the efficacy of communication in group decision making. See Dean E. Hewes, "Small Group Communication May Not Influence Decision Making: An Amplification of Socio-Egocentric Theory," in *Communication and Group Decision Making, 2nd ed.,* Randy Hirokawa and Marshall Scott Poole (eds.), Sage, Thousand Oaks, CA, 1996, pp. 179–212 .

2 Randy Hirokawa, "Avoiding Camels: Lessons Learned in the Facilitation of High-Quality Group Decision Making Through Effective Discussion," Van Zelst Lecture in Communication, Northwestern University School of Speech, Evanston, IL, May 24, 1993.

3 Dennis Gouran, "Group Decision Making: An Approach to Integrative Research," in *A Handbook for the Study of Human Communication,* Charles Tardy (ed.), Ablex, Norwood, NJ, 1988, pp. 247–267.

4 Proverbs 15:22, Revised Standard Version of the Bible.

5 Dennis Gouran, Randy Hirokawa, Kelly Julian, and Geoff Leatham, "The Evolution and Current Status of the Functional Perspective on Communication in Decision-Making and Problem-Solving Groups," in *Communication Yearbook 16,* Stanley Deetz (ed.), Sage, Newbury Park, CA, 1993, p. 591.

6 Randy Hirokawa and Dirk Scheerhorn, "Communication in Faulty Group Decision-Making," in *Communication and Group Decision Making,* Randy Hirokawa and Marshall Scott Poole (eds.), Sage, Beverly Hills, CA, 1986, p. 69.

7 Hirokawa bases the distinction between rational and political logics on the work of Peter Senge, *The Fifth Discipline,* Doubleday, New York, 1990, p. 60.

8 Dennis Gouran and Randy Hirokawa, "The Role of Communication in Decision-Making Groups: A Functional Perspective" in *Communications in Transition,* Mary Mander (ed.), Praeger, New York, 1983, p. 174.

9 Randy Hirokawa, "Understanding the Relationship Between Group Communication and Group Decision-Making Effectiveness from a Functional Perspective: Why 'It's Not All Bad' Isn't Quite 'Good Enough,'" Thomas M. Scheidel Lecture, University of Washington, Seattle, WA, April 24, 1998.

10 Randy Hirokawa and Poppy McLeod, "Communication, Decision Development, and Decision Quality in Small Groups: An Integration of Two Approaches," paper presented at the annual meeting of the Speech Communication Association, Miami, November 18–21, 1993.

11 Randy Hirokawa, "Functional Approaches to the Study of Group Discussion," *Small Group Research,* Vol. 25, 1994, p. 546.

12 Marc Orlitzky and Randy Hirokawa, "To Err Is Human, To Correct for It Divine: A Meta-Analysis of the Functional

Theory of Group Decision-Making Effectiveness," paper presented at the annual meeting of the National Communication Association, Chicago, November 19–23, 1997.

13 See, for example, J. Richard Hackman, "Work Teams in Organizations: An Orienting Framework," in *Groups That Work (and Those That Don't),* J. Richard Hackman (ed.), Jossey-Bass, San Francisco, CA, 1990, pp. 1–14.

14 Ivan Steiner, *Group Process and Productivity,* Academic Press, New York, 1972, p. 9.

15 Randy Hirokawa, "Avoiding Camels," p. 8.

16 Dennis Gouran and Randy Hirokawa, "Counteractive Functions of Communication in Effective Group Decision-Making," in *Communication and Group Decision Making,* p. 82.

17 Randy Hirokawa, "Group Communication and Problem-Solving Effectiveness I: A Critical Review of Inconsistent Findings," *Communication Quarterly,* Vol. 30, 1982, p. 139.

18 Gouran, Hirokawa, Julian, and Leatham, pp. 574–579.

19 Robert Craig, "Treatments of Reflective Thought in John Dewey and Hans-Georg Gadamer," paper presented at the 1994 Convention of the International Communication Association, Sydney, Australia, July 11–15, 1994.

20 John Dewey, *How We Think,* Heath, New York, 1910.

21 My analysis of Habermas' discourse ethics has been greatly informed by Theodore Glasser and James Ettema, "Ethics and Eloquence in Journalism: A Study of the Demands of Press Accountability," presented to the Media Ethics Division of the Association for Education in Journalism and Mass Communication, Miami Beach, FL, August 2002.

22 Sonja Foss, Karen Foss, and Robert Trapp, *Contemporary Perspectives on Rhetoric,* Waveland Press, Prospect Heights, IL, 1991, pp. 241–272. (Like all interpreters of Habermas, Foss, Foss, and Trapp refer to his dense writing style. For that reason, all citations in this ethical reflection are from secondary sources. For an overview of Habermas' thinking, see Jane Braaten, *Habermas's Critical Theory of Society,* State University of New York, Albany, NY, 1991. For a primary source, see Jürgen Habermas, "Discourse Ethics: Notes on a Program of Philosophical Justification," Shierry Weber Nicholsen and Christian Lenhardt (trans.), in *Communicative Ethics Controversy,* Seyla Benhabib and Fred Dallmayr (eds.), MIT Press, Cambridge, MA, 1990, pp. 60–110.

23 Theodore Glasser, "Communicative Ethics and the Aim of Accountability in Journalism," *Social Responsibility: Business, Journalism, Law, Medicine, Vol. 21,* Louis Hodges (ed.), Washington & Lee University, Lexington, VA, 1995, pp. 41–42.

24 Ibid., p. 49.

25 John Cragan and David Wright, "Small Group Communication Research of the 1980s: A Synthesis and Critique," *Communication Studies,* Vol. 41, 1990, pp. 212–236.

26 Cynthia Stohl and Michael Holmes, "A Functional Perspective for Bona Fide Groups," in *Communication Yearbook 16,* Stanley Deetz (ed.), Sage, Newbury Park, CA, 1993, p. 601.

27 See John Cragan and David Wright, "The Functional Theory of Small Group Decision-Making: A Replication," *Journal of Social Behavior and Personality,* Vol. 7, 1992 (special issue). Reprinted in John Cragan and David Wright (eds.), *Theory and Research in Small Group Communication,* Burgess International, Edina, MN, 1993, pp. 87–95.

28 B. Aubrey Fisher, "Decision Emergence: Phases in Group Decision Making," *Speech Monographs,* Vol. 37, 1970, pp. 53–66.

29 B. Aubrey Fisher, *Small Group Decision Making,* 2nd ed., McGraw-Hill, New York, 1980, p. 149.

30 Dennis Gouran, "Reflections on the Type of Question as a Determinant of the Form of Interaction in Decision-Making and Problem-Solving Discussions," *Communication Quarterly,* Vol. 53, 2003, pp. 111–125.

Chapter 18: Symbolic Convergence Theory

1 Robert Bales, *Personality and Interpersonal Behavior,* Holt, Rinehart, and Winston, 1970.

2 Ernest G. Bormann, John Cragan, and Donald Shields, "Three Decades of Developing, Grounding, and Using Symbolic Convergence Theory (SCT)," *Communication Yearbook 25,* William Gudykunst (ed.), Lawrence Erlbaum, Mahwah, NJ, 2001, pp. 274–276.

3 Ernest G. Bormann, *Small Group Communication: Theory and Practice,* 3rd ed., Harper & Row, New York, 1990, p. 122.

4 Ernest G. Bormann, John Cragan, and Donald Shields, "In Defense of Symbolic Convergence Theory: A Look at the Theory and Its Criticisms After Two Decades," *Communication Theory,* Vol. 4, 1994, p. 280.

5 James Olufowote, "Rousing a Sleeping Giant: Symbolic Convergence Theory and Complexities in the Communicative Constitution of Collective Action," *Management Communication Quarterly,* Vol. 19, 2006, p. 455.

6 Ernest G. Bormann and Nancy C. Bormann, *Effective Small Group Communication,* 5th ed., Burgess International, Edina, MN, 1992, p. 124.

7 Ernest G. Bormann, "Fantasy and Rhetorical Vision: The Rhetorical Criticism of Social Reality," *Quarterly Journal of Speech,* Vol. 58, 1972, p. 397.

8 Alan D. DeSantis, "Smoke Screen: An Ethnographic Study of a Cigar Shop's Collective Rationalization," *Health Communication,* Vol. 14, 2002, p. 185.

9 Ernest G. Bormann, "Symbolic Convergence Theory and Communication in Group Decision Making," *Communication and Group Decision Making,* Randy Hirokawa and Marshall Scott Poole (eds.), Sage, Newbury Park, CA, 1986, p. 221.

10 DeSantis, "Smoke Screen," p. 193.

11 Bormann and Bormann, p. 124.

12 Alan D. DeSantis, "A Couple of White Guys Sitting Around Talking: The Collective Rationalization of Cigar Smokers," *Journal of Contemporary Ethnography,* Vol. 32, 2003, p. 462.

13 Olufowote, p. 456.

14 Bormann, "Symbolic Convergence Theory and Communication in Group Decision Making," p. 222.

15 Bormann and Bormann, p. 119.

16 Bormann, Cragan, and Shields, "In Defense," p. 290.

17 John Cragan and Donald Shields, *Symbolic Theories in Applied Communication Research: Bormann, Burke, and Fisher,* Hampton Press, Cresskill, NJ, 1995, p. 39.

18 Sonja K. Foss, *Rhetorical Criticism: Exploration and Practice,* 4th ed., Waveland, Prospect Heights, IL, 2009, pp. 97–136.

19 Jessi McCabe, "Resisting Alienation: The Social Construction of Internet Communities Supporting Eating Disorders," *Communication Studies,* Vol. 60, 2009, p. 3.

20 Ibid., p. 8.

21 Sanitarium (website), accessed 2004.

22 The Ana Hotline (website), accessed 2004.

23 Blue Dragon Fly (website), accessed 2004.

24 Sanitarium, accessed 2004.

25 Jessi McCabe, p. 11.

26 Pro-Ana Suicide Society (website), accessed 2004.

27 Ibid.
28 Jessi McCabe, p. 13.
29 Bormann, *Small Group Communication,* p. 123; Bormann and Bormann, p. 122.
30 Cragan and Shields, pp. 46–47.
31 Ernest G. Bormann, *Communication Theory,* Sheffield, Salem, WI, 1989, p. 254.
32 John Cragan, "Obituary #10694," *Communication, Research and Theory Network,* January 6, 2009, http://www.natcom.org/CRTNET, accessed January 12, 2009.
33 Bormann, *Communication Theory,* p. 190.
34 Olufowote, p. 460.
35 Bormann, Cragan, and Shields, "In Defense," p. 267.
36 Olufowote, pp. 460–461.
37 Bormann, Cragan, and Shields, "In Defense," pp. 275–276.
38 Ibid., p. 282.
39 Bormann and Bormann, p. 122.

Organizational Communication

1 Gareth Morgan, "Organizations as Machines," in *Images of Organization,* 2nd ed., Sage, Thousand Oaks, CA, 1997, pp. 11–31.

Chapter 19: Cultural Approach to Organizations

1 Clifford Geertz, "Thick Description: Toward an Interpretive Theory of Culture," in *The Interpretation of Cultures,* Basic Books, New York, 1973, p. 5.
2 Michael Pacanowsky and Nick O'Donnell-Trujillo, "Organizational Communication as Cultural Performance," *Communication Monographs,* Vol. 50, 1983, p. 129. (Pacanowsky's early work was co-authored with Nick O'Donnell-Trujillo from the communication department at Southern Methodist University. Because Pacanowsky was the lead author in these articles and Trujillo's scholarship took a critical turn, I refer only to Pacanowsky. For an example of critical ethnography, see Nick Trujillo, "Interpreting November 22: A Critical Ethnography of an Assassination Site," *Quarterly Journal of Speech,* Vol. 79, 1993, pp. 447–466.)
3 Michael Pacanowsky and Nick O'Donnell-Trujillo, "Communication and Organizational Cultures," *Western Journal of Speech Communication,* Vol. 46, 1982, p. 121.
4 Pacanowsky and O'Donnell-Trujillo, "Organizational Communication," p. 146.
5 Ibid., p. 131.
6 Pacanowsky and O'Donnell-Trujillo, "Communication and Organizational Cultures," p. 116.
7 Clifford Geertz, "Deep Play: Notes on the Balinese Cockfight," in *Myth, Symbol, and Culture,* Norton, New York, 1971, p. 29.
8 Geertz, "Thick Description," p. 5.
9 Gareth Morgan, *Images of Organization,* Sage, Newbury Park, CA, 1986, pp. 130–131.
10 Clifford Geertz, "A Life of Learning" (ACLS Occasional Paper No. 45), American Council of Learned Societies, New York, 1999, p. 14.
11 Pacanowsky and O'Donnell-Trujillo, "Communication and Organizational Cultures," p. 127.
12 Jeffrey C. Alexander, "Clifford Geertz and the Strong Program: The Human Sciences and Cultural Sociology," *Cultural Sociology,* Vol. 2, 2008, p. 166.
13 Joseph G. Ponterotto, "Brief Note on the Origins, Evolution, and Meaning of the Qualitative Research Concept 'Thick Description,'" *The Qualitative Report,* Vol. 11, 2006, pp. 538–549.
14 Michael Pacanowsky, "Communication in the Empowering Organization," in *Communication Yearbook 11,* James Anderson (ed.), Sage, Newbury Park, CA, 1988, pp. 357, 362–364. For an update on the culture of W. L. Gore & Associates two decades later, see Alan Deutschman, "The Fabric of Creativity," *Fast Company,* December 2004, pp. 54–62.
15 Ibid., p. 357.
16 Ibid., p. 358.
17 Michael Pacanowsky, "Slouching Towards Chicago," *Quarterly Journal of Speech,* Vol. 74, 1988, p. 454.
18 *Mad Men,* Lionsgate, AMC, 2007, Season 1, Disc 1.
19 Pacanowsky and O'Donnell-Trujillo, "Communication and Organizational Cultures," p. 123.
20 Geertz, "Deep Play," pp. 5, 26.
21 Pacanowsky and O'Donnell-Trujillo, "Organizational Communication," p. 137.
22 Linda Smircich, "Concepts of Culture and Organizational Analysis," *Administrative Science Quarterly,* Vol. 28, 1983, pp. 339–358.
23 William Gardner, Brian Reithel, et al., "Attraction to Organizational Culture Profiles: Effects of Realistic Recruitment and Vertical and Horizontal Individualism–Collectivism," *Management Communication Quarterly,* Vol. 22, 2009, pp. 437–472.
24 Bryan Taylor and Nick Trujillo, "Qualitative Research Methods," in *The New Handbook of Organizational Communication,* Fredric Jablin and Linda L. Putnam (eds.), Sage, Thousand Oaks, CA, 2001, p. 169.
25 Geertz, *The Interpretation of Cultures,* p. 15.
26 Adam Kuper, *Culture: The Anthropologists' Account,* Harvard University, Cambridge, MA, 1999, pp. 112–113.
27 Estelle Jorgensen, "On Thick Description and Narrative Inquiry In Music Education," *Research Studies in Music Education,* Vol. 31, 2009, p. 71.
28 T. M. Luhrmann, "The Touch of the Real," *London Times Literary Supplement,* January 12, 2001, p. 3.

Chapter 20: Communicative Constitution of Organizations

1 Nick Wingfield, "Game Maker Without a Rule Book," *The New York Times,* September 9, 2012, p. BU1.
2 Wendy's Company, "2012 Annual Report," http://ir.wendys.com/phoenix.zhtml?c=67548&p=irol-reports annual, accessed October 7, 2013.
3 *Valve Handbook for New Employees,* Valve Press, Bellevue, WA, 2012, p. 55.
4 Ibid., p. viii.
5 Ryan S. Bisel, "A Communicative Ontology of Organization? A Description, History, and Critique of CCO Theories for Organization Science," *Management Communication Quarterly,* Vol. 24, 2010, pp. 124–131.
6 Karl Weick, *Sensemaking in Organizations,* Sage, Thousand Oaks, CA, 1995, p. 12.
7 Ibid., p. 12. Weick attributes the story to Graham Wallas, *The Art of Thought,* Harcourt Brace, New York, 1926, p. 106, and repeatedly refers to it as the core idea of retrospective sensemaking.
8 William Harris, *Heraclitus: The Complete Fragments,* http://community.middlebury.edu/~harris/Philosophy/heraclitus.pdf, accessed October 7, 2013.
9 Robert D. McPhee and Pamela Zaug, "The Communicative Constitution of Organizations: A Framework for Explanation," in *Building Theories of Organization: The Constitutive Role of Communication,* Linda L. Putnam and Anne Maydan Nicotera (eds.), Routledge, New York, 2009, p. 29.

10 The largest council for men's Greek organizations is the North American Interfraternity Conference. The National Panhellenic Conference is the counterpart for women's Greek organizations. Statistics were obtained from the websites of these organizations: http://www.nicindy.org/press and https://www.npcwomen.org/resources/pdf/Annual%20Report%202011.pdf, accessed October 7, 2013.
11 *Valve Handbook,* p. 6.
12 William Poundstone, "Answers to Google Interview Questions," *The Wall Street Journal* online, December 24, 2011, http://online.wsj.com/article/SB100014240529702045523045771130037050897744.html, accessed October 7, 2013. According to Poundstone, the answer is, "Start both hourglasses at 0 minutes. Flip over the four-minute glass when it runs out (at 4:00); ditto for the seven-minute glass (at 7:00). When the four-minute glass runs out the second time (at 8:00), the seven-minute glass will then have one minute of sand in its lower bulb. Flip the seven-minute glass over again and let the minute of sand run back. When the last grain falls, that will be nine minutes."
13 J. Kevin Barge and David W. Schlueter, "Memorable Messages and Newcomer Socialization," *Western Journal of Communication,* Vol. 68, 2004, pp. 233–256.
14 *Valve Handbook,* p. 16.
15 Ibid.
16 François Cooren and Gail T. Fairhurst, "Speech Timing and Spacing: The Phenomenon of Organizational Closure," *Organization,* Vol. 11, No. 6, 2004, pp. 793–824.
17 Valve Corporation website, http://www.valvesoftware.com/company/, accessed October 7, 2013.
18 *Valve Handbook,* p. 40.
19 Ibid., p. 39.
20 Sarah J. Tracy, Karen K. Myers, and Clifton W. Scott, "Cracking Jokes and Crafting Selves: Sensemaking and Identity Management Among Human Service Workers," *Communication Monographs,* Vol. 73, 2006, p. 302.
21 Ibid., p. 300.
22 "Friendship and Philanthropy Drive Pi Phi Satisfaction," *The Arrow of Pi Beta Phi,* Vol. 128, Fall 2011, p. 33.
23 Statistics obtained from the websites for the National Interfraternity Conference (http://www.nicindy.org/press) and National Panhellenic Conference (https://www.npcwomen.org/resources/pdf/Annual%20Report%202011.pdf), accessed October 7, 2013.
24 St. Jude Children's Research Hospital, http://www.stjude.org/stjude/v/index.jsp?vgnextoid=56297ff0be118010VgnVCM1000000e2015acRCRD, accessed October 7, 2013.
25 Michelle Shumate and Amy O'Connor, "Corporate Reporting of Cross-Sector Alliances: The Portfolio of NGO Partners Communicated on Corporate Websites," *Communication Monographs,* Vol. 77, 2010, pp. 207–230.
26 Ken Fisher, "Valve Triumphs Over Vivendi with Settlement," *Arstechnica,* May 1, 2005, http://arstechnica.com/uncategorized/2005/05/4868-2/, accessed October 7, 2013.
27 "One Year Later: Occupy in Disarray but Spirit Lives On," *CBS News,* September 16, 2012, http://www.cbsnews.com/8301-201_162-57513826/one-year-later-occupy-in-disarray-but-spirit-lives-on/, accessed October 7, 2013.
28 Robert D. McPhee and Joel Iverson, "Agents of Constitution in Communidad: Constitutive Processes of Communication in Organizations," in *Building Theories of Organization,* p. 52.
29 Larry D. Browning, Ronald Walter Greene, S. B. Sitkin, Kathleen M. Sutcliffe, and David Obstfeld, "Constitutive Complexity: Military Entrepreneurs and the Synthetic Character of Communication Flows," in *Building Theories of Organization,* pp. 89–116.
30 McPhee and Zaug, p. 29.
31 Pamela Lutgen-Sandvik and Virginia McDermott, "The Constitution of Employee-Abusive Organizations: A Communication Flows Theory," *Communication Theory,* Vol. 18, 2008, p. 304.
32 Ibid., p. 307, italics added for emphasis.
33 Ibid.
34 Ibid.
35 James R. Taylor, *Rethinking the Theory of Organizational Communication: How to Read an Organization,* Ablex, Norwood, NJ, 1993, p. ix. As quoted in François Cooren, "Communication Theory at the Center: Ventriloquism and the Communicative Constitution of Reality," *Communication Theory,* Vol. 62, 2012, p. 4.
36 James R. Taylor, "Organizing From the Bottom Up? Reflections on the Constitution of Organization in Communication," in *Building Theories of Organization,* p. 154.
37 James R. Taylor and Elizabeth J. Van Every, *The Emergent Organization: Communication As Its Site and Surface,* Lawrence Erlbaum, Hillsdale, NJ, 2000.
38 Timothy Kuhn and Karen Lee Ashcraft, "Corporate Scandal and the Theory of the Firm: Formulating the Contributions of Organizational Communication Studies," *Management Communication Quarterly,* Vol. 17, 2003, p. 41. This definition of co-orientation is very similar to Taylor and Van Every, p. 50: "Two actors who are attitudinally related to some object in the same way."
39 Bisel, p. 128.

Chapter 21: Critical Theory of Communication in Organizations

1 Stanley Deetz, *Transforming Communication, Transforming Business: Building Responsive and Responsible Workplaces,* Hampton, Cresskill, NJ, 1995, p. 33.
2 Stanley Deetz, *Democracy in an Age of Corporate Colonization: Developments in Communication and the Politics of Everyday Life,* State University of New York, Albany, NY, 1992, p. 349.
3 http://www.aflcio.org/Corporate-Watch/CEO-Pay-and-You, accessed May 1, 2013.
4 Deetz, *Democracy,* p. 43.
5 Deetz, *Transforming Communication,* p. 68.
6 Deetz, *Democracy,* p. 129.
7 Deetz, *Transforming Communication,* p. 4.
8 Stanley Deetz, "Future of the Discipline: The Challenges, the Research, and the Social Contribution," in *Communication Yearbook 17,* Stanley Deetz (ed.), Sage, Newbury Park, CA, 1994, p. 577.
9 Deetz, *Democracy,* p. 222.
10 Philip Zimbardo, *The Lucifer Effect: Understanding How Good People Turn Evil,* Random House, New York, 2008.
11 Deetz, *Democracy,* p. 217.
12 Ibid., p. 235.
13 Ibid., p. 310.
14 Deetz, *Transforming Communication,* p. 114.
15 Ibid., p. xv.
16 Ibid., p. 85.
17 Stanley Deetz, "The Rise of Stakeholder Governance Models and the Redesign of Communication Necessary for Them," in *Revista Organicom 7: A Comunicação na Gestão para Sustentabilidade das Organizações,* M. Kunsch (ed.), Difusão, São Paulo, Brazil, p. 2.
18 Deetz, *Democracy,* p. 47.
19 Deetz, *Transforming Communication,* p. 3.
20 Ibid., pp. 50–51.

21 Ibid., p. 2.
22 Deetz, *Democracy*, p. 169.
23 Deetz, "The Rise of Stakeholder Governance," p. 4.
24 Ibid., p. 7.
25 Stanley Deetz, "Power and the Possibility of Generative Community Dialogue," in *The Coordinated Management of Meaning: A Festschrift in Honor of W. Barnett Pearce*, Stephen Littlejohn (ed.), Fairleigh Dickinson, Madison, NJ, 2013, in press.
26 Deetz, "The Rise of Stakeholder Governance," p. 8.
27 Stanley Deetz and Elizabeth K. Eger, "Developing a Metatheoretical Perspective for Organizational Communication Studies," in *The New Handbook of Organizational Communication: Advances in Theory, Research, and Methods*, 2nd ed., Fredrick Jablin and Linda L. Putnam (eds.), Sage, Thousand Oaks, CA, 2013, in press.
28 Tim Newton, Stan Deetz, and Mike Reed, "Responses to Social Constructionism and Critical Realism in Organizational Studies," *Organizational Studies*, Vol. 32, 2011, p. 22.
29 "Message from the Chairman," *The National Diet of Japan Fukushima Nuclear Accident Independent Investigation Commission*, http://www.nirs.org/fukushima/naiic_report.pdf, accessed May 7, 2013.
30 Personal conversation with Stan Deetz, April 22, 2013.
31 Robert McPhee, "Comments on Stanley Deetz' Democracy in an Age of Corporate Colonization," paper presented at the 1995 Annual Convention of the Speech Communication Association, San Antonio, November 15–18, 1995.
32 Deetz, "Future of the Discipline," p. 581.
33 Personal correspondence from Stanley Deetz, March 17, 2010.
34 Stanley Deetz, "Critical Theory," in *Engaging Organizational Communication Theory: Multiple Perspectives*, S. May and Dennis Mumby (eds.), Sage, Thousand Oaks, CA, 2004, p. 101.
35 Ibid., p. 103.

Public Rhetoric

1 Aristotle, *On Rhetoric: A Theory of Civil Discourse*, George A. Kennedy (ed. and trans.), Oxford University Press, New York, 1991, p. 36.
2 Plato, *Gorgias*, Lane Cooper (trans.), Oxford University Press, New York, 1948, p. 122.
3 1 Corinthians 2:4, New Revised Standard Version of the Bible.
4 1 Corinthians 9:22, New Revised Standard Version of the Bible.
5 Hugh C. Dick (ed.), *Selected Writings of Francis Bacon*, Modern Library, New York, 1955, p. x.

Chapter 22: The Rhetoric

1 Clarke Rountree, "Sophist," in *Encyclopedia of Rhetoric and Composition: Communication from Ancient Times to the Information Age*, Theresa Enos (ed.), Garland, New York, 1996, p. 681.
2 Aristotle, *On Rhetoric: A Theory of Civil Discourse*, George A. Kennedy (ed. and trans.), Oxford University Press, New York, 1991, p. 35.
3 David J. Garrow, *Bearing the Cross*, William Morrow, New York, 1986, p. 284.
4 Aristotle, p. 33.
5 Lloyd Bitzer, "Aristotle's Enthymeme Revisited," *Quarterly Journal of Speech*, Vol. 45, 1959, p. 409.
6 Attributed to Ralph Waldo Emerson by Dale Carnegie, *How to Win Friends and Influence People*, Pocket Books, New York, 1982, p. 29.
7 James McCroskey and Jason Teven, "Goodwill: A Reexamination of the Construct and Its Measurement," *Communication Monographs*, Vol. 66, 1999, pp. 90–103.
8 Jeffrey Walker, "*Pathos* and *Katharsis* in 'Aristotelian' Rhetoric: Some Implications," in *Rereading Aristotle's Rhetoric*, Alan Gross and Arthur Walzer (eds.), Southern Illinois University, Carbondale, IL, 2000, pp. 74–92.
9 Aristotle, p. 122.
10 Lane Cooper, *The Rhetoric of Aristotle*, Appleton-Century-Crofts, New York, 1932, introduction.
11 Aristotle, p. 258.
12 Ibid., p. 244.
13 Ibid., p. 223.
14 Sara Newman, "Aristotle's Notion of 'Bringing-Before-the-Eyes': Its Contributions to Aristotelian and Contemporary Conceptualizations of Metaphor, Style, and Audience," *Rhetorica*, Vol. 20, 2002, pp. 1–23.
15 Amos 5:24, Revised Standard Version of the Bible.
16 Theodore White, *The Making of the President, 1964*, Atheneum, New York, 1965, p. 288.
17 Aristotle, *Nicomachean Ethics*, H. Rackham (trans.), Harvard University, Cambridge, MA, 1934, book 4, chapter 7.
18 Alan Gross and Marcelo Dascal, "The Conceptual Unity of Aristotle's Rhetoric," *Philosophy and Rhetoric*, Vol. 34, 2001, p. 288.
19 Voltaire, *Dictionnaire Philosophique*, "Aristotle," Oeuvres Complètes de Voltaire, Vol. 17, Librairie Garnier, Paris, p. 372.

Chapter 23: Dramatism

1 Kenneth Burke, "Dramatism," in *International Encyclopedia of the Social Sciences*, Vol. 7, David Sills (ed.), Macmillan/Free, New York, NY, 1968, p. 446.
2 Edward C. Appel, *Language, Life, Literature, Rhetoric and Composition as Dramatic Action: A Burkean Primer*, Oar Press, Leola, PA, 2012, pp. 5–6.
3 Matthew Josephson, *Life Among the Surrealists: A Memoir*, Holt, Rinehart and Winston, New York, 1962, p. 35.
4 Marie Hochmuth Nichols, "Kenneth Burke and the New Rhetoric," *Quarterly Journal of Speech*, Vol. 38, 1952, pp. 133–144.
5 Kenneth Burke, *A Grammar of Motives*, University of California, Berkeley, 1969, p. xv.
6 David Bobbitt, *The Rhetoric of Redemption: Kenneth Burke's Redemption Drama and Martin Luther King Jr.'s "I Have a Dream" Speech*, Rowman & Littlefield, Lanham, MD, 2004, p. 49.
7 http://www.americanrhetoric.com/speeches/gwbush911jointsessionspeech.htm, accessed December 29, 2012.
8 Burke, *Grammar of Motives*, pp. 127–320.
9 Ibid., pp. 3–20.
10 Appel, p. 4.
11 Kenneth Burke, *Rhetoric of Religion: Studies in Logology*, Beacon, Boston, 1969, p. 19.
12 Bobbitt, pp. 89–90.
13 Kenneth Burke, "Definition of Man," in *Language as Symbolic Action: Essays on Life, Literature, and Method*, University of California, Berkeley, 1966, p. 16.
14 Paul Dickson, *The Official Rules*, Dell, New York, 1978, p. 165.
15 Kenneth Burke, *Permanence and Change: An Anatomy of Purpose*, Bobbs-Merrill, Indianapolis, IN, 1965, pp. 69–70, also entire Part II; Burke, *Attitudes Toward History*, Hermes, Los Altos, CA, 1959, pp. 308–314.
16 Burke, *Permanence and Change*, p. 283.
17 Burke, *Rhetoric of Religion*, pp. 190, 206.

18 Kenneth Burke, *Philosophy of Literary Form: Studies in Symbolic Action*, Berkeley, CA, 1973, pp. 39–40, 203; see also Kenneth Burke, *Language as Symbolic Action*, pp. 435, 478.
19 Daniel Aaron, "Thirty Years Later: Memories of the First American Writers' Congress," *American Scholar*, Vol. 35, 1966, p. 499.
20 Adolf Hitler, *Mein Kampf*, Educa, Ottawa, Ontario, 2006.
21 Kenneth Burke, "Rhetoric—Old and New," *Journal of General Education*, Vol. 5, 1951, p. 203.
22 See, for example, Marshall Prisbell and Janis Anderson, "The Importance of Perceived Homophily, Levels of Uncertainty, Feeling Good, Safety, and Self-Disclosure in Interpersonal Relationships," *Communication Quarterly*, Vol. 28, 1980, No. 3, pp. 22–33.
23 Kenneth Burke, *A Rhetoric of Motives*, University of California, Berkeley, 1969, p. 55.
24 Ruth 1:16, Revised Standard Version of the Bible.
25 Malcolm X, "The Ballot or the Bullet," in *Great Speakers and Speeches*, 2nd ed., John Lucaites and Lawrence Bernabo (eds.), Kendall/Hunt, Dubuque, IA, 1992, pp. 277–286.
26 Nichols, p. 144.

Chapter 24: Narrative Paradigm

1 Walter R. Fisher, *Human Communication as Narration: Toward a Philosophy of Reason, Value, and Action*, University of South Carolina, Columbia, 1987, p. 24.
2 Ibid., p. xi.
3 Walter R. Fisher, "Toward a Logic of Good Reasons," *Quarterly Journal of Speech*, Vol. 64, 1978, pp. 376–384; Walter R. Fisher, "Narration as a Human Communication Paradigm: The Case of Public Moral Argument," *Communication Monographs*, Vol. 51, 1984, pp. 1–22.
4 See the book of Ruth in the Torah or Old Testament.
5 Frederick Buechner, *Peculiar Treasures*, HarperCollins, New York, 1979, pp. 166–168.
6 Fisher, *Human Communication as Narration*, p. 58.
7 Walter R. Fisher, "Clarifying the Narrative Paradigm," *Communication Monographs*, Vol. 56, 1989, pp. 55–58.
8 Thomas Kuhn, *The Structure of Scientific Revolutions*, University of Chicago, IL, 1962.
9 Fisher, *Human Communication as Narration*, p. 194.
10 Ibid., p. 20.
11 Ibid., pp. 59–62.
12 Ibid., pp. 62–69.
13 Ibid., p. 66.
14 Ibid, pp. 105–123.
15 Ibid., p. 109.
16 Ibid., pp. 187–188.
17 Ibid., p. 188.
18 Ruth 1:16, New Living Translation of the Bible.
19 Fisher, *Human Communication as Narration*, p. 76.
20 Barbara Warnick, "The Narrative Paradigm: Another Story," *Quarterly Journal of Speech*, Vol. 73, 1987, p. 176.
21 William G. Kirkwood, "Narration and the Rhetoric of Possibility," *Communication Monographs*, Vol. 59, 1992, pp. 30–47.
22 Fisher, *Human Communication as Narration*, p. 66.
23 Kevin McClure, "Resurrecting the Narrative Paradigm: Identification and the Case of Young Earth Creationism," *Rhetoric Society Quarterly*, Vol. 39, 2009, pp. 197, 208.
24 Fisher, *Human Communication as Narration*, p. 67.
25 Walter R. Fisher, "The Narrative Paradigm: An Invitation, Not a Demand; A Proposal, Not a Panacea," paper presented at the Speech Communication Association Annual Meeting, San Francisco, 1989.

Media and Culture

1 David Lyon, *Postmodernity*, 2nd ed., University of Minnesota, Minneapolis, 1999. For a fictional introduction to postmodernism, see Arthur Asa Berger, *Postmortem for a Postmodernist*, Alta Mira, Walnut Creek, CA, 1997.
2 Jean Baudrillard, "On Nihilism," *On the Beach*, Vol. 6, Spring 1984, pp. 38–39.
3 Jean-François Lyotard, *The Postmodern Condition: A Report on Knowledge*, University of Minnesota, Minneapolis, 1984, p. xxiv.
4 Jean Baudrillard, *America*, Verso, London, 1988, p. 166.
5 Lyotard, *The Postmodern Condition*, p. 76.
6 Fredric Jameson, "Postmodernism and Consumer Society," in *The Anti-Aesthetic: Essays on Postmodern Culture*, H. Foster (ed.), Bay Press, Port Townsend, WA, 1983, p. 113.

Chapter 25: Media Ecology

1 Rachael Dretzin and Douglas Rushkoff (eds.), "Digital Nation," *Frontline*, WGBH, Boston, February 2, 2010.
2 Marshall McLuhan, "*Playboy* Interview: A Candid Conversation with the High Priest of Popcult and Metaphysician of Media," March 1969, p. 53ff. Reprinted in *Essential McLuhan*, Eric McLuhan and Frank Zingrone (eds.), BasicBooks, New York, 1995, p. 238.
3 Marshall McLuhan, *Understanding Media: The Extensions of Man*, Gingko, Corte Madera, CA, 2003, p. 31.
4 http://www.nfl.com/videos/nfl-super-bowl-commercials/0ap2000000134659/Brotherhood, accessed June 5, 2013.
5 Marshall McLuhan and Quentin Fiore, *The Medium Is the Massage: An Inventory of Effects*, Touchstone, New York, 1989, p. 26.
6 Ibid., pp. 84–85.
7 Ibid., p. 50.
8 John 8:32, New International Version of the Bible.
9 McLuhan and Fiore, p. 40.
10 Maurice Charland, "McLuhan and the Problematic of Modernity: Riding the Maelstrom of Technological Mediation," unpublished manuscript.
11 Neil Postman, *Amusing Ourselves to Death*, Penguin, New York, 1985, p. 6.
12 Ibid., p. 7.
13 Neil Postman, "The Humanism of Media Ecology," Keynote Address, Inaugural Media Ecology Association Convention, Fordham University, New York, June 2000. Available at http://www.media-ecology.org/publications/MEA_proceedings/v1/humanism_of_media_ecology.html, accessed November 20, 2010.
14 Neil Postman, "Informing Ourselves to Death," German Informatics Society, Stuttgart, Germany, October 11, 1990. Available at http://w2.eff.org/Net_culture/Criticisms/informing_ourselves_to_death.paper, accessed October 21, 2013.
15 Neil Postman, *The Disappearance of Childhood*, Vintage, NewYork, 1994, p. 73.
16 McLuhan, *Understanding Media*, p. 17.
17 Dan M. Davin in *McLuhan: Hot & Cool*, Gerald Stearn (ed.), Dial, New York, 1967, p. 185.
18 Dwight Macdonald in *McLuhan: Hot & Cool*, p. 203.
19 Christopher Ricks in *McLuhan: Hot & Cool*, p. 211.
20 George N. Gordon, "An End to McLuhanacy," *Educational Technology*, January 1982, p. 42.
21 Thomas W. Cooper, "The Medium Is the Mass: Marshall McLuhan's Catholicism and catholicism," *Journal of Media and Religion*, Vol. 5, 2006.

22 Marshall McLuhan, *Letters of Marshall McLuhan*, Matie Molinaro, Corinne McLuhan, and William Toye (eds.), Oxford University Press, Toronto, 1987, p. 384.
23 Marshall McLuhan, *The Medium and the Light: Reflections on Religion*, Eric McLuhan and Jacek Szklarek (eds.), Stoddart, Toronto, 1999, p. 103.
24 Tom Wolfe in *McLuhan: Hot & Cool*, p. 31.
25 Kenneth Boulding in *McLuhan: Hot & Cool*, p. 57.
26 Robert Putnam, "Bowling Alone: America's Declining Social Capital," *Journal of Democracy*, Vol. 6, No. 1, 1995, pp. 65–78.

Chapter 26: Semiotics

1 Roland Barthes, *The Semiotic Challenge*, Richard Howard (trans.), University of California, Berkeley, 1994, p. 4.
2 James R. Beniger, "Who Are the Most Important Theorists of Communication?" *Communication Research*, Vol. 17, 1990, pp. 698–715.
3 Umberto Eco, *A Theory of Semiotics*, Indiana University, Bloomington, 1976, p. 7.
4 Ferdinand de Saussure, *Course in General Linguistics*, Wade Baskin (trans.), McGraw-Hill, New York, 1966, p. 16.
5 Roland Barthes, "The World of Wrestling," in *Mythologies*, Annette Lavers (trans.), Hill and Wang, New York, 1972, p. 17.
6 Ibid., pp. 19, 24.
7 See Barthes' use of this phrase in *The Semiotic Challenge*, p. 85. Barthes used these words to describe rhetoricians' efforts to categorize figures of speech—alliteration, hyperbole, irony, etc. The phrase is even more appropriate to characterize his book *Elements of Semiology*, Annette Lavers and Colin Smith (trans.), Jonathan Cape, London, 1967.
8 Donald Fry and Virginia Fry, "Continuing the Conversation Regarding Myth and Culture: An Alternative Reading of Barthes," *American Journal of Semiotics*, Vol. 6, No. 2/3, 1989, pp. 183–197.
9 Irwin Levine and L. Russell Brown, "Tie a Yellow Ribbon Round the Ole Oak Tree," Levine and Brown Music, Inc., 1973.
10 Barthes, "Myth Today," in *Mythologies*, p. 118.
11 W. Thomas Duncanson, "Issues of Transcendence and Value in a Semiotic Frame," paper presented to a joint session of the Religious Speech Communication Association and the Speech Communication Association Convention, San Francisco, November 19, 1989, p. 29.
12 Kyong Kim, *Caged in Our Own Signs: A Book about Semiotics*, Ablex, Norwood, NJ, 1996, p. 189.
13 Daniel Chandler, *Semiotics: The Basics*, 2nd ed., Routledge, New York, 2007, pp. 13–57.
14 Anne Norton, *Republic of Signs: Liberal Theory and American Popular Culture*, University of Chicago Press, Chicago, 1993, p. 60.
15 Douglas Kellner, "Cultural Studies, Multiculturalism, and Media Culture," in *Gender, Race and Class in Media: A Text-Reader*, Gail Dines and Jan M. Humez (eds.), Sage, Thousand Oaks, CA, 1996, p. 15.
16 Stuart Hall, "The Work of Representation," in *Representation: Cultural Representations and Signifying Practices*, Stuart Hall (ed.), Sage, London, pp. 13–74.

Chapter 27: Cultural Studies

1 www.rasmussenreports.com/public_content/politics/current_events/healthcare/health_care_law, accessed September 3, 2013.
2 Stuart Hall, "Ideology and Communication Theory," in *Rethinking Communication Theory, Vol. 1: Paradigm Issues*, Brenda Dervin, Lawrence Grossberg, Barbara J. O'Keefe, and Ellen Wartella (eds.), Sage, Newbury Park, CA, 1989, p. 52.
3 Stuart Hall, "The Problem of Ideology—Marxism Without Guarantees," *Journal of Communication Inquiry*, Vol. 10, No. 2, 1986, p. 29.
4 Jorge Larrain, "Stuart Hall and the Marxist Concept of Ideology," in *Stuart Hall: Critical Dialogues in Cultural Studies*, David Morley and Kuan-Hsing Chen (eds.), Routledge, New York, 1996, p. 49.
5 Lawrence Grossberg, "History, Politics and Postmodernism: Stuart Hall and Cultural Studies," *Journal of Communication Inquiry*, Vol. 10, No. 2, 1986, p. 72.
6 Hall, "The Problem of Ideology," pp. 28–44.
7 Antonio Gramsci, *Selections from the Prison Notebooks of Antonio Gramsci*, Quintin Hoare and Geoffrey Nowell Smith (eds. and trans.), International Publishers, New York, 1971.
8 Stuart Hall, *Representations: Cultural Representations and Signifying Practices*, Sage, London, 1997, p. 2.
9 Michel Foucault, *Madness and Civilization: A History of Insanity in the Age of Reason*, Random House, New York, 1965.
10 Michel Foucault, *The Archaeology of Knowledge*, Tavistock, London, 1982, p. 46.
11 Herbert Gans, *Deciding What's News: A Study of CBS Evening News, NBC Nightly News,* Newsweek, *and* Time, Northwestern University, Evanston, IL, 1979.
12 From the CIA World Factbook shown in http://en.wikipedia.org/wiki/List_of_countries_by_infant_mortality_rate, accessed September 8, 2013.
13 http://www.usatoday.com/story/money/business/2013/08/22/report-medicare-physician-access/2682301/, accessed September 7, 2013.
14 Stuart Hall, "The Neo-Liberal Revolution," *Cultural Studies*, Vol. 25, 2011, pp. 705–728.
15 Luke Winslow, "Comforting the Comfortable: *Extreme Makeover Home Edition's* Ideological Conquest," *Critical Studies in Media Communication*, Vol. 27, 2010, p. 269.
16 After a 10-year run, the final program aired on December 16, 2012. http://www.abc.go.com/shows/extreme-makeover-home-edition/episode-guide, accessed September 8, 2013.
17 Winslow, "Comforting the Comfortable," p. 271.
18 Ibid., p. 276.
19 Ibid., p. 280.
20 Ibid., p. 286.
21 Stuart Hall, "Notes on Deconstructing 'The Popular,'" http://www.udel.edu/History/suisman/611_S05_webpage/Hall_Notes-decon-popular.pdf, p. 453, accessed September 3, 2013.
22 Grossberg, "History, Politics and Postmodernism," p. 65.
23 James Anderson and Amie Kincaid, "Media Subservience and Satirical Subversiveness: *The Daily Show, The Colbert Report*, The Propaganda Model and the Paradox of Parody," *Critical Studies in Media Communication*, Vol. 30, 2013, pp. 171–188.
24 Ibid.
25 Cornel West, *The American Evasion of Philosophy: A Genealogy of Pragmatism*, University of Wisconsin, Madison, 1989, p. 86.
26 Ibid., p. 239.
27 Reinhold Niebuhr, *Christian Realism and Political Problems*, Charles Scribner's Sons, New York, 1953, pp. 1–14.
28 See Cornel West, *Prophecy Deliverance*, Westminster Press, Philadelphia, PA, 1982, pp. 95–127.
29 West, *American Evasion*, p. 233.
30 The Good Samaritan, Luke 10:25–37.

31 Clair Alexander, "Introduction: Stuart Hall and 'Race,'" *Cultural Studies*, Vol. 23, 2009, p. 457.
32 Stuart Hall, "On Postmodernism and Articulation: An Interview with Stuart Hall," Lawrence Grossberg (ed.), *Journal of Communication Inquiry*, Vol. 10, No. 2, 1986, p. 45.
33 Cited by Helen Davis, *Understanding Stuart Hall*, Sage, Thousand Oaks, CA, 2004, p. 128.
34 *Parekh Report of the Commission on the Future of Multi-Ethnic Britain*, Profile/The Runnymede Trust, London, 2000, p. 169.
35 Clifford Christians, "Normativity as Catalyst," in *Rethinking Communication Theory*, p. 148.
36 Samuel Becker, "Communication Studies: Visions of the Future," in *Rethinking Communication Theory*, p. 126.

Media Effects

1 Paul Lazarsfeld, Bernard Berelson, and Hazel Gaudet, *The People's Choice*, Duell, Sloan and Pearce, New York, 1944.
2 A. W. van den Ban, "A Review of the Two-Step Flow of Communication Hypothesis," in *Speech Communication Behavior*, Larry L. Barker and Robert Kiebler (eds.), Prentice-Hall, Englewood Cliffs, NJ, 1971, pp. 193–205.
3 Dolf Zillmann, "Excitation Transfer in Communication-Mediated Aggressive Behavior," *Journal of Experimental Social Psychology*, Vol. 7, 1971, pp. 419–434.
4 Albert Bandura, *Social Learning Theory*, Prentice-Hall, Englewood Cliffs, NJ, 1977.
5 Igor Pantic, Aleksandar Damjanovic, Jovana Todorovic, Dubravka Topalovic, Dragana Bojovic-Jovic, Sinisa Ristic, and Senka Pantic, "Association Between Online Social Networking and Depression in High School Students: Behavioral Physiology Viewpoint," *Psychiatria Danubina*, Vol. 24, 2012, pp. 90–93.
6 Lauren Jelenchick, Jens Eickhoff, and Megan Moreno, "'Facebook Depression?' Social Networking Site Use and Depression in Older Adolescents," *Journal of Adolescent Health*, Vol. 52, 2013, pp. 128–130.
7 Maria Kalpidou, Dan Costin, and Jessica Morris, "The Relationship Between Facebook and the Well-Being of Undergraduate College Students," *Cyberpsychology, Behavior, and Social Networking*, Vol. 14, 2011, pp. 183–189.

Chapter 28: Uses and Gratifications

1 "Man Dies After Playing Video Game for 32 Hours," *The Sydney Morning Herald*, October 20, 2002, http://www.smh.com.au/articles/2002/10/19/1034561356377.html, accessed September 11, 2010.
2 "S Korean Dies After Games Session," *BBC News*, August 10, 2005, http://news.bbc.co.uk/2/hi/technology/4137782.stm, accessed September 11, 2010.
3 Paul and Alex are hypothetical roommates invented for this chapter, but the stories of the men who died playing video games are well-documented, real-life cases.
4 Aliyah Shahid, "Xbox Addict, Chris Staniforth, Killed by Blood Clot After Marathon Gaming Session in England," *Daily News*, July 30, 2011, http://www.nydailynews.com/news/world/xbox-addict-chris-staniforth-killed-blood-clot-marathon-gaming-session-england-article-1.162095, accessed August 13, 2013.
5 Elihu Katz, "Mass Communication Research and the Study of Popular Culture: An Editorial Note on a Possible Future for This Journal," *Studies in Public Communication*, Vol. 2, 1959, pp. 1–6.
6 Bernard Berelson, "The State of Communication Research," *Public Opinion Quarterly*, Vol. 23, 1959, pp. 1–6.
7 Paul Lazarsfeld, Bernard Berelson, and Hazel Gaudet, *The People's Choice*, Columbia University Press, New York, 1948.
8 Werner J. Severin and James W. Tankard Jr., *Communication Theories: Origins, Methods, and Uses in the Mass Media*, Longman, New York, 2001, pp. 293–294.
9 The core ideas of the theory detailed here are presented in Alan M. Rubin, "Uses and Gratifications: An Evolving Perspective of Media Effects," in *The Sage Handbook of Media Processes and Effects*, Robin L. Nabi and Mary Beth Oliver (eds.), Sage, Los Angeles, CA, 2009, pp. 147–159.
10 Elihu Katz, Jay G. Blumler, and Michael Gurevitch, "Utilization of Mass Communication by the Individual," in *The Uses of Mass Communications: Current Perspectives on Gratifications Research*, Jay G. Blumler and Elihu Katz (eds.), Sage, Beverly Hills, CA, 1974, p. 21.
11 Zizi Papacharissi and Alan M. Rubin, "Predictors of Internet Use," *Journal of Broadcasting & Electronic Media*, Vol. 44, 2000, pp. 175–196.
12 Seth Finn, "Origins of Media Exposure: Linking Personality Traits to TV, Radio, Print, and Film Use," *Communication Research*, Vol. 24, 1997, pp. 507–529.
13 Glenn G. Sparks and Cheri W. Sparks, "Violence, Mayhem and Horror," in *Media Entertainment: The Psychology of Its Appeal*, Dolf Zillmann and Peter Vorderer (eds.), Lawrence Erlbaum, Mahwah, NJ, 2000, pp. 73–91.
14 Jay G. Blumler and Denis McQuail, *Television in Politics*, University of Chicago Press, Chicago, IL, 1969.
15 Jack M. McLeod and Lee B. Becker, "Testing the Validity of Gratification Measures Through Political Effects Analysis," in *The Uses of Mass Communications*, pp. 137–164.
16 Alan M. Rubin, "An Examination of Television Viewing Motives," *Communication Research*, Vol. 8, 1981, pp. 141–165.
17 Bradley S. Greenberg, "Gratifications of Television Viewing and Their Correlates for British Children," in *The Uses of Mass Communications*, pp. 71–92.
18 Robert Kubey and Mihaly Csikszentmihalyi, "Television Addiction Is No Mere Metaphor," *Scientific American*, Vol. 286, No. 2, 2002, pp. 74–80.
19 David Giles, *Illusions of Immortality: A Psychology of Fame and Celebrity*, Macmillan, London, 2000, p. 64.
20 Alan M. Rubin, Elizabeth M. Perse, and Robert A. Powell, "Loneliness, Parasocial Interaction, and Local Television News Viewing," *Human Communication Research*, Vol. 12, 1985, pp. 155–180.
21 Public Broadcasting System, *On Television: The Violence Factor*, video directed by Mary Magee, distributed by California Newsreel, San Francisco, CA, 1984.
22 Maane Khatchatourian, "The Memory of Cory Monteith Lives On (and On) Via Social Media," *Variety*, July 31, 2013, http://variety.com/2013/digital/news/the-memory-of-cory-monteith-lives-on-and-on-on-social-media-1200569547/, accessed August 13, 2013.
23 Alan M. Rubin, "Uses-and-Gratifications Perspective on Media Effects," in *Media Effects: Advances in Theory and Research*, Jennings Bryant and Mary Beth Oliver (eds.), Lawrence Erlbaum, New York, 2009, pp. 165–184.
24 William J. Brown and Michael D. Basil, "Media Celebrities and Public Health: Responses to 'Magic' Johnson's HIV Disclosure and Its Impact on AIDS Risk and High-Risk Behaviors," *Health Communication*, Vol. 7, 1995, pp. 345–370.
25 Jiyeon So, "Uses, Gratifications, and Beyond: Toward a Model of Motivated Media Exposure and Its Effects on Risk Perception," *Communication Theory*, Vol. 22, No. 2, 2012, pp. 116–137.
26 Philip Elliott, "Uses and Gratifications Research: A Critique and a Sociological Alternative," in *The Uses of Mass Communications*, pp. 249–268.
27 Alan Rubin, "Ritualized and Instrumental Television Viewing," *Journal of Communication*, Vol. 34, No. 3, 1984, pp. 67–77.

Chapter 29: Cultivation Theory

1 George Gerbner and Larry Gross, "Living with Television: The Violence Profile," *Journal of Communication*, Vol. 26, 1976, No. 2, p. 76.
2 Ibid., p. 77.
3 Jerome H. Skolnick, *The Politics of Protest*, Simon and Schuster, New York, 1969, pp. 3–24.
4 Michael Morgan, James Shanahan, and Nancy Signorielli, "Growing Up With Television," in *Media Effects: Advances in Theory & Research*, Jennings Bryant and Mary Beth Oliver (eds.), Routledge, New York, 2009, pp. 34–49.
5 George Gerbner, Larry Gross, Michael Morgan, and Nancy Signorielli, "Charting the Mainstream: Television's Contributions to Political Orientations," *Journal of Communication*, Vol. 32, No. 2, 1982, p. 103.
6 Morgan, Shanahan, and Signorielli, p. 35.
7 Ibid., p. 38.
8 Glenn Sparks and Robert Ogles, "The Difference Between Fear of Victimization and the Probability of Being Victimized: Implications for Cultivation," *Journal of Broadcasting & Electronic Media*, Vol. 34, 1990, No. 3, pp. 351–358.
9 L. J. Shrum, "Media Consumption and Perceptions of Social Reality: Effects and Underlying Processes," in *Media Effects: Advances in Theory & Research*, pp. 50–73.
10 Gerbner, Gross, Morgan, and Signorielli, p. 117.
11 George Gerbner, Larry Gross, Michael Morgan, and Nancy Signorielli, "The 'Mainstreaming' of America: Violence Profile No. 11," *Journal of Communication*, Vol. 30, No. 3, 1980, p. 15.
12 Gerbner, Gross, Morgan, and Signorielli, "Charting the Mainstream," p. 103.
13 Michael Morgan and James Shanahan, "Two Decades of Cultivation Research: An Appraisal and a Meta-Analysis," in *Communication Yearbook 20*, Brant R. Burleson (ed.), Sage, Thousand Oaks, CA, 1997, pp. 1–45.
14 Anthony Doob and Glenn Macdonald, "Television Viewing and Fear of Victimization: Is the Relationship Causal?" *Journal of Personality and Social Psychology*, Vol. 37, No. 2, 1979, pp. 170–179.
15 Morgan and Shanahan, p. 5.

Chapter 30: Agenda-Setting Theory

1 Maxwell McCombs, "News Influence on Our Pictures of the World," in *Media Effects: Advances in Theory and Research*, Jennings Bryant and Dolf Zillmann (eds.), Lawrence Erlbaum, Hillsdale, NJ, 1994, p. 4.
2 Maxwell McCombs and Donald Shaw, "A Progress Report on Agenda-Setting Research," paper presented to the Association for Education in Journalism and Mass Communication, Theory and Methodology Division, San Diego, CA, April 18–27, 1974, p. 28.
3 Walter Lippmann, *Public Opinion*, Macmillan, New York, 1922, p. 3.
4 Bernard C. Cohen, *The Press and Foreign Policy*, Princeton University, Princeton, NJ, 1963, p. 13.
5 Theodore White, *The Making of the President, 1972*, Bantam, New York, 1973, p. 245.
6 Paul Lazarsfeld, Bernard Berelson, and Hazel Gaudet, *The People's Choice*, Duell, Sloan and Pearce, New York, 1944.
7 Maxwell McCombs and Donald Shaw, "The Agenda-Setting Function of the Mass Media," *Public Opinion Quarterly*, Vol. 36, 1972, pp. 176–187.
8 Ray Funkhouser, "The Issues of the Sixties: An Exploratory Study in the Dynamics of Public Opinion," *Public Opinion Quarterly*, Vol. 37, 1973, pp. 62–75.
9 Shanto Iyengar, Mark Peters, and Donald Kinder, "Experimental Demonstrations of the 'Not-So-Minimal' Consequences of Television News Programs," *American Political Science Review*, Vol. 76, 1982, pp. 848–858. The experiment reported is only one of a series of studies conducted by Iyengar and Kinder at Yale and the University of Michigan.
10 Maxwell McCombs and Tamara Bell, "The Agenda-Setting Role of Mass Communication," in *An Integrated Approach to Communication Theory and Research*, Michael Salwen and Donald Stacks (eds.), Lawrence Erlbaum, Hillsdale, NJ, 1996, p. 100.
11 James Tankard et al., "Media Frames: Approaches to Conceptualization and Measurement," paper presented at the annual meeting of the Association for Education in Journalism and Mass Communication, Boston, August 1991.
12 Maxwell McCombs, "New Frontiers in Agenda Setting: Agendas of Attributes and Frames," *Mass Communication Review*, Vol. 24, 1997, pp. 32–52.
13 Robert Entman, "Framing: Toward Clarification of a Fractured Paradigm," *Journal of Communication*, Vol. 43, No. 3, 1993, p. 52.
14 Maxwell McCombs, Esteban López-Escobar, and Juan Pablo Llamas, "Setting the Agenda of Attributes in the 1996 Spanish General Election," *Journal of Communication*, Vol. 50, No. 2, 2000, pp. 77–92; Toshiro Takeshita and Shunji Mikami, "A Study of Agenda Setting," *Keio Communication Review*, Vol. 17, 1995, pp. 27–41; Sebastián Valenzuela and Maxwell McCombs, "Agenda-Setting Effects on Vote Choice: Evidence from the 2006 Mexican Election," paper presented at the Political Communication Division of the International Communication Association, San Francisco, CA, May 2007.
15 Salma Ghanem, "Media Coverage of Crime and Public Opinion: An Explanation of the Second Level of Agenda Setting," unpublished doctoral dissertation, University of Texas at Austin, 1996. The study is also described in McCombs, "New Frontiers in Agenda Setting," pp. 11–12.
16 Kihan Kim and Maxwell McCombs, "News Story Descriptions and the Public's Opinions of Political Candidates," *Journalism and Mass Communication Quarterly*, Vol. 84, 2007, pp. 299–314.
17 McCombs, "New Frontiers in Agenda Setting," p. 48.
18 Craig Trumbo, "The Effect of Newspaper Coverage of Influenza on the Rate of Physician Visits for Influenza 2002–2008," *Mass Communication and Society*, Vol. 15, 2012, pp. 718–738.
19 John Fortunato, *The Ultimate Assist: The Relationship and Broadcasting Strategies of the NBA and Television Networks*, Hampton, Cresskill, NJ, 2001.
20 Young Jun Son and David Weaver, "Another Look at What Moves Public Opinion: Media Agenda Setting and Polls in the 2000 U.S. Election," *International Journal of Public Opinion Research*, Vol. 18, 2006, pp. 174–197.
21 Maxwell McCombs, *Setting the Agenda*, Polity, Cambridge, UK, 2004, p. 140.
22 McCombs, "News Influence," p. 11.
23 Maxwell McCombs and Marcus Funk, "Shaping the Agenda of Local Daily Newspapers: A Methodology Merging the Agenda Setting and Community Structure Perspectives," *Mass Communication and Society*, Vol. 14, 2011, pp. 905–919.
24 Scott Althaus and David Tewksbury, "Agenda Setting and the 'New' News: Patterns of Issue Importance Among Readers of the Paper and Online Versions of *The New York Times*," *Communication Research*, Vol. 29, 2002, pp. 180–207.
25 Ibid., p. 197.

26 Adam Shehata and Jesper Strömbäck, "Not (Yet) a New Era of Minimal Effects: A Study of Agenda Setting at the Aggregate and Individual Levels," *Harvard International Journal of Press Politics*, Vol. 18, 2013, pp. 234–255.
27 Renita Coleman and Maxwell McCombs, "The Young and Agenda-less? Exploring Age-Related Differences in Agenda Setting on the Youngest Generation, Baby Boomers, and the Civic Generation," *Journalism and Mass Communication Quarterly*, Vol. 84, 2007, p. 505.
28 Clifford Christians, John Ferré, and Mark Fackler, *Good News: Social Ethics and the Press*, Oxford University Press, New York, 1993.
29 Richard Rorty, *Philosophy and the Mirror of Nature*, Princeton University, Princeton, NJ, 1979, p. 373.
30 Christians, Ferré, and Fackler, p. 192.
31 Martin Buber, *I and Thou*, 2nd ed., R. G. Smith (trans.), Scribner's, New York, 1958, pp. 60, 69.
32 Christians, Ferré, and Fackler, pp. 69, 73.
33 Ibid., p. 89.
34 Ibid., pp. 78, 111–113.
35 Clifford Christians and Kaarle Nordenstreng, "Social Responsibility Worldwide," *Journal of Mass Media Ethics*, Vol. 19, 2004, pp. 3–28.
36 Christians, Ferré, and Fackler, p. 92.
37 McCombs, "News Influence," p. 6.
38 Gerald Kosicki, "Problems and Opportunities in Agenda-Setting Research," *Journal of Communication*, Vol. 43, No. 2, 1993, p. 113.
39 Donald Shaw and Maxwell McCombs (eds.), *The Emergence of American Political Issues*, West, St. Paul, MN, 1977, p. 12.
40 McCombs, "New Frontiers in Agenda Setting," p. 9.

Intercultural Communication

1 Gerry Philipsen, *Speaking Culturally: Exploration in Social Communication*, State University of New York, Albany, 1992, p. 7.
2 Gerry Philipsen, "Speaking 'Like a Man' in Teamsterville: Cultural Patterns of Role Enactment in an Urban Neighborhood," *Quarterly Journal of Speech*, Vol. 61, 1975, pp. 13–22.
3 Donal Carbaugh, "Communication Rules in *Donahue* Discourse," in *Cultural Communication and Intercultural Contact*, Donal Carbaugh (ed.), Lawrence Erlbaum, Hillsdale, NJ, 1990, pp. 119–149.
4 See chapter on cultural variability in William B. Gudykunst and Stella Ting-Toomey, *Culture and Interpersonal Communication*, Sage, Newbury Park, CA, 1988, pp. 39–59.
5 Edward T. Hall, *Beyond Culture*, Anchor, New York, 1977, p. 91.
6 Ibid., pp. 85–128.
7 Personal correspondence from Gerry Philipsen, August 2, 2009.

Chapter 31: Communication Accommodation Theory

1 Howard Giles, "Accent Mobility: A Model and Some Data," *Anthropological Linguistics*, Vol. 15, 1973, pp. 87–109.
2 Cindy Gallois, Tania Ogay, and Howard Giles, "Communication Accommodation Theory: A Look Back and a Look Ahead," in *Theorizing About Intercultural Communication*, William B. Gudykunst (ed.), Sage, Thousand Oaks, CA, 2005, p. 123.
3 Nikolas Coupland, Justine Coupland, Howard Giles, and Karen Henwood, "Accommodating the Elderly: Invoking and Extending a Theory," *Language and Society*, Vol. 17, 1988, p. 3.
4 Angie Williams and Howard Giles, "Intergenerational Conversations: Young Adults' Retrospective Accounts," *Human Communication Research*, Vol. 23, 1996, p. 237.
5 Ibid., p. 239.
6 Howard Giles, Nikolas Coupland, and Justine Coupland, "Accommodation Theory: Communication, Context, and Consequence," in *Contexts of Accommodation: Developments in Applied Sociolinguistics*, Howard Giles, Justine Coupland, and Nikolas Coupland (eds.), Cambridge University, England, 1991, p. 10.
7 Howard Giles, Kimberly Noels, et al., "Intergenerational Communication Across Cultures: Young People's Perceptions of Conversations with Family Elders, Non-Family Elders and Same-Age Peers," *Journal of Cross-Cultural Gerontology*, Vol. 18, 2003, p. 9.
8 Jake Harwood, Priya Raman, and Miles Hewstone, "The Family and Communication Dynamics of Group Salience," *Journal of Family Communication*, Vol. 6, 2006, pp. 181–200.
9 Williams and Giles, "Intergenerational Conversations," p. 233.
10 Giles, Coupland, and Coupland, "Accommodation Theory," p. 46.
11 Ibid., p. 42.
12 Henri Tajfel and John C. Turner, "The Social Identity Theory of Intergroup Behavior," in *The Psychology of Intergroup Relations*, L. Worchel and W. Austin (eds.), Nelson Hall, Chicago, IL, 1986, pp. 7–24.
13 Jake Harwood, "Communication as Social Identity," in *Communication as . . . Perspectives on Theory*, Gregory Shepherd, Jeffrey St. John, and Ted Striphas (eds.), Sage, Thousand Oaks, CA, 2006, p. 89.
14 Giles, Noels, et al., "Intergenerational Communication," p. 24.
15 Williams and Giles, "Intergenerational Conversations," p. 238.
16 Ibid., p. 221.
17 Cynthia Gallois and Victor Callan, "Interethnic Accommodation: The Role of Norms," in *Contexts of Accommodation*, p. 249.
18 Cynthia Gallois, Arlene Franklyn Stokes, et al., "Communication Accommodation in Intercultural Encounters," in *Theories in Intercultural Communication*, Young Yun Kim and William B. Gudykunst (eds.), Sage, Newbury Park, CA, 1988, p. 166.
19 Gallois, Ogay, and Giles, "Communication Accommodation Theory," p. 128.
20 Giles, Coupland, and Coupland, "Accommodation Theory," p. 28.
21 Gallois, Ogay, and Giles, "Communication Accommodation Theory," p. 126.
22 Fritz Heider, *The Psychology of Interpersonal Relations*, John Wiley, New York, 1958; Harold Kelley, "The Process of Causal Attribution," *American Psychologist*, Vol. 28, 1973, pp. 107–128.
23 Ellen B. Ryan, Ann P. Anas, and Melissa Vuckovich, "The Effects of Age, Hearing Loss, and Communication Difficulty on First Impressions," *Communication Research Reports*, Vol. 24, 2007, pp. 13–19.
24 Howard Giles, Anthony Mulac, James Bradac, and Patricia Johnson, "Speech Accommodation Theory: The First Decade and Beyond," in *Communication Yearbook 10*, Margaret L. McLaughlin (ed.), Sage, Newbury Park, CA, 1987, p. 26.
25 Howard Giles, Michael Willemyns, Cindy Gallois, and Michelle Chernikoff Anderson, "Accommodating a New Frontier: The Context of Law Enforcement," in *Social Communication*, Klaus Fiedler (ed.), Psychology Press, New York, 2007, p. 130.
26 Michael S. Schmidt and Joseph Goldstein, "Even as Violent Crime Falls, Killing of Officers Rises," *The New York*

Times, April 9, 2012, http://www.nytimes.com/2012/04/10/us/defying-trends-killings-of-police-officers-are-on-the-rise.html, accessed October 29, 2013. (Also published on p. A1 of the April 10, 2012 edition, titled "Killing of Police Continues Rising as Violence Falls.")

27 Travis Dixon, Terry Schell, Howard Giles, and Kristin Drogos, "The Influence of Race in Police–Civilian Interactions: A Content Analysis of Videotaped Interactions Taken During Cincinnati Police Traffic Stops," *Journal of Communication*, Vol. 58, 2008, p. 530.

28 Giles, Willemyns, Gallois, and Anderson, p. 148.

29 Gallois, Ogay, and Giles, "Communication Accommodation Theory," p. 134.

30 Ibid., p. 130.

31 Cindy Gallois and Howard Giles, "Accommodating Mutual Influence in Intergroup Encounters," in *Progress in Communication Sciences: Vol. 14*, M. T. Palmer and G. A. Barnett (eds.), Ablex, Stamford, UK, 1998, p. 158.

32 Gallois, Ogay, and Giles, "Communication Accommodation Theory," p. 134.

33 Jordan Soliz and Howard Giles, "Relational and Identity Processes in Communication: A Contextual and Meta-Analytical Review of Communication Accommodation Theory," in *Communication Yearbook 38*, Elisia L. Cohen (ed.), Thousand Oaks, CA, in press.

Chapter 32: Face-Negotiation Theory

1 Stella Ting-Toomey and Atsuko Kurogi, "Facework Competence in Intercultural Conflict: An Updated Face-Negotiation Theory," *International Journal of Intercultural Relations*, Vol. 22, 1998, p. 190.

2 Harry C. Triandis, *Individualism & Collectivism*, Westview, Boulder, CO, 1995, pp. 10–11.

3 Ting-Toomey and Kurogi, p. 190.

4 Ibid., p. 196.

5 Hazel Markus and Shinobu Kitayama, "Culture and the Self: Implications for Cognition, Emotion, and Motivation," *Psychological Review*, Vol. 2, 1991, pp. 224–253.

6 John Oetzel, "The Effects of Self-Construals and Ethnicity on Self-Reported Conflict Styles," *Communication Reports*, Vol. 11, 1998, p. 140. See also William B. Gudykunst et al., "The Influence of Cultural Individualism–Collectivism, Self-Construals, and Individual Values on Communication Styles Across Cultures," *Human Communication Research*, Vol. 22, 1996, pp. 510–540.

7 Ting-Toomey and Kurogi, p. 218.

8 John Oetzel and Stella Ting-Toomey, "Face Concerns in Interpersonal Conflict: A Cross-Cultural Empirical Test of the Face-Negotiation Theory," *Communication Research*, Vol. 30, 2003, p. 619.

9 Ting-Toomey and Kurogi, p. 187.

10 Penelope Brown and Stephen Levinson, "Universals in Language Usage: Politeness Phenomenon," in *Questions and Politeness: Strategies in Social Interaction*, Esther N. Goody (ed.), Cambridge University Press, Cambridge, UK, 1978, p. 66.

11 Lin Yutang, *My Country and My People*, John Day, Taipei, Republic of China, 1968, p. 199.

12 Stella Ting-Toomey, "Intercultural Conflict Styles: A Face-Negotiation Theory," in *Theories in Intercultural Communication*, Young Yun Kim and William B. Gudykunst (eds.), Sage, Newbury Park, CA, 1988, p. 215.

13 M. A. Rahim, "A Measure of Styles of Handling Interpersonal Conflict," *Academy of Management Journal*, Vol. 26, 1983, pp. 368–376.

14 Robert Blake and Jane Mouton, *The Managerial Grid*, Gulf, Houston, 1964; Ralph Kilmann and Kenneth Thomas, "Developing a Forced-Choice Measure of Conflict-Handling Behavior: The 'Mode' Instrument," *Educational and Psychological Measurement*, Vol. 37, 1977, pp. 309–325.

15 Stella Ting-Toomey, John Oetzel, and Kimberlie Yee-Jung, "Self-Construal Types and Conflict Management Styles," *Communication Reports*, Vol. 14, 2002, pp. 87–104.

16 Stella Ting-Toomey, "Translating Conflict Face-Negotiation Theory into Practice," in Dan Landis, Jane Bennett, and Milton Bennett (eds.), *Handbook of Intercultural Training*, 3rd ed., Sage, Thousand Oaks, 2004, pp. 229–230.

17 Ibid., p. 230.

18 Ting-Toomey, Oetzel, and Yee-Jung, pp. 87–104.

19 Stella Ting-Toomey, "The Matrix of Face: An Updated Face-Negotiation Theory," in *Theorizing About Intercultural Communication*, William B. Gudykunst (ed.), Sage, Thousand Oaks, CA, 2005, p. 86.

20 Roger Fisher, William Ury, and Bruce Patton, *Getting to Yes: Negotiating Agreement Without Giving In*, 2nd ed., Penguin, New York, 1991.

21 Ting-Toomey and Kurogi, p. 194.

22 Stella Ting-Toomey and Jiro Takai, "Explaining Intercultural Conflict: Promising Approaches and Directions," in *The Sage Handbook of Conflict Communication: Integrating Theory, Research and Practice*, John G. Oetzel and Stella Ting-Toomey (eds.), Sage, Thousand Oaks, CA, 2006, p. 698.

23 Ting-Toomey, "The Matrix of Face."

24 Ting-Toomey and Takai, p. 702.

25 Stella Ting-Toomey, *Communicating Across Cultures*, Guilford, New York, 1999, p. vii.

26 Oetzel and Ting-Toomey, p. 599.

27 Ibid., p. 617.

28 Gerry Philipsen, "Some Thoughts on How to Approach Finding One's Feet in Unfamiliar Cultural Terrain," *Communication Monographs*, Vol. 77, 2013, pp. 160–168.

29 Adrian Toomey, Tenzin Dorjee, and Stella Ting-Toomey, "Bicultural Identity Negotiation, Conflicts, and Intergroup Communication Strategies," *Journal of Intercultural Communication Research*, Vol. 42, 2013, pp. 112–134.

Chapter 33: Speech Codes Theory

1 Gerry Philipsen, "Speaking 'Like a Man' in Teamsterville: Culture Patterns of Role Enactment in an Urban Neighborhood," *Quarterly Journal of Speech*, Vol. 61, 1975, pp. 13–22; Gerry Philipsen, "Places for Speaking in Teamsterville," *Quarterly Journal of Speech*, Vol. 62, 1976, pp. 15–25.

2 Dell Hymes, "The Ethnography of Speaking," in T. Gladwin and W. C. Sturtevant (eds.), *Anthropology and Human Behavior*, Anthropological Society of Washington, Washington, DC, 1962, pp. 13–53.

3 Gerry Philipsen, "Cultural Communication," in *Handbook of International and Intercultural Communication*, 2nd ed., William B. Gudykunst and Bella Mody (eds.), Sage, Thousand Oaks, CA, 2002, p. 56.

4 Ibid., p. 60.

5 Tamar Katriel and Gerry Philipsen, "'What We Need Is Communication': Communication as a Cultural Category in Some American Speech," *Communication Monographs*, Vol. 48, 1981, pp. 302–317.

6 Gerry Philipsen, *Speaking Culturally: Explorations in Social Communication*, State University of New York, Albany, 1992, p. 7.

7 Ibid., p. 4.

8 Ibid., p. 6.

9 Gerry Philipsen, "A Theory of Speech Codes," in *Developing Communication Theory,* Gerry Philipsen and Terrance Albrecht (eds.), State University of New York, Albany, 1997, pp. 119–156.
10 Gerry Philipsen, Lisa M. Coutu, and Patricia Covarrubias, "Speech Codes Theory: Restatement, Revisions, and Response to Criticisms," in *Theorizing About Intercultural Communication,* William B. Gudykunst (ed.), Sage, Thousand Oaks, CA, 2005, p. 59.
11 Dell Hymes, "Ways of Speaking," in *Explorations in the Ethnography of Speaking,* Richard Bauman and Joel Sherzer (eds.), Cambridge University, London, 1974, pp. 433–451.
12 Erving Goffman, *The Presentation of Self in Everyday Life,* Doubleday Anchor, Garden City, NY, 1959.
13 Philipsen, "A Theory of Speech Codes," p. 139.
14 Philipsen, *Speaking Culturally,* p. 110.
15 Ibid., p. 113, citing P. Berger, B. Berger, and H. Kellner, *The Homeless Mind: Modernization and Consciousness,* Vintage, New York, 1973, p. 89.
16 Ibid., p. 76. See also Katriel and Philipsen, "'What We Need Is Communication,'" p. 308.
17 Philipsen, "A Theory of Speech Codes," p. 140.
18 Philipsen, "Mayor Daley's Council Speech," in *Speaking Culturally,* pp. 43–61.
19 Philipsen, *Speaking Culturally,* pp. 77–80.
20 Philipsen, "A Theory of Speech Codes," p. 148.
21 Dwight Conquergood, "Poetics, Play, Process, and Power: The Performance Turn in Anthropology," *Text and Performance Quarterly,* Vol. 1, 1989, pp. 82–95.
22 James Clifford, *Predicament of Culture,* Harvard University Press, Cambridge, MA, p. 49.
23 Conquergood, p. 87.
24 Dwight Conquergood, "Ethnography, Rhetoric, and Performance," *Quarterly Journal of Speech,* Vol. 78, 1992, p. 90.
25 Gerry Philipsen, "Coming to Terms with Cultures," 2008 NCA Carroll C. Arnold distinguished lecture, Allyn & Bacon, Boston, MA, 2010, p. 7.
26 Stella Ting-Toomey, "Applying Dimensional Values in Understanding Intercultural Communication," *Communication Monographs,* Vol. 77, 2010, pp. 169–180
27 Gerry Philipsen, "Speech Codes Theory: Traces of Culture in Interpersonal Communication," in *Engaging Theories of Interpersonal Communication,* Leslie A. Baxter and Dawn O. Braithwaite (eds.) Sage, Thousand Oaks, CA, 2008, pp. 269–280.
28 Ibid., p. 278.

Gender and Communication

1 Robin Lakoff, *Language and Women's Place,* Harper & Row, New York, 1975.
2 Kathryn Dindia, "Men Are from North Dakota, Women Are from South Dakota," paper presented at the National Communication Association convention, November 19–23, 1997.
3 Julia T. Wood and Kathryn Dindia, "What's the Difference? A Dialogue About Differences and Similarities Between Women and Men," in *Sex Differences and Similarities in Communication,* Daniel Canary and Kathryn Dindia (eds.), Lawrence Erlbaum, Mahwah, NJ, 1998, pp. 19–38.
4 Sandra L. Bem, "Androgyny vs. the Tight Little Lives of Fluffy Women and Chesty Men," *Psychology Today,* Vol. 9, 1975, pp. 58–62.
5 Cheris Kramarae, "Gender and Dominance," in *Communication Yearbook 15,* Stanley Deetz (ed.), Sage, Newbury Park, CA, 1992, pp. 469–474.

Chapter 34: Genderlect Styles

1 Deborah Tannen, *You Just Don't Understand*, Ballantine, New York, 1990, p. 42.
2 Deborah Tannen, *Conversational Style: Analyzing Talk Among Friends*, Ablex, Norwood, NJ, 1984.
3 Ibid., p. vii.
4 Tannen, *You Just Don't Understand*, p. 259.
5 Ibid., p. 279.
6 Ibid., p. 16.
7 Ibid., p. 108.
8 Julia Wood, *Gendered Lives*, Cengage, Boston, MA, 2009, p. 126.
9 Daniel Maltz and Ruth Borker, "A Cultural Approach to Male–Female Miscommunication," in *Language and Social Identity*, John Gumperz (ed.), Cambridge University Press, Cambridge, UK, 1982, pp. 196–216.
10 Wood, pp. 127–128.
11 Tannen, *You Just Don't Understand*, p. 48.
12 Louann Brizendine, *The Female Brain*, Random House, New York, NY, 2006.
13 Tannen, *You Just Don't Understand*, p. 212.
14 Ibid., p. 62.
15 Ibid., p. 72.
16 Ibid., p. 150.
17 Susan Pease Gadoua, "To Connect, Women Want to Talk and Men Want Sex—How Do Straight Couples Reconcile?" *Psychology Today*, February 7, 2010, http://www.psychologytoday.com/blog/contemplating-divorce/201002/connect-women-want-talk-and-men-want-sex-how-do-straight-couples-r, accessed September 24, 2013.
18 William Labov, *Sociolinguistic Patterns*, University of Pennsylvania Press, Philadelphia, 1972.
19 Wood, p. 126.
20 Louise Cherry and Michael Lewis, "Mothers and Two-Year-Olds: A Study of Sex-Differentiated Aspects of Verbal Interaction," *Developmental Psychology*, Vol. 12, 1976, pp. 276–282.
21 Tannen, *You Just Don't Understand*, pp. 120–121, 298.
22 Carol Gilligan, *In a Different Voice: Psychological Theory and Women's Development,* Harvard University, Cambridge, MA, 1982.
23 Seyla Benhabib, "The Generalized and the Concrete Other: The Kohlberg–Gilligan Controversy and Feminist Theory," in Seyla Benhabib and Drucilla Cornell (eds.), *Feminism as Critique,* University of Minnesota, Minneapolis, 1987, p. 78.
24 Lawrence Kohlberg, *Essays on Moral Development, Volume 1: The Philosophy of Moral Development,* Harper & Row, San Francisco, 1981, p. 12.
25 Gilligan, p. 18.
26 Carol Gilligan, "In a Different Voice: Women's Conceptions of Self and Morality," *Harvard Educational Review,* Vol. 47, 1977, p. 484.
27 Tannen, *Conversational Style*, p. 38.
28 J. W. Santrock, A. M. Minnett, and B. D. Campbell, *The Authoritative Guide to Self-Help Books*, Guilford, New York, 1994.
29 Adrianne W. Kunkel and Brant R. Burleson, "Social Support and the Emotional Lives of Men and Women: An Assessment of the Different Cultures Perspective," in *Sex Differences and Similarities in Communication*, Daniel Canary and Kathryn Dindia (eds.), Lawrence Erlbaum, Mahwah, NJ, 1998, p. 116.
30 Senta Troemel-Ploetz, "Review Essay: Selling the Apolitical," *Discourse & Society*, Vol. 2, 1991, p. 497.
31 Ibid., p. 491.
32 Ibid., p. 495.

Chapter 35: Standpoint Theory

1 Julia T. Wood, *Communication Theories in Action,* 1st ed., Wadsworth, Belmont, CA, 1997, p. 250.

2 Sandra Harding, "Comment on Hekman's 'Truth and Method: Feminist Standpoint Theory Revisited': Whose Standpoint Needs the Regimes of Truth and Reality?" *Signs: Journal of Women in Culture and Society,* Vol. 22, 1997, p. 384.

3 Sandra Harding, *Whose Science? Whose Knowledge? Thinking from Women's Lives,* Cornell University Press, Ithaca, NY, 1991, pp. 269–270.

4 Meenakshi Gigi Durham, "On the Relevance of Standpoint Epistemology to the Practice of Journalism: The Case for 'Strong Objectivity,'" *Communication Theory,* Vol. 8, 1998, p. 117.

5 Julia T. Wood, "Gender and Moral Voice: Moving from Woman's Nature to Standpoint Epistemology," *Women's Studies in Communication,* Vol. 15, 1993, p. 13.

6 Julia T. Wood, "Feminist Scholarship and the Study of Relationships," *Journal of Social and Personal Relationships,* Vol. 12, 1995, p. 110.

7 Georg Wilhelm Friedrich Hegel, *The Phenomenology of Mind,* Macmillan, New York, 1910, pp. 182–188.

8 Friedrich Engels, "Socialism: Utopian and Scientific," and "The Origin of the Family, Private Property, and the State," in *The Marx–Engels Reader,* Robert Tucker (ed.), W. W. Norton, New York, 1978, pp. 701–702, 734–736. See also Sandra Harding, "The Instability of the Analytical Categories of Feminist Theory," in *Sex and Scientific Inquiry,* Sandra Harding and Jean O'Barr (eds.), University of Chicago, IL, 1987, p. 292.

9 Harding, "Comment on Hekman's 'Truth and Method,'" p. 389.

10 Wood, "Feminist Scholarship," p. 111.

11 Jean-François Lyotard, *The Postmodern Condition: A Report on Knowledge,* Geoff Bennington and Brian Massumi (trans.), University of Minnesota Press, Minneapolis, 1984, p. xxiv.

12 Kathryn Stockett, *The Help,* Amy Einhorn Books/Putnam, New York, 2009.

13 Ibid., pp. 79–80.

14 Ibid., p. 4.

15 Ibid., flyleaf.

16 Ibid., p. 386.

17 Rachael A. Griffin, "Problematic Representations of Progressive Whiteness (?) and Post Racial Pedagogy: A Critical Race Reading of *The Help,*" paper presented at the Central States Communication Association Convention, Kansas City, MO, April 3–7, 2013.

18 Julia T. Wood, "Engendered Relations: Interaction, Caring, Power and Responsibility in Intimacy," in *Social Context and Relationships,* Steve Duck (ed.), Sage, Newbury Park, CA, 1993, p. 37.

19 Wood, "Feminist Scholarship," p. 112.

20 Stockett, p. 173.

21 Ibid., p. 304.

22 Julia T. Wood, *Communication Theories in Action,* 3rd ed., Wadsworth, Belmont, CA, p. 212. See also Harding, *Whose Science? Whose Knowledge?* p. 59.

23 Wood, "Gender and Moral Voice," p. 8.

24 Stockett, p. 418.

25 Ibid., pp. 8–9.

26 Harding, *Whose Science? Whose Knowledge?* p. 192.

27 Donna Haraway, "Situated Knowledges: The Science Question in Feminism and the Privilege of Partial Perspective," *Feminist Studies,* Vol. 14, 1988, p. 3; Sandra Harding, "Introduction: Standpoint Theory as a Site of Political, Philosophic, and Scientific Debate," in *The Feminist Standpoint Theory Reader,* Sandra Harding (ed.), Routledge, New York, 2004, p. 4.

28 Harding, *Whose Science? Whose Knowledge?* pp. 159, 58.

29 Ibid., p. 59.

30 Wood, *Communication Theories in Action,* 1st ed., p. 257.

31 http://www.nytimes.com/2009/05/15/us/politics/15judge.text.html?pagewanted=5, accessed November 22, 2010.

32 Harding, *Whose Science? Whose Knowledge?* pp. 149–152.

33 Ibid., p. 270.

34 Wood, *Communication Theories in Action,* 1st ed., p. 254.

35 Ibid.

36 Harding, *Whose Science? Whose Knowledge?* p. 167.

37 Sandra Harding, "Introduction," p. 9; Julia T. Wood, "Feminist Standpoint Theory and Muted Group Theory: Commonalities and Divergences," *Women and Language,* Vol. 28, 2005, pp. 61–64.

38 Stockett, p. 277.

39 Julia T. Wood, *Who Cares? Women, Care, and Culture,* Southern Illinois University Press, Carbondale, 1994, p. 4.

40 Ibid., p. 6.

41 Ibid., pp. 8–9.

42 Ibid., p. 163.

43 Patricia Hill Collins, "Learning from the Outsider Within: The Sociological Significance of Black Feminist Thought," in *The Feminist Standpoint Reader,* p. 103.

44 Pearl Cleage, *Deals with the Devil and Other Reasons to Riot,* Ballantine, New York, 1993, pp. 55.

45 The wording of the four criteria of black feminist epistemology and the quotations that accompany them are from Patricia Hill Collins, *Black Feminist Thought: Knowledge, Consciousness, and the Politics of Empowerment,* 2nd ed., Routledge, New York, 2000, pp. 257–266.

46 Seyla Benhabib, *Situating the Self: Gender, Community and Postmodernism in Contemporary Ethics,* Routledge, New York, 1992, p. 4.

47 Ibid., p. 2.

48 Jean-François Lyotard, *The Postmodern Condition: A Report on Knowledge,* 1984.

49 Benhabib, *Situating the Self,* p. 209.

50 Ibid., p. 229.

51 Ibid., p. 14.

52 Benhabib's critique of Habermas draws on Nancy Fraser, "Rethinking the Public Sphere," in *Justice Interruptus,* Routledge, New York, 1997, pp. 69–98.

53 Benhabib, *Situating the Self,* p. 3.

54 Benhabib, "The Generalized and the Concrete Other: The Kohlberg–Gilligan Controversy and Feminist Theory," in *Situating the Self,* pp. 148–177.

55 Susan Hekman, "Truth and Method: Feminist Standpoint Theory Revisited," *Signs,* Vol. 22, 1997, pp. 341–365; Nancy Hirschmann, "Feminist Standpoint as Postmodern Strategy," *Women and Politics,* Vol. 18, No. 3, 1997, pp. 73–92.

56 John Michael, "Making a Stand: Standpoint Epistemologies, Political Positions, Proposition 187," *Telos,* Vol. 108, 1996, pp. 93–103.

57 Lynn Worsham, "Romancing the Stones: My Movie Date with Sandra Harding," *Journal of Advanced Composition,* Vol. 15, 1995, p. 568.

Chapter 36: Muted Group Theory

1 Cheris Kramarae, *Women and Men Speaking,* Newbury House, Rowley, MA, 1981, p. 1.

2 Barrie Thorne, Cheris Kramarae, and Nancy Henley (eds.), *Language, Gender and Society,* Newbury House, Rowley, MA, 1983, p. 9.

3 Cheris Kramarae, "Folklinguistics," *Psychology Today*, Vol. 8, June 1974, pp. 82–85.
4 Edwin Ardener, "Belief and the Problem of Women," in *Perceiving Women*, Shirley Ardener (ed.), Malaby Press, London, 1975, p. 2.
5 Shirley Ardener, "The Nature of Women in Society," in *Defining Females*, Halsted, New York, 1978, p. 21.
6 Edwin Ardener, "The 'Problem' Revisited," in *Perceiving Women*, p. 22.
7 Ibid., p. 25.
8 Kramarae, *Women and Men Speaking*, p. 3.
9 Simone de Beauvoir, *The Second Sex*, H. M. Parshley (ed. and trans.), Bantam, New York, 1964, p. xv.
10 Kramarae, *Women and Men Speaking*, p. 3.
11 Julia P. Stanley, "Paradigmatic Women: The Prostitute," in *Papers in Language Variation*, David L. Shores and Carole P. Hines (eds.), University of Alabama, Tuscaloosa, 1977, p. 7.
12 Kramarae, *Women and Men Speaking*, p. 1.
13 Virginia Woolf, *A Room of One's Own*, Hogarth (Penguin edition), 1928, p. 45.
14 Dorothy Smith, "A Peculiar Eclipsing: Women's Exclusion from Man's Culture," *Women's Studies International Quarterly*, Vol. 1, 1978, p. 281.
15 Kramarae, *Women and Men Speaking*, p. 3.
16 Tillie Olsen, *Silences*, Delacorte/Seymour Lawrence, New York, 1978, p. 23.
17 Kramarae, *Women and Men Speaking*, p. 19.
18 Ibid., p. 12.
19 Ibid., p. 4.
20 Cheris Kramarae and Paula Treichler, *A Feminist Dictionary: Amazons, Bluestockings and Crones*, 2nd ed., Pandora, London, 1992, p. 17.
21 Keith Wagstaff, "Men Are from Google+, Women Are from Pinterest," *Time* magazine, http://techland.time.com/2012/02/15/men-are-from-google-women-are-from-pinterest/, accessed November 6, 2013.
22 Kramarae and Treichler, p. 4.
23 Dale Spender, *Man Made Language*, Routledge & Kegan, London, 1980, p. 87.
24 Cheris Kramarae, "Punctuating the Dictionary," *International Journal of the Sociology of Language*, Vol. 94, 1992, p. 135.
25 Kramarae and Treichler, p. 4.
26 Cheris Kramarae, "Harassment and Everyday Life," in *Women Making Meaning: New Feminist Directions in Communication*, Lana Rakow (ed.), Routledge, New York, 1992, p. 102.
27 Julia T. Wood (ed.), "Special Section—'Telling Our Stories': Sexual Harassment in the Communication Discipline," *Journal of Applied Communication Research*, Vol. 20, 1992, pp. 383–384.
28 Ann Burnett, Jody L. Mattern, Liliana L. Herakova, David H. Kahl Jr., Cloy Tobola, and Susan E. Bornsen, "Communicating/Muting Date Rape: A Co-Cultural Theoretical Analysis of Communication Factors Related to Rape Culture on a College Campus," *Journal of Applied Communication Research*, Vol. 37, 2009, pp. 465–485.
29 Mark P. Orbe, "From the Standpoint(s) of Traditionally Muted Groups: Explicating a Co-Cultural Communication Theoretical Model," *Communication Theory*, Vol. 8, 1998, p. 1.
30 "Biography," J. K. Rowling's website, http://www.jkrowling.com/en_US/#/about-jk-rowling/accessed August 23, 2013.
31 Orbe, p. 10.
32 Mark P. Orbe and Christopher R. Groscurth, "A Co-Cultural Theoretical Analysis of Communicating on Campus and at Home: Exploring the Negotiation Strategies of First Generation College (FGC) Students," *Qualitative Research Reports in Communication*, Vol. 5, 2004, pp. 41–47.
33 "First Generation Students in Postsecondary Education: A Brief Portrait," National Center for Education Statistics of the U.S. Department of Education, http://nces.ed.gov/ssbr/pages/postsec.asp, accessed November 6, 2013.
34 Christopher R. Groscurth and Mark P. Orbe, "The Oppositional Nature of Civil Rights Discourse: Co-Cultural Communicative Practices that Speak Truth to Power," *Atlantic Journal of Communication*, Vol. 14, pp. 123–140; Marsha Cohen and Susan Avanzino, "We are People First: Framing Organizational Assimilation Experiences of the Physically Disabled Using Co-Cultural Theory," *Communication Studies*, Vol. 61, 2010, pp. 272–303.
35 "Muted Group Theory Excerpts," in *Women and Language*, Vol. 28, 2005, p. 50.
36 Karen A. Foss and Sonja K. Foss, "Incorporating the Feminist Perspective in Communication Scholarship: A Research Commentary," in *Doing Research on Women's Communication: Perspectives on Theory and Method*, Kathryn Carter and Carole Spitzack (eds.), Ablex, Norwood, NJ, 1989, p. 72.
37 Cheris Kramarae, "Muted Group Theory and Communication: Asking Dangerous Questions," in *Women and Language*, Vol. 28, 2005, p. 58.
38 Ibid., p. 59.
39 Deborah Tannen, *Conversational Style: Analyzing Talk Among Friends*, Ablex, Norwood, NJ, 1984, p. 43.
40 Kramarae, "Punctuating the Dictionary," p. 146.

Integration

1 Robert Bostrom and Lewis Donohew, "The Case for Empiricism: Clarifying Fundamental Issues in Communication Theory," *Communication Monographs*, Vol. 59, 1992, pp. 109, 127.
2 Stuart Hall, "Ideology and Communication Theory," in *Rethinking Communication, Vol. 1*, Brenda Dervin, Lawrence Grossberg, Barbara O'Keefe, and Ellen Wartella (eds.), Sage, Newbury Park, CA, 1989, pp. 52, 42.
3 Richard Rorty, *Consequences of Pragmatism*, University of Minnesota, Minneapolis, 1982, p. 197.
4 George Gerbner, "The Importance of Being Critical—In One's Own Fashion," *Journal of Communication*, Vol. 33, No. 3, 1983, p. 361.
5 Marie Hochmuth Nichols, *Rhetoric and Criticism*, Louisiana State University, Baton Rouge, 1963, p. 18.

Chapter 37: Common Threads in Comm Theories

1 To access a chapter on Heider's attribution theory that appeared in a previous edition of this text, click on Theory List at *www.afirstlook.com*.
2 Raymond Bauer, "The Obstinate Audience," *American Psychologist*, Vol. 19, 1964, pp. 319–328.

INDEX

B

D

E

F

G

H

I

J

K

L

N

Q

R

S

T

U

V

W

Y

Z

CONVERSATIONS WITH COMMUNICATION THEORISTS

The "Conversations" sections at the end of the chapters listed below connect the theories to 17 original video interviews conducted and produced by the authors. These videos appear on the book's Online Learning Center, *www.mhhe.com/griffin9e,* and the author-driven website, *www.afirstlook.com.*

Chapter 6	Barnett Pearce—Coordinated Management of Meaning (Em)
Chapter 7	Judee Burgoon—Expectancy Violations Theory (Em)
Chapter 9	Chuck Berger—Uncertainty Reduction Theory (Em)
Chapter 10	Joe Walther—Social Information Processing Theory (Em)
Chapter 11	Leslie Baxter—Relational Dialectics (Em)
Chapter 12	Sandra Petronio—Communication Privacy Management Theory (Glenn)
Chapter 17	Randy Hirokawa—Functional Perspective on Group Decision Making (Em)
Chapter 21	Stan Deetz—Critical Theory of Communication in Organizations (Em)
Chapter 30	Max McCombs—Agenda-Setting Theory (Em)
Chapter 31	Howie Giles—Communication Accommodation Theory (Andrew)
Chapter 32	Stella Ting-Toomey—Face-Negotiation Theory (Em)
Chapter 33	Gerry Philipsen—Speech Codes Theory (Em)
Chapter 36	Cheris Kramarae—Muted Group Theory (Em)
Archive	Scott Poole—Adaptive Structuration Theory (Em)
	Jesse Delia, Brant Burleson & Jim Applegate—Constructivism (Em)
	David Buller—Interpersonal Deception Theory (Em)
	Byron Reeves & Clifford Nass—Media Equation (Em)